also by

Melville J. Herskovits

The Human Factor in Changing Africa

Man and His Works

Economic Anthropology
a revised and enlarged edition of
The Economic Life of Primitive Peoples

Life in a Haitian Valley

The American Negro

Trinidad Village
with Frances S. Herskovits

These are Borzoi Books
published by
Alfred A. Knopf

Cultural Anthropology

Cultural Anthropology

Melville J. Herskovits

An
Abridged
Revision
of
Man and His Works

Alfred A. Knopf
New York

L. C. catalog card number: 55-5171
© Melville J. Herskovits, 1955

This is a BORZOI BOOK
Published by ALFRED A. KNOPF, INC.

FIRST ABRIDGED AND REVISED EDITION MARCH 1955; REPRINTED
1955, 1958, 1960, 1963, 1964, 1965, 1966, 1969

To My Students,

from whom

I have learned

many things

Each fresh start on the never-ending quest of Man *as* he ought to be *has been the response of theory to fresh facts about* Man *as he is. . . . Meanwhile, the dreams and speculations of one thinker after another— even dreams and speculations which have moved nations and precipitated revolutions—have ceased to command men's reason, when they ceased to accord with their knowledge.*

Sir John Myres, "The Influence of Anthropology on the Course of Political Science," *University of California Publications in History,* Vol. 4 (1916), No. 1, pp. 75–6

Preface

This abridgement and revision of *Man and His Works* has been undertaken at the request of many of my fellow anthropologists, who, in making the point of view and the materials of the larger book available to their students, have felt that a briefer presentation would be more in accord with their needs in shorter elementary courses. *Man and His Works*, as indicated in its Preface, was written both for "students in institutions of higher learning, who follow formal courses in anthropology," and for "the many persons who, having completed their formal education in institutions where anthropology was not yet offered, wish in their mature years to learn about the subject." Its reception has, I think, demonstrated that both these objectives reflected a felt need.

The changes in organization that differentiate this book from its larger predecessor, however, have been made with the pedagogical requirements of students in introductory courses in anthropology primarily in mind. To this end, the chapters that deal with empirical data have been concentrated in the first half of the book, while the discussions of concept, method and theory have been brought together in later sections. And because, especially for students taking their first course in the subject, access to the facts and the organization of data are of primary importance, the abridgement of the theoretical chapters has been more extensive than of the chapters that now come at the beginning.

The present book, however, is by no means an exercise in subtraction. On the other side of the balance, I have expanded the discussion of the relation between physical type and culture into two chapters, one on the nature of race, and the other on the modes of interaction between physical type and learned behavior. In addition, this revision has made it possible for me to indicate such developments in the fast-moving anthropological scene as the exposure of the Piltdown "hoax"; certain methodological advances in the field of psychoethnography; and the increasing attention being given to the role of value-systems, especially as these are manifested in the debate, gratifyingly stimulated by the chapter in the earlier book, over the propositions implicit in the philosophy of cultural relativism. With all these changes, I have kept unaltered my care that documentation of citations and bibliographic references be as accurate as I can make them. One cannot begin too early to inculcate in the student the importance for scholarship of the care for detail that is of the essence of scientific presentation.

The task of revision of my earlier book has made it possible for me to profit from the suggestions of those who, in reviewing *Man and His Works*, indicated ways in which it could be improved. For these thoughtful comments I am deeply grateful. For the rest, I can but repeat here the thanks I gave in the Preface to the earlier volume to my friends, associates, and students; and to those institutions which aided me in preparing it. To that list I should like to add the names of Mrs. Virginia Smith and Robert P. Armstrong, whose work in the preparation of the manuscript of this revision has been of much help to me.

Melville J. Herskovits

Evanston, Illinois
25 March, 1954

Contents

IV. *Cultural Structure and Cultural Dynamics*

V. *Conclusion*

Bibliographies

Figures in Text

Plates

Part One

The
Setting
of
Culture

Chapter **One**

Anthropology: the Science of Man

The science of anthropology is divided into two broad fields, *physical* and *cultural anthropology*. Physical anthropologists study such matters as the nature of racial differences; the inheritance of bodily traits; the growth, development, and decay of the human organism; the influences of the natural environment on man. Cultural anthropologists study the ways man has devised to cope with his natural setting and his social milieu; and how bodies of custom are learned, retained, and handed down from one generation to the next.

In addition to the study of man's physical type and his cultural behavior, anthropology also includes *prehistoric archaeology* and, as a specialized subdivision of cultural anthropology, *comparative linguistics*. The prehistoric archaeologist investigates and analyzes those aspects of the study of man that throw light on the early development of the human race, during that period of a half-million years or more before the discovery of writing; while the linguistic anthropologist deals with the many varieties of that uniquely human attribute, speech.

When we consider the diversity of this subject matter, we may well ask: What is the unity of anthropology? The answer lies in the fact that anthropology takes into account all phases of man's existence, biological and cultural, past and present, combining these varied materials into an integrated attack on the problem of human experience. Unlike the disciplines that deal with more restricted aspects of the human being, anthropology emphasizes the principle that life is not lived by categories, but as a continuous stream. In practice, no anthropologist today studies all the divisions of his subject, but he is aware of their interrelations. The physical anthropologist, for example, recognizes the influence of social convention on mating as a factor in determining the physical type of a people. The linguistic anthropologist is alert to the social significance of speech forms. The prehistorian makes his contribution to the understanding of how basic technological devices used by men to underwrite their social life were developed and how the present races of mankind evolved. The cultural anthropologist is continuously aware that human traditions and ways of life are the expression of behavior based on the learning process and thus, in the broadest sense, are derived from man's biopsychological make-up.

It has been stated that when all its subdivisions are taken into account, anthropology, in its totality, is to be thought of as one of the most highly specialized of the sciences and at the same time one of the broadest. Physical anthropology is the most specialized aspect; cultural anthropology the one that ranges widely.

In anthropology as a biological science, the anthropologist, as human biologist, is interested in *Homo sapiens* alone. He studies a single form out of the vast range of creatures that claim the attention of the general biologist.

Cultural anthropology, on the other hand, has a far wider breadth of interest than related fields in the social sciences and the humanities, each of which takes up some one segment of human activity. The cultural anthropologist generally studies peoples who are outside the stream of European cultural history and attempts, as far as he can, to investigate a given body of custom as a whole. Or, if he concentrates on any one aspect of a culture, he takes as a primary objective the analysis of the interrelation of that aspect with the other phases of the life of the people. He analyzes these aspects not only as each is to be distinguished from the others, but as all form a functioning system that adapts the people to their setting. In this, the anthropologist differs from the economist, the political scientist, the sociologist, the student of comparative religions or of art or literature.

The anthropological linguist takes all languages as his province, though in practice he concentrates on unwritten tongues, studying them as cultural as well as purely linguistic phenomena.

The prehistorian finds evidence appertaining to the physical type and the cultural achievements of the people who lived during the time before writing was developed. He not only integrates such different materials but also employs skills developed to meet the special problems of the geologist and the paleontologist.

A comprehensive definition of anthropology as "the study of man and his works" is thus justified, because anthropology centers its attention on man, whether the focus of concern is broad or narrow. The great range of its subject matter has made it necessary for anthropology to develop special techniques and objectives to give unity to its aims and methods. At the same time, this very range brings anthropology into relation with many other subjects. It will be of substantial aid to us in understanding the nature of anthropological science to explore its relation to other disciplines.

2

We may begin by recalling some relevant facts about the development of science. Like charity, science begins at home. In the social sciences particularly, problems of an immediate nature that called for solution were self-evident points of attack. As a result, practical issues have been prominent in the interests of social scientists. The general principles advanced by them have been based largely on the study of materials from a single country or, at most, a series of countries with similar historical traditions.

It was only after the great epoch of discovery and European expansion into the Near and Far East, the Americas, and Africa, that it became apparent that other modes of behavior than those known to ourselves, other forms of linguistic expression, and other ways of worshipping the gods existed among peoples living in these newly visited regions of the world. The impact of this knowledge had far-reaching results. This is to be seen, for example, in the political philosophy of Rousseau, whose concept of the social contract still finds repercussions in our day. These early speculations and theories were often based on misconception rather than fact, for it is difficult to reach out of our own background and, without systematic training, understand the motives, the aims, the values of another people. This skill, which lies at the heart of anthropological method, developed late. For, though by then the other social-science disciplines had their established techniques, these were not adequate for the study of broader, cross-cultural topics.

Though in this book we are most concerned with cultural anthropology, it is nonetheless important that we also realize how the human biologist, the linguistic anthropologist, and the prehistorian, no less than the student of custom, are to be differentiated by this factor of specialization in method from those working in related disciplines.

The difference in the controls exerted over his data marks off the physical anthropologist from the general biologist, who can employ laboratory techniques forbidden the student of human biology. The student of general genetics, working with the fruit fly, *Drosophila melanogaster*, can count a numerous new generation every nine days. To study human genetics, one must work with a creature as long-lived as himself, who produces very few offspring in each mating and ordinarily gives birth to only one individual at a time. The student of human growth finds that to follow the development of an individual requires years, rather than the relatively short period needed for the lower forms to mature. But a greater handicap is the simple fact that, of all biologists, the physical anthropologist alone deals with a creature that has a voice in determining whether or not he is going to be studied at all!

The student of human prehistory studies problems closely related to those of paleontology and geology, but he must, in addition, be equipped with his own special methods. A paleontologist may find his knowledge of an entire extinct species restricted to a single bone, a unique fossil; but this is commonplace for the student of human evolution, for whom the find of a whole skull, to say nothing of a series of complete skeletons, is most unusual. The establishment of chronology through the study of geological strata is standard practice for the student of the earth sciences. The prehistoric archaeologist must, however, go on to infer an entire civilization from the fragments of artifacts he is able to recover from the earth. He must correlate these with the physical type of the early humans who produced them, if skeletal material is associated with the cultural remains; with the flora and fauna that are indicated in the site; and with the data that tell not only when these people lived but the environmental conditions to which they had to adapt their ways of life.

The anthropological linguist is similarly faced with special problems of method that he must solve before he can successfully attack the questions all linguists consider. Like other linguists, he is interested in forms of speech, phonetic patterns and the consistency of their use, dialectic variation, the relation of one language to another, the symbolism in languages. But the anthropological linguist must, first of all, reduce the speech he hears to systematic phonemic forms, transcribing such sounds as the "clicks" of the Bushmen and Hottentots, or incorporate into his grammatical system the use of different sounds spoken at different pitch. He must be prepared for genders based not on sex but on movement, or tenses that refer to duration of time rather than points in time. He must at times even determine what the language he is studying regards as a word. It is apparent that such tasks as these require methods quite different from those used in studying written languages.

3

We have thus far seen that despite the diversity of its interests, the unity of anthropological science derives from its concern with the rounded study of man. Through its concentrated attack on the fundamental question of the nature of man and his works, anthropology has become the synthesizing discipline we must recognize it to be. This brings us again to its relation to the other fields of scholarship with which it has problems in common, or from which it has borrowed methods for the study of its special problems.

Most bodies of subject matter fall into one of the three or four principal categories into which all knowledge is divided: the exact and natural sciences, the humanities, and the social sciences. Not so anthropology; for man is obviously a creature of many facets, and those who would understand him must disregard conventional boundaries as they pursue their problems into whatever fields these may lead.

Let us suppose, for example, that an anthropologist undertakes to study a people who inhabit an island in the South Seas, or an Indian tribe, or an African community. To the extent that he is concerned with their physical form and racial affiliation, he is working on a biological problem. But, if he analyzes the patterns of selection in mating, or the effects of a particular form of diet, he must take into account the factor of tradition, which we know can deeply influence genetic and physiological endowment. He must understand their reaction to their habitat, so here the anthropologist encounters the kind of problem treated by human geographers. When our student investigates their language, his research is in the field of the humanities, as it is when he collects their myths and tales, or records their music, or analyzes their art, or films their dances, or seeks to know their philosophy. But the same student is a social scientist when his problem is an analysis of their kinship system, or their economy, or when he investigates how their rulers govern, or describes the forms of their religious life.

Cultural anthropology has wider affiliations with other disciplines than has any other phase of anthropological science. Because it treats of the "works" of man in all their variety, it has experienced greater difficulty in standardizing its terminology than have other branches of the discipline. On the continent of Europe, indeed, it is not called "anthropology" at all. There "anthropology" is reserved for the study of physical type. In the United States cultural anthropology is customarily divided into *ethnology* and *ethnography*, the first being the comparative study of culture and the investigation of the theoretical problems that arise out of the analysis of human custom, the second the description of individual cultures. Some students in England and the United States give it the name "social anthropology." In this case, "ethnology" becomes the description of individual cultures, which we shall call "ethnography," while to "social anthropology" is assigned something of the role we give ethnology.

Among the social sciences, cultural anthropology is most often identified with sociology. Social institutions and the problems of the integration of the individual into his society are obviously of great importance in the study of man. In assessing the relation between the two disciplines, however, we must remember that the definition of what constitutes sociology differs substantially in continental Europe and England and in the United States, to mention only two areas. Thus an English study of the political institutions of native Africa, offered as "an attempt to bring into focus one of the major problems of African sociology," involves a use of the word "sociology" strange to American ears. On the other hand, the interest of sociologists in the United States in the problems of adjustment and integration of groups in their own society and their utilization of statistical techniques are not in accord with either the English tradition or that of continental Europe, which lays stress on social philosophy. But when questions of the development and functions of institutions, general principles of human group behavior, and problems of social theory are involved, sociology and cultural anthropology work together with a give and take that is solidly rooted and has proved mutually helpful.

Geographers have stressed the interaction between habitat and culture more than have anthropologists, who have tended to take the natural setting for granted. The influence of habitat should not, however, be minimized. For just as man is a member of the biological series, so he lives in a setting that exists independently of him and out of which he derives the raw stuff for the material objects he uses in getting a living; both circumstances must be continuously held in mind.

Active recognition of the problems common to anthropology and other social sciences, such as economics and political science, has been relatively slight. Communication between anthropologists and economists is steadily increasing, especially since anthropologists have become aware of the need to record as fully as possible the economic mechanisms of the societies they study. Economists, on their part—particularly those interested in economic institutions—are discovering that a comparative analysis of the different ways in which men solve their economic problems reveals relations and mechanisms hitherto overlooked.

This holds for the study of political institutions, too, though here definition is more difficult. Non-European peoples have often devised controls that differ so markedly from the political institutions of Euroamerican and other historical societies as almost to defy recognition. A system of regulating conduct such as that found among some Plains Indian tribes, for example, where certain degrees of cousinship permit public joking at the expense of a person who has transgressed accepted custom, can only be tenuously defined as political. But an understanding of the entire range of political institutions, which includes such complex systems as those of Africa and Polynesia, points the way toward a deeper comprehension of the nature, meaning, and functioning of governmental forms in human groups everywhere.

Many elements common to cultural anthropology and the humanistic disciplines have yet to be fully explored. This is partly because the phases of cultural anthropology related to the humanities employ techniques that require special preparation to master, as in linguistics or music. It is also because of a long-standing tradition whereby the comparative study of social institutions has received far more attention than other aspects of culture. This emphasis has tended to ignore the broader, more inclusive base for generalizing about human social life that a rounded, balanced study of all aspects of culture provides.

In the humanities, however, the tie between anthropological linguistics and the study of written languages, especially of Indo-European stock, needs only mention to become apparent. In the field of art, students have in recent years sought knowledge of the widest possible range of aesthetic expression among all peoples of the earth. Creative artists have visited many non-European societies for stimulation and study. In our art galleries, African wood carvings take their place with French modernist paintings and sculpture, on whose style they have had so profound an influence. Art students analyze Navaho sand paintings, or Peruvian pottery and textiles in much the same way as they study the classical forms of our own past. The field of the social role of art, which is a kind of no man's land between art and sociology, has been brought to the fore by students of nonliterate cultures. They have not only reproduced exotic art forms and explained their symbolism but, in integrating all manifestations of the culture that produced them, have sought the meaning of the art to the people, the drives that actuate the artist, and the functioning of the art in its society.

Analysis of the literary forms with which the anthropologist deals proceeds on much the same lines as does the study of any literature. Problems of style, narrative sequences, devices to heighten suspense or reach a climax; problems of variation in a tale as it has moved from one people to another, and the way in which this reflects mutations in literary patterns; problems of the origin and of the spread of tales, are all familiar to those who deal with written literature. Here we also move into the field of drama, which has been far too neglected by anthropologists and students of the drama alike. Yet drama is among the universals in human experience, and failure to study any of the universals in a society inhibits proper perspective.

Comparative musicology is another field that, though related to the conventional study of music, has yet to be accorded full recognition. All people make music, and they make music in obedience to patterns to which they give little conscious thought —as little as men give to the grammatical or phonetic systems of the languages they speak. Mechanical recording of melodies and rhythms of peoples in all parts of the world provides an accurate instrument with which to test problems of cultural stability, of individual variation in performance, of reworking of old melodies in a new cultural setting. These songs, furthermore, furnish composers with fresh thematic and rhythmic materials.

Since human biology is essentially a specialized form of general biology, the closeness of the relation between physical anthropology and the study of other living beings is apparent. In the analysis of human evolution, paleontology plays an important role, while the line between anatomy and physical anthropology is so fine that both disciplines have traditionally shared in the examination of many problems. Anatomy is essential in conventional studies of the human form, especially in the analysis of racial differences, so that physical anthropology is often studied and taught in departments of anatomy. It has even been said that no one can specialize in physical anthropology without prior training in anatomy—to which some have added the need for medical training, as well.

The study of human genetics, another branch of physical anthropology, requires knowledge of the findings of geneticists in general. The physical anthropologist must also be able to use mathematical tools, since biometrics, the statistical analysis of data from living creatures, is of critical significance. However, the human biologist remains an anthropologist, employing the aids given him by these other disciplines, but carrying the common problems into the total area of human living.

The affiliation of prehistoric archaeology with the earth sciences is intimate. Only geology can provide an answer to the critical question of the relation in time of a find to other remains. For example, the information necessary for dating the worked stone "points," discovered at Folsom, New Mexico, embedded in the vertebrae of an extinct species of bison, concerned the geological stratum in which the remains lay. The archaeologist could tell us that the points differed from other previously recovered. The paleontologist could identify the bison skeleton as that of an extinct form. But only a geologist could answer the questions: When did the form become extinct? When were the points made?

4

We have seen that anthropology, as a specialized biology, has drawn significantly on the exact and natural sciences out of which, in a very real sense, it has developed. In its relation to the humanities and the social sciences, however, anthropology is essentially the contributor, the synthesizing agent. This is as true of method as of objectives. To illustrate, the methods of anthropology used in studying human physical type are refinements of techniques of such older disciplines as anatomy and statistics, in this case adapted to the narrowed field in which physical anthropology specializes. The same principle applies also to prehistory, when considered in terms of the methods it employs that come from related fields. In the relation of anthropology to the social sciences and the humanities, however, it is the older disciplines that are the more restricted in scope, and have the more specific methods of attack. Anthropology thus brings to them a wider frame of reference within which surer generalizations can be erected, together with methods that represent radical departures from earlier techniques.

This brings us to three subjects that stand in a peculiarly close relation to anthropology. As a dynamic field of investigation that would understand the whole development of man and study the many varieties of culture that are the result of changes over long periods of time, anthropology is *historical*. As a science that seeks to understand the mainsprings of social behavior and the role of culture in making for human adjustment, it is *psychological*. Finally, as a discipline that considers the nature and range of the value-systems by which all men live, their explanations of the universe, and the relations between institutions and those who live in accordance with them, it is *philosophical*.

This is not the place to develop the relations between anthropology and these three disciplines, as has been done for the others. They are too fundamental, and, especially in their philosophical implications, too little examined. In a sense, much of the remainder of this book will be germane to this point, since our approach to an understanding of the cultures that have been evolved by man will be in terms of many concepts and findings of these disciplines. Like anthropology, they are concerned with syntheses of broad areas of human experience. All have a common point of departure and common objectives that give added meaning to the results of cross-disciplinary cooperation between them.

Thus we once more express the fundamental unity of anthropological science and its primary contribution to knowledge. The comprehensive approach of anthropology to the study of man that arises out of the diversity of its materials, and the analysis of them achieved through utilizing the special methods it has developed, must always be held in mind. In depicting man in the round, anthropology affords perspective not only in time but also in terms of the possible range of human behavior. It widens the world stage on which man has played his many roles, projecting our view beyond the scope of written history and into societies where conventions, never dreamed of in our culture, regularize and give meaning to behavior. In making possible this broadening of our perspective, we are permitted to peer out over the rim of our own culture and then to look back at our way of life with an objectivity not otherwise to be gained.

Chapter **Two**

The Evolution of Mankind

Where man first appeared, and when, is still under investigation. Some authorities hold that he originated in northern India, some in Africa, some in other regions. Most scholars believe that the earliest forms are those that have been recovered from sites in the Far East that reach from Java to Choukoutien, near Peking. Java yielded to Eugene Dubois, one of the early students of paleoanthropology, the famous *Pithecanthropus erectus*, or the Java ape man, which was held to be the "missing link" between man and ape. The passage of time, however, brought discoveries that taught us that no such simple formulation could explain the complexities of human development, as is to be seen from the increasing number of early remains from South Africa.

One of the most dramatic of these problems was posed when some enormous teeth were discovered in Chinese apothecary shops in Hong Kong, where they awaited use as medicine in accordance with the Chinese custom of grinding fossils to employ in this manner. What could these teeth, whose form indicated they were human molars, signify? Several times the size of the largest molars of living or fossil men, did they imply that man in the earliest days had been gigantic in proportion? Or could they have grown in jaws more in size like those of present-day human beings; and, if so, what appearance would creatures with such teeth have presented?

Yet there they are—and they epitomize the difficulties in archaeological research that pose its greatest challenge and give it its greatest fascination. No branch of anthropology requires more exercise of the scientific imagination. No matter how logical an hypothesis may seem, one specimen taken out of an undisturbed place in the ground may disprove it. From the positive point of view, the existence of a human or protohuman type, hitherto unrecognized, must be assumed on the basis of fragmentary remains, such as these great teeth.

What constitutes the greatest aid to the student in reconstructing the prehistoric development of man's physical type is that human morphology, like other natural phenomena, has a regularity that can be counted on. A given bone, or a complex of skeletal elements, will differ from species to species. The limits of variation within a given species, however, are relatively slight. The relation of form to function, moreover, is such that even in different species the way in which one element is mortised into the whole is so consistent that much information can be gained from even a part of a single bone. Thus we do not attribute tallness to a form that has a short thighbone, while one that is curved tells us its owner had a stooping rather than an upright posture.

The regularity of the process of biological evolution is also a factor of the greatest importance. This regularity is attested in the work of the paleontologists who have described the development of many animal forms in the same way as the paleoanthropologist does for man. One of their most notable achievements is the reconstruction of the process by which the horse, a small three-toed quadruped, evolved into the large-hoofed form known to us today.

By utilizing the logic of structure and the logic of evolutionary development, it has been possible to achieve what seem almost miracles in reconstructing the characteristics of the earlier, extinct forms of mankind. No one claims perfection for these reconstructions, which are always subject to revision on the discovery of more precise data than were at hand when any one reconstruction was made. Yet with the complete skull, let us say, of a Neanderthal man, it is possible to make clay replicas of the muscles that, under the logic of structure, must have been of a given length and thickness; and then over this reconstructed

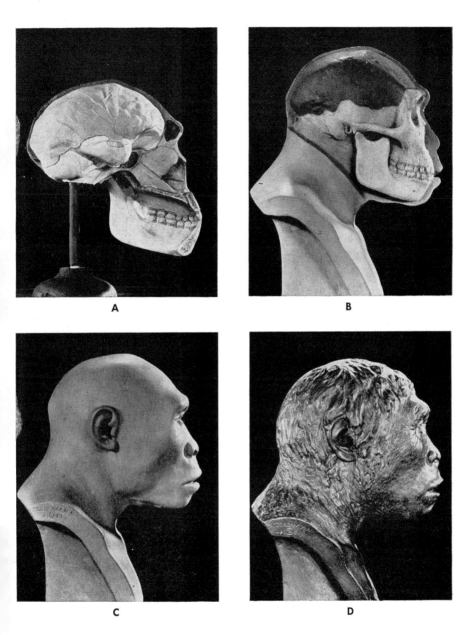

Plate 1a *Stages in the restoration of* Pithecanthropus erectus *by J. H. McGregor.*
(A) Half-skull and brain; (B) skull with flesh modeled on one side; (C) half-skull
with flesh modeled on; (D) complete restoration. See p. 13. (Photographs courtesy
American Museum of Natural History, New York.)

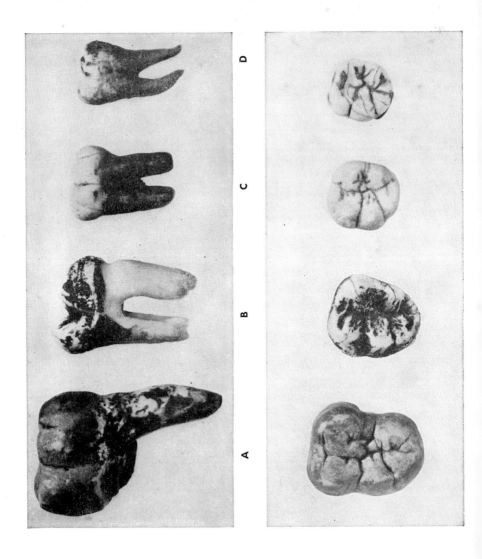

Plate 1b (*A*) *Third lower molar of* Gigantopithecus blacki *compared with* (*B*) *same tooth of male gorilla,* (*C*) *first lower molar of* Sinanthropus pekinensis, *and* (*D*) *the same tooth of modern man. Upper, lateral; and lower, occlusal orientation. See p. 20. (Photographs courtesy F. Weidenreich and American Museum of Natural History, New York; cf. also F. Weidenreich, 1946, Figs. 57 and 58.)*

musculature to place another covering that represents the skin. Or, with more fragmentary remains, such as a part of a jaw-bone, it is possible, using both logical systems, and taking into account not only the bone itself but the period when a given creature lived, to achieve the same result, though in these instances the skull itself must first be "restored."

Certain cautions must always be kept in mind when looking at such restorations. The first example we have cited will have far greater chances of being a correct approximation than the second. In restorations from partial materials, too, those parts of the skeleton closest to the recovered bones will be handled more surely than where the skeletal base is hypothetical. Certain "soft parts"—fleshly protuberances like the nose and ears—must always be guesswork. When they disintegrate, they leave no clues to what their shape had been. The same is true of hair. In some of the earlier restorations, only the fully human types were represented as clean-shaven, with hair parted. The psychological effect of the contrast of these forms with the unkempt earlier protohumans expresses the transparent, though unconscious, ethnocentrism—in this case, anthropocentrism—of those who made them! Yet such restorations make it possible for those unaccustomed to looking at skulls, or evaluating differences in skeletons, to understand, along broad lines, the development of *Homo sapiens*, the species to which all living mankind belongs.

2

A century before Darwin, it was realized that the similarities between man and certain other animal forms were so great that they could not be overlooked in setting up classifications of animal types. Linnaeus, therefore, grouped man, the great apes, and the monkeys in a single order, called *primates*. Within this order, New and Old World forms are to be distinguished. In the New World, evolution went no further than certain small monkey forms. This is why there is no question of the New World origin of man, since in the New World there was nothing from which he could have evolved. Furthermore, all man's closest relatives, the anthropoid apes, today exist in the areas where man has lived longest. Gorilla and chimpanzee are found in Africa, orangutan and gibbon in Malaysia.

That man represents the end product of a process of change characteristic of all living creatures is today beyond dispute. This process of change is what is meant when the word "evolution" is used. It occurs as the result of the variations which every living form exhibits. The importance of this factor of variability has been recognized since the time of Darwin. The variants a form produces offer the possibilty of change, and have been the instruments through which all living types and the many more extinct ones were enabled to appear through the millennia life has existed on earth.

As for the relation between man and other forms, we study not only paleontological evidence but the similarities in structure and functioning of the living representations of related types. Such a demonstration as has been given by Gregory [1] in tracing the bones of the face, item by item, from the fish, through intermediate types, to man, shows how wide-spread are these resemblances. Many similarities between man and his closest primate relations, the great apes, have been described.[2] That none of these forms has a tail, that they alone have the vermiform appendix, that they have similar blood-types, have almost the same structure of uterus and placenta, are omnivorous, having the dental equipment to chew either meat or herbivorous foods, have stereoscopic vision, and possess the opposable thumb, indicate how numerous are these resemblances. Most important is the fact that only man and the anthropoid apes share the tendency to upright posture and bipedal locomotion. Though man is the only true biped, and the apes employ their arms to assist them in walking, yet only man and the great apes have posterior extremities that can be put to such use.

The attainment of upright posture was fundamental in bringing about the changes that made of man the erect, speaking, tool-using, culture-building creature he has become. We cannot here debate the question whether or not the forms that preceded man began the march toward erect posture by coming out of the trees to lead a terrestrial rather than an arboreal life. The play of cause and effect is much too obscure, much too complex to permit any conclusive answer. It is quite possible, however, that a period of arboreal life did encourage the development of upright posture by shifting the axis of support to a line between the great toe and the rest of the foot. What is important here is to trace the consequences that followed when man's anterior extremities came exclusively to function as grasping organs, and his legs and feet came to be his only means of support and locomotion.

Morton has given a diagram which demonstrates how the human foot differs from that of the two forms most closely re-

---

[1] W. K. Gregory, 1929, *passim*.
[2] One of the most detailed of these is A. Schultz, 1936.

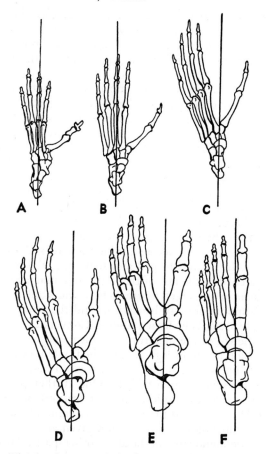

Fig. 1 *The development of the human foot, from* **(A)** *lemuroid and* **(B)** *simian (macaque) types of feet through* **(C)** *gibbon,* **(D)** *chimpanzee, and* **(E)** *gorilla to* **(F)** *man. The terrestrial adaptations of gorilla and human feet are seen in the more massive development of the heel and the increased development of the inner border of the foot, with a shortening of the toes. (After Morton, 1927, Fig. 3.)*

lated to man, the chimpanzee and the gorilla.[3] In man the great toe is firm and fixed, and has lost most of the opposability that in the other primates permits it to be employed as we and they use the thumb. This rigidity is essential to upright posture, as those who in accidents or otherwise have lost this organ demonstrate.

[3] D. J. Morton, 1927, p. 179, Fig. 3.

The great toe of the gorilla and chimpanzee give them stance in the approximations of upright posture they achieve. But because their great toes are not rigid they soon tire, and resume their characteristic position in which they support themselves with their arms.

With the assumption of upright posture, concomitant changes in many other parts of the body took place. The changes that comprise the outstanding differences between men and the forms closest to them are in accordance with certain principles of physics the violation of which would have rendered upright stance impossible.

If we depict in diagrams, as in Figure 2, the basic skeletal structure of a quadruped, of an upright brachiating form, and of an erect type, we can reduce this structure to the following elements: the head, the vertebral column, the extremities, and two girdles—one at the shoulder and the other at the hip—to which the extremities are attached and which are related to the vertebral column. In the quadruped and semiupright forms, the head must be attached to the rest of the body by a much stronger musculature than in the erect figure, where the skull benefits from having its support directly beneath it, and therefore can be kept in balance by relatively light muscles. Conversely, the posterior girdle, the pelvis, in the quadruped is not much more than something to which the hind legs are attached, while in an erect animal it must support the organs of the torso. In all this, the semiupright forms will be intermediate. One further point must be made here before we explore the implications of these simple principles. We have used the term "musculature," and spoken of heavier or lighter muscles needed in a given area of the body to retain and accommodate the head or other parts. Most muscles attach themselves to bones at roughened places. The harder the work which the muscle must perform, the rougher the place of attachment and the heavier the bone.

When man stood up on his feet, the femur (thigh-bone) became straighter and longer, and the articulations between the bones of the leg and foot underwent alterations at knee and ankle and thus allowed more effective adjustment to erect posture. The ridge or crest at the back of the human femur also became emphasized to allow for the stronger musculature that was necessary for walking and bending. The pelvis broadened and flattened, to become a kind of basin for the support not only of the internal organs that were now above it, but also of the upper girdle, arms and head, that pressed down upon it. The triple curvature of the spine made the vertebral column a kind of springlike structure that cushioned, for the head, the shock the entire body experiences with walking. Though less change is apparent in the anterior girdle, it also broadened and flattened into the human scapulae, the forearm lengthened in proportion to the total length of the body, and the thumb and fingers became specialized as grasping organs.

Fig. 2 *Basic skeletal structure of a quadruped, upright brachiating type, and erect form, highly stylized to show balance of head in* Homo.

The changes in the head and face were profound. The jaw became much lighter, and the teeth, especially the canines, became smaller. The jawbone, or mandible, is attached to the skull by the muscles that move it, and its lighter character meant that it could be manipulated by lighter muscles. Lighter muscles meant that there was more room inside the jaw for the tongue, while the bones of the skull could become less rugged, when they were no longer called upon to provide the surfaces that heavy muscles require as points of attachment. The significance of this is apparent when we compare the smooth vault of the human skull with that of the gorilla skull, with its bony crest to which the muscles that operate the mandible are attached. Finally, brains of a size distinctive of man alone could develop.

It must be emphasized again that the process sketched here leaves aside the problem why the changes occurred that resulted in *Homo sapiens*. One scholar will argue that these came about from need, another from chance, another from the physical forces involved, another from selection. The data do not reveal the causes. But they are emphatic that these, and many other alterations in detail not given here, do exhibit a pattern of consistency down the ages that is discernible when man is compared with other living forms. We can best see this consistency by tracing the evolutionary process in which the early hominid forms, far more like their primate relatives than any living human being, gradually assumed the characteristics of present-day man.

3

We shall here first consider the forms that derive from the Far East, and then those that have been recovered from Africa and Europe. While they cannot be placed with finality in their geological order, it is evident that in structural form most specimens thus far recovered from sites in the Far East are closer to the anthropoids than are those from Europe and Africa. In geological time, all these forms came into being in the Pleistocene so that, from the beginning of the Pleistocene epoch of the Cenozoic era until the present, the earth has continuously had a protohuman or human population. Man has been on earth for a matter of some million years, more or less—it being always understood that dates of this kind, when applied to geological time periods, are tentative.

The order given here, which follows that of Weidenreich, must be regarded as tentative. Especially as concerns the first three forms, there is much dispute as to their precise significance. They are given here, then, subject to such reservations as may be made regarding them by other students.

1. *Gigantopithecus blacki* ("*Gigantanthropus*").[4] Only the great molars, found in a Chinese apothecary shop in Hong Kong, represent this form. The first tooth was acquired in 1935 by von Koenigswald, a Dutch colonial officer. Later two more teeth were recovered in other apothecary shops of the same city. Because the teeth were initially considered the dentition of a giant anthropoid, the name first indicated above was given to the form.

[4] The materials on which this classification was drawn are most fully considered in G. H. R. von Koenigswald, 1952. Von Koenigswald concludes that *Gigantopithecus* "might be regarded, with reservation, as a gigantic member of the human group," but as a specialized offshoot of the human line, and not "ancestral to man" (p. 323).

However, closer examination suggested that they had belonged to a hominid and not an anthropoid form. The second name has been urged by Weidenreich as more appropriate, "if only the iron rule of scientific nomenclature" would permit the change.

2. *Meganthropus palaeojavanicus.* One and perhaps two mandibles belonging to a giant early form were recovered in 1939 and 1941 by von Koenigswald in the Sangiran district of central Java.

3. *Pithecanthropus robustus.* Found in 1938, also by von Koenigswald, at Trinil, Java, where the original *Pithecanthropus* discovery was made, this form, of which a skull cap and upper jaw have been recovered, was first regarded as a large *Pithecanthropus* male. But, after the subsequent discovery of the other *Gigantopithecus* teeth, it was given this name by Weidenreich, the better to denote its place in the evolutionary sequence.

We now move to surer ground as we consider those types for which the documentation is more adequate and concerning which there is a greater consensus of opinion.

4. *Pithecanthropus erectus.* The first hominid form to be recovered from Java, it was for almost three decades the only early form from the Far East, and served as a constant challenge to students of early man. It was discovered by Dr. Eugene Dubois, a Dutch physician, in 1891–2, and received its name "erect ape-man of Java" because its discoverer felt that its characteristics marked it as a form midway between apes and living man, something in the nature of a "missing link." Since the two series of *Pithecanthropus* remains were discovered by von Koenigswald (in 1938 and 1939), its position, as determined by considerations of comparative morphology, has been revised to give it a later place in the human evolutionary series than these giant types. Besides three skull parts, the remains now in hand consist of six femora, a mandible, and two teeth of questionable affiliation.

5. *Homo modjokertensis.* A juvenile skull, found in 1936, is difficult to assign to a place in the paleoanthropological series, since the younger the individual, the more generalized its traits and the more difficult its identification. Weidenreich believes that its place in the evolutionary scale cannot be determined "without a thorough investigation, but also in this case the answer will probably remain doubtful because of the infantile character of the specimen." [5]

6. *Sinanthropus pekinensis.* This form, first found in 1929 by W. C. Pei, reopened the whole problem of early man in the Far

[5] F. Weidenreich, 1945, p. 388.

East. As the years passed, fresh discoveries were made of this type which, well documented by the finds, became as important as *Pithecanthropus* for the understanding of the story of human evolution. Portions of the skulls of fourteen individuals, including entire brain cases, facial bones of six individuals, and long bones and teeth that give us parts of almost forty more have been recovered from a cave at Choukoutien. Its relation to *Pithecanthropus* has been remarked from the first, and it is quite likely that the two forms existed at about the same period of the Pleistocene.

7. *Homo soloensis.* A series of skulls found in 1931 near the Solo River, at the village of Ngandong, represents this form. The correspondences of this find with *Pithecanthropus* and *Sinanthropus* materials are too numerous to permit it to be sharply differentiated from them, yet there are too many differences to allow it to be placed in the same category with them. It is classed by Weidenreich as "an enlarged *Pithecanthropus* type on the way to an advanced form." He adds: "The fact that the geological level in which the Ngandong skulls were found is higher than that of the Trinil specimen also fits into this morphological picture."⁶

8. *Homo wadjakensis* (Wadjak man). The two skulls of this form were found in 1891 by Dubois, the discoverer of *Pithecanthropus*, but an account of the find was not published until 1920. They have greater cranial capacity than the earlier types and take their importance from their resemblance to the skulls of the modern aboriginal Australian, whose ancestors they have been claimed to be. This, however, remains controversial. The difficulties in assigning these skulls arise from the fact that they were badly crushed when recovered, while their discovery was announced so long after they were found that further investigation at the site was impossible.

Turning now to the west, we must, first of all, discuss a form on whose position, nature, even validity, there was never agreement, until the astounding discovery that it was "a most elaborate and carefully prepared hoax" put an end to the argument.⁷ In 1924, MacCurdy stated: "The prehistoric archaeologist sometimes uncovers strange bedfellows; no other discovery is quite so remarkable in this respect as the assemblage from Piltdown. Nature has set many a trap for the scientist, but here at Piltdown she outdid herself in the concatenation of pitfalls left behind."⁸ What he did not realize was that the trap was set by man, not nature.

⁶ F. Weidenreich, 1943, p. 274.
⁷ J. S. Weiner, K. P. Oakley, and W. E. LeGros Clark, 1953.
⁸ G. G. MacCurdy, 1924, Vol. I, p. 333.

This form, called *Eoanthropus dawsoni* (Piltdown man), was discovered in Sussex, England, in 1911–12 by Mr. Charles Dawson. Later finds, made some two miles from Piltdown in 1915, were held to validate the original remains. The great difficulty was that the cranial fragments, which if found alone would have been named those of a modern man, and are now dated as being 50,000 years old, lay near half of a lower jaw that was essentially anthropoid; fluoroscopic analysis showed it to have been that of a modern chimpanzee, skillfully colored and abraded to give the appearance of great antiquity. The difficulty of reconciling jaw and skull, as belonging to the same individual, which those who defended the appellation *Eoanthropus* (Dawn man) insisted on doing, was the basis for the controversy. The exposure of the hoax completely validates the position taken by Weidenreich in 1943, for which he was severely attacked, since he dismissed the entire find as "an artificial combination of fragments of a modern-human braincase with orang-utan-like mandible and teeth" and termed it a "chemaera" that should be "erased from the list of human fossils." [9] In actuality, as Weiner and his associates state: "The elimination of the Piltdown jaw and teeth from any further consideration clarifies very considerably the problem of human evolution." For it now seems that the line of human development moves from the bipedal *Australopithecenes*, the South African precursors of true men,[10] through *Pithecanthropus* and the other Far Eastern forms to the later types named below.

Piltdown "man" now being out of the series, we take up the progression which, in the West, tells the tale of human evolution there.

9. *Africanthropus njarasensis.* The first of the western forms is also controversial, though the dispute in this case concerns its place in the evolutionary series rather than its validity. It was found in 1935, in Tanganyika, East Africa, in a Pleistocene deposit, by a Norwegian, Kohl-Larsen. The find consisted of many fragments of several skulls. These were reconstructed by Weinert, who related the reconstructed form to the *Pithecanthropus-Sinanthropus* group. Needless to say, if this were true it would be a fact of the first order of importance. Granting the validity of

[9] F. Weidenreich, 1943, p. 220.

[10] The role of Africa in the early development of man has been underscored by the work of Dart, Broom, and others who, beginning in 1924, recovered the *Australopithecenes*, named after the first one, found by Dart, and called *Australopithecus africanus* Dart. For an early summary of South African paleoanthropology, see Galloway, 1937, and, for later developments, Barbour, 1949.

the reconstruction, however—which by no means all students do —the most that we can say is that this is morphologically an early type, which lived during the Pleistocene epoch, and which is transitional in the sense that it shares some traits with the Far Eastern early group, but more with the later Neanderthals.

10. *Homo heidelbergensis.* Though discovered in 1907, this form has taken on a new importance with time. It consists only of a large and very heavy mandible—so heavy that it most probably would have been classified as that of an ape had not the teeth also been preserved. These, and the manner in which they are set in the jaw (the "dental arch"), are, however, so definitely human that the classification of this type as *Homo* was required. Whether or not it is to be regarded as ancestral to Neanderthal man cannot be said, though this claim has been raised, and has been justifiably argued on the basis of certain traits of this jaw-bone and the teeth. The disparity between teeth and jaw, and the massiveness of this bone, make us think at once of the Far Eastern forms. With other finds that combine traits morphologically earlier and later, it indicates that such protohuman types as are represented by Heidelberg man and the Far Eastern group may have been widely distributed.

11. *Homo neanderthalensis.* We now reach the immediate forerunner of modern man, Neanderthal man. The type had many variations which, following the usage of a number of students, we may call by the name "Neanderthals." This is because no single find can be regarded as typical for the considerable number of representatives that have been discovered in localities not only widely dispersed over Europe, but in North Africa, southeastern Africa, Palestine, and central Asia. They are too numerous to describe individually. Rather, following Weidenreich, we may distinguish them as more or less falling into four subgroups, on the basis of a scale that takes into account the degree of resemblance to anthropoid forms or to modern man.

11*a.* The "Rhodesian group," represented only by the find from Broken Hill, Northern Rhodesia, in southeastern Africa. Of all the Neanderthals it lies nearest the anthropoids. Like many others, it has been a subject for controversy, but since its affiliation with the Neanderthal group has in some measure been recognized by most students, it may be regarded as a transitional form, related more closely to the Neanderthal than to any other type.

11*b.* The forms termed "Mousterian" by Morant or "Spy group" by Weidenreich, including the skulls found at La Chapelle,

La Quina, Spy, Neanderthal, Gibraltar, Krapina and Le Moustier, to name the outstanding instances.

11*c*. The "Ehringsdorf group," which besides the Ehringsdorf skull includes skulls from Tabun, from Steinheim, and other places.

11*d*. The group closest in type to modern man, including the Skhūl Mount Carmel finds of T. D. McCown and Sir Arthur Keith, and the Galilee skull. Their discoveries in the late 1920's forced the conclusion that the transition from Neanderthal man to *Homo sapiens* was gradual, and not due to the clash of two species that resulted in the extinction of the less advanced. As McGregor puts it: "The combination of definite neoanthropic (i.e., modern) with paleoanthropic features in human types which antedate the Neanderthals of western Europe . . . raises perplexing questions regarding the definition of *Homo neanderthalensis*, the relationship of the two types, and the origin of the neoanthropic type." [11]

Neanderthal remains were first found in 1848, at Gibraltar. Their real significance was not recognized until much later, and this particular specimen was not studied in detail until 1936. The find that gave the type its name was recovered in 1856, in a cave of the Neanderthal ravine near Düsseldorf, Germany. It was recognized as a new species and named in 1864, though the dispute over whether this was a pathological example of modern man or an early human type went on for many years. Today, with parts of more than one hundred individuals at hand, long bones as well as skulls, the type is well enough known so that not only have reconstructions been made of its head, but of the entire body, both male and female Neanderthal having been sculptured.

The career of this form on the earth was a long one. The earliest examples of Neanderthal remains that can be dated by the geological strata from which they were recovered are about one hundred thousand years old, the latest some twenty-five thousand years. The span of time during which the Neanderthal types lived was thus far greater than the period that has elapsed since the most recent specimen died. It is therefore apparent why the line of division between the Neanderthals and their successors, the Cro-Magnon men, is to be loosely drawn. The best opinion now holds that crossing between these two types was not only possible, but probably occurred to a considerable degree. This hypothesis is borne out by the fact that in museum and laboratory

[11] J. H. McGregor, 1938, p. 68.

skull collections, specimens of present-day individuals appear with distinct Neanderthaloid traits that have been carried by persons whose physical characteristics while living were not measurably distinct from the others among whom they lived. It is now beyond dispute that the first *sapiens* type to appear, Cro-Magnon man, was for long generations a contemporary of the Neanderthal types who, on the basis of comparative morphology, are their immediate ancestors.

What kind of creatures were these Neanderthals? Even with the variations in the many specimens of this type we have, they are homogeneous enough to be described in terms of average values, much as living races are described. Neanderthal man was short, about five feet three inches tall. He was somewhat stooped and walked with semiflexed knees, which means that he did not attain completely upright posture. He was heavy-set, with a short, thick neck. Whether he was hairy, as restorations depict him, or not, cannot be said, since hair, like soft parts, completely disappears with the passage of time. He had a large head, characterized by a rugged skull, a low forehead, marked brow ridges and a heavy, chinless jaw. His nose was broad, and the orbits of his eyes were large and deeply set in the skull. On first glance there is a temptation to associate his receding forehead with small brain-size, but this is not justified by the facts. The capacity of his cranium, which varies between 1220 and 1610 cubic centimeters, in general exceeds that of modern man both in range and on the average.

12. *Cro-Magnon.* Our final prehistoric type, is the equivalent of living man in every respect. It takes its name from the rock shelter at the village of Les Eyzies, in southern France where, in 1868, the original discovery of this form was made. There was never any question but that it was an early manifestation of *Homo sapiens*, whose career on earth has been regarded as antedating this form since the discovery in 1935, at Swanscombe, England, of parts of a skull, which lay in a middle Pleistocene deposit. Swanscombe man, if not *Homo sapiens*, was at least closer to modern man than the Neanderthal forms.[12] Since the original discovery of Cro-Magnon, much more skeletal material and skulls of this type have been excavated, so that we have a fully adequate idea of its physical characteristics. The males were tall, some of them reaching six feet. They were considerably taller than the female Cro-Magnons seem to have been, even when the sex differences in stature are compared to those between the sexes in mod-

[12] G. M. Morant and others, 1938.

ern humans. Their average cranial capacity was larger than the average for modern man. The forehead was high, the chin prominent, and the facial angle upright (orthognathous), in striking contrast to the jutting maxillae and jaws of earlier prognathous forms.

What transitions from these earlier forms gave rise to present-day races we cannot say. Some students relate Cro-Magnon to the Caucasoid (European) type, which, in truth, he most resembles. The Negroid race is on occasion referred to ancestral forms represented by the Grimaldi skeletons, unearthed in 1874–5 near Monaco. Certainly these, and the mixed Neanderthal–Cro-Magnon remains, excavated at Brünn and Předmost in Czechoslovakia show that even some twenty-five thousand years ago the variations in the physical types of men then existing were pronounced. Weidenreich holds that the racial divisions of mankind reach back into middle Pleistocene periods. He speaks of a "continuous line leading from *Pithecanthropus* through *Homo soloensis* and fossil Australian forms to certain modern primitive Australian races. Rhodesian man seems to be linked, through types like the Florisbad Man, to certain South African races of today." [13] The implications of such an argument for the importance of racial differences are far reaching, but these conclusions are still conjectural. Thus while Dobzhansky,[14] on the basis of these findings, argues that all races of living men belong to a single species, Ruggles Gates,[15] using the same data, holds that present-day races represent distinct species.

4

Certain conclusions from this brief discussion may be pointed out before we proceed to consider the development of culture in prehistoric times. We may, first of all, reaffirm the proposition of the complexity of the process of human development, that makes for many difficulties when we seek to establish more than its broadest outlines. It is clear, however, that this developmental process began with more or less anthropoid-like forms. On the basis of the study of his hominid ancestry, no less than from the comparative analysis of present-day anthropoid and human forms, man is seen to be a full-fledged member of the biological series.

This is perceived when comparative figures for such an important index of humanness as cranial capacity are considered. It

[13] F. Weidenreich, 1943, p. 276.
[14] T. Dobzhansky, 1944, *passim*.
[15] 1944, *passim*.

will be remembered that the development of a larger brain, indicated by the size of the brain case, is one of the most significant traits that mark man as different from other forms. Cranial capacity is especially useful for comparative purposes, since the calvarium, the top part of the skull, has been found more frequently and in a better state of preservation, than those other more fragile bones that make up the skeleton of the face, or elements of the skeletal structure of the body and the extremities.

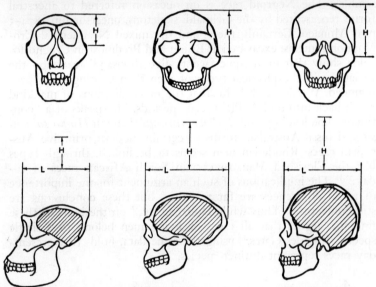

Fig. 3 *Skulls of gorilla,* Sinanthropus, *and* Homo sapiens *(Chinese), showing differences in height and length of skull. (Adapted from Weidenreich, 1946, Figs. 9 and 32.)*

We may again turn to Weidenreich's study for a compilation of the cranial capacity of various hominid and human types.

	Minimum-Maximum Values	Average
Anthropoids	300– 585 cc.	415 cc.
Pithecanthropus	775– 900	860
Sinanthropus	915–1,225	1,043
Homo soloensis	1,035–1,255	1,100
Neanderthals	1,220–1,610	1,400
Modern man	1,225–1,540	1,300 [16]

[16] F. Weidenreich, 1943, p. 120. Weidenreich does not state where he derives this last average. R. Martin, whose work is the standard manual of

Or, as another example of this consistency of change, the index between the height of the skull (at the vertex) and its length may be cited. Here, the greater height of the head is indicated by the larger figure; the low skull, almost without any forehead, being characteristic of the anthropoids in contrast to man.

	Minimum-Maximum Values	Average
Anthropoids	50.6–56.2	54.0
Pithecanthropus II	....	64.2
Sinanthropus	67.7–71.6	69.4
Homo soloensis	65.5–74.6	69.0
Neanderthals	64.4–92.0	77.7
Modern man	84.3–98.4	91.0 [17]

Certain traits manifest the characteristics of modern man earlier than others. The teeth, for example, become humanoid long before the jaw. Yet, for still other traits, such as the facial

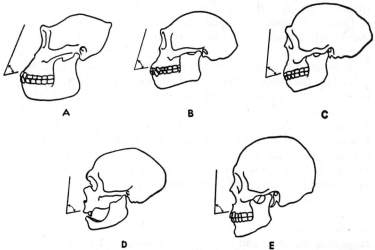

Fig. 4 *Increase of facial angle from anthropoids through hominids to* Homo. **(A)** *female gorilla;* **(B)** Pithecanthropus erectus; **(C)** Sinanthropus pekinensis; **(D)** *Neanderthal (La Chapelle aux Saints);* **(E)** Homo sapiens *(modern Chinese).*

physical anthropology, gives (p. 746) larger maxima and minima and states the averages for Europeans to be 1450 cc. for males and 1300 cc. for females. Weidenreich himself (1946, p. 94) recognizes this larger average, mentioning the figure of 1500 cc. for "modern man," but feels that this is "much higher" than the "1300 cc. for males when all races are included."

[17] *Ibid.*, p. 121.

angle, or the prominence of brow ridges, or a more and more erect posture as indicated by the leg bones, the later specimens are successively closer to modern man than the older ones.

We must take care, however, not to think of this developmental process in terms of "lower" to "higher," or use any analogous series of evaluative concepts. It will be remarked that in our discussion even the use of such a word as "primitive," a valid term when employed to denote earlier biological forms in comparison with later ones, has been avoided.

Above all, this long and fascinating tale of human evolution is not to be correlated with the successive changes in culture that we shall consider in the following chapter. Only when we approach this relation in the broadest terms is even an approximation of such a correlation to be found, and it is questionable whether it exists even then. This is what Movius implies when he lays stress on the fact that "the field of archaeology, though it utilizes and synthesizes the conclusions of the natural sciences, is directly related to the social sciences." [18] Even such an early form as *Pithecanthropus* developed a technique of making stone implements, while *Sinanthropus* knew the use of fire. In Europe, while graphic art showed a steady development during the Upper Paleolithic, it disappeared at the onset of the Neolithic, to be replaced by the crudest kind of aesthetic expression. So independent of each other were physical and cultural changes, indeed, that some students stress the fact that culture, as expressed in stone artifacts, remained relatively stable in contrast to the many different hominid forms that made these implements; but that, in the comparatively brief period since the appearance of *Homo sapiens*, culture has so proliferated that present ways of life may lie beyond the powers of human control.

Without going into the merits of either position, it can be stated that the story of man's development affords but few materials for those who would correlate physical type and culture. We recognize that man had need of the brains, the tongue, the hands to create and manipulate culture. Once begun, however, the process of culture-building continued on the basis of learning and not of instinct. And this means that, at any given moment, the cultures even of the early forms comprised bodies of accepted modes of behavior which, developing out of their own traditional bases, equipped the human groups who lived in accordance with them to meet the demands of the natural and psychological setting in which they moved.

[18] H. L. Movius, Jr., 1944, p. 8.

Chapter **Three**

The Prehistoric Development of Culture

In reconstructing the physical development of man, the student can call upon the logic of structure and the regularity of the evolutionary process to help him in his difficult task. No such aid is at hand when the prehistoric development of culture is studied. When a flaked flint point is found in the earth, it can mean no more than that a human being was present either to make it or to use it. But what it was used for, or how, can merely be conjectured. It might have been hafted to a long thin stick and employed as an arrow, or it might have been thrown by hand, or used to make fire, or it might even have been an object of ceremonial usage.

This range of variation in the employment of man-made objects, or *artifacts*, as they are termed in archaeology, is only a beginning of the problems faced by the prehistorian in his quest for an understanding of the origin and development of culture. This is why it is imperative to understand when conclusions are based on fact, and when they are but hypotheses based on inference from the facts.

An example will make the difference clear. Deep in the cave

of Trois Frères, in the Dordogne region of southern France, is a famous wall painting of the Magdalenian period, perhaps twenty thousand years old. In the reproduction given here, it is to be seen that this figure stands erect on human feet, for all its stag's antlers, head and body. The remoteness of the gallery where it was made, the fact that it is high on the wall, that people did not live in this gallery have caused archaeologists to speculate whether it was not a symbol to control supernatural forces. So reasonable does this seem, that the figure has become known as a worker of magic, and has been named "Le Sorcier de Trois Frères."

What are the facts? The painting exists, and its remoteness is a fact. That the cave was not used for human occupancy is a reliable deduction from fact, since evidence of occupancy in the gallery, such as the remains of fire or gnawed bones are absent. The rest is inference, based on the customs of present-day, living "primitive" peoples. Yet we read in popularized versions of prehistory that the Magdalenian folk who occupied the cave of Trois Frères are known to have practiced magic!

Inference is a workable and useful tool if held within its limitations. Thus in caves inhabited during the Mousterian epoch, remains of fire are found to a great depth. In some of these caves, human skeletons are present. On some of the bones are flecks of red ocher, while the thighbone of a horse and a beautifully worked flint implement were also recovered in association with one such skeleton. The depth of the ash could only mean that the cave was consistently inhabited over a very long period of time. The further inference is irresistible, that the inhabitants, in order to leave remains of fire to this depth, formed a social group that also existed continuously over a very long period. The position of the skeleton indicates that it was buried at the place it was found. The ocher, obviously, must have settled on the bones after the flesh had disintegrated. This means that the body was decorated before it was buried. The horse's thigh and the stone implement were also obviously buried with it. We may assume, then, that, as with many living peoples, the purpose of these objects was to provide food and protection for the dead. Since the cult of the dead figures as an integral part of religion over most of the world, and can consequently be assumed to have had a long existence, we may infer that some form of belief concerning life after death, and thus some type of religious concept, existed at this early date.

However, it must be stressed that, in assuming a social group living in our cave over many generations, no claim has been made whether a man had one wife or a number of them; whether a woman had one husband or several; whether there was any family life at all; or whether the entire group lived promiscuously. Such a matter as the position in this society of the individual whose burial we have noted we likewise can never know; we cannot even

Fig. 5 *The "Sorcerer" of the cave of Trois Frères, Ariège, France. (After MacCurdy, 1924, Fig. 151, from photograph by Count Begouin.)*

speculate with profit on whether he was a secular chief or a religious leader. Nor can we make assumptions concerning the nature of the beliefs these people may have had. There are only the cave, the ashes, the bones, the artifact. They argue a social life and formal disposal of the body of at least the individual whose remains were found.

In essence, then, we perceive that, except by inference, prehistoric archaeology can tell us no more than the story of the development of man's physical type and of certain aspects of his *material* culture. The intangibles that are so large a proportion of human civilization can never be recovered. Even in the realm of material objects, our knowledge for earlier periods is restricted to things fashioned of inorganic matter. Primeval man often inhabited caves, but he also lived in open country. Did he have skin tents? Did he use skins at all? Did he make utensils of wood? Until a chance find of some fossilized implement made of organic material provides an answer to such questions, we can do no more than speculate about them.

All the more remarkable, then, that the archaeologists have been able, with such fragmentary data, to give us in so short a time a picture of the development of man and his culture. That blank spaces exist in the picture, especially where the development of culture in specific areas is in question, does not detract from this achievement. Enough is known of the story of man's prehistoric past to warrant all confidence that, in its principal outlines, no serious revision of the tale, as thus far written, will have to be made. That early prehistoric sites have been investigated more extensively in Europe than in other parts of the world is only a reflection of the fact that archaeologists, whose studies are but a part of the broader stream of Euroamerican scientific thought, found it easier to work at home than abroad. This is why so much of the archaeological data from Paleolithic times comes from France, for it was here that scientific prehistory developed, and where, among the rich sites available for study, research has been most intensively cultivated. By the same token, and for the same reasons, the archaeology of the Americas is incomparably better known than that of Africa.

2

It has not been found possible to devise a single series of classifications to cover all prehistoric cultures. As in all studies of prehistoric phenomena, the timetable on which reliance must be placed to order our data is phrased in terms of geological epochs. In Europe the various glaciations left deposits that afford a convenient chronology. But such a timetable does not exist for many other parts of the world, notably the tropics. Furthermore, as we have seen in discussing the unfolding tale of human physical development, additional discoveries make for added complexities. As a result, periods that were at first set up on the basis of European prehistory and were long held to be applicable everywhere were found not to hold for Africa or Asia, to say nothing of the New World where, as we shall see, human occupancy has been relatively recent.

One of the best statements of the difficulty of establishing world-wide sequences has been given by Movius, who says:

> The material brought to light during the last ten years in Asia has opened up a new approach to the problem of Palaeolithic archaeology. . . . Since the classic Western European sequence is absent in the Far East, it is clear that, at the dawn of the Lower Palaeolithic, we have to deal with independent groups of . . . cultures that have followed different patterns of growth. In each, the basic rate of change, as judged by the technique of manufacture and form of the stone tools used over a span of perhaps five hundred thousand years, varies enormously.[1]

As a consequence, in the Lower Paleolithic, he differentiates East and West in terms of what he has called the "hand-ax cultures" of the West and the "chopping-tool cultures" of the East, deriving his classification from the imperishable implements that alone have been preserved out of the total cultural equipment of the early peoples of these two great areas.

The accepted classification of prehistoric cultures for many years was drawn in terms of Paleolithic (Old Stone), Mesolithic (Transitional), Neolithic (New Stone) ages, and the Bronze and Iron ages. The Paleolithic was in turn divided into Lower, Middle, and Upper. Work from 1925 onward, however, has tended to show that even for Europe such a classification, employed in the customary sense, is not valid. Garrod says:

> In the old system, the palaeolithic cultures appeared as a straightforward succession with clear-cut horizontal divisions as in a diagrammatic geological section. For the pioneers of prehistory these cultures developed logically one from the other in an orderly upward movement, and it was assumed that they represented world-wide stages in the history of human progress. Today prehistory has suffered the fate of so many of the component parts of the orderly universe of the nineteenth century. New knowledge has given a twist to the kaleidoscope, and the pieces are still falling about before our bewildered eyes. The main outline of the new pattern is, however, already beginning to appear. We can distinguish in the Old Stone Age three cultural elements of primary importance. These are manifested in the so-called hand-axe industries, flake industries, and blade indus-

[1] H. L. Movius, Jr., 1944, pp. 104–5.

tries, and we know that the first two, at any rate, run side by side as far back as we can see, and we are beginning to realize that the origins of the third may have to be sought much farther back than we had suspected. Only a moment of reflection is needed to see that we have here the old divisions of Lower, Middle, and Upper Palaeolithic, but with a new axis; we must be careful, however, not to make these divisions too rigid. In fact, these culture-streams do not run parallel and independent; such a view of human history would be absurdly artificial. They are perpetually meeting and influencing each other, and sometimes they come together to produce a new facies." [2]

We may thus consider the prehistoric development of human culture in western Europe as one instance of the process by means of which man reached the condition of life in which he is discovered as the curtain of history rises. For thousands of generations he lived without domesticated animals, or the wheel, or agriculture, or pottery, to say nothing of metal tools. It took hundreds upon hundreds of generations for man to learn to put a decent edge on a flint knife. Millennia went by before his aesthetic impulses had even the crudest means of expression in enduring form.

The table of prehistoric correlations given on page 38 should be continually consulted during our discussion. It includes both the older terminology and the revisions that later research has introduced. As will be apparent from our table, the most drastic revisions of terminology have come in designating the periods of the Paleolithic. This is not only, as the citation from Garrod indicates, because, as in all scientific research, the persistent search for the solution to a problem reveals new facets of that problem and causes earlier solutions to be recognized as inadequate in the light of more abundant data. In addition, a more specific factor has been operative in the case of European prehistory, the growing realization that the prehistorian does not study *cultures*, but *industries*. This was forced by the nature of the data; the fact that the intangibles in the early life of man cannot be recovered, so that only the things made in imperishable materials are available for study.

The primary kinds of tools found in Paleolithic sites fall into three categories. For the earlier and longer part of the epoch, *core* (chopping) and *flake* types are present. The characteristic implement of the later portion is the *blade*. It is on the basis of the predominance of one or the other of these types—for none is exclusively present in any period—that the newer nomenclature has

[2] Dorothy A. E. Garrod, 1938, p. 1.

been worked out. By this means, an over-all series of designations for prehistoric data has been reached within which local variants, named after specific sites, can be discerned or, in the future, can be designated in accordance with later finds.

Childe has given one of the clearest short descriptions of the techniques of flint-working that produced these basic forms. "Core tools," he says, "were made by knocking bits off a large lump or *core* until this was reduced to one of four or five standard

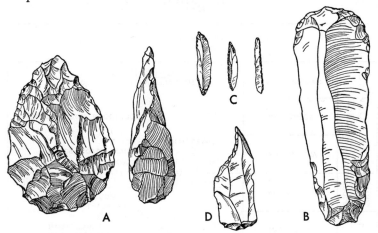

Fig. 6 *Core, flake, and blade tools.* **(A)** *Acheulean hand-axe;* **(B)** *Aurignacian end scraper;* **(C)** *Aurignacian backed blades;* **(D)** *graver. (After Burkitt, 1933, and Leakey, 1934.)*

forms. The products can all be classified as *core* tools and are currently designated hand-axes." Of *flake tools*, he says: "Their makers do not seem to have cared much what shape was ultimately assumed by the parent lump or core; they were primarily interested in the flakes detached and trimmed these up to form implements less rigorously standardized than hand-axes." With the passage of time, skills increased, and the nodule off which pieces were struck was preworked so as to yield implements of greater precision and efficiency. During the Upper Paleolithic man "had learned to prepare a lump of flint or obsidian so that a whole series of long narrow flakes, termed blades, could be struck off a single core once the long preliminaries had been executed." Typical of these periods, too, was the *burin* or graver, "a blade pointed by removing a facet along one edge in such a way that it can be repeatedly repointed by simply removing another facet." [3]

[3] V. G. Childe, 1946, p. 24, pp. 29–30.

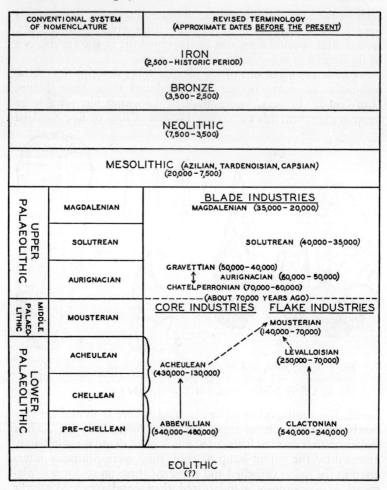

CONVENTIONAL SYSTEM OF NOMENCLATURE		REVISED TERMINOLOGY (APPROXIMATE DATES BEFORE THE PRESENT)
IRON (2,500 – HISTORIC PERIOD)		
BRONZE (3,500 – 2,500)		
NEOLITHIC (7,500 – 3,500)		
MESOLITHIC (AZILIAN, TARDENOISIAN, CAPSIAN) (20,000 – 7,500)		

Fig. 7 *The prehistory of western Europe. (After Garrod, Zeuner, Braidwood, and others.)*

3

The beginnings of human culture are matters of great controversy. The eoliths, or "dawn-stones," found on the continent of Europe and in England, and named in the 1880's, have never received the same acceptance as tools made and used by early man that is granted the artifacts of later prehistoric cultures. The question is whether these objects were actually made and used by man, or were merely shaped by the elements into what seemed to be the forms of crude tools.

There is no question, however, that human beings manufactured the tools found in later archaeological horizons. The earliest artifacts are crude, indeed. Some of these hand-axes and flakes closely resemble naturally fractured stones. Hand-axes are large and unwieldy; their edges and points exist more by definition than functionally. As we move into later stages of the *Lower Paleolithic*, however, hand-axes become smaller and better balanced; they fit the hand, and they have an edge and a point that make them recognizably useful for incising and cutting. Early flaking-tools also have a crudity that is quite comparable to the crudeness of the earliest core-tools. It is obvious that flakes must come from stone nodules, but it is by no means certain that the first flakes were by-products of a core industry. Clactonian tools are primarily flakes, as Abbevillian tools are primarily cores. But the Clactonian flakers were apparently little interested in the cores from which the flakes came. As time goes on, the flakes, like the cores, reflect growing skill in the techniques of their preparation and manufacture.

The stages that for Europe have variously been termed the *pre-Chellean* and *Chellean* or *Abbevillian*, the *Acheulean*, and the *Clactonian* and *Levalloisian*, lasted for periods variously estimated at from half a million to a quarter of a million years. What life was like in those times, with their alternations of cold and warm climates as the glaciers advanced and retreated, is not known. That the early beings who made these implements had the ability to learn can be seen by inspecting in any museum a sequence of artifacts of the Lower Paleolithic. But of the broad repertory of culture as we know it, we cannot hint even as to the basic forms of economic life, except sparsely, and in negative terms. That is, we can say with confidence that the early European Lower Paleolithic beings did not have fire, or the remains of ash would have been present where they lived. They had no domesticated animals or plants, for the faunal remains are those of wild forms only. They were hunters and gatherers of fruits, nuts, roots, and berries, like all those who lived later during the Paleolithic.

The *Mousterian*, which was also conventionally called the *Middle Paleolithic*, is now known to include a number of differentiated industries. The "typical" Mousterian takes its name from the rock shelters in the Dordogne region of southern France, from which came so much important material bearing on the prehistory of Europe. It will be remembered that the Mousterian, as earlier conceived, was the culture of Neanderthal man, who is so closely associated with this form that the name "Mousterian man" has been suggested for him. The use of the striking platform on the prepared nodules made possible the production of the smaller, more finely shaped hand-axes that mark their ultimate form, before they gave way entirely to different tools, some of which were made out of different materials.

The number of sites, the length of time many of these sites were occupied, the remains of fauna, and the disposition of skeletal materials permit us to infer much about other aspects of life at this time. It is plain that the people were hunters, and that, hav-

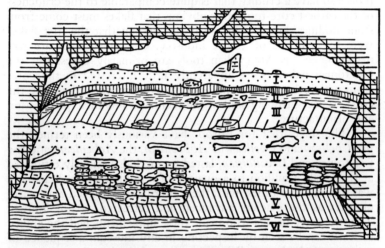

Fig. 8 *Cave at Drachenloch.* **(A)** *Hearth with charcoal;* **(B)** *"altar" with cave-bear skulls;* **(C)** *flat stones. The various strata indicated by Roman numerals presumably bear the remains of different periods of occupation. I and VI have no artifacts. (After Mac-Curdy and Bächler.)*

ing the use of fire, their livelihood was more assured than it would have been without fire. It is possible, from the position and location of certain skeletal and cultural remains of the period that have been found in association, to infer a belief in life in an afterworld. Of similar significance would seem to be the remains of cave-bear skulls, arranged somewhat like an altar, in the cavern of Drachenloch, high above the present snow line in the Swiss Alps. In this cavern, too, we come on some of the earliest European bone tools. Cave-bear fibulae seem to have been favored. They were broken in two, the broken surface polished, and the joint used as a handle. Still other bones, marked by use, could have served as vessels for holding liquids and are found in quantity, while bone splinters were employed as points.

4

As we move to the *Upper Paleolithic,* the stone technique becomes refined through the utilization of blades, and core tools virtually disappear. The production of blades becomes more and more precise, until we find tiny pieces of flint, some less than half an inch long, an eighth of an inch or less wide, retouched by subsidiary flaking to give a fine edge and a sharp point—a far cry from the crudities of the Lower Paleolithic. Bone and ivory were used for such specialized implements as harpoons, while it may be assumed that some of the small flint points may have been set in wooden or bone clubs or staves to make composite weapons or implements.

The period represents a broadening and deepening of human resources that go beyond the use of stone and the introduction of bone and ivory tools. The environment in which the Cro-Magnon men of the period lived was cruel. This was the height of the final glaciation, and these people had to cope with such animals as the mammoth, the woolly rhinoceros, the cave-bear, cave-lion, cave-hyena, wild boar, and other great beasts. Implements that look like spear throwers have been found, probably used to propel barbed harpoons. Deep deposits of debris and ash in the inhabited caves show that caves afforded protection against both weather and predatory animals. The people probably clothed themselves with the skins of the beasts they killed, and their clothing may even have been sewed, since buttons and toggles have been recovered from Magdalenian sites, while awls and bone needles are also present. Not all these are found throughout the Upper Paleolithic, of course. Each of its periods, moreover, is marked by different features in its lithic industry. Among *Aurignacian* tools (*Chatelperronian and Gravettian*), end scrapers and side scrapers predominate; the *Solutrean* produced the beautiful, delicate "laurel-leaf" flints, with overall flaking on both sides; the many specialized implements of the *Magdalenian,* and its bone and ivory work, are noteworthy.

The greatest achievement of the Upper Paleolithic in Europe, however, was its art. Before this time no embellishment of artifact is to be found, no attempt to depict any object on walls of caves, no scratching of lines to make a crude design. How the superb accomplishments of the Upper Paleolithic artists began, and where they had their origin, are unknown. The three-dimensional figurines of the Aurignacian, which are among the earliest specimens, represent a sureness in the handling of form and the organization of mass that few modern sculptors surpass. These figurines disappear with the epoch, and no developmental sequence has been established for them. Pictorial art, on the other hand, shows a gradual development from crude outline drawings or more skilled sketches to the impressive realistic cave paintings, in color, of bison, reindeer, and mammoth. The Aurignacian "Venuses" are especially interesting figures, always representing the female form, the secondary sexual characteristics accentuated, the long curled hair occasionally depicted, the face never modeled realistically.

Fig. 9 *Line drawing, showing superimposition of cave paintings of the Magdalenian period. To be seen in this figure are bison, mammoth, horse, and reindeer. (After MacCurdy, 1924, Fig. 130.)*

Drawing and painting show a longer development, and a more orderly one, than sculpture. Yet they, too, are cut off at their zenith. For when the Magdalenian is ended its art disappears, to give way to the scratchings and crude daubs of the Mesolithic.[4] We see, when we follow through this art, how the earliest attempts tried, with but little success, to master the problem of

[4] Further aspects of the development of this art, and some of the problems in art theory it poses, are considered in Chap. 13.

perspective.[5] The polychrome paintings of the Magdalenian, despite the fact that like the drawings they are at times superimposed on one another, have the faithfulness of portraiture. Incised representations on reindeer bone show the animal with its head turned backward—a difficult design element to master—while on certain wands we find a full-face, head-on engraving of various animals. An impressionistic technique was also employed to represent whole herds of reindeer or wild horses.

Because the subject matter of the paintings is almost exclusively animal, these representations have been explained by referring to the concepts of sympathetic magic that are today found among many living peoples. The paintings are thus thought of as having been endowed, under terms of the concept of "like to like," with the "essence" of the beasts they depicted. Magic rites performed in their presence, this theory runs, would ensure success later in the hunt. It is a good theory, but has little to support it except reference to customs practiced many hundreds of generations and thousands of miles removed from where the paintings were made. The theories of art for art's sake, or of a prohibition against depicting animals, which drove these artists deep into the caverns to work in secret, offer alternatives that are perhaps less acceptable. Such alternatives, however, are supported by exactly the same amount of objective evidence—that is, none at all—as the explanation in terms of magic.

The *Mesolithic* has been regarded as a transitional period between the Paleolithic when, in the terms used by the early archaeologists, stone was chipped, and the Neolithic, when stone was polished. This classification was one of the first to break down, however, for Magdalenian deposits yield polished implements, while perhaps the finest overall flaked artifacts ever made were manufactured during the Neolithic in Scandinavia. Moreover, the Mesolithic is distinguished neither for its polished nor chipped implements, though both are present. Its outstanding form is the tiny microlithic flake, retouched, and set in bone or perhaps wooden spears as darts, or used for other purposes. The bone industry continues, though it declines in importance, and ivory disappears with its source, the great mammoths that inhabited Europe during the Ice ages. The glaciers were receding, and like the reindeer, these great beasts followed them, the reindeer to continue in Northern Europe and Asia, the mammoth to wander northeast to extinction.

In this "transitional" period, also, as we have noted, art forms

[5] See Pl. 11 and Figs. 27-33, 35-9, below.

degenerate and disappear. Painting is reduced to a few geometric figures, and to designs on pebbles. Some have said that the painted pebbles foreshadowed the alphabet, others have again referred to religion—divining—for explanation, and still others have held them to have been some game of chance. The Mesolithic, represented by the Azilian in Southern France, the Tardenoisian in Central France, the Maglemosean on the island of Zealand in Denmark, may perhaps some day come to be thought of as a series of

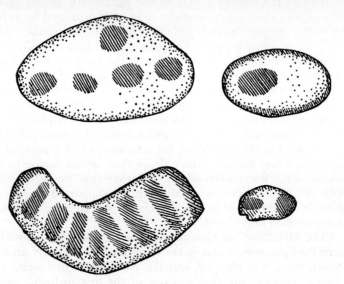

Fig. 10 *Painted pebbles of the Azilian (Mesolithic) period. (Drawn from specimens in the Chicago Natural History Museum.)*

local developments that represent an extension of the Upper Paleolithic. As Movius puts it:

> In a positive sense the Mesolithic defines a stage in cultural development basically founded on the economy of the Upper Palaeolithic, but profoundly modified by the changes in environment induced by the recession of the ice at the close of the Glacial Period. . . . With the coming-in of the new food-producing Neolithic civilization, bringing its associated elements —pottery, domestication of animals, agriculture and polished stone—there is a break in the sequence. Certain elements from the earlier phase, however, continued in use, as no new forms displaced them, but these cannot be regarded as evolutionary. Instead, they represent the survival of types of implements for

which there was still a need and in place of which no innovations were introduced by the new culture.[6]

With the *Neolithic*, the richness of the archaeological record makes it possible to reconstruct a fuller picture of material culture, and to infer much more about the nonmaterial aspects of life than for earlier periods. Neolithic culture, indeed, would not be too strange to many persons living in Europe today; and it has even been said that the peasant of Eastern and Central Europe would find himself more at home in a Neolithic settlement than in a modern industrial city. The plants raised for food, and even the manner of raising them, would be familiar to him. The animals on his farm would all be about, available for similar purposes. Spinning and weaving, the construction of houses, and the making of pottery would be going on. The flint-working technique would be unknown to him, but he would find certain of the metal tools he is accustomed to using, in stone or bone—knives, axes, chisels, sickle blades, and weapons such as daggers and spears. He would find the mining industry devoted to producing flint, with miners working in underground tunnels, using picks of antler-horn to detach nodules to be worked later. He would be able to utilize well-established trade-routes. For example, Pressigny, where a kind of "beeswax" flint was mined, was a trading center which sent this distinctive type of flint over all of what is now France, and eastward as far as Switzerland. He might encounter strange forms of religious worship, though the cult of the dead would offer familiar associations. The great megalithic monuments, called "dolmens" or "menhirs," such as are found at Stonehenge in England or Carnac in France, could not but impress him.

In the *Bronze* and *Iron Ages*, the complexity of cultural development becomes ever more clear. As is the case with the introduction of writing, which opens the historic period, we find that the use of metal appears at different times in various parts of Europe and the Near East. The discovery of the use of metal was one of the major developments of human history. With the continuing mastery of this technique, man diminished the degree of his dependence upon his natural setting and thus achieved new adaptations to his environment. But the productivity that the use of metals permitted did more than release human societies from the immediate pressure of their habitat. With other techniques, such as irrigation, it made possible an increase in the goods produced beyond anything previously possessed, and thus opened

[6] H. L. Movius, Jr., 1942, p. xxiii.

the way to the production of what we term an "economic surplus." In this manner, the basis was laid for the differences in the control of wealth that underlie class structures wherever found. It was the Bronze and Iron Ages, in short, that set the stage for the cultures we encounter as the curtain of history rises.

5

We have devoted the preceding sections to tracing the development of the prehistoric cultures of Western Europe because of the availability for study of the longest series of successive industries and the cultures associated with them. However, this series must not be given world-wide application. As Movius says:

> Since prehistoric archaeology is . . . by itself utterly incapable of establishing a reliable system of Pleistocene chronology on the basis of a classification of the types of implements found in a given series of deposits, the more exacting disciplines of the natural sciences cannot be applied to it. . . . Far from being constant, human culture is an extremely variable factor; man was repeatedly faced with new situations and he was continually experimenting with new methods of adapting his way of life to the environmental factors which confronted him.[7]

We see how pertinent these qualifications are when we shift our attention from the European scene to other continents. We have indicated how, in the Far East, the category of core (chopping) and flake tools has been employed. Both the sequences in which the tools are found, and the local terms applied to these sequences, however, call for fresh mastery by the specialist in European archaeology. The series of "three stages" of Stone, Bronze, and Iron Ages is interrupted in Negro Africa by a transition to metal-working which, except for Egypt, entirely omits any period when bronze was used. Again, the pictographic art of Africa, which falls quite outside the problem of succession of industries, offers many difficulties. Similarities of treatment between modern Bushmen rock paintings and those in some of the caves in Spain and France have often been noted. A chain of pictographs disclosing many common features stretches the length of the African continent. Since paintings of this type found in Europe are Upper Paleolithic, are the cultures of modern African Bushmen to be classified as belonging to this epoch? Or, to turn elsewhere, are the contemporary "stone-age" cultures of Australia and New Guinea to be classed with European counterparts that

[7] *Ibid., pp.* 106–7.

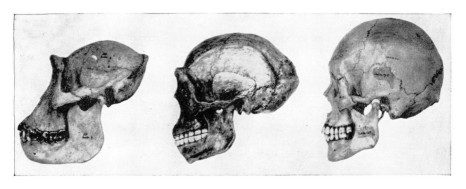

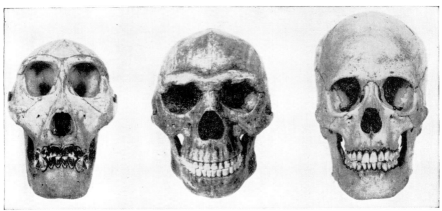

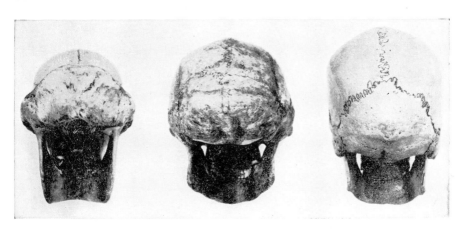

Plate 2a *Evolutionary changes in the skull. Left to right, female gorilla, female of*
Sinanthropus pekinensis, *modern man (male) from North China, lateral view. See
p. 22.* **Plate 2b** *Same skulls as in Pl. 2a, front view. See p. 22.* **Plate 2c** *Same skulls
as in Pl. 2a, rear (occipital) view. See p. 22. (Photographs courtesy F. Weidenreich
and American Museum of Natural History, New York; cf. also F. Weidenreich,
1946, Figs. 9, 32, and 33.)*

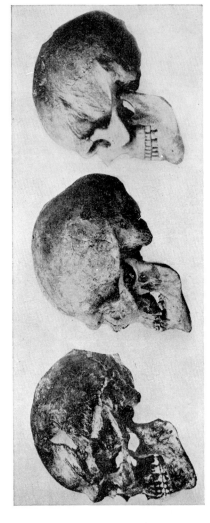

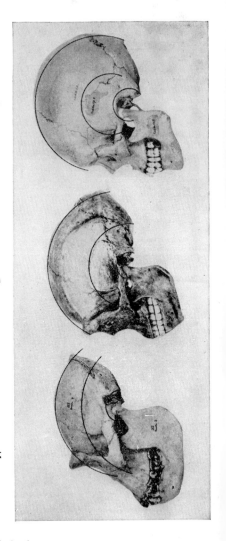

Plate 3a *Upper Paleolithic skulls, lying structurally between Palestine finds and modern man. (A) Male, from Předmostí; (B) male, from Beni-Segoual (Algiers); and (C) male from Obercassel. See p. 27.* **Plate 3b** *(A) Gorilla; (B) Sinanthropus; and (C) modern skulls in lateral view, with circles at identical levels, showing tendency of human skull to assume globular form. See p. 28. (Photographs courtesy F. Weidenreich and American Museum of Natural History, New York; cf. also F. Weidenreich, 1946, Figs. 36 and 42.)*

existed a thousand generations earlier, on the basis of the forms of stone implements these people make? One archaeologist, W. J. Sollas, has seriously proposed such affinities and, on similar grounds, has also equated the Eskimo with the Magdalenian peoples.

The archaeology of the Americas offers perhaps the best example of how different areas pose different problems and demand different nomenclatures. When Europeans first came into contact with the aboriginal Indians, the Indians were a full stone-age people. Some could be classified as Paleolithic, as, for the example, the Paiute; some, like the Iroquois, as Neolithic. These terms are occasionally encountered in the older literature. Yet all Indian tribes, whether their stonework was crude or finished, had domesticated plants and thus knew agriculture, which in Europe is a Neolithic trait. On the other hand, except for the dog, the turkey, the llama, and the vicuña, the Indians had no domesticated animals, despite the fact that in Europe the domestication of plants and animals occurred at about the same time.

During the thousands of years that the prehistoric physical types and cultures of the Old World were developing, the New World remained uninhabited by man and his forebears, or by any primates except certain monkeys. Some human remains that have been found in association with extinct Pleistocene animal forms have forced the reconsideration of the date earlier accepted for the coming of man to the Americas. This was originally placed at about ten thousand years ago. It is now argued, however, that the migration may have occurred during the last glaciation, in late Pleistocene times, perhaps fifteen to twenty thousand years ago. But none of the forms that reach to this earlier epoch is prehuman; as a matter of fact, none is markedly different from the Indian of today.

It is generally agreed that the ancestors of the American Indians reached their new habitat over the Bering Straits and the Aleutian Islands, though there are those who press the claim of some migration across the Pacific. The contributions of the Pacific islands to the peopling of the Americas must have been small and relatively late, however, and must have occurred after the migrants from Asia had established their physical types and cultures. If man came to the Americas during the last glaciation, there was a corridor east of the Rocky Mountains that would have permitted migrants from the Asiatic continent to move southward despite the ice. It would have been this Pleistocene migration that left the skeletal remains that have been found in Gypsum Cave,

Nevada, or in Browns Valley, Minnesota; or such artifacts as the famous Folsom points, the finding of which reopened the entire question of the antiquity of man in the Americas.

In any event, basic discoveries, such as working flint or using fire, were made long before the ancestors of the Indians began their journey down the length of two continents. These migrants came equipped with such techniques, and they also brought the dog with them. It has been established that their dogs are related to no New World canine form, but are of the same species as the dogs of Europe, Asia, and Africa. The new inhabitants were essentially hunters, and so effectively did they hunt that it is believed their coming brought extinction to many Pleistocene fauna that may have persisted into the Recent.

The problems of New World archaeology are very different from those of Old World prehistory. The Indians developed cultures that, for variety in form, differences in the complexity of different aspects, and types of adjustment to habitat, compare with the cultures of any other large region anywhere. They domesticated the enormous variety of plants found by the European explorers who had first contact with them. They had, in Central and South America, developed the technique of pottery making to a degree unsurpassed elsewhere. From what is now New Mexico, southward to Peru, great aggregates of population formed political units and had a standard of living that impressed all the Europeans.

So specialized are the problems of New World archaeology that new techniques of study have had to be devised to investigate them—techniques that are difficult, if not impossible, to employ over the great stretches of time that confront the Old World archaeologist. Naturally the basic methods of excavation, whereby the geological setting is fully taken into account, the careful recording of stratification is noted, and the classification of finds in accordance with their relative depth is made, must be used. But a smaller canvas needs finer brushes.

This New World setting has also made for a welding of history to prehistory as a special approach to archaeological research. One important development is the study of documentary materials for information about peoples now extinct, or who inhabited a locality they no longer live in. As a corollary, materials dug out of the earth have in many instances offered confirmation or necessitated reinvestigation of documents bearing on the peoples who occupied the site of a given excavation. This method has been used for many years by those who have worked in Mexico and Central and South America where the great kingdoms of Aztec and Toltec and Maya and Inca flourished. The writings of Sahagún, of Garcilaso, and the other early Spaniards who set down their experiences and described the lives of the natives conquered by the first expeditions have been continuously employed by the archaeologists. They have thus had a surer base for projecting the developments of the past behind the period of writing. The skill with which they have employed these sources has done much to help them reconstruct the development of the many cultures that came into being in the New World during the relatively short period that elapsed between the time of its original discovery by the migrating Asiatics, and its rediscovery by voyagers across the Atlantic fifteen to twenty thousand years later.

6

Our debt to prehistoric man is an impressive one. Practically all the discoveries of basic techniques that mark present-day modes of life and that are now commonplace—excepting only metal-working, power-driven machinery and electricity—were made during the time when man's economy was characterized by the use of stone tools. In recapitulating these achievements, we may follow MacCurdy's summary of what he has called the "stone age culture complex." [8] Fire was tamed early in man's existence, when techniques of hunting and fishing were also perfected. Man learned how to use rivers and other waterways as means of transport; he later devised the wheel, which ranks with fire and the use of metals as basic patents for human social existence; he also learned the technique of pottery manufacture. The domestication of plants and animals included most species known today. In the case of animals, indeed, it is probable that almost all species subject to domestication were brought under man's control during the Neolithic period. These, in turn, made possible agriculture, with the use of the plow, and herding. Commerce, which meant the establishment of trade routes, had appeared, and many settlements were established that much later developed into the towns and cities of the present. The medical arts were initiated, and some religious concepts were developed. Finally, to be counted among the finest achievements of prehistoric man were the aesthetic manifestations of his culture, which included both graphic and plastic forms.

These developments can be thought of as comprising the first

[8] G. G. MacCurdy, 1924, Vol. II, pp. 133–69.

of several great revolutions that have marked the course of human experience. Childe [9] has shown how, after the earliest period of human culture, when man lived in terms of a hunting, food-gathering economy, the "Neolithic revolution" made possible economic and social systems that could only exist on the basis of an assured and abundant food supply resulting from the domestication of plants and animals. Then, with the discovery of metalworking and the further development of wheeled transport, sailing vessels, irrigation, better farming techniques, and more efficient employment of domesticated animals, came a second, or "Urban revolution." This was marked by the growth of cities, of regular foreign trade, of dynasties and empires and social stratification that included slavery, and a greatly extended system of industrial specialization. The third revolution, a matter of historic record, does not concern us here; this came with the invention of the power-driven machine and is generally known as the Industrial Revolution. Whether man's latest technological achievement, the conquest of the atom, marks a fourth, or Atomic Revolution, only the future student of man can tell. To contemplate the possibility is but the more fascinating, however, when the potentialities of this force are projected against the backdrop of the whole story of the growth of culture.

[9] V. G. Childe, 1946, *passim.*

Chapter **Four**

The Races of Man

What is a race? Scientific anthropology answers the question in this way: *A race is a principal division of mankind, marked by physical characteristics that breed true.* In this sense, the word is a biological term, restricted to the bodily characteristics that distinguish one group of human beings from another. This, in turn, sets off the concept as one of emphasis on the inborn as against the learned aspects of human behavior.

A group of physical anthropologists and geneticists, called together under the auspices of the United Nations Educational, Scientific and Cultural Organization (UNESCO) in Paris during June 1951 to consider the problems of the nature of race and race differences, phrased their observations in this manner: "In its anthropological sense, the word 'race' should be reserved for groups of mankind possessing well-developed and primarily heritable physical differences from other groups." They stressed the utility of the concept for the analysis of the differences between human aggregates when they stated that it is "unanimously regarded by anthropologists as a classificatory device providing a zoological frame within which the various groups of mankind can be arranged. . . ." However, a caution, whose importance cannot be overstressed, is also included. Noting that in terms of the definition, "many populations can be so classified," the reservation is also clearly entered that "because of the complexity of human history, there are also many populations which cannot easily be fitted into a racial classification." [1]

Even in strict biological terms, the use of the word "race" is subject to certain reservations. Not all anthropologists are agreed on the size of the groups to which it should be applied. The races of man, in the conventional sense, are three, this being the number recognized by the UNESCO committee, or four—the Caucasoid, the Mongoloid, the Negroid and, for some, the Australoid. Yet subdivisions in each of these, such as the Alpine, Nordic, Mediterranean and Dinaric divisions of the Caucasoid race, can be differentiated. These are often called "races," too, though it would seem better to call them "sub-racial types," or "sub-races." The UNESCO Statement introduces a variation on this theme. "Existing mankind," it first observes, by anthropological agreement, is classified "into at least three large units, which may be called major groups (in French *grandes-races;* in German, *Hauptrassen*)." Within these "major groups," then, "races" are stated to be less large aggregates, which constitute in their totality these more widely spread ones. Races are to be distinguished from one another by "heritable physical differences" that characterize each, but are not exclusive to any one of them, since, "the differences between individuals belonging to the same race are greater than the differences that occur between the observed averages for two or more races within the same major group"—a point to which we shall return shortly. However, since the word "race" has been employed for so long to designate the larger groupings, we shall, in the conventional manner, call the principal types of mankind *races* and use the term *sub-race* to designate the subordinate aggregates.

Certain traits, which cannot be accurately measured or measured at all, have come to hold great importance because they are so prominently before the observer. One is pigmentation, which has played a preponderant role in racial designation, since for many years it alone was employed for this purpose. The fivefold racial color scheme of the White, Black, Yellow, Brown, and Red races is widely known. Yet no one has ever seen a human being who is really white, or black, or red. "White" people are actually

[1] UNESCO, 1952, Par. 1, p. 11. This document makes interesting reading, since it is followed by comments, both critical and commendatory, made by anthropologists and geneticists from all parts of the world.

pink, "black" ones are brown, and so are "red" ones. The so-called yellow, brown, and red "races" are all Mongoloid, and should never have been separated.

More important, however, is the principle that no one trait can be relied upon to establish a racial category. If skin color is taken as an example, one will find Caucasoids, from Northern India, quite as dark or darker than many persons who belong to the Negroid race. Australoids will also be well within the Negroid range of pigmentation. Another example of the same sort of error is the oft-used trait of head-form, long held to be the prime racial criterion, as when the "long-headed Nordic" is the subject of description. Yet if head-form is taken as the determining trait of racial differences, not only would Nordics and Mediterranean sub-groups of the Caucasoid race have to be classed together, but most Negroids as well, since, except for some populations that inhabit the Congo basin, most of the Negro race who live in Africa are also long-headed!

We may consider briefly some of the traits that have been employed in differentiating racial types. We shall be able to indicate only a small number of those that have been taken, or that can be used, for in actuality there is a very large number of points on the human body and head that yield landmarks for anthropometric measurements, as they are termed. In addition to these are the observation of form, color and general configuration noted by the anthropologist studying living populations—traits such as hair type or shape of the eyes or the degree to which the so-called Darwinian point on the ear exists, which are not susceptible to quantitative analysis, and hence are termed "observations." Finally, we have the physiological characteristics, like blood-type, in which populations have been found to differ significantly from each other. The anthropologist also makes measurements and observations on the skeleton, of particular importance in tracing the affiliations of living peoples with ancestral populations, in classifying types, and in assessing the relation between the bony structure and the soft parts that overlie it, this being especially relevant in research on the dynamics of child development. Measurements on the bony structure, moreover, have the advantage of being more precise than their counterparts on the living.

Out of this great range of possible dimensions to be studied the anthropologist selects those that are the most significant for a given problem. Thus, measurement of the dimensions of the head would be important where a population geographically intermediate between a long- and a short-headed people was being investigated. On the other hand, where crossing between long-headed Negroid and long-headed Caucasoid groups had taken place, such a trait as thickness of the lips would be critical, while head-form would be relatively unimportant. Where a hitherto unstudied population, especially a stable one, is to be described, it is obvious that the student will seek to make as many measurements and observations as he can, and this is also true where skeletal collections are under study. A general principle is to measure as large a number of traits as considerations of time and resources permit, selecting, where selection is necessary, those that are of known or likely significance for the problem in hand, or that will be especially helpful for an understanding of the physical characteristics that mark off the population under analysis as a distinctive unit. Physical anthropologists have learned from experience that it is often as important to establish lack of relevance for a given trait in a given instance as it is to ascertain that one is germane to a particular problem. It is a good working principle that data once shown not to be significant can be discarded; but where materials of possible relevance have not been collected, a question always remains that cannot be resolved until new research is undertaken.

Head-form, the trait probably most measured by physical anthropologists, may be described to give an idea of how measurements are taken and classified for further analysis. It was one of the first to be used in scientifically describing and differentiating human types. It is relatively easy to measure, and has a high degree of accuracy. Because it has been recorded for most populations that have been studied, and hence is available for extensive comparative analysis, it is almost always included in programs of anthropometric research.

The form of the head is described as a ratio between two measurements, the greatest dimension of the head or skull in length and breadth. The ratio between the two gives what is called the cephalic index. Both measurements are made with an instrument termed the spreading calipers, so constructed as to permit the distance to be measured in a straight line between two points on a rounded surface. To ascertain the greatest length of the head, one measures from the glabella, the protrusion just over the bridge of the nose, to the opisthocranium, that place on the occipital protrusion at the back of the head, in a median line that is empirically determined to be the farthest removed from the first point. For head-breadth, the calipers are held at right angles to their previous position, and moved about in the region of the head or skull that is over and a little behind the ears, until the maximum reading is ascertained.

The index is calculated in accordance with the formula:

$$\text{C.I.} = \frac{\text{Width of head} \times 100}{\text{Length of head}},$$

the resulting figures being most often divided into three categories, though finer divisions can be used if the problem calls for this. Since the larger the length in relation to the width the lower the resulting figure, it has been possible to set up classes of long-, medium-, and short-headed individuals and populations. The following figures give the limits for each class. They are for measurements on the living, since those taken on the skull, when combined, give indexes one point lower in each category.

Dolichocephalic	x–75.9
Mesocephalic	76.0–80.9
Brachycephalic	81.0–x

Other traits frequently measured and observed in studying human physical type may be sketched. The *height* of the subject, and his *weight*—not always an easy figure to obtain, where clothing is a consideration—are recorded when possible. Other dimensions of height are taken to show how total stature is distributed over the different parts of the body, since this can be an important diagnostic point in differentiating racial and sub-racial types. One of these length measurements is shoulder height; another is the distance from the ground to the tip of the middle finger, with the arm hanging perpendicularly, at full length. *Sitting height,* as its name implies, is the distance between the top of the head and the table, flat stool or box on which the subject is seated. Anthropologists are not entirely in agreement on how sitting height is to be measured, though in any event the degree of error shown by differences in repeated measurements of the same subject in this trait is likely to be somewhat larger than in the case of the dimensions we have previously named. Nonetheless, sitting height is important; for, when subtracted from stature, it shows the length of the legs in the living as no other means of measuring this can do. And, presented in terms of proportion of total body-height, it has not only been found to be of significance in racial diagnosis, since the bodily proportions of persons of different races have been found to differ, but also reveals to those concerned with problems of growth how the differential development of torso and legs makes for the characteristic bodily form of the human organism at different periods in its pre-adult life.

Shoulder width, breadth and *depth of chest,* and *width of hip* are measured where possible, though among many peoples social conventions place difficulties in the way of realizing this objective. All these, and other dimensions not named here, are cast into indexes, to be used to supplement statistical comparisons of the gross measurements employed in assessing similarities and differences in bodily form between populations and racial groupings.

The traits measured on the head and face are more numerous than those taken on any other part of the body. For one thing, facial characteristics have long been used in diagnosing type. This is evidenced, for example, in the manner in which such traits as eye form and color, hair form, shape of nose and form of the lips, to name but a few, have been invested with sociological significance as marking off national, tribal or class affiliation in many different parts of the world, and for as long a time as recorded history gives us information on the matter. For the anthropologist, in addition, dimensions of the head and face are of value because of the relatively high degree of precision with which many of them can be measured. Moreover, in terms of practical considerations, there is often less objection on the part of subjects to having them taken than there is to submitting to bodily measurements where, as we have seen, taboos of a sexual or other nature may enter.

In addition to length and breadth of the head, the *minimum frontal breadth* and the *maximum facial breadth* are customarily taken. The first measures what may be termed forehead width, the distance between the temporal ridges that can be felt if the fingers are moved to and fro somewhat above and inside the point marked by the outer corners of the eyes, or can be readily seen on a skull. Facial breadth is the distance between the zygomatic arches—the cheek-bones, in popular parlance. It is measured at its maximum value, which is found to be not near the eyes, as most beginners expect on the basis of what is customarily heard about people with broad faces having "high cheek-bones," but slightly in front of the ears. The *bigonial width,* or width of the jaw, is the distance between the right and left borders of the angle of the lower jaw, from gonion to gonion, whence comes the technical name for this diameter. Because of the striking racial differences in the horizontal dimensions of the face—the wideness of the Chinese or Polish face as against the narrowness of that of the

Scandinavian or the Nilotic African—these characteristics are of obvious importance in classifying racial types.

This is especially true when such traits are combined into indexes with measurements of facial length. The height of the face is sometimes measured in its totality, from the hair-line to the lowest point at the center of the chin, the gnathion. However, because factors of a sociological nature often dictate manipulation of the hair, because in males baldness makes it impossible in many instances to determine the hair-line, and because the dimension cannot be taken at all on the skull, a shorter measurement, the *morphological facial height*, is preferred. This is the distance between the gnathion and the nasion, the mid-point on the suture between the frontal bone (the forehead) and the two nasal bones, which also meet here. This measurement presents certain difficulties in the living, since the nasion cannot be felt; but on the skull, where the lower jaw has not been lost and a reasonably full complement of teeth is present, it can be obtained with great accuracy. Most satisfactory of all, from this point of view, is the *upper facial height*, taken from the nasion to the lowest point on the upper gum (or upper jaw, on the skull) between the two central teeth.

Of equal importance in the analysis of physical type are measurements of the width and height of the nose, physiognomic height and width of the ear, the distance between the inner and between the outer corners of the eyes, the thickness of the lips, and the breadth of the mouth. Details of these need not be given here, since the techniques of measurement, as in the case of the many other measurements that are taken on the face, head and body can be found in manuals of physical anthropology, where such technical matters are discussed.[2] The preceding discussion will suffice to give an idea of how the student of race goes about obtaining quantitative data on which to base his conclusions regarding the differentiation of human types, and his classification of populations in terms of their racial affiliation.

We may next indicate some of those traits that are qualitatively evaluated, before moving to a brief discussion of the characteristics that are of a physiological rather than an anatomical order.

[2] The most important work of this kind, the standard reference used by physical anthropologists over the world, is R. Martin's great three-volume compendium. Shorter discussions are to be found in M. F. Ashley Montagu, pp. 257–75, E. A. Hooton, pp. 715–69, and Louis R. Sullivan, *passim*.

The importance of *skin-color* has been mentioned. What is not ordinarily realized is that the chemical that yields the observed racial differences in this trait is the same in all human beings, regardless of race. The differences derive primarily, though not exclusively, from the amount of pigmentation, which is relatively slight in the blond peoples of northern Europe and very heavily deposited in Negroid and other dark types. Many attempts have been made to study the trait quantitatively, but the results have either not given the degree of accuracy that would be desired, or they have required ponderous apparatus that cannot be used outside the laboratory, and would thus be unavailable for the field. Felix von Luschan, a German anatomist and anthropologist, developed a skin-color chart consisting of a series of rectangles of different colors to match various shades of pigmented skin. These rectangles were made of opaque glass, so that the sheen of the skin would be simulated, as well as the color given, since not only the amount of pigment but also the reflection of light enters into the perception of skin-color. Results from the use of this chart, or of later variants of it, could not, however, be expressed other than in percentages of the number of persons in a given group studied whose skins matched particular units of the color scale. Color-tops—in one case, black, red, yellow and white are combined to reproduce the color of a given skin—have yielded somewhat more satisfactory results of a quantitative nature, but this is still a relatively crude measuring device. The problem of studying skin-color, moreover, is complicated by the fact that it differs considerably on different parts of the same individual, being darkest in the pubic region and on the outer arm and leg, lightest inside the arm and leg and in the region of the breast; while all skin darkens when exposed to the rays of the sun. Pigmentation of the face is rarely recorded, unless the effect of exposure to climatic conditions is under study.

The matching process is also used where the color of the hair and of the eyes is being investigated. *Hair-form*, also, is matched to samples that permit its classification in categories ranging from straight through wavy and curly to frizzled, woolly and tufted, as in the "peppercorn" hair of the Bushman and Hottentot of southern Africa. The *shape of the eye*, another important trait for racial differentiation, is observed in terms of the presence or absence of the epicanthic fold, which gives what is popularly called the "slant-eyed" appearance of the Mongoloid peoples. Actually, however, the eyeballs of the members of all races are set in the skull in the same fashion; the slanting appearance is given by this fold of skin attached to the upper lid that covers its inner corners, concealing the red tear-gland to be observed in the eyes of those who do not possess the fold.

Of the physiological traits that are employed in racial classi- fication, *blood-types* have been most studied, both as classificatory devices and in research on human genetics. Other traits in this category, such as the presence or absence of certain taste reactions, and the functioning of the endocrine glands, have also received some attention. Boyd has described blood-types in these terms:

> The four classical blood groups, . . . depend upon the circumstance that the red blood corpuscles of certain individuals are acted upon by substances present in the fluid part of the blood (i.e., plasma or serum) of certain other persons in such a way that they stick together to form clusters and clumps. . . . The chemical substances in the red corpuscles which permit their being agglutinated in this way are called antigens, and there are two of them, designated A and B. In serum, substances which re- act with these substances may be formed, and there are two of these, designated anti-A and anti-B. The division of all persons into four blood groups depends upon the fact that two different blood corpuscle characteristics, A and B, can be present singly or together, or can be absent. . . . These four possibilities cor- respond to the four blood groups which are now by international agreement designated briefly by the above mentioned letters, thus: O A B AB.[3]

The practical importance of this fact of differences in blood- types, for such a matter as blood transfusion, is well known. For scientific purposes, its significance is that here we have a trait that is hereditary, not subject to the influence of environmental fac- tors, and capable of being studied in terms of objective criteria. As in the case of other traits, when their utility for the study of ra- cial differences was first discerned, early enthusiasts held that this fact of differential types of agglutinative reactions of blood would provide the solution to problems in classifying human groups. As far as classification is concerned, however, blood-typing has since taken its place as another trait whose analysis aids in drawing more accurate lines in differentiating racial and sub-racial types. In addition, however, the study of blood-types has led to a more adequate understanding of the hereditary processes under- lying the formation of population types, and the changes to be observed in their physical characteristics over time.

[3] W. C. Boyd, 1950, p. 212.

A question that arises as a result of the tendency to analyze physical differences in human groups through the study of individual traits should be noted. As we will see, it is not unlike the problem encountered in analyzing cultures, where a comparable attempt to break down a total way of life into analogous units for purposes of study has been made. Yet are we not concerned, it is asked, with the total entity that we are studying—in this case, the human being as a whole? Is the individual but a summation of those traits that can be measured and observed, or is he more than their sum? Various attempts to meet this challenge have been made—composite photographs made from pictures of a large number of subjects, for example, assembled to portray the characteristics of the group through the resultant single picture. More systematic has been the approach through the study of *constitutional types*. This was initiated, in its present form, by a German psychologist, Kretschmer, who distinguished three principal divisions—the pyknic, of short, stocky build; the athletic, large and brawny; and the leptosome, tall and slender. To each of these he assigned propensities of a psychological—more precisely, of a psychiatric—order. This attempt, however, like the attempts of others who have elaborated on Kretschmer's method and refined his terminology and concepts, has been the subject of such extensive controversy regarding its theoretical and methodological validity in the light of the data that have been employed in studies of constitutional type that we need here pursue the question no further. That the problem posed is a valid one is not to be denied, but it is clear that the difficulties it presents are far from resolved, especially where racial classification is the end in view.

2

If we consider the ways in which human aggregates differ in these, and in the large number of other traits that are to be measured, observed and analyzed, we find that, in reality, no single group of human beings has a monopoly of any single trait, or cluster of traits. Every major grouping runs a scale from short to tall, from broad to narrow, from light to dark. This is why, with the years, it has become increasingly evident that the outstanding factor in the study of physical types is *variability*. No two human beings are exactly alike, nor two families, nor two local populations, to say nothing of two races. To differentiate races, therefore, by defining them in terms of their physical traits is thus a statistical problem. It brings into play those methods that have been devised for describing and delimiting any variable quantities;

consequently, how members of a given group vary must figure fully when we set off that group from another.

It follows, therefore, that the phenomenon of *overlapping* bulks large in the study of racial differences. For it must never be forgotten that, by overwhelming consensus of competent opinion, man comprises a single species. This means that the differences between races are differences of detail that play upon the basic form we recognize as man. We see this illustrated in the fact that specialized groups such as pygmies, whose stature is so short that it sets them off from most other human forms, are the exception and not the rule. Even here a tall pygmy will reach a stature that is within the range of non-pygmy groups. But were we to attempt to differentiate other populations on this basis of stature, let us say, with the degree of overlapping as great as it is, we would need to make full use of such concepts as the average and the variations about it in making our comparisons.

It is a commonplace that the noses of Europeans are narrow, those of Africans broad. Among the broadest-nosed Negroes are the Kajji of the Niger Delta of West Africa; among the Caucasoids with narrowest nostrils are the Swedes. If we set down the average values of this measurement for these two populations, a striking difference between them is to be seen:

55 Kajji   45.5 mm.[4]

260 Swedes   30.2 mm.[5]

Yet when we take into account the variability of these two populations in this trait, we see that even such a marked difference in

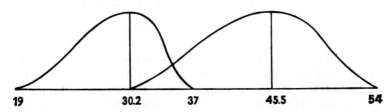

19   30.2   37   45.5   54

Fig. 11 *Distribution curves (stylized) of Swedish and Kajji noses.*

nose-form does not prevent *some* Swedes from having broader nostrils than *some Negroes,* and that *some* Negroes have narrower nostrils than *some* Swedes. Kajji noses vary between about 30 to

[4] A. J. N. Tremearne, 1912, p. 145.

[5] H. Lundborg and F. J. Linders, 1926, p. 102.

54 millimeters, while Swedish noses range from about 19 to 37 millimeters. Therefore, if one were to draw a line between 30 and 37 millimeters long, and present it to an expert, asking him to designate whether this line represented the nose-width of a Negro or a Swede, he could not tell from which group it had been taken. This would be true in spite of the fact that we are dealing here with populations that represent extreme forms taken by their respective races in the characteristic being measured.

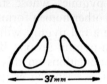

Fig. 12 *Nose, 37 mm. wide.*

This demonstration could be continued for trait after trait, and only in a few of them would we find an absence of overlapping between groups. Such groups would be discovered to be those wherein the most emphatic manifestation of a given aspect was found. Differences in average values will always be apparent, as when we say that Americans are taller than Filipinos. Yet in this trait, as in the one just discussed, we will find that some Filipinos are taller than some Americans, since each group varies from shortness to tallness, and the number of either group who are taller or shorter than any individual member of the other is small indeed. Consequently, we may state as a general principle that *greater differences exist in the range of physical traits that characterize any single race of mankind, than between races taken in their entirety.*

Does this mean, as is sometimes said, that there is no such thing as a race? A statement of this sort can hold only by definition. Common sense tells us that different types of human beings are marked off from each other by a range of perceptibly different manifestations of the same traits. A Chinese, an African, an Englishman will exhibit physical differences that will distinguish each from the other, and it would merely be a denial of objective reality to ignore the existence of these differences. Nonetheless, races must be recognized for what they are—categories based on outer appearance as reflected in scientific measurements or observations that permit us to make convenient classifications of human materials. As we shall see later, this is an important initial step in assessing the biological nature of man and the relation this aspect holds to his culture-building tendencies; but it is scarcely an end in itself. Failure to recognize that in setting up these classifications we have but sorted our data as a means to studying other problems has done much to bring about the widespread misunderstanding which confronts us of the nature of race.

3

As we have seen, the major groupings of mankind most frequently named as races are the Caucasoid, the Mongoloid, and the Negroid. Their distributions can be indicated in a general way as centering in Europe, Asia and the Americas, and Africa, respectively. This does not tell the whole tale, however, for we may also think of them as being distributed about various bodies of water. The Caucasoid race, which is found not only in Europe but along the northern belt of Africa and eastward through Palestine, Asia Minor, and Iran to Baluchistan and northern India, can in these terms be said to be distributed about the Mediterranean Sea. The Mongoloid race, which includes the peoples of all areas of Asia not inhabited by Caucasoids and all aboriginal inhabitants of the Americas, can be thought of as clustering about the Pacific. The Indian Ocean bears a similar relation to the Negroid race, which includes not only all Africans living south of the Sahara desert, but the pygmy groups of Indonesia and the inhabitants of the great region of New Guinea and Melanesia, habitat of the Papuan type, the so-called Melanesian Negroids. A word may also be said here about the Australoids, though there is less agreement concerning their identity as a race than there is concerning the others we have just considered. If we accept the designation "Australoid," for which a good case can be made, then this race will include all the aboriginal inhabitants of Australia, and the autochthonous Dravidian folk of southern India as well.

The physical characteristics of the three principal races and their subraces have often been described. Haddon's scheme[6] is perhaps the most elaborate that has been drawn, and can be consulted with profit. The table given by Krogman,[7] however, will enable us more effectively to envisage the manner in which we may, in broadest terms, distinguish the several races from one another. With a slight change in terminology to accord with our usage here, this table is as follows:

[6] A. C. Haddon, 1925, pp. 15–36.
[7] W. M. Krogman, 1945, p. 50.

Trait	Caucasoid	Mongoloid	Negroid
Skin color	Pale reddish white to olive brown	Saffron to yellow brown; some reddish brown	Brown to brown black; some yellow brown
Stature	Medium to tall	Medium tall to medium short	Tall to very short
Head form	Long to broad and short; medium high to very high	Predominantly broad; height medium	Predominantly long; height low to medium
Face	Narrow to medium broad; tends to high, no prognathism	Medium broad to very broad; malars "high" and flat; tends to medium high	Medium broad to narrow; tends to medium high; strong prognathism
Hair	Head hair: color, light blonde to dark brown; texture, fine to medium; form, straight to wavy	Head hair: color, brown to brown black; texture, coarse; form, straight	Head hair: color, brown black; texture, coarse; form, light curl to woolly or frizzly
	Body hair: moderate to profuse	Body hair: sparse	Body hair: slight
Eye	Color, light blue to dark brown; lateral eye-fold occasional	Color, brown to dark brown; medial epicanthic fold very common	Color, brown to brown black; vertical eye-fold common
Nose	Bridge usually high; form, narrow to medium broad	Bridge usually low to medium; form, medium broad	Bridge usually low; form, medium broad to very broad
Body build	Linear to lateral; slender to rugged	Tends to be lateral; some linearity evident	Tends to be lateral and muscular, but some linearity evident

Each of these races comprehends a number of sub-races, a fact that emphasizes the range of differences within each of them that is so important an aspect of such groupings. The Caucasoid—the *-oid* ending means *-like,* and is used to underscore the inclusiveness of such classifications—is most generally held to be composed of four sub-races, the northern European, or Nordic; the central European, or Alpine; the southern European and north African Mediterranean sub-race and, eastwardly, the Dinaric. The Mongoloid sub-races have been less well defined than the others, but the Malayan groups of Indonesia are recognized as one, the southern Chinese as another, the northern Chinese and Mongolians as a third, the Siberians as a fourth; and, in the Americas, the American Indians as one sub-race, the Eskimo another. The African

Negroids are divided into the inhabitants of the Sahara, of mixed Negroid-Caucasoid descent, the "true Negroes" of the Guinea Coast, the heterogeneous Bantu-speaking populations of the Congo Basin and East Africa, the Khoisan peoples of South Africa, (a term that includes both the Hottentots and Bushmen), the Nilotics of the Lakes region of East Africa, and the Hamites of the Ethiopian peninsula and the region southwest of it. In addition, the Negroid race includes all pygmies (inhabitants of the Congo forest, Andamanese, Veddas of Ceylon, Negritos of the Philippines, Aëta of Sumatra, and the like) and, as a final sub-race, the Melanesian Negroids we have already mentioned.

Even so general a scheme of differentiating human types as we have presented omits certain groupings about which there is no agreement. The inhabitants of the islands of the Pacific Ocean, the Polynesians, are an example of this. Where did they come from? What is their descent? These are questions that cannot be answered in the present state of our knowledge. Perhaps they represent the spent force of an eastward migration from the Old World land mass that made of them an amalgam of all the principal races. Some students, because of the Caucasoid appearance of these Polynesians, have assigned them to that category. The Ainu of the island of Sakhalin, north of Japan, are another such group. "The hairy Ainu," they are called, from the heavy deposition of body-hair of the males. Because of this, and of other traits, they have at times been classed as Caucasoid. Yet when we consider the distance between them and the Eurasiatic area where the Caucasoid race is located, the problem of how they came to their present habitat without leaving traces of their migration appears an unsurmountable barrier to any assumption of a genetic relation between them and the other members of the race to which they are sometimes assigned.

In truth, problems such as these are historical. They cannot be satisfactorily solved on the basis of observed similarities or differences between living populations. This is another way of saying that racial classification tells us nothing except what types exist, and where. In these two last instances resemblances may validly give rise to hypotheses concerning biological relations. But these hypotheses can never be more than hypotheses until archaeological evidence, for instance, shows a path of migration, or until the genetic processes by which such groups made their appearance and were maintained down the generations to the present, in the setting in which they are found, are described. The reality of differences in human physical types must not be dismissed, but all care must be taken that this reality is not given disproportionate weighting. Groups that exist by definition only are as much a departure from reality as is any claim of the nonexistence of those physical characteristics that differentiate groups of men and mark them as members of one race or another.

4

Our next step in understanding the nature of the differences in physical type between human groups is to consider these differences in terms of the final phrase of our definition. This phrase, it will be remembered, stated that the traits that mark off one race from another *breed true*. The implication of this statement is that these characteristics are hereditarily stable. It follows, then, that the very essence of the study of race, once classification has been achieved, lies in the field of human genetics. In truth, it is only from this point of view that we can analyze the dynamic processes of human biology that lie at the crux of our problem. These processes explain such matters as the purity of racial or population types, how new types have developed or may develop, and, above all, the manner in which cultural sanctions and the behavior that is their expression can influence the physical form of the populations.

Speciation is a dynamic process, and mere classification can never explain how different forms have come to differ. To hold that man comprises a single species, therefore, entails at once the assumption that crossing between the subspecific forms—races—is possible. It is needless to stress that this assumption can be proved valid merely by looking about, no matter where on the earth the casual observer happens to be. This leads us at once to the question whether or not pure races are found among man.

If we turn to the UNESCO Statement on race once again, we find the following:

> There is no evidence for the existence of so-called "pure" races. Skeletal remains provide the basis for our limited knowledge about earlier races. In regard to race mixture, the evidence points to the fact that human hybridization has been going on for an indefinite but considerable time. Indeed, one of the processes of race formation and race extinction or absorption is by means of hybridization between races. As there is no reliable evidence that disadvantageous effects are produced thereby, no biological justification exists for prohibiting intermarriage between persons of different races.[8]

[8] UNESCO, 1952, Par. 7, p. 14.

This does not mean that theoretically man, like any other form, could not produce strains through inbreeding that, after generations without contact and hence crossing with other types, would be homogeneous and, given the proper historical circumstances, even large enough to be called pure races. In actuality, however, a pure *race*, that is, one of those major groups that includes no members whose ancestry was drawn from other races, is not to be found. But if we look at *populations* rather than races, and think in terms of the geneticist's concept of "pure strain" rather than pure races, it is possible to state that inbreeding, whether due to geographical or sociological isolation, has induced differing degrees of homogeneity and heterogeneity in different populations.

The fact that all human groups are mutually fertile is of the greatest importance in this connection, since this made possible the interbreeding between populations that has marked the existence of man from his earliest days on earth, and has produced the types that, when we think in racial terms, we speak of as race mixtures. Crossing under contact has been so widespread, indeed, that one of the few axioms about the human animal we can accept is that *no two human groups meet but that they produce mixed offspring*. It seems to make little difference how strict may be the rules against contact. Penalties may be assessed in this world or in eternity; they may involve ostracism, or even death. Yet love, so to speak, will find a way. This is one reason why the range of variation in human groups is so great. In short, this is why we can say that there are no pure races, why man is probably as mongrelized an animal as is to be encountered in the biological world.

Here the matter of relative variation is extremely important. It is conceivable that two populations could be identical in the average measurements they yield for a given trait, and yet be genetically quite different. Figure 13 illustrates this. Both populations are seen to have the same average value. The distribution about the average of *A*, however, is broad; and this population is a heterogeneous one. *B*, on the other hand, with its high, narrow curve indicates an inbred group whose ancestry is homogeneous.

There is, in all probability, little difference in the variability of the major races in those traits that are susceptible of measurement, but there is a vast difference in the variation that any single population may manifest. The Eskimos, for example, are understandably inbred; local differences are to be found, but all the members of any single Eskimo group are closely related and, therefore, appreciably resemble one another. Let us see how such a result was achieved. The natural environment of the Eskimo holds each group to a population of fixed size, to which there are few accessions from the outside. This results in a *loss of ancestry*. Sooner or later—in this case sooner rather than later—persons mate who are related and who in greater or lesser degree share ancestors. In certain mountaineer communities of Kentucky, marriage records show that every person is at least the third cousin of every other, while many persons are more closely related. The

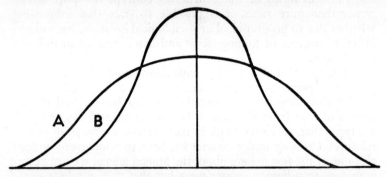

Fig. 13 *Distribution curves from homogeneous and heterogeneous populations.*

number of ancestors theoretically required is thus reduced for their descendants. This principle can be clarified by an example. Brother-sister mating is rare among humans, but if a brother and a sister should have a child, that child would have two rather than four grandparents, since the parents of his father and his mother would be the same individuals.

Thus two forces are constantly at work in determining the character of population mixture between groups of different types: mixture is predominant when there is contact; inbreeding occurs when there is isolation. The first makes for *heterogeneity* —at least after an initial cross—the second for *homogeneity*. The racial history of man, in a very real sense, is the result of the interplay of these two forces.

One of the significant contributions to the study of human physical types was the development, by F. Boas, of a technique for the mathematical expression and the statistical analysis of these mechanisms. Because of its importance, we may outline the reasoning he followed in determining, through the consideration of the relative homogeneity or heterogeneity of populations, the story of how their particular physical types were developed.

We begin with the fact that, as observed at any given moment, a population is made up of individuals of both sexes and all ages, no two of whom are exactly alike. The physical anthropologist, ordinarily, when faced with the need to describe a group, measures adult males or females, or both—since sex differences must always be taken into account—in sufficient numbers to give him an adequate sampling. He then computes his averages and variabilities for the traits he has elected to study, and sets down his results as those that describe this people. These statistical constants, as they are called, permit him to assign the people he has studied to one or another racial or sub-racial category. What he has done, however, is to measure individuals, who, though they may be representative of the entire population, are the end-result of the processes of heredity and growth and have been subject to the influence of their environment and of their culture since their birth.

Yet this population, like any other, is more than an aggregate of individuals. The variation they manifest is only expressed as a gross figure that does not distinguish any of the dynamic factors that have made of them what they are. To achieve this, our population must be analyzed rather as a series of families—the living representatives of the family lines that, as we have already mentioned, are the essential genetic components of any human group, racial or otherwise. To attack the problem of analyzing our population from this point of view, however, it is essential that our anthropologist measure not only adults, but entire families, children as well as grown members. He will then have data that approximate the actual composition of his population, for he will have men and women, boys and girls, of all ages and of various degrees of relationship.

For the purpose of this discussion we need not be concerned with the involved statistical treatment to which the data must be subjected before the measurements of different sex and age components are reduced to a common value, or the weighting to be accorded families having different numbers of children. The final result, which is our concern, is to resolve the gross, or total variability of the population into two terms. One represents the differences *between* families. The other indicates the differences, on the average, that exist *within* families. The first of these is called family variation, the second fraternal variation. The proposition at which we arrive is that *the variability of a population in a given trait is composed of the family variability, plus the fraternal variation in that trait.*

This approach yields two very important facts about the biological history of a given population. The lower the family variability of a given group, the more inbreeding it has experienced; the lower the fraternal variation, the more homogeneous the stock from which it is descended. Thus free mating in a population of mixed origin such as a modern American city where class lines are not institutionalized—at least among the white component—produces high family and fraternal variability. An inbred population, such as lives in an isolated mountain valley, will show low values in both. Let us look at a table of such figures for head-form, the trait that has been most utilized in analyses of this sort.

Population	Variability of Family Lines	Variability within Families
Potenza, Italy	2.41	2.52
Central Italians	2.39	2.72
Bohemians	2.37	2.61
Worcester, Mass.	2.36	2.36
East European Jews	2.29	2.52
Scottish	2.17	2.66
New York mixed Negroes	1.85	2.93
Blue Ridge Mountaineers	1.85	2.09
Chippewa Indians	1.77	3.32
Bastaards (S. Africa)	1.26	2.52 [9]

For the moment we shall consider only the first two of these sets of figures. Potenza is in southern Italy, where the long-headed Mediterranean type prevails. In central Italy, however, Rome has attracted folk from all parts of the peninsula—from the long-headed southern populations, and from the north, where the short-headed, Alpine sub-racial type predominates. Italy is an old country, so that the populations in all these areas are relatively stable. The figures in the first column of our table indicate that free mating and inbreeding have occurred to about the same extent in both central and southern Italy, and these results are substantiated by the historical records. But if the figures for fraternal variation are considered, it is apparent that in Potenza, the breeding between persons who were all long-headed gives a lower value in this trait than we find for central Italy, where groups originally long- and short-headed mingled. We consequently see how this biohistorical analysis explains the homogeneity of the

[9] F. Boas, 1916, p. 9. The figures for the New York Negroes (M. J. Herskovits, 1924b) and the Blue Ridge Mountaineers (I. G. Carter, 1928) have been added to the original table, since they are the result of researches that occurred after the publication of Boas's original paper.

southern Italian peoples in head-form, as against the heterogeneity of the people of central Italy.

From the genetic point of view, a race is thus to be considered not as an aggregate of individuals whose physical characteristics are similar, but as a series of *family lines*. These produce offspring who, when they are adults, resemble each other because they are the product of similar genetic strains. As we have seen, the degree to which all adult members of the group will be similar in physical form will depend on the amount of inbreeding that has occurred. It is thus the *population* that is significant from the point of view of achieving an understanding of the processes of stability and change in human physical type. *Race*, that is, remains a classificatory device, lying on an elementary level of scientific analysis, and affording few insights, once the task of classification has been carried out.

Yet to state this is but to pose the problem, for it is simpler to frame a question of this sort than it is to answer it. The analysis of populations in terms of homogeneity and heterogeneity of family lines represents one approach; a later one, which derived from animal genetics rather than from human biometrics, the field in which Boas worked out his formulae, employs the concept of the *breeding isolate*. This approach attacks the problem by analyzing the opportunities of an individual for mating within a given social group, in terms of its relative isolation, or the access its members have to persons who belong to other groups. The number and situation of those of the opposite sex whom a given individual meets in the course of his sexually active life obviously limits the number of those with whom he can mate; it is equally obvious that this, in turn, is further limited by considerations of personal taste and social custom. The study of these limitations, both by calculating the probability of opportunity and by ascertaining the number of individuals who have been considered by specific persons as possible mates, supplements the approach we have discussed in the previous sections by adding a new dimension to the analysis.

All these studies of the dynamics of the formation of human physical types take as their basic assumption the regularity of the hereditary processes. These, in turn, trace their conceptual genealogy in modern genetics to the work of Gregor Mendel, the Austrian scholar who, in 1866, published his discoveries of the principles governing the inheritance of various characteristics of peas. Tested and clarified by long years of research, the generalizations derived from his initial researches are accepted as basic for an understanding of hereditary processes in all members of the biological world, plant or animal, human or infrahuman. Intensive and extended study has revealed complexities unrealized in the earlier years of genetic science; but this is merely to state that investigations in this field have followed the usual course of scientific growth.

What Mendel discovered was that the heritable traits of the peas he studied were unit characters that bred true under crossing, and that even where there is an apparent blending of an observed trait crossed with another, as in the case of color, in later generations the shades will be sorted out; that is, two traits, when crossed—let us say round and wrinkled peas—produce in the first generation only peas that are smooth and rounded. Yet when plants grown from these seeds are cross-fertilized, approximately one fourth of the next generation (the F_2, or second filial generation), will be wrinkled.

The inheritance of color in the red and white flowers of cross-fertilized plants can be cited to clarify the way in which the process operates. Of the first generation after the cross, all flowers are pink; when these are interbred, one half will be pink, one quarter red, one quarter white. Red of this generation bred with red gives only red flowers, and the same is true of the plants that produced white blooms; but each succeeding generation of pink will yield red, pink and white in the ratio of 1:2:1. In the case of round and wrinkled peas, the round peas are not all genetically the same. After the second filial generation, the one quarter that is wrinkled will always breed true, producing only wrinkled peas. But of the three quarters that are round, one out of every three has genetic carriers for the wrinkled trait, though precisely which of the round peas are in this category cannot be told by inspection. In such cases the trait of roundness is *dominant*, that of being wrinkled *recessive*, only appearing when two round peas that genetically carry the recessive determiners for the wrinkled trait are crossed.

Attempts to apply Mendelian formulae to human heredity have met with many difficulties, especially of a methodological nature. As has been mentioned, man, unlike plants and most animal forms, is a slow-breeding animal, and a given mating produces but few offspring. Hence to follow through the actual inheritance of specific traits, generation after generation, is not possible in human beings. This is why the *biometric* approach, as the statistical study of measurements taken on living beings is called, takes on such great importance in the case of the study of man. The biometric analysis of data from populations descended from ancestral stocks that differ in given traits studied is one possible attack on the question of human heredity that has yielded significant results. Students of human genetics have also paid much attention to tracing the inheritance of various pathological traits of an hereditary character, such as polydactylism, or the inheritance of more than the customary number of digits on hand or foot, or haemophilia, the tendency to bleed more than the normal person does when the skin is cut, due to an inherited inability of the blood to coagulate.

Continuing research has, however, taught that we must be wary of thinking of human racial traits as unit characters, inherited in terms of the classical formulae of early Mendelism. Research on insects and infrahuman mammalian forms has shown that the units that determine a given trait are, in most cases, numerous, and that it is the manner in which, in the genetic structure, these units combine and recombine that yields the variation in a given characteristic manifested in a particular animal or human population. Thus, for example, to think of the effect of Negro-white crossing on the inheritance of skin-color in simple Mendelian terms is unrealistic, since there is every indication that multiple determiners combine and recombine to produce the particular degree of pigmentation that characterizes a given individual. To establish that the 1:2:1 ratio does not hold in such cases needs no more than casual observation of the blends in skin-color of a mixed group.

What is essential for us to understand is that in all their variations, the inherited traits that mark off any population from others breed true within the limits set by the physical characteristics of its ancestry. If, in racial terms, the derivation is from one stock, variations will be less in a group of racially mixed ancestry, which can draw on a wider range of determiners, than in a racially unmixed group. This, then, is what is meant when it is maintained that the concept "race" is a genetic one; but, by the same token, the mechanisms that have made for less variation can also make for more. With all human groups mutually fertile, we thus come once more to the historic fact of contact between peoples to account, in the final analysis, for the many aggregates of differing physical type found on earth to which the various terms that are used to mark them off from each other as racial or sub-racial forms apply.

5

We may here summarize the points that have thus far emerged from our discussion:

1. Man comprises a single species, *homo sapiens*.
2. Human beings manifest differences in certain physical traits that breed true and thus permit the differentiation of various races and subraces.
3. Since man represents one species, and hence all members are mutually fertile without regard to race, lines of delimitation are blurred.
4. Race being a matter of classification, descriptions of racial types tell us nothing of the processes that have made races what they are.
5. These processes are of a genetic character.
6. The analysis of human genetics can be profitably approached through the study of family lines in various local groupings.
7. This leads to the study of homogeneity or heterogeneity within and between family lines, as indices of inbreeding or mixture.

All these, it is evident, have to do with problems of human existence that are of a biological character. We must look to continuing investigations that are in accord with an approach implied by such statements for far more definite answers than we can now give to such fundamental questions as the incidence and effect of mutations, chromosomal change and permutation and combination of gene frequencies in establishing, maintaining, and changing the types of human beings found on the earth. Yet even when the answers to vexing questions such as these have been found, we shall have resolved but one part of the total problem. We must of course understand the full significance of the fact that man, as a member of the biological series, resembles the other animals in his physicochemical reactions and in the genetic and physiological mechanisms which make of him the kind of being he is. But we must also assess the implications of the further fact that he, alone of all the animals, has the capacity to develop and maintain the cultures that influence his behavior so profoundly that they constitute for some students a force outside himself.

Chapter **Five**

Physical Type and Culture

The uniqueness of man's place in the biological series arises from the fact that he is the only culture-building animal. Like other animals, his physical form is determined by his genetic composition; but unlike them, he learns *cumulatively*, from one generation to the next. If we expand this observation somewhat, we find that man alone orders his behavior in terms of the traditions of his group, that these traditions are historically, not biologically derived, and that each society has modes of conduct that differ from those of other societies. This leads us to the principle, whose implications will be discussed at length in a later chapter, that man is the only biological organism which has developed the sensitive, plastic instrument of language as a means of communication, and has learned to extend the inherent capacities of his physical endowment by the use of tools. In essence, then, our problem is to gain some insight into the interplay between two facets of the human being, the biological and the cultural.

This problem of the relation between physical type and culture—or race and culture, as it is more commonly phrased—most often turns on the question of the degree to which the former influences the latter. This is an important question, and the wrong answer given it can have tragic consequences, as the history of the period between the two world wars demonstrates. Because it is so vital we must consider it carefully, first treating the aspect of the relation that comprehends the influence of culture on physical type. For the answers to the "why" of race cannot be encompassed in biological terms alone. If they could be, there would be little need for human biologists who, as we have seen, differ from other biologists only insofar as they are specialists in the method of dealing with their particular subjects. The answers are to be had only when the biological factors are studied as they interact with the cultural ones, influencing and being influenced by them in the life of the single entity we term man.

With this point in mind let us again turn to the table of family and fraternal variabilities given in the preceding chapter. We can see how inbreeding makes for low variability in a population; that each family will have about the same ancestry and thus be like every other one; that within each family brothers and sisters will resemble one another, on the average, more or less according to whether their ancestry incorporates similar or divergent strains. But why should the Potenza district of Italy attract relatively few outsiders, thus making its population homogeneous, and Rome attract many, with resulting heterogeneity? This, clearly, is due to what we call the "importance" of Rome—an historical, cultural fact that, from a biological point of view, is quite fortuitous. Why should there be nonselective, "free" mating, to take another point of considerable biological importance, in one population, and assortative mating—along class lines, let us say—in another? This also is a matter of tradition, not of biology; but it sets the lines within which the genetic strains of a population are formed and continued. It introduces a factor that may, as in England, for example, or in Sweden, result in the formation within the same population, according to class, of two strains that are distinct enough so that in many instances one need but glance at a man to tell of which group he is a member.

Here we come to the basic significance of the study of these breeding isolates within large population units, which are increasingly attracting the attention of human biologists. We can see how the conventions of mating, influenced by such factors as locality, class differentials, religious groupings or clan affiliations, affect choice in marriage and thus set the limits within which genetic mechanisms can operate. This is especially the case where the nature of sub-groups, "in terms of inbreeding, size, migrations, and selective mating" determined by "the attitude of the population . . . as it ascribes values to certain body features," as one student of human genetics puts it, enhances "reality and understanding . . . in . . . subsequent analysis." [1]

Another set of figures from our table can profitably be analyzed with this position in mind. That the Negro population of New York City manifests the same degree of family variability as the Blue Ridge Mountaineers is striking. Yet how heterogeneous the ancestry of these Negroes actually is becomes apparent when it is pointed out that their forebears include not only Africans and Europeans, but American Indians as well. This means that they represent in their genetic composition all the three principal human races. This is made evident by the degree of their fraternal variability, one of the highest listed. In this, however, they stand sharply in contrast to the Mountaineers, whose ancestry is exclusively Scotch-Irish, and who have the lowest figure in the second column.

The answer to the question "why" here lies in the different factors in the situations of these two populations that have caused inbreeding. In the Blue Ridge Mountains, geographical isolation has been reinforced by a convention that encourages suspicion of strangers, and a tradition of not leaving the valley where one was born. In the case of the Negroes, the isolation has been social; the feeling that mating across the color line is undesirable has here been paramount, making for a force whose strength may be understood when it is made clear that the wall of tradition erected against cross-mating is a double one. For Negroes are quite as reluctant to marry whites as whites are to marry Negroes, and the sanctions imposed on those who violate this prescript are of the same kind and exacted where possible to about the same degree by the Negroes as they are by the whites. A similar explanation may be given for the figures of the South African Bastaards. These people are the result of crossing, many generations back, between Hottentots and Boers. Here not only has convention frowned on acceptance of the mixed blood by the whites, but a certain degree of geographical isolation has reinforced the social segregation that these persons experience.

Facts such as these show with great clarity how important an influence ideas can have in setting the stage for the operation of the biological processes in man. So powerful are ideas, indeed, that we have the phenomenon of whole groups that exist by definition only. Thus the word "Negro," as employed in the United States, has no biological meaning. This is why its use is so baffling

[1] F. P. Thieme, 1952, p. 508.

to Europeans or South Americans, who give the word its correct
biological sense by applying it only to those whose appearance is
that of unmixed members of the Negroid race. In the United
States, however, any degree of African ancestry makes one a
"Negro." As a result, the phenomenon of the "white" Negro
appears—a contradiction in terms, but used with naïve uncon-
sciousness of this fact, because a social definition takes precedence
over the biological reality.

From the point of view of the influence of ideas, it is obvious
that a culturally drawn definition, in this case the definition of
the word "Negro," despite its arbitrary character when thought
of in biological terms, can deeply influence the composition of a
population. Where "Negro" takes its proper genetic significance,
mixed-bloods are designated as such and, in Latin countries, are
classed with the majority group of predominant non-Negroid
ancestry. As a result, this group becomes racially heterogeneous,
while those called "Negroes" remain without much crossing. In
the United States, in contrast, the majority population has remained relatively, though by no means entirely, free of Negro
ancestry. Racial heterogeneity, however, is accentuated among
the Negroes, who because of social conventions receive in their
number all the mixed-bloods.

2

How far-reaching the influence of culture on physical type
can be emerges as we consider the extreme variability that marks
man when he is contrasted with other animal species. We refer
here to the hypothesis that man is to be considered as a domesticated form, and that *domestication* and the *social selection* that
has resulted from it have afforded the mechanisms whereby the
multiplicity of local and sub-racial human types, if not the major
races themselves, have been molded into the many forms we find
at the present time.

Just where or when this differentiation into the present racial
types took place cannot be said with any degree of certainty. The
problem, already mentioned, whether man comprises a single
species or whether the major races belong to different species,
turns to a considerable degree on this point. Thus Klaatsch, an
early German anthropologist, held that the races of the present
day had evolved from different anthropoid forms, espousing a
polygenetic position, as against the monogenetic point of view
regarding the origin of racial differences taken by most students
of the problem. Weidenreich, who accepted the unity of man-

kind as a single species, explains that "evolution went on wherever man may have lived, and each step may have been a center of both general development and special strains." Thus he not only finds, as we have seen, "typical features of Australian aborigines . . . in Pithecanthropus and Homo soloensis," but also points out that the so-called "shovel-shaped" incisor teeth that characterized Sinanthropus are the same as those found in Mongoloids at the present time. Nonetheless, he enters his caution concerning "how far back the characters of living races are traceable," when he points out that in attempting to answer this question, "we meet with the difficulty that the striking features are those of skin and hair, while we are entirely dependent on skeletal parts for the identification of past races, especially fossil ones," and that "bone structures are more difficult to define than the soft parts of the body." [2]

Certainly, when the historical scene opens, the races of man as we know them today are found to be well established. Egyptian paintings depict figures having different colors of the skin—red, yellow and black—that can be interpreted only as portraying different Mediterranean and African types. The sub-races of Europe were well known to the early Greeks and to the Romans, though here, as in the case of all other historical documentation, the materials are so recent, as the history of man on earth goes, that they are of minor significance. In truth, the differentiation of existing races is so obscure that we can agree with McGregor when he says: "It is perhaps no exaggeration to say that less is known about the immediate origin of *Homo sapiens* than of *Homo neanderthalensis*." [3] It is as though we stood before a tree and could see only the lower trunk, the lower branches, and the top, with our view of the intermediate portion blocked out by some obstacle. The presence of this obstacle is recognized, and paleo-anthropologists are working to remove it to clear the way for resolving the complex questions of where and when present-day races were differentiated.

It will be noted, however, that all attempts to discuss the problem of racial differentiation have lodged on the biological level, with disregard for the possible influence of cultural factors. Yet we have seen that man, from the onset of his career on earth, has manifested cultural behavior; and we know that culture can be powerful in influencing the processes that shape the physical characteristics of the human organism. Let us, therefore, with this

[2] F. Weidenreich, 1946, pp. 84-5.
[3] J. H. McGregor, 1938, p. 76.

in mind, inquire into some of the implications of the hypothesis that man is to be considered a domesticated form, and that domestication operated as an effective mechanism in the differentiation and genetic segregation of those traits that mark off human racial types.

We can say that man is a domesticated animal both because he shares the physical traits peculiar to domestication with the other domesticated forms, and because his mode of life fulfills the objective criteria of domestication. What are the physical traits in which domesticated species differ most from related wild ones? They are, first of all, an extreme range of color differences. Blondness, especially, is restricted to them; there are no true wild blonds. Such a form as the polar bear, whose white pelt represents an adaptation to arctic conditions, has brown eyes, unlike light-colored dogs or cats or horses. Coloring of pelt ranges from white to black, with greys and browns and tans and other shades in profusion. Spotted animals also appear, but unlike wild forms such as giraffes and leopards, the spotted condition is inherited by strain and does not mark off a domesticated species as a whole. Hair form of wild types is usually wiry and short. Among domesticated forms it ranges from tightly curled to straight. Body build and size likewise vary greatly—contrast the Pekinese with the Great Dane or the Saint Bernard. The same is true of facial features and form of the head, for noses will be long or short, ears of bewilderingly different sizes, eyes set in the head in many different ways.

It is hardly necessary to point out that the traits in which domesticated animals vary are the very ones in which men likewise differ most—the very ones, indeed, that most often mark off races and sub-races from each other. The blond, blue-eyed Nordic or Alpine Caucasoid thus has his counterpart among dogs and cats, horses and cows, pigs and chickens, both in the blueness of his eyes and in the lightness of his hair. The hair forms of the principal races of man can be duplicated in such a domesticated animal as the dog—the wavy, soft hair of the setter is like Caucasoid hair, the short, wiry hair of the Airedale resembles the Mongoloid type, the kinky hair of the poodle is the counterpart of Negroid hair. The difference between the Shetland pony and the Norman draft horse parallels the difference between the Negroid pygmy and the Caucasoid Scot—and in both horses and men, all intermediate sizes are to be found. The nose of the Russian wolfhound is no more extreme for dogs than is that of the Nordic for men; the pug-dog, in contrast, is scarcely more removed from its long canine counterpart than is the extremely broad Negroid nasal form. It is unnecessary to labor the point—it should be clear that, on the basis of mere observation, striking parallels exist between man and the domesticated forms, not only in the distinctive physical traits that mark them off as such, but in the variation found in each of these traits.

There are four criteria of domestication:

1. restricted habitat;
2. regular supply of special foods;
3. protection against weather and predatory animals;
4. controlled breeding.

It must be pointed out that, as in all phenomena of the natural world, there are differences in the degree of domestication under which an animal may live. This depends on whether controls sit lightly or are drawn tight. If we contrast the life of the mustang of the western American plains with that of the blooded racehorse, the difference between *loose* and *close* domestication becomes clear. But both kinds of horses are domesticated varieties.

The controls imposed on the domesticated lower animals are exercised by man who, as far as we know, has brought practically all the creatures able to be domesticated under the conditions that have placed them in association with him. It is man who builds fences, or cages, or makes other devices to keep his animals from roaming. He raises and provides them with food, often as far different from what their wild ancestors ate or that the present-day wild forms related to them eat, as is the dog biscuit from the kill of the wolf pack. He makes barns and other kinds of shelters that protect them from the weather, and watches to see that wild beasts do not prey on them. Finally, especially where domestication is close, he also watches to see that casual mating does not prevent the continuance of the pure lines he has developed, often at the expense of any survival value the animal may originally have had. This is especially significant. If there is any one word that summarizes the criteria of domestication and the conditions under which domesticated animals live, it is *protection*. And protection alone makes possible the substitution of artificial for natural selection.

In human groups, under the protective devices man commands through his cultures, *social selection* has made it possible for the many different human types found over the earth to be perpetuated once they appeared. Through his cultural proclivities, man has been able to do for himself, albeit without realizing the fact, what he has done in breeding the animals he has domesticated.

The initial domesticating factor for man was, in all probability, a knowledge that we know from archaeological remains goes back to the time of *Sinanthropus pekinensis*. Fire established the hearth which, in conjunction with the fear of unknown predatory beings—human, animal, and supernatural—must have served as a powerful force in creating a frame of mind and habit of life that came to be symbolized by the concept "home." Fire certainly made possible the preservation of foods that would otherwise have spoiled and allowed man to devise cooking techniques that yielded end-products vastly different from antecedent forms of foodstuffs. Fire, too, afforded protection against the weather and, in a measure, against wild animals. Fire, and the use of tools—the basis of material culture, and with language, of human economic, social, intellectual and aesthetic life everywhere—thus made social life possible.

Selection in mating is an aspect of social life. Custom generally rules that marriage within a group is more desirable than marriage outside it. Elaborations are devised on this theme so that all kinds of restrictions of an economic, social, religious, magical, and aesthetic variety become operative. One marries or not in accordance with his resources, selects a mate because he or she belongs to a given class in society, accepts or rejects an individual as the gods are favorable or not, or in accordance with some physical trait held to be associated with some supernatural power, falls in love, all unconscious that he is reacting to culturally sanctioned ideals of beauty. We must stress again how fortuitous these reasons are; yet, as we have seen, their effect is powerful in influencing the physical type of a given population. They are just as fortuitous as the decision of a breeder of animals that he will elect to breed for a long- rather than short-haired variety of dog, or horse, or cow, and quite comparable in their effectiveness.

An example of this is the selection in marriage on the basis of color differences found among American mixed Negroes, one of the few instances of social selection that has been studied as such.[4] The facts given in the following table are of the comparative color of mates: first, of parents as judged by their children; second, through objective study of pigmentation by the use of the color-top:

[4] M. J. Herskovits, 1928, pp. 51–66.

	Estimate of Parents by Children	Color-Top Findings
Husband lighter	30.3%	29.0%
About the same color	13.2	14.5
Mother lighter	56.5	56.5

The reasons for the selection in mating shown here are historical, psychological, and cultural. Historically, mixed Negroes were often manumitted by their white fathers during the period of slavery and sent North to establish themselves in some trade or to find some other gainful occupation. Their light color was associated with the favorable economic position this group attained with the years, and with the resulting advantageous social position they came to occupy within the Negro community. Psychologically, there has been a transfer of the values set by the Caucasoid majority of the American population, whose white color is associated in the minds of the Negroes with freedom from the disabilities under which they live. Culturally, the American tradition that the woman marries a man who can care for her, while the man seeks a woman who can enhance his self-esteem among his fellows, is here translated into terms of color difference.

What is the biological consequence of the play of all these nonbiological forces? Selectivity has reduced the number of full-bloods in the community, and increased its racial heterogeneity. But because of the barriers to crossing with the whites, a type of inbreeding exists that, as we have seen, has caused the American Negro population to achieve its own homogeneity. This permits it to be described as a distinctive type that lies about halfway in its physical traits between the characteristics that differentiate its Caucasoid and Negroid ancestry.

3

Through the protection afforded man by technology and social institutions, the perpetuation of mutants that might otherwise not have survived has been encouraged. Their descendants form not only the present-day local types and sub-races of *Homo sapiens*, but perhaps even the major human races that are to be distinguished. What, however, of the other aspect of our problem? What is the influence of physical type or, as it is more often expressed, what is the influence of race on culture?

The scientific truth of the matter is that *culture influences physical type far more than physical type influences culture*. Full recognition of this is all the more cogent since so much of the discussion concerning the relation between race and culture sees the problem as the determination of the degree to which race is instrumental in shaping the culture of a people and does not consider at all the influence of culture on physical type. Thus we meet with the first of the several determinisms of which we take account in studying culture.

Racial determinism, as the position which holds that physical type determines culture is called, easily slips into the political field, where this approach is called *racism.* In its most extreme form, it is exemplified by the racial doctrines of Nazism, which maintained the existence of a so-called "Aryan race," a kind of mystic grouping superior to all others, and, for political reasons, another presumed "racial" entity, the Jews, who were singled out for special indignities.

Neither the word Aryan nor the term Jew has scientific validity as a racial designation. Aryan is the name of the language from which most European tongues have been derived. Warning against its use as the name for a presumed racial entity was never more deeply nor more bitterly expressed than by F. Müller himself, the philologist who first used it, when he said: "There is no more an Aryan race than there is a dolichocephalic (long-headed) dictionary." As for the term Jew, its meaning, except when it is applied as a name symbol for a group called Jews, who possess in common a certain historic continuity, is extremely tenuous. No traits have been distinguished that characterize the Jews as such everywhere they are found. A rich store of evidence, on the other hand, demonstrates that the Jews of a given region resemble the general population of the region they inhabit.[5] The difference between the Jews of Germany and France, for example, is about that between the other elements in these two countries.

This being the case, we may profit from a somewhat more extended consideration of the concept of a presumed Jewish race, as this bears on the problem we are now considering, the relation between physical type and culture. It throws into high relief the difficulties that are encountered, beginning with the task of adequately defining the group being studied. For even where all possible designations seem to have been exhausted—race, people, nation, cultural entity, ethnic group, historic type, linguistic unit —we find students, still not satisfied, searching for other, more precise terms. All attempts, however, have come to grief because

[5] This has been made apparent for central Europe in G. M. Morant's discussion (1939, pp. 72–4, 80–7).

they attempt to encompass, at one time, both the biological and cultural characteristics of the people they are trying to differentiate.

The operation of a psychological mechanism called the stereotype makes possible a belief in the existence of fixed racial differences in physical type that is the basis for the assumption that so-called "racial" groups, such as the Jews, differ in aptitudes and ability. For example, Frenchmen are commonly visualized as dark, short, brown-eyed, vivacious people who gesticulate as they talk. That there are, in northern France, Norman French who are tall, blond, and blue-eyed, or in the east the stocky, blond Alpine French, is overlooked. When such persons are recognized as Frenchmen at all, they are dismissed as exceptions. On the other hand, every person who answers the preconceived description reinforces the conception of what a Frenchman should look like. Such stereotyped concepts are misleading in that they are highly selective. More than that, they are also fallacious, for they confuse cultural traits—in this instance vivacity and the use of the hands in speaking—with such biological characteristics as stature and eye color.

In the case of the Jews, there is enough similarity in physical characteristics to allow the development of a stereotype that, in the minds of laymen, receives daily reinforcement; and has even been called on to justify classifications drawn for certain Jewish sub-groups by physical anthropologists. Yet when we examine the traits that make up the stereotype, in the light of the individual variations in these traits among those to whom the term "Jew" is applied, the untenability of designating such traits as typically Jewish becomes apparent.

As far as can be ascertained, the Jews derive, historically and biologically, from that special type of the Mediterranean sub-race of the Caucasoid race that was formed several thousands of years ago along the eastern shores of the Mediterranean Sea. This original stock, related by students variously to the early Hittites, or to an "Iranian Plateau type," experienced three dispersals from the area they originally inhabited. The first was during the captivity of the Jews in Babylon, which took them into Mesopotamia and Iran; the second, under Hellenistic influence, distributed them eastward to Asia Minor and westward about the eastern Mediterranean; while the third, under the Romans, eventually saw their spread over most of Europe.

Two principal Jewish types are most often named in the literature. These are the Ashkenazim—the German, Russian and

Polish Jews—and the Sephardim, who came to live in the Balkans and Turkey after their eviction from Spain in 1492. The groupings distinguished by these terms are, however, differentiated no less on linguistic than they are on historic grounds, since many of the Ashkenazim speak a language based on German, while the Sephardim employ one derived from Spanish; both, however, being written with Hebrew characters. When we study their physical form, two points become apparent—that the two groupings differ a great deal from each other, and that each resembles the Caucasoid sub-type that inhabits the area where it also lives. Thus, if we consider the trait of head-form in Spanish and Russian Jews, we find the following percentages:

	Spanish Jews	*Russian Jews*
Long-headed	19.7%	1.0%
Medium-headed	65.5	29.0
Short-headed	14.8	70.0

The average of the cephalic index for males of the Spanish group is 78.1, as against 82.5 for the Russian Jews; for females, the figures are 78.9 and 82.4. Yet, as Krogman observes: "The contrast between the Ashkenazim and the Sephardim is really one between an Alpo-Dinaric (or Armenoid) and a Mediterranean racial type." That is, the Jews of the Mediterranean area have the longer heads that mark off the Mediterranean sub-race as against the broader heads, with correspondingly higher cephalic indices found among the general population of eastern Europe as well as among the Jews of that region.

We may see further how the point, both as regards differences between the principal Jewish types, and as concerns the resemblance of each to the population of which it forms a part, can be documented when we consider a table of averages in cephalic index for Jews and non-Jews of certain other countries, based on measurements made at the turn of the century.

	Jews	*Non-Jews*
Lithuania	81.05	81.88
Rumania	81.82	82.91
Poland	81.91	82.13
Hungary	82.45	81.40
Little Russia	82.45	82.31
Galicia	83.33	84.40

It becomes obvious when we scrutinize these figures that the average head-form of Jews and non-Jews in the several territories varies from less to greater width in much the same way. This is also apparent in another table, which presents averages for the same trait computed for certain other Jewish and non-Jewish populations of Europe.

	Jews	Non-Jews
England	80.0	78.0
Bosnia	80.1	85.3
Frankfort, Germany	80.8	81.4
Southern Russia and Ukraine	82.5	83.2
Warsaw, Poland	82.9	82.0
Bavaria	83.5	84.1
Bukovina	84.3	86.3

As might be expected in populations where social conventions make for the selection of mates within the group, in terms of the various communities of Jews as breeding isolates inside the larger aggregates of which they form a part, the over-all range of values in the Jewish column (80.0–84.3), as Coon has pointed out, is less than that of the non-Jewish groups (78.0–86.3).[6] However, the way in which the two tend to vary together indicates that cross-breeding as well as inbreeding has taken place. Since most of the data at hand are derived from head measurements, it should be added that Morant has found that comparative figures for stature confirms "in a striking manner the similarity of the stature of the Jews to that of their neighbors."[7]

The problem, then, is how to ascribe causation to physical type when, in the case of such a people, one finds in them the degree of variation that is apparent from materials such as have just been given. Moreover, as we move from the consideration of inborn traits to those that are learned, we find even less relation between the various groupings of Jews classed according to physical traits. This is the case whether we consider the relation from the point of view of the languages they speak, or of their customary modes of behavior in general, or even of such a specific feature of their culture as their religious beliefs and ritualistic patterns.

In truth, race, nationality, language and culture in its various manifestations are independent variables. They meet only in the persons of given individuals who belong to a particular race, are citizens of a specific nation, speak a certain language, and live in

[6] Coon, 1942, pp. 20–37.
[7] For more extended discussion of this point, and for the relevant bibliographic references, see M. J. Herskovits, 1949, *passim.*

accordance with the traditions of their society. The word "French" can mean any of these. Only the phrase "French race" is unacceptable. Northern Frenchmen are Nordics, eastern French Alpines, southern and central French Mediterranean. All are Caucasoids—if they come of stock originating in France itself. But a Negro from Senegal may have French citizenship, an Arab from Tunis may speak French, an Annamese from Indo-China, who grew up among Frenchmen in Paris, will behave and think in ways indistinguishable from those of Caucasoid Parisians. The same argument will hold for the word "Jew," or for any other human grouping that has been designated by the word "race."

A negative position is difficult of proof, so that it is too dogmatic to state flatly, as is sometimes done in controversy, that there is no influence of any kind exerted by physical form on cultural behavior. Yet all testimony in hand seems to indicate that any normal human being, *if given the necessary opportunity*, can learn the way of life of any people existing on the earth today. Everyday experience in the United States richly corroborates this. Second-generation Japanese, called "nisei," dress, talk, and otherwise behave as do their fellow Americans. Their thought processes, value systems, and goals are those of the country in which they live. The same is true of those Negroes whose disadvantages have not been so serious as to deny them the same avenues of self-realization as are enjoyed by others among whom they live. The evidence, in short, demonstrates that every large human group, even of the order of a sub-race, just about runs the gamut of human capability, whether in intellectual capacity, or in those particular abilities that are represented by special sensitivity to sound waves (musical aptitude) or to light waves (artistic ability) or some other aspect of behavior in which individuals surpass their fellows in excellence of perception or performance.

How a given society, sub-race, or race uses its human endowment, that is, is a matter of history, not biology. Language, for example, as we have seen, is learned, like any other aspect of culture. On occasion, such linguistic terms as Aryan, Semitic and Bantu are applied to what are called racial groups. When used in a manner of speaking, or for convenience, the fault is merely one of bad logic. Too often, however, the idea becomes fixed that the two phenomena, really found only in association, are causally related. Then a given physical type comes to be identified with a specific language, and the conclusion is drawn that the members of a given race are especially and innately endowed to use the language which they, as a race, are presumed to speak. Yet nothing could be further from the truth. As in other aspects of culture, any normal human being, no matter what his race, can speak any language, provided he begins to learn it early enough in life and has full opportunity to master it. Neither the thin lips of the Nordic nor the thick lips of the Negro of themselves condition the manner of speech of an individual of either group who, for all we know, may learn to speak an excellent Chinese!

4

We have seen that culture exerts a very real, if largely unrealized influence on the formation of physical type and, through this, on the development of major racial groupings of man. Let us now turn to the other side of the question, the influence of physical type, or race, on culture. Here we examine the degree to which differences in physical form between human groups is to be considered a causal factor in making for differences in their behavioral propensities, as manifested in their total bodies of cultural traditions, beliefs and values.

It is important to distinguish clearly between the scientific study of race and racial differences, with which most physical anthropologists are concerned, and the use of the concept of race as something that determines cultural behavior to achieve political ends, which, as we have seen, is called racism. We will consider the development of racist philosophies shortly; here we need only recall their culmination in the racial interpretation of history, translated into political policy by Nazi Germany, which was one of the causes of World War II.

Because of this distortion of scientific truth for ulterior ends, and its tragic consequences, the UNESCO Statement, to which reference has already been made, was drawn to clarify the position of scientists on the question. This is stated as follows:

> The scientific material available to us at present does not justify the conclusion that inherited genetic differences are a major factor in producing the differences between the cultures and cultural achievements of different peoples or groups. It does indicate, on the contrary, that a major factor in explaining such differences is the cultural experience which each group has undergone.

In the summary to the statement, two of the five items underscore this point. "Available scientific knowledge provides no basis for believing that the groups of mankind differ in their innate capacity for intellectual and emotional development." Moreover, "Vast social changes have occurred that have not been connected in any way with changes in racial type. Historical and sociological studies thus support the view that genetic differences are of little significance in determining the social and cultural differences between different groups of men." [8]

This, as a matter of fact, has been the point of view taken by almost all physical anthropologists on the practical issues involved in their study, though statements such as this have not been made frequently. As scientists, physical anthropologists have been occupied with the study of problems remote from such issues, studies that laid the foundation in earlier times for the scientific analysis of human types, or more recently sought an understanding of the dynamic processes that underlie the differentiation and perpetuation of these types. Counts, who has sketched the historical development of physical anthropology, traces the change from early concern with the original cause of racial differences, through the employment of techniques of measurement as a means toward attaining greater exactitude in drawing racial classifications and the genetic approach, to current interests in new classifications based on studies in constitution and of blood-types.[9] Some of these approaches have been considered in preceding pages; all the earlier ones have left a residue of sound data and method that are continually being employed in the study of man's physical form and will continue to be used effectively to this end. They hew close to the scientific line, properly maintaining that race is a biological phenomenon and that the traits that mark off one group of men from another cannot be held inferior or superior except insofar as they do or do not function adequately. After the mode of science, that is, the traits studied are described and analyzed, not judged.

When we come to the problem of superiority in racial characteristics, we are thus outside the limits of scientific concern, since the question is essentially one of evaluation. As a matter of fact, it is a problem of the same order as that of cultural evaluation, and partakes of all the difficulties that inhere in attempts to implement preconceived judgment with fact. Every people, that is, feels it enjoys superiorities over others. Such a point of view, as we shall see, when it expresses gratification at the positive qualities of one's own group, serves as an important integrating factor for the individual, and makes for adjustment and co-operation in

[8] UNESCO, 1952, Par. 6, Par. 9 (b), (d), pp. 14–15.
[9] E. W. Counts, pp. xix–xxvii.

intergroup relations. Only when this conviction gives rise to theories of biological superiority that find expression in aggressive desires to impose an inferior status on others does it become socially disruptive. Then this essentially constructive pride turns into destructive motivations and behavior, and we find racism rampant. It is this racism which, it cannot be too often stressed, must always be held in contrast to the scientific study of racial differences. Supported by arguments that distort science and sanctioned by force, it seeks to impose the dictum of a self-styled "superior" race on all who fall outside its arbitrarily fixed limits.

Histories of racism name as the earliest expressions of racist philosophy the *Essay on the Inequality of the Human Races* by the Frenchman Count Arthur de Gobineau, and the work entitled *The Foundations of the Nineteenth Century* by Houston Stewart Chamberlain, the German-English son-in-law of Richard Wagner. The writings of these men and the host of others who have followed them have without doubt had wide influence in shaping racist doctrines. But New World chattel slavery gave an added impetus to racism by providing some of the earliest studies of race. Made with the objective of justifying slavery, these studies consequently emphasized the importance and inevitability of racial differences. The vigorous arguments of those who supported the abolitionist position were countered by apologists for slavery on both sides of the Atlantic, in France and England as well as in the United States, where the abolitionist campaign brought counter-arguments that took the form of the rationalizations of early American racism.

A certain relation between Old and New World currents of racism can be traced. During the middle of the nineteenth century, two societies existed in England for the study of man. One was pro-slavery, one anti-slavery. The former was the Anthropological Society of London, headed by Dr. James Hunt, a distinguished scholar. His paper "On the Negro's Place in Nature" in the *Memoirs* of the Society for 1863–4 asserted that "we may safely say that there is in the Negro that assemblage of evidence which would, *ipso facto*, induce an unbiased observer to make the European and Negro two distinct types of man." It went on to argue that "it is not alone the man of science who has discerned the Negro's unfitness for civilization as we understand it." These are sentiments quite familiar to those who know opinions current during the period and who have followed racist writings of later years; opinions that have persisted despite their lack of scientific validity. What is often overlooked in discussions of this and other racist writings is the number of American citations employed by Dr. Hunt to document his case.

In the same volume the paper that follows that of Dr. Hunt underscores this point—"Some Observations on the Past and Present Populations of the New World," by William Bollaert. In the fashion of latter-day racist thought, Bollaert holds that the races of man represent different species, and he lays much stress on the evils of race mixture. In his paper, we find him commenting on the work of the Americans who plead that Negro and white are creatures of a different order. He writes:

> I cannot help the expression of surprise that we do not hear our anthropologists and ethnologists refer oftener to Knox on the *Races of Mankind*, Nott and Gliddon's *Types of Mankind*, and their *Indigenous Races*. The first work is thoughtful and original; the second, elementary; but the *Indigenous Races* is one of the most valuable anthropological contributions we have as yet in our language . . .

It is not without interest, even now, to take down this last volume, published in Philadelphia in 1857, scan its drawings of crania and living racial types and read its controversial upholdings of the polygenist position against the monogenists, who held that mankind had been created one. But most interesting of all is to turn to the "Alphabetical List of Subscribers" at the back of the volume and to note in it the name "le Comte A. de Gobineau."

Nott, Gliddon, Knox, van Evrie are only a few names of those who were first in the United States to give racism the forms of science. Their work fell into deserved oblivion as the frontier claimed the attention of Americans, but the seed they had planted by no means died, though it was not until the end of World War I that systematic expression of racism appeared once more. The names of Madison Grant and Lothrop Stoddard are outstanding in this connection, Grant's *The Passing of the Great Race* and Stoddard's *Rising Tide of Color* being two of the most widely read works of the period. These books sought to phrase racial prejudice in scientific terms in order to achieve political ends. Their authors are often cited by European proponents of racism, and it is worth noting that in a work by such an outstanding exponent of German "race science" as Hans F. K. Günther, translated as *The Racial Element of European History*, tribute is paid to their writings.

The results of psychological testing in the American army during World War I also influenced world racist thought. "Intelligence" tests, they were called and though we know better today, they have been used again and again to "prove" the presumed superiority of the north European types that stood highest in them. They constituted one of the most effective arguments of the racists; so that this unhappy contribution of scholars, who were responding to a tradition whose existence they perhaps did not even suspect, became a mainstay for those who have called upon science to serve ends that are anything but scientific. Yet it is a commentary on the working of scientific method that objective analysis of the data on which these claims were made, and reappraisal of the methods used, caused psychologists to reject the concept of racial "intelligence" a few years later.

Chapter **Six**

Habitat and Culture

Whether we study man or any other living creature, the dimension of space is no more to be disregarded than that of time. In the case of man, where culture, as Forde puts it, intervenes as "a middle term . . . between the physical environment and human activity," [1] the problem becomes essentially one of assessing the interaction between the natural environment in which a people live and their culture. Human ecology has thus come to signify the study of this relation rather than the investigation of how man, the biological organism, has adapted himself to his geographical setting.

The word "environment," in its specialized usage, refers to the natural setting and is so used by geographers whose primary interest is in this aspect of the physical world. This is the meaning it holds in the phrase "environmental determinism," which expresses the position that the natural environment of a culture not only sets the cultural stage but determines the action that takes place on this stage. Interestingly enough, though "environment" is interpreted as meaning the natural setting of life, much more than its social setting, those students who have been concerned

[1] C. D. Forde, 1934, p. 463.

with the social setting have only recently fixed their attention on the problems that arise out of the interaction between ways of life of a people and the scene in which these ways are brought into being and are continued from generation to generation.

We can best achieve clarification by recognizing that the *natural* and the *cultural* elements in man's total setting are to be differentiated in terminology, as they are in fact. To this end, we shall employ the following terms:

> *Habitat,* to designate the *natural* setting of human existence —the physical features of the region inhabited by a group of people; its natural resources, actually or potentially available to the inhabitants; its climate, altitude, and other geographical features to which they have adapted themselves.

> *Culture,* to refer to that part of the total setting that includes the material objects of human manufacture, techniques, social orientations, points of view, and sanctioned ends, which are the immediate conditioning factors underlying behavior.

> *Environment,* in its full dictionary significance—"the aggregate of all the external conditions and influences affecting the life and development of an organism"—in this case, man in his natural and cultural setting.

With these definitions in mind, we may now turn to a discussion of how man reacts to his habitat. To what degree is man's individual life and his culture shaped by it, or how do the individual and his culture employ the habitat in achieving their own ends? And finally, what are the mechanisms whereby these adjustments are reached?

2

Man cannot exist unless he meets the challenge of his habitat. When cultures with relatively simple technologies and limited economic resources are seen from the point of view of their relation to their habitat, this challenge seems so powerful, and the influence of the natural setting so pervasive, as to make the conclusion appear inescapable that habitat exercises a decisive influence in shaping ways of life. This holds especially when we take as our example peoples whose habitat is harsh, such as those who live in Arctic or desert regions. Descriptions of the cultures of such groups necessarily place considerable stress on the means by which they achieve their adaptation.

The aboriginal Australians offer an excellent example of such a people. Little seems to be passed over by them in the way of edible foodstuffs. In northwest central Queensland they find seeds, roots, fruits and vegetables, flowers and honey, insects and crustaceans, frogs, lizards, fish and crocodiles (where there are streams), turkey-bustards, pigeons, emus, bandicoots, opossums, and kangaroos. They have no hoes, do no agriculture; their weapons are rudimentary. Some of their hunting techniques show great resourcefulness. Thus, on occasion, when a kangaroo is sighted, the native may set out after it on the run. He keeps after it all day, and at night both he and his prey settle down to sleep where they find themselves. By the next morning, the muscles of the kangaroo are so stiff from the unaccustomed steady pace he has been forced to keep that the hunter soon catches up with him. It is then a question of closing in for the kill with the club that is the weapon the native uses in hunting this animal—a feat calling for bravery—and then waiting for the rest of the group, who have been following the trail left by hunter and hunted, to come up for the feast.

The technique of coping with a difficult habitat used by a people having but the crudest equipment is also illustrated by the pygmy Bushman of South Africa. With his small bow and arrows in hand, the Bushman hunter conceals himself by placing over his crouched body the skin of an ostrich, mounted on a frame. Moving cautiously toward the herd, he imitates the movements of these great birds so cleverly that they do not suspect his presence until one of them falls under his arrow. The need of this people for water is paramount, since the Kalahari Desert they inhabit is one of the most inhospitable desert habitats in the world. They fill ostrich-egg shells during the short season when the water holes are not dry, or use their intimate knowledge of the country to find the roots, bulbs and melonlike fruits that contain moisture or store up liquids. Not even the most stagnant pool daunts them, for in such cases they place grass filters at the bottom of the hollow reeds they use in sucking up water.

One of the finest adaptations of culture to habitat is revealed by the Eskimos. Their dome-shaped snow houses, called igloos, are models of the exercise of effective engineering techniques, using the materials at hand. This is evidenced by the ease with which an igloo can be constructed, its durability, and the manner in which it fulfills its function of providing shelter and comfort in the savage cold of the Arctic winter. The uses of walrus ivory—for sled runners, or for eyeshields to protect against the driving blizzards or against the glare of the sun on the snow—are other instances of this adaptation. The detachable heads of the spears used in hunting walrus or whale allow the precious wooden handles to float away unharmed once a strike has been made, to be recovered by the hunter later. Or we may cite the blown-up walrus bladders that are attached to a spearhead to irritate a struck whale when it dives and, by weakening the whale with loss of blood, force it to the surface for the kill. Even such an implement as the snow-beater has been thought of to free fur clothing of snow so that it will not deteriorate from moisture when taken into the warm igloo.

3

The systematic study of human geography, or *anthropogeography*, as it is sometimes called, dates from the time of Friedrich Ratzel. This German scholar was impressed by the influence of the natural setting on the ways of life of peoples, and his great work, in its English translation called *History of Mankind*, assembled much of what was known at the time of its writing about peoples over all the earth. Ratzel's position, however, which held that the habitat of a people could not be neglected in assessing those influences that play on the formation and functioning of culture, was destined to be changed to a more rigid formulation by some of his followers. These students transmuted his earlier and quite acceptable position into one held that the habitat is the *determining* factor in shaping a way of life.

This, in brief, is the position called *environmental determinism*, the next of the determinisms that must be examined in our search for an understanding of what culture is and how it works. An uncompromising expression of this point of view is to be found in the opening pages of a standard work on the geography of North America, wherein the hypothesis of environmental determinism is stated as the framework for the discussion that follows it. "To understand what man has wrought we must study the place, the environment, in which he has wrought," [2] states this author. Then, after rejecting such aspects of culture as government, economics, social ideals, and race as causal factors in explaining the achievements of a society—in this case, the people of the United States—we are told that ". . . natural resources, climate and accessibility are the stuff of which industry, trade, religion, national policy and to some extent civilization, are made . . ." [3]

[2] J. Russell Smith, 1925, p. 3.
[3] *Ibid.*, p. 10.

Students of culture have reacted strongly against environmental determinism. They maintain that since many forces—geographical, biological, psychological, historical—play on culture, no one of them should be overemphasized, but the role of each should be investigated and weighed. In practice, however, this has led to an emphasis on the negative objective of showing that the habitat does not play the all-important part in shaping culture that environmental determinism claims for it.

It is not difficult to frame a refutation of environmental or any other determinism, if only because of its vulnerability in terms of logic. That is, if a determinism is to be *deterministic*, the operation of other forces is inadmissible. Consequently, in the case of environmental determinism, if it can be shown that two cultures found in the same habitat differ, or that the same kind of culture exists in two different settings, some other force than that assumed as the determinant must have exerted a measure of influence. With this established, habitat becomes only one of a number of forces that shape culture.

Let us recall some well-known instances that illustrate this point. We have already commented on the effectiveness of the adaptation made by the Eskimo, especially the eastern Eskimo, to their habitat. It has been pointed out with what efficiency they employ the materials at hand. The efficient use they make of their dogs, their only domesticated animal, in pulling their sleds, the waterproof boats called *kayaks* in which they can turn over completely and still survive, and other skills of adaptation that have for years intrigued students might also have been mentioned. It is accepted as a truism that anyone who would live in this harsh habitat must follow the ways of the Eskimo, adapting himself to the Arctic winter as they do, if he would survive.

Yet when we turn to the Siberian Arctic, inhabited by such tribes as the Chukchi and Koryak and Yukaghir, though the rigors of the climate are the same as in northernmost North America, we find quite a different type of culture. The igloo is unknown, and shelters are made of skins that are attached to a framework of wood, even though wood is as scarce here as elsewhere above the Arctic Circle. The Siberians are herders rather than hunters, their economic mainstay being reindeer, not walrus, and this, again, despite the fact that many of them are not too far removed from the sea coast to be hunters like the Eskimo.

Early in a wintry Arctic day, when the reindeer have exhausted the tundra on which they feed, the encampment must be changed. With the thermometer thirty degrees or more below zero, the men drive off the herd to its new feeding ground, leaving behind the women and children. It is the women's task to break camp. They get to work at once, dismantling the tents and loading skins, tent poles, utensils and the young children on the pack reindeer that must transport them. The men and the herd reach the new feeding ground long before the women. They do not put up a snow shelter as the Eskimo would, however, and they have no wood to make a fire to warm themselves. So they sit about in the cold, waiting until the pack animals arrive and the skin tents can be erected by the women, for the men would demean themselves by doing this kind of work.

Here in the difficult circumpolar habitat, then, we have two quite different ways of life, one based on hunting, the other on herding. The adaptation of both peoples is equally successful, inasmuch as the only test of success in adaptation is survival, and Siberians no less than the Eskimo have managed to cope with their Arctic setting for untold generations. The efficiency of Eskimo adaptation over that of the Siberians *strikes us* as greater, but this does not mean that the Siberians would concur in this evaluation. It is clear, therefore, that factors other than habitat enter in this varied adaptation. Once we perceive this, the all-powerful influence of the environment in shaping culture, posited by the hypothesis of environmental determinism, is seen to call for qualification.

An instance taken from the American Southwest has frequently been used to test formulations of environmental determinism. Here the life of the Pueblo Indians is contrasted with that of their neighbors, the Navaho. The Pueblo folk are communal village dwellers, their economic life is based on agriculture. The Navaho live in individual huts and are preoccupied with their sheep herds. Or finally another case, from the Pacific, might be considered. The Polynesians are all island dwellers, and, being expert navigators and sailors in their outrigger canoes, have been able to make of the sea a highway rather than a barrier. The striking unity of Polynesian culture over the vast sweep of the central Pacific indicates that this contact between the peoples living there has exerted a comparable influence over all the area in which they live. Yet the differences between the habitat afforded by such localities as the Hawaiian Islands, the Tuomotos, and New Zealand are very great. In this instance culture tends to be the constant, while the environment varies. This again implies something less than a one-to-one relation between the two.

4

The position of those who qualify the extreme enviromentalist point of view has been that *the habitat of a people acts as a limiting rather than a determining factor in influencing culture.* In this, they express an approach that brings them much closer to the facts.

This position is not restricted to anthropologists alone, but is much closer to the position of the majority of geographers than is the deterministic one. The reason we have considered the deterministic approach at length, indeed, is that the writings of the minority of geographers who hold to it have had an appeal out of proportion to their representativeness. This appeal is attributable to the fact that their thesis is at once simple, appears convincing —until analyzed in the light of all the facts—and is dramatic. Living in a complex world, we welcome simple explanations. It seems plausible that skyscrapers are found in Manhattan because Manhattan, an overpopulated island, had to reach toward the heavens to accommodate its activities, and that this was made possible by its rocky substructure. We tend to forget that bridges and tunnels and ferryboats connect Manhattan to the mainland and to Long Island, where so large a proportion of Manhattan's daytime millions live; or that in Chicago, where the substratum is clay, skyscrapers are erected on piles driven deep into the ground. We may overlook the fact that, in the plains of central United States, where there is neither lack of space nor pressure of local population, skyscrapers still are built. We may fail to see that in Rio de Janeiro not alone the desire of many persons to enjoy the magnificent bay and ocean front, but also the belief that skyscrapers symbolize "civilization," have caused this architectural form to dominate the skyline of that city.

In discussing the life of people whose cultures are attuned to difficult habitats, moreover, it is their technologies and economic activities that are given most attention. Yet when we wish to analyze the relation of culture, considered as a whole, to habitat, we must range the entire gamut of custom, taking its nonmaterial aspects into account as well as those concerned with getting a living. What, for example, is the relation between decorative design and the habitat of the artist? What interaction is there between political structures of a society and its natural setting?

Phrased in this manner, the complexities of what seems at first glance a matter of simple statement are seen to emerge. Nonrepresentational decorative designs afford a good instance of this.

These designs do not portray any objects and most commonly are found to consist merely of a series of lines, curved or angular, which embellish some object to make it more pleasing to the eye than if it were unornamented. What interpretations these lines will be given, if they are given any at all, depend on the tradition of the people among whom this art is found. Thus, among the Indians of the Plains in the United States such a series of lines as

 has been variously interpreted as a tent with people

standing in front of it, as a cloud with rain falling from it, or as a mountain with streams running down its side. In West Africa,

a design such as 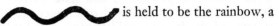 is held to be the rainbow, a

path through the bush, or a snake. The only conclusion we can draw regarding the effect of the habitat on such designs is that where interpretations are given, the explanations are couched in terms of the experience of those who make or look at them. In this experience, the natural setting, as it figures in the life of the people, always enters. But whether or not an explanation of design is referred to the natural setting is a matter of pure chance. Of one thing we can be certain—those who have never seen or heard of a mountain will never interpret any design by such a symbol. But this merely restates the principle that interpretation does not go outside experience; it helps us but little in the process of analyzing relations.

The influence of habitat on political structures, though somewhat less removed from the influence of the natural setting than decorative art, is to be discerned only after several intermediate steps have been traced. Complex political structures exist in large aggregates of population, small ones understandably having little need for them. Concentrations of populations, however, are found where the basic economy of the people is agriculture rather than hunting or herding. But basic economies are tied in more closely with the habitat than any other aspect of culture. Consequently, in general terms, the development of self-conscious political institutions that can be made explicit in description because they are personified in rulers, or are typified in well-recognized systems of law, tends to be found in those areas where sedentary populations produce enough goods to support these specialists.

An analysis of the statements set down in the preceding paragraphs indicates that the flexibility permitted cultural institutions by any habitat is a crucial point in our consideration. Turning again to the principle of the limiting role of the habitat, we perceive that even such a formulation is too simple to provide a conclusive answer to the problem of the relation between culture and habitat. On the central plains of the United States, hunting Indian bands once followed a nomadic existence and lived under systems of government that were little institutionalized. Three hundred years later, by the historic circumstance of a change in basic culture brought in by European migrants, this same area presents an entirely different picture. Agriculture has replaced hunting and even herding; cities dot the region. The political structures of those who live in the area differ from those of the aboriginal Indians. Today, city, county, and state governments, courts and law-enforcement officers, and other agencies of control operate as units of the larger political entity called "the United States." But the natural setting has changed not at all in the past three hundred years, except as it has been changed by the hand of man.

To assign to habitat merely a *limiting* role is thus not enough for our purpose. This explanation, it is patent, has outlived its usefulness, since it essentially expresses a negative point of view that can be called on only to refute positive claims that exceed the facts. As a negative approach, it cannot guide analysis of the habitat-culture equation that will lead to positive findings. We must, first of all, thus recognize that just as the total range of human activities is not equally affected by habitat, any analysis of the relation must be concerned with the differing *responsiveness of the various aspects of culture* to their natural setting, rather than with attempts to erect generalizations affecting total cultures.

We may, therefore, summarize here the degree of relation of several aspects of culture to the habitat. It is evident that the technological and economic elements in the life of a people are far more responsive to the habitat than the form of the dance, or religious rituals, or decorative art. Social and political structures, insofar as they maintain or encourage economic or technological functions, or are dependent upon them, also show some measure of response. This was seen in the examples of political structures in the American plains at two different periods. Yet many elements, even in these aspects of culture, cannot be correlated with habitat at all. Types of kinship systems, or the presence of secret societies, for instance, seem to bear little or no relation to the natural setting. Even less does the form of religion, despite the fact that everywhere its effective functioning lies in adjusting man to the universe. The universe to which it adjusts him, however, is one of his own devising, for which the actual habitat provides a background. The portrayals in the earlier literature of the beliefs of such West African folk as live in the Niger Delta or Cross River jungles are a case in point. Their belief in magic and their stark fear of supernatural powers were held to reflect the hardships and dangers of life in these dark forests. A more sophisticated technique of study, however, shows that the constant fear these people have been said to live under because of their habitat is more a construct of the observer than a fact in their lives. The dangers, to be sure, are real enough, but they are no greater than the dangers of living in a world where electricity and automobiles and other mechanical devices injure or kill thousands every year. Though the comparative psychological effect of living amid these hazards is still to be studied, it is not too rash to conjecture that both the Niger Delta groups and ourselves achieve a parallel measure of integration to life as they and we live it.

5

The fact that the total environment provides men with the raw stuff of experience and that habitat is an integral and constant element in this environment must thus never be lost sight of. We should also, however, understand that the degree of latitude in possible variation is greater in art or religion or story-telling than in agriculture or herding. The symbolism of decorative art *may* draw on the habitat; the gods are customarily related in some way to the forces of nature; stories about animals rarely refer to creatures found outside the habitat of the tellers. Yet in the play of the imagination, the permitted variation is undeniably greater in such cultural phenomena than where the seasons dictate the agricultural cycle, or the habitat restricts the crops that may be planted, or a limited supply of grass makes it necessary for a herding people to be constantly on the move. Habitat, then, is a limiting factor, but it *selectively* limits behavior.

This principle must be still further refined, however. For it becomes clear, as we study the relation between culture and habitat, that man not only adapts himself to his natural setting, but as his adaptation becomes more effective, he is freed from the demands of his habitat, making it possible for him at times to challenge or even defy its limitations.

Rice cultivation in the Far East affords an excellent instance of how this operates. Though there are types of rice that grow where the ground is dry, the species of rice used in this part of the world is grown in irrigated paddies. It would seem obvious that flat land is essential for this sort of cultivation, for where else could the necessary pools of shallow water be maintained? Obviously, as the tradition of "wet" rice growing and the taste for rice spread, either through borrowing or migration, or both, to regions where the land is rugged, a choice of adaptation or renunciation was forced.

Rice cultivation as carried on by the Ifugao of the Philippines shows how the knowledge of terracing, a technological development, permitted the growing of irrigated rice in a terrain that, on the face of it, would seem absolutely to forbid this. Rice grows to an altitude of five thousand feet, and the terraces that have been built up the mountainsides to reach this limit sometimes soar three thousand feet from the floor of the narrow valleys that lie between the mountains. With these terraces, the only requirement for growing "wet" rice is that the water begin its flow at a point higher than the highest terrace. Then the stream can be directed as needed from its source to the highest terrace, then to the next, and so on until all the "fields" have the water they need. And the water, having finally dropped its silt in the calm pools through which it has been directed, joins the river in the valley bottom. The labor that goes into constructing these terraces and in maintaining them is grueling. On steep slopes, stone-retaining walls have to be built. Each rock used in these walls must be carried up the mountainside from the valley floor. Sometimes terrace walls have to be twenty feet high to permit the utilization of land about eleven feet wide. Elsewhere in the Philippines, where the mountains are steeper, the terraces rise fifty feet to allow this much space for cultivation.[4]

The manner in which the technological devices of Euroamerican culture allow a far greater latitude in ways of living in the tropics than could ever be dreamed of without them, may also be mentioned as a case in point. Electrical refrigeration, for example, and air conditioning, to cite only two of the more striking developments, permit a wider variety of foodstuffs to be utilized and a more effective escape from high temperatures than a tropical habitat of itself could ever permit. Technological achievements such as vaccines and other inoculations have freed inhabitants of tropical areas from endemic diseases and have thus

[4] R. F. Barton, 1922, *passim.*

directly contravened what had become limitations set by the habitat.

Culture, especially in its technological aspects, can moreover be thought of as influencing habitat in a manner analogous to the way in which we have seen it influence physical type. Though we rarely conceive of culture as altering the natural setting, it needs but little reflection to see that this is commonplace in human history. All groups who have built irrigation systems have changed the physical structure of their habitat in thus extending its potentialities. We need but recall the example of how the Ifugao and many other Far Eastern rice-growing folk have changed the physical features of the mountainous country they inhabit, for corroboration of the point. To go from these manipulations of the habitat to such engineering feats as the Suez and Panama canals, which have severed whole continental land masses, or to the great dams that create man-made lakes covering hundreds of square miles, is but to traverse a series of steps that reflect an increasing technological competence.

We have thus far seen that, though the habitat limits man's culture, it influences cultures not as wholes but to different degrees in different cultures, and variously in their several aspects. It should be emphasized that though technology and economics respond most readily to the demands of the natural setting, this does not mean that habitat does not affect nonmaterial as well as material elements. In the main, it can be said, as a refinement of earlier phrasings of the relation between habitat and culture, that *the more adequate the technology of a people, the less direct will be the demands made by the habitat on them.* We are here expressing a principle analogous to the one advanced in our discussion of the relation between race and culture. The fact that culture acts as a buffer between man and his habitat is a phenomenon of the same order as that which permitted us to state, on the biological level, that man, as a culture-building animal, in large measure replaced natural selection with social selection. What we perceive is that the relation of culture to either of these facets of human existence is a *reciprocal* one. Culture, that is, can in no wise be thought of as a passive element, to be molded by the impact of race or habitat. We need, therefore, to examine in this context certain of the implications that the reality of culture is psychological.[5]

[5] For the development of this point, see Chap. 16, below.

6

The environment, under the definitions given at the outset of this chapter, is the total setting of human life, encompassing both culture, or what is learned, and habitat, or the natural setting. In their interplay, the two components react selectively on each other. That is, just as differing aspects of culture are influenced to different degrees by the habitat, so within the limits imposed by its habitat in terms of its technological competence, a culture defines the effective elements of the natural environment that enter into its total setting, and indicates to what extent the habitat must continuously be taken into account by the individual in his daily life. This is what has been termed the behavioral world of the individual. It is this psychological environment that provides him with his defined concept of reality.

But is it possible, one may ask, to tamper with such immutable elements in experience as time and space and direction? The sun, the moon, the stars, the planets—are they not fixed, unchangeable realities in the life of a man? Can these, and the rivers and mountains and forests exist only by definition? Such an approach, even when questions of this order are merely posed, strikes so deep into our thinking that the very questions seem inadmissible as subjects of discussion.

We here turn to a principle to be considered later in this book, that of cultural relativism.[6] There it will be seen how the Indians of the Southwest and zenith and nadir, up and down, to our north, east, south and west. The convention of map reading in our own culture shows us how the reality of direction is culturally defined. It is this that makes it difficult for us to think of the *upper* Nile as *south* and the *lower* Nile as *north*. Or again, while the spectrum can be objectively verified, perception of its colors is culturally conditioned. In West Africa, among the Yoruba—to cite only one example out of the many that might be mentioned—any blue as dark or darker than indigo is identified as black. Colors, on the spectrum, merge from one to another imperceptibly; it is culture that interprets these data of experience by drawing the distinguishing lines.

Mountains may exist as barriers, as suppliers of raw materials, as elements in the landscape, as factors in influencing climate, or in other capacities; and so with rivers and other aspects of the habitat. Nor must we, for a moment, in sketching the environment of man, neglect those unseen beings that people the habitat.

[6] Chap. 19, below.

Myth carries quite as much conviction to those who count it as a part of their heritage as the rocks they come upon in preparing a field—rocks which, in their concept of reality, may have been placed in the way of the gardener by the creatures whose existence the myth explains. It is a commonplace that in any culture where belief is strong one can actually encounter those who have seen supernatural beings. In our mechanistic universe, multitudes still people graveyards with ghosts whose presence, even for those who do not acknowledge them, is sufficiently a part of that particular detail of their habitat to make them reluctant to visit such a spot late at night.

The problem in studying the relation between culture and habitat is thus to determine the degree of integration of experience achieved by a people as they adapt themselves to the conditions under which they live—how, as Gayton phrases it, the culture is "enmeshed with its natural surroundings." [7] After describing the "fundamental culture-environment relationship" of the California Indian Yokuts and Western Mono tribes, this student points out that here "the cultural concern with natural surroundings was not limited to utilitarian concern." Rather, "a culture-environment form of integration of more than a merely mechanical sort" is found, so that "features of the environment which are not essential to basic subsistence are caught up in the ceremonial, social and religious superstructure." From this, various modes of attack on the question appear. "Does this mean," we are asked, "that a culture which carries more environmental references is less subject to change—is more stable—than one which has less?" [8] The study of the dynamics of culture-habitat interaction is indicated; as is the study of how the natural setting is integrated into the behavioral world of the members of a given society, and how the reaction to habitat differs among peoples who live in a single natural setting but whose cultures differ.

In accepting the role of the habitat as a factor in shaping culture, as something to which culture must respond, however selectively, we thus also recognize that the total environment of man, drawing on both the traditional heritage of his way of life and the habitat in which he lives, is made up of no more than can be comprehended in the definition of reality that he and his fellows draw out of their experience and the experience of those from whom they have descended.

[7] A. H. Gayton, 1946, p. 254.
[8] *Ibid.*, p. 264.

Part Two

The

Aspects

of

Culture

Chapter **Seven**

The Universals in Culture

One of the earliest postulates of anthropological science was that the ends achieved by all human ways of life, or cultures, are basically similar. This universality in the general outlines of cultures supported the theory, advanced by such early anthropologists as Herbert Spencer and E. B. Tylor, of the "psychic unity of mankind," which held that the similarities to be found in the institutions of different cultures are to be accounted for by the similar capacities of all men. The resemblances in structure actually found in one culture after another are an expression of similarities in individual behavior, transferred to the level of the social group. Wissler, one of the first to direct attention to this problem, inclined toward a biological interpretation of cultural universals, or a "culture scheme," as he called it.[1] "It seems reasonable to suppose that what all men have in common is inherited," he stated at one point. He also held that men "have a type of behavior as inevitably fixed as that of any social insect." That is, "man builds cultures because he cannot help it; there is a *drive* in his protoplasm that carries him forward even against his will."[2]

[1] C. Wissler, 1923, p. 74.
[2] *Ibid.*, pp. 260, 265.

This drive is then shaped by the conditioning process, the process of cultural learning that causes an infant to manifest the behavior of his group. The variants in cultural behavior, it follows, become "largely variants in the conditioning of inborn responses." The "content of culture" is thus to be differentiated from the universal pattern. "The former is, in the main, acquired behavior, the latter is an expression of inborn behavior." [3]

Certain cultural uniformities do arise out of the similarities in the situations all human beings must cope with, such as some kind of family to care for the young, or even some system of belief with which to achieve a sense of security in an otherwise overpowering universe. But admitting this is far from postulating inherent drives to account for such uniformities. A genetic basis for culture implies a genetic mechanism; and this has never been discovered. Man is a "tool-using animal," as Tylor called him, because his physical type makes it possible to devise the extensions of his hands and arms we call "tools." He is a "speaking animal" because he has the anatomical and neurological structures to make speech possible.

The most elaborate attempt to account for the universality of certain aspects of culture appears in a posthumous work of B. Malinowski. Here is set forth the function which each of the cultural responses is held to fulfill in satisfying what are termed the basic needs of men. His scheme is as follows:

Basic Needs	*Cultural Responses*
1. Metabolism	1. Commissariat
2. Reproduction	2. Kinship
3. Bodily comforts	3. Shelter
4. Safety	4. Protection
5. Movement	5. Activities
6. Growth	6. Training
7. Health	7. Hygiene

This list, its author holds,

> has to be read with each pair of horizontal entries regarded as linked up inseparably. The real understanding of our concept of need implies its direct correlation with the response which it receives from culture. . . . The needs for food, drink, and oxygen are never isolated, impelling forces which send the individual organism or a group as a whole into a blind search for food or water or oxygen. . . . Human beings under their con-

[3] *Ibid.*, pp. 267–9.
[4] B. Malinowski, 1944, p. 92.

ditions of culture wake up with their morning appetite ready, and also with a breakfast waiting for them or else ready to be prepared. . . . It is clear that the organism becomes adjusted, so that within the domain of each need specific habits are developed; and, in the organization of cultural responses, these routine habits are met by an organized routine of satisfactions.[5]

Basic human needs, manifest in the cultural activities of men, in turn set up a series of "derived needs," which means that "culture supplies man with derived potentialities, abilities, and powers." From the derived needs come a series of "cultural imperatives," which give form to the institutions of a culture that go to make up those broadest divisions that we shall here term "aspects." In the following table Malinowski indicates how these are built up.

Imperatives	*Responses*
1. The cultural apparatus of implements and consumer's goods must be produced, used, maintained, and replaced by new production.	1. Economics
2. Human behavior, as regards its technical, customary, legal or moral prescription must be codified, regulated in action and sanction.	2. Social control
3. The human material by which every institution is maintained must be renewed, formed, drilled and provided with full knowledge of tribal tradition.	3. Education
4. Authority within each institution must be defined, equipped with powers, and endowed with means of forceful execution of its orders.	4. Political organization [6]

In scrutinizing these two tables, however, we cannot but be struck with the omission of any reference to religion or the aesthetic elements of culture. Is the universality of these aspects less securely established than are the domains of economics or social organization?

Later in this same volume Malinowski did include these facets of custom. He there defines culture as "essentially an instrumental apparatus by which man is put in a position the better to cope with the concrete specific problems that face him in his environment in the course of the satisfaction of his needs." Then, he continues, its "activities, attitudes and objects are organized around important and vital tasks into institutions such as the family, the clan, the local community, the tribe, and organized teams of eco-

[5] *Ibid.*, pp. 93-4.
[6] *Ibid.*, p. 125.

nomic cooperation, political, legal and educational activity." Finally, he states that "from the dynamic point of view, that is, as regards the type of activity, culture can be analyzed into a number of aspects such as education, social control, economics, systems of knowledge, belief and morality, and also modes of creative and artistic expression." [7] But what needs are satisfied by these "systems of belief" or "modes of creative and artistic expression" we are not told.

Murdock, who has drawn up one of the most elaborate listings of cultural elements, posits that "only a small proportion of men's actions in any society spring directly from any of the demonstrable basic drives," citing as illustration how acquired appetites channel reactions of hunger toward certain foods, or taboos stand in the way of satisfying hunger drives.[8] He then sets forth a second reason for "rejecting the impulse factor." This arises out of the fact that "most social institutions or culture complexes actually give satisfaction to several basic impulses as well as to a variety of derived drives"—as when marriage becomes as important for the prestige it confers as for the sexual satisfactions it affords. He therefore refers cultural behavior to two mechanisms. The first is instinct, defined as "a precise organization of behavior developed through natural selection and transmitted through heredity," which man shares with all other organisms. The second is habit formation, which man shares with the higher forms. These operate "to mediate between two types of situations in which organisms find themselves, namely, those in which impulses are aroused and impulses are satisfied." The satisfaction of an impulse results in the reduction of the drives that stimulated the activity.

Culture lends itself to this end, we are told, both through directly satisfying basic needs, and by means of secondary, or "instrumental," responses. Finally, culture comprehends "a third and very large category of cultural habits . . . in which behavior is followed by rewards that bear no relation, or only an incidental one, to the impulses prompting the behavior." Such a sequence occurs when a rain-making spell evokes a storm, for instance, or a magic charm "works." The establishment of these patterns is referred to a kind of selective process, whereby the institutions best fitted to achieve their ends survive at the expense of those less fitted.[9]

[7] *Ibid.,* p. 150.
[8] G. P. Murdock and others, 1945.
[9] G. P. Murdock, 1945, pp. 128–33.

In referring cultural *universals* to processes of this kind, however, the problem of accounting for the similarities in basic organization found in all cultures is merely moved to a different plane. That is to say, if we envisage our universals as satisfying basic biological needs, out of which the acquired cultural responses arise, then we find ourselves exactly where all other hypotheses have taken us. If, on the other hand, we stress the secondary responses, and refer the broad aspects of human culture to them, we must treat universals as historic phenomena, having their origin so early in man's life on earth as to have caused them to be passed on from one generation to the next, and to be preserved everywhere mankind traveled as the earth became populated.

The question in the comprehensive study of culture with which we are concerned here is thus a most difficult one. Answering it involves weighing fundamental points concerning the origin and development of culture on which we have no information, and as far as we can tell at present are unlikely to have. Each of the theories advanced to explain it is persuasive until we study it closely and become aware of its incompleteness. Incontrovertibly, there are biological bases for the behavior of individuals that fashion culture, and there are requirements of the habitat that must be met, a fact already pointed out and one that will enter again in later pages. We have seen how the fact that man is a member of the biological series and that he must meet the demands of his habitat, deeply influences his cultural proclivities. The story of his development in prehistoric times was seen to be the story of how these phases of man's existence were reconciled in the development of his culture. But "life is not lived by bread alone," and accounting for "the arts of life" but leads us into rationalizations rather than scientifically verifiable explanations.

Most students recognize that the institutions in which these broad adjustments are manifest in given societies are by no means to be explained in simple terms. Does not culture often seem to defeat its ends, as when food taboos interpose a cultural restraint that entails deprivation, rather than the satisfaction of hunger? Wissler phrases this distortion by tradition in terms of the conditioning process, Malinowski speaks of the resulting psychological drives as derived needs. There can be no doubt that, viewed in the large, culture does fulfill the needs of man, psychic no less than biological; that it solves for him problems whose solution is demanded both by the character of his biopsychological make-up and the need to meet the demands of his habitat. He does this by setting up institutions which, for each society, exact conformities from the individuals who compose it, in the interest of adjustment and survival. That institutions vary so widely from one society to another only means that multiple solutions stemming from an underlying universal base characterize human culture.

2

It is impossible for any single study to describe more than a portion of the aspects of the life of a people. Even those whose aim is to give the most rounded portrayal possible find limits which, for technical reasons of time, space and competence they cannot exceed. In practice, language is left to the specialist, and so is music. If any attempt is made to include the literary arts, this material must commonly be reserved for separate treatment because of its bulk. Some aspects of culture are rarely studied as such; forms of dramatic expression, for instance, since in non-literate societies drama is customarily a part of ritual. The dance, also, has too rarely been analyzed, because of the technical difficulties of valid recording.

It is worth while noting how a rounded study of a culture has been organized in terms of its principal aspects. For this purpose, we may turn to the study of a Mexican village community, Cherán, a Tarascan group in the state of Michoacán, west of Mexico City.[10] The discussion opens with a description of the natural setting of this village, its size and its physical organization, which is documented with detailed maps illustrating house types and political subdivisions. The culture itself is treated under five principal headings, entitled technology, economics, the community, religion and ceremonial, and the individual and his culture.

The first heading considers how the natural resources are utilized—minerals, forests, water supply; how agriculture is carried on, and the crops that are raised; the use of domesticated animals; how various manufacturing processes—ceramics, textiles, woodworking—are carried on; and how foods are prepared and used. Under economics, we learn about the organization of production, in terms of the use of land, labor, and capital; the costs of production and the income yielded by those who work at the various specialties whose technical aspects were discussed earlier; the mechanisms of distribution; such matters as consumption, as reflected in family budgets or in the values and prices of various goods and services; and how wealth is distributed and regarded. The social structure and the governmental instrumentalities of the

[10] R. L. Beals, 1946.

community are described, while the section on religion and ceremonial treats of the place of the Catholic Church in the lives of the people, and the particular forms which its rites take in this Mexican Indian community. Here, too, the secular dances are described, and witchcraft and other beliefs outside the purview of the Church are discussed. The description of the life of the individual follows the principal events in the life-cycle, and the analysis ends with a discussion of certain problems in the study of culture raised by this body of materials.

The assumptions that underlie the progression of topics in such a presentation are those of most descriptive studies. The description moves from consideration of those aspects that supply the physical wants of man, to those that order social relations, and finally to the aspects that, in giving meaning to the universe, sanction everyday living and, in their aesthetic manifestations, afford men some of their deepest satisfactions.

On the basis of the pooled experience of students of culture, the following organization of cultural universals, to be followed in the ensuing chapters, is suggested:

> *Material Culture and Its Sanctions*
> Technology
> Economics
> *Social Institutions*
> Social organization
> Education
> Political structures
> *Man and the Universe*
> Belief systems
> The control of power
> *Aesthetics*
> Graphic and plastic arts
> Folklore
> Music, drama and the dance
> *Language*

It must be stressed that in dividing cultures in this way, we are but utilizing a scientific device whose justification is its utility in throwing light on the problems that are the subject of study. Ideally, cultures should be considered as wholes, but in fact as entities they are too complex and present too many interrelations to permit such a comprehensive attack. With this in mind, for example, it is clear we will not be deceived into regarding material culture as distinct from the nonmaterial aspects of civilization. We will recognize that there is no single object, no matter how tangible it may seem, but has a cultural existence by definition. A cartwheel that serves as a chandelier is no longer a cartwheel but a lighting device. The batik cloth that is an article of clothing in Java becomes translated, in another culture, into a wall hanging. Even the hardest-bitten engineer includes "know-how" as part of the technical equipment of his profession. But "know-how" is the nonmaterial aspect of technology.

Graphic and plastic arts offer another instance of how data cast even in the broadest categories can refuse to stay within the scholar's bounds. Painting and sculpture do not exist apart from their expression, and this expression can only be given in some tangible form—the painting on a cave wall, the decoration on a pottery jar or on a woven basket, the figurine carved of wood, or the statue hewn out of stone. For this reason art follows material culture and technology in many cultural schemes. But we find that in monographs dealing with specific tribal cultures, art rarely stands in this relation to the description of the tangible objects used in everyday life. The ethnographer disregards the fact that art is manifested in material objects. His approach strikes through to the cultural reality that the essence of art, that which gives the tangible object its appeal and its meaning, to say nothing of the impulse to create it, cannot be touched. These qualities constitute what we call the aesthetic conventions of a people, which, in the last analysis, find realization in the genius of the individuals who decorate the pot, or paint the wall, or carve the statuette.

What, then, of our categories of culture? Does this mean that they, too, vanish on examination? All experience with the study of culture indicates that this is not the case. To maintain that the approach by categories is fruitless would be to disregard the basis on which the various scholarly and scientific disciplines have been erected. He would indeed be a hardy advocate of the study of whole cultures who would insist that the economic aspects of life failed to present problems that could not be studied in disregard of the fact that at some few points the economic system might be involved in matters of religious, or aesthetic, or even sociological import. Problems of composition, color, and mass are problems of art and do not impinge on questions about government.

Chapter **Eight**

Technology and the Utilization of Natural Resources

By means of their *technology*, men wrest from their habitat the foodstuffs, the shelter, the clothing, and the implements they must have if they are to survive. The objects they make and use for these purposes are generally classified under the heading of *material culture*.[1]

The study of technology is essential to an understanding of culture, just as the comprehension of the material basis of social life is indispensable to an understanding of human group behavior. More than this, we have seen that the technological equipment of a people figures more than any other aspect of their culture when judgments of advancement or retardation are drawn. This is due to the fact that technology is the only aspect of culture susceptible of objective evaluation. These evaluations follow a pattern that, with the rise of a system of production based on the power machine, has become exceedingly congenial to our culture.

The machine, however, is by no means unknown to non-literate peoples. As Digby points out, the essential problem of the machine is "to convert and *guide* the movements of four prime -

[1] M. J. Herskovits, 1952, *passim*.

movers into channels whereby they would perform useful work." Most of this work, he shows, is done by the use of stationary man power as the prime mover, and in this the hands are used far more often than the feet. Also found as movers are human or animal power combined with the force of gravity or used tractively, water power, and wind power—though the last is employed so rarely that it need not be taken into account, except in the use of sails.

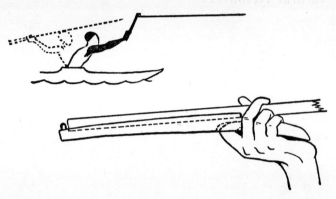

Fig. 14 *Eskimo spear thrower, showing manner of holding and using.*

The methods of application are two, the first of which is found in by far the greater numbers of instances: a reciprocating or unidirectional motion "as a result of constant repetition and less need for muscular control," and the second, rotary motion. Instances of the rotary method of applying the force of man power are not numerous. They include the Tibetan prayer wheel, the Eskimo stringmaker, and the New Guinea drill. Direct motion is employed in the fireplow, the pestle and mortar, the bellows, and the loom. Wedges are used for lifting weights, levers in deadfalls and, with the auxiliary power of gravity, in the cassava squeezers of the South American Indians. Rollers are employed in spinning, while nonliterate folk utilize the principle of the axle and bearing, converting power by a means of a cord or crank, as in such devices as the Eskimo bow drill or the Samoan rope twister.[2]

Even peoples whose equipment is of the simplest, who have no machines such as these, employ mechanical principles that are

[2] A. Digby, 1938, p. 73.

quite complex. The boomerang of the Australian, the heavy knob-kerrie of the South African Bantu, the spear-thrower—all show a shrewd utilization of physical forces that give the individual added flexibility and power in using his physical capacities. The use of

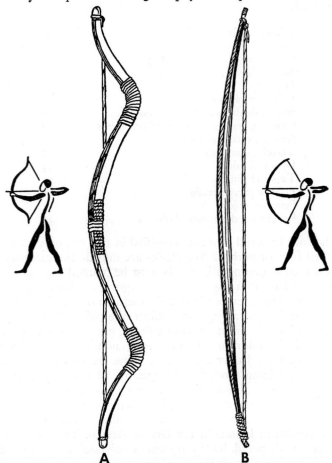

Fig. 15 **(A)** *Eskimo compound bow;* **(B)** *Sauk and Fox simple bow.*

the principle of the spring in the manufacture of the compound bow is another instance of this. Even the simpler type of bow, made of one piece of wood, recognizes and allows for the elasticity of wood, while the bow-string compounds the same principle, and the feathered arrow insures better aim.

It should be noted that the technological equipment of a peo-

ple comprises most of the man-made elements in culture that have
a physical existence of their own. Because of this they form the
greater part of ethnographic museum collections. Osgood's classification of the items in Ingalik material culture documents this
point well.

Primary tools	40
Lines	15
Containers	41
Miscellaneous manufactures	60
Weapons	11
Fishing implements	23
Snares, deadfalls and other traps	12
Clothing, cradles and personal ornaments	46
Shelters, caches and racks	29
Travel implements	25
Dyes and paints	13
Tags and games	22
Puberty paraphernalia	8
Funerary objects	14
Religious and ceremonial objects	41

Of the four hundred elements classified in this list, only those of
the final four or perhaps five classes are outside the category of
objects used in getting a living. It must be pointed out, however,
than an implement in Osgood's first category, a primary tool such
as an awl or a bark scraper, is equally useful in making a food container or in manufacturing some object of a puberty rite.[3]

Not all the items in material culture, nor all the elements of
technological equipment found among nonliterate peoples are
equally distributed over the world. Some are ubiquitous—techniques of obtaining food, for example, are of necessity a part of
the equipment of all societies. Such a technique as fire making,
which is not essential to survival, is present in all human cultures,
with one or two exceptions such as the culture of the inhabitants
of the Andaman Islands in the Bay of Bengal. The building of
shelters is widespread, but by no means universal, and the same is
true of clothing, though there are few peoples who do not cover
some portion of the body on certain occasions. Other technical
processes, for a variety of reasons, have still more restricted distributions. In some instances, the habitat lays its prohibition, as it
does for basketry or wood carving in the arctic. Sometimes considerations of utility enter, as is evidenced by the almost complete
absence of cumbersome and fragile pottery vessels among nomadic

[3] C. Osgood, 1940, *passim.*

peoples. On occasion historical reasons explain why the distribution of a given technique is restricted, as in the instance of ironworking, which was developed in the Old World but was never worked out in the Western Hemisphere.

Certain principles of universal applicability may be abstracted from the data. First, every society has worked out a material culture and techniques of exploiting the natural resources of its habitat that provide the basis for the nonmaterial aspects of the culture. Second, every group evinces a hardheaded approach to the problems of exploiting the resources of their habitat. Their techniques are in accord with the physical principles involved, and are based on processes of inference from cause to effect. These techniques demonstrate ingenuity and inventiveness, and show that the people are quite able to profit from the method of trial and error.

The reasoning with which "primitive" man approaches his practical problems, and the fact that in this he manifests no special type of mentality that inhibits his powers of reasoning objectively where questions of utility are at issue, should be stressed. Skills such as are involved in making a boomerang or a compound bow are displayed by peoples whose "level of culture," as this is phrased, is low indeed. We scarcely expect to find the pygmies of the Congo forests constructing suspension bridges, but they do. Some of the more complex achievements of science also have their parallels among nonliterate peoples. Examples often cited are the precision of the Maya calendar or the architectural skills of the pre-Spanish Peruvian structures. Not so well known is the indigenous practice among certain African tribes of smallpox vaccination; or the use by the Polynesians of rattan charts to indicate prevailing winds and currents, thus incorporating full sailing directions for their long voyages.

The picture of nonliterate man we draw from studying his technology and material culture is of a hard-working individual who effectively calls on the skills that he has learned, and that are adequate to gain him the living he desires. Thus, nonliterate man, like men who live in literate societies, is practical, seeing an advantage when it is presented to him—provided it is not too far removed from the technological patterns of his culture—and using it if he is convinced that it will accomplish the results he desires.

2

Foodstuffs are of two kinds, animal and plant, used either in their wild state, or in a state of domestication. The fourfold classification that results from these alternatives was for a long time used as the basis for distinguishing the different economic systems of nonliterate peoples, in this manner:

Economy	Foods
food gathering	plant (wild)
hunting	animal (wild)
herding	animal (domesticated)
agriculture (cultivation)	plant (domesticated)

The order in which these are given was believed to be that in which the economies of human societies evolved. However, Forde's caution must be remembered: "People do not live at economic stages. They possess economies; and again we do not find single and exclusive economies but combinations of them." For the conventional classification he substitutes collecting, hunting, fishing, cultivation, and stock raising,[4] stressing the fact that none is exclusive in any society.

This follows from the nature of dietary requirements. A diet restricted to meat would be monotonous indeed. Even the Eskimo, forced by their habitat to eat nothing else during the long winter, in summer become food gatherers and taboo eating the flesh of sea mammals. Similarly, it is difficult to think of any people, even with a well-advanced agricultural system, who do not supplement their garden produce by hunting. As in all aspects of culture, we find that clear-cut classifications are difficult. Man draws on the food resources at hand and employs the techniques that are known to him. He is rarely committed to any one way of doing anything.

There can be little question that gathering, hunting, and fishing existed long before herding or cultivation. This is well established by the archaeological evidence. Before the beginning of the Neolithic, life was lived on the basis of finding and utilizing the foods offered by the habitat, with no way to control the supply except by knowledge of the location of roots, nuts, and berries, or of the habits of game animals. There are many peoples who, to the present, have neither domesticated plants nor domesticated food animals. Among these gatherers are the Indians of the California and Great Basin areas, the peoples having "marginal" cultures in the eastern and southern open country of South America, the pygmies of central Africa and elsewhere, the aboriginal inhabitants of the Andaman Islands. Hunting peoples include the Eskimo, most of the Canadian Indians and Plains Indians, the

[4] C. D. Forde, 1934, p. 461.

South African Bushmen, and the Australian aborigines—though these last two are as much food gatherers as they are hunters.

Despite their simplicity, food-gathering and hunting economies require considerable technical competence. To find and gather wild roots, nuts, seeds, and berries, to trap or hunt the food animals, takes knowledge not only of the terrain but of the most favorable times and the best conditions under which to obtain these foods, to say nothing of preserving them for future use. The life of the wild-rice gatherers of the Upper Great Lakes strikingly demonstrates this. During March, April, and May these Indians lived principally on the maple sugar they made, then they ate early berries, and later green corn. In the autumn and later, the wild rice that was stored for early winter use was consumed. During the spring and summer they supplemented their diet with the wild fowl to be found in the rice fields; in the late winter they subsisted on the meat of the animals they hunted, and pemmican, a compound of dried meat and berries. Peoples who live on what their habitat yields must also have containers for what they gather, and traps, snares, spears, bows and arrows, nets, and other paraphernalia for hunting and fishing. The list of material objects we have already quoted from Osgood provides us with one example of how many things such an economy requires.

Relatively few animals have been domesticated, and most herding economies are based primarily on the predominance of a single one of these forms. The principal domesticated animals are the horse, ox, reindeer, camel, and sheep; and, like all the domesticated types except the llama, vicuña, and turkey, they were domesticated in the Old World, to which their aboriginal distribution was confined. Reindeer form the basis of the economies of most Old World peoples living in the circumpolar zone, from Lapland to eastern Siberia, while on the Asiatic steppes to the south, horses, and in East Africa, cattle, predominate. In the Sahara and Arabian deserts, the camel and the horse are the principal animals. Most herding folk have sheep and other smaller forms, which furnish them with food to supplement the yield from the larger animals. The camel and the horse, however, are rarely sources of meat.

In contrast to the limited number of animals that has been domesticated, the number of domesticated plants is legion. As regards the cultivation of cereals, students speak of three principal areas. The first includes Europe, northern Africa, and the Near East, where wheat, oats, and barley are the most important crops. The second, where rice predominates, comprehends Asia, Malaysia, and Indonesia. The third, or maize area, is the New World. Africa is more eclectic, with maize, millet, yams, and cassava all having important places in the food economy of various parts of the continent. In Polynesia, taro, yams, breadfruit and sugar cane predominate, no cereals being cultivated.

The techniques of cultivation are numerous. The simplest agricultural implement is the digging stick, a pointed branch hardened by fire. In Australia the women use it to loosen the earth about the roots of the wild tubers to facilitate the growth of the plants. Elsewhere, however, in Africa, the Americas and the South Seas, the digging stick is employed as a kind of hoe, while among the Maori of New Zealand and the Zuñi a crosspiece is attached, or a crotch provides a footrest so that the implement can be utilized as a crude spade.

Essentially an Old World tool, the hoe represents a vast improvement. It exhibits a wide variety of forms. Thus the African broad-bladed, short-handled iron hoe contrasts with the European narrow-bladed, long-handled implement. When placed in the competent hands of an experienced user, it is almost as effective for breaking the ground as a plow. The latter, which puts the domesticated animal to work, is a Euro-Asiatic implement and is not found elsewhere.

Many nonliterate cultivators fully recognize that continuous use of a plot of ground exhausts the soil. Where land is plentiful, this presents no problem, since new gardens can be prepared from virgin soil. Where land is not plentiful, however, a technique especially used in tropical countries is to burn off the growth of the preceding year to supply ash as fertilizer for the next crop. The Indians of eastern United States who planted their maize in hills put a fish in each hill as fertilizer. These Indians also practiced multiple planting. In each hill, squash and bean seeds were placed, so that the bean plants might climb the corn stalks, and the squash vines run along the ground. The same principle is operative in West Africa, where gourds take the place of squashes. The native theory that governs this practice indicates how native peoples reason about such matters. They hold that a plant that grows erect, one that climbs, and one that hugs the earth each takes different foods from the ground—a deduction not too much at variance with the principles of soil chemistry. Notable techniques in growing crops are irrigation and terracing. An outstanding example of irrigation is found in the American Southwest, where it has been practiced since early pre-Spanish times. The terracing in the Philippines has been discussed in an earlier chapter. Another example of terracing as an aid to agriculture is afforded in the Andean highlands.

Whether plants or animals were domesticated first, a question that has aroused much controversy, derives theoretical importance

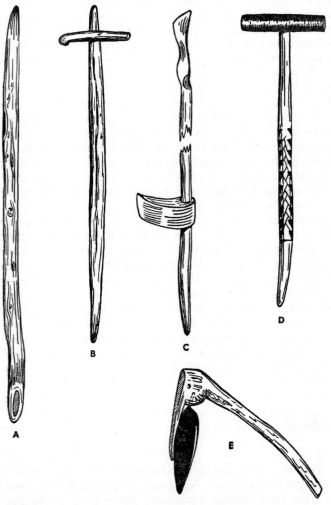

Fig. 16 *Agricultural implements.* **(A)** *Australian digging stick (length, 3¾ ft.);* **(B)** *Cowichan hafted digging stick (length, 3 ft.);* **(C)** *Maori dibble with footrest (length, 5 ft.);* **(D)** *Thompson Indian dibble (length, 2½ ft.);* **(E)** *African (Nigerian) broad-bladed hoe (length of handle, 20 in.).*

from its bearing on the hypothesis of stages in the development of food economies. For, if the sequence gathering-hunting-herding-agriculture is valid, the domestication of animals must have preceded that of plants. Various researches, however, seem to indicate that the domestication of animals followed the beginnings of agriculture. Another unresolved question is how plants and animals came to be domesticated. It is reasonable to assume that the domestication of plants may have resulted from the astute observation of some unknown culture-hero—or, more likely, heroine—of how dropped seeds reproduce themselves. As for the domestication of animals, the answers range between two extremes—that the earliest animals to be domesticated freely associated with man, or that man conceived the idea of domestication and experimented until he achieved the desired result. Quite possibly both of these processes were involved. What we know is that practically all the domesticated animals were brought to the service of man in a very short period of time. With this accomplished, few others susceptible of living under domestication, and complying with its conditions, have since been discovered.

One result of the domestication of animals seems to have been to bring men prominently into the field of agricultural activities, while the domestication of plants seems to have extended women's gathering activities to include the work of caring for the crops. Whether men in those early days took over the hard labor of breaking the ground and preparing it for planting cannot be said. Most societies today assign this work to men. The discovery of the plow that called for a domesticated animal to pull it posed a problem: either the beast, whose care was in the male sphere of the economy, had to be transferred to the economic sphere of women, or agricultural work, heretofore the concern of women, had to be transferred to men. The latter is what did occur. The world over, in plow cultures, women have a minor role in agriculture, whereas in cultures where the plow is not used, their role is a dominant one.

3

Though a food supply is indispensable, it is quite possible to get along without *shelter*. Not many peoples, it is true, omit this item from their cultural equipment, but it always surprises the novice in the study of culture to what a minimum it can successfully be reduced.

That a rough correlation does exist between habitat and shelter may be readily granted. Extremes of temperature make imperative demands and press upon the limits of human endurance. Yet the Siberian Chukchi and the Eskimo can function under conditions of extreme cold that both astound the visitor from warmer regions and would be beyond his endurance if he tried to imitate them. Bogoras tells of Chukchi women sitting out of doors sewing without gloves when the temperature was at its lowest. That the hands should be so exposed is sufficient cause for remark; but it must not be overlooked that the rest of the body was warmly clothed, and that a skin tent stood nearby to provide shelter when it was needed. Similarly, there is frequent comment on the imperviousness of the inhabitants of the tropics to the rays of the sun. Living in a tropical milieu does undoubtedly make the indigenous dweller better able to resist the sun than is the case with those who come from more temperate zones, yet the student will soon observe that natives seek the shade of a tree or the dark coolness of a thatched hut at midday, until the period of the most severe heat has passed. In actuality, we find that the minimum of shelter necessary to preserve life is lower than casual consideration would indicate. Conversely, the maximum degree of shelter attained by most societies is so much greater than necessary for survival that we must seek other reasons to account for it.

Absence of constructed shelters marks the life of peoples with limited technologies and without materials from which shelters can readily be constructed. Certain South African Bushmen tribes inhabit caves or rock shelters. The Australian aborigines use fire screens to give them some shelter. A fire screen is a shield made of skin attached to two sticks placed upright in the ground; this construction protects from the wind those who huddle between the skin and the fire. Both these folk inhabit desert areas, which are marked by wide fluctuations in temperature, so that one can be as uncomfortable in the cold of the night as in the heat of the day.

The saving grace in all these situations is a knowledge of the use of *fire*. This aspect of the technology, a well-nigh universal possession of mankind, is as important in affording protection against the elements as it is in preparing and preserving foodstuffs. Its revolutionary role in the life of man is widely recognized. A vast number of myths recount the bringing of fire by a culture-hero. Many peoples assign ritual significance to the hearthstone, and a rich imagery accompanies the symbolism of an undying fire. The use of matches, and even of flint, has so improved competence in fire making that those unfamiliar with the methods of most nonliterate societies cannot guess how difficult it is to make fire. Peoples who use these methods do not underestimate the task, however, as witness the fact that many of them take the greatest pains to ensure that once a fire has been started, it will not be allowed to die out.

Two basic methods are employed to make fire. Harrison classifies these as the wood-friction method, which predominates, and the percussion method. The former is of three types, "boring or *drilling* one piece of wood into another, . . . rubbing or *ploughing* along the grain, and . . . *sawing* across the grain." The first is the most often encountered. It consists simply of twirling one piece of wood in another until wood dust is produced and ignited. A variant of the drilling method employs the bow

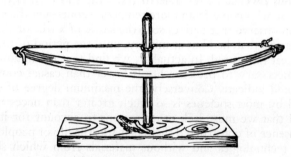

Fig. 17 *Bow drill.*

drill; a bow cord is wound about the drilling stick, while pressure is applied by means of a socket into which the top of this stick fits. The socket may be held by the hand or, as it is among the Eskimo, in the mouth. The fireplow is identified with Polynesia, the fire saw with Malaysia, though both have wider distributions. Percussion usually employs flint and tinder, though Harrison reports that in southeast Asia, two pieces of bamboo or a fragment of china and a length of bamboo are used.[5]

Let us return now to the contribution fire making has made to the increased effectiveness of shelter. Though the Australian fire screen shields people from the wind, it is the fire on the other side that protects them from the cold. In the forests of tropical South America, the natives sling their hammocks inside their shelters over a bed of coals or a low fire. The snugness of the Eskimo igloo is enhanced by its blubber lamp; the smoke of the fire in the African's thatched house keeps the insects away. Without fire, indeed, housing would be no more than protection from

[5] H. S. Harrison, 1925, pp. 32–4.

the elements where, in warm and temperate zones, people could huddle, miserable from the cold, while areas with extremely cold climates would be forbidden to them.

The simplest shelters are the cave, the windbreak, the hut. More complex types to be differentiated vary between the simple skin tent of the American Indian or the wooden lean-to erected in many parts of the world, and the truly architectural structures of Peru and Mexico, West Africa and Indonesia. In North America are found the birch-bark wigwam and the skin tipi, the multi-family dwellings of the southwestern Pueblos, the dugout, or half-underground sod-covered dwelling used by the Mandan of the Upper Missouri and other tribes, the plank house of the Northwest Coast, the Iroquois long house. In South and Central America we find the monumental achievements of the Peruvian and Mexican builders, and the lean-to and the beehive hut of the south; the thatched dwelling of the Guianas; the communal structure of the Amazonian tribes, made with timbered framework and covering space up to ten thousand square feet; and the simple rectangular dwelling of the mountainous areas. The thatched rectangular or round house characterizes Polynesia, but in Melanesia types vary from the lean-to to the great gable-roofed men's house, with the front peak of its roof sometimes rising to a height of more than a hundred feet. Africa runs the gamut from the simple beehive type shelter of the Hottentots, consisting of poles bent over to intersect at the top as a framework for a covering of skins, through the thatched round houses of East Africa and the rectangular ones of the western part of the continent, to the architectural structures of such Sudanese cities as Kano and Timbuctoo, where the arch and the dome were incorporated in buildings made of sun-dried, plastered brick.

It is customary to think and write of most nonliterate folk as though their cultures were characterized each by a single house type. This again oversimplifies the problem. Frequently the kind of housing depends on the season, or the function a given kind of dwelling is to fulfill. The Mandan half-underground house, like the Eskimo igloo, gives way to the skin tent for summer use. Men and women may inhabit quite different kinds of houses, especially where men have a communal dwelling, while women live with their children in individual shelters. Nor is the term dwelling by any means synonymous with shelter, or building. The magnificent Central American structures, or those of the "lost" civilizations of Malaysia were not dwellings at all. They symbolized the power of the ruler, the splendor with which the gods were worshipped.

Men build for less tangible reasons than mere protection against the elements. Reasons of prestige enter, and aesthetic motivations, as shown by the decorations that are so frequently lavished on all kinds of structures. More than this, and not to be overlooked, are the emotional ties that bind men and women to their places of residence and cause them to regard their dwellings as havens of security and often sources of beauty.

4

Clothing can be tailored, that is, sewed and fitted to the contours of the body, or it may consist of materials loosely draped over the human frame. Again, there is no essential correlation between the amount of clothing worn by a people and the nature of their habitat. It is possible to generalize, however, that fitted clothing is found among peoples who live in colder areas, while draped cloths are used by those who inhabit warmer regions.

Clothing requires materials that are pliant and reasonably soft, and that lend themselves readily to stitching or decoration. The available materials seem to be quite few—woven fabrics, skins, and bark-cloth. Exceptions are especially found in the materials of ritual garb, or of garments that are marks of status, as, for example, feather capes, or capes made of finely woven matting, or the metal armor of the medieval knight, or armor made of thick, spiked fishskin, such as is worn by the warriors of the New Britain archipelago.

With a few exceptions, such as leaves and grasses, we find that the materials that clothe mankind cannot be used in their natural state, so that various processes must be employed to fit them for use as clothing. The most complex of these are the processes whereby cloth is manufactured from threads spun from fibers of some kind, either animal or vegetable. Sheep and goats in the Old World, and llamas and vicuñas in South America are the principal sources of animal fibers. Cotton and flax are the most widely used vegetable ones. Extraneous materials are first removed, after which the mass is "carded" so that the fibers will lie approximately parallel to each other. Then the fibers are spun into yarn by twining them together so that they make a strong, continuous cord. The simplest method, widely distributed among nonliterate peoples, is to roll the fibers on the thigh. The cord is gathered on a spindle, which supplies the tension needed to make thread of varying degrees of fineness. Spindles are twirled by twisting with the hand, and are usually weighted to provide continuous motion and even tension.

The loom, the prime implement in clothmaking, consists of a frame across which parallel strands of yarn—the warp—are stretched. The weft threads are then inserted at right angles between these strands, once over and once under, or in any combination of them. Warp strands customarily are placed vertically or, if the loom is parallel to the ground, stretch away from the weaver. In the simplest looms the warp strands are free, but it apparently did not take long to discover that time could be saved

Fig. 18 *Simple loom used with twilling stick (Cowichan tribe of the Pacific Northwest, North America).*

by attaching half—or any required number—of warp threads to a device whereby they could be raised with one motion, leaving a clear space through which the yarn could be passed. In still more complex looms, the rod by which the strands are elevated or depressed may be attached to a foot-pedal, or treadle. A sword, or beater, is often passed through the space thus made. Turned on its side, the sword enlarges the opening through which the weft strand passes, and its edge is used to press down each cross strand on the preceding ones, so as to give the finished cloth a firmer texture. In many looms of nonliterate people, too, a shuttle is employed to carry the weft strand across the warp. Sometimes this is no more than a stick to which the weft is attached—in which case it is used like a large needle. Sometimes, however, it encloses a spool that supplies the weft yarn as the shuttle is passed across the loom.

Skins must be dressed before they can be used for any purpose that requires a pliant material. In many instances, skins are pegged on the ground, so that the hair may be shaved or cut off. Accretions of meat and fat, and the inner layers of the skin itself, which

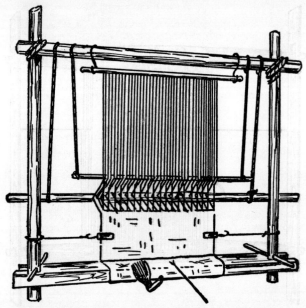

Fig. 19 *Loom with treadle (Arabs of North Africa).*

would render the resultant material too unwieldy, are also removed. Sometimes the skin is soaked in materials containing wood ash, that supply a natural alkali. More often the tanning process is carried out by rubbing the skin with brain tissue, and working it with the hands, or with an instrument such as an iron or wooden beater, or even by chewing it until it is quite soft.

Bark-cloth is derived from the inner bark of certain trees whose fibers cross each other at right angles, as do the warp and weft of true cloth. It is found only in the South Seas, central Africa, and tropical South America, where the requisite trees grow. The manufacture of bark-cloth is relatively simple. The bark is first soaked in water and then beaten on a smooth log to loosen the fibers and, in some instances, to separate it into layers. Beating also thins out the bark, and gives it a firmer texture. Beaters take either the forms of clubs, as in the South Seas, or hammers, as in Africa. Their macerating effect is increased by the grooves that are cut at right angles across the working surfaces. The resulting material is soft, and becomes softer with washing. It lends itself readily to decoration, as is evidenced by the painted and block-printed designs on South Seas tapa cloth displayed in most ethnographic museum collections.

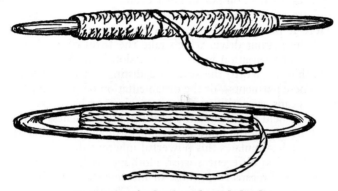

Fig. 20 *Simple shuttle and spool shuttle.*

Though more than one of these materials is used for clothing in most cultures, it is rare when one or the other of them is not predominant. Textiles are woven in Africa, in Mexico, Central America, and the Andean highlands, and in Eurasia except in the arctic and steppe areas, where skin clothing is found. Skins also predominate in the southern and eastern parts of Africa. In the American arctic and subarctic and in the Plains area, skin clothing is tailored, while in the wooded region east and southeast of the Plains and in southeastern South America, skin robes prevail. Elsewhere, clothing is not worn at all, or is rudimentary, consisting of a brief covering of the genitalia or other portions of the body that custom requires be concealed. Where temperatures are high, clothing may be held to a minimum while a person is at work. This does not militate against his wearing a substantial amount of clothing when rank or circumstance requires it, as in parts of West Africa, where the toga-like man's cloth is seven or eight feet long, four or five feet wide, and of appreciable weight.

Why clothing is worn cannot be answered by any simple formula. We have but to consider the canons of taste, of conduct, of occasion that rule the use of clothing in our own society to make this clear. As with housing, there is, of course, a rough correlation with the nature of the habitat. Yet convention on occasion seems to defy requirements of this sort, as is clear when we consider the pitifully inadequate protection the long skin mantle of the tribes of Tierra del Fuego affords against the penetrating cold of this region. Or one need not stray far from home to see how inappropriate is the clothing of women in our culture, worn on formal occasions on the coldest nights, or, conversely, the formal dress of men on hot summer evenings.

Of great importance also is the association of clothing with sex. Here it plays a dual role, providing those mechanisms that channel the mating drive, which take the form of *modesty* and *coquetry*. The variation in their expression is endless, but wherever clothing is worn, the sexes are distinguished by their garments. These garments—or the ornamentation of the human body by such means as scarification, or tattooing, or hairdressing—are everywhere held to enhance the physical attractiveness of the individual, by giving the body concealment or heightened aesthetic appeal, which stimulates this powerful inherent drive.

Where class differences exist, clothing marks off individuals of position and means from those of inferior status. This prestige factor can be expressed in various ways. Clothing of those in high position may be more lavishly decorated, as are the feather capes of the Hawaiian nobles; or may be of a different type from others, as where the uniforms of officers differ from those of the common soldier; or may, in subtlest form, reflect the control of resources by extreme simplicity and restraint where the accepted means of display are within the reach of all. By extension, through the association of clothing with both the sex drive and status, dress carries a strong aesthetic appeal that is a powerful factor in maintaining the patterned form and degree of bodily covering that, in each culture, influences the reactions of men and women to the fellow members of their society.

5

Other than weaving, the crafts most often found in the nonliterate world are basketry and pottery making. Neither of these techniques, with the possible exception of basketry, has anything like the universality of those that supply the needs for food and shelter, or even of clothing. It must not be assumed, however, that this exhausts the list of the technological resources of nonliterate man. He works stone, wood, metal, and leather; he has developed medical skills that extend to surgery, and he practices the arts of navigation.

It is plausible that before baskets and pots were devised, man had recourse to natural objects, such as skins, gourds and shells for his belongings. Peoples like the Australians or the Bushmen, who make neither pottery nor basketry, employ such objects as their habitat affords them for these purposes. The most striking instance of this is the use of ostrich-egg shells by the Bushmen to store water.

Basketry is made by three processes, weaving, twining or twilling, and coiling. If the material used in weaving a basket is broad and flat, there is little that can be done except to pass the strands alternately over and under, producing a checkerboard design, like the ordinary American market basket. When narrow strands are used, however, the weaving may be very complex indeed, as is to be seen in the traylike cassava-meal sifters manufactured by the Amazonian and Guiana Indians. Twilled or twined baskets, made by weaving pliant strands about a framework of twigs or other rigid materials, can be woven so finely and tightly that they can hold water. In such cases, the basket becomes a cooking vessel, since water can be boiled in it by the simple device of dropping heated stones in the water. Wissler notes that in North America most of the tribes who use the twining and coiling techniques in making their baskets are "stone boilers."

Coiled baskets may be termed "sewn basketry," because of the technique of making them. The description given by Mason of how they are manufactured by California Indians makes this clear:

> The elements are a stiff root or rod for the fundamental coil, and a soft splint or strip of the same material for the sewing. In making her basket, the woman starts in the centre of the bottom, coiling the rod and wrapping it as she proceeds with the split root or rattan, so as to bind it to the preceding turn, drawing her splint between the spirals. When the rod comes to an end, she neatly splices the end to that of a new one and proceeds as before, carefully concealing the joint. When the splint is exhausted, the end is tucked in behind the spiral and another one started in the same manner, but so carefully joined as to defy detection.[6]

Sometimes the "rod," as Mason terms the foundation, is a bundle of twigs or grasses, about which the wrapping material is passed in such a way that each turn takes a stitch through some of the

[6] Otis T. Mason, 1895, p. 235.

preceding coil, thus anchoring the whole firmly together. In the New World the California Indians are notable for the quality of their sewn baskets; this form predominates in Africa, where outstanding examples are also found. Coiled basketry has great flexibility. There are, for example, limitations on the size of woven or twined baskets, but coiled basketry is produced that ranges from miniature specimens to such forms as Pima or VaHanda storage baskets, large enough to hold a man.

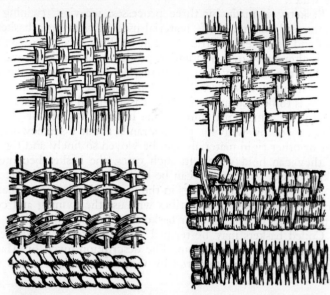

Fig. 21 *Details of basket-making techniques: weaving, twining, coiling.*

It is not difficult to envisage how early man, by intertwining grasses and twigs, came to the discovery of basketry. To discover pottery, however, was quite another matter, since the finished product can only result after several operations, whose relation to each other and to the resulting utensil is by no means obvious. The first step in making a pot is to find clay which contains sand or some other siliceous material, but no stones. This is then kneaded to give it the proper consistency, after which it is shaped to form the desired vessel. This step presents no problem, nor the next, in which it is allowed to dry. It can now be handled, but is still useless, since the dry clay will shred at the touch. It must, therefore, be fired—baked in a fire to fuse the siliceous material with the clay to make the final utensil. The firing is a critical test of the potter's skill, since too much heat will crack a pot, while too little will leave it soft and brittle.

Once this step has been achieved, the clay has been transformed into a material that is durable, despite the ease with which the objects made out of it can be broken. Broken pottery produces only potsherds that never return to clay, but remain unaltered for an indefinite time. This is why pottery is so important for the archaeologist. Given a pottery-making people, the shards they leave behind them tell much about the nature and contacts of their culture. Pottery remains, for example, allowed Reisner, in his excavations at Karma, on the Upper Nile, to reconstruct the history of the contacts this outpost of Egypt had with the Nubians, and to tell the story of how these contacts influenced the technique of both Egyptians and Nubians, bringing into existence new pottery forms.[7] Similarly, the study of pottery has permitted the New World archaeologists to tell the tale of the successive civilizations of the Andean and South American West Coast regions, that culminated in the Inca Empire; or of the development of Pueblo culture in the southwestern part of the United States.[8]

The distribution of pottery is restricted by various factors we have already mentioned. It is not found at all in Polynesia, for coral islands provide no materials from which it can be made. As far as is known, few peoples with simple technologies possess pottery. It was probably never known in Australia and Tasmania, and is lacking in most pygmy groups and in the simpler North and South American cultures. Its quality varies from extremely crude, soft products, as in certain parts of New Guinea, to the technically perfect pottery made in the Andes, Central America, Mexico, and the southwestern part of the United States. Indeed, the pottery of these regions, which include the polychrome portrait jars of pre-Spanish Peru, rank among some of the finest ceramic achievements of any culture.

Handmade pottery is fashioned in three ways, by molding, by modeling, and by coiling. Molded pottery, the least frequently encountered, is made by spreading the clay over a basket or an old pot in order to give it the desired shape. Potsherds showing the indentations of basketry molds, recovered in pueblos of pre-Spanish occupancy, demonstrate that this was long practiced in the New World; and the use of pots as molds is reported from

---

[7] G. A. Reisner, 1923, Chap. XXXII.
[8] P. S. Martin, G. I. Quimby, and D. Collier, 1947, Part IV.

Africa. Modeling is far more widely distributed. An example of this technique can be taken from an early report of the process as observed among the Hottentots.

> The clay was obtained from termite heaps, cleared of sand and gravel, and kneaded together with the ants' eggs mixed in it. A lump was placed on a smooth flat stone and modelled into the shape required. Next it was carefully smoothed inside and outside by hand, and exposed to the sun for a couple of days. When perfectly dry, it was finally put in a hole in the ground and burned by a fire around and inside it, till it was baked through and hard.[9]

Coiled pottery is made by a process first of pinching a rope-like length of clay on to a base, and then by continuing the process so as to build up the vessel until it has the desired shape and size. The Southwest has provided many examples of this. A very small coil, pinched on with consistent force and at regular intervals, can result in a pleasant design. Generally, however, the pinching is smoothed over, and no sign of the process remains in the finished pot.

One of the remarkable facts about the pottery of nonliterate peoples is the sureness with which the potters shape their vessels. Not only do they achieve a perfect circular form without the use of any measuring device, but their vessels are so shaped as to be objects of aesthetic as well as utilitarian value. This quality of aesthetic form arises only after training yields motor skills that permit the play of such creative ability as the potter may have.

The two broadest categories of pottery making are those that distinguish pottery made by hand, and by the use of the potter's wheel. The potter's wheel, however, is not found outside the literate cultures of Europe and Asia. Almost everywhere that pottery is produced with the aid of a potter's wheel, men make it, but where it is made by hand, it is woman's work. Here we meet another of those irrationalities in culture that so often confront the student. They are of historical derivation, and document a concept in the study of culture known as *adhesion*—the fact that two apparently unrelated aspects of culture become associated and take on a functional relationship.

To understand this particular instance, we return to the division of labor in early human society, when men hunted the larger game animals, while women, remaining nearer home, were occupied with gathering activities. It will be remembered that this

[9] I. Schapera, 1930, pp. 313–4.

association is believed to be the historical and logical antecedent of the fact that while cultivation with hoe or digging stick is customarily woman's work, plowing is invariably allotted to man's sphere of activity. In the case of pottery, it is not known whether this was initially the work of men or women, but everything points to the conclusion that it was woman's responsibility. The wheel was discovered during the Neolithic, probably in connection with transport. With the wheel, it was possible to utilize domesticated animals to pull carts; and since, as we have seen, the care of the larger domesticated forms is the concern of men, it is understandable how the manufacture and use of wheeled vehicles likewise became their province.

When the utility of the wheel for pottery making became apparent, this activity also became a male task. But where the wheel was employed as a device for spinning, women retained the spinning and weaving functions, and continued to hold them until the advent of the power loom. Men are potters in the plow cultures of Eurasia; elsewhere women make the pottery. The logic of this is the logic of history, and its implications present some of the more difficult problems with which the student of culture must cope.

Of such techniques as metalworking and wood carving we need only make mention. Metalworking for other than aesthetic and prestige ends was a rarity among the nonliterate peoples of the New World, despite the skills in fashioning silver and gold that gave to the empires of Mexico and Peru their fabled quality and in the end aroused the cupidity of the invading Europeans and brought on their downfall. New World metalwork as a distinctive element in technology is thus significant for its aesthetic rather than its utilitarian values.

Old World metalworking began in prehistoric times, with what was long termed the Age of Bronze. Ironworking soon appeared, and is outstanding today in the cultures of most of Africa and those of the nonliterate folk of southern and eastern Asia. So prevalent are the smelting of iron ore among African peoples and the use of indigenously manufactured iron implements, that it was held for many years that the original discovery of the processes of smelting and forging iron must have been made by the people of that continent. More recent evidence, however, points to Asia Minor as another region where this may have occurred. Whatever the point of origin, the distribution of ironmaking in Africa is impressive, especially in view of the varied and distinct processes through which particular kinds of ore-bearing rock must be put before they can be transformed into quite different material, which in turn must be heated to allow its being shaped into knives, hoes, spearheads, pins and many other durable and efficient tools. Small wonder that this knowledge is so frequently kept in the hands of family guilds, whose power is believed to come from the supernatural controls they exercise, quite as much as from their technological knowledge.

Plate 4a   *Terraced valley, showing method of cultivating rice in the Philippines.*
Plate 4b   *Close-up of rice terraces. See p. 104. (Photographs by R. F. Barton, courtesy F. Eggan.)*

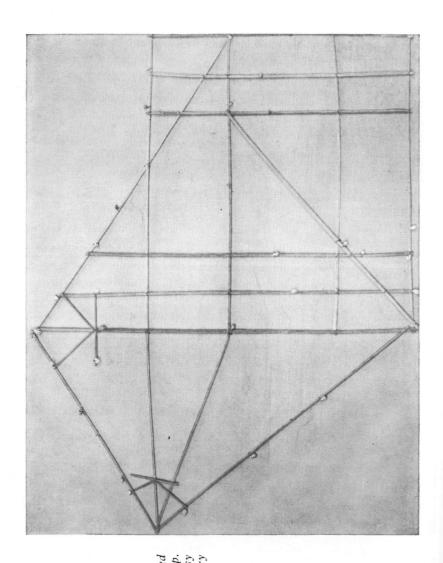

Plate 5 *Sailing chart used by Marshall Islanders. See p. 123. (Photograph courtesy Chicago Natural History Museum.)*

Chapter **Nine**

Economics and the Fulfillment of Wants

The need to economize, in the broadest sense of the term, derives from the existence of wants in excess of the capacity to produce. Economists call this maximizing satisfactions through the utilization of "scarce means." In societies where a machine technology pours out an abundance of goods, and where an economic system based on the use of money imposes many steps between the producer of goods and the ultimate consumer, the processes are complex indeed. For the student of culture, however, the economic system of the peoples who live by the machine constitute only one of the many different ways that man has devised of utilizing scarce means. It is, so to speak, an extreme case, resting at one pole of a series that stretches in an order of diminishing complexity to the societies whose economies are so immediate, so simple, that the problem of survival is paramount.

Certain general economic principles that have been worked out by the economists for our economy hold everywhere. There is no society without methods of production, distribution, consumption, and some form of exchange. There is no group without some expression of value, even though value may not be formulated in terms of some commonly accepted monetary symbol. Some specialization in effort is manifest, some concept of reward for labor is found.

What marks off our economic system from all others is the special relation between a machine technology and a pecuniary orientation. This relation has given rise to certain institutions found in no other culture. A unique focusing of economic effort on production for profit has had repercussions on all other aspects of life. Technological unemployment is one such result, the business cycle is another; both are related to a system that requires scarcity, artificially produced if necessary, for its functioning. This, in turn, makes it difficult, especially in times of stress, for many persons, without regard to their ability or willingness to perform a required task, to obtain the fundamental necessities of life. In almost all nonmachine societies, and in all nonliterate ones, this is unknown. Resources may be meager, and subsistence difficult to obtain, but where there is not enough to go around, all go hungry, as all participate when seasons of plenty provide abundance. "No one ever went hungry," among the Baganda of East Africa, "because everyone was welcome to go and sit down and share a meal with his equals," is a good expression of the tradition.[1]

The specialization of labor that is a commonplace in our own culture is not found among nonliterate groups, nor are capital goods often controlled by those who do not use them. The difference in specialization is one of degree rather than of kind. Some specialization is found in every culture, if only along the lines of sex division of labor. Experts in some craft or other are to be encountered in all societies, except where the economies are on the level of subsistence, with only enough produced to provide for basic physiological needs. The control of capital goods in our culture by those who profit from them without using them, however, represents a difference of kind. Capital goods, it is true, are concentrated to unequal degrees in the hands of different individuals in nonliterate communities. The economic basis of differences in status is known wherever the technology permits production to rise above subsistence requirements. Thus slavery is found in many nonliterate societies, though this almost always involves personal control of the slave by the master who benefits from his toil. But such an institution as the labor market is not found even in cultures where individuals occasionally work for others for pay, using tools not their own. Such work, in non-

[1] J. Roscoe, 1911, p. 12.

literate groups, supplements income; it is not the primary source of income, essential to existence.

Other differences between our own economy and the economies of small groups that command simple technological resources may also be mentioned. Money, as we have said, is widely used outside Euroamerican culture, but nowhere does it have so exclusive a function in expressing value. If to the factors of population mass and specialization of labor we add that of money as a medium of exchange, we arrive at the complexities of the market, with its paraphernalia of credit mechanisms, the interposition of middlemen between producer and consumer, the vastness of the apparatus that channels goods to buyer and reward to producer, and the like. All this, which comes under the head of business enterprise, represents an elaboration of economic phenomena developed to a degree not found elsewhere.

The role of the pecuniary symbol in establishing prestige has similarly been carried to a point far beyond anything found in any other culture. Whereas in many societies subsistence and prestige economic systems are distinguished from each other by the use of different symbols of value, or by the use of different means of exchange, or by the different ends to which the means of exchange are put; such distinctions do not hold for our culture. Money is the symbol of prestige, as well as the means of acquiring commodities. The prestige dollar or pound sterling or cruzeiro or franc that buys oil paintings or pays for a debut are no different from the tokens with which the humblest citizen buys groceries.

2

Among the stereotypes most widely held about "primitive" man is the belief that he works as little as possible, and that, where natural conditions permit, he works almost not at all. The facts are quite otherwise. The knotty problems nonliterate peoples must solve in coping with desert or arctic habitats are obvious, and it is not difficult to see how even the temperate zone, with its changing seasons, presents problems that call for sustained effort and planning. The tropics, which seem to offer a life of ease, provide a harsh, not a benign setting. The dweller in the Amazon forests, the Congo Basin, or New Guinea is beset by many vexations. When he prepares a field, he must clear dense forest growth; as his plants mature, he must protect them against rapidly growing parasitic vines that thrive on tender vegetation; his crops must be guarded from voracious insects, wild animals and birds.

A study that shows how a nonliterate people work comes

from the island of Wogeo, off the north coast of New Guinea near the mouth of the Sepik River. Hogbin's discussion of this economy [2] includes two schedules of gardening. That given here concerns a clearing made by a man named Waru. This garden "was a level area of 1,300 square yards which when planted eventually contained nearly 3,000 taro, 65 bananas, and a few tobacco plants, yams, sweet potatoes, herbs and greens." The time consumed in making and planting this plot was as follows:

Day 1. Waru left home accompanied by Gris at 7:30 a.m. Arrived at the garden site at 7:50 a.m. Both worked till 12:10 p.m. cutting down trees. Gris returned to the village, but Waru rested till 2:15 p.m. Worked cutting down trees till 5:04 p.m. During the afternoon he had two rests totalling twenty-five minutes.

Day 2. Waru left home accompanied by Gris at 7:26 a.m. Arrived at garden site at 7:45 a.m. Both worked till 11:56 a.m. cutting down trees. Gris returned to the village but Waru rested till 2:17 p.m. Worked at cutting down trees till the whole area cleared at 4:31 p.m.

Days 3–12. Timber left to dry.

Day 13. Waru and Mujewa arrived at garden at 8:02 a.m. Picked over timber together till noon, with a rest for twelve minutes at 10:56 a.m. Rested till 1:58 p.m. Picked over timber till 2:38 p.m., when work was abandoned on account of rain.

Day 14. Raining.

Day 15. Waru fencing 8:01 a.m. to 12:03 p.m. and 1:50 p.m. to 4:16 p.m. Mujewa burning rubbish and clearing ground 8:01 a.m. to 12:03 p.m. and 1:50 p.m. to 3:04 p.m. Both rested for twenty-two minutes.

Day 16. Waru fencing 7:56 a.m. to 11:59 a.m. and 2:01 p.m. to 4:21 p.m. Mujewa clearing ground 7:56 a.m. to 12:04 p.m. and 2 p.m. to 2:40 p.m.

Day 17. Waru finished fencing and divided the area into allotments 7:40 a.m. to 11:58 a.m.

Day 18. Waru and two youths cleared away stones 8:30 a.m. to 10:20 a.m.; 11:04 a.m. to 12:16 p.m.; and 3:01 p.m. to 4:02 p.m. Long pauses due to rain.

Day 19. Waru brought banana suckers and Mujewa taro shoots.

Day 20. Raining.

Day 21. Waru planted banana suckers 8:00 a.m. to 12:10 p.m. and 2:02 p.m. to 4:05 p.m. Several pauses, totalling thirty-five minutes, to chat to passers by. Mujewa planted taro shoots 8:05 a.m. to 12:05 p.m. and 2:01 p.m. to 3:29 p.m.

Day 22. Both Waru and Mujewa occupied elsewhere.

[2] H. I. Hogbin, 1938–9, pp. 286–96.

Day 23. Mujewa planted taro shoots 8:02 a.m. to 12:20 p.m. Waru planted yams 8.02 a.m. to 8:50 a.m.

Day 24. Mujewa finished planting taro shoots, greens, etc., 8:14 a.m. to 2:17 p.m.

Waru's family group was small. He had one wife, Mujewa, an infant, and Gris, an orphan boy seventeen years old who lived with him. To make this garden Waru gave forty-two hours of labor over eight working days, Mujewa thirty hours over six days; there were eight hours from Gris, and four from each of the two youths who helped in the work. This was only one of six garden plots Waru made. These provided his small family with the very substantial amount of 7,000 taro and approximately 70 bunches of bananas, or about 4,200 of this fruit, in addition to sugar cane, vegetables, and tobacco.

Hogbin compares the work on this garden with that on one twice as large belonging to the head of a polygynous household. The latter required a total of seventy-nine hours' work from the men and sixty from the women, as against fifty-eight and thirty, respectively, on that of Waru. These data would seem to testify to the efficiency of cooperative group as against individual labor. In this case, it is given expression by the natives themselves:

> A man who toils by himself goes along as he pleases: he works slowly and pauses every time he feels like having a smoke. But when two men work together, each tries to do the most. One man thinks to himself, "My back aches and I feel like resting, but my friend there is going on: I must go on too, or I shall feel ashamed." The other man thinks to himself, "My arms are tired and my back is breaking, but I must not be the first to pause." Each man strives to do the most, and the garden is finished quickly.[3]

One element in the effort of those not living in machine cultures is what Richards, in her study of the Bemba of Northern Rhodesia, has called "the rhythm of work." She points out that this African people is dependent on seasonal change of "light, dark and temperature" to a degree unknown in machine cultures, and that the "work-time interval which dominates our activities and calculations" does not exist for them. She continues:

> We, after all, can hardly conceive of time except in terms of energy expenditure and, to many of us, a fixed money value as well. But the Bemba, in his unspecialized society does different

[3] *Ibid.*, p. 296.

tasks daily and a different amount of work each day. . . . The working hours also change in what seems to us a most erratic manner. In fact I do not think the people ever conceive of such periods as the month, week or day in relation to regular work at all. The major agricultural tasks have to coincide with certain seasons and moons, and that is all. A man says he has to cut trees between such-and-such climatic changes, but not that he has so many hours of work to get through, and daily work, which has become from habit almost a physiological necessity to many Europeans, only occurs at certain times of the year. The whole bodily rhythm of the Bemba differs completely from that of a peasant in Western Europe, let alone an industrial worker. For instance at Kasaka, in a slack season, the old men worked 14 days out of 20 and the young men 7; while at Kampamba in a busier season, the men of all ages worked on an average 8 out of 9 working days. The average working day in the first instance was 2¾ hours for men and 2 hours gardening plus 4 hours domestic work for the women, but the figures varied from 0 to 6 hours a day. In the second case the average was 4 hours for the men and 6 for the women, and the figures showed the same daily variation.[4]

The amount of work done in nonliterate societies can also be gauged by productivity. Wild-rice gatherers in the Great Lakes region of North America are reported as harvesting substantial amounts of this crop. In 1864 three Chippewa groups having a total population of 3,966 individuals gathered 5,000 bushels, while in addition they obtained, by hunting, a large quantity of valuable furs and produced 150,000 pounds of maple sugar, besides growing potatoes and maize.[5] The members of one kin group in Umor, a settlement of the Yakö of Eastern Nigeria, composed of 97 "adult able-bodied men" and their families, planted gardens whose estimated average size was an acre and a half, each having about 2,440 yam hills, with a mean yield of 2,545 yams. The harvest ranged from 235 to 11,410 tubers. In addition, coco-yams, corn, pumpkins, okra, three varieties of beans, sugar cane, gourds, cassava, and peanuts are grown.[6]

The problems of division of labor and specialization, because of their importance in the cycle of production, merit further examination. In nonliterate societies such division of labor as exists is by whole industries, and rarely, if ever, represents the kind of intra-industrial specialization that the term signifies in our own society. In all nonliterate groups, as we have seen, certain work is

---

[4] A. I. Richards, 1939, pp. 392–4.
[5] A. E. Jenks, 1900, pp. 1,074–5, 1,078.
[6] C. D. Forde, 1937, pp. 32–4, 41.

done by men and other work by women. One may, therefore, speak of the universality of sex division of labor. Within this category many societies exist whose technologies call for a division of labor by crafts. In such cultures, some men will be iron-workers or wood carvers or canoe builders; some women will make pottery or baskets or weave cloths. But outside the machine cultures we practically never encounter a people among whom, for instance, one man mines ore, another smelts it, and a third fashions it into hoes; or among whom one woman gathers withes and a second strips the bark from them, while a third fashions baskets out of them.

Craft specialists in nonliterate societies seldom engage exclusively in one particular kind of work. Rather, only those who are "specialists" carry on a given craft. Craftsmen do other things —in particular, they provide for their subsistence, at least in part, by working in the fields, producing crops that they and their families will consume. Craft specialization in these societies does not provide a living in the sense that the much narrower intra-industrial specialization of machine cultures does. But in those societies where there is enough subsistence goods produced to release some members from a portion of the task of producing for their own primary needs, craft specialization is widespread.

Specialization of this kind can be based on hereditary calling, as with the California Indian basket makers, or African iron-workers, or South Sea Island canoe builders. The presence of these specialists makes for a greater variety of goods, and goods of better workmanship. On occasion, as in Melanesia, a type of regional or tribal specialization is found. That is, an entire group may manufacture pots and exchange them for the fishing nets another people make, and so on. This is but another way in which the same ends are met; in this case, the benefits of the technical proficiency that comes with specialization accrue to societies so small in number that, of themselves, they could not support specialists of any kind.

A question that inevitably arises when the productive cycle is being investigated is why men work. Men work, of course, because they must. But this simple answer by no means suffices. In the discussion we have earlier cited, Hogbin says:

> I began this paper by stating that these natives depend for their subsistence on tillage and collection. Though this remains true, they have many additional motives for the practice of agriculture and gathering of the fruits of the forest: food has become associated with personal prestige, status and vanity; with the de-

sire for immortality; and even with aesthetics. In Jaua's words, it is the most important thing in Wogeo.[7]

No discussion of the motivations that underlie the drive to work may omit the satisfactions that come when a craftsman can point to an object and say, with pride, "I made it." Herein lies one of the most difficult problems of an industrialized society, where specialization of labor has been carried so far that this identification with the finished product is not possible. It is only under such circumstances that labor becomes distasteful. We become aware with astonishment that the concept "vacation" is unique to our society, until we reflect how, in other cultures, the rhythm of labor is set by sanctions accepted by all; the ends of labor are the possessions of the one who makes the goods, to dispose of as he desires; and the laborer can identify himself with what he has wrought with his skill and his strength. We tend to overlook that a vacation is no release from the expenditure of effort, but that it affords an opportunity to expend energy without outside intervention. This, and this alone, is what makes it desirable.

3

Often no more is involved in the distribution of goods in many nonliterate societies than allocating what is available within the households of the producers. Even where there is some degree of specialization, and exchanges are effected, these are personal, direct, and specific. Only where population density is appreciable, and some degree of specialization is present, do we find the market as a formal element in the economy. Since among nonliterate peoples these conditions are relatively rare, market operations usually facilitate the exchange of goods between members of different communities rather than within a given society.

It is unlikely that the origin of the tradition of exchange of goods or services will ever be established. Mauss has derived it from the psychology of gift giving; that is, a present, however freely given, entails an obligation of reciprocal return.[8] Countless instances of this are to be found all over the world. In our own culture, the obligation to return a dinner invitation or a wedding present comes to mind at once. The ritualized gift giving of the Kwakiutl, Haida and other tribes of the Northwest Coast of North America, classical in the literature of anthropology, affords an

[7] H. I. Hogbin, 1938–9, p. 325.
[8] M. Mauss, 1923–4, *passim*.

outstanding instance. So do the ceremonial exchanges of Melanesia, or the funerary gifts of West Africa, or the passing of presents in northern Australia, which serve notice that a future return is expected.

The significance of *gift exchange*, as such forms are called, or *covert exchange*, as Firth terms it,[9] is patent if one but traces the flow of valuables from their source, most often and most strikingly through the channel of the ritual exchange, to their destination, and back again. Buck states that "reciprocal feasts and presents form the standard pattern of Polynesian weddings."[10] In Mangaia, social position was determined by the quantity and quality of the gifts proffered by the family of a bride on the occasion of a marriage, and by the elaborateness of the bridal feast. For the family of the bridegroom not to reciprocate with a feast that surpassed the original in the amount of food provided and the quantity of gifts presented was to admit inferior status. In Tonga, when marriage gifts were exchanged between the families of the principals, the father of the bridegroom remembered what each relative had contributed, and undertook to return twice this amount. He would strip his house of all its possessions to do this, lest the social position of his family suffer, and his remaining children, as well as their offspring, be unable to make desirable marriages.

Trade, properly speaking, consists of the direct exchange of values, designated either in terms of one another or of a least common denominator, such as money. In societies where institutions are not sharply differentiated, gift giving shades imperceptibly into trade. The logical categories drawn to designate the different forms taken by exchanges of various sorts are, therefore, at times extremely difficult to distinguish in a given instance. They are, besides gift and ritual exchange, barter, money barter, and exchanges based on the use of money.

Barter is the direct exchange of goods for goods. A special form, the "silent trade," has been known for many hundreds of years. Herodotus mentions it as the way the Carthaginians traded with Africans who lived beyond the Pillars of Hercules—that is, on the west coast of Africa. Ibn-Batuta, the Arabian traveler, tells how it was the means of carrying on trade for furs in the far northern "Land of Darkness." Modern instances have been cited between the Chukchi of Siberia and the Alaskans, between the Congo pygmies and their Bantu neighbors, and in California,

[9] Raymond Firth, 1939, p. 310.
[10] P. H. Buck (Te Rangi Hiroa), 1934, p. 91.

Malaysia, New Guinea, and elsewhere. Essentially the procedure is as follows: One party to a transaction leaves goods at a stated place, either going away or withdrawing to a vantage point, to watch unobserved. The other party then comes, inspects what he finds, and if satisfied leaves a comparable amount of another commodity.

Face-to-face trading of goods for goods is the most prevalent form of exchange in nonliterate societies. Bargaining may or may not be present. Barter seems to be carried on between different tribes more than within a society. North and South America knew numerous instances of this form of intertribal exchange, such as when the Tewa of the Southwest trafficked corn, corn meal, and wheat bread for the buffalo hides of the Comanche, or the Choroti of the Chaco bartered dried fish for maize, red paint, and necklaces. Melanesia is replete with instances. Even in Africa, intertribal exchanges take on more importance than intra-tribal ones.

In order to trade, a person must want something he does not himself have, but that another individual does. To effect an exchange, some agreement about the relative value of these goods must be reached. Hence the problem of how value is expressed, and of how values shift as goods move from one hand to the next, is critical in this connection. One of the reasons why the study of economies that are self-sufficient or where exchange is based on barter requires special methods is because there is no way in which values can be expressed except by detailing each instance where a good was produced, or exchanged, or consumed. Values may be quite capricious, as among the Arawak in South America, where the value of each object bartered is dictated by the strength of its appeal at the moment it is offered. Sometimes values of one commodity are expressed in terms of another, as in Buka, in the Solomons, where a bundle of six or seven carrying baskets is traded for a basket full of taro. Here the implication of shifting value is interesting, since a basket maker exchanging with a strong woman who can carry a heavy load will obtain more taro than if she did business with a smaller, weaker woman. There seems to be no seeking out of larger trading partners, however, and no haggling.

Money-barter occurs when some consumption good is used as a least common denominator of value. One of the best examples of this has come from the Ifugao of the Philippines, where, in addition to pure barter, rice acts as money. Barton provides a table of 1922 values, with their equivalence in Philippine dollars:

Unit	Number of Bundles of Rice	Unit	Value during Harvest and Spading (Pesos)	Value in Season of Growing Rice (Pesos)
1 botek	1	. . . . . .	.02½	.05
5 botek	5	1 hongal	.12½	.25
4 hongal	20	1 dalan	.50	1.00
5 dalan	100	1 bongale	2.50	5.00
10 dalan	200	1 upu	5.00	10.00
4 upu	800	1 lotak	20.00	40.00
2 lotak	1,600	1 gukud	40.00	80.00
10 upu	2,000	1 { nabukene / pigil	50.00	100.00

Here we see how the introduction of a token of common value brings order into calculations; how a commodity of this sort, used as money, can reflect its different values as a commodity in terms of its function as money. Rice is, of course, more plentiful at harvest-time than during the growing season. Not only is this apparent when translated into terms of money, strictly speaking (the Philippine peso), but it is reflected in the prices of the commodities it buys. A fowl that in growing season brings one hongal of rice, will at harvest-time, when rice is plentiful, bring two hongal, and so on.[11] Many other examples of societies where money-barter figures in the exchange of goods have been reported. Iron objects, such as rods, hoes, axes, double gongs, and other commodities, were used for this purpose in the Congo, salt in West Africa, tobacco in Siberia, cacao in pre-Spanish Mexico.

To so great an extent do commodities used as money act like money, that it is difficult to distinguish them in their functioning from those objects whose worth as a commodity, if they have any, has been lost sight of in their specialized use as tokens of value. *Money*, properly speaking, has the characteristics of homogeneity, portability, divisibility, and durability. In this it differs from the goods used in money-barter, or from "valuables" that are symbols of wealth, like the great stone wheels that are repositories of "congealed values" on the island of Yap, or the cattle of East Africa. In nonliterate societies, distinctions such as those between the use of money in trade and the use of commodity tokens in money-barter are very difficult to draw. This need not trouble us greatly, however, since both effectively perform the functions of money.

[11] R. F. Barton, 1922, pp. 427–31.

The distribution of those nonliterate peoples in whose economy money, properly speaking, functions is relatively restricted. The use of money was found in the aboriginal cultures of West Africa and the Congo, of Melanesia, and of western North America. The cowry-shell was current in Africa before European occupation. In recent times the cowry has given further testimony that it is actually money. In 1883 the value of the cowry in French West Africa was about five hundred to the franc, which was then worth twenty cents. Later it fell to eight hundred to the franc, where it remained until 1918. After 1918, however, when the franc depreciated, the cowry increased in value, until by 1930 it had stabilized to the figure of six hundred for a five-franc note, or one hundred and twenty cowries to the franc.[12] Among the Yurok of California dentalium shells were employed as money, and farther south, clamshell disks. In Melanesia the media of exchange are so numerous as almost to defy enumeration. In some instances they are true money, as in the case of dog's teeth in the Admiralty Islands, where they not only express the values of other commodities, but, like any medium of exchange, are subject to manipulation in the money market.

Tax has clearly shown how, in the Guatemalan Indian society of Panajachel, the presence of money, in the European sense, makes for ways of determining value quite in line with the demands of economic theory. These people who "enter in minor ways, into the world economy of firms" have "a money economy . . . with a strongly developed market that tends to be perfectly competitive." Because production as well as consumption is "organized in single households," it follows that "a large proportion of what is consumed has to be purchased," and bought for cash. Sales are made on the basis of cost estimates which analysis of actual cases shows to be remarkably accurate, and the life of the community is permeated with a "spirit of business enterprise."[13] This would seem to indicate how important a role money plays in making for the type of economic system that has classically occupied the attention of economists in studying Euroamerican economies.

The business activities of nonliterate peoples—for so they may be termed—have characteristics that relate them to business dealings everywhere. Markets and middlemen are found, and mechanisms of credit are widespread. One of the clearest state-

[12] See M. J. Herskovits, 1952, pp. 247–50, for a fuller discussion of this point.

[13] S. Tax, 1953, pp. 13–14, and *passim.*

ments of this has been given by Boas. Of the Indians in British Columbia he says:

> This economic system has developed to such an extent that the capital possessed by all the individuals of the tribe combined exceeds many times the actual amount of cash that exists; that is to say, the conditions are quite analogous to those prevailing in our community: if we want to call in all our outstanding debts, it is found that there is not by any means money enough in existence to pay them, and the result of an attempt of all the creditors to call in their loans results in disastrous panic, from which it takes the community a long time to recover.[14]

Credit, as in Euroamerican culture, is usually extended for a consideration, and interest rates, in many cultures, are very high. Pawning of children was a recognized means of obtaining money in West Africa, and palm groves are still pledged where a man is hard pressed for funds.

Money is a repository of value as well as a medium of exchange. In nonliterate societies, the two economic systems reflected by this dual function of money are often made explicit. The subsistence economy may be carried out on a barter basis, for instance, while the prestige system operates with the aid of money. Du Bois first made this distinction explicit in studying the Tolowa and Tututni Indians of California. Here, while the dentalium shell and other "treasures" were employed "in the purchase of social protection and prestige, in sex, and in maintaining familial status, . . ." they "entered hardly at all into the subsistence equation." [15] The blanket of the Northwest Coast Indians was a token in the prestige economic system, and figured but little in exchanges of subsistence goods.[16] In Melanesia, such symbols of value as the arm bands and necklaces of the Kula ring of the Trobriands are restricted to the prestige system.

There are no hard and fast differences between prestige and subsistence systems. Thus, on Rossel Island, the prestige currency also figures in regular trading operations. The essential thing is that their existence, however expressed, should not be overlooked. The fact that our economy employs only one unit of value masks the dual nature of our system. The purchase of a consignment of wheat and of a precious jewel are both effected by means of money. But the wheat is for food, while the jewel is a repository

---

[14] F. Boas, 1898, pp. 54–5.
[15] C. Du Bois, 1936, p. 51.
[16] F. Boas, 1897, pp. 341 ff.

of value, designed to bring the prestige that goes with owning it. It is striking that in so specialized a society as our own these two phases of the economy, functionally so distinct, should be blurred. Our one set of value tokens, however, has made it difficult for us to distinguish between them, either in the forms in which they manifest themselves, or in their dynamic aspects of gift-exchange as against the buying and selling of more ordinary, workaday commodities.

4

The technological capacity of any people is directed toward making consumption goods, production goods (or what has been termed "auxiliary capital"), and depositories of value. Like all categories, these must be interpreted in accordance with the actual functioning of a given element in the economy of a given culture. The first of these categories has to do principally with the economics of consumption, the second with the processes whereby capital goods are acquired and used, the third with the broad category loosely termed property or wealth. The first two have been little studied among nonliterate peoples, but anthropologists have devoted much attention to the third, principally because of its function of maintaining kinship structures.

Food and clothing are the primary *consumption goods*. In most nonliterate societies the economic processes by which they are distributed are relatively simple. Here the real problem largely lies outside the economic sphere. We have seen how even peoples living on the subsistence level do not utilize all available foodstuffs, either because of patterned concepts of what is fit for human consumption, or because of special taboos of a religious or sociological character. The same kind of selectivity is found in clothing, as among groups where the productive capacity permits class differentiation and clothing becomes a mark of rank.

One aspect of the economics of food in nonliterate societies is the relation of the consumption of food to the immediate needs of the people. Studies of this kind are few, but they already have thrown light on certain aspects, previously not understood, of the consumption economy of nonliterate folk. Thus the production of the Tallensi of the Gold Coast, when balanced against seasonal needs, yields the following conclusion:

> It will be seen that domestic food-supplies are at the lowest at the time—recognized as such by the natives—of the most strenuous output of physical labour, i.e., in May–June, and high-

est when there is least agricultural work. In other words, it would seem that food consumption is inversely correlated with food requirements, if we may assume that more food is needed to sustain the arduous agricultural labour of the rainy season than the leisure months of the dry season.

Yet it is precisely in the dry season that feasting occurs. Despite the recognized need of the period when hard work will require more food, and the fact that these people know how to store foodstuffs and have the concepts of frugality and thrift, customary habits take precedence in an ordered and regular manner over physiological needs.[17]

Richards has described the relation of food supply and requirements among the Bemba:

> The most pronounced feature of this dietary is its alternation between hunger and plenty, a characteristic common to African peoples in areas where the distribution of rain allows only one season of cultivation a year, and where one staple crop is relied upon. In this territory the existence of a definite scarcity is noticed at once by the most casual observer. The Bemba constantly talk about "hunger months" as distinguished from the food months. . . . When the scarcity becomes marked the whole appearance of village life is changed. For adults meals are reduced from two to one a day, and beer is rarely if ever brewed. Children who seem to munch extras all day long in the plentiful season (April to October) are reduced to a single dish late in the day. . . . Most adult natives can remember occasions when they went two days without food, and "sat in the hut and drank water and took snuff."[18]

It must be remembered that this, like the former instance, has to do with a particular situation, differing from those in other cultures having different technological bases and economic orientations. Thus the Malayan fishermen of Kelautan, even "during the difficult period of the monsoon" live above the subsistence level. "It seems probable," we are informed, "that the fisherman's family enjoys a diet which at most times of the year is sufficient for the energy needs of the people, not too unvaried, and, prima facie, not badly balanced."[19] Seasonal variations may cause differences in diet at different periods of the year, rather than a cycle of plenty and want. This is what is found among peoples as dif-

---

[17] M. and S. L. Fortes, 1936, pp. 260–1.
[18] A. I. Richards, 1939, pp. 35–6.
[19] Rosemary Firth, 1943, p. 136; C. Wagley, 1941, pp. 51–5.

ferent as the Mexican Cherán, the Minnesota wild-rice gatherers, and the Eskimo.

Another phase of consumer economics in nonliterate societies concerns the budgeting of family resources. Here we may cite one budget from the series of detailed accounts collected by Harris among the Nigerian Ibo who inhabit the village of Ozuitem. This budget was given by an elder, who was the head of a large rela-

Income	£	s.	d.
1. Share of bride-price of various girls of kindred		3	0
2. Sale of yams	3	0	0
3. Sale of coconuts, oranges and kola		5	0
4. Fees from rental of land		5	0
5. Interest on loans		10	0
6. Rec'd from elder son		10	0
Total cash income	£4	13	0

Expenditures	£	s.	d.
1. One-fourth of son's government tax		0	
2. School tax			6
3. Contribution for purchase of cows eaten at Bende Division Union meeting			2½
4. Contribution for sacrifice to the deity Kamálu			2
5. Contribution for annual sacrifice to Earth Deity			2
6. Food for household	1	0	0
7. Clothes for self		4	6
8. Meat, palm wine, and kola to greet visitors		5	0
9. Contributions to burials of those in his kindred, his mother's kindred, and affinal relatives		5	0
10. Stockfish, meat, and			

Expenditures (continued)	£	s.	d.
money to women who gave him food during "famine" period		1	6
11. Soap		1	0
12. Blood sucked when ill		2	0
13. Sacrifices for well-being, medicines and purgatives		3	0
14. Calendric ceremonial sacrifices to ancestors, deities, and other supernatural agencies		4	9
15. Kerosene		3	0
16. Tobacco, potash, and snuff		2	6
17. Hired workers to clear bush and plant —wages and food		7	0
18. Fine and costs of case against younger son, who ran away (fine 2 *s.*, 10 *s.* bribe to court members)		12	0
19. Meat, palm wine, and food to relatives who worked for him		6	0
20. Contribution to bride-price of wife his elder son is marrying		10	0
21. Church fees for "wife" of elder son			3
Total cash expenditure	£4	9	6½

tionship group and a member of two secret societies. He was a widower, with two sons, a daughter, and his eldest son's young "wife" living in the household. The eldest son was a trader and laborer, the younger a worthless young man who refused to work. The daughter, about thirteen years old, was going through the year's "fattening" period that follows first menstruation and precedes marriage. The family head was not well, so "most of the work is done by the nine-year-old 'wife' of the elder son."

In addition to these items, the non-monetary returns from the harvesting of certain crops, food exchanges, cooperative labor, and the like, should rightly be calculated, as well as the reserves of food, clothing, and personal property owned by this man. Despite these omissions, however, "because so much of the life entails monetary transactions of one sort or another, these budgets present not only a sharp insight into the economic life of the Ibo individual but they cast into relief many other aspects of his culture." [20]

The *capitalization* of resources among nonliterate peoples is simple and, in the main, obvious. Tools make up the bulk of their capital goods. In all but the poorest cultures, too, more permanent works are found. More complex economies permit the centralization of capital goods in the hands of certain members of society, so that "capital" in its specialized sense is present, as where the phenomena of credit and interest accompany the presence of money capital. In the main, however, the capital goods of nonliterate societies include those items comprised in the material culture, plus such permanent improvements as terraces, irrigation ditches, and other "public works."

As in all societies, *property* in nonliterate communities consists of land, material goods, and intangibles such as "rights." There has been much discussion of whether "primitive communism" is not manifest in the ownership of any or all of these among "primitives," but on examination we find that the problems of ownership in societies that vary so greatly cannot be encompassed under any such simple formula. Where land is plentiful, it becomes a kind of "free good," since where there is no scarcity, considerations of fixed ownership need not enter. Among hunting and herding people, the ownership of land is almost never in the hands of individuals, but in that of some group—a family hunting band, or a clan, or a tribe.

The formula for land ownership in nonliterate societies—and also for property in general—is that title rests on use. It is a gen-

[20] J. S. Harris, 1944, pp. 303–5.

eral rule that land under cultivation is free from trespass, while the tools, clothing, and other objects used or made by an individual are generally recognized as his, whether or not convention requires that what he owns be made available to other members of his tribe. This is well illustrated by the way in which trees in various parts of the world are held to be private property. Coconut trees in Polynesia; mango, lemon, and other trees in Mexico; palm-trees in Africa; maple-sugar trees utilized by the Ojibwa of the Eastern Woodland area—all are owned as any property is owned, without regard to who may be cultivating the land on which they grow. In all such cases, access to the trees must be permitted the one who planted them, and who continues to own them though his fields may now be elsewhere.

Intangibles form an important category of property in all societies, as witness the economic value placed on patent rights, on good will, and on copyright in our own culture. The knowledge of ironworking, retained jealously in East African families, or of curing processes, restricted to members of certain societies among the American Indians, furnish analogous instances among non-literate groups. Another example of the importance of incorporeal property includes an assortment of rights called *topati* by the Nootka of British Columbia—knowledge of family legends, a ritual for spearing fish, honorific names of many kinds, the right to carve certain designs on totem poles and grave posts, to sing certain songs, to dance certain dances, to perform certain specific parts of certain rituals.[21] Membership in many Melanesian men's societies is another valuable good, which can only be acquired by the expenditure of considerable wealth. In the South Seas, personal names, incantations, songs, charms, and family traditions all figure as family wealth.

5

We have seen that most societies have a dual economy, one for the satisfaction of material needs, and one directed toward satisfying the desire for prestige. The *prestige economy* can only operate where production provides more than is needed for the requirements of living. We must, therefore, examine the circumstances under which such a surplus is produced, before we inquire into its nature and functioning.

The comparative analysis of data from different cultures seems to indicate that the production of an economic surplus is a function, first of all, of population size. The nature of the habitat

[21] E. Sapir and M. Swadesh, 1939, note to p. 222.

and technological competence also enter. It is apparent from the facts cited earlier in this chapter that the problem of survival is most pressing in the smallest societies, living in harsh environments. Conversely, specialization that is required to produce more goods than necessary for the mere support of the population is to be found in larger groups, living in more favorable habitats. This means that the larger groups reach a per capita productivity that is greater than their needs, while the smaller ones do not. The excess that is produced is called the *economic surplus;* in giving partial release from the work of gaining subsistence it provides *social leisure.*

The correlation that exists between population size and excess productivity can be exemplified by comparing peoples living at and near the subsistence level, whose habitats and cultures are otherwise enough alike so that some of the numerous variables that enter into the equation may be held constant. The Bushmen and Hottentots of South Africa are two such peoples. The former, in pre-European times, are estimated to have totaled about ten thousand individuals, split into minute tribal groupings. The latter, as late as 1900, were enumerated at the figure of fifty thousand. The Bushmen, as has been pointed out, produce little more than the necessities of life; the Hottentots are a cattle-keeping people and live on a more secure economic level. The Bushmen have no chiefs, except in a most rudimentary sense. They likewise have no priests nor other specialists; rituals in honor of their gods or other ceremonial observances are quite simple. The Hottentots, on the other hand, were organized into bands that recognized wider affiliations to clan and tribe, and each tribe had its chief and his headmen. The chief was generally the wealthiest man of the group and could levy fines, which he shared with his councilors, in criminal and civil cases. Priests or other specialists the Hottentots do not have, but their religious rites were on occasion marked by large feasts.[22] Other examples from the Americas and Melanesia could be cited that make the same point—where there is no economic surplus, there can be no specialization. For specialization implies that the specialist who is not producing immediate subsistence goods is supported by the excess his fellows produce over survival needs, while he works at his particular craft.

The specialists who are thus supported render outstandingly two types of services, the exercise of administrative functions, and control of the supernatural. That is why, in comparing the Hottentots with the Bushmen, the point was made that the former

[22] I. Schapera, 1930, *passim.*

have chiefs and the latter none. Both are so close to the subsistence level that neither can afford priests. But in richer societies, these two functions are in time separated, except where a priest-ruler, as chief executive by divine right, fulfills the functions of both offices. In accounting terms, this signifies that the primary charges on income over and above the costs of subsistence are those of management and of insurance.

The cost of government is met by taxes, and taxation is found in all societies having rulers, though it may not be recognized as such at first glance. In the West African kingdoms of Ashanti [23] and Nupe [24] and Dahomey [25] specific mechanisms of taxation have been reported, and among the BaVenda [26] and Losi [27] of southeastern Africa. Peru and Mexico have long been known for the taxes levied by the rulers in the pre-Spanish kingdoms. In the Pacific, where institutions of government are less sharply outlined, and the problem of getting a living is relatively simple, contributions to the chief may take the direct form of labor, or first fruits and the first catch of fish may be the ruler's share. Even among the essentially democratic North American Indian tribes, certain individuals customarily received gifts from persons of lesser standing. In the Southeast and Northwest, where governing hierarchies were well established, the customary rule prevailed of allotting labor, or a portion of the harvest, or part of the yield from the hunt to those in office.

It is more difficult to discover the mechanisms whereby those who serve the supernatural are remunerated. The fact that the office of priest and ruler are often combined in cultures where there is little specialization complicates the problem. It must also be apparent that the basis on which the power of the priests rests differs from that of the ruler, and that this makes the levying of fees the primary means of return for his services. In many cases the priest is clearly subordinate to the chief, but most often the two work in harmony. Many examples of close, and not disinterested cooperation have been recorded. Thus, among the Yokuts and Western Mono tribes of California, the shaman would cause illness to come to one who refused to contribute to a dance ordered by the chief, from the contributions to which both benefited. Or in Dahomey, the priests, by proclaiming the anger of the

[23] R. S. Rattray, 1929.
[24] S. F. Nadel, 1942a.
[25] M. J. Herskovits, 1938b.
[26] H. A. Stayt, 1931.
[27] M. Gluckman, 1943.

gods, would ordain minute offerings for each goat a man owned. Thus they made available to the royal tax gatherers a count of goats, village by village, so that levies could later be laid with precision.

As we move to more complex economies, we find those who participate in the allocation of excess resources more numerous, and their functions more varied. In societies as large and as productive as our own, or in India and China, the disparities in distribution make possible a large group whose primary occupation is the utilization of this excess productivity, while at the other end of the scale are those whose bare survival needs are scarcely met.

What use, we may ask, is made of this surplus by its beneficiaries? What are the drives underlying the economic functions of such persons? The classical study of this problem has been made by Thorstein Veblen, who analyzed that "differentiation in consumption" which, he held, was made possible by the "specialized consumption of goods as an evidence of pecuniary strength." In many societies, this process produced experts who have so developed techniques of utilizing goods and services that this aspect of their socioeconomic roles becomes an art, and an end in itself. This process Veblen termed "conspicuous consumption," a phrase that penetratingly summarizes what seems to be a universal process in human society, and that has come to be a part of everyday speech.

The concept "conspicuous consumption" gives profound insight into the psychology that underlies prestige economies. The economic surplus can be distributed in two ways. There can be a spread of the socialized leisure over a whole population, thus releasing all members from some part of the manual labor they would otherwise perform in growing crops, working forges, and doing other tasks of the subsistence economy. Or it can be concentrated in various non-subsistence callings in which individuals maintain their position by expending, as conspicuously as possible, the surplus that is produced by others, because it is expected of them. The psychological processes of *identification* so function that those who do not participate in the economic surplus, even though they produce it, derive satisfaction from this conspicuous expenditure rather than resent it.[28]

Examples of the process in nonliterate societies are manifold. Veblen's exposition of its operation in historic cultures shows us how, with greater productivity, consumption becomes more conspicuous, as in the coronation of a monarch, or the debut of a

[28] T. Veblen, 1915, *passim*.

millionaire's daughter. "Social Advancement in Guadalcanal" is the telling title of a paper [29] that details the elaborate expenditure of foodstuffs that marks the rise of a man from common status to that of a leader in his community. We see in this account how he works, with his wives and relatives, to amass resources that make possible increasing participation in the reciprocal feasting essential for the attainment of a more favorable social position. Then, when he can afford it, he proffers a feast where gifts of food are so lavish that, in the words of the natives, "We eat till we sicken and vomit." This feast, if elaborate enough when compared with other feasts, marks his arrival at the desired stage in his progression, where he remains until he is in a position to resume the continuing process of giving and receiving gifts that marks the man of recognized position.

During the Kwakiutl potlatch, literally thousands of valuable blankets were burned, several canoes broken, and a slave killed to establish a chief's prestige. At African upper-class funerals, the goods placed in the grave of a family head or of a chief, or given to participants outside the family, or destroyed, represent substantial wealth. The houses of Samoan chiefs reflect the position of their owners. The degree of elegance associated with a structure is determined by the elaborateness with which those who built it were entertained while engaged in this work. Clothing differentials that mark rank are common—the Ashanti chief ceremonially wears a silk cloth of exclusive pattern, the commoner wears one of cotton. The elaborateness of religious rites is also a part of the complex of conspicuous consumption, and represents the allocation of surplus goods to those who control this aspect of a culture.

The prestige economy is a system in which gain comes through expenditure rather than through saving, and the highest position is reserved for those who most conspicuously spend the contributions of the less privileged, for the vicarious enjoyment of the contributors. That this phenomenon should be so widely spread as to make it almost a universal in human experience illuminates the nature and functioning of culture, and, beyond this, of the human psyche. Every people, we have said, have wants in excess of their technological competence. There could be no better evidence that such "wants" are culturally established. Their expression is only remotely related to the requirements of the biological organism, or to the natural setting in which they are found. Their rationale is one of convention, their sanctions wholly those of tradition.

[29] H. I. Hogbin, 1937–38.

6

All this has direct bearing on one much discussed problem—economic determinism. Here we come to the last of the trio of deterministic theories that have entered into the study of culture; the first, it will be recalled, having been biological, the second environmental, determinism. The problem of economic determinism has been particularly obscured by a failure to distinguish it from the concept of historical materialism, both of which derive from the writings of Karl Marx. In a single passage, Marx, who did not himself employ the terms, gave expression to the concepts. "The method of production in material life determines the general character of the social, political and spiritual processes of life"—this is *economic determinism.* "It is not the consciousness of men that determines their being," he then goes on to say, "but, on the contrary, their social being determines their consciousness." [30] This is *historical materialism.* It is not difficult to see that the second theory underlies all scientific study of culture, while the former is the proclamation of a position that is open to the same criticism lodged against any single, and therefore simplified, explanation of the complexities of human social life.

Innumerable instances from subsistence economies controvert the economic deterministic position, even if the patterns of prestige economic systems did not of themselves do this. Thus among the tribes of Travancore, India, the rigidity of the religious rites makes the Urali more successful farmers than their neighbors, the Paliyan and Mannan, whose rituals are "casual and haphazard." [31] The productivity of Dahomean ironworkers could be increased appreciably if every eighth instead of every fourth day were reserved to the god of iron. The material resources of the Navaho Indians would be greater if the house and personal effects of a man were not destroyed at his death.

This is not to deny the role that the economy and its technological base play in shaping the mode of life of a people, a role that is especially large where a group is small, technology simple, resources scarce, and the problem of survival paramount. But there are too many societies whose dominant orientations lie in non-economic aspects of life for us to attribute to the economic phases of culture more than the influence they exert in providing the material base, without which no human activity could be carried on.

[30] Cited by G. D. H. Cole, 1933, p. xvi.
[31] D. G. Mandelbaum, 1939.

Chapter **Ten**

Social Organization and the Educational Function

Social organization designates the institutions that determine the position of men and women in society and thus channel their personal relations. As Eggan has put it:

> Such relationships may be characterized both in terms of the individuals or groups represented and by the type of relation involved. . . . These social relations between individuals and groups form a network which we can call the social structure, the organizational or configurational aspect of society. Institutions partake of both aspects: they are composed of individuals organized in a social structure, with a set of attributes and behavior patterns through which the structure is exemplified and the institutional ends achieved.[1]

The study of social organization was one of the early emphases of early anthropology, and gave rise to what, in England, was termed "comparative sociology." Under the influence of A. R. Radcliffe-Brown, this concern with social institutions and their

[1] F. Eggan, 1950, p. 5.

functioning developed, especially in England, into the sub-discipline of *social anthropology*, which in time came almost exclusively to have to do with the study of social structures. Firth, a social anthropologist, has defined the term "social organization" as "the systematic ordering of social relations by acts of choice and decision." [2] In this view, social organization is the dynamic phase of social structure, "the continuity principle of society." Firth's view, while differing from that of most students of the social aspects of culture, essentially rephrases and sharpens an interrelation between social structure and function long accepted by students of society; though, as with all social anthropologists, his organizing concept is society and not culture.

Social organization is customarily studied in terms of two broad classes of institutions—those that grow out of kinship, and those that result from the free association of individuals. Kinship structures include the family and its extension into broader relationship groupings such as the clan. The association of individuals who are not kin gives rise to a wide range of forms that vary from blood brotherhood and institutionalized friendship to secret and non-secret "societies" of various kinds. Age-groupings, though more often than not informal in character, can play important roles in societies where they hold the formal position of age-grades. In a still broader sense, social structures include relations of a political character based on locale and status. The educational function of various social institutions, especially the family, is also of signal importance.

In this chapter, we shall be concerned with these institutionalized ways in which human groups are organized and function. How men and women conventionally seek their mates, the lines along which mating is permitted, and the resultant family structures—these are fundamental to our discussion. How these primary groupings proliferate into the broader units we have already mentioned, and what the recognized sanctions of these larger structures are, will also be considered. The non-relationship categories, based on age and free association, will claim our attention. Finally, we will treat the role of all these social units in training the young to become functioning members of society. In these, as in all other aspects of culture, we will seek to obtain a sense of the variety of means employed to achieve common ends. But we will also bear in mind how, in reaching these ends, neither logic nor patterned coherence is sacrificed by those who, in each society, achieve integration in living their culture.

[2] Raymond Firth, 1951, p. 40.

2

The biological and social family may be two distinct entities. The biological fact is simple—two parents are required to produce offspring, and the number of ancestors doubles with each ascending generation. Some societies do institutionalize this fact of *bilateral* descent, as it is technically termed. More often, however, descent is counted in accordance with a *unilateral* pattern, whereby a person belongs to his father's or to his mother's family. In the former case, descent is *patrilineal*, in the latter, *matrilineal*. In either instance, in counting descent, only one significant ancestor appears in each generation.

Even in cultures where the bilateral system prevails, ancestry is not counted in accordance with biological reality. Thus, while Euroamerican conventions of descent are bilateral, in that relationship to both mother's and father's families is fully acknowledged, the spirit of the system is patrilineal as regards family names. The phenomenon of the "hyphenated name" is known in Spain and in upper class usage elsewhere, but it persists for only a generation or two. This unilateral aspect of our descent system, while it facilitates genealogical identification, tends to obscure the contributions to our ancestry of our female antecedents, whose "maiden names," as we term them, were given up on marriage.

There is no doubt that different traditions of descent influence the psychosocial relation between members of families. One aspect of our family convention is the father's role. He is what has been termed the "surrogate" for society—he is the family head, the arbiter of its destiny, and in some countries controller of its economic resources. His function as court of last resort is important in the disciplining of children. Because of all this, he stands in a relation to his offspring and collateral relatives that differs from that of his wife. Outside the home, he customarily speaks for the group; while inside it, the wife's role, allowing for differences in forcefulness of character, is a softer, gentler one.

The organization and functioning of the matrilineal descent-group, and the relations that exist between its members, are quite different. Where matriliny prevails, the family head is commonly the mother's brother, rather than the father. In some cases, the matrilineal tradition may be associated with *matrilocal* residence, under which the man takes up his residence in his wife's village. When the wife comes to live at her husband's home, this is called *patrilocal* residence. Where matrilocal residence is associated with matriliny, the feeling about the primacy of women in the family may be so strong that the husband is regarded as a kind of outsider in his wife's family and may, as among the Zuñi Indians, live in it on sufferance. Among these people, there is no question in anyone's mind but that the home of a man, for all his life, is that of his mother or, after her death, of his sisters. In what *we* would term "his own home," the dwelling of his wife and his children, he has no status at all, except the position he may enjoy as a result of long residence and the personal regard in which he may come to be held by his wife's kin. It is obvious that relations within the family will be deeply influenced by all this. Functions held by the father as family head in patrilineal societies are transferred to the mother's eldest brother under matriliny. The mother's brother controls family finances, speaks for the family, and exercises authority over the children.

It must be stressed that the grouping of father, mother and children is universal. Even in the few instances where the physiological role of the father in reproduction is not comprehended, the immediate family grouping is a fully functioning element in society. Furthermore, there is a vast store of data that proves beyond any doubt that, whatever unilinear convention of descent may obtain, both parents, and their families, however these may be defined, have a full place in the regard of all members of the family group. In those parts of Australia, for example, where patrilineal descent is found, the ties that bind a child to its mother, no less than its father, are extended to collateral relatives.

> Since there is a close bond between a child and its mother, and another bond between the mother and her brother the child is brought into a close personal bond with the mother's brother. The latter is not treated in any way as similar to the father or father's brother, but is treated as a sort of male "mother." Similarly the father's sister is treated as a sort of female "father." In all Australian tribes the actual mother's brother and the actual father's sister of an individual have important places in his life, and the whole system can be understood only when this is fully recognized.[3]

The immediate family can be either *monogamous* or *polygamous*. There is, however, no society where polygamy is countenanced that does not have a large proportion of monogamous families, and few monogamous societies where what would be called in Euroamerican culture extra-legal plural matings, often of some stability, are not present. The incidence of polygamous

[3] A. R. Radcliffe-Brown, 1931, p. 100.

families in a society that sanctions plural marriage is held down by biological and economic circumstances. Except where infanticide is practiced, the equivalence of the sexes in numbers permits only relatively few individuals to have multiple spouses. Otherwise, a sizable proportion of one sex would be deprived of all chances to marry; and this situation is found in no culture that has been studied. Even where infanticide is practiced, the expense of marriage makes it difficult for most persons to meet the costs of more than one mate. This is why in societies that produce little economic surplus, monogamy is the practice, even though it is not the required form of marriage.

Polygamous marriages are of two types, *polygynous*, where a man has more than one wife and *polyandrous*, where a woman has more than one husband. The latter type in fully institutionalized form is restricted to the aboriginal tribes of India, and to Tibet. One of the best-known examples of polyandry is that of the Todas, who practice female infanticide and thus artificially create a differential in sex ratio. Here a woman who marries a man becomes the wife of his brothers; if it is a child marriage, the privilege of being her husband is reserved to any brothers yet to be born. When a wife becomes pregnant, the eldest brother ceremonially presents her with a bow and arrow, and "for all social purposes," becomes the father of the child, continuing, even after death, to be the "father" of all children born to the common wife until another husband performs the rite of giving the bow and arrow.[4]

Polygyny exists in all parts of the world, though because of the economic factors (that do not seem to be operative in polyandrous matings) and the absence of significant differences in the number of men and women, the incidence of these plural marriages in different polygynous societies varies greatly. Even though in plural marriages the problem of personal adjustment figures prominently, friction seems less prevalent than is expected by those living under monogamous patterns. A first wife will urge her husband to add another spouse to the household, because it brings the family prestige and also brings her aid in domestic tasks and companionship. In many societies, friction is lessened by a system whereby each wife has her own dwelling place, where she lives with her children. In such cases, the husband may stay with his wives in turn, or they may alternate in visiting him.

Marriage inevitably involves far-reaching personal adjustments. Not only are new responsibilities incurred, but a new and

[4] W. H. R. Rivers, 1906, pp. 516–18.

intimate association with another individual must be established. Many societies ease this personal adjustment by permitting a period of experimentation before marriage. In some instances, wide-scale experimentation is sanctioned, as among the Masai of East Africa. In other societies, a marriage is not concluded until a child has been born to the girl.

Relations of a new kind must also be established with the mate's family, who often have the determining voice in deciding whether a marriage is to take place. The customary forms of behavior between a man or woman and a father-in-law or a mother-in-law have been the subject of much pseudo-psychological speculation. The misinterpretation of the mother-in-law taboo is an example of this. The avoidance, requiring, among other things, that a man turn his back when he meets his mother-in-law on the path and that he never be alone in the same dwelling or converse directly with her, is usually interpreted as hostile behavior; whereas these conventions signify respect. Whether or not, in addition, unconscious hostility is sublimated in this fashion cannot be said, though a logical argument can be raised to support the position. Speculation has also centered about the meaning of the joking relations that are widely found in nonliterate groups between brothers- and sisters-in-law, especially where the *levirate* or *sororate* makes potential mates of the younger sisters or brothers of a husband or wife.

Local and kinship affiliations govern the choice of a mate. Since more often than not these matters are controlled in nonliterate societies by the rules of larger kinship units, discussion of them must be deferred until the following section. Irrespective of the lines that dictate choice in marriage, however, the family in all societies is distinguished by a stability that arises out of the fact that it is based on marriage; that is to say, on *socially sanctioned mating entered into with the assumption of permanency.*

3

Unilineal descent systems not only simplify the process of indicating ancestry and relationships, but also facilitate placing a given nuclear family group in a much wider context of kinship than is customary in bilateral aggregates. Figure 22 shows the ramifications of kinship in a matrilineal relationship group, carried through five generations. *Ego*, a male, traces his descent through his mother (*17*), his mother's mother (*9*) and his mother's mother's mother (*4*), which is as far as our genealogy takes us. He has a sister (*33*) and a younger brother (*35*); his sister's children

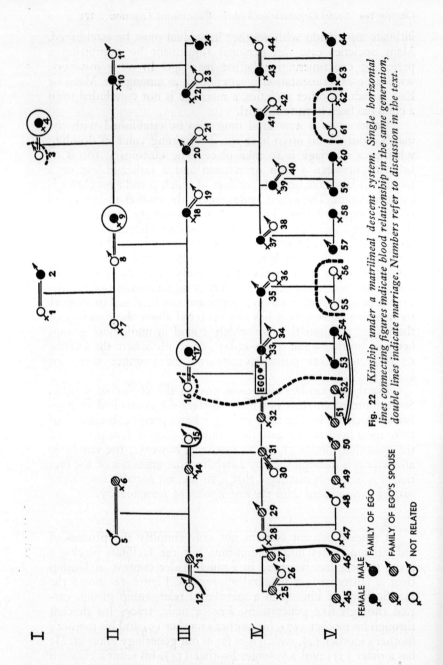

Fig. 22 *Kinship under a matrilineal descent system. Single horizontal lines connecting figures indicate blood relationship in the same generation, double lines indicate marriage. Numbers refer to discussion in the text.*

FEMALE MALE
● ○ FAMILY OF EGO
◉ ⊘ FAMILY OF EGO'S SPOUSE
○ ○ NOT RELATED

I
II
III
IV
V

(*53* and *54*) are under his control, but he is not related to his brother's children (*55* and *56*) at all. His mother's sister (*18*) and his mother's mother's sister (*10*) are related to him, as are their descendants in the female line—that is, the children of his mother's sister's daughters (*37* and *39; 57, 58, 59* and *60*), but not the offspring of this woman's son (*41; 61* and *62*). Similarly, collaterals descended from (*10*) are members of his relationship group.

Study of our chart demonstrates that it would actually be most unwieldy, if not impossible, to specify by separate relationship terms all the facts of descent, marriage ties, generation, age, and the like. Moreover, every people thinks its own system, however complicated to the outsider, is obvious, logical, and simple. We are no exception, yet numerous points in our kinship terminology might well puzzle a Crow Indian, or an Australian, or a Vandau of East Africa. A person's male parent (*16*) is "father," female parent (*17*) "mother." These terms are precise, and each applies only to one individual. But when we say "grandfather" do we mean "father's father" or "mother's father"? Descent line is here neglected, as age is neglected in other terms we use. "Brother" means the male child of my father and mother; we do not name age differentials by indicating whether a particular individual called "brother" was born before or after the person speaking. But many peoples hold it important to indicate this difference. Our term "cousin" carries this grouping of individuals of different sex, age, and generation so far that we ourselves find it cumbersome and confusing.

Anthropologists study kinship terminology for many purposes, of which the most important is the insight into the underlying social structure that regularizes behavior, gained from listing kinship terms and analyzing the rights and duties identified with those called by the various terms.

One of the most widely spread types of unilateral kinship terminology is the *classificatory* system, in which generation is paramount and degree of relationship is subordinated. In our diagram, under such a system, *Ego* calls his grandmother's sister (*10*) by the same term as he calls his grandmother (*9*); he calls his mother's sister (*18*) "mother" and also the daughter (*22*) of his mother's mother's sister (*10*). All the daughters of his "grandmothers" are his "mothers" and all the children of his "mothers" are his "sisters" and "brothers." That is, he would not only call *33* "sister," but use this term for *37, 39,* and *43;* he would call *41* "brother" as well as *35*. Because he is a man in a matrilineal system, what he would call his younger relatives would vary, but it would probably not be "son" or "daughter." That is what *33*, a woman, would call *57* and *58*, *59* and *60*, *63* and *64*, as well as *53* and *54*. Some terms such as "sister's son" and "sister's daughter" would be *Ego*'s name for these individuals, and they would probably call him "mother's brother," the term by which he would call *20* and *24*.

It would be pointless to indicate even a portion of the different systems of kinship nomenclature that have been recorded. The important thing for the student to recognize is how such a framework influences the lives of those who live within it. Its function in regulating marriage is perhaps its best-known role. The ease with which incest lines can be drawn in a unilineal system is striking. Any child of any "mother"—or of any "father" in a patrilineal system—is my "brother" or "sister." To marry a brother or sister is incestuous. Therefore, when a match is under consideration, the genealogies of the principals are examined to discover if the descent line of either party contains the name of a "significant ancestor" found in the other. If this is discovered, they are "brother" and "sister," and to mate would therefore be incestuous.

The broadest extension of a unilinear descent group has been given various names. *Clan* is widely employed. However, anthropologists, especially in the United States, have also used the word "clan" to distinguish groups in which descent is counted on the mother's side. Those counting descent on the father's side have been called *gens*. Lowie chose the word *sib* as a common term, making possible the differentiation of the two types into *mother-sibs* and *father-sibs*.[5] "Sib" will be used here to denote these broad unilineal kinship aggregates.

The sib performs numerous functions, but its most common task is to regulate selection in marriage. One instance of this is to be found in systems of *preferential mating*, usually occurring between *cross-cousins*—that is, the children of a brother and a sister, real or classificatory. This is possible because these offspring belong to different sibs. In our diagram, *54* and *55* are cross-cousins; *54* belongs to the sib of her mother, *33*, while *55* belongs to the sib of *his* mother, *36*. He is not sociologically related to *54*, though she is the child of the sister of *35*, and *35* is the father of *55*. Technically, it can be noted, cross-cousins are the opposite of *parallel cousins*, children of two brothers or two sisters. Ego is the parallel cousin of *37* and *39*, and it would be incestuous for him to marry either of these women. Indeed, in some societies, he

[5] R. H. Lowie, 1920, pp. 111–12.

late 6a *Inca masonry: wall of fortress above Cuzco, Peru.* **Plate 6b** *Inca ma-*
onry: pre-Spanish walls still used as house walls in Cuzco. See p. 123. (Photograph
ourtesy Wendell Bennett.)

A   B

C

Plate 7a   *Yoruba masked dancer, showing manner of wearing mask.* **Plate 7b***Closer view of same masked dancer. (Photographs 7a and 7b courtesy W. Bascom*
Plate 7c   *Yoruba mask in position customarily exhibited. See p. 236. (Collection
W. Bascom; photograph by Mary Modglin, Chicago.)*

would be at considerable pains to avoid social contacts with them as much as possible.

Chief among the sanctions that give the sib its power are the sib mythologies. These sacred tales recount the origin and history of these groupings and explain codes regulating marriage or other conventions, such as taboos of various sorts. Though by no means a universal aspect of the sib, the sanctions behind sib regulations are in many instances derived from a mythological being technically called a *totem*. *Totemism* is the belief that a mystical relationship exists between a group of human beings who make up a kinship unit and a species of plant or animal or, less commonly, some natural phenomenon.

There are many definitions of totemism, and controversy at one time was acute over the meaning of the term, the origin of the institution, and its sociological significance. Totemism is as often designated a religious as a social phenomenon. The imposition of food taboos on totemites, their taking the name of the totem animal as an *eponym*, and their duty of assuring the propagation of the totem animal are some of its features that have at various times been emphasized as essential to it. Frazer tended to see all totemic practices as typified by the Australian belief in the reincarnation of the totemic spirit, associated with a given locality, in each child.[6] Goldenweiser, however, established that so many different manifestations of the relationship between men and animals are to be found that none of these, by itself, can be used to characterize the phenomenon in general.[7]

The practice of assuming a symbolic relationship between men and animals is not to be thought of as an odd quirk of the "primitive" mind. The eponymous feature of totemism, for example, is more prevalent in American culture than is realized. It is present when a lodge member proclaims himself a Moose or an Elk, or when a college man or woman is spoken of as a Bulldog or a Gopher or a Wildcat. Its development in more specific form during World War I in the American Expeditionary Force, as recounted by Linton, shows that this mystical relationship could develop to a point lacking only exogamy to make it fit the totemic pattern of nonliterate societies.[8]

In concentrating on the problems of the family and the sib,

[6] Sir J. G. Frazer, 1910, *passim*, Cf., however, Vol. IV, p. 5, where Frazer speaks of "pure totemism, such as we find it among the Australian aborigines."

[7] A. A. Goldenweiser, 1910; reprinted in Goldenweiser, 1933, pp. 213–332.

[8] R. Linton, 1924, pp. 296–300.

anthropologists have tended to neglect other intermediate social groupings between the immediate family and the sib. In African societies, however, where tribal populations are large, the sib is too unwieldy to stand without the support of such intermediate institutions. Thus, among the Beni-Amer of the Sudan, Nadel reports that, in the upper classes, "the genealogical pattern repeats itself, with diminishing range, throughout the social structure of the tribes down to the smallest unit. Each clan is subdivided into kinship groups . . . , in turn . . . composed of a number of families, each under its family head." [9] Or, in West Africa, the forty-eight sibs and sub-sibs of Dahomey seem a considerable number, until it is realized that there are about a million Dahomeans. In Nigeria and the Gold Coast, towns are divided into quarters, each predominantly inhabited by the local representatives of some of the sibs spread over the total tribal area. The concept of the *extended family* was developed in Africa, therefore, to designate these local groups, composed of a series of *immediate*, or nuclear families inhabiting the same locale. When large enough, the extended family is to be thought of as a *sub-sib*, which can develop into a full-fledged sib.

The institution of the extended family has now been found to exist in many parts of the world. It would seem as though it were essential, as a matter of fact, to the functioning of society. For if the clan is too broad a grouping, the immediate family is too small to stand alone. Thus in modern Peru "the extended family is the basic unit in Aymara society and the most important economic group." It includes a man and his brothers, their wives, sons, and unmarried daughters, and each "conjugal family" (that is, immediate family) has its own cluster of houses within the compound where the entire group lives.[10] Drucker states that among the Indians of the North Pacific Coast, "when we come to examine the constitution of the typical local group of the area, a more striking fact appears: everywhere this social division was no more and no less than an extended family (slaves, of course, excluded) and was so considered by its members." [11] Goodwin's analysis of the Western Apache includes groupings of "several households choosing to live together because of blood, clan, marital, and economic ties," which he designates as "the extended family, or 'family cluster.' " [12]

[9] S. F. Nadel, 1945, p. 6.
[10] H. Tschopik, Jr., 1946, pp. 542–3.
[11] P. Drucker, 1939, p. 58.
[12] G. Goodwin, 1942, p. 123.

It is becoming apparent, moreover, that not even a tripartite scheme of dividing kinship aggregates is adequate to express all the social structures based on kinship. Groupings of kin within a sib and without reference to size vary considerably from one society to another in the number of sub-units they comprise. This has been demonstrated by Evans-Pritchard, who describes four orders of such groupings among the East African Nuer. "A Nuer clan," that is, a sib, "is the largest group of agnates who trace their descent from a common ancestor and between whom marriage is forbidden and sexual relations considered incestuous." It is "a highly segmented genealogical structure." The genealogical segments are of four degrees, *maximal, major, minor,* and

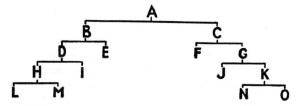

Fig. 23 *Relationships between Nuer lineages. (After Evans-Pritchard, 1940.)*

minimal. Their relationship is shown in Figure 23. Sib A "is segmented into maximal lineages B and C and these bifurcate into major lineages D, E, F and G. Minor lineages H, I, J, and K are segments of major lineages D and G, and L, M, N and O are minimal lineages which are segments of H and K." [13] These aggregates are recognized in native terminology and practice, yet each stands as a unit "only in relation to each other" and in contradistinction to another of the same degree. Thus "M is a group only in opposition to L, H is a group only in opposition to I, D is a group only in opposition to E." Conversely, "there is always fusion of collateral lineages of the same branch in relation to a collateral branch, e.g. in the diagram L and M are a single minor lineage H, in opposition to I," and so on. This means that "a man is a member of a lineage in relation to a certain group and not a member of it in relation to a different group." [14]

It is apparent from this analysis that the institutions of family and sibs are but points of reference in a continuum that may, in terms of form and function, extend beyond these points and

[13] E. E. Evans-Pritchard, 1940, pp. 192-3.
[14] *Ibid.*, pp. 197-8.

be composed of elements far more complicated than is often realized. Where families are polygynous and wives inhabit separate houses, this seemingly minimal unit may be broken down into smaller ones, each consisting of a woman and her children, as in the case in large West African compounds. At the other end of the scale, sibs may be combined into clusters called *moieties,* as in North America and Australia.

4

In addition to the various groupings based on kinship are those human aggregates that derive from other criteria, such as sex, or age, or common interest. To all these the term best applied is *associations.* The size of associations and the ends they seek are even more varied than those of kinship structures. Earlier students, emphasizing kinship groupings, quite disregarded these others, and it was not until the turn of the century that this oversight began to be corrected. Even then, however, attention turned to the factor of sex differences, as expressed in the separation of the sexes in secret "societies," age grades, and men's houses, all of which were held to reflect the greater importance of the role of men in society. Thus the variety of significant functions of non-relationship groupings was neglected. Nonetheless, the mere fact that these associations were brought to the attention of students was of importance in placing the study of social organization in proper perspective. The exclusive concern of earlier studies with larger nonrelationship groupings gradually gave way to the investigation of more modest types.

Institutionalized friendship, first described as such for Dahomey, offers an excellent example of this. As late as 1920, Lowie could write of the "diminutive association" represented by "the union of two unrelated friends pledged to mutual support and lifelong comradeship" as something "of altogether peculiar character" among the Dakota Indians and related tribes. With the leads furnished by the African material, however, data, either gathered independently or recovered from older sources, have established the importance and indicated the functions of institutionalized friendship in the social organization of many peoples. Mandelbaum, giving details of such friendships among the Plains Cree Indians of Canada, also cites ten earlier references to various types of friendship alliance in North America.[15] In Malekula, an island of the New Hebrides group in Melanesia, the ceremonial significance of friendship is stressed. In this society, currency in

[15] D. Mandelbaum, 1936.

the ritual and prestige economy is the pig. At funerals, the rites "may be said to depend essentially upon the killing and giving of one pig." This animal, which must have belonged to the dead man, is produced, and then, "his greatest friend . . . steps forward with a spear and seizes hold of the rope to which the pig is tied, as though for the moment he were about to kill it." He hands the rope and spear to the second-best friend of the dead man, who turns to the third-best friend, and so on, until they reach "a man who was not a friend of the deceased and who, therefore, is going to accept the pig." He kills the animal, and takes it and the banana and yams given him to his village, where they are eaten. This refusal to perform the duty arises out of the "very intense bond . . . something that may be described almost as love," experienced by "two men who habitually eat together, sharing a common meal." [16]

In the example of institutionalized friendship from Dahomey, West Africa, a man has three friends, the *honton daho*, or first friend; the second, whose name is derived from the fact that at one point in the funeral ceremony, he takes his place against a wall; and the third, "the friend who stands on the threshold." The relation demands complete mutual confidence, the more striking because of the circumspectness that usually marks relations between Dahomeans. A man withholds nothing from his first friend; to his second he tells no more than half of what he knows; while the third "stands at the door and hears what he can." The first friend transmits the desires of his dead friend concerning the disposal of his property, and confirms the heir; he is the first after the eldest son to make funerary gifts; when an ancestor is deified, the soul of his best friend is summoned to possess a descendant, who makes the proper offering. The deep emotional tone that marks this relation is reflected in the following explanation of a Dahomean tale: "In the life of man, when the choice must be made between the father-in-law, diviner, or best friend, a man must always be closest to the best friend. The others a man may leave to one side, but the best friend of a man is first." [17]

These examples show that the distribution of institutionalized friendship is wide, though it remains for later studies to demonstrate its full incidence. Some of this information will come from fresh ethnographic research. Much, however, is to be gained from hints in the literature, such as Mandelbaum found, and from citations where more striking aspects of friendship, such as blood

[16] A. B. Deacon, 1934, pp. 537–40.
[17] M. J. Herskovits, 1938b, Vol. I, pp. 88 ff., 239–42, 361 ff., *passim*.

brotherhood, have been described. There is the likelihood that these are but ceremonial phases, which bring into relief an association that, over the years, plays a constant role in the complex of personal relations shaped by the social organization of a people.

Larger groupings are better known. Among the Plains Indian tribes, in addition to the friendship relations are associations "based on a common supernatural experience," feasting societies, dance societies, and military societies. We note also the Cheyenne women's crafts guilds, Hidatsa bundle fraternities, and the Tobacco order of the Crow. If this list is extended to other parts of the world, we find groupings with police or executive functions, societies with insurance features, or those dedicated to cooperative labor, as well as religious orders and age sets. Though by no means all, many of these are restricted to men. One exception already mentioned is a woman's society, while still others, such as West African associations that pool savings for a common end or for ultimate redistribution, may include both men and women.

Nonliterate societies are thus no different from our own in the number, or type, or functions of associations. Neither they, nor we, for all the specialization that marks our culture, have clear-cut objectives that permit precise classification. Our lodges, too, have supernatural sanctions; the Knights Templar division of the Masonic order, for example, could easily be classed by a visiting Melanesian ethnographer as a religious grouping. Labor unions are often called lodges, with passwords and ritual, and recreational as well as economic functions.

It would seem we can do little more than note that in all human societies men and women form attachments and set up groupings that transcend the lines of kinship. Propinquity is perhaps one reason for this, community of interests another, the possession of the same skill a third, and the establishment of status by exclusiveness a fourth. Specific hypotheses about their development, such as that secret societies have sprung from the initiatory rites which, in many nonliterate cultures, boys and sometimes girls must undergo at puberty, are interesting but impossible to document. The multiplicity of forms and purposes of such groupings demonstrate that no study of the social organization of any people is adequate unless they are taken fully into account.

5

Education is a process whose function is to bring individual behavior into line with the specific requirements of a culture. In stating this, we need not take sides in the debate over theories of learning. Controversies over the role of imitation *versus* conditioning, of reward and punishment *versus* association have stimulated study and sharpened perceptions of the problems involved. Since most persons of Euroamerican culture tend to regard education as synonymous with schooling, anthropologists have been confronted with statements such as, "The *X* tribe has no system of education." What is meant by such a statement is almost always revealed to be something quite different—that the people in question have no *schools*. The significance of the distinction between "schooling" and "education" is grasped when we learn that while every people must train their young, the cultures in which any substantial part of this training is carried on outside the household are few indeed.

When we consider education, we must again take into account the important place specialization plays in machine cultures. What we call "vocational training" affords an excellent example. Nonliterate societies have no need for special buildings stocked with intricate machines that young men and women learn to operate. Within the limits of sex lines of division of labor, the child has from his early years been continuously engaged in learning the processes he must later employ in getting his living. He may be more effective in one activity than in another, but his opportunities to learn embrace all the techniques which, as a grown man or woman, he will be called upon to handle.

An outstanding contrast between education in nonliterate and Euroamerican cultures is found in our attitude toward learning and teaching. Thus, in Wogeo, New Guinea, "The children are in most cases even more eager to learn than the elders are to teach." For example:

> Sabwakai took up the adze on his own initiative [to help his father make a dugout] and on another occasion asked permission to come along with his father to one of our conferences at my house. "By listening to what I tell you," the father explained to me with a smile, "he thinks he'll find out about the things he'll have to do when he's a man.[18]

The urge to learn, basic in all children, is in nonliterate societies pointed toward much broader culturally sanctioned ends in relation to the cultural resources than in a culture such as our own where, because of intense specialization, choices are numerous and training must be along narrower lines. Among nonliterate peoples there are few square pegs in round holes. Yet knowledge

[18] H. I. Hogbin, 1946–47b, p. 282.

must be acquired by learning, and it is not sufficient to lay it before even the most eager learner without organization and direction. Therefore, though formal schooling is not a factor in the education of the young of most nonliterate peoples, there is no lack of educational techniques to encourage, to discipline, to punish. Methods of arousing interest by rewards for the performance of duties laid on a child, or by dramatizing the right to learn these duties, are frequently reported. Where a culture stresses competition, the play of competitive drives will be utilized to induce learning. Where competition is not important in ordering behavior, other methods of stimulating a child to strive for competence will be found. The process of educating the young, that is, like any other aspect of culture, is patterned and institutionalized.

Educational techniques used by nonliterate peoples vary as widely as any other aspect of their cultures—overt training by elders, emulation of older children, observation at ceremonies where only the mature are active participants, or while a parent or elder relative goes about his daily tasks. They include the inculcation of moral values and conduct by direct instruction, the correction of an infringement of an accepted code by admonition, ridicule, or corporal punishment. Positive as well as negative measures are employed in bringing up a child. In many cultures, praise is lavished on the child who successfully performs an act, and various other ways of encouragement have been recorded, as in West Africa where bells are attached to the ankles of an infant who is learning to walk.

Within the family, education is principally carried on by the members of a household. Where family units are small, as among ourselves, this means that the father and mother, with perhaps a grandparent or uncle or aunt who is for a time a member of this grouping, discharge this obligation. In unilineal systems, where the classificatory relationship pattern prevails, the immediate contacts of the child will be far different. Under a classificatory kinship structure, there will be several "fathers" or "mothers" concerned with the upbringing of a child. All of these, by right, can admonish, encourage, punish, or reward in ways that uncles and aunts in our own culture would rarely presume to do. Thus in a survey of the educational practices of American Indian tribes north of Mexico, Pettitt [19] names forty-three groups in which the mother's brother plays a principal part in the education of the child.

[19] G. A. Pettitt, 1946, pp. 19–22.

In Zuñi, Li assigns this broad base of supervision an important place in the "working mechanism" of educational discipline to which the child is subjected.

> All the members of the family besides the parents coöperate to see that the child behaves well. In fact, any member of the community who happens to pass by will say something to correct some misbehavior of a child. Confronted with this united front of adults, so to speak, the child does not have much chance in trying to play one against the other. And if he is not unduly constrained, why should he make it unpleasant both for himself and for others? It is often observed that a very obstreperous child is easily hushed by a slight sound of any adult, in fact, by any facial expression which is seen by the child.[20]

Here we have an extension of the function of correction from classificatory relatives to the other adults of the community. This, again, entails no difficulty. The homogeneity of the culture makes for a unity of teaching objectives that reflect unity of cultural aims and methods, leaving little room for conflict between the directives of different preceptors.

This conflict in directives is perhaps the source of the most serious difficulties in larger, less homogeneous societies, where the total educational process includes schooling as well as training in the home. Deep-seated maladjustment may result from education received at the hands of persons whose cultural or sub-cultural frames of reference differ. The educational processes of nonliterate societies by no means make for perfect adjustment, or reflect complete cultural homogeneity. Such terms are always relative, and since culture is never static, continuous changes imply everywhere some measure of departure from the utter homogeneity that has mistakenly been held to characterize nonliterate societies. There are sources of conflict and maladjustment other than imbalance in the educational system of a people, and many instances of these are reported in the ethnographic literature. Nonetheless, where a single agency—the family, however constituted—has for all practical purposes the sole responsibility for training a child, there is little opportunity to introduce the contradictions that can arise where multiple channels exist.

The varied techniques of teaching and disciplining the young found in nonliterate societies make a point that controverts two stereotypes about the relation between parents and children in "primitive society." One is that "primitive man" is brutal toward

[20] Li An-che, 1937, p. 70.

children, regarding them as wealth and exploiting them to his advantage; the other is that he permits them to grow up without correction, giving in to their every whim, until they metamorphose as full-fledged, responsible adult members of their group. Either view can be documented by examples from the literature, but not from the studies of those who in their field-work have been trained to record variation in custom even to the point of setting down practices that seem quite at odds. Thus, among the Chiricahua Apache, whose educational system has been studied in detail by Opler,[21] a pattern of using the gentlest methods of correction and the heartiest encouragement does not preclude the use of corporal punishment when this is held to be necessary.

A wide range of educational procedures and methods of correction has been reported from every culture where careful studies of the training of children have been made. The South African Kgatla, for example, employ "exhortation and reprimand, as well as . . . chastisement, as the occasion arises. Mistakes are corrected, ignorance is dispelled, good behavior is applauded, and insolence or disobedience are immediately followed by punishment." This is generally a scolding or whipping, but sometimes a beating is administered. "The Kgatla say that thrashing makes a child wise, and helps it to remember what it has been taught." But they also say that "a growing child is like a little dog," and even though it may annoy grown-ups, it must be taught proper conduct with patience and forbearance.[22]

Whiting gives numerous instances to show that the Kwoma, a New Guinea people of the Sepik River area, use all the customary teaching techniques. They motivate by punishing, scolding, threatening, warning, and inciting; they guide by leading, instructing, and demonstrating; they reward by giving gifts, helping, and praising. A blow of a stick or the use of a word having associations of disgust or danger will punish or scold. Showing a younger boy how to light a fire in a strong wind is instructing. Giving presents to young boys who participate in cooperative labor is training by reward for meritorious behavior.[23]

We see, then, how, in the nonliterate world, the education of the young is accomplished by the use of no single device. Rather, each society calls on the resources of persuasion and compulsion to develop its young into the kind of individual it holds desirable. Children nowhere "just grow," like Topsy. The elders watch,

[21] M. E. Opler, 1941, pp. 27–34.
[22] I. Schapera, 1940, p. 253.
[23] J. W. M. Whiting, 1941, pp. 180 ff.

guide, supervise, correct. That all of them can perform this function is one of the reasons why, in nonliterate societies, education is so integral a part of day-to-day life that for many years students overlooked its existence as a ubiquitous aspect of culture.

6

Some aspects of education are universal. Every people conditions the infant to control his bodily functions. All encourage linguistic communication, and see to it that the semantic values of the words in a language are properly used and understood. All instruct the young in how to interpret the behavior of their fellows, and how to act in specific situations and toward persons to whom they stand in particular kinds of relations. There is none that does not teach ways of getting a living, and inculcate a sense of the economic values accepted by the group. Moral codes are everywhere emphasized, and those methods whereby an individual not only gets on with his fellows, but comes to be esteemed by them. Etiquette, in the widest sense of the term, is given continuous attention. As an extension of this, the meaning of the rituals of all kinds, and knowledge of how to conduct such of them as will fall to a given individual are taught, as are the causes and cures of sickness, and the facts of birth and death.

Certain widespread emphases in the education of the young in a great many nonliterate cultures are touched on with relative lightness by literate peoples, particularly by those societies in the Euroamerican cultural stream. Two of these can be considered here. One is the importance of learning proper attitudes and behavior-patterns toward relatives; the other has to do with education for accepted sexual behavior.

When we read of the complex order of kinship terminology in most nonliterate cultures, we know that the intricate system reflects certain sanctioned forms of polite conduct, certain emotionally toned affects, certain duties and obligations between individuals that have to be learned. Radcliffe-Brown writes:

> At every moment of the life of a member of an Australian tribe, his dealings with other individuals are regulated by the relationship in which he stands to them. His relatives, near and distant, are classified into certain large groups, and this classification is carried out by means of the terminology, and could apparently not be achieved in any other way. Thus in any part of the continent when a stranger comes to a camp the first thing to be done, before he can be admitted within the camp, is to determine his relationship to every man and woman in it, i.e., to determine

what is the proper term of relationship for him to apply to each of them. As soon as he knows his relation to a given individual he knows how to behave towards him, what his duties are and what his rights.[24]

These things obviously are not just absorbed. An Australian aborigine has to be taught the complicated kinship structure of his people, without which he would literally be unable to function as a member of his society. No sharper contrast could be cited to the way in which a man or woman in Euroamerican society may, without affecting his life, take only the closest relatives into account.

The Chaga child, in East Africa, must first of all learn the difference between the use of his parents' personal names and the terms of address he must use in speaking to them. This is much the same as the convention of our society, where the child is taught that though his mother addresses his father as "John," he must call him "Father" or "Daddy" or by some other appellation. The Chaga child, as he grows, must learn that terms are used in the singular for reference, and in the plural when addressing those of the parental and grandparental generation to whom reverence must be shown. We are told:

> From birth the child is taught the proper terms for addressing his relatives. He is told about paternal and maternal grandparents, uncles, and aunts before he understands one word of his language. It is the mother and nurse who teach the child to use the terms in appropriate situations. . . . Father, mother, elder siblings and nurse admonish the impolite child and advise it. . . . It is not to be wondered at that children are masters of kinship etiquette when they are six years old and that at fourteen they know most of the terminological subtleties.[25]

In most nonliterate societies, as we have seen, the knowledge and practice of sex is not left to chance. Some of the mechanisms employed demonstrate deep insight, as, for instance, the practice in West Africa of requiring a newly circumcised youth to have sexual relations with a woman who has passed the menopause, "to take off the burn of the knife." By her experience she aids him in the technique of sexual performance and helps overcome any traumatic shock that may have resulted from the operation. The premarital experimentation that many nonliterate cultures sanction plays a definite role in inculcating skill and finesse in sex

[24] A. R. Radcliffe-Brown, 1931, p. 95.
[25] O. F. Raum, 1940, pp. 169-75.

behavior. There are, however, nonliterate societies where the conspiracy of silence in matters of sex is as strong as was ever the case in Europe or America in mid-Victorian times. Yet these are in the minority. Most peoples, in numbering the facts of life, do not draw the line this side of the problems of reproduction.

Training in sexual habits can be given formally or informally, or both methods may be utilized even in the same culture. Much of the formal schooling given nonliterate boys and girls in the various "initiation" rites they undergo at puberty is concerned with preparation for marriage. A mother, or more often a grandmother, may inform the nubile girl about the conduct of sexual relations and the behavior expected of her as a married woman, just as later she will attend her on the first night of her marriage, officiate at the birth of her child, and teach her how to care for it. The men of the family will instruct the boy how to behave toward his female companions. In many societies, the maternal uncle is especially charged with imparting this information to his sister's sons. The attitude toward instruction in sex is generally marked by consciousness of a serious duty on the part of the older people, rarely by lasciviousness. Lasciviousness, like obscenity, is found among all people. Both the occasions permitting their expression and the forms this may take are often institutionalized and channeled. Their universality attests the psychological release they afford, and their stimulus to sexual play. But situations where sex instruction is given differ in setting and tone from the lighter moods of the young folk as they go about the business of satisfying their sexual desires, before they eventually enter into an arrangement whereby they establish families and in turn take up the parental role.

7

Education carried on by means of schooling in the hands of specialists cannot be overlooked in considering the training of the young among nonliterate peoples, even though this is only a minor aspect of their educational systems. In the aggregate, the variety and number of these forms are greater than earlier studies have recorded. They vary from rather temporary groupings, meeting informally, as when a Plains warrior takes some boys with him to learn to hunt, to the long periods of seclusion and intensive courses of instruction of some of the African "schools."

Africa and Polynesia provide most instances of schooling, properly speaking, in nonliterate cultures. African examples vary considerably in the period of seclusion and in the rites they practice, but differ little in their objectives, since all mark the transition from the status of child to that of adult and demand the proofs of competence and endurance that set off the social life of the adult from that of the child. Among the BaVenda, the boys' schools are attended by every boy in the eighteen districts where they are located. Attendance begins when the lad is eight or nine years old, and continues until after he has attained puberty, when he completes his initiation and his age-set is recognized. The boys live at the *thondo*, as their school is called, undergoing the discipline that will make of them a military unit. Instruction is given in such techniques of warfare as ambush, night attack, and spying. Such tasks as matmaking that are assigned them must be finished on time. The rules of tribal etiquette must be carefully observed, otherwise a severe beating is inflicted. The youths also practice dancing while in school. They emerge from their training "hardened and disciplined, ready to shoulder the responsibilities as well as to share the privileges of a fighting man of the tribe."

The Venda girls' schooling, lasting only six days and nights, marks the passage of girls from childhood to adolescence, and occurs shortly after initial menstruation. Tribal rules of etiquette and obedience, dancing, and sexual behavior are the principal subjects taught. Further formal instruction, in a mixed school called *domba*, is described as "general preparation for marriage." Its intricate ceremonial, "by means of symbols and metaphors," teaches boys and girls "to understand the true significance of marriage and childbirth," and warns them "of the pitfalls and dangers that they are likely to encounter during the course of their lives." [26]

From the western part of Africa many examples of schools have been reported, of which the *poro* and *sande* schools of Liberia and Sierra Leone, the first for boys, the second for girls, may be cited. The boys' school involves protracted training; periods varying from eighteen months to eight years are mentioned for different tribes. Circumcision precedes entry into the school, which is under the general supervision of a leader whose position in the community reflects the importance of his office.

> The boys are divided into groups according to their ages and aptitudes, and receive instruction . . . in all the arts, crafts and lore of native life. . . . It is by this means that the character is molded and a youth is prepared to take his place among the generation of adults. . . . The first instruction involves a series of tests in order to determine individual differences, interests, and

[26] H. A. Stayt, 1931, pp. 101 ff.

ambitions. . . . A youth who shows special aptitude for weaving, for example, is trained to become a master of the craft; while those who show distinctive skill and interest in carving, leather-work, dancing, "medicine," folklore, etc., are developed along these specialized lines. This early training also includes work in the erection of the structures which are used while the session lasts. . . . All the laws and traditions of the tribe are taught, as well as duty to the tribal chief, tribe and elders, and the proper relations to women. Training is given in the recognition and use of various medicinal herbs, their curative powers, and various antidotes. Also, the secrets of wild animals are taught—how they live, how to recognize their spoor, and how to attack them.

Finally, "all this training is tested out in the laboratory of 'bush'-school life," as when warfare is simulated, and the boys are called on to utilize their training in planning and executing a campaign. The *sande* school, for girls, parallels in the organization of its staff and in other characteristics, the *poro* training for boys. Its curriculum is directed towards training girls in their duties as grown women—wives and mothers—and thus with different content fulfills the same educational ends.[27]

Formal courses of higher learning have also been reported from many parts of Polynesia, such as the Hawaiian college of heraldry. In general, we are told, "the hallmark of any well-born and well-trained chief was his ability to give orations with an abundance of religious and historical allusions, metaphors, similes, and proverbs"—which obviously required special training; and such training was also required if a person was to qualify as a member of the companies of dancers, or as an entertainer, of the kind found in Hawaii. For the most part, those who received training "in composition, narration and chanting were usually of noble birth . . ." though they "did not form a special, intellectual class except in Mangareva, Marquesas and Easter Island." On the other hand, Polynesians of all ranks and both sexes might cultivate the art of oral literature, and some became specialists in reciting the long and complicated narratives about "a single favorite character." Furthermore, "daily life in Polynesia . . . required knowledge of many incantations, chants, traditions, proverbs, and fables. Every craft and occupation had its magical formulae, religious history, myths, and traditions. Besides their practical value in gaining the assistance of the gods, these gave dignity, prestige, and background to the worker and those who used the results of his work."[28] These motivations would seem

[27] M. H. Watkins, 1943, pp. 670–1, 673–4.
[28] K. Luomala, 1946, pp. 772–5.

largely to explain why, here, the tradition of specialized training that marked the area developed and maintained itself as an important part of the culture.

One further trait of education among nonliterate peoples must be mentioned. It has been said that in such societies education continues until adolescence, or shortly after, but that the process is somewhat longer among literate peoples. Concerning the "everyday business of life" this is true. Yet when we touch the supernatural we come to a phase of the transmission of knowledge that is substantially confined to mature adults. The importance of religion in the daily life of nonliterate peoples will become fully apparent when we discuss this aspect of culture. The control of the powers of the universe is conceived as essential to the successful solution of most of their problems. But children, whose physical power is slight, are rarely conceded any greater amount of spiritual power. Therefore, not until they become older are they taught the theological concepts and the ritual practices of their tribe. For the most complete account of any religion we go to the elders, who, even though they are not specialists, are the ones versed in the supernatural sanctions of their society, and the accepted means of propitiation and expiation.

The education of nonliterate peoples, then, must not be thought as reaching its completion with the assumption of adult status. Not even formal teaching ends then. But in the sense of education as *the process whereby the knowledge of a people is passed from one generation to the next*, a man or woman is fitted to carry on in his culture at an earlier age, and without the prolonged institutionalized training that exists where writing and the machine technology condition modes of living. In affairs of the spirit, however, this is but a beginning point. Those charged with the direction of affairs continue to be taught by their elders as long as there are those older than themselves to teach them.

Chapter **Eleven**

Political Systems: the Ordering of Human Relations

There was a time when scholars held that early man lived in a kind of beneficent anarchy, in which each person was granted his rights by his fellows, and there was no governing or being governed. Various early writers looked back to this Golden Age, but the point of view that man was originally a "child of nature" is best known to us in the writings of Rousseau and Locke and Hobbes. These men developed the concept of the "social contract," which put an end to the "state of nature" in which earliest man is supposed to have lived.

Lewis H. Morgan and Sir Henry Maine were among the first to attempt the comparative study of political institutions on the basis of facts established through systematic investigation of ways of life outside their own culture. Morgan worked primarily with materials from nonliterate societies, Maine with historical data from Ireland and India and early England and with materials garnered from his profound knowledge of the classical writers of Greece and Rome. Their findings were in essential agreement. Both held that kinship was the bond that brought earliest men together, and that only the more advanced aggregates formed states, properly speaking, which were based on territory. Maine wrote:

> From the moment when a tribal community settles down finally upon a definite space of land, the Land begins to be the basis of society in place of the Kinship. . . . For all groups of men larger than the Family, the Land on which they live tends to become the bond of union between them, at the expense of Kinship, ever more and more vaguely conceived.

He puts his point pithily, in these words: "England was once the country which Englishmen inhabited. Englishmen are now the people who inhabit England."[1]

This point of view dominated political theory for many years. Students of politics, particularly in England and on the continent of Europe, tended to ignore the fresh materials made available to them through the development of scientific ethnography. Only by implication was any concern shown for the range of variation of political phenomena in human societies.[2] In addition, this approach is marred by two methodological faults. As has been stressed, the origins of intangibles such as political institutions can only be inferred. Furthermore, attempts to reconstruct the prehistory of political development, in which living "primitive" man is equated with his prehistoric forerunners, violate a basic principle of anthropological method, which holds that present-day nonliterate peoples are not our "contemporary ancestors."

Very few, if any, students of politics have made comparative studies of political institutions outside the literate world. Theories of government are therefore framed in terms of the political forms of the historic societies of Europe and America, with occasional reference to those of Asia. As a result, anthropologists studying political institutions in nonliterate cultures have had to collect and analyze their data on the basis of rough-and-ready judgments of what are to be classed as political phenomena. Instruments of political control were described as part of the total range of social institutions, without preconception about whether the unifying principle of a given system was kinship, common interest, age, language, or territory.

The scope of political mechanisms, and hence the function of governments, has been indicated in the following terms:

[1] Sir H. S. Maine, 1888, pp. 72–4.
[2] Cf. E. M. Sait, 1938, pp. 99–136.

In studying political organization, we have to deal with the maintenance or establishment of social order, within a territorial framework, by the organized exercise of coercive authority, through the use, or the possibility of use, of physical force. In well-organized states, the police and the army are the instruments by which coercion is exercised. Within the state, the social order, whatever it may be, is maintained by the punishment of those who offend against the laws and by the armed suppression of revolt. Externally the state stands ready to use armed force against other states, either to maintain the existing order or to create a new one. In dealing with political systems, therefore, we are dealing with law, on the one hand, and with war, on the other.[3]

From a cross-cultural point of view, any institutions by which the affairs of a society are directed and the conduct of its members is regulated must be regarded as governmental institutions, however informal they may seem. Llewellyn and Hoebel preface their analysis of Cheyenne law with this statement by High Forehead, one of their informants, which might well serve as a definition of police function anywhere: "The Indian on the prairie, before there was the White Man to put him in the guardhouse, had to have something to keep him from doing wrong." [4] Nadel, discussing the organization of the small Nuba tribe inhabiting the Kadero hills of Kordofan, in northeastern Africa, says:

> Primitive political organization is essentially an organization for war and peace—war without, and peace within. Attacks on human life outside the political unit are conceived of as legitimate warfare and entail no sanction—save the diffuse, voluntary sanction of the revenge which chances of war might offer. Within the political unit, such attacks are branded as crime: the society imposes penalties upon the perpetrator, or lays down compulsory acts of retaliation (in the form of blood feud) or expiatory rites, which will restore the peace that had been broken.[5]

Radcliffe-Brown's designation of the political organization of society as "that aspect of the total organization which is concerned with the control and regulation of the use of physical force," [6] despite the narrowness with which it is drawn, thus does give a frame of reference within which many different forms of this aspect of society may be treated.

Certain other questions of terminology which inevitably arise

[3] A. R. Radcliffe-Brown, 1940, p. xiv.
[4] K. N. Llewellyn and E. A. Hoebel, 1941, p. 2.
[5] S. F. Nadel, 1942b, p. 59.
[6] *Op. cit.*, p. xxiii.

in the study of government will of necessity require careful consideration. A long tradition in the study of law and politics makes definition "of the essence." Perhaps, *by definition*, it can be said that groups with rudimentary political organization, who manage their lives in terms of common consent, "lack government." Even with the sharpest definition, however, one would be hard put to it to draw the line between intermediate cases. There would be agreement, in all probability, that the Papuan Keraki are in these terms without government, despite the fact that each group does have a local headman, who, though "he does not issue orders to be obeyed, . . . is none the less definitely the leader of the group." [7] But what of the South American Chaco tribes considered by Métraux? These people have chiefs of considerable power, responsible for the welfare of the community, with "vague judiciary powers" that may force a thief to return stolen goods. In external affairs, these chiefs represent their people in dealings with groups outside the tribe. Yet they dare not give orders that are contrary to the will of the people, and a chief will readily lose his followers if his regime is not successful. [8] The classification of the political organization of these people as "government," or "pre-government," or as "rule by custom"—to use various terms that have been employed—would require far sharper delimitation of terms than has yet been achieved.

When is the political structure of a people to be designated as a state? Is the state something different from a tribe? If so, then when, we might ask, does the tribe become a nation? One possible answer to such questions has been given by Fortes and Evans-Pritchard in their study of African native political systems, some of which have "centralized authority, administrative machinery, and judicial institutions, . . . and in which cleavages of wealth, privilege, and status correspond to the distribution of power and authority," while others do not. "Those who consider that a state should be defined by the presence of governmental institutions will regard the first group as primitive states and the second group as stateless societies." [9] Yet even these students speak of the first group as having governments, and the second as lacking them, thus once more throwing the question open to debate!

2

Of the areas inhabited by nonliterate peoples, Africa exhibits the greatest incidence of complex governmental structures. Not

[7] F. E. Williams, 1936, p. 113.
[8] A. Métraux, 1946a, p. 303.
[9] M. Fortes and E. E. Evans-Pritchard, 1940, p. 5.

even the kingdoms of Peru and Mexico could mobilize resources and concentrate power more effectively than could some of these African monarchies, which are more to be compared with Europe of the Middle Ages than referred to the common conception of the "primitive" state, though it must be recognized that not all the political structures of Africa were so complex.

It is interesting to speculate what the effect would have been on the development of political philosophy if, during the late seventeenth and early eighteenth centuries, the writings on Africa had received the attention that was given the accounts of travelers in North America, the West Indies, and the South Seas. Why the works of Dapper and Barbot and Bosman and others were not used is a problem for the historian of the intellectual currents of the period. Their works might have prevented writers from reaching the conclusion that "not merely . . . a pre-social state had once existed, but that some barbarous peoples had not yet emerged from it," [10] as Myres summarizes the misconceptions of the period that arose out of preoccupation with the "noble savage" as personified in the Iroquois, the Huron, the Carib, the Pacific Islander.

The longest known of these African kingdoms, has also received the most careful analysis by means of modern field study. The Gold Coast was a center of the slave trade, and the traders wrote a number of descriptions of the Ashanti and Fanti nations with whom they trafficked for their human goods, and whose customs it was to their advantage to know. That these kingdoms, like those of Dahomey, the Yoruba, and Benin to the east, had stability and permanence is apparent from a historic record of more than three hundred years. So vital are the political mechanisms of these kingdoms that even their extinction as autonomously functioning institutions has not been able to eradicate certain of their aspects. The clarity with which they can be detailed by young persons who have never known anything but foreign control attests this vitality.

Rattray lays down three basic principles of Ashanti government: that the Ashanti were governed "patriarchally rather than aristocratically," that a man named to any office "succeeded to obligations rather than to rights," and that every "lesser loyalty" was fostered as a means to achieving a greater.[11] The "little democracy" of the household was the core of the broader controls exercised by the people. Grouped into larger entities, each social

[10] Sir J. L. Myres, 1916, p. 51.
[11] R. S. Rattray, 1929, pp. 401-3.

unit was represented by its head in the councils of the group immediately superior to it. Every "concentric circle of loyalty" had its own tradition, its own genealogical record, its own officers.

Emphasis on local authority was thus the rule. Only in times of danger, when resources had to be mobilized efficiently and unity of action had to be based on quick decisions, did the seeming autocracy of the political hierarchy function as such. Otherwise, a chief who acted without the full consent of the members of his council, which in turn only gave an opinion after consultation with their subordinates, and so on down the line to the individual family member, was liable to be deposed. This does not mean that the Ashanti state was utopian. Rulers had power and knew how to exercise it to maintain their preferred economic and social status. Yet this power always had to be exercised within the limits of the conventions set for it, and with an eye to the obligations it entailed toward those of lesser place in the hierarchy. In the final analysis, the structure was such that every Ashanti male sensed and exercised his right to participation in government.

In the Ashanti political structure as it existed at the time of its fall, each of the five territorial divisions was headed by a Paramount Chief. He was guided in the administration of his stool—the Ashanti synonym for the word "throne"—by a group of Elders analogous to the senior members of a kinship unit who act as advisers to its head. The honorific titles borne by these men reflected their position in the military organization headed by their Paramount Chief, since each territorial unit had its own army, in which every adult male had his place. Under the Paramount Chief were the chiefs of divisional units and subunits, each with his own court, attendants, and war organization, which stood in the same relation to the Paramount Chief as he stood in relation to the king, the *Asantehene*. The officeholders in a territorial division may be listed as follows:

1. The Chief (*Ohene* or *Omanhene*), like all other officers, selected by the elders from possible candidates in the matrilineal line. He had a certain sacred quality that lasted, however, only as long as he held office, since on destoolment he again became an ordinary individual, liable for his misdeeds.

2. The Queen Mother, a powerful personage, described tellingly by Rattray as " 'the whisper' behind the Stool." She was consulted by the Chief on all important occasions, and her voice carried weight far beyond the modesty of her outward bearing.

3. The *Ko'ntire* and *Akwamu* Chiefs, the deputy commander

of the army and his second. They figured importantly in the native tribunals, and took a prominent place in the enstoolment of the Chief.

4. The Clan Chief, who looked after the interests of members of the kinship group to which the Chief belonged. He took from the Chief the necessity of passing on cases involving those who were of the royal sib, and thus freed his superior from charges of nepotism.

5. The Military Officials, which included the leaders of the right and left wing of the army. The leader of the advance-guard, the commander of the main body, the head of the Chief's personal body-guard, and the commander of the rear-guard were next in rank.

6. The *Gyase Hene*, chief of those who made up the "palace" organization, the heads of particular departments of the Chief's household. These are named to show how large and complex a ceremonial organization he headed:

Spokesmen	Hammock-carriers
Stool-carriers	Floor-polishers
Drummers and horn- blowers	Treasurers and sub- treasurers
Umbrella carriers	Eunuchs
Caretakers of the Royal Mausoleum	Heralds
Bathroom attendants	Sword-bearers
Chief's "soul-washers"	Gun-bearers
Elephant-tail switchers	Shield-bearers
Fan-bearers	Minstrels
Cooks	Executioners [12]

The functions of officials named *Birempon* and *Adamfo* must be understood to grasp the lines of authority along which the kingdom of the Ashanti was administered, and on which the hierarchy of local divisions still rests. The *Birempon* is an official who is Chief of a smaller unit in respect to his immediate superior. These men are not members of their superior's Council, but have their own. The *Adamfo* is the patron of a given *Birempon* at court, since etiquette demands that an inferior present himself to his superior only with due ceremony, and through the intercession of an intermediary. The *Adamfo* is therefore that member of a Chief's Council who sponsors a given lesser chief, a *Birempon*, in his dealings with the superior.[13]

Rattray's diagram,[14] which presents the organization of a

[12] *Ibid.*, pp. 81–91.
[13] *Ibid.*, pp. 93 ff.
[14] *Ibid.*, p. 97.

territorial division, and permits the lines of authority and the relations of groups composing it to be traced, will be useful.

The outer circle, A, represents a Territorial Division under a Head-Chief . . . and a Queen Mother, who are represented by the centre of this circle. Inside the circle A, and concentric with it is another lesser circle, B, with figures 1, 2, 3, and 4 marked on

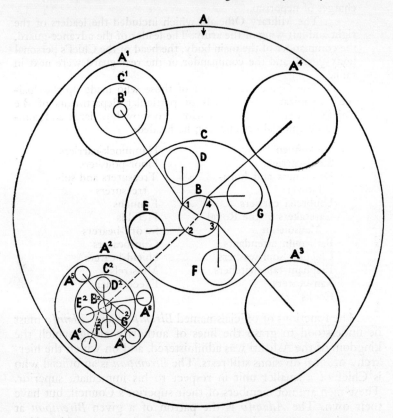

Fig. 24 *Ashanti political organization.* (*After Rattray, 1929.*)

its circumference. These are supposed to stand for four of the Head-Chief's Elders, who [with others] surround him and form the royal *entourage*. Just outside circle B, but not concentric with it, lie four smaller circles, D, E, F, and G. These circles represent smaller outlying villages which owe direct allegiance to the Head-Chief. Circle C surrounds all, and within it lies the hub, as it were, of the Territorial Division. Outside this circle C, but eccentric from it, lie four slightly smaller circles, marked A^1, A^2, A^3, and A^4, which represent four subdivisions of four *Birempon*, each of whom owes allegiance to the Head-Chief. Within these lesser circles A^1 to A^4 lies an organization exactly similar, if on a somewhat smaller scale, to that which is embraced in the great circle, A. Each has its own local head-chief, councillors, villages under these councillors, and finally there are towns outside the circles C^1, C^2, &c., which are represented by the circles A^5 to A^8 and are under Chiefs of lesser importance than the *Birempon;* these are subject to him directly, and thus subject indirectly to the Head-Chief. With respect to the *Birempon* of circle A^2, the lesser Chiefs of A^5 to A^8 are in the nature of miniature *Birempon*.

All lines lead eventually to the Head-Chief, the center of circle A. The chain of communication that brings a lesser official to the Head-Chief is traced by the dotted line in the diagram.

It commences from the centre of the circle A^6 and represents a Chief of a town directly under the *Birempon* of Division A^2. Commencing from the centre of A^6, the line goes directly to a point on the circumference of the circle B^2, which is its first point of contact. This point represents one of the Elders of the Chief of the Division represented by the circle A^2 . . . the *Adamfo* of the Chief who rules over A^6. Thence the line passes straight to the centre of the circle A^2, i.e. to the *Birempon* of the Head-Chief. From here it leads to a point marked '2' on the circumference of circle B. This point stands for one of the Elders of the Head-Chief, who is the *Adamfo* of the *Birempon* of circle A^2. Thence the line connects directly with the centre of circle A, i.e., with the Head-Chief of the whole Territorial Division.

A further point is revealing. "It should be observed that the only line of communication between the centre of a circle and that of any other circle lies by the way of the centre of the circle A. Remove this central point of common contact, and all that remains is a series of greater or smaller disconnected circles." This principle held for the entire kingdom, which was but a more complicated extension of the diagram given for a division. Any attempt to pass over any of the contact points where an official of one jurisdiction, for instance, had a dispute with another, "would be deeply resented by all the persons concerned, and systematic attempts to ignore any of the intermediaries would lead to such dissatisfaction as eventually to throw out of gear the smooth working of the Administrative machine." This is why, as Rattray puts it, "To understand this diagram . . . is . . . to possess the key to an understanding of the decentralized Constitution of Ashanti." [15]

The Ashanti kingdom had most of the appurtenances of a modern state—a well-defined system of collecting revenue, a system of finance, courts to administer the laws of the realm and adjudicate disputes, and an army. Revenues were derived from a complicated system of death duties, from certain kinds of temporary trade monopolies that gave the rulers an advantage in the disposal of seasonal goods, taxes (or rather, toll charges) on imports, court fines, and fees, and a percentage of all gold mined. Special levies might also be laid to cover the expenses of a chief's funeral, a proportion of the spoils of war, a war tax, treasure-trove, fees assessed on the enstoolment of a chief, and levies of foodstuffs, game, and fish. Revenues were distributed among officials in accordance with an established series of proportions, while the remainder was employed for buying arms and powder, paying for regalia, and entertaining. This last constituted a heavy charge on the income of any official, since all who came to a chief's palace must be provided with food and drink. This meant that every chief, in effect, had to hold continuous open house for the many who took advantage of his hospitality. A record of income and expenditures was kept by this nonliterate people through the use of cowry-shells, aided by the prodigious memories of those charged with taking care of the exchequer.

Something of the organization of the army has been indicated in naming certain of the chiefs attached to a stool. It was undoubtedly due to the care given the army that the Ashanti owed their success in warfare, a success that made them among the best-known and most-feared peoples of all West Africa. Court cases were heard by a chief and his elders, and appeal could be made through the chain of higher authority. Offenses brought before these tribunals were murder, suicide (that is, the dead was tried for offenses it was believed he must have committed), certain sexual offenses, such as incest, certain kinds of abuse, insult, or stealing, the invoking of a curse on a chief, treason and cowardice, the practice of evil magic, and the violation of tribal taboos or of an oath. Cases involving land tenure and alienation—a complicated matter—were also brought before the courts for judgment, as well as cases involving pawning, loaning, and the recovery of debts. Punishment was severe. Execution, mutilation, and flogging were some of the penalties, while in earlier times a culprit could

[15] *Ibid.*, pp. 96–101.

be sold into slavery. Court procedures included the taking of testimony and submission to the ordeal.

What did this apparatus of government mean to the individual Ashanti? It is apparent that he could go about his affairs with the knowledge that, if he followed the rules of procedure set down by custom, he would not be molested. He was assured, furthermore, that the demands of the supernatural powers would be cared for, and he would not be liable to indiscriminate manifestations of their ill will. If he were unjustly charged with crime, or if a dispute with one of his fellows arose, he could have recourse to the orderly processes of law. His family was protected against foreign enemies; as an Ashanti, he had a sense of participation in the affairs of his tribe that, though exercised remotely, gave him some say in the determination of his fate. It must be emphasized again that this state was no nearer perfection than any other political system that has been devised by human beings. The ordinary man was exploited, sometimes brutally, by his superiors. Courts on occasion failed to function, and the Elders were not always scrupulous in rendering justice. To overlook these defects would be to erect a fiction of the kind that led to the concept of the carefree life of the untrammeled savage. Yet within its human limits, the Ashanti state—it would be difficult not to accord it that term—functioned well, and performed efficiently its task of regulating the behavior and assuring the peace of its many citizens.

3

The Ashanti represent an extreme degree of complexity in governmental institutions among nonliterate societies. Variation moves from cultures such as this to the point where, in small societies with simple technologies, political structures exist only by definition, and law and custom are almost impossible to differentiate.

Among the Bushmen, some of the larger bands have a chief, but in most of them the "common affairs," such as migration and hunting, are under the direction of men whose skill alone earns them the respect and obedience of their fellows. Where chiefs are found, they seem only to direct the group as it moves from one locality to another, to see to the burning over of the hunting territory, and to lead in combat. This "official" is thus a leader, with authority only as he demonstrates his ability to use it. He does not judge his fellows and does not even control the grown members of his own family. There is no code of law except the customary habits and beliefs of the group. Adultery, theft, and homicide are punished by blood vengeance; as for other offenses, the supernatural powers whose taboos have been broken can be expected to exact their own punishment. Each band is a unit conscious of its own identity, with a hunting territory whose boundaries are recognized and within which it confines its activities. The relations between them that result from marriage, trade, and common need suggest that their contacts do not go entirely unregulated. Feuding can occur between bands when an individual of one band commits an offense against a member of another.[16]

Is this government? Can we speak of such a small, loosely organized group as a "state"? Is their adherence to customary sanction to be termed "law"? Can their feuds be called "warfare"? These questions become more pointed when we compare these rudimentary forms of political mechanism with the robust institutions of the Ashanti. And such questions, together with those that have been raised in earlier pages, become more puzzling as we turn to still another African people, the Nuer. They number some two hundred thousand individuals, divided into several tribes. According to Evans-Pritchard, they live in an "ordered anarchy" that makes of their political system an "acephalous kinship state" lacking legal institutions or developed leadership.[17]

Tribes are split into segments, segments into lineages, and identification of an individual with any component of his tribe depends on the situation of the moment, particularly whether a group to which he potentially belongs happens to be in opposition to another corresponding one. We have seen how Nuer segmentation operates in its social structures; in the political aspect of tribal life it gives rise to "the principle of contradiction in political structure." Again, a diagram will aid in clarifying the point.

> When Z^1 fights Z^2, no other section is involved. When Z^1 fights Y^1, Z^1 and Z^2 unite as Y^2. When Y^1 fights X^1, Y^1 and Y^2 unite, and so do X^1 and X^2. When X^1 fights A, X^1, X^2, Y^1, and Y^2 all unite as B. When A raids the Dinka A and B may unite.

In the political structure of the tribe,

> a member of Z^2 tertiary section of tribe B sees himself as a member of Z^2 in relation to Z^1. . . . But he regards himself as a member of Y^2 and not of Z^2 in relation to Y^1 and is so regarded

[16] I. Schapera, 1930, pp. 149–59.
[17] E. E. Evans-Pritchard, 1940, p. 181.

by members of Y^1. Likewise he regards himself as a member of Y and not of Y^2 in relation to X, and as a member of the tribe B, and not of its primary section Y, in relation to tribe A. . . . Political values are relative and . . . the political system is an equilibrium between opposed tendencies toward fission and fusion, between the tendency of all groups to segment, and the tendency of all groups to combine with segments of the same order.[18]

This is a fighting people, made up of arrant individualists. No authority exists to whom a man can appeal when he has suffered a wrong, so a duel is the only way out, and this may develop into a feud. But when one man has slain another, he can seek sanctuary with a personage known as a leopard-skin chief until negotiations can be completed looking toward compounding the offense. The larger the group involved, the more difficult his task. Yet he is usually successful, if the groups are not too large. Other disputes involving damage to property, adultery, and loss of limb, are

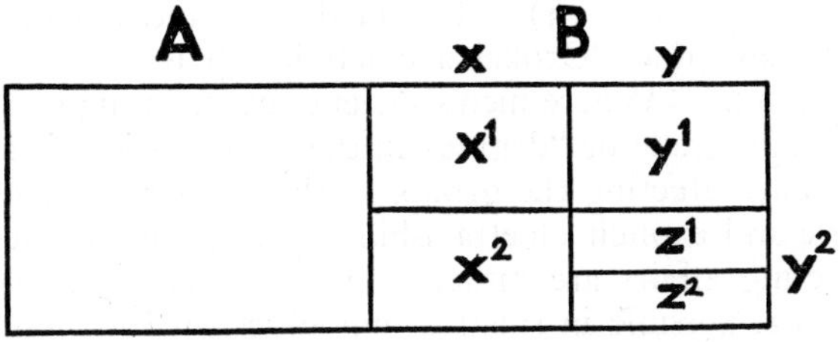

Fig. 25 *Nuer political segmentation. (After Evans-Pritchard, 1940.)*

settled by compensations, the amounts of which are fixed by common usage. Except for the good offices of the leopard-skin chief as mediator, however, there is no legal source such as a court, to which a man can look for redress. Nuer law, then, exists as "a moral obligation to settle disputes by conventional methods, and not in the sense of legal procedure or of legal institutions."

We turn once again to our questions. On the African continent alone, a vast number of tribal regulatory systems run the scale between explicit and tightly knit integration to little more than sanctions enforced by the personality of a leader and the accepted traditions of the people. Despite their differences, all these systems are means whereby a people, whose affiliation transcends kinship groupings, and which identifies itself with an area it inhabits or dominates, is enabled to regulate the conduct of its mem-

[18] *Ibid.*, pp. 143-4, 147.

bers and direct its affairs when it must treat with another autonomous group. More than this, however, we cannot say and still comprehend the diversity of form found in the functioning units that achieve these ends which we term political.

4

This same principle of flexibility in definition must guide the study of political phenomena as we move from the African continent to consider their forms among nonliterate peoples elsewhere. In Polynesia the political structures can be said to be almost theocratic in their base, the descent of the chiefs from the gods being an outstanding sanction of their position. They emphasize rank more than power, and the taboos that go with rank, plus the display that validates position, are dominant factors in establishing and maintaining them. In Melanesia and New Guinea political institutions are weak. Williams tells us that in Papua the tribe is defined by "(1) a common territory, (2) certain idiosyncrasies of custom, (3) a distinct dialect, and (4) its common enmities," and that "Orokaiva chieftainship is of the most elementary kind." [19] Where men's societies exist, an important member of a high grade or "degree" in the men's society is looked to for decisions affecting the group. In the islands of eastern Melanesia true and explicit chieftainship appears, but the mechanisms for directing affairs are rather simple, and ruling is a personal matter, as is possible in small communities. In Indonesia, on the other hand, population mass necessitates more complicated controls.

The democratic nature of government in aboriginal North and South America has long been recognized. The exceptions are notable, however. Even outside the Inca Empire of Peru, Ecuador, and Colombia, and the Maya, Toltec, and Aztec kingdoms of Mexico, non-democratic peoples existed, having well-institutionalized governing structures administered by persons who had the right to govern because of inherited status. The stratification of Northwest Coast society has long been an anthropological byword, though "the strictly political powers of a chief were disproportionately small when compared with his social eminence." [20] The Natchez of the Southeast had a government furthest removed from the prevalent democratic patterns of North American Indian tribes. Here the equalitarian principle seems to have disappeared completely. An absolute sovereign, held sacred

[19] F. E. Williams, 1930, pp. 156, 325.
[20] R. H. Lowie, 1920, p. 383.

by the subjects over whom he exercised absolute power of life and death, administered the controls that enabled him to command blind obedience.

The League of the Iroquois, the federation known as "The Five Nations," represented a governmental form more common in eastern North America. The five tribes that formed the league were the Mohawk, Oneida, Onondaga, Cayuga, and Seneca. Each was autonomous in local affairs, but in matters involving relations between tribes, or with groups outside the federation, a Council of fifty representatives acted for all. Due to pre-confederacy conditions, the tribes were not represented equally on this body, the number of representatives ranging from eight to fourteen. Since unanimous decisions were required, the difference did not involve any surrender of tribal rights. The council was highly responsive to public opinion, since anyone could argue before it concerning any matter it was considering. It was charged, in the main, with keeping the peace, making treaties, and deciding all disputes between tribes, with the warpath as a final resort. It must be noted, however, that each tribe had its own internal organization, with a council composed of its League delegates plus appointed war chiefs. The sib-groups that composed each tribe were represented in the tribal council, and the fact that sibs cut across tribal lines gave firmness to the confederation by providing a weft of kin affiliation to bind together the separate tribal political strands that made up the political warp.

Particular interest attaches to this confederation because of the role of the women in it. So important were the "matriarchs," as they have been called, that it has often been cited as an instance of female government. This, however, is something of a distortion of the facts; the women were more in the nature of the power behind the throne than the active administering agencies. Thus the members of the tribal councils were men, but they were named by the matriarchs of their families and could be removed for cause by them. Women also appointed the sib-chiefs who became the tribal representatives in the League. But the actual decisions were reached and effected by these men.

Generally, government in the Americas was informal. Ridicule by cross-cousins, for example, was an effective mechanism in regulating conduct in the Plains, where, during communal buffalo hunts or tribal gatherings, war societies or other organizations that fulfilled police functions were more formal instruments for imposing order. These amorphous institutions could take on form and stability, as among the Cheyenne, with its Council of

Forty-Four and its military societies. This Council was "a self-perpetuating body of tribal trustees," and the term of office was ten years, when a rite of "renewing" the chiefs took place. Five of the group were head chiefs, whose functions were religious as well as political. They were responsive to public opinion, and were expected to be exemplary in conduct and models for other members of the tribe. The officers of the military societies were the war chiefs, who held their offices nominally for life. In practice, however, they turned their posts over to younger men as they advanced in age. Their authority could be coercive in times of emergency, and they were known to impose penalties, such as whipping, on erring followers. Yet their power was held in check by the force of opinion.

In considering the total range of political structures, another problem of terminology confronts us. Plains Indian institutions were democratic, runs the formula. And, as labels go, it is not a bad designation. In economic and social, no less than in political aspects of life, class stratification was at a minimum, and opportunity to enjoy the rewards the culture held important was limited only by ability. But when the African monarchies are labeled autocratic, as they often are, we must pause. We have seen how, beneath the seeming power of the Ashanti king lay the broad base of considered popular consent to his decrees. Moreover, in African societies with rudimentary political institutions, such as the Bushmen and Nuer, the same absence of class stratification and special privilege is found that distinguish American Indian cultures.

The designation "socialistic," often applied to the Inca Empire, must be given particular scrutiny. This great organization, headed by its absolute ruler, saw to it that every man, woman, and child was cared for, and that each labored according to the capacities with which his age, strength and training endowed him. But when we investigate this system more closely, we find it marked by features that no student of political theory would term "socialistic." Class lines were strictly drawn, neither economic nor political democracy existed. Punishment for refusal to obey orders was severe. It would be more accurate to term this government "authoritarian." In it man lived for the State, which controlled his every move by means that were striking counterparts of twentieth-century dictatorships, complete with secret police and youth movements. Communication never moved across the levels of the governing hierarchy, but reports passed up the line of control to the central authority, and orders were handed down. Consultation among equals was unknown; there were, in this sense, no equals, but only those who stood at identical levels on steps of different stairways.

The lesson from such facts is again one of caution in applying a term that describes a particular kind of phenomenon or system of ideas and institutions, to something analogous to it. For though the need for concepts and the importance of classifying data so as to compare, analyze, and thus comprehend their nature and functioning is real, it cannot be too often emphasized that to apply terms cross-culturally, without due regard for cultural meanings beyond outer form, is scientifically hazardous.

4

Political systems order the relations between groups by means of diplomacy and warfare. They control conduct within the group by the exercise of law. We may briefly consider these important phases of the political concerns of nonliterate folk before we turn to other aspects of culture.

Diplomacy is the peaceful resolution of disputes between autonomous groups. That nonliterate peoples, in their dealings with each other, had and still have techniques of settling differences is known. Numelin has compiled data from the literature which show how various peoples went about accomplishing these ends. We read of ambassadors being sent to other tribes by such aggregates as the League of the Iroquois or certain African kingdoms. Such matters as the immunity enjoyed by envoys, the ceremonial with which a case was debated, and the method of arriving at compromises have been but little investigated. The materials, though scattered and sparse, indicate, however, that many of the mechanisms of modern international negotiation were operative among autonomous nonliterate peoples.[21]

War was waged on a level of simplicity that, according to Turney-High, scarcely permits it to be called by that name. Most students tell, in a general way, how fighting was carried on, but weapons have been described much more meticulously than the uses to which they have been put in combat. Perhaps, as Turney-High says, this is "a civilian failing," the counterpart of the ethnographer's earlier tendency to describe technological culture but give little attention to the economic processes that governed the production and distribution of goods. Turney-High's criteria for the conditions that divide war from "sub-military combat" can be given to differentiate these two levels of operations. War,

[21] R. Numelin, 1950, *passim.*

he says, is marked by tactical operations; by definite command and control; by the ability to conduct a campaign for the reduction of enemy resistance if a first battle fails; by clarity of motivation, which must move a group rather than be a matter of individual or family differences; and by adequate supply of forces in the field.[22]

These criteria differentiate warfare from feuds and raids and other operations of short duration that have as their end the attainment of limited objectives. They make it clear why warfare, thus defined, was as rare among nonliterate peoples as are legislative bodies constituted like those of Euroamerican states. Demographic considerations alone forbid a small people to have an army. There is no man-power to enable them to do more than raid an enemy, or, over time to sustain more than feuding operations. Simple economies cannot provide supplies for campaigns, and warriors cannot always count on their ability to live off the land. The Zulu armies, or those of Ashanti and Dahomey, or, in the New World, of Peru and Mexico were, however, armies in every sense, and they carried on war. We would apply the term "soldiers" to the men who composed them, as against "warriors," which, significantly enough, we use for those who carry on most combats of nonliterate peoples.

The study of *law* in nonliterate societies was for many years made difficult by the distinctions drawn between codified and customary law. Difficulties were imposed, also, by the fact that the stated rules and regulations of a people, literate or nonliterate, by no means conform to observed customary behavior. "To seek a definition of law is like the quest of the Holy Grail," says Hoebel, in discussing the relation between law and anthropology.

Where, then, does custom end and law begin? This same student has given us a useful ethnological definition of law. "A social norm is legal," he states, "if its neglect or infraction is met by the application, in threat or in fact, of the absolute coercive force by a social unit possessing the socially recognized privilege of so acting." [23] Here the essential element is authority. "The legal has teeth," say Hoebel and Llewellyn. "What it protects is *protected;* if its prohibitions be disregarded, somebody can *do* something about it." And, while a custom that prevails need not be legal, it becomes so if it comes to appertain to what these students term "part of the going order" of the group.[24]

[22] H. H. Turney-High, 1942, pp. 21-2.
[23] E. A. Hoebel, 1946, p. 839; 1940, p. 47.
[24] K. N. Llewellyn and E. A. Hoebel, 1941, pp. 283-4.

No precision in the study of unwritten law could be attained until the case method was applied. Otherwise, only a kind of ethnographic statement of ideal or normative procedures could be arrived at. Such an early study as that of Dundas on the Kikuyu is replete with statements that report a consensus of behavior, much in the manner of any student of culture laying down the patterns of conduct in a society he is studying. These studies had, and still have, their value. No one can read Barton's report on Ifugao law and maintain that "primitive" people live only by the rule of force, or that they have no concepts of justice and no means of enforcing just resolutions of disputes or of punishing crimes. These studies, too, have had the result of sharpening perceptions of how varied and arbitrary are the categories of offenses recognized in different communities.

The variety of ways in which justice can be administered also gives impressive testimony of how differently the same ends can be achieved in different societies. The use of religious sanctions, such as the ordeal or the oath, or of secular ones, such as citing proverbs or weighing testimony about the facts, everywhere enter into the determination of justice. Courts with presiding officials who render judgment, advisers who act as a kind of jury, and even special pleaders who perform the functions of the lawyer are known in nonliterate cultures. The lack of specialization nonetheless makes procedures more direct and participation more general, for in this, as in all other phases of political structures, lines we draw sharply are blurred. Hence the need to enlarge categories and make flexibility the outstanding characteristic of definition becomes particularly important.

Chapter Twelve

Religion: the Problem of Man and the Universe

In 1871 E. B. Tylor offered as a "minimum definition of Religion, the belief in Spiritual Beings." To this "deep-lying doctrine," he applied the term animism. He says:

> It is habitually found that the theory of Animism divides into two great dogmas, forming part of one consistent doctrine; first, concerning souls of individual creatures, capable of continued existence after death or destruction of the body; second, concerning other spirits, upward to the rank of powerful deities. . . . Thus Animism, in its full development, includes the belief in souls and in a future state, in controlling deities and subordinate spirits, these doctrines practically resulting in some kind of active worship.[1]

Many criticisms have been lodged against this hypothesis, especially against the position that animism is the basis of all religion. The most telling of these criticisms has pointed to the purely intellectual processes Tylor assumed to have produced the basic animistic concept of "soul." In religion, as in any other

[1] E. B. Tylor, 1874, Vol. I, pp. 424-7.

aspect of tradition, the power of conditioned emotional drives is so strong that rational thought tends usually, if not invariably, to be rationalizing rather than exploring. It is thus apparent why such statements as the following became especially vulnerable:

> In spite of endless diversity of detail, the general principles of this investigation seem comparatively easy of access to the enquirer, if he will use . . . two keys . . . first, that spiritual beings are modelled by man on his primary conception of his own human soul, and second, that their purpose is to explain nature on the primitive childlike theory that it is truly and throughout "Animated Nature." [2]

The question was also raised whether broader, more undifferentiated beliefs must not have preceded animism. The answer to this question was believed to have been found when Bishop Codrington described the Melanesian belief in the impersonal force called *mana*, and McGee discovered the comparable Siouan Indian *wakanda*. For Marett, the concepts of *mana* and its counterpart, *tabu*, represented the most generalized, and hence the basic, force of religious belief. This he held to be especially true when mana was compared to animism which was intellectualistic and lacked "the emotions of awe, wonder, and the like." To the sense "of the attribution of life and animation which many peoples have toward inanimate objects," Marett gave the name "animatism." Thus he distinguished this belief from the narrower category of the *animae*, the spirits that actuate men and beasts and objects of nature and which, for Tylor, constituted animism.[3]

We do not hold the service these scholars have performed in shaping concepts the less valuable because we reject those of their findings that appear untenable in the light of subsequent knowledge. We can agree with Marett, who disclaimed any intent of depreciating the contribution of Tylor: "I am no irreconcilable foe who has a rival theory to put forward concerning the origin of religion." [4] Neither animism nor animatism is now regarded as an earlier, or original, or universal form of religion, any more than is the conception of Durkheim that religion has grown out of the social experience of men; [5] or the theory of Andrew Lang, that religion was first manifest in the belief in High Gods; [6] or Father Schmidt's extension of this concept by adding the corol-

[2] *Ibid.*, Vol. II, p. 168.
[3] R. R. Marett, 1914, pp. 119–22.
[4] *Ibid.*, p. xi.
[5] E. Durkheim, 1915, p. 10 and *passim*.
[6] A. Lang, 1887, Vol. I, pp. 327 ff.

lary that present beliefs of nonliterate peoples represent a degeneration from this purer form.[7]

Each of these scholars has provided evidence to document his theory and to satisfy any who will read what he has written; that is, until the evidence for some other theory is studied. Their contributions lie not in their having solved the riddle of how religion originated, or the steps by which it developed, or its social or psychological roots; but rather in the different phenomena of religion each emphasized and, by so doing, imprinted indelibly on all future discussions. The controversies over the nature and origin of religion have produced, almost as a by-product, an awareness of the range of religious beliefs and practices, and of their role in the lives of the people. This awareness has stimulated field workers to look for all these forms, and to investigate all the ways in which they influence a culture as a whole.

We shall consider each of these established categories of religious experience in classifying and organizing our materials. Animistic and animatistic beliefs, the concepts of spirits and ghosts, polytheism and monotheism, and magic—all characterize types of religious phenomena that must be understood. The order in which they are discussed is a matter of no importance, since we are taking them as no more than different forms of belief concerning the universe that, in part or in their entirety, may be found in any specific culture at a definite period of its existence.

2

Beliefs that not only human beings, but animals and inanimate objects are actuated by spirits that give them volition and purpose —that is, the beliefs we call animistic—are no monopoly of "primitive" man, or of children. Even in a machine culture, where physical causation is well understood, the owner of an automobile will berate it for the stalled engine or the punctured tire that interrupts his journey. The responses of children to objects that cause them harm have been used repeatedly as examples of animistic thought. But to correlate a "civilized" child with an adult "savage," as has often been done in this connection, is not admissible. The child who says, "Bad rock!" when he stubs his toe, or beats the chair against which he bumped himself is the precursor of the man who berates his stalled car. He is in no way to be equated with the nonliterate man who stands in awe before a magnificent waterfall, or a great tree, or a rock of striking formation.

[7] W. Schmidt, 1931, pp. 283 ff.

There are few peoples living today who do not have the concept of soul or spirit. Everywhere we encounter the postulate of an incorporeal thing that gives man his being, makes him the individual he is, and persists after his death. We may conjecture how primeval man must have been filled with fervor when a person, apparently dead, arose from his trance and told of his visions. To observe a man's body at rest, sleeping, and yet have the sleeper awaken and recount how he talked to a father long dead, or how he visited with a friend in the next village, or met a monstrous creature must have elicited some kind of explanation of the dream experience. Since the teller had not left the habitation, must there not have been some part of him that wandered away, some part that could not be seen, that was able to detach itself at will?

A few examples will document the widespread belief in a soul.

> In the religious system of the Montagnais-Naskapi the soul of the individual is the focal center of attention. Whatever we mean by the term "soul" its lexical equivalent in the language of these nomads . . . designates one's shadow. Another native term embracing the same word element . . . is met in the term for "mirror" . . . "see-soul-metal." It is interesting to observe that over much of the territory in America where Algonkian languages are spoken, the same stem and even most of the linked concepts are found. . . . Another term . . . in frequent use . . . means "spirit" in the sense of "intellect, comprehension"; hence, "mind."

In addition, we are informed, the Naskapi use a proper name "which is more descriptive of the soul's function." "Great Man" is the name given the "soul in its active state." This provides "guidance through life and . . . the means of overcoming the spirits of animals in the life-long search for food." The customary and significant usage is to employ the word for "my friend" when speaking of the soul, so that when a hunter has performed some act that gives him satisfaction, he will declare, "I wish to content myself," which, literally translated, means "I wish to make my friend (my soul) feel good." [8]

The Keraki of New Guinea distinguish the soul from the ghost, "the spiritual part of a living man and the spiritual substitute for him which survives his death," and may plague those who are left behind.[9] In Malekula, while every person has one soul that

[8] F. G. Speck, 1935, pp. 41–2.
[9] F. E. Williams, 1936, p. 361.

exists after death and can return to the land of the living, certain sacred plants that play an important ceremonial and economic role also are believed to have souls. A pig with a well-developed tusk curvature, the index of its value, has much spiritual power. If a small boy eats of its flesh, the spirit of the child is held to be in danger of being devoured by this more powerful spirit, and it is believed that the lad will die.[10]

Soul concepts of African peoples are highly elaborated, as in Dahomey, where all persons have at least three souls, and adult males have four. One is inherited from an ancestor, and is the "guardian spirit" of the individual. Before this spirit assumes his role of guardian, however, he finds the clay for molding the body it is to guard. The second is the personal soul, while the third is the small bit of the Creator that "lives in every person's body." The first, in terms of Euroamerican thought, is to be conceived as the biological aspect of a man, the second his personality, and the third his intellect and intuition. The fourth soul of adult males is associated with the concept of Destiny. This soul occupies itself not alone with the affairs of the individual who has established its formal worship, but also with the collective destiny of his household, since "the Dahomean reasons that when a man reaches maturity, his own life cannot know fulfillment apart from the lives of those who share that life with him." [11]

To the Aymara of the Peruvian highlands, "the world is so densely populated with supernatural beings that it is literally impossible to enumerate them. They exist almost everywhere in nature and vary from vaguely defined 'powers' to clearly personified supernatural beings." All unusual natural phenomena are held to be inhabited by good or evil spirits, though the word applied to such phenomena is also used for twins, and for persons with a harelip or other abnormalities. Plants and animals, being "owned" by supernatural beings of a higher order, are not believed to have spirits of their own. The spirits associated with places such as mountains and rivers can do much harm or much good. Conceived as old folk, principally men, who live under the earth, they punish evil-doing, and cause people to fall ill for reasons of their own. A class of evil beings inhabits ruins and caves, and house spirits guard property left in the house.[12] Among these people, the concepts of soul and ghost are not sharply differentiated. Ghosts

[10] A. B. Deacon, 1934, pp. 547–8.
[11] M. J. Herskovits, 1938b, Vol. II, p. 238.
[12] H. Tschopik, Jr., 1946, pp. 558–9.

are greatly feared, however, since the spirits of the dead can return to earth to reward or punish their living relatives.[13]

Except when used in the loosest fashion, the term "animistic" cannot be applied to the total system of belief of any people. To characterize a religion in such terms is so broad as to be meaningless. Christianity is animistic in that the belief in the human soul is an integral part of it, but Christians do not officially believe that automobiles have spirits. On the other hand, a belief that a waterfall or a rock or a bear or moose has a spirit does not necessarily exclude belief in a pantheon of gods who direct the larger concerns of the universe, or in quite impersonal supernatural forces. Both these, in turn, can and in most instances do coexist, as part of the same system, with ghosts and other manifestations of the spirits of the dead, perhaps formalized as an ancestral cult.

Wherever students have investigated the interrelations of these coexisting beliefs, they have found all such forms to be integrated into a unified world-view. This world-view, moreover, is not to be taken as evidence of a deficient or even a particular kind of mentality; it is the expression of a system of logic that moves with sureness from accepted premises concerning the nature of the world and man. It is not difficult to see how a people who believe in a human spirit can attribute spirits to animals, and even to inanimate objects. Just as an obdurate person may be regarded as having a "strong spirit," or a compliant one may be thought to have a weak soul, so animals and objects can be obstinate or compliant, friendly or hostile. The dog will refuse to track the animal being hunted, or the prey will defy the best efforts of the hunter. The knife that for years has performed its task will of a sudden turn on its user and cut him. How explain these happenings? Out of the many possible ways to account for them man, everywhere, has attributed to the animal or inanimate object the same willfulness in action he has observed in human beings.

The high gods of nonliterate cultures may be few or many. They may be immanent or removed from men. They may personify the forces of nature or be abstractions. But their concern is with the affairs of the universe and all things living and inert it contains, to the end that friction may be eliminated and harmony achieved. This is not to say that a belief in gods who reward and punish necessarily implies that religion must have an ethical content, for there is good evidence that such a criterion is by no means universally applicable. There are societies, for example,

[13] *Ibid.*, p. 552.

where reward and punishment are cared for quite satisfactorily by human agencies, without the aid of supernatural sanctions.

Conversely, there is no justification for holding that only the "higher" religions have ethical content. The gods of too many peoples are marshaled for the support of sanctioned behavior and the suppression of evil to permit systems of belief to be distinguished on these grounds. In a majority of nonliterate cultures, it is true, the gods have many preoccupations, in addition to the support of an ethical system. They must see to it that the crops grow, that children thrive, that their worshippers prosper, that wars are won, that trade flourishes. The suppression of evil is but one of their duties, and it lies on the level of these others. Yet what is more natural than that in a world where everything is endowed with a spirit, and man is the dominant creature, the spirit of man, or his soul, should be the most powerful of all? And that the spirits of those who exert the most power while on earth should continue to manifest their power in the world of the dead, finally coming to dominate, as gods, the very universe?

There are gods that are removed from men, however, even among peoples with the simplest technologies—those whose cultures are held by some to be the living examples of primeval man's way of life. Thus Father Schmidt, the most emphatic opponent of Tylor's point of view, holds that the primeval systems must essentially have been the worship of the high gods. Hence spirits and ghosts, and the souls of animals, plants, and inert objects are to Father Schmidt but manifestations of a degeneration from the high level of presumed aboriginal monotheistic world view. Yet, as Marett has argued, from what could the concept of high gods have developed? Either there had been a forerunner to the idea of deities, or we must assume that the different gods revealed themselves in the early days of man on earth. But were this the case, how do we account for religions in which deities are but minor expressions of the power phenomenon that, impersonal as the rain, permits all controls to function?

Once again we must stress the futility of the search for the absolute origin of any nonmaterial element in culture, or of seeking simple explanations for the complexities of custom. Animism is an important part of the world view of so many peoples, that to regard it as the irreducible minimum of belief is persuasive until we look at all the facts. The high gods and their complementary beings are found in cultures simple and complex, but many other kinds of beliefs are found in association with them. The categories of animatism, animism, polytheism, and monotheism are important as classifications of religious phenomena, but not as a developmental progression.

3

The supernatural force that gives power to gods and ghosts, and makes it possible for inanimate objects to become entities motivated by good or ill will, is among many peoples a humanly controllable essence. Sometimes benefiting from the prompting of the spirit-gods, and sometimes by his own discovery, man has learned to influence even the highest spiritual beings, through supplication, propitiation, expiation. *Mana, wakanda, orenda, manitou* are, however, not anthropomorphized. They represent what is best termed blind power, and there is little point in petitioning them.

Mana, the name most commonly given this phenomenon, is found in Melanesia, but the ideas it expresses are by no means restricted to that area. Together with other religious beliefs, it exists in many cultures, under many guises. We ourselves are not without it; in our culture, it is called "luck." For what is luck if not an uncontrollable force, which comes and goes as it wills, without regard to the wishes of those whom it may at one moment favor, at another abandon? Some people, our idiom goes, are just "lucky," and they are often "touched" by others who hope thus to acquire some power. Try as we will, however, luck cannot be induced to come to us. Those who have played cards know how desperately the loser—at poker, let us say—will walk about his chair, blow on the cards, turn three times before taking his seat, to "change his luck." To no avail, luck will not be petitioned or coerced. The mathematician can tell us about probability, but we know better. The luck either was there, or it wasn't.

That this is not a far-fetched analogy is patent when we turn to Codrington's classical description of mana. The Melanesian mind, he says,

> is entirely possessed by the belief in a supernatural power or influence, called almost universally *mana*. This is what works to effect everything which is beyond the ordinary power of men, outside the common processes of nature; it is present in the atmosphere of life, attaches itself to persons and to things, and is manifested by results which can only be ascribed to its operation. When one has got it he can use it and direct it, but its force may break forth at some new point; the presence of it is ascertained by proof.

A stone of uncommon shape may have mana if, when it is buried in a garden, the yield is bountiful; and its power can be transferred to other stones. Songs can have mana, also.

> This power, though itself impersonal, is always connected with some person who directs it; all spirits have it, ghosts generally, some men. If a stone is found to have a supernatural power, it is because a spirit has associated itself with it; a dead man's bone has with it *mana*, because the ghost is with the bone; a man may have so close a connexion with a spirit or ghost that he has *mana* in himself also, and can so direct it as to effect what he desires; a charm is powerful because the name of a spirit or ghost expressed in the form of words brings into it the power which the ghost or spirit exercises through it. Thus all conspicuous success is a proof that a man has *mana;* his influence depends on the impression made on the people's mind that he has it; he becomes a chief by virtue of it.[14]

This passage has been quoted at length because it shows how no single formula can encompass the beliefs of a single people. In the quotation we find the power that is mana is not only lodged in stone but is also to be found in a bone because the bone of a dead person has associated with it the ghost of the dead. Furthermore, Codrington names a second category of beliefs in spirits found among these same people, "beings personal, intelligent, full of *mana*, with a certain bodily form which is visible but not fleshly like the bodies of men." [15] Such spirits are different from ghosts, which are the disembodied spirits of men. In some of the islands, beings even more difficult to describe, called *viu*, enter into the system of belief.

Though mana is neither god nor spirit, its power, in the areas studied by Codrington, can be manipulated. It "attaches itself to persons and things" and can be transmitted from one individual to another. Its use to maintain power in the family of a certain chief exemplifies this. This man, who was "the most conspicuous chief" in the island of Florida at the time of first European contact was a native of a different island. But as a young man staying there he had played a prominent part in successfully fighting the enemies of the people of Florida. His reputation as a man of power was thus established, and it increased with the years. Like other chiefs, he was presumed to have access to a powerful ghost, a *tendalo*, so that, like them, he could utilize the power of this spirit for his own ends and might pass it on to his successor.

[14] R. H. Codrington, 1891, pp. 118–20.
[15] *Ibid.*, p. 120.

Various mana-like power manifestations have been reported from the North American continent, the Algonkian concept of *manitou,* the Siouan *wakanda,* the Iroquois *orenda.* An Algonkian Montagnais-Naskapi version of this power is illuminating:

> The background upon which rest the supernatural relationships of the Montagnais-Naskapi must be understood in the term *mɘntú,* variants being *manɘtú* (Lake St. John), *mantú* (Mistassini). The term cannot be adequately translated, since it is an abstraction having no definite compass in the genius of a vague philosophy. . . . Everything not understood is implied in it. . . . One informant will try to illustrate the meaning of the term by comparing it to natural physical force observable in electricity, gravity, heat, steam, while another will liken it to psychic principles operating in thought, invention, memory, coordination, in animal generation and human procreation, in heredity, and especially in supernatural control. . . . In the sense of "spiritual being" or "deity" . . . it has been adapted . . . to Christian theism. In the sense of "power" we find it in common use in the translations given by thoughtful Indians in explaining the miracles of the shaman or conjuror. It often appears, moreover, in terms expressing mental states which result in producing physical effects.[16]

The power concept among American Indians is not always as completely impersonal and as sharply definable in terms of mana as the Algonkian *manitou* and similar beliefs, as we see if we turn to the Puyallup-Nisqually of the Pacific Coast. "Every individual characteristic and every cultural complex, except those related to sexual life, was understood and was thought to operate through power. Adult life without power was inconceivable and childhood was viewed as a period of preparation . . . for the reception of power." This preparation, under the control of the trainer, lasted from the age of five to six until puberty, and was essentially a process of physical hardening. At puberty, most boys went on a power quest, though this was not the exclusive means of obtaining power; girls, who might also receive power, never went on these quests, but bathed and fasted as a part of the isolation enjoined at initial menstruation.

There were two kinds of power: those associated with some trait of personality or aptitude, and shamanistic powers. The first type was very generally distributed, and made of a person a good hunter, fortunate in economic pursuits, or a lucky gambler. The

[16] F. G. Speck, 1914, p. 35.

shamanistic power was of a sterner quality. It came without regard for a person's wishes, and "failure to meet the ceremonial requirements of one's power caused a friction which resulted in the illness or ultimate death of the human who was thus stubborn in refusal." Furthermore, "weakness of the body through fatigue or physical illness might cause the power to become detached or dislodged, a state, again, which involved illness and ultimate death if the power could not be recovered." These shamanistic powers, like other powers that were associated with animal or abstract beings, were widely distributed, but "in the average person were overbalanced and held in check" by the possession of stronger powers.

Numerous powers are recognized by these people. Chicken-hawk power, to take an example at random, makes a good gambler; grizzly-bear power makes a man "apt to be mean and always brave"; snake power "is just a 'cuss.' You can't do anything with a man who has it, he just goes off and lives away from the others. People don't like him, and he doesn't like them." There are more generalized powers. One, for example, protects the home, another is the principal wealth power, another gives a man the ability to dance, another makes a man brave. The variety of powers is confusing, but the general principle underlying them all is clear. All powers represent the force in the universe that endows men and women with ability, with aptitudes, with insights that make of them the persons they are.[17]

The idea of impersonal power also seems to be present in Africa, but here the role of polytheistic worship and the ancestral cult is so important that beliefs in non-anthropomorphic forces appear in the literature only by implication. A hint of this same feeling of power in the impersonal sense is given in the following passage from Stayt:

> On inquiring minutely into the history of a small piece of wood, worn as a charm round the neck of a MuVenda for protection when travelling, it transpired that this wood was taken from a bough of a tree overhanging a difficult climb in a well-frequented path. This bough was grasped by every passerby in order to assist him over the difficult place. In this way the power of that particular bough was inordinately increased by helping the wayfarer, and it became the obvious source from which effective charms for the timid traveller could be obtained.

[17] M. W. Smith, 1940, pp. 56–75, 189–95.

This illustrates "the belief that every object, animate or inanimate, possesses a kinetic power for good or evil," a belief that is basic to the medico-magical arts of the BaVenda.[18]

This brings us to the idea of magic. The important point stressed here is that magic, which for many years was held to be without relation to religion, is actually an integral part of religion. We cannot even distinguish it fully from the worship of the gods, in terms of criteria often met with—that magic is effected by formula, while the gods are moved by prayer; or that magic is always used with reference to a specific problem, while the gods are petitioned for general well-being.

Magic has been differentiated from religion in other ways. Frazer held it to be antecedent to the worship of the gods. With somewhat better reason, he also equated magic with science, though to call magic "primitive science" [19] will not bear too close scrutiny. There can be no question that the element of direct causation of specific ends does characterize many of the magical practices of man, as it does the routine of the scientist. The differences between them, however, are important. The scientist works in a closed, mechanistic system, where causation is effected by putting into operation forces invariably of a material nature. In magical operations, however, while a given combination of factors must produce a desired result, the system is not a closed one, but departs from the natural to include and account for the play of supernatural forces.

Magic is no more the exclusive property of nonliterate peoples than is monotheism the monopoly of certain literate cultures, so that a word may be said about how we designate the magical practices we employ. We call them "superstitions"; and then extend the meaning of the word to include any form of belief we do not hold, or that is not officially recognized by a particular body of doctrine in which we find satisfaction. Superstitions are, however, but beliefs of which there is no longer a wholehearted acceptance. They are practices that are followed without conviction, but with an uneasy feeling that it will do no harm to carry them out, if by chance we thus get on the good side of powers whose existence we may at times doubt.

From this comes the rather shamefaced attitude toward magic, which is familiar to us and which has given rise to rationalizations that have become standard explanations of behavior

[18] H. A. Stayt, 1931, p. 262.
[19] Sir J. G. Frazer, 1935, Vol. I, pp. 220–5.

that can be interpreted as belief in "superstitions." We avoid walking under a ladder, and then explain that we fear it will fall, or that a bucket of paint will come down on us. We fail to note audibly that our hotel, following standard practice, has no thirteenth floor. A man carries a buckeye "as a pocket piece" rather than as a preventive for rheumatism; he surreptitiously raps three times on wood for good luck when he thinks no one is looking, or makes a game of it. This attitude toward beliefs held without conviction is by no means unique to Euroamerican culture. The same feeling about superstitions was shown by the West African who, expressing scepticism at the belief of his fellows in the power of the earth, nonetheless knelt, touched his hand to the ground and kissed his fingers as he discussed the earth deity whose windstorms destroyed the crops.

If we recognize that magic is an integral part of most belief systems, we may then distinguish it from other forms of religion. All are like parts of a single mechanism that helps to assure man his place in a scheme of things so vast, and so complex, that without these varied controls he would be hard put to it to make meaning out of his life, or to achieve a sense of security in it.

4

The narrowness with which we define religion stems from the intense specialization of our culture. Without prescribed training, we approach the powers of the universe with no more feeling of competence than if we were called on to operate a power lathe, derive a formula for the manufacture of gasoline, or compose a tone poem for orchestra. Religion, for vast numbers of us, has become a matter of adherence to an accepted world-view. In this we approach as near to the point of being entirely passive in our religious experience as, in all probability, the history of man has ever known. Performance is left to the experts; in proffering our faith, we lend our presence and our ears, but not a hand. Other cultures, however, move from this extreme to a state of affairs where every adult has some competence in dealing with the supernatural, even though specialists may be called on to aid in solving particular problems.

Most nonliterate peoples take belief for granted. The powers that rule the universe are known, and the ways in which they are approached are part of the routine of living. To make a token offering of food to gods or ancestors before eating, to murmur a formula before the arrow leaves the bow, or to strengthen the power of a charm by sprinkling it with palm-wine, takes no more thought, and occurs as frequently as our conventional "excuse me" or "thank you." For people living in terms of a system of thought that takes a symbolic group of invisible forces into daily account, belief will not be narrowly framed, and attitudes will be relaxed and natural. Many students have commented on the absence in other cultures of the hushed voice and the restrained movements that mark our approach to the forces of the universe. Where these forces are thought to be all about and never aloof from any part of life, there is no place for such attitudes.

The ways in which men seek to bring themselves into harmony with the powers of the universe are many. They may be intensely personal, or require participation by the entire group. They may be public, or private. They may involve highly keyed emotional improvisation, or demand precision of movement, set by an ancient tradition. They may call for the recitation of elaborate formulae, or may be wordless. They may utilize special objects, carefully made and of intricate form, or they may be restricted to nonmaterial expression in word or song or dance. Any of these, moreover, may be found alone or in combination with others. And any of them, or all, may be used to petition or compel action by powers whose resources transcend those of the human being who invokes them.

Prayer is one of the principal categories of worship. It may be defined as the use of words to bring about the favorable intervention of the powers of the universe in the affairs of men. It can vary from casual address to formalized plea, and may be specific or general in its reference. "The gods are like children; they must be told what to do," said a Dahomean. This expresses a widespread attitude toward the relation between men and supernatural beings that can make a prayer informative (with the implication that being informed, the divine agent will feel disposed to friendly intercession), or can be an admonition, or even a compulsive prompting. Prayer is often phrased with such beauty of imagery that some of the finest poetic expressions of nonliterate peoples have been collected in the form of prayers.

Let us cite some prayers that have been recorded from various parts of the nonliterate world. On the Polynesian island of Mangareva, an annual ceremony celebrated the appearance of the first or second breadfruit crop. Like all rites in Polynesia, this involved long preliminary preparation and the participation of many persons. At sunrise of the first day, the trumpeter sounded the shell trumpet, and the high priest invoked the deity, bidding him to come to the festival and to clear the path, that the breadfruit trees, awakened by the call of the trumpet, might produce their fruit:

> Behold, this is the announcement
> An announcement of much to do,
> To invoke Tu,
> Tu-of-the-outer-space, Tu-eater-of-people,
> Tu-who-floats-up-the-land . . .

The priest continued his recital of the ritual names of the god, and then, after the offerings were made, he went to the plantations and spoke the following lines, directing his words toward the bark cloth streamer that had been erected:

> The streamer! Streamer for us,
> Streamer for the gods,
> Streamer that protects the back,
> That protects the front.
> The interior was void,
> The interior was empty.
> Let (productivity) appear
> And spread to the foothills.
> Grant the smell of food,
> Grant the growth of food,
> A portion of fatness,
> A breeze that calls for fermentation.

Finally, the names of the ancestors were called. Here the end sought was clearly expressed. That the prayer was spoken in the elaborate setting that marked its use did not alter the spirit that motivated it.[20]

An Ashanti who marries a widow addresses this prayer to the ghost of the late husband:

> *Asumasi*, they say that when a cutlass breaks, they put a new shaft to it; today they have taken your wife and given her to me, I beg you to look well after me and her. Let these children prosper and serve me, and let me beget others to add to your own.[21]

From the Bushmen of South Africa comes this prayer, spoken when the sacred New Moon appears:

> Ho, my hand is this
> I shoot a springbok with my hand
> By an arrow.

[20] P. H. Buck (Te Rangi Hiroa), 1938, pp. 434–5.
[21] R. S. Rattray, 1929, p. 28.

I lie down
I will early kill a springbok
Tomorrow.

Ho Moon lying there,
Let me kill a springbok
Tomorrow,
Let me eat a springbok;
With this arrow
Let me shoot a springbok
With this arrow;
Let me eat a springbok,
Let me eat filling my body
In the night which is here,
Let me fill my body.

Ho Moon lying there,
I dig out ants' food
Tomorrow,
Let me eat it.

Ho Moon lying there,
I kill an ostrich tomorrow
With this arrow.

Ho Moon lying there,
Thou must look at this arrow,
That I may shoot a springbok with it tomorrow.[22]

Here the directness of the appeal bespeaks a sense of close relation between the Bushman and the being he worships. The urgency of the food quest causes the petitions of this people to be phrased in terms of the basic necessity, food.

It is apparent that the techniques of *magic* stand in contrast, though by no means in opposition, to prayer. That is, it is reasonably safe to conclude that magical and religious practices are to be differentiated if, for example, distinguishing words are used for prayer and for the magic spell, or to designate the powers of a deity as against the power of a magic charm, or to name those who serve the gods as apart from those who work the charms.

This is demonstrated in Evans-Pritchard's analysis of magic among the Azande, who live just north of the Congo Basin, west of the East African area. In studying their methods of controlling the supernatural world, this student has been "mainly concerned with following Zande thought." "I have classed under a single

[22] D. F. Bleek, 1929, p. 306.

heading," he says, "what Azande call by a single word, and I have distinguished between types of behaviour that they consider different." These people have a well-developed system of bringing injury to a person or his belongings. Divination is employed to discover who has set evil against a man, and magic is the principal means of combating this evil. Evans-Pritchard states that "witchcraft, oracles, and magic are like three sides to a triangle." It testifies to the complexity of the phenomenon that even in a discussion restricted to the practices of a single people, and drawn strictly in terms of their concepts, we learn that "in Zande opinion some magic is to be classed, from the legal and moral standpoint, with witchcraft." [23]

Two kinds of magic are often distinguished by students. First named by Frazer, they are "imitative" ("homeopathic") and "contagious." Both are held to operate in accordance with a principle of "like to like," also called a "principle of sympathy." "Contagious" magic is exemplified when a hunter drinks the blood of his kill to acquire its craftiness or its strength. "Imitative" magic would, let us say, be found in the performance of a dance in which the simulated killing of an animal was enacted so as to assure success in hunting. These categories, however, while valid as far as they go, neither constitute the entire field, nor are they absent from certain practices to which the term "religious" is customarily given.

The charm and the spell are widely spread devices employed in magic. A specific power, held to reside in a specific object, is set in operation by the pronouncement of a formula that of itself can wield power. The magic charm takes innumerable forms. It most often includes some part of the object over which its power is to be exerted, or some element that, because of outer resemblance or inner character, habitually achieves the desired result. One word applied to charms is *fetish*, and no term has proved more troublesome than this and its companion, *fetichism*. The derivation is from the Portuguese *feitiço*, "something made," and was used by the early Portuguese to denote the charms and images of African peoples. These terms appear often in the literature, as when it is said "fetichism is the religion of Africa." If used at all, they should designate "charm" and "magic"; but they are better omitted from discussions of control of the supernatural.

Magic is often divided into "black" and "white," the first being of evil intent, the second beneficent. In the literature, emphasis tends to be laid most heavily on the first category. The reason for

[23] E. E. Evans-Pritchard, 1937, pp. 9–11, 387.

this is twofold. There is the challenge to the investigator to uncover what his informants are least willing to divulge. More than this, though, is the dramatic appeal of "black" magic for the people themselves. Once a willingness to talk about it is established, informants will dwell on the subject with relish and exuberant detail, leaving "white" magic as something taken for granted.

Nonetheless, it is evident from the innumerable instances of magic reported from other parts of the world, that the practice of "black" magic by no means predominates. The category of "white" magical devices, indeed, must be extended to include much of native medicine; just as "black" magic includes the use of devices, such as poison, that we would term anything but supernatural. The categories of good and evil magic, as a matter of fact, in large measure arise out of the patterns of Euroamerican thought. Nonliterate peoples are usually more realistic than we. They recognize neither black nor white, but a series of grays of varying shades. The magic I set to prevent my house from being robbed will harm the robber; his thieving magic will benefit him and does hurt to me. From this one moves to the extremes. The magic rites of fertility that are to assure bountiful crops, or charms that are designed to safeguard the pregnant woman and ensure her a safe delivery, are good. Magic that kills is bad, and the worker of such malevolent devices is everywhere feared, and in most cultures regarded as a criminal and punished as such when apprehended. And at this point, we come again the full circle to the gods, who in many instances themselves empower magic and punish its misuse to attain evil ends.

5

The need to ascertain and interpret the will of the gods and to negate the factors of time and distance is felt by many peoples. Various techniques have been devised to accomplish these ends. *Divination*, the general term for them, must be considered as another way in which the control of the supernatural is attained. The phenomenon takes two forms. One is the use of devices in which chance is the principal element. The second is contact with a divine spirit, which displaces the personality of a priest or medium and speaks through him. Both are of wide distribution in the Old World; in the New World, the second type predominates.

Techniques of divination are many. One, the scrutiny of the entrails of animals killed for the purpose, is found everywhere in the Old World. Often an autopsy is performed on the human dead to the same end. Another method is the inspection of scapulae. These bones are placed in the fire until they crack, whereupon the diviner inspects the lines and makes his interpretation. Perhaps as complex a series of systems of divination by mechanical means as is found anywhere in Africa exists. In one small region of the Cameroons, for example, palm-leaf cards with special markings are thrown, other kinds of cards are placed at the hole of a trained tarantula so he may scatter them, cowry-shells are cast to attain combinations of open and closed sides, human and animal entrails are inspected, states of possession are induced to permit the gods to speak.[24] Each of these techniques could be duplicated in many other areas of the continent. New World divining practices, which extend also to Siberia, are generally of the shamanistic variety and are concerned with healing and the quest for power. The shaman is an individual endowed with supernatural power to heal, or one who can call his spirit to find out what is beyond time and space. There is conjuring of the "non-inspired type" wherein the spirits speak *to* or *in the presence* of the shaman, rather than enter his body and speak *through* him,[25] and "inspirational shamanism," which is predominant in Siberia but is also found to a lesser degree among American Indians.

Possession, however, is more than a mode of ascertaining the will and intent of supernatural beings. Held by some students to be the supreme religious experience, it is an awesome performance, and presents many baffling psychological problems. It is framed by the conventions of worship of the individual to whom it comes and in these terms is never haphazard, but patterned. It may come in solitude, or during a public ceremony to which a supernatural being has been called. Under states of possession, devotees experience a change in their customary behavior, even the timbre and pitch of their voices may alter. They may speak "in tongues" or remain silent, prophesy and cure, be acquiescent or recalcitrant. As the spirit, the human being possessed may walk on burning coals, chew glass, lash himself with thorny bushes, or otherwise castigate himself, without apparent harm. Many such cases have been recorded by competent observers.

Rapport with the supernatural, unattainable by ordinary persons, is vouchsafed the worshipper who experiences possession. Whether a guardian spirit, a ghost, or a deity comes to him, he has a sense of personal security and power, and, in many societies, a

[24] From an unpublished study by Paul Gebauer.
[25] A. I. Hallowell, 1942, pp. 9–13.

preferred social position. His visions enable his fellows the more confidently to face the forces of the universe; the pronouncements of the god, spirit, or ghost who speaks through him may indicate the way to fortune, to good health, and to those other ends men strive for.

Ceremonialism calls on the pageantry of ritual to reinforce belief. Not all ceremonialism is religious; for every culture also has secular rites of various sorts. Religious ceremonies, however, provide the widest opportunity for group worship. Here are to be found the elaborate costumes, the decorated wands, the masks and other paraphernalia that yield aesthetic as well as religious satisfaction. Ceremonialism is a powerful agent in uniting a people. Whether as active participants in the worship or as spectators, the bonds that bind them to their fellows are strengthened by ceremonialism. Therefore, though Durkheim's hypothesis that the origin of all religion is to be sought in ceremonial must be substantially modified, it is by no means to be completely dismissed. But we cannot define the sacred as strictly as Durkheim does when he describes religion as activity exercised in institutions analogous to churches. It requires but little experience in the field to discover that among the vast majority of nonliterate peoples, the line between religious and nonreligious rites, between the sacred and the secular, is as blurred as are such divisions in all cultures, even where a high degree of specialization is present.

The ceremonial aspects of religion are the first to strike the outsider; and most descriptions of the religion of nonliterate peoples, given by people without anthropological training, are in actuality no more than descriptions of ceremonies. As almost nowhere else in the range of culture, it is here essential to call into constant play the "why" that is the primary tool of the field worker. Rituals, however, are but the implementation of belief. Not only must the rite itself be detailed with care, but the sanctions for it must also be probed. Why does one dancer wear red beads, another white? What does it mean that all the participants in a ceremony have a vertical streak painted in the center of the forehead? For what reason does the action move in a clockwise direction? The observed fact, of itself, tells us nothing; it is not until we learn the reasons for the observed behavior that we begin to comprehend the ritual we record.

Usually the "why" of the ethnographer leads to mythology. Myth is the "charter of belief," and gives point and meaning to the ritualistic behavior that derives from its sanctions. Very often the myth will itself take on a sacred quality which can render the ethnographer's task most difficult. The story, conceived as partaking of the power of the characters of which it treats, then becomes not only sacred but secret, and is not to be imparted to the outsider—not because he is an outsider, perhaps, but because, like the younger members of the tribe, he does not have the strength to render its spiritual impact harmless to himself.

If mythology gives belief its charter, ritual is the instrument by which conviction is renewed and strengthened. For initiate and noninitiate, and even for those who may be forbidden to witness certain rites, the mere knowledge that the proper ceremonies have been performed gives assurance that the favor of the benevolent powers of the universe has been won. Thus added to the sociological significance of ritual as a binding force for the group as a whole is its psychological importance as the mechanism that validates belief.

6

It is easier to say what religion is not than to frame a positive definition of it. We have seen that Tylor's "minimum definition" as the belief in spirits comprehended only a segment of religious beliefs and practices. Moreover, to define religion in terms of any particular system of belief or dogma restricts our view, since in such terms religion can only exist by definition. Some have sought to find the basis of religion in fear; others have stressed ethical content as its essential element; and we have commented on the hypothesis that it developed out of ritual.

All these are but partial answers. The mere fact that powers greater than man are conceived to exist in the universe means that some element of fear enters, especially when there is a complementary belief that some act of human omission or commission may provoke retaliatory acts. The ethical role of the so-called "great" religions has been advanced as the primary factor that sets them off from the religions of nonliterate peoples. But concepts of right and wrong can be found in the systems of belief of all groups.

Marett and Goldenweiser, approaching the problem of the nature of religion from somewhat different points of view, have agreed in holding that supernaturalism is the essence of all religious phenomena.

> Magic and religion . . . belong to the same departments of human experience—one of the two great departments, the two worlds, one might almost call them, into which human experience, throughout its whole history, has been divided. Together

they belong to the supernormal world, the *x*-region of experience, the region of mental twilight.[26]

Goldenweiser divides beliefs in the supernatural into the tenet of
animistic faith and the tenet of *magical faith*, underlying both of
which is "the third and most important tenet of supernaturalism,"
the *faith in power*. But all these are given reality through the experience of the *religious thrill*, which is "the concrete living participation of the individual in this world of supernaturalism." [27]

Here, however, we must enter still another qualification. For
though, as Goldenweiser says, the "thrill" is the essence of religious participation, this thrill is the exceptional rather than the
common religious experience. It stands out as a mountain peak
seen from the plain of everyday religious practice. But the less
spectacular phases of everyday religion are, in point of fact, the
ones that pervade religious behavior. All men, at all times, have
sensed frustration and fear when faced with problems that their
own human resources could not solve. Such frustrations and fears
come not alone with dramatic displays or the havoc of nature.
They also arise, in everyday life, in the give and take of human
relations, in encounters with fellow humans who deny, forbid,
dominate, challenge, or inflict pain. The Freudian explanation of
religion, the unconscious desire for the security of childhood, is
too simple to be fully acceptable; but it does give us an important
insight into probable motivations that lead to religious expression.

The propensity for intense mystical experiences is no more
the same among men than is the length of their noses. Some human
beings reach an accord with the supernatural powers that is denied their more stolid fellows. The Dahomeans recognize these
differences in the reaction of individuals to mystical religious
experiences.

> Skeptics among the Dahomeans themselves state that many
> of the cult-initiates derive nothing deeper from their experiences
> in the cult-house than the enjoyment of freedom from routine
> and, after emergence, the pleasure of appearing before acquaint-
> ances in the fineries of a cult-member. It is also said that particu-
> larly in the case of women is it advantageous to have gone through
> the initiatory rites of the cult-house, because this gives a woman
> certain advantages in her relation to the other members of her
> family, and a certain favorable position with her husband. It is
> said, further, that some go through the initiatory experience

[26] R. R. Marett, 1912, p. 209.
[27] A. A. Goldenweiser, 1922, pp. 231-3.

merely to satisfy curiosity. Yet even skeptics admit that there are some who experience the real "mystery." . . . Such persons feel an exaltation, a sense of awe and of unity with the god that, though held in check between ceremonies, wells forth at once if the proper songs or drum rhythms are heard. On such occasions, as the cult-initiates stand ready to dance, a figure taller than any human stands before them, the left hand outstretched to touch their heads. This is the *vodũ* (the god). And when the hand touches them they feel a great strength. As they dance, they are no longer themselves, and they remember nothing of what happened when the *vodũ* leaves them. But, when they regain consciousness of the world outside and are themselves once more, they feel as though something heavy had left them.[28]

In defining religion in terms of crises or of the religious thrill, we must remember that crises are by no means always severe; that the thrill is manifested only at intervals, and not to every member of a society. Our definition, therefore, must allow for the less dramatic, quieter, everyday forms of religious belief and prac-tice that tend to be overlooked. We must, also, in drawing our definition consider the emphasis on supernaturalism that plays so prominent a part in most discussions of religion.

Among most peoples, literate or nonliterate, belief in super-natural forces of the universe does undoubtedly comprise the core of religious belief. Yet if we approach the phenomena of religion from the point of view of their essentially emotional character, we recognize that many reactions that have no basis in super-naturalism must be thought of as religious.

In our mechanistic culture, the emotional drive, the deep faith in the transcendental importance of what is undertaken, the dedi-cation to the experimental tradition, which mark the scientist in his laboratory, are essentially religious in its psychological orienta-tion. The thrill that comes when the formula is discovered to be correct or when the last stroke of the adding machine proves the validity of the mathematical calculation is probably little different from that experienced by the nonliterate man when he comes face to face with his deity. The crusading spirit of the convinced atheist, or the intransigent selflessness of the political revolution-ary must, in psychological terms, be thought of as falling in the same category, if we consider the phenomenon from the point of view of its motivating drives and not in terms of the forms in which it manifests itself. One of the reasons it is so difficult for those in the stream of Euroamerican culture, especially for in-

[28] M. J. Herskovits, 1938b, Vol. II, pp. 199–200.

tellectuals, to grasp the essential homely, everyday nature of religion is that we think of religion as supernaturalism, while our religious emotions are lavished on aspects of our experience we label as secular.

In broadest terms, then, religion may best be defined as *belief in, and identification with a greater force or power.* A belief may so pervade attitude and action as rarely to enter the stream of conscious thought, except in moments of crisis when it is called upon to steady a world that seems to be falling about one's head. The greater force or power that stands for order and protection in the life of the individual may be a supernatural being or beings, an impersonal force, a concept such as society, or science. It is enough that man have faith in its unfailing potentialities, that he feel that it can be called on when needed, that it will not fail him when his own resources are insufficient.

Above all, religion implies the emotional response to the power that rules the universe, however it may be conceived. Though the supreme religious experience, the "thrill," is felt by relatively few persons, and by them but sporadically, yet the raw material of emotion is ever present. On a less intense scale, it is experienced by all those whose emotional susceptibilities are keyed to a religious response.

Chapter **Thirteen**

The Aesthetic Drive: Graphic and Plastic Arts

The search for beauty is universal in human experience. Its innumerable forms have sprung from the play of the creative imagination, and afford some of the deepest satisfactions known to man. To understand how closely integrated with all of life, and how expressive of a way of living art can be, is again not easy for members of the highly specialized societies of Euroamerican culture, where we are confronted with the effect of compartmentalization. We have observed this in the case of religion, of politics, of education—to cite but three examples. In the analysis of art, when we differentiate "pure" from "applied" art, we similarly restrict the play of our aesthetic appreciation. Furthermore, we set up invidious distinctions between the "artist" who produces this "pure" art and the "craftsman" whose art, if it is admitted that he has one, is held to be of a different category, of a quality that we call "applied."

It can safely be said that there are no nonliterate societies where distinctions of this order will prevail. Art is a part of life, not separated from it. This by no means implies that specialization does not exist in such cultures; for wherever the creative drive comes into play, individuals are found to excel, or to be inept, in their performance. Even in a small group, for example, a visitor will be directed to some one person who is an outstanding wood carver. The other men, however, and the women, who may be forbidden by tradition to work in wood, will be able to appreciate and make informed judgments about any carved piece. All will know stories, but a particular old woman will be pointed out as the best storyteller in the village.

In the widest sense, then, art is to be thought of as *any embellishment of ordinary living that is achieved with competence and has describable form.* Competence can become virtuosity, which is the supreme control over technique that gives every society its finest aesthetic products and, as we shall see, is a significant factor in the creative process itself. Even where no question of virtuosity arises, however, the artist must be competent if he is to be effective in the expression of his art. Form, function, and design are also necessary to the execution of any art form. Within these limits, however, the student of culture must regard as art whatever a people recognizes as manifestations of the impulse to make more beautiful and thus to heighten the pleasure of any phase of living.

2

The artist's interpretation of experience is the quintessence of artistic expression. This fact, that art involves the interpretation of experience, at once brings us to one of the most controversial matters in the field of art study—the problem of realism as against conventionalization, of representation as against symbolism in art. The problem has two facets. The first is how the tradition of a people, in defining the framework within which reality is perceived and in supplying the materials with which the artist works, influences both the composition and the interpretation of that which is carved, woven, painted, or modeled. The second has to do with the play of the individual artist's creative impulse and technical skill as these find expression through the accepted styles and media of his culture and exert an influence in changing these patterns by introducing new elements into what he creates.

It is not too much to say that no work of art achieves complete realism. If realism were the end of artistic striving, then the most perfect example of it would be a three-dimensional, colored, talking motion picture. More than one ethnographer has reported the experience of having shown a clear photograph of a house, a person, or a familiar landscape to people living in a culture innocent of any knowledge of photography, and having had the picture held at all possible angles, or turned over for an inspection of its blank back, as the native tried to interpret this meaningless arrangement of varying shades of gray on a piece of paper. For even the clearest photograph is only an *interpretation* of what the camera sees. We are too accustomed to looking at pictures to be conscious of the fact that they interpret a three-dimensional world in two dimensions, or that they change a setting of color into a composition in black and white. Because a photograph is an interpretation, the person who looks at it must have a clue to the arrangement of forms and shadings if he is to grasp the meaning of what it reproduces. That this is easier for photographs than for other art forms, once the clues are grasped, merely means that the photograph is more realistic than forms whose interpretation is more arbitrary.

Realism is thus best defined as an attempt to *approach* reality in art. But this attempt is, as we know, always made in terms of cultural definitions, so that a cross-cultural interpretation of the intent of the artist is very apt to be overlaid with misinterpretation. An outstanding example of this is furnished by certain conventions of African wood carving. The type of Yoruba dance mask reproduced in Plate 7 is invariably discussed by Euroamerican art critics as a conventionalization of the human face, wherein the skillful manipulation of masses is achieved through a reworking of the proportions of face and head. Invariably, too, the discussion is based on study of the mask as it is fixed in a perpendicular position, a perspective that does, indeed, bring out the distortions that give rise to the elaborate analyses of much art criticism. It happens, though, that this mask is actually a realistic reproduction of the Negro face, when looked at in the horizontal position in which it is intended to be used. For it is a "mask" only in the sense that it is worn by a person whose identity it aids in concealing. It is worn atop the head, and concealment is achieved by long fiber strands that descend from it to cover the whole body of the wearer. The second photograph of it shows how the Yoruba see it, and how the artist intended it to be seen. Here the "distortion" turns out to be skillful foreshortening, which makes of the presumed stylized presentation an artistic, realistic portrayal. The current interpretation thus becomes a well-intentioned misstatement.

There are numerous examples of forms that are meaningful only by cultural definition, and that lie far toward the more abstract pole of the scale from realism to conventionalization. In some instances, a single motif may be given different interpretations by different artists, or by the different members of the same society who are presented with a design and requested to explain it. Thus, among the Yurok and Karok Indians of California, O'Neale obtained differing explanations for various individual motifs used to decorate their basketry. In the accompanying figure, *A* is called "flint" or "flint-like"; *B* is a snake or a long worm; *C* is "spread finger" or "frog hand"; *D* is variously interpreted as "sharp tooth" or "points."

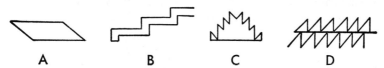

Fig. 26 *Yurok-Karok basketry design elements.* (*After O'Neale, 1932, Fig. 13.*)

Extreme conventionalization in design is found in the art of regions where an attempt is only exceptionally made to achieve realistic portrayal. A striking example of this is found in the wood carvings of the Bush Negroes of Dutch Guiana, where conventionalization is carried to such a degree that, though not difficult to interpret when clues have been provided, the motifs are impossible to understand until the natives themselves can be induced to reveal the significance of the designs traced in low relief or cut through the wood.

These carvings, decorated with symbols that, for the most part, are concerned with fertility, are made by men, and most forms are for presentation to their wives or sweethearts. The tray used for winnowing rice (shown on Plate 8) affords a good example of this type of conventionalization. When first seen by a stranger, the tray suggests nothing; one only perceives the beauty of the individual motifs and the mastery with which the circular space is utilized. To ascribe the meaning given by the Bush Negroes to the total composition or to any of the elements in it defies the most agile imagination.

Yet any Bush Negro can independently interpret this carving in realistic terms. The two large figures on either side of the central line are women. The outer units of these figures are their arms, the inner corresponding elements are their legs. Of the rest of the body, only the vulva is represented, while the small triangular figure represents the male organ. The opposed series of alternating squares cut into the border outside the figures is the hair of the woman, the tacks inserted in the incised design are the cicatrized cuts that are made on the bodies of men and women for purposes of beautification. The two small figures represent the twins it is hoped will be born to these women, for twins are prized in this culture as the bearers of good fortune. The twins, however, are of different sex. At the top of the illustration is the male figure, with a fine line traced about it; the female has no line. Here is an instance of how purely arbitrary conventionalization can be.

At the other end of our scale, we find that realism is by no means absent from the art of nonliterate societies. It tends to be manifest more in three-dimensional figures than in graphic forms,

Fig. 27 *Middle Aurignacian, mural engravings of elk, France. (After MacCurdy, 1924, Fig. 114.)*

though the realistic portrayals of Eskimo engravings caution against too sweeping a generalization in this regard. Often realism and conventionalization are combined by those who work in the same medium, even in the same piece. The metalwork of West Africa illustrates this, as can be seen in the Dahomean brass figures shown in Plate 9. The man hoeing is a realistic presentation; the elephant is conventionalized, and so is the human figure he holds in his trunk, though the agony of the victim is convincingly depicted.

That nonliterate art can, in effect, be portraiture, is shown by the Ife bronze heads that were recovered from the West African Yoruban town of Ife in 1938.[1] Of lifelike dimensions, they have frequently been compared, in the quality of their execution, to Greek sculpture of the classic period. The striations on the face represent the markings that, though no longer made in this form by the Yoruba, are today found among various tribes in northern Nigeria. The male head has a series of holes that mark the line of head hair, moustache, and beard, and it is possible that the realism of the figure was enhanced by inserting hair in these apertures

[1] W. R. Bascom, 1939. These are reproduced in Pl. 10.

Plate 8 *Bush Negro tray used for winnowing rice. See p. 237.*

Plate 9 *Dahomean brass figures. Man in grasp of elephant (height, 6 in.) and mar hoeing (height, 3¾ in.). See p. 238. (Photograph by Mary Modglin, Chicago.)*

much as is done today with masks carved out of wood. The meaning of the woman's diadem with its front ornament can only be conjectured. It might be just a head ornament, or it might be a decoration of ritual significance or a mark of rank.

The question of realism and conventionalization has prominently entered into discussions of the development of art forms. The realism of the Paleolithic cave paintings, which followed earlier strivings toward representational portrayal of animals, has

Fig. 28 *Aurignacian drawing of mammoth on cave wall, Santandar, Spain. (After MacCurdy, 1924, Fig. 116.)*

been stressed as an argument for the beginnings of art in realism. On the other hand, the importance of conventionalization in the art of nonliterate peoples has been urged in support of the opposite position. The problem posed is well worth investigating.

If we look closely at a series of drawings and paintings from the Paleolithic period in France, we see how, beginning with the early Aurignacian and proceeding through the Magdalenian, a continuously greater skill in realistically depicting the upper Paleolithic animals is to be observed. The earliest engravings and drawings on the walls of French and Spanish caves show how realism was limited only by technical inability to suggest depth. The treatment of figures in profile particularly—as the elk in Figure 27, and the mammoth in Figure 28—and the unsolved problem posed by the need to draw all four of the animal's legs, disclose the absence of skill rather than the absence of desire to achieve realistic portrayals.

The wall engraving of a mammoth (Figure 29) and the drawing of a woolly rhinoceros (Figure 30) indicate more flexibility

Fig. 29   *Aurignacian mammoth, from cave wall in the Dordogne, France. (After MacCurdy, 1924, Fig. 117.)*

in the direction of realism. All four legs of each animal are either depicted or suggested, while hair is also indicated and posture is more adequately shown. The end of the mammoth's trunk is especially well done. Yet in both animals the eye is schematized,

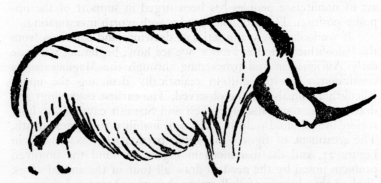

Fig. 30   *Aurignacian wooly rhinocerous, Font-de-Gaume, Dordogne, France. (After MacCurdy, 1924, Fig. 119.)*

and in the case of the mammoth the problem of drawing the trunk so as to conceal the tusk behind it, while concealing the trunk by the tusk in front, was too much for this artist. The treatment of the hind legs also merits scrutiny. The one farthest away from the observer is seen, as it were, through the leg closest to him. This is in contrast to the fidelity with which the hind legs of the rhinoceros are shown.

Later, when Paleolithic art afforded us masterpieces such as the polychrome paintings of bison, reindeer, and other creatures,

Fig. 31 *Magdalenian mural engraving of mammoth, cave of Font-de-Gaume, France. (AfterMacCurdy, 1924, Fig. 122.)*

variation in the artist's skill or conception of how a design is to be executed makes for marked differences in the degree to which realistic portrayal is achieved. Thus the Magdalenian mammoth of Figure 31 may be contrasted with our Aurignacian example. The ear and eye, the treatment of the hair, and the outline of the body indicate a sure hand. Yet the trunk shows through the tusk in front of it, the end of the trunk is not depicted at all, one of the forelegs is barely suggested, and one of the hindlegs is so spindly as to give us a feeling almost of discomfort. Nonetheless, this mammoth was drawn during the period when the techniques in use permitted one prehistoric artist to engrave on horn a stag looking backward, or to demonstrate a greater command of perspective by engraving a moose as viewed from the front (Figures 32 and 33).

The hypothesis of A. C. Haddon, that art styles change from realistic portrayal to symbolic form, is perhaps the best known of those theories that draw on materials from nonliterate peoples for illustrative data. Asserting that "we may recognize three stages of artistic development—origin, evolution, and decay," Haddon develops his conception of the process in the following terms:

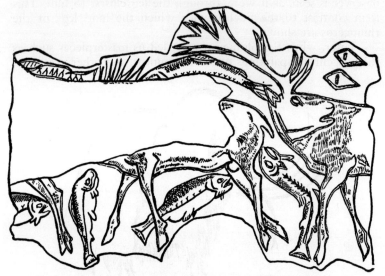

Fig. 32 *Magdalenian stag and salmon, engraved on reindeer horn, France. (After MacCurdy, 1924, Fig. 127.)*

The vast bulk of artistic expression owes its birth to realism; the representations were meant to be life-like, or to suggest real objects; that they may not have been so was owing to the apathy or incapacity of the artist or to the unsuitability of his materials. Once born, the design was acted upon by constraining and restraining forces which gave it, so to speak, an individuality of its own. In the great majority of representations the life-history ran its course through various stages until it settled down to uneventful senility; in some cases, the representation ceased to be—in fact, it died.[2]

This quasi-biological approach was so heavily documented with materials from both historic and non-historic cultures that its wide acceptance by students of art is scarcely surprising. The current of thought at the time it was enunciated was especially hospitable to this view, as evidenced by such earlier studies as those of Holmes on American pottery,[3] or Balfour's analysis of decora-

[2] A. C. Haddon, 1914, p. 7.
[3] W. H. Holmes, 1886, pp. 445 ff.

tive art in general.[4] Best-known of Haddon's illustrative data are the arrows from the Torres Straits area, decorated with carvings representative of the crocodile. The series given in Figure 34 shows how such arrows can be arranged to demonstrate change from realism to conventionalization. In the first of these, marked *A* in Haddon's sketch reproduced there, the long snout can be

Fig. 33 *Magdalenian moose, engraved on reindeer horn, France. (After MacCurdy, 1924, Fig. 136.)*

discerned, though the nostrils projecting above the smooth line that delineates the top of the head are placed one after the other. Behind the head, at the thickest part of the arrow, are the forelimbs, shown as an acute angle, with cross lines at the bottom indicating the claws. Then come the body, represented by vertical lines between which are short horizontal ones; the hind legs, given as an angular line that balances, and is opposed to the forelegs; and finally the tail, indicated by the cross lines or protuberances.

[4] H. Balfour, 1895.

Every part of this design can be followed through from *A* to *F*, each showing a greater degree of conventionalization. In *F*, indeed, it would be impossible for the most assiduous seeker after realistic interpretations to discover any clue to its meaning. As Haddon phrases it: "The front part of the mouth has disappeared; . . . the forelimbs and body are absent. The hindlimbs are narrow, but retain their characteristic forward bend; the dorsal caudal scutes are replaced by numerous parallel transverse lines." [5]

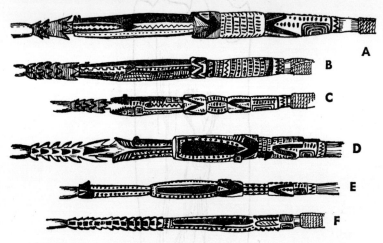

Fig. 34 *Torres Straits "crocodile-arrows and derivatives," as arranged in a presumed developmental series. (After Haddon, 1894, Fig. 19.)*

Does not a series of this sort, then, demonstrate how variations in a design indicate the way in which conventionalization must have developed out of realism? Is this case not made the stronger by the fact that the materials from prehistoric sites, such as the forms we have reproduced, show that the development of art in these early times represented a striving toward ever greater command of techniques that would perfect an ability to portray realistically the creatures that shared man's habitat with him?

Like all other attempts to devise developmental formulae of universal applicability, this one fails both because of its faulty method and its failure to take all the facts into account. Haddon's arrows, or Holmes' pots were arranged in accordance with a scheme that existed *in the mind of the student.* The postulated development has validity only in terms of the hypothesis. All the

[5] A. C. Haddon, 1894, p. 57.

objects belong to the same epoch and do not represent a developmental series in the sense that one item can be shown to have preceded the other.

The development of European Paleolithic art is itself not nearly as clear as would seem from an analysis of the cave paintings alone. Representations of the human figure executed in the round, for example, not only fail to exhibit a parallel develop-

Fig. 35 *The Aurignacian "Venus" of Willendorf, Austria.*

mental sequence, but are restricted to a single period, the Aurignacian. The Aurignacian "Venuses" that date from this epoch are varying conventionalizations, in bas-relief or full sculpture, which always stress them out of all semblance to reality. The head is treated in summary fashion, as are the arms and legs; at most, the hair of the head is indicated by a series of lines. Most famous is the so-called "Venus of Willendorf" (Figure 35). This statuette is intermediate, as regards its degree of realism, between Figure 36, wherein the female figure is treated in a way that approaches normal proportions, and the extreme stylization of Figure 37. In the latter the remarkable handling of masses and proportion that gives

Fig. 36 *Aurignacian "Venus" carved in low relief, from Laussel,*
Dordogne, France. (After MacCurdy, 1924, Fig. 162.)

it its great distinction entails so wide a departure from reality that its character as a human form must be read into it.

A similar range is to be found in the graphic arts of the Upper Paleolithic. The developing realism of the several epochs, culmi-

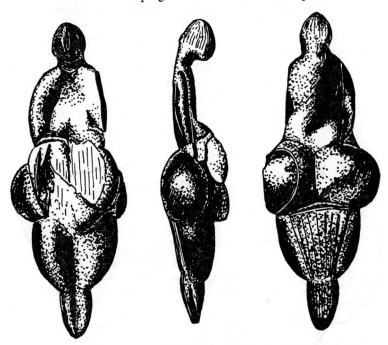

Fig. 37 *Aurignacian figurine in ivory, known as the "Venus" of Lespugue, Haute-Garonne, France; front, side and rear views. (After MacCurdy, 1924, Fig. 159.)*

nating in the polychrome paintings of the Magdalenian, takes an impressionistic turn in engraving on stone, bone, and horn. The herd of reindeer depicted by a Magdalenian artist on the wing bone of an eagle (Figure 38) is justly famous. Except for the three

Fig. 38 *Upper Magdalenian engraving of reindeer herd on wing bone of an eagle, France. (After MacCurdy, 1924, Fig. 131.)*

front animals shown in this composition, and the one at the rear, a realistic portrayal is not even attempted. The similar treatment of a herd of horses (Figure 39), engraved on stone, from a different locality than that in which the other composition was found, is evidence that it was more than a local development or the idiosyncrasy of an individual artist.

Boas has shown how, in Mexico, "factory production and . . . slovenly execution" have operated to effect a cycle from realism, through meaningless form, to realistic execution in the decoration of certain types of wooden and calabash dishes. These dishes are painted orange and then overlaid with designs in green. Older specimens, made of wood, wherein the motifs consist of animal forms or fish, are excellently executed. Later workmanship,

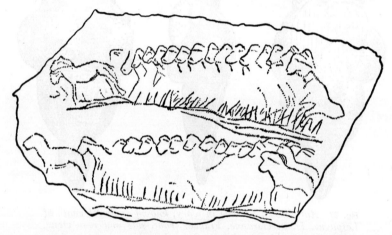

Fig. 39 *Upper Magdalenian herd of horses, engraved on stone, Vienne, France. (After MacCurdy, 1924, Fig. 132.)*

however, is far inferior and shows a decided change in the original design. In some cases, there seems to be a reinterpretation, though whether through misunderstanding or the process of "the substitution of new subject matter for old, in which process the new subject was rightly controlled by the old, stereotyped form" [6] cannot be stated. The series Boas has reproduced demonstrate how changes of this order can occur. In the instance of these plates (Figure 40), the fish that in the earlier forms were painted lying horizontally within a circular frame broke down into an almost meaningless design. This design then seems to have been reinterpreted as an equal number of leaves, placed

[6] F. Boas, 1927, p. 131.

about the outer edge of the circle, this time enclosing an inner circle within which a new, flowerlike unit has been introduced.

It is apparent from our discussion that no developmental principle of universal applicability concerning any tendency to move toward conventionalization from realism, or toward realism from abstract design, can be established. Rather the principle of consistent change in either direction, or both, is the rule. Hasty manufacture, ineptitude in the use of the medium, calculated "abbreviations" of various kinds may, as we have seen, cause a form

Fig. 40 *Transformation of designs painted on calabash dishes, Oaxaca, Mexico. (After Boas, 1927, Fig. 122.)*

realistically conceived to break down into conventionalized, symbolic variants. On the other hand, a combination of lines, the protuberances on a rock, or any other kind of fortuitous form may have significance read into it by the imaginative mind and gradually come to be accepted as meaningful by all members of a society, who thereupon may move toward realism in its portrayal. In this, as probably in all other instances of change in art convention, the considerations of an established style and the customary media prevail. We, therefore, turn next to a discussion of art style, since this is one of the central problems in the study of any art.

3

The art of one people, one epoch, one artist, even, is marked off from another essentially by its style. Under situations that might be considered conducive to change, an art style can often show great tenaciousness. Yet, its resistance to change does not preclude continuous developments that may markedly alter a

Fig. 41 *Analysis of forms of Admiralty Island wooden bowls. (After Reichard, 1933, Vol. I, Fig. 1.)*

style over a relatively short period of time. In the art of Euroamerican societies we are accustomed to trace the "periods" in the work of certain individual artists, as for example when we describe the art of such painters as Renoir, Picasso, or Braque. Even in cultures more stable than that of Europe and America of the twentieth century, changes in artistic style are everywhere discernible, as in the decorations on the pottery of the Indians of southwestern United States.

The analysis of style, it must be clear, can be carried on quite without reference to the significance of art forms to the people of the culture where they are produced. We have, in this particular instance, a parallel to our dual approach to the study of culture as a whole—the psychological and the institutional. In the first of these approaches, as in the study of symbolism in art, meaning is indispensable to comprehension. In the second, we are concerned with the forms institutions take—forms that, like elements in style, can be analyzed without reference to their meaning for the people who live in terms of them.

A study of the stylistic conventions of Melanesian art offers an excellent illustration of how the graphic and plastic arts can be analyzed from this objective point of view. Admiralty Island natives carve wooden bowls which can be divided into three formal types. The first of these types are round bowls, resting on feet or stands of different kinds (Figure 42). The unity of style these bowls show in their outline can be seen in the diagram given here, as well as the variation found within the limits of this style, and

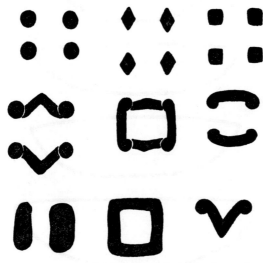

Fig. 42   *Analysis of rests of Admiralty Island wooden bowls. (After Reichard, 1933, Vol. I, Fig. 2.)*

the variety of their feet and stands. Bowls of the second type have realistic handles carved from the same piece of wood as the bowl, and thicker rims. A third type has carvings of birds and animals, executed in realistic enough fashion to make possible their identification. These bowls, in their outline as well as their decoration, follow a style that is distinct from the style of similar bowls, shown in Figure 43, from the small island of Tami (Cretin) off eastern New Guinea. Here the form of the bowls is round; they rest on no legs and have no handles. The outlined forms show their contrast with the Admiralty Islands types.

The style of an art is what permits the expert to tell where a given piece was made, or from what period of a given culture it derives, or the "school" to which he belonged, or even the name of the individual artist who produced it. It is possible, on the basis of style, to set off art provinces in terms of the distribution of forms similar to each other.[7] This broad view of style is especially useful where the differentiation of specimens of unknown provenience is involved. A Southwest pot among a collection of Guiana Indian pottery stands out in unmistakable contrast; but one who knows the pottery of the Southwest can do more than recognize

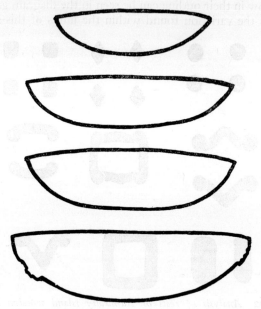

Fig. 43 *Analysis of shapes of wooden bowls from Tami Island. (After Reichard, 1933, Vol. 1, Fig. 13.)*

it as coming from that area. He can identify the pueblo from which it derived, and perhaps even the period when it was made.

In one early work on African art, its author included four illustrations of carved pieces that, to one familiar with the various styles of carving done by nonliterate peoples, were obviously not from the continent of Africa but rather from the Marquesan Islands.[8] Certainly, the proportions of head and body, and the treatment of arms, legs, and torso in pieces of the type illustrated in that work (reproduced in Figure 44), bear enough surface resemblances to trick the unwary. No sooner, however, do we inspect certain outstanding details of the carvings than critical

[7] Cf., P. S. Wingert, 1950, *passim.*
[8] C. Einstein, 1920, pp. 42, 43, 79, 86.

differences appear. The African wood carver does not stylize the hand and fingers in the manner of the Marquesan carver, nor does he represent the ear in the same way. No one who has handled any appreciable number of carvings can mistake the art of one area in this medium for that of the other.

How tenacious stylistic elements may be is apparent when art forms from one culture are treated by artists of another. The style of wood carving of the New Zealand Maori is characterized by the application of intricate patterns, derived from tattooing, to the object that is to be decorated. A piece from the Chicago Natural History Museum, which shows a bone carving, and a wooden figure, now in the Copenhagen Ethnographic Museum, shown in Plates 11b and 11c, illustrate the basic pattern. A striking example of this is from Benin, in West Africa, a culture whose bronzes and ivory carvings are famous in the world of art. Benin was first visited by Europeans in the fifteenth century. Its workers in bronze had such mastery of their medium and such disciplined perceptiveness of significant detail that they have left realistic portrayals of the Portuguese harquebusiers of the period —helmet, breastplate, short pleated tunic, and weapons. In the treatment of the face in representations of Europeans in those bronzes, the long, narrow nose is accurately portrayed, but the nostrils flare after the African conventions of this art.

A Benin container is shown in Figure 45 and Plate 12; the top has been lost, but holes for its attachment remain. The central figure is Christ on the cross. The head is carved with representations of the type of moustache, beard, and hair style of the sixteenth century; the body proportions are those of European art of the period. Two doves, representing the Holy Ghost, are found in the squares above the upper arms of the cross, stylized in a manner more African than European. Below them, on the left, is Mary, in an attitude of prayer; to the right, Saint John with his chalice. The bonnet of the female figure and the ruff of the male are recognizable as the European dress of the time. From left to right, the four other figures that fill the rest of the space represent saints, each being marked by his appropriate symbol—Saint Paul, with a sword; Saint John (a second time), with his chalice; Saint Andrew, with the particular type of cross associated with him; and Saint Peter, with the key. All this is mainly European. The total composition, however, is conceived in a manner quite African, while the decorations that frame the figures and outline the cross, and particularly the intercrossed curving lines at the bottom, can be seen in many Benin pieces.

Fig. 44 *Marquesan carved figure (right) included in a work on African art, and an African figure (left) from same work. (After Einstein, 1920, Pls. 79 and 86.)*

The directives laid down by any traditional style govern the artist even as he introduces change into its art forms. In every society the artist is the experimenter, the innovator, the rebel. But he is an innovator only within bounds, for he is all unwittingly influenced by factors that guide him in his creative experience, as they guide the behavior of all human beings in every aspect of their lives. Indeed, just because in playing with his technique the artist inevitably experiments, as a result of his virtuosity, he effec-

Fig. 45 *Designs on Benin container.*

tively reveals to the student of culture the force of cultural conditioning.

It is important to stress this function of the artist in inducing change, especially where the art of nonliterate peoples is under discussion, because stability, rather than change, is generally emphasized when these art forms are being considered. It has even been seriously contended that the nonliterate carver, potter, or painter is not a creative artist at all, but rather a copyist, who slavishly follows the designs laid down for him by some gifted ancestor. Nothing, however, could be further from the truth, as any field investigator can attest.

For an example of change in a specific form, we may take the appliqué cloths of Dahomey. These cloths are made as wall hangings for chiefs, with motifs drawn from the life of the people. The sewing is done by men who belong to a cloth sewer's hereditary guild. The guild has in its possession the patterns of a large series of motifs. When a cloth is being designed, the subject matter and its thematic sequence are first decided upon; then, the requisite motifs are grouped and regrouped on the ground until a satisfying composition is realized.

Reproduced in Plate 13 are four cloths that show how a subject has been successively altered in its treatment by men of four generations. The theme is a lion hunt. The first of the series was made by the grandfather of the contemporary chief of the guild for the Dahomean king who reigned from 1858 to 1889. The son of the originator criticized the earlier conception on the ground that it paid insufficient honor to this feline, associated as it is with royalty, to have it attacked by men armed only with clubs. He therefore placed bows and arrows in their hands and also omitted the prey held in the mouth of the animal in the original. The chief from whom the series was acquired felt, in his turn, that the cloth made by his father lacked dramatic quality, and he radically altered the composition to show one of the hunters caught by the beast. He also emphasized its power and heightened the struggle between hunters and hunted by equipping the hunters with guns and machetes; and he portrayed the lion with greater realism. The final revision was made by the son of this man, his potential successor as chief of the guild. Among other changes, the young man added a third human figure to the attacking group and improved the treatment of the lion by outlining it with a strip of cloth so as to separate the black of the lion's body from the gold of the background.

The problem of the artist as experimenter within the limits set by the conventions of the art of his society has been exhaustively studied among the Pueblo Indians by Bunzel. Writing of the Zuñi, she says.

> Although the women do not recognize any very definite proprietorship in designs, every potter claims that she can distinguish readily between the work of her fellow artists. "I can always tell by looking at a jar who made it." One Zuñi woman was more explicit: "If I painted my bowls like every one else, I might lose my bowl when I took dinner to the dancers in the plaza. I am the only person who makes a checkerboard design around the rim, so I can always tell my bowl by looking at the edge." [9]

A Hopi Indian potter described the sources of her design in this way: "I am always thinking about designs, even when I am doing other things, and whenever I close my eyes, I see designs in front of me. I often dream of designs, and whenever I am ready to paint, I close my eyes and then the designs just come to me. I paint them as I see them." An Acoma artist remarked: "I like all

[9] R. Bunzel, 1929, pp. 64–5.

kinds of designs. My jars are all different. I don't make the same
design twice. Sometimes I make two or three alike, but not often.
I don't like to do that." [10] Statements of this kind must be taken
in conjunction with the criticisms leveled against designs that lie
outside the range of the accepted pattern, as recorded from these
Indians and from artists of other societies. They thus further
clarify how, whatever the talents of an artist, his creativeness will
express itself along lines laid down by the established art style of
his culture, within the limits of which he must work.

4

The elements that go to make up a style are termed the formal aspects of art. They include all manifestations of form that
can be expressed graphically or plastically—rhythm, symmetry,
the use of color. Designs may be conceived as horizontal or vertical—though this is less often found. They may be adapted to a
circular form, as in a pot or a basket; in such instances their movement may be clockwise or counterclockwise. The medium is itself a determinant of form. This is apparent when attempts are
made to reproduce figures realistically in such media as basketry
or weaving. The representations of human and animal forms
woven by the Cayapa Indians of Ecuador (Figure 46) offer a
case in point. Here conventionalization is imposed by the difficulties inherent in weaving a curved line. This control over expression is to be contrasted with the relative freedom of the artist
to depict figures realistically—always in terms of the stylistic
patterns of his art—when he paints designs on pottery or wood
or some other background or when he carves.

The supreme mastery of technique of the outstanding artist
of any culture permits him to experiment with the formal elements
recognized by the conventions of the art of his society. Without
this virtuosity in the use of the materials at the artist's command,
there could be no great art. Much of the appeal of art arises out
of this fact. What attracts the person who sees specimens of an
art unfamiliar to him is the skill with which they have been executed—the juxtaposition of color values, the manipulation of elements of form that comes from the long acquaintance of the
creator of a given piece with the materials he employs.

One point to be stressed, however, is that virtuosity in one
medium or one art style does not by any means imply command
of another. This is particularly true when the new medium is
strange to the artist and derives from the conventions of a different

[10] *Ibid.*, pp. 51–2.

culture. When an artist in a nonliterate culture, therefore, is given pencil and paper and asked to sketch a scene, he produces a series of crude outlines. Such drawings have too often been cited to bolster the specious identification of "primitive art" with the productions of our children, or of psychoneurotics. Yet the

Fig. 46 *Stylizations of human and animal forms woven by Cayapa Indians of Ecuador.* (A) *and* (B) *human beings;* (C) *monkey;* (D) *horse;* (E) *deer;* (F) *dog;* (G) *spider;* (H) *toad.* (*After Barrett, 1925, Pl. 123.*)

"primitive" man's crudities are no more crude than the drawings of artistically untutored "civilized" men and women. This has been demonstrated by Cameron, who asked "scientifically trained adults," in this case staff physicians of The Johns Hopkins Hospital, to draw "certain objects from memory" when each was alone and at leisure. These drawings were to be of "a girl pushing a baby-carriage" and of "a man on horseback." [11] When presented

[11] N. Cameron, 1938, *passim.*

with this novel request, these scientifically but not artistically trained men did what the nonliterate artist who is unaccustomed

Fig. 47 *"Girl Pushing a Baby Carriage." Drawing by a scientifically trained adult. (After Cameron, 1938, Fig. 1.)*

to pencil and paper does—they produced drawings that, as can be seen from the reproductions of them given here, are essentially childlike in character. However skilled the artist may be in his

Fig. 48 *"Girl Pushing a Baby Carriage." Drawing by a scientifically trained adult. (After Cameron, 1938, Fig. 6.)*

own medium, virtuosity counts for nothing in one foreign to him. He is a novice in this new form, and he draws like one.

The skill of the artist will not be called on vainly if he is given enough opportunity to master the new medium. There is

Fig. 49 *Two drawings, "Man on Horseback," by scientifically trained adults. The one on the right is by an experienced horseman. (After Cameron, 1938, Figs. 4 and 5.)*

substantial evidence in hand from various cultures to illustrate this. For example, the Indians of the Southwest, through contact with the whites, have come to know the use of water colors and have learned to be at ease in this medium. They paint the masked figures of their sacred rites, the *kachinas*, singly or in groups, and

Fig. 50 *Basic double-curve motifs in Northeastern Algonkian art. (After Speck, 1914, Fig. 1.)*

paint them so well that these representations have become collectors' items. In other words, proficiency in a medium is built on experience, and a long tradition in its use frees the artist to achieve mastery and to express himself creatively. Some media taken over

Fig. 51 *Elaboration of two basic double-curve Northeastern Algonkian motifs. (After Speck, 1914, Pls. 1, 2, 4, and 17.)*

cross-culturally will lend themselves to ready adaptation by artists working in a culture that is hospitable to playing with new techniques; some will be rejected or will be used crudely. But regardless of the degree of responsiveness to a foreign medium or art style, the criterion of success or failure in taking over something new involves neither a problem of inherent competence nor of maturity.

Within a culture, the way elements of form are built up into a composition that is in consonance with the patterns of a particular style is to be seen in the intricate designs that mark the decorative art of the Northeastern Algonkian Indians. The basic motif is a "double-curve" unit, "consisting of two opposed in-curves as a foundation element, with embellishments modifying the enclosed space, and with variations in the shape and propor-

Fig. 52 *Elaboration of Northeastern Algonkian double-curve motif as found on Penobscot cradleboard. (After Speck, 1914, Fig. 3.)*

tions of the whole." Some of the varieties of the "primary foundation element" are given in Figure 50. This simple beginning, we are told, is "capable of being subjected to such a variety of augments, not infrequently distortive, as to become scarcely recognizable at first or second sight." [12] This, in a very real sense, represents the playing of the virtuoso with the thematic materials of the style in which he works. It can be seen further if series of double-curve designs are graded in accordance with their complexity, as in Figure 51. How far the process can go is shown by the modifications introduced in this decoration of a Penobscot cradleboard:

A discussion of art forms brings up the question of the relation between form and function in art, or, as it is sometimes phrased, between the forms of a given art and the media in which they are expressed. "Primitive" art, it is sometimes maintained,

[12] F. G. Speck, 1914, p. 1.

does not stray outside the requirements of the media in which the artist works—the wood carver emphasizes mass and does not attempt delicate traceries. The fact of the matter, however, is

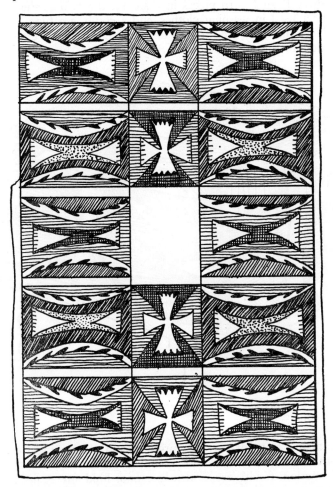

Fig. 53 *Design on Sauk and Fox Indian rawhide box before folding. (After Boas, 1927, Fig. 13.)*

that such an assumption is no more valid than any generalization about nonliterate cultures considered as a whole and in opposition to the historic cultures.

No carving could be less characterized by solidity than the

ceremonial wooden statues of New Ireland (Plate 14), which quite refute statements that "primitives" in some mystical way "feel" certain qualities of the medium in which they work. Of the three Bush Negro pieces in Plate 15, the two at the top, a pounder used in washing clothes, and a comb, are functional in the sense that they are fitted to do the things they were made to do, despite the embellishments they bear. But the piece at the

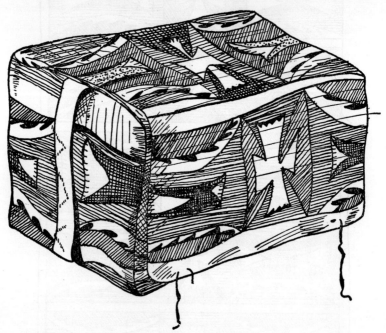

Fig. 54 *Sauk and Fox Indian rawhide box, folded. (After Boas, 1927, Fig. 12.)*

bottom is a tray for carrying produce and winnowing rice. Its cut-through designs, therefore, completely rule out the winnowing function, for it very evidently cannot hold any grain. From the standpoint of the villagers, however, it was one of the most beautiful examples of their art, both because of the excellence they recognized in its design and the artistry of its execution.

If the concept of art for art's sake is unique to our culture, in practice all cultures produce examples of art forms where utilitarian needs are disregarded, or where the aesthetic impulse refuses to be bound by the distortions of design in an object destined for use. Two instances cited by Boas afford illustrations of this. The first has to do with the rawhide boxes made by the Sauk and Fox Indians, which are decorated with symmetrical units that make a pleasing design on the hide as it lies flat. However, once these hides are folded to make the box, only a portion

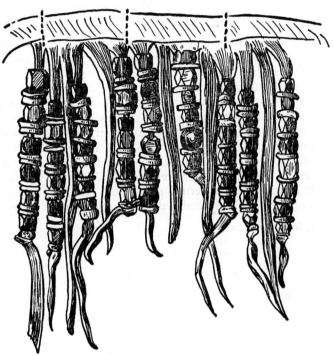

Fig. 55 *Fringe from legging, Thompson Indians, British Columbia. (After Boas, 1927, Fig. 16.)*

of the design is visible. The units that are then seen stand in no artistic relation to each other, since the totality of the composition is quite lost.

The second instance concerns the beadwork decorations on the fringe along the outer seam of leggings of a Thompson River Indian.

These strips are decorated in rhythmic order, a string decorated by one glass bead and two bone beads in alternating order is followed by a plain string, next by one alternating glass and bone beads, then a plain one and finally one like the first. When we indicate the plain and decorated strips by letters, we find the arrangement . . . /ABCBA/ABCBA/ . . . repeated over and over again. The important point to be noted is, that when in use, the fringe hangs down without order along the outer side of the leg so that the elaborate rhythmic pattern cannot be seen. The only way in which the maker can get any satisfaction from her work is while making it or when exhibiting it to her friends. When it is in use, there is no aesthetic effect.[13]

We may say, then, that in all societies the aesthetic impulse finds expression in terms of the standards of beauty laid down in the traditions of the people. Where art is close to life, as it is in all nonliterate cultures and in many strata of literate societies, the technical virtuosity of the artists will be lavished on objects of everyday use, far more than may be the case with the forms we classify as "pure" art. But whatever forms art may take, however it is manifested, it will be present. No art, that is, is haphazard or chaotic. It is the expression of the desire for beauty that finds fulfillment in the application of technical skill through sanctioned form, in terms of the patterned perceptions and imaginative resources of the artistically endowed members of every society.

[13] F. Boas, 1927, p. 29.

Chapter **Fourteen**

Folklore, Drama, and Music

The folklore of nonliterate peoples consists of their myths, tales, proverbs, riddles, and verse, together with their music; and comprises the least tangible expression of the aesthetic aspects of culture. To varying degrees, these forms combine with each other and with the graphic and plastic arts, to make up the rituals, dances, and other means of group expression we term drama.

The separation of stories into such general categories as myth and tale cannot be done validly for folklore as a whole. The tale of the ant and the grasshopper, made familiar by La Fontaine, is a moralizing fable, its moral conveyed, and its climax reached, when the hard-working ant says to the carefree grasshopper: "He who sings in summer will not eat in winter." A tale told by the Shuswap Indians of western North America is obviously derived from this story. Like other American Indians, the Shuswap only rarely moralize in their tales. The La Fontaine fable here becomes an explanatory myth. As the Shuswap tell it, a grasshopper-man refuses to help his tribe catch salmon for the winter—he prefers to dance and to eat grass. When winter comes, and the grass is covered with snow, he goes everywhere begging for food, but he is told to go and eat grass. Half-dead of hunger, he transforms himself into the creature that bears his name. And it is ordained that ". . . since you are lazy, you shall eat only grass and you will pass your existence jumping here and there as you make your noise." [1]

Another instance of change, in this case showing how a tale can lose its sacred character and become explanatory, is found in the Zuñi Indian version of the Biblical account of the Flight into Egypt and the birth of Jesus. In a culture where stress is laid on fertility, Jesus is translated into twins. Where the original re-counts the persecution of Herod, Mary, who becomes a Mexican girl, is pursued by "soldiers"—volunteers who, in Zuñi ritual practice, guard the saints. The tale is as follows:

> In the West, there lived a Mexican girl who never went out. She staid all the time in her own house. She would sit where the sun shone in. The sun . . . "gave her a child." At this time, the soldiers were guarding her. One of the soldiers saw her, and said to the others, "The one we are guarding is pregnant. If she does such things, what is the use of guarding her? Let us kill her!" The next day in the morning she was to die. That evening the Sun by his knowledge came into her room, and said, "Tomorrow you are to die."—"Well, if it is to be, I must die," she said. He said, "No, I won't let you die, I will get you out." The next morning early by his knowledge he lifted her up out of the window. "Now go to where you are to live." So she went on till she came to a *sipaloa* planting. She said, "What are you planting?" He said, "Round stones." Because he did not answer right, she did some-thing to the seed, and his corn did not come up. She went on a little ways, and she came to another one planting. She asked him what he was planting. He said, "I am planting corn and wheat." Because he answered her right, she did nothing to his seed, and they all came up. Then the soldiers found she was gone, and they came on after her. They asked the first man if he had seen a girl coming. He said, "Yes, she has just gone over the hill." They said, "Well, we must be nearly up with her, we will hurry on." So they went on over the hill, and they saw no one. They came to another little hill, and they could not see her. They came to a river, and it was very deep. They cut some poles, and they said, "We'll see how deep it is." They stuck the poles down, and they said, "It is too deep. There is no use in hunting any more for her." So they turned back. But the girl had crossed the river, and went on until she came to Kluwela, and there she lay in. She had twins. The pigs and dogs kissed her. That is why the pigs and the dogs have children. The mules would not kiss her. That is why the mules have no children. [2]

[1] This tale is recounted by A. Van Gennep, 1920, p. 74.
[2] E. C. Parsons, 1918, pp. 258-9.

All stories are composed of three elements—character, incident, and plot. These elements are independently variable, and can move in new groupings and in any combination. Even in the same culture, different characters will be found performing the same sequence of acts that constitute the incidents which, in turn, make up a specific plot. Or a given character may move from tale to tale, and become involved in the most diverse kinds of situations that are combined into many plots. This is why the cataloging of *motifs* and the analysis of *variants* is so important a part of the work of the folklorist.

Tales are great travelers. One of the most fascinating and profitable tasks in the study of folklore is to see how, in their travels, they have been altered to fit a new natural setting and a new cultural matrix. Some stories have a distribution that is almost literally world-wide. For instance, the "Magic Flight" tale is found in Europe and Asia, in aboriginal North and South America, in Africa and among New World Negroes. Basically the story concerns a girl, or two sisters, pursued by an evil being. The only protection the girls have is a comb, a glass, and one other object, such as a red cloth, that have magic power. As the pursuer, steadily gaining on the fugitives, is heard to approach, first the comb is thrown down, whereupon a forest appears through which the ogre must cut his way. As he again gains in his pursuit, the glass is thrown down, and becomes a lake he must cross. Eventually, the pursuit fails and the girl or sisters live in peace.

It should be apparent from those examples that folk tales are more than the literary expression of a people. They constitute, in a very real sense, their ethnography; if systematized by the student, they give a penetrating picture of a given way of life. This was demonstrated by Boas in his study of the myths of the Tsimshian Indians of the Pacific Northwest. From this great collection of myths are abstracted descriptions of Tsimshian material culture, economy, social structures, and religious beliefs, accounts of the life cycle of the individual, of secret societies, of the prestige-giving contests of economic waste known as the potlatch; of their ethical concepts and emotional life.[3] Thus literary expression, in whatever form it exists, draws its materials from the experience of its creators, giving us what Boas termed an "autobiography of the tribe." The artist who uses words as his medium, no less than the artist who works with paints or in wood or stone, acts as a creature of his culture; his responses are always relative to its formal patterns, and his values reflect its underlying values.

[3] F. Boas, 1909–10.

A folk tale that incorporates details of an earlier period in the history of the people who tell it, documents that earlier life. The stories of the Pueblo Indians, where the characters go in and out of rooms by the use of ladders, describe an earlier period when Pueblo structures had no doors or windows. Many of the fairy tales we ourselves tell, of kings and queens, princes and knights, represent the living lore of an earlier period of our own culture. It is interesting to speculate, for instance, on the age of such a story as "Little Red Riding Rood," which, because of its forest setting, makes us wonder whether it is perhaps not a legacy of late prehistoric times.

In addition to reflecting the life of a people as of the period when a given story of a living lore is told, folklore also reveals much about their aspirations, values, and goals. It has been seen how the emphasis on fertility of the Zuñi Indians is reflected in the turn these people give the Biblical nativity tale. Many other instances, drawn out of tales that are not the result of contact with a foreign people, can be given. The myths of the inhabitants of the Pacific Islands stress rank, a consideration that dominates their lives. Different forms of address are employed for chief and commoner. The demands of protocol strictly regulate the place of each individual at ceremonies and at secular gatherings. Polynesian mythology treats the universe in terms congenial to this fundamental pattern. Creation is conceived as an orderly process, having a kind of evolutionary character, wherein each phenomenon appears in proper sequence, to achieve a stratified universe that begins with chaos and ends with the existing order of things. Among most North American tribes, in contrast, there is no hierarchy of beings, no chaos to be ordered into the present scene by the will of a creator. And this, it is not too much to assume, is not unrelated to the absence of ruling classes.

The flexibility in personal relations that marks the Indian's contacts with his fellows, organized as these people are in small tribal units, is further reflected by the absence of the moralizing tale and the proverb. These forms, in contrast, dominate African folklore. Particularly in West Africa, the mythology reveals the underlying motivations and drives that support the highly integrated social structures characteristic of the continent. Here, too, are reflected the attitudes of a sophisticated and perhaps cynical view of human relations, which dictate probing for the underlying motive for an act, even when it is in no way hostile. We understand this attitude better, for instance, when, as in Dahomey, we hear the widespread myth that tells how, in creating the world,

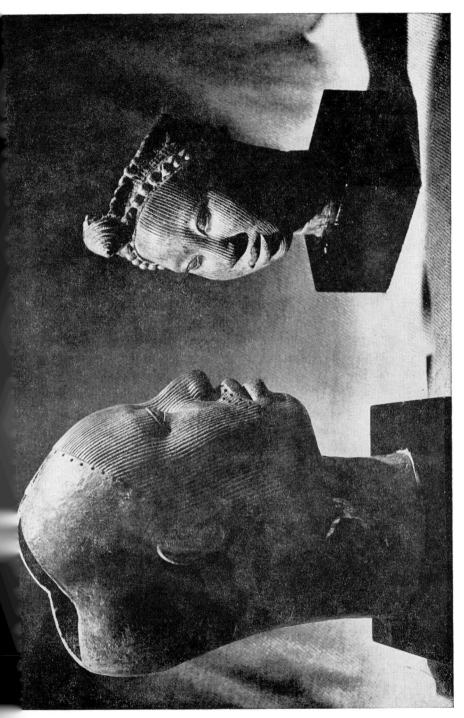

e 10 *Bronze heads from Ife, western Nigeria, collected by W. R. Bascom. Fe-*
e head (height, 9¾ in.) and male head (height, 12½ in.). See p. 238. (Photograph
Mary Modglin, Chicago.)

A

B

C

Plate 11a *Admiralty Island bowl. See p. 251.* **Plate 11b** *Maori bone carving. S p. 253. (Photographs 11a and 11b courtesy Chicago Natural History Museum* **Plate 11c** *Maori carving, showing tattooing designs. See p. 253. (Photograph co tesy Royal Ethnographic Museum, Copenhagen.)*

and dividing the work of administering it to lesser gods, the Creator, whose children these deities are conceived to be, gave each a separate language to ensure that no conspiracy be formed to take over ultimate power. Or, again, it is revealing to learn that though the Creator endowed these lesser beings with extensive powers, especially of discipline and destruction, the power to create was never given over, lest terrible creatures might be given life, to prey on mankind.

Folklore also gives us clues to the hidden reactions to social sanctions that on the surface seem to be complied with willingly enough. In this, indeed, we find a psychoanalytic mechanism at work, wherein customary behavior is often distorted in a manner that tells us much about the desires individuals must suppress in order to conform. It is enough in this connection to mention how, in Indonesian and Melanesian groups where rigid brother-sister sexual taboos obtain, the origin-myths often tell of the beginning of mankind in the incestuous relation of a brother and sister.

One of the earlier folklorists, Andrew Lang, was so struck by this phenomenon of ascribing to deities conduct abhorrent to mortals, that he considered at length the problem of the bestial traits of the godly characters in many of the mythologies. Though his resulting theory has with time come to be rejected, there is little question that the gods of many a mythology do violate the codes of behavior by which men must live. As we see it today, these stories afford an impressive documentation of the hypothesis that we derive powerful satisfactions from identifying ourselves, all unconsciously, with characters who transgress the codes we ourselves may not violate.

Another manifestation of how folklore creates a world where vindications that the world of reality denies are granted is to be found in the stories wherein the weak prevail over the strong, where evil meets an avenger, or where the less pleasant conditions of life are resolved in ways that are not of the workaday world. This is no different from the release afforded in Euroamerican culture by the novel, the theater, the motion picture. By transporting men and women into a realm where problems are solved as they rarely are in actual life, folklore shows itself as a many-faceted vehicle of psychological release and creative self-expression on both the conscious and unconscious levels.

2

When we define folklore as the literary arts, or better, the language arts, of a culture, we depart from the conventional definition which, particularly in England, the continent of Europe, and Latin America, has tended to hold closely to the implications of its original statement.

The word "folklore" was first employed in a letter signed by Ambrose Merton, published in *The Athenaeum* of London, August 22, 1846. Its writer, who used this pseudonym for his real name, William J. Thoms, urged that accounts of "the manners, customs, observances, superstitions, ballads, proverbs, &c. of the olden time" be recorded so that later students could turn for information to these dying remnants of the unrecorded past that were termed "popular Antiquities, or Popular Literature." In Europe, where peasant populations preserved customs of an earlier period, there was a real place for the systematic, scholarly investigation of ways of life that no longer survived among urban people. In the United States, however, the customs of peasant Europe had been given over in the westward thrust of the frontier.

When, therefore, in 1888, the American Folklore Society was founded, of the four categories of "the fast-vanishing remains of Folklore in America" that were set up as the objects of study, only one, "Relics of Old English Folk-lore (ballads, tales, superstitions, dialect, etc.)," was equivalent to the content of folklore as it was conceived in the Old World. The "Lore of Negroes in the Southern States of the Union," turned out to comprise literary forms to a predominant degree, and so, in practice at least, were the materials collected under the heading "Lore of French Canada, Mexico, etc." But the other category, "Lore of Indian Tribes of North America, (myths, tales, etc.)," made it necessary to distinguish between literary and other aspects of culture. The original statement reads:

> Here the investigation has to deal with whole nations, scattered over a continent. The harvest does not consist of scattered gleanings, the relics of a crop once plentiful, but, unhappily, allowed to perish ungarnered; on the contrary, it remains to be gathered, if not in the original abundance, still in ample measure. Systems of myth, rituals, feasts, sacred customs, games, songs, tales, exist in such profusion that volumes would be required to contain the lore of each separate tribe.[4]

The validity of this conclusion came to be recognized even by those students of folklore who accepted the original formulation

[4] For an extended account of this development, see M. J. Herskovits, 1946. The quotations are from the *Journal of American Folklore*, Vol. I (1888), pp. 2–5.

of the field, once they went to those parts of the world where nonliterate peoples lived in accordance with aboriginal custom. In these instances, vestiges of ways of life no longer current could not be found, as they could for the rural dwellers of Europe. The Maypole dance, the Christmas tree, wishing on the new moon, beliefs about witches and black cats, the rituals at the laying of cornerstones—all these manifestations of earlier European belief were legitimately to be regarded as "folk-custom" and studied in terms of the frame of reference laid down by Ambrose Merton. But in Africa and Australia and the South Seas, as among the North American Indians, the distinction between folklore and other aspects of culture—that is to say, the distinction between folklore and ethnography—had to be drawn. This, from the anthropological point of view, is the basis for the limitation of folklore to the forms indicated in the beginning of this chapter.

Yet these forms—myth, tale, proverb, riddle, and verse—are not by any means to be thought of as a monopoly of nonliterate peoples. All societies have their lore. The tenacity of such tales, even where writing is prevalent and formal literary values dominate, is impressive. Consider, for example, the "moron" stories that were popular during World War II, of which a typical instance follows:

> Two morons were fishing. They pulled in lots of fish. In the evening one said, "You'd better mark this place." When they got to the pier, the first one asked, "Did you mark it?" "Yes, I put a cross on the side of the boat just over the fishing hole." "You fool! How do you know we'll get this boat tomorrow?" [5]

Almost exactly the same tale is heard in Brazil, where stories that parallel many "moron" tales are told to make sport of the Portuguese:

> João and Manoel were out fishing, and found a spot where the catch was especially good. "Be sure and mark the spot, so we can come here tomorrow," said João. Manoel took a piece of chalk from his pocket, and made a large "X" on the side of the boat. As they were rowing in, João asked, "Did you mark the spot carefully?" "Yes, see the cross on the side of the boat?" "You fool, you! Don't you know we'll have a different boat tomorrow?"

Few who laugh at these stories realize their age. Yet we find this very tale in the European Till Eulenspiegel trickster cycle,

[5] L. J. Davidson, 1943, p. 101.

popular since the Middle Ages. In the equivalent version, Till tricks a man, who thinks he hears the drums beating war, into joining him in raising a false alarm in the city of Schoppenstadt. The burghers fear that the beautiful new bell in the courthouse steeple, if captured, will be melted to make gun barrels. Till advises that it be sunk in the sea.

> Another of the councilmen spoke. "How will we be able to tell where we have sunk the bell, when the time comes to bring it up again?" he asked. "You need have no worries on that account," answered Till. "Come with me and I will show you how to mark the place." All the men of Schoppenstadt gathered together and in a short time they had unfastened the bell. They put it into a boat and rowed a little way out to sea. Here they lifted the bell and lowered it over the side of the boat. "Now," said Till, "I will show you how we will mark the spot." He took a knife from his pocket and cut a notch on the side of the boat. "When you want to raise the bell, you need only to row out here again, and you will find the bell right under the notch in the side of the boat." [6]

There are a number of problems in the study of folklore, especially those that treat of its purely structural values, of which considerations of space forbid more than passing mention. One problem bearing on folklore as a cultural phenomenon, whose study aids significantly in understanding the culture of which it is a part, concerns the distribution of tales and their constituent parts. Each tale, in itself a cluster of elements that are independently variable, yields materials for the understanding of how any complex of cultural traits can vary in transmission from one people to another. Again, because of the stability and tenaciousness of folk tales, we are appreciably aided in reconstructing the contacts of nonliterate folk by the use of methods we will treat when discussing historical reconstruction. [7]

Out of the study of distributions we derive the concept of the principal folklore areas of the world, which can be briefly outlined here. These areas are three in number—the Old World (Africa, Europe, and Asia), the South Seas, and North and South America. The unity of the folklore in these great regions, each of which, of course, has its local sub-areas, is very striking. The distribution of recognizably similar animal-trickster or moralizing tales over all of the Old World is a case in point. Equally significant is the use of the proverb and riddle that marks off this

[6] T. Yoseloff and L. Stuckey, 1944, pp. 57–9.
[7] Cf. S. Thompson, 1932–1936.

region from the North and South American and South Seas areas. Another distinction of this Old World area is the prevalence of the concept of the universe as directed by pantheons of gods who stand in relation to each other as members of a family of supernatural beings, as the study of Greek, Roman, African, Norse, and Asiatic myths reveals.

The South Seas area is characterized by the presence of elaborate creation myths of a formal, fixed structure, and of great length, so that their narration calls upon the services of specialists. It is perhaps the only area in the nonliterate world that has produced what may be regarded as epic poetry. The tales are searchingly philosophical in content, as has been commented on by those who have recorded them from the earliest contact of the Polynesians with Europeans. In Melanesia, as elsewhere in the South Seas, the creation is of lesser concern, and the culture-hero is not as important as in Polynesia. Less formalized "fairy tales" are employed for magical purposes, while cycles of stories that recount the adventures of dualistic heroes—one wise and the other foolish, one good and the other wicked—take on a place that such tales, if they exist at all in Polynesia, do not have.[8]

In the Americas, the explanatory tale plays a prominent role, while the myths everywhere show a preoccupation with celestial phenomena. Trickster tales, especially of the trickster-transformer type, abound in western North America. Boas, in his analysis of North American Indian folklore,[9] distinguishes the mythologies of various regions in terms of their degree of systematization, noting the loose grouping of Plateau tales concerning a single hero, or the absence of migration legends in the northern part of the continent, where the people regard themselves as always having lived in their present habitat. He also contrasts the characters—raven, mink, blue jay, coyote—who in different areas play the trickster. Tales of the same general categories—of tricksters and cultures-heroes, of transformation of men into animals or animals into men—also abound in South America. The number of categories is not very great. Métraux gives the most important types of South American Indian tales as:

> Creation myths, in which are included the adventures of the Culture Heroes that gave the world its present physiognomy; myths about cataclysms, which may or may not be related to the Culture Hero cycle; transformation; star myths; myths purport-

[8] Cf. B. Dixon, 1916; K. Luomala, 1946.

[9] F. Boas, 1914, 1940, pp. 451–90; see also S. Thompson, 1929, and E. W. Voegelin, 1946.

ing to explain the origin of institutions; myths validating a rite or charm; ancestor stories; ghost and spirit tales; animal stories, properly speaking.[10]

To comprehend and adequately assess the literary qualities of the folklore of nonliterate peoples, large numbers of tales and myths from a single society must be studied with the criteria and concepts of any literary form. In these terms the mechanisms employed by nonliterate folk to develop plot, sustain interest, and achieve characterization will be found not too far at variance with those used by any skilled teller of tales, whether his medium be the oral folk tale or the written narrative. Yet one distinction between the stylistic conventions of the written and the unwritten tale must be drawn. The fact that the folk tale is recited gives it certain values that the written story can never achieve—just as certain features of the written story are necessarily absent in the tale. These nuances can only be recorded by a phonograph— pauses in speech, interjections, intonation, stress; or by the motion picture—gesture, facial expression, and the like. Oral literature, that is, as the instrument of the able teller of tales, is dramatic in form. To this point we turn, as we consider the drama among nonliterate folk.

3

The drama in nonliterate societies affirms some of the deepest sanctions of living. The myths declaimed and acted, the choreography of the dances, the rhythms of the drums, the verses sung and spoken, call forth responses from participants and onlookers that bear profoundly on the value system of the individuals who compose the group, and on their adjustment within this system. They give assurance that the rains will come, that crops will be abundant, that calamity will not befall, that the group will continue. Our own reaction to a deeply moving dramatic presentation, one that gives a sense of identification with a problem we feel more or less consciously is close to our own experience, yields a like response. But we respond largely as spectators, whereas the members of nonliterate societies may actually take part in the figures of a dance, the telling of myths, the acting out of a dramatic sequence.

Participation in dramatic presentations may range from complete participation to performances by trained specialists that, in effect, differ from those familiar to us only in that they are not

[10] A. Métraux, 1946b, Vol. I, p. 851.

performed in a theater. We may cite, as examples of each, the initiatory rites of the Australian aborigines, which no one except candidates and initiates may witness, and in which all have roles to play; and the elaborate dance dramas of Bali, with their highly trained, professional performers, whose entire lives are pointed toward these skills.

Yet there is one feature that all forms of dramatic expression have in common, whether simple or complex, performed by specialists or the group as a whole, manifested in the open-air performances of nonliterate folk, or in the modern theater. All performances have structure; all manifest the unities that distinguish any artistic production. There is a beginning and an end. There is a sequence in time and in incident. There is a sense of progression—of climax—whether the tradition of the group orders heightening or diminishing of effect, or conceives it in a more flexible mold. Furthermore, all such performances, however they may be integrated in nonliterate cultures with other aspects of living, are clearly differentiated from the ordinary round of life. They are special, anticipated, often calling for the amassing of provisions and ceremonial regalia. Whether the theme is comedy or tragedy, their presentation is a break in the customary routine. It is not chance that in West Africa, English-speaking natives use the word "play" to designate their dances, and any of the wide variety of the dances in the area may be taken as an instance of the structured drama of these performances.

One learns, let us say, when among the Ashanti, that a dance is to take place the next afternoon. The village is small and remote; the dancing space offers but little shade to protect the spectators from other villages. As one arrives, the drums are sounding, and the dancers are already circling the enclosure. There are perhaps ten or twelve of them, some men, some women. All are in or near a state of possession. A shriek is heard—and a woman falls to the ground, rolls along it, attempts to get up. Others come to her asistance, but she signals for a stick; then, painfully rising, begins to crawl about the enclosure, barely able to use one foot. Another dances violently about the circle, arms swinging, facial muscles working, pausing before the drums to dance backward and forward, backward and forward, always facing the instruments whose tone is the compelling voice of the god. The rhythms of the percussion orchestra, the massed voices and hand clapping of the singers, the vividly colored silk and cotton cloths of the spectators, the red of the earth and green of the forest background, the constant movement of dancers and attendants, and, over all, the brilliance of the afternoon sun—these make up the settings for the action to follow.

One man, a priest, now becomes possessed. All follow his magnificent dancing with an intentness revealing tensions hitherto unremarked. He goes about the dancing space several times, dances to the drums, circles again, and then, with a cry, breaks out of the ring and runs into the village. Some—but only those qualified—follow him, and from them soon comes a shout echoed by the spectators as the drums take up a quickened beat, and those left behind go on with their dancing with renewed energy. The woman with the staff throws it from her, dancing as energetically as the rest. She is joined by the priest, who, returning with something in his hands, leads the others in dancing to the drums until he is escorted to the cult-house. The dance lasts well into the night, but the priest does not rejoin the dancers; the end of the dance comes when there are no more possessed by the gods.

A simple enough rite, this. Yet, if one reaches beneath outer form and touches the meaning of the performance, the dance becomes an episode in the drama of expunging an evil that threatened the village. For some time before this dance, misfortune dogged the group. Crops were bad, houses burned, children died. Divination revealed magic laid against the people. The dance, which brought the gods of the village to the heads of their worshippers, was to seek out and drive away the evil. When the god of the priest possessed him, he revealed the hiding place of the charm that actuated the evil. This was why tensions mounted with his possession, why anxiety followed his dancing and his muttered utterances, why the shout announcing that the cause of the evil had been found was followed by the vigorous dancing of the devotees remaining behind. The situation was resolved; the plot had worked to its conclusion. But for all its simplicity of form and directness of line, the dramatic quality of the dance was of the highest, carrying performers into states of possession, and holding spectators taut with excitement and expectancy.

Plots may vary in complexity of organization. Where, as in Polynesia, rituals dramatize portions of a complicated mythological system, a performance may rival in intricacy of organization and delineation of character those with which we are familiar. One essential difference between such representations in nonliterate society and our own follows upon the presence or absence of writing. The drama of native peoples has been developed by the people; for us, a play is written out by one specialist for other specialists to stage. Much of dramatic form among nonliterate peoples consists of ceremonies that enact various myths, or recapitulate group experience of an earlier day; or that comprise rituals demanded by the current system of belief to achieve ends held imperative for survival, such an ensuring rainfall, or fertility, or victory in combat.

The Indians of southwestern United States offer many examples of ritual drama in highly developed form. A simple rite illustrating Navaho dramatic expression will serve our purpose—a curing "sing" or a private sand painting. The "sing" is an all-night affair; its setting, the inside of a dimly lit hogan. The patient sits facing the priest, who leads the singing, continuing without interruption until the climax at dawn, when the door is thrown open and the priest moves outside to perform the concluding rites alone. The sand-painting sessions similarly work to their climaxes with the destruction of the beautiful, stylized images of the gods on which the one for whom the rite has been given has been placed to obtain power and aid from the spirits.

The Pueblo Indians have the same feeling for drama in their ritual. The snake dance of the Hopi is perhaps the most famous of these rites, though this very fame brings so many tourist spectators to witness it that much of the artistic unity of the ritual is lost to the observer. Far more impressive artistically, because it is free of intrusive strangers, is the antelope dance of the preceding day, when the beauty of the setting can be appreciated, the singing heard, the movements of the priestly dance followed.

In considering the ritual drama, the spectacles connected with religious rites, it is important not to take the point of view often encountered, that the dramatic expressions of nonliterate peoples are all ritualistic. That this hypothesis should have been accepted so widely is understandable. For one thing, ritual performances bulked large in the early stages of our own drama. Then, too, dramatic expression in nonliterate societies is, in fact, much more frequently found in association with religious than with secular rites. And finally, since cause and effect are so closely related in the drama of these societies, few students have been on the watch for secular drama, even when they have been conscious of the drama as a subject for study.

In many instances, the classification of a given performance is difficult. We may consider another dramatic spectacle of the Ashanti people, partially religious, partially secular—the Kwasi-dae rite. This is held once a month, and its purpose is to strengthen the "stool," or throne, of the ruler of a village, a province, or the Ashanti kingdom as a whole. Here the pageantry is so lavish as to beggar description—the golden ornaments and emblems; the ornate palanquin in which the chief is carried to the market place, as his drums, sounding rhythms of praise to his ancestors, precede and follow him; the great lavishly ornamented state umbrellas, twirled by their dancing bearers; and the throngs of subjects in their colorful cloths who, excluded from the rituals inside the compound of the chief, line the route and crowd the market place where dancing societies from many outlying villages and towns compete for the ruler's approbation. It may be argued with cogency that this rite is secular, since it is an integral part of native political life, and with equal validity that it is religious, in that it figures in the ancestral cult. But it is of the essence of ancestral rites that secular dances and songs figure prominently, and improvisation is encouraged as a special prerogative of the powerful dead. The student of the drama, naturally, does not make such a problem his primary concern. Yet it is important, if only because the accepted position tends to focus attention on religious rites to the exclusion of secular ones.

Secular drama, it is true, customarily takes on humbler forms than religious performances. There is less pageantry, a smaller group; yet drama it nonetheless is. Let us return to the field of folklore, and take as an instance an evening of storytelling in a West Indian village. The setting is the hut of some member of the community, in front of which the storyteller and his audience, many of them children, sit about in dim lamp light or in the brilliance of the moon. "Cric-crac!" begins the leader, and points to some member of the group who "pulls a riddle," demanding an answer from his neighbor. As the storytelling proceeds, the teller acts out each detail of the developing plot. His voice becomes high and whining when the trickster, in difficulty, pleads for help; it is stern when the victor in a contest speaks. But the audience, whites of eyes gleaming, is more than audience. The tale is broken by exclamations, and from time to time a song sung by one of the characters enters—a song that the audience, now fully participating, carries as a chorus to the solo of the storyteller. It is a humble occasion, but it has all the elements of theater; the story furnishes the plot, and the acting is superb. Properties only are lacking, but they are no more needed than by the *diseuse*, who holds her audience with a monologue despite the bareness of the platform on which she stands.

One further point may be made concerning the drama in nonliterate societies. If the unified character of life has made drama an integral part of the daily round, this same unity has joined dramatic art the more firmly to other artistic forms. Song, dance, myth, poem—all these are integrated closely in perform- ances in the worship of the gods, the burial of the dead, marriage, or other events in the life cycle. Just as poetry exists as words to music, and music and words are essential parts of the dance, so all these contribute in giving to the dramatic performances of non- literate folk their aesthetic appeal and artistic validity.

We have numerous instances of the poetry with which drama is embellished; two examples may be taken from the rituals of the West African Dahomeans. The first is from rites for the Earth God, the second from a funeral ceremony.[11]

> Thy need is great,
> And great our need to sing,
> For days of trouble are upon us.
> The bullock of Abomey
> Says to him of Cana,
> It is the day of trouble;
> The carrier of grain,
> Says to the bearer of salt,
> Thy load is heavy, brother,
> And this the day for carrying;
> The bearer of the dead
> Says to the carrier of ladders,
> It is the day for carrying loads,
> It is the day of trouble.

*   *

> *Leader:* Do not weep,
> Nothing stays Death
> Nor the day of its coming.
>
> *Chorus:* Death troubles us—o!
> Death troubles us.
>
> As the flies fret our backs,
> Returning, and returning,
>
> So Death troubles us—o!
> Death troubles us.
>
> As the pigeons alight
> On a housetop,
> And dance, and dance,

[11] F. S. Herskovits, 1934, p. 76; 1935, p. 95; reprinted by permission.

So Death dances—o!
Death dances.

Ai—yo!
Ai—yo—o!

In addition to music, poetry, and dance, moreover, we must not forget the contributions of the graphic and plastic arts to the drama of nonliterate groups—the variety of masks, of costumes in all forms and of all kinds of materials, of other paraphernalia of various sorts. All these are used in combination with other art forms, and do their part in carrying on the action and providing the setting that make drama of the total performance.

4

The comparative study of the music of peoples outside the stream of Euroamerican culture, on a scientific, objective basis, leads us to some of the most fundamental truths about the nature and functioning of culture. The music of non-European peoples has long attracted the attention of travelers and others who have had occasion to hear it. In the eighteenth century, for example, the African explorer, Mungo Park, set down and published some of the songs he heard among the peoples of the Senegal River area. Folk-music of European groups and of American Indians and Negroes has been copied down. Yet today we know that transcriptions of non-European music are only approximations of the songs and rhythms actually heard by those who note them down. We hear music, no less than we produce it, in terms of very subtle conditionings that make up our musical enculturation.

An interesting exercise for one who hears a melody from a musical tradition not his own is to attempt to reproduce it. The greater his musical training, the less he will succeed; for, quite unconsciously he will translate it into his own idiom. The recording phonograph alone can render a song as it is actually sung, or catch the rhythmic complexities of a musical style dominated by rhythm rather than melody. The standard notation of Euroamerican music in terms of the eight-note scale with a series of accidentals that allows no place, let us say, for quarter tones, requires special adaptations before it can even begin to permit the transcription of music in modes where finer intervals are the rule. Our relatively simple system of time signatures, with fixed measures, is less than satisfactory when, for example, a piece played on the xylophone must be set down that has a 4/4 beat in the left hand and a 5/4 in the right, making a "measure" that is more than we are trained to carry as a unit.

Euroamerican music, as a matter of fact, is almost unique in the stress it lays on pitch. This derives from the predominance of mechanically tuned instruments, such as the piano, something that conditions us to react in terms of notes that stand in a fixed relation to each other. The importance we attach to proper intonation where deviation from a fixed tone is possible, as in singing or in playing the violin, is only the most obvious aspect of this tradition. In most cultures, not only is singing in a fixed key not the rule, but deviation from true pitch causes the listeners no discomfort. That is, the intervals of a song are relatively, not absolutely, the same when different singers render it, or the same performer repeats it. On different occasions, when the song begins on a still different note, it will be transposed from key to key without difficulty.

Differences in tonal values make up only one element in musical style that renders it difficult for those trained in the music of one culture to appreciate or comprehend that of another. Thus, our music is polyphonic in conception. An orchestra, a band, a choir, is made up of units, each of which plays or sings in such a way that at a given moment the sounds made by all will be in harmony, as we call it. These sounds will be separated from each other by intervals, culturally determined, that by definition are within the range of differences that notes heard at one time may have. From this come the various degrees of manipulation of thematic materials—that is, of tunes—that lead to the elaborations of the developmental sections in symphonies and, outstandingly, in that most sophisticated musical expression of our culture, the fugue.

Let us return for a moment, in contrast, to the simplicity of our rhythms. In Euroamerican music, beats are regular and phrases are short. As von Hornbostel has said, the syncope, where emphasis lies on the off-beat (one-*and*, two-*and*, and so forth, instead of *one*-and, *two*-and . . . , as in a march tune), an African commonplace, is a European achievement. We count in two, three, four, six, eight, and occasionally, where beats are rapid and units of time small, in twelve, as in 12/16 time, which in essence reduces itself to 3/4. Many other possibilities remain that we do not utilize at all. Those conversant with symphonic literature will think of the difficulties of counting 5/4 time, as in one of the Tschaikowsky symphonies, which for many resolves itself into 2/4 and 3/4 counts.

A simple test of this may be made by anyone. We are all familiar with the way we divide into units—"measures"—a steady beat, like the ticking of a clock, or the click of the wheels of a train on the rails. It is interesting to try to break down this regular beat into units of five rather than three ("waltz-time") or four ("march-time"). It is difficult, but it can be done. But then, this accomplished, one should next try to hear this regular beat as though it were separated into units of *seven*. In most cases, it will soon either slip into units of six or eight, or, if by resolution we hold to sevens, it will become a combination of threes and fours. The next step is even more difficult. When one has trained himself to hear units of seven, then he should make up some tune to go with this rhythm—that is, a tune that would have the time signature of $7/4$ or $7/8$. This, it has been found, will, in Euroamerican culture, frustrate all but the most determined experimenter, who is willing to give much time to the reconditioning process necessary.

The importance of rhythm in nonliterate societies is reflected in the relative number of instruments that are used for percussion as against the number employed to carry melody. One may almost say that for melody to be carried by other than the voice is the exception rather than the rule. Not only this, but melody in these societies is relatively simple. It is not quite true, as some students of comparative musicology have claimed, that the music of "primitive" peoples is marked by an absence of part singing. There are enough instances on record to demonstrate the presence of sustained singing in stated intervals, and thus to refute so sweeping an assertion. But the statement is true in so many cases that it is easy to understand how the principle was reached. Unison singing is thus the rule, rather than the exception.

The great number of musical instruments that have been devised by nonliterate peoples can only be discussed briefly here. They can be classified into the categories with which we are familiar—string, wind, and percussion—of which the first have the most restricted distribution and the fewest types, the last the greatest number of different forms and the widest spread. Stringed instruments, found aboriginally only in the Old World, may be plucked or played with a bow, and are provided with some resonating device to amplify the resulting weak sound. These devices may take the form of calabash or wooden attachments to the instrument; the chest of the player will also serve the purpose. The musical bow, a single string plucked with one hand while the other varies the length of the portion permitted to vibrate and thus produce changes in pitch, is the simplest form of stringed instrument; more complex forms are harps and lyres.

Wind instruments include various kinds of flutes, flageolets, and trumpets. They are made of different materials—wood, horn, bamboo, bone, pottery—and they range in flexibility from the trumpet, with its fundamental note and the limited number of tones that can be played without valves, to the flute, which has considerable compass. Wind instruments are not always employed for musical purposes alone. The trumpet, particularly, is widely used for signaling. Where a language has meaningful patterns of tone and stress, the trumpet joins the drums in transmitting messages. Forms of wind instruments such as the nose flute of the South Seas require the use of techniques different from any method known to Euroamerican culture. Pan-pipes, which have Old and New World distributions, likewise require special technical ability, since it is necessary to blow over them, rather than into them. Here, melody is achieved by using pipes of different length to obtain different tones.

Between tonal and percussion instruments are various "transitional" forms. One such is the xylophone (marimba); another the aggregates of bells having different tones. In this transition category the "African piano" or *sanza* is noteworthy. This is an instrument having strips of metal or of bamboo of different lengths suspended over a resonator in such a way that each, as its end is pressed and released by the thumb, gives off a different note.

Even when we consider purely percussion types, such as the drum, the element of tonality is by no means entirely lacking. African hollow-log drums, headed with skins, are tuned, and if struck different types of blows, at different places on the drumhead, as many as four distinct tones can be produced by a single drum. The wooden slit-drum of the Congo Basin and, perhaps derivatively, of the Amazon, gives various tones, also depending on where it is struck. Rhythms are also produced by rattles, by beads worn on the ankles of a dancer, by calabashes or wooden blocks with striations cut in them over which a stick is rubbed or, most simply and universally, by hand clapping.

It is evident that the difference between the musical culture of nonliterate peoples and our own is not as much a difference in means or complexity of expression, as in the extent to which it is a subject for analysis by those who compose, perform, or listen to it. As Herzog has stated it, the musical theory of nonliterate groups comprehends comparatively few analytical statements and a modest technical vocabulary. . . . The units distinguished . . . are not as minute as ours. They are apt to differentiate music according to general differences in the melodic and rhythmic configuration, which in turn tend to become connected with differences in usage and social function. They are, however, very concise and definite when it comes to questions which we are at some loss to answer: the origin and ultimate meaning of music.[12]

Now that the mechanical devices necessary for the adequate recording of unwritten music have been developed, and a more effective analysis of this music has thus been rendered possible, the student of culture can use these materials as he has employed the patterns of language in his study of human behavior. Music, like language, has basic structural forms that are only revealed after their manifestations in the everyday life of a people are objectively investigated. On analysis, however, they go far in disclosing the cultural factors, in both pattern and process, from which they take on their ascribed form and meaning. Everywhere man sings, and in singing experiences the satisfactions that go with all forms of self-expression. But in singing, too, he all unwittingly provides precious data by the use of which the student of culture, transmuting artistic expression into scientific analysis, can extend our knowledge and understanding of the life of man.

[12] G. Herzog, 1938, p. 5.

Chapter **Fifteen**

Language: the Vehicle of Culture

The nature and social functioning of language is indicated in the following definition: *A language is a system of arbitrary vocal symbols by which members of a social group coöperate and interact.*[1] This signifies that in its organization it is regular and not haphazard—that is, it is a system; and that as a series of symbols its meanings must be learned as must all other cultural phenomena. The definition, however, stresses the social functions of language. So that the full significance of language as an aspect of culture may be grasped, we must therefore add, ". . . *and by means of which the learning process is effectuated and a given way of life achieves both continuity and change.*"

Without language, the accumulations of knowledge that mark off human from other animal aggregates could not have been developed or maintained. Through language man has been able to devise, continue, and change the great variety of his material and nonmaterial cultural institutions. If a phenomenon has cultural relevance, it is because it holds *meaning* in thought and in behavior. This, in turn, is because men have the linguistic equipment to grasp and express its significance. The importance

[1] E. H. Sturtevant, 1947, p. 2.

of language in furthering the creative aspects of culture is obvious. There is much reason, furthermore, to believe that the very nature of reality itself, as conceived by a people, is a reflection of the categories of their thought, categories that stem from their linguistic usages.

It comes as a surprise to the novice in the study of speech that language is not instinctive. Undoubtedly, many individual acts of speaking *seem* instinctive, as when we emit cries of great emotion under stress. An analogy can be drawn between language and man's tool-using propensities. Upright stance and the release of the anterior extremities as grasping organs have made it possible for man to use tools. Yet we have seen that we are hardly justified, for that reason, in saying that the tools man does use derive from a "tool-using instinct." As with language, the variety of tools he uses and, above all, the fact that he must learn to use the tools put into his hands by those of his society who have preceded him, make any assumption of inherent aptitude untenable.

The forms of any speech system, it must also be emphasized, have no relation to structural peculiarities that mark off the physical characteristics of those who employ it. Any human being can make any sound or any combination of sounds that any other person can make, no matter what his racial affiliation, provided he has the opportunity to do so at an early enough age. Whether lips are thick or thin, noses broad or narrow, every sound made in any language is within any individual's range of possible use.

For purposes of study, every language is to be divided into three parts. The first consists of its sounds, and makes up its phonemic system. The second is the combinations of sounds into units that have distinct significance, its vocabulary. The third is the manner in which these sound combinations are themselves combined and recombined into larger units, and is what is ordinarily meant when we speak of grammar. There is no system of speech that lacks any of these.

Like any other aspect of culture, languages are to be studied both from the point of view of form and of function. The former type of analysis, which inquires what language *is*, has the importance the study of form holds in any other phase of culture. Its significance in this respect is heightened, however, by the fact that the forms of speech are so deeply imbedded in the habits of people that they afford especially good materials for the study of the objective manifestations of culture as a whole.

The second approach, which is concerned primarily with what language *does*, presents considerable difficulties of method.

This approach includes what one student has termed "the conception of speech as a mode of action, and not merely of expression." [2] It is what Sapir meant when he characterized "the fundamental ground-work of language" not only as "the development of a clear cut phonetic system," but also "the specific association of speech elements with concepts, and the delicate provision for the formal expression of all manner of relations." [3] It is to be regarded as one of the outstanding accomplishments of anthropological linguistics that it has laid emphasis on function, no less than on the study of forms.

Of similar import is Bloomfield's concept of the *speech-community*—a "group of people who interact by means of speech." [4] The speech-community, Bloomfield holds, "is the most important kind of social group," since "all the so-called higher activities of man—our specifically human activities—spring from the close adjustment among individuals which we call society, and this adjustment, in turn, is based upon language." Speech-communities vary enormously in size, and merge sometimes imperceptibly into one another, as in the case of minor dialectic differences, such as distinguish the speech of the South from that of the Middle West in the United States.

2

The study of the sound-making devices of the human organs of speech and of their total range of sounds is called *phonetics*. In a given language, the significant sounds that are combined to convey meaning are called *phonemes*. In a sense, analysis of the phonemic structure of a speech system is one of the most revealing phases of linguistic research, especially as it holds significance for the study of culture. To understand this, we need only refer to the contributions made by the early students of Indo-European tongues. Through the comparative study of sound-shifts, it was possible to discover historic relationships between tongues as seemingly different from each other as Russian and English. This, in turn, forced a reconsideration of the processes in the development, through contact, of the cultures of Europe and the areas which contributed to them.

To comprehend how wide is the range of possibilities in any phase of linguistic expression we must, however, broaden our perspective and move outside the literate societies. Only by doing

[2] G. A. de Laguna, 1927, p. 21, note.
[3] E. Sapir, 1921, p. 22.
[4] L. Bloomfield, 1933, p. 42.

this can we perceive how man can use differing means to achieve the same ends. The fact of linguistic variability is blurred for us because, for one thing, the symbols used in writing are conventionalized approximations of phonemes rather than representations of them. In English, for example, the symbol *a* stands for sounds as different as the *a* in f*a*r, in h*a*t, in c*a*me, in *a*bove. Not only that, but the same phoneme can be represented by different letter symbols, as, for instance, the *a* in f*a*r, which is the same phoneme as the *o* in Midwestern h*o*t. The series given by Bloomfield makes the point. "The words *oh, owe, so, sew, sow, hoe, beau, though* all end with the same phoneme, variously represented in writing; the words *though, bough, through, cough, tough, hiccough* end with different phonemes but are all written with the letters *-ough*." [5]

In the scientific study of language, special symbols are used so that each sound unit has its particular sign. This permits the student, whether he is studying a new tongue or a local dialect, to approximate the sounds of speech closely enough so that a trained linguist, reading these signs, can reproduce sound combinations quite accurately in pressing his analyses or comparing the speech habits of different groups.

A simple exercise will show how a certain group of the sounds we conceive as separate and distinct, the vowels, are actually no more than points on a continuous scale. First purse the lips so as to sound a *u* as in yo*u*. Then, expelling the breath and continuously activating the vocal cords, gradually open the mouth through *o* as in h*o*pe until a broad *a* as in f*a*r is reached. Continue the process, extending the corners of the mouth to attain *e* as in th*e*y until the phoneme *i*, the *ee* of f*ee*t is heard. Finally return slowly to the pursed lip position through the German *ü* until the original *u* is once more being pronounced.

These stopping points are indicated on the vowel chart on the next page. Such stopping points, however, are quite arbitrary. In the actual speech of any group, many minor variants of these points are found, most of which are ignored by those who speak a given language. Try once again to run the gamut of sounds, but stop halfway between *o* and *a*. The result will be a sound that we indicate by the *au* in c*au*ght but that students of language write *ɔ*. About halfway between the *a* and the *e* we reach *a* as in h*a*t, which phoneticians denote by the symbol *ä*. Between *e* and *i* lies *ι*, the sound made when the word h*i*t is pronounced. Still another progression, ignoring the full opening of *a*, produces the sequence

[5] *Ibid.*, p. 85.

o→ö→e, the middle term being one foreign to English, but heard in Scandinavian tongues. With practice, finer shadings can be pronounced, at will; and linguists have found that many of those sounds have significance—that is, have phonemic value—in lan-

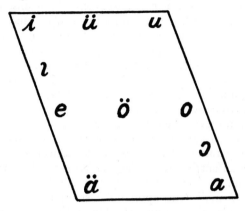

guages that, in turn, disregard some of the points on the progression we utilize.

Vowels are produced by permitting air that actuates the vocal cords to flow through the mouth unimpeded by tongue or glottis. When the breath is obstructed, we produce the sounds classified as consonants. They, too, have a range that extends far beyond the usage of any single speech system. They are customarily classified under one of five headings. First are the stops, made when the stream is halted for an instant. If the vocal cords are actuated, then voiced stops such as *b* or *d* result; if not, then corresponding voiceless sounds, in these cases *p* or *t*, are heard. Another category is made up of the fricatives, or spirants, sounded when the breath comes through a narrow passage. Voiced sounds in this class would include *v* and *z*, whose unvoiced correspondences are *f* and *s*. Trills are exemplified by the rolled *r*, familiar in Latin tongues, usually voiced; laterals by *l*; and nasals by *m* and *n* and their variants. These may be voiced or unvoiced; in Indo-European languages, however, only voiced forms of them are significant.

Other phonemic elements exist that are not included in the above categories. Outstanding is the group comprised by the "clicks" of the Bushman and Hottentot languages of South Africa. These differ from all other phonemes of human speech in that they are made by creating a vacuum in the mouth, into which the air is introduced, making a sharp sound. When they employ the lips, a kissing-like sound results. When the middle part of the tongue is pressed against the palate and released, a sound much like the reproachful one we have in mind when we write "tut, tut" is obtained. The tip of the tongue, held against the middle palate and quickly released, makes a third, while mid-tongue and mid-palate combine in the sound used to urge on a horse. How complicated the resulting phonetic combinations of this language can be becomes apparent when it is realized that these clicks join with other consonants, and vowels, voiced and unvoiced, nasalized and free from nasalization in differing pitch registers, to form the words it uses to convey its meanings.

This by no means tells the entire story. Devices such as the glottal stop are of paramount importance in Polynesian tongues—that is, the separation of the vowels pronounced when a mother reproves her infant by exclaiming "*A-a-a-a-a!*" The name of the island Hawaii, pronounced *Hawaya* on the American mainland, is actually *Hawai'i* (the apostrophe standing for the stopped breath after the diphthong *ai*). The mainland pronunciation, *Hawaya*, indicates what happens to such a form in a speech community where the glottal stop is not the rule; where stops only occur when two words that begin and end with the same consonant, as in the phrase *this ' song*, must be pronounced separately. Stress and duration and tone are other phonemic elements. The initial consonant *s* in the combination *sŏ*, in the Kru language of Liberia gives it the meaning "two"; but when the *s* is prolonged, the word *s·ŏ* means "to be rotten." In Ibo, another African language, the word *ákwá*, in which each vowel is pronounced with high pitch, means "cry"; when the first vowel is high and the second low (*ákwà*) it means "cloth"; first low and second high (*àkwá*) is "egg"; while both low (*àkwà*) signifies "bridge."

Thus we see how different languages use different series of sounds and accessory devices to build up the sound-clusters to which are assigned specific meanings, but also we see how each series represents, in its totality, only a selection of the possibilities presented by the vocal equipment of human beings. This leads us to two salient facts about the phonemic system of every language, *consistency* and *limitation*. Boas has phrased the point in these words: "One of the most important facts relating to the phonetics of human speech is that every single language has a definite and limited group of sounds, and that the number of those used in any particular dialect is never excessively large." [6] Both principles are

[6] F. Boas, 1911, p. 16.

essential if the function of language as a means of communication is to be served. This is why we encounter the phenomenon of standardization that enables the hearer to disregard the minor idiosyncrasies of individual pronunciation, and "hear" only in terms of the limited number of sounds that make the exquisite pattern we call a language.

3

What is a word? Various definitions of the concept have been advanced. Boas has defined a word as "a phonetic group which, owing to its permanence of form, clearness of significance, and phonetic independence, is readily separated from the whole sentence." [7] There are many languages, however, in which we come upon combinations of phonemes that look like words but are what we would term sentences, despite the fact that in the whole complex there is no element that can stand alone any more than can the English suffix -*ed* which means time past (*depart, depart-ed*).

Sapir gives an example of a "word-sentence" from the language of the Paiute Indians of Utah. *Wii-to-kuchum-punku-rügani-yugwi-va-ntü-m(ü)* means "they who are going to sit up and cut up with a knife a black cow (or bull)." In the order of its elements, its literal translation is: "knife-black-buffalo-pet-cut up-sit (plur.)-future-participle-animate plur." Sapir, however, raises the question whether this really is a word in the sense we think of the term; or, by implication, whether any combination of this sort can be comprehended under such a definition as that given by Boas. "In truth," he says, "it is impossible to define the word from a functional standpoint at all, for the word may be anything from the expression of a single concept—concrete or abstract or purely relational (as in *of* or *by* or *and*)—to the expression of a complete thought (as in Latin *dico* 'I say' or, with greater elaborateness of form, in a Nootka verb form denoting 'I have been accustomed to eat twenty round objects [e.g., apples] while engaged in [doing so and so]'). In the latter case the word becomes identical with the sentence." [8]

Linguists have adopted the concept of the "morpheme" in analyzing language. The morpheme, which is the unit of linguistic form, consists of one or more units of sound (phonemes) plus a unit of meaning. Two important types of morphemes are recognized: "free morphemes," which can be used alone, like words;

[7] *Ibid.*, p. 28.
[8] E. Sapir, 1921, pp. 32–3.

and "bound morphemes," such as prefixes and suffixes, which "are genuine linguistic forms and convey a meaning, but . . . occur only in construction, as part of a larger form." [9] Bound morphemes are never used as sentences. Examples of them are to be found in the -*ess* in "countess," or the -*ish* in "greenish," or the -*s* in "hats," while in the same words "count," "green," and "hat" are free morphemes, since they can be used separately. The difficulties of analyzing the word-sentences cited above from Paiute and Nootka disappear when the unit of analysis is the morpheme, which does not necessarily have the "phonetic independence" usually attributed to a word.

It is thus possible to define a word as "a minimum free form," or "a free form which does not consist entirely of (two or more) lesser free forms." [10] In terms of this definition, words are to be classed as secondary and primary, each having two sub-types. Secondary words are compound or derived. Compound words, such as "hat-rack," have more than one free morpheme, since both "hat" and "rack" are susceptible of independent use. Derived secondary words are composed of one free morpheme and one or more bound morphemes, as in "boy-ish." Primary words are those that do not contain a free morpheme in combination with bound morphemes. They may be "morpheme-words," such as "man," "boy," "cat," "run," or "see," where the word is identical with the morpheme; or derived primary words that are composed of two or more bound morphemes, such as "re-ceive" or "re-tain." [11]

Word structure is so basic in linguistic study that it has been set up as the criterion for one of the most widely employed systems of language classification devised by linguists, that which counts languages as isolating, agglutinative, inflective, and polysynthetic. Chinese exemplifies the first, where independent units merely follow each other as a series of concepts are expressed. An instance of a word from a so-called isolating tongue would be *namímanawè*, from the Fõn language of West Africa, which means "wife exchange." Broken down, it is found to consist of the following components: *na*, give; *mí*, us; *ma*, we; *na*, give; *wè*, you —"give-us-we-give-you." Agglutinating languages bind these separate forms together in words that follow each other or are used with prefixes and suffixes. In inflectional languages, meanings are changed by adding such elements as prefixes or suffixes to free forms; Indo-European tongues are inflectional. The polysyn-

[9] L. Bloomfield, 1933, pp. 177–8.
[10] *Ibid.*, p. 207.
[11] *Ibid.*, p. 209.

thetic languages are those in which ideas are expressed by synthesizing to an elaborate degree. Some American Indian tongues are assigned to this category, and the examples of word-sentences that have been given can be taken as illustrating the type. That this classification is no more satisfactory than others that have been set up on the basis of word forms, or grammatical structures, or any other single aspect of language is aside from the point. Here we merely mention this system to indicate the importance of word formation in the study of language.

The devices employed to shade meaning vary greatly from language to language, but each follows well-marked and clearly patterned usage. English, for example, is rich in prefixes and suffixes, but does not use the infix, a phonetic combination that is inserted within a form to change its meaning. In Portuguese, for example, the future, third-person, singular of the verb *diser*, to say, is *dirá*. In this tense, the pronomial form is inserted between the syllables of the future verb, resulting in *dir-lhe-á*, "he will say to him." In the language of the Bontoc Igorot, of the Philippines, where *tengao* means "to celebrate a holiday," *tumengao-ak* (*t-um-engao-ak*) means "I shall have a holiday." In Sioux the verb *cheti* "to build a fire" gives *chewati* "I build a fire," in which the infix -*wa*- means "I."

Reduplication, though uncommon in English usage, is found in such forms as "so-so," or "boom-boom." It is more prevalent in the speech of English-speaking children who are not linguistically enculturated, as when "far, far" is used to indicate considerable distance. In the language of the Kwakiutl Indians reduplication regularly expresses the idea of occasional repetition of an action: *mēxa*, "to sleep"; *mēxmēxa*, "to sleep now and then"; *hanʟa*, "to shoot"; *hant-hanʟa*, "to shoot now and then." In the speech of the Saramacca Bush Negroes reduplication transforms a verb into a noun: *hesi* "to go fast"; *hesihesi* "speed"; *nyam* "to eat," *nanyam* or *nyamnyam* "food."

Internal vowel changes are frequently used to alter meaning, such as "man—men" or "sing—sang" found in English. Consonantal change occurs much less often, but is occasionally employed in various tongues as where, in English, we pronounce "rise" with a *z* (*riz*) when it is used as a verb, and with a terminal *s* (*ris*) when we speak of "the rise of a statesman to power," employing the word as a noun.

"Significant tone," which involves the pronunciation of the same phonetic complex at different registers, is much more widely employed than is ordinarily thought. It may have both semantic and grammatical use, changing the meaning of a word or affording the basis for paradigm systems. Chinese is the language most often thought of when tone is mentioned, but many American Indian tongues have significant tone, and most African languages are marked by pitch variation that gives them their "musical" character. In the language of the Shona of southern Africa, for example, *rudzí* (rising tone) is a "bark rope," while *rudzì* (falling tone) means "tribe"; *edzá* is "to try"; *edza* (even tones) signifies "fish." Other examples are *rambá*, "to be sterile"; *rambà*, "refuse"; *chúro*, "orphan"; *churò*, "have." In Zulu, a neighboring tongue, *ńyaga* means "moon"; *nyàgà*, "doctor."

4

The study of word forms and of grammar differs from the analysis of the sounds of a language in that the sounds, by themselves, are meaningless, while words and combinations of words always convey meaning. Linguists have therefore come to distinguish the study of phonemics, on the one hand, from grammar. Grammar, in turn, is divided into *morphology*, which has to do with word structure, and *syntax*, which is concerned with the manner in which words are combined into the larger groupings of phrases and sentences.

As with other aspects of culture, the syntactic constructions of a language seem to its speaker utterly obvious, logical, exclusive, and irrevocable. One's own language seems to offer the only possible series of valid categories by which experience can be interpreted and transmitted from person to person. Let us consider, however, the forms that the verb "to cut" can take in Kru, the Liberian tongue we have already mentioned. We can do this without reference to the native words, since we are here concerned with the categories, which can be given by the translations alone.

Present:
    I cut now.
    I am through cutting just now.
    I am continuing to cut now.
Recent Past:
    I did cut a little while ago.
    I cut several times a little while ago.
    I kept on cutting a little while ago.
    I had the purpose in mind of cutting a little while ago, but didn't.

Distant Past:
I did cut a long time ago.
I cut several times a long time ago.
I kept on cutting a long time ago.
I had the purpose in mind of cutting a long time ago, but didn't.
Near Future:
I will cut pretty soon.
I will cut again and again pretty soon.
I will keep on cutting pretty soon.
Indefinite Future:
I will cut in an indefinite time in the future.
I will cut again and again at an indefinite time in the future.
I will keep on cutting at an indefinite time in the future.
Present Reflexive:
I cut myself.
I am through cutting myself.
I am keeping on cutting myself.
Recent Past Reflexive:
I did cut myself a little while ago.
I cut myself several times a little while ago.
I kept on cutting myself a little while ago.

The way action is conceived in this series of tenses and modes is clearly different from English. We here encounter the past, present, and future familiar to us, but distance in time is also taken into account. Furthermore, it is specified whether action is continuing or intermittent, whether it is to take place at a given moment in the future or at an indefinite period; while, in one mode, intent is indicated. It is interesting to note that the reflexive of our verb is not represented by future forms, though they can, of course, be constructed by following the pattern for forming future tenses in other verbs. But the particular verb used as an example carries a connotation. It means "to cut," it is true, but intent is implied in it. Therefore, to the Kru, for a person to declare "I will cut myself intentionally"—the future reflexive—makes no sense and is apparently not employed.

Similar ranges of difference are found in other forms of speech. Consider, for example, the demonstrative pronoun, expressed in English only as "this" and "that" (with their plurals). These really indicate "position-near" and "position-away." In Tlingit, a language of the Northwest Coast of North America, however, *he* indicates an object very near and always present; *ya* one very near and present, but a little farther away; *yu* something still farther away, almost in the indefinite sense such as the English article "the chair," "a horse"; while *we* is used for something very remote and quite invisible.

Gender offers another example of variation in categories that seem fixed by experience which, to speakers of English, dictates distinctions drawn on the basis of sex. This is by no means the only type of gender-classification that can be made. Many languages of West Africa have no words to express difference in sex, such as our pronouns "he," "she," "it." Sex must be specifically distinguished, in particular instances, by the use of different words, such as "father" or "mother," or by adding words for "male" or "female." But these same languages have forms that set the categories of "big" and "small," or distinguish between living and nonliving beings, or between persons and things. This is like Fox, an American Indian language of Algonkian affiliation, in which the rigid classification of experience into things animate and inanimate dominates all forms. Thus *i'nig'* is "they (an.)". while *i'nin'* is "they (inan.)." The word for "dog" is A*'nemō'·ᵃ*. "My dog" is *ne'*tΛnemōhe*'mᵃ*. "Rock" in this language is A*'sen'*; "my rock" becomes *net*Λ*'*seni*'m'*. The final vowel, that is, is *-a* with animate possessed nouns, *-i* with inanimate.

Still another grammatical device, used by the many millions who inhabit the heart of the African continent and speak the Bantu languages, is an elaborate pattern of prefixing, which gives rise to the principles of *classification* and *concordance*. The prefixes indicate the place of a word in the classificatory system that includes all phenomena, drawn up in accordance with some descriptive criterion. Some of these classes include "human beings (males); trees and plants, wooden things and long objects; round, bulky objects, stones, and abstract nouns; leaves and fibres, with objects made from them, and flat, thin objects in general; boughs of trees; forked branches; human and animal extremities." [12] The word *bantu* itself illustrates the principle of classification: *ntu* means "a living thing"; *mu-ntu*, "a man"; *ba-ntu*, "people."

Various numbers of prefixes have been recorded for various Bantu tongues, but it is safe to put the quantity for any given dialect at between fifteen and twenty. Their utility is increased, and their use made easier by the fact that the normal Bantu word stem is of two syllables, to which prefixes, suffixes, and on occasion infixes can be added to give subject-pronoun, tense, and object-pronoun. How much flexibility the use of suffixes gives can be seen from the following forms, which are derived from the verb *kang-a*, "to tie": *kangema*, "to be tied"; *kangela*, "to tie for,

[12] A. Werner, 1930, pp. 39–40.

by"; *kangana,* "to tie each other"; *kangia,* "to cause to tie"; *kangola,* "to untie"; *kangomela,* "to be tied for"; *kangenela,* "to tie each other with"; *kangolela,* "to untie for or with"; and so forth.

These are only a few of the many different ways in which languages convey meaning with precision, and thus ensure communication. Principles such as word order or stress, which Sapir hypothetically advanced as "the primary methods for the expression of all syntactic relations," and out of which "the present relational values of specific words and elements" become "but a secondary condition due to a transfer of values" [13] may lead to a deeper comprehension of the nature of language than we now have. Yet this is not as yet achieved. For the student of culture, the fact of variation in linguistic phenomena, regarded in world perspective, and the regularity of the particular structure assumed by each tongue are the most significant features of the grammatical, phonemic and lexical aspects of speech.

5

The importance of studying language as an aspect of culture becomes apparent when we realize that its use is one of the two criteria by which man is differentiated from other creatures, as when we say that man is the only speaking, tool-using animal. This does not mean that man is the only creature that can communicate with his fellows, or even communicate so as to convey to others different shades of meaning. A dog, for example, quite effectively conveys his caution when he growls, while a bark can be playful, or friendly, or hostile. Animals have quite elaborate systems of signaling by the use of sounds that are, in effect, ways of communicating with each other.

But while man is like many other forms in that he can communicate, his mode of communication differs fundamentally from theirs. Being non-instinctive, the symbols he employs are, as we have seen, arbitrary in their selection though systematic in their combination. Animal sounds, on the other hand, are fixed, instinctive, and exhibit only the most limited range. Language is to infrahuman communication what human social institutions are to the social structures of other animals. Like all other aspects of culture, language not only varies greatly but, since it is learned, is capable of the same sort of accumulation over periods of time that is manifested by culture as a whole.

This factor of accumulation presents a problem that, in general, is no different from the one faced by the student of change

[13] E. Sapir, 1921, p. 119.

in any other aspect of culture. There is, however, one point that we must consider here, since it is primarily, though by no means exclusively, a problem of linguistic usage. That is the question of the effect the presence of writing has on linguistic change. There is no question that writing is a much more effective way to store up knowledge, so to speak, than are other mnemonic devices or memory alone. Yet the buttressing of memory by writing has apparently little to do with whether or not, in a literate society, linguistic change is retarded or hastened. If we go back but a relatively short time in our history, we find that, though our culture has been literate for many centuries, change has not always been rapid. Certainly the development of the many different written languages found today is a demonstration of the fact that change in them does occur. Conversely, however, the consistency of unwritten tongues also implies a high degree of stability. Their regularity refutes the idea, held by many persons unacquainted with them, that since they are unwritten, they must be cast in less durable molds than speech that is channeled into forms set by written expression.

Obviously, one cannot investigate the problem of change in unwritten languages with the same resources that the study of change in written modes of speech can be made. Because it is unwritten, we must, on the one hand, rely on such fragments of data as are found in words or phrases (often very poorly transcribed), as set down by early explorers; or, on the other hand, make more reliable reconstructions of the past of present-day languages. But, where written languages are concerned, we can investigate the problem from fuller records as well as by reconstructions. Thus we can compare meanings of words used in Elizabethan times and today. Such a word as "fist," for example, then meant no more than we mean by "hand," so that the poet could write a sonnet to "my lady's dainty fist." Slang is a good example of how new meaning can be read into old words of a written language, while the anguish of old-fashioned grammarians over their inability to stem the tide of such usages as "It's me" offers further illustrations of the process. Trade tongues, the languages of various "speech-communities," such as those of the theater or of musical circles devoted to jazz, offer further documentation of the change in written language.

Linguistic change, it would seem, is thus influenced relatively little by the circumstance of writing, even though, to those who are literate, writing and language are often regarded as synonyms. Yet beyond the written forms are the spoken ones; and language, expressed in speech, constantly changes. Individual differences in pronunciation or in the use of words tend to be taken over by others, and thus variants occur that may develop into different dialects and even into those mutually unintelligible modes of speech we call languages. Writing, though one of the great achievements of mankind, follows rather than determines changes in the speaking habits of peoples who employ it.

The problem of *meaning* is fundamental to the comprehension of the function of language as a basic, even a determining, element in culture. For it is through the emission and consequent comprehension of meaningful complexes of sound that men express their desires, transmit their knowledge and inculcate the values by which they live. In essence, however, the sound-complexes that symbolize experience and the projections of experience are so arbitrary that we can do little more than wonder what has caused men to identify the most abstract concepts with a given group of sounds and to transmit ideas through the manipulation of words.

To the student of culture, language, it must now be evident, offers rich resources for his investigations. Its manifold and complex forms are subject to analysis in terms of their structures and modes of change, like the forms of any other aspect of culture. In addition, the symbolic values of language lead to a comprehension of the least tangible elements in any body of custom—the values, the goals, the ideals that direct conduct and order convention—while at the same time they reveal some of the deepest roots of culture itself. In truth, symbolisms of this order justify us in regarding language as "an index to culture," as it has been called; in thinking of it, in the widest sense, as the vehicle of custom.

Part Three

The
Nature
of
Culture

Chapter **Sixteen**

The Reality of Culture

Definitions of culture are numerous. Kroeber and Kluckhohn, reviewing these definitions and the conceptions of culture associated with them, list over one hundred and sixty different formal delimitations of the term.[1] There is general agreement that culture is learned; that it allows man to adapt himself to his natural and social setting; that it is greatly variable; that it is manifested in institutions, thought patterns and material objects. One of the best early definitions was given by E. B. Tylor, who described culture as "that complex whole which includes knowledge, belief, art, morals, law, custom, and any other capabilities and habits acquired by man as a member of society." [2]

A short and useful delineation of the concept is: *Culture is the man-made part of the environment.* Implicit here is the recognition that man's life is lived in a natural habitat and a social "environment." It also implies that culture is more than a biological phenomenon. Culture includes all the elements in man's mature endowment that he has acquired from his group by conscious learning or by a conditioning process—techniques of various

[1] A. L. Kroeber and C. Kluckhohn, 1952, *passim.*
[2] E. B. Tylor, 1874, Vol. I, p. 1.

kinds, social and other institutions, beliefs, and patterned modes of conduct. Culture, in short, can be contrasted with the raw materials, outer and inner, from which it derives. Resources presented by the natural world are shaped to meet existing needs; while inborn traits are so molded as to derive out of inherent endowment the reflexes that are preponderant in the overt manifestations of behavior.

The concept of culture used as a tool in the study of man differs from the popular meaning of the term "cultured," so that the application of the concept "culture" to a digging stick or a cooking recipe necessitates some readjustment in thinking. The popular concept of culture comes within the terms of what may be called a boarding-school definition, and is the equivalent of "refinement." Such a definition implies the ability of a person who has "culture" to manipulate certain aspects of our civilization that are principally the possession of those persons who have the leisure to learn them.

For the scientist, however, a "cultured person," in the popular sense, commands but a specialized fragment of our culture. He shares more than he suspects with the farmer, the bricklayer, the engineer, the ditchdigger, the professional man. The comparative study of custom shows us this very clearly. In small isolated groups, there is no room for the social stratification that must be present if a person, "cultured" in the popular sense, is to have the economic resources essential for his support while he devotes himself to his avocations.

2

Those who would comprehend the essential nature of culture must resolve a series of seeming paradoxes, which may be stated here as follows:

1. *Culture is universal in man's experience, yet each local or regional manifestation of it is unique.*
2. *Culture is stable, yet is also dynamic, and manifests continuous and constant change.*
3. *Culture fills and largely determines the course of our lives, yet rarely intrudes into conscious thought.*

We shall see later how fundamental are the problems raised by these formulations, and how difficult it is to reconcile their seeming contradictions. Here we may consider them as they bear on the immediate question of the reality of culture.

1. The concept of man as the only organism that is a "culture-building animal" recognizes that culture is universal, that it

is an attribute of all human beings. All cultures, at least when viewed objectively, possess a restricted number of aspects into which they are conveniently divided for study, as has been shown in the preceding section of this book where the aspects have been taken up, one by one. Let us, at this point, review these aspects briefly so as to grasp how the concept of the universality of culture is extended to include all those broad subdivisions of human experience it invariably comprehends. In the first place, we found that all people have technological equipment, which they use to wrest from their natural environment the means to sustain life and carry on their daily activities. They have some way of distributing what they thus produce, an economic system that allows them to make the most of those "scarce means" that require them to economize. All give formal expression to the institution of the family or various kinds of broader kinship structures, and to associations based on other than blood ties; none lives in complete anarchy but maintains some kind of political control. All have a philosophy of life, that is, a religious system. With song and dance and tale, and graphic and plastic art forms to give aesthetic satisfaction, language to convey ideas, and a system of sanctions and goals to give meaning and point to living, we round out this summary of these aspects of culture which, like culture as a whole, are attributes of all human groups.

Yet anyone who has had contact with persons of a different way of life from his own, even with a group living in another part of his own country, knows that no two bodies of custom are identical in detail. This is why it can be said that every culture is the result of the particular experiences of its population, past and present, that every body of tradition must be regarded as the living embodiment of its past. It follows that a culture cannot be understood unless its past is taken into account, using every available device—historical sources, comparisons with other ways of living, archaeological evidence—to probe its background and development.

In reality, then, our first paradox is to be resolved by accepting both of its terms. The universality of culture is an attribute of human existence. Even its division into a series of aspects has been proved wherever cultures have been studied. On the other hand, that no two cultures are the same is equally susceptible of objective proof. When observations of this fact are translated into the dimension of time, it means that each culture has had a unique development. The universals in culture, we may thus say, provide a framework within which the particular ex-

periences of a people are expressed in the particular forms taken
by their body of custom.

2. When we weigh cultural stability against cultural change,
we must, first of all, recognize that the evidence in hand proves
that culture is dynamic. The only completely static cultures are
dead ones. We have but to look at our own experience to see how
change comes upon us, frequently so softly that we never suspect
it until we project the present on the past. The instance of a
photograph of ourselves, perhaps only a few years old, which
amuses us because of the difference in the style of clothing makes
the point. The same phenomenon is to be studied among any people. Change may only be manifest in small details of their culture,
such as a variation on an accepted pattern of design, or a new
method of preparing foods. But some change will always be apparent if a people can be studied over a period of time, if remains
of their culture can be excavated from the earth, or if their ways
can be compared with those of some neighboring group whose
culture is like theirs in general, yet varies in detail.

This is how we escape from our second apparent dilemma.
Culture is *both* stable and everchanging. *Cultural change can be
studied only as a part of the problem of cultural stability; cultural stability can be understood only when change is measured
against conservatism.* Furthermore, both phenomena must be considered in relation to each other. The conclusions reached concerning permanence and change in a given culture are dependent
to a very considerable extent on the stress laid by the particular
observer of that culture on its conservatism or its flexibility.

The matter is of immediate importance, since it is widely
held that Euroamerican culture is more receptive to change than
any other. How relative such a point of view is may be seen from
the expressions of opinion of those who variously hold that
change is desirable, or is to be deplored. Contemporary patterns
of thought accept change in material aspects of our civilization
as, on the whole, good. On the other hand, change in such elements in our culture as the moral code, family structure, or underlying political sanctions is frowned upon. As a result, technological developments are so emphasized that the changes in this
area of our life symbolize for us a tendency to change in our
culture as a whole. Our culture is then differentiated from others
on this basis of receptivity to technological change, so that its
stability, in contrast to its propensity to change, is minimized.

3. In resolving the third paradox, that culture fills our lives,
yet we are largely unconscious of it, we are confronted with basic

psychological and philosophical questions. We must seek to understand the psychological problem of how human beings learn their cultures and function as members of society, and to find an answer to the philosophical question that asks whether culture is thus a function of human mentality, or exists by and of itself.

We here face the issue that, while culture, a human attribute, is restricted to man, culture as a whole, or any individual culture, is more than any individual human being can grasp. A case can thus be made for studying culture as though it were independent of man. Yet an equally strong case can be made for conceiving culture as having no more than psychological reality, existing as a series of constructs in the mind of the individual. Philosophically, here is but another instance of the age-old clash between realism and idealism, a clash that defines a fundamental cleavage of concept and approach to the nature of the world and of man. Both points of view, however, hold much that is essential to an understanding of culture, and we shall examine the arguments advanced by the proponents of each.

3

There is little doubt that culture *can* be studied without taking human beings into account. Most of the older descriptions of ways of life of given peoples are written solely in terms of institutions. Most diffusion studies—those which give the geographic spread of a given element of culture—are presented without any mention of the individuals who use the objects or observe given customs. It would be difficult even for the most psychologically oriented student of human behavior to deny the value of such research. It is essential that the structure of a culture be understood if the reasons why a people behave as they do are to be grasped; unless the structure of custom is taken fully into account, behavior will be meaningless.

The argument for the objective reality of culture—granting that it is possible to study custom as though it had objective reality—turns on the point that culture, being extra-human, "superorganic," is beyond the control of man and operates in terms of its own laws. Here we are analyzing *cultural determinism*, another of the several determinisms that have been advanced to explain the nature of culture.

Let us examine the statement that "any culture is more than any individual human being can grasp." At the present time, many millions of people in our society behave in certain predictable ways, within describable limits. To illustrate: we can count on the word "yes" to mean an affirmative answer to a question; on our farms, women will not do the plowing except under exceptional circumstances. "Yes" has meant an affirmative for many centuries; plowing has for countless decades been recognized as the work of men; and so with a vast number of items. But it is apparent that no person who two hundred years ago used the vocable "yes" to mean the affirmative or plowed his field is alive today.

Those who hold that culture exists by and of itself emphasize that traditional ways of life continue generation after generation, without reference to the span of life of any given person. Such an argument is undeniably impressive. We can almost envisage two entities—the everchanging group made up of human beings who enter it at birth, live their lives, and die; and the solid body of custom that flows on, its identity intact. That interrelations exist between people and culture not even the most confirmed determinist would deny, just as those who hold culture exists only as ideas in the minds of individuals who live it grant the need to study its institutionalized forms. It cannot be too strongly stressed, therefore, that we are discussing emphases rather than exclusive alternatives.

Not only when considered in the large, over the centuries, can culture be shown to be more than men; within a given group, at a given moment in its history, no individual is competent in all details of the ways of life of his group. More than this, no individual, though he be a member of the smallest tribe, with the simplest culture, knows his cultural heritage in its entirety. To take but the most obvious example, we need go no further than the fact of sex differences in accepted modes of behavior. Not only is an economic division of labor between men and women everywhere present, but we find in most cultures that the activities of men differ from those of women in the nature of their occupations within the family, in religious activities, or in the types of aesthetic satisfactions they find. Sometimes this is a matter of habit. That in West Africa women should make pottery and men sew cloth is neither more nor less rational than that, among ourselves, men are potters and women seamstresses. Or the division may be one consciously imposed and penalized if transgressed, as in the case of unauthorized manipulation of the supernatural among the Australian aborigines, or the wearing of women's clothing by men in our own society.

In populations of considerable size, with a high degree of specialization and a class structure, it is beyond the capacity of any one person to know his entire culture. Both the Chinese peasant of the nineteenth century and the Mandarin scholar lived according to the dictates of a common culture, but they went their separate ways, each following his particular mode of life, and probably not concerned with questions of how their lives differed. When priests are set off from laity, rulers from commoners, industrial specialists such as East African native ironworkers or Polynesian canoe builders from those who follow other trades, the individual, to an even greater degree, knows only a segment of his total culture, despite the fact that the individual's total culture describes the basic orientations in terms of which his group, as a whole, regularize their day-to-day conduct.

Culture, viewed as more than man, forms the third term in the progression of inorganic, organic, and superorganic that was first formulated by Herbert Spencer. More than half a century later, the word *superorganic* was used by Kroeber to stress the fact that, since culture and biological endowment are different, though related, phenomena, culture must be regarded as existing by and of itself. Kroeber says:

> Mohammedanism—a social phenomenon, in stifling the imitative possibilities of the pictorial and plastic arts, has obviously affected the civilization of many peoples; but it must also have altered the careers of many persons born in three continents during a thousand years.

Or, again,

> Even within one nationally limited sphere of civilization, similar results are necessarily bound to occur. The natural logician or administrator born into a caste of fishermen or street sweepers is not likely to achieve the satisfaction in life, and certainly not the success, that would have been his lot had his parents been Brahmins or Kshatriyas; and what is true formally of India holds true substantially for Europe.[3]

Much more documentation of his position is now at hand than existed when Kroeber wrote his paper, but his examples still illustrate his point well. Darwin's discovery of the concept of evolution, paralleled by Wallace, who was working on the other side of the globe, is one of his most striking illustrations. Of Darwin, Kroeber says:

> No one can sanely believe that the distinction of Darwin's greatest accomplishment, the formulation of the doctrine of evolution by natural selection, would now stand to his credit had he

[3] Reprinted in A. L. Kroeber, 1952, pp. 47–8.

been born fifty years sooner or later. If later, he would have been infallibly anticipated by Wallace, for one thing; by others, if an early death had cut off Wallace.

The case of Gregor Mendel's work in heredity, lost sight of because, according to this point of view, our culture was not ready for it, is equally well known. Published in 1865, it was ignored until 1900, when three students, independently, within a few weeks of each other, discovered the discovery of Mendel, and a new turn was given to biological science.

The study of women's dress styles made by Kroeber and Richardson, based on an earlier exploratory study of the subject by Kroeber,[4] is one of the most careful analyses of change in a specific element of culture that has been made. From various fashion guides, measurements and calculated ratios for certain traits in the female dress pattern were computed, year by year, from 1787 to 1936. For the period 1605 to 1787 they gathered the same information for such years as data were available. They analyzed length and width of skirt, position and diameter of the waist, and length and width of the decolletage, finding changes in regular sequence that would seem to transcend the operation of any factors due solely to chance. Yet what is the significance of the activities of the Paris dress designers, who, from year to year, make it their business to invent new modes, and who have, to a high degree, perfected techniques of inducing the acceptance of change in women's dresses? It is precisely because the elements of conscious planning and choice bulk so large that this phenomenon was selected as a test case. It is because of this, too, that the results cannot but be impressive as evidence of how man is swept by the historic stream of his culture, whether he desires it or not.

4

The case for the psychological reality of culture rests largely on the undesirability of dividing human experience so that man, the organism, is set off from those aspects of his behavior that make up the "superorganic" elements in his existence. Any culture observed over the years has a vitality that transcends the life of any member of the group that manifests it. Yet without man, culture could not exist. Therefore, to objectify a phenomenon that can have no manifestation except in human thought and action is to argue a separate existence for something that actually exists only in the mind of the student.

[4] Reprinted in A. L. Kroeber, 1952, pp. 332–6, 358–72.

A parallel is to be drawn between the "superorganic" conception of culture and the hypothesis of the group mind which, in earlier years, was made famous by such men as Le Bon and Trotter. The group mind was conceived as something more than the reactions of all the individuals composing, let us say, a mob. The question raised concerning the seat of this group mind, since it was held to be more than the sum of the reactions of individuals composing the group, led to the rejection of the hypothesis as not susceptible to the kind of proof required by scientific method.

The clearest definition of culture in psychological terms states: *Culture is the learned portion of human behavior.* Here the word "learned" is essential. All students recognize that whatever forms may compose a culture, they must be acquired by succeeding generations if they are not to be lost. Otherwise, it would be necessary to assume that not only is man an animal equipped with an innate culture-building drive, but with drives so specific as to orient his behavior along invariable lines. This was the view taken by the "instinct" psychologists, who postulated one instinct after another to account for reactions that were later found to be reactions so effectively assimilated that they had become automatic.

The arguments of the instinctivist school carried conviction because human beings actually do learn their cultures well, and by means of a process that is as pervasive as it is thorough. We use the word "education" when we refer to directed learning. But most culture, among all groups, is acquired by a process termed habituation, or imitation, or, perhaps best, unconscious *conditioning*, a form of learning related to the other types where conscious conditioning (training) is applied.

This process can be extraordinarily subtle. Thus, though a human being must, for organic reasons, periodically refrain from activity, the manner in which he takes his rest is culturally determined. Where people sleep on mats spread on the ground, it is intolerable for them to sleep in beds on soft mattresses. The reverse is equally true. Where wooden headrests are used, down pillows become oppressive. Should circumstances force readaptation, then a process of relearning, or *reconditioning*, accommodates one to the new circumstances.

Language offers an endless variety of instances of how meticulously speech is conditioned. Regional differences, such as the broad *a* of Boston as against the flat one of Cleveland; or status differences, as the speech of the London cockney when contrasted to that of the upper-class Londoner, afford excellent examples. Some forms are so slightly shaded that they are never heard, except by a trained, sensitive ear, as in the transmutation, in Chicago, of the flat middlewestern *a* in such a word as *cab* into *keb*, with the short *e*. Other examples, such as motor habits in walking or the manner of sitting down, are but two more of the many instances that might be cited to show how, without giving any thought to the process and without conscious teaching, man learns his culture.

The effectiveness, then, with which techniques, accepted modes of behavior, and various beliefs are handed down from one generation to the next gives to culture the degree of stability that permits it to be regarded as having an existence of its own. Yet what is handed down is never so rigidly prescribed as to leave no choice to the individual. One of the primary factors in cultural change is the variation that every society accepts in any given mode of behavior. Thus most people in our own culture habitually rest by sitting on chairs. But some chairs are soft and others hard, some rock and some do not, some have straight backs and some are rounded. We do not ordinarily sit cross-legged at low tables, however, nor on small stools, nor relax by standing on one leg.

Does not the conception of behavior as conditioned by tradition again argue that man is but a creature of his culture? The answer to this lies in the fact of permitted variation. In every culture there is always room for choice, even, it must be stressed, among the simplest, most conservative groups. For though much of man's behavior is automatic, we do not thereby conclude that man is an automaton. When some aspect of his culture that he has always taken for granted—a belief about a particular deity, perhaps, or the validity of a certain way of doing business, or some item of etiquette—is challenged, he makes his defense with a degree of emotion that eloquently bespeaks his feeling.

This signifies that culture is *meaningful*. Though behavior may be automatic, and sanctions taken for granted, yet any accepted form of action or belief, any institution in a culture, "makes sense." Herein lies the principal argument of those who hold that culture is a summation of the beliefs, habits and points of view of people, rather than a thing in itself. *Experience is culturally defined*, and this implies that culture has meaning for those who live in accordance with it. Even for material goods definition is essential. An object such as a table figures in the life of a people only as it is recognized as such. To a member of an isolated New Guinea tribe it would, of itself, be as incomprehensible as the symbolism of his designs would be to us. Human behavior, indeed, has been defined as "symbolic behavior." Working back from this factor of symbolism, we see that the use of symbols gives meaning to life. Through them man culturally defines his experience, which he orders in terms of the ways of life of the group into which he is born and, through the learning process, grows to become a fully functioning member of it.

5

Must we choose between the view that culture is an entity in its own right, moving irrespective of man, and the one that holds that culture is but a manifestation of the human psyche? Or is it possible to reconcile these two points of view?

So deeply do the conditionings of the individual lodge in human behavior, so automatic are his responses, so smooth the historic line to be traced when changes in a given culture are followed over a period of years, that it is difficult not to treat culture as a thing outside man. It is difficult, indeed, even to speak or write of culture without implying this. Yet, as we have seen, when culture is closely analyzed, we find but a series of patterned reactions that characterize the behavior of the members of a given group. That is, we find *people* reacting, *people* behaving, *people* thinking, *people* rationalizing. Under these circumstances, it becomes clear that what we do is to reify, that is, objectify and make concrete, the experiences of individuals in a group at a given time. These we gather into a totality we call their culture. And, *for purposes of study*, this is quite proper. The danger point is reached when we reify similarities in behavior that only result from the similar conditioning of a group of individuals to their common setting into something that exists outside man, something that is *superorganic*.

This does not mean that we deny the usefulness, for certain anthropological problems, of studying culture *as if* it had an objective existence. But we must not allow the recognition of a methodological need to obscure the fact that we are dealing with a construct—and that, as in all science, we erect this construct as a guide to our thinking and as an aid to analysis.

Chapter **Seventeen**

Culture and Society

In the study of man and his works, it is necessary to distinguish "culture" from its companion term "society." *A culture is the way of life of a people; while a society is an organized, interacting aggregate of individuals who follow a given way of life.* In still simpler terms *a society is composed of people; the way they behave is their culture.*[1] Can we, however, thus separate man as a social animal from man as a creature who has culture? Is not social behavior actually cultural behavior? Indeed, have we not seen that the ultimate reality in the study of man is man himself, rather than the ideas, the institutions, even the material objects that have come into being as a result of man's association in the aggregates we call "societies"? Let us consider these three points, briefly, in succession.

In stating that man is a social animal who lives only in organized aggregates, we touch on an aspect of his existence that, as we shall see, is shared by many other creatures in the biological

---

[1] S. F. Nadel (1951, pp. 79–80) phrases the distinction in this way: "Society, as I see it, means the totality of social facts projected on to the dimension of relationships and groupings; culture, the same totality in the dimension of action."

world. Except for a few instances whose significance is not entirely clear, man is the only creature that has achieved culture. Once we realize that man shares with many other social animals the propensity to live in aggregates, but is the sole culture-building animal, the distinction between the terms "society" and "culture" is at once apparent. Consequently, as a step in achieving understanding, the two must be considered separately as well as in their interrelations.

Much the same argument enters when we consider our second question, whether social behavior is not also cultural behavior. Here, too, when we say that man is a social animal, we must recognize that this is not the whole story. Social institutions may be broadly interpreted to include economic and political orientations as well as those based on kinship and free association. But only with difficulty can they be extended to include religion, the arts, and language, to say nothing of the unspoken sanctions that underlie all conduct. Social organization is the technical anthropological term for the basic aspect of human group life that comprises the institutions in which all other behavior, both social and individual, is set. To recognize the fact that man, in interacting with his fellows, provides a setting for these other types of institutions, means that the sanctioned patterns of behavior can be differentiated from the motives out of which they have arisen.

Yet, in the final analysis, are not *people*—society—the reality rather than their ways of life? Are not these latter intangibles merely inferences from the behavior that is to be observed when we visit a community of Eskimo, of Africans, of Frenchmen, and follow the comings and goings of the people, seeing how they react to each other, studying the pattern of these reactions, and thus charting the institutions that channel this behavior? This, indeed, is the case; and the process of observing people, termed field research, is the tool by which ethnography obtains its primary data.

The concept "society" as used in this sense is, nonetheless, subject to all the reservations that must be held in mind when the concept "culture" is used. Just as any culture was seen to be a reification of individual behavior, so any human society is similarly reified out of the succession of human beings who compose a group. The point will be remembered that culture, because it persists from one generation to another, is more than any individual who lives in it. In the same fashion, no society is made up of the same people for very long. Births and deaths constantly change its personnel. When a whole generation has passed, all that links a society to the past are the patterns of behavior that have been handed down to the people who now comprise it. It is apparent that, in assuming *social* continuity, we must call into play the same methodological departures from reality as when we assume the continuity of culture.

We have already seen that the study of society is important for us because it is essential to understand how the fact that man lives in organized aggregates affects his behavior. We must, however, take into account not only the social institutions man has created to permit human societies to function, but also the drives that cause him to set up these aggregates, and the manner in which the individual is integrated into the society into which he is born. These latter points will be discussed in this chapter, since they bear most importantly on the relation between society and culture.

2

The considerable degree to which man shares his propensity for social living with other animal forms is not generally realized. The systematic study of animal sociology is quite new. Allee, who has perhaps treated the subject most comprehensively, tells why it developed so slowly. In 1878 the French scientist Espinas published a work, *Des Sociétés Animales*, in which he affirmed, "that no living being is solitary, but that, from the lowest to the highest, each is normally immersed in some sort of social life." [2] Granting Espinas' statement was more sweeping than the facts justify, it was nonetheless important because "the scientific world was then . . . under the spell of the idea that there is an intense and frequently very personal struggle for existence so important and far reaching as to leave no room for so-called softer philosophies." [3]

In reaction against this philosophy of the fang and claw, Kropotkin stressed mutual aid as a factor in evolution:

> Two aspects of animal life impressed me most during the journeys which I made in my youth in Eastern Siberia and Northern Manchuria. One of them was the extreme severity of the struggle for existence which most species of animals have to carry on against an inclement Nature. . . . And the other was, that even in those few spots where animal life teemed in abundance, I failed to find—though I was eagerly looking for it—that bitter struggle for the means of existence, *among animals belonging to the same species*, which was considered by most Darwinists (though not always by Darwin himself) as the domi-

[2] W. C. Allee, 1938, p. 25.
[3] *Ibid.*, p. 26.

nant characteristic of struggle for life, and the main factor of evolution.

A lecture Kropotkin heard in St. Petersburg in 1880, delivered by the Russian zoologist Kessler, stimulated the formulation of his later ideas; for Kessler, as Kropotkin reports it, held, "that besides the *law of Mutual Struggle* there is in Nature the *law of Mutual Aid*, which, for the success of the struggle for life, and especially for the progressive evolution of the species, is far more important than the law of mutual contest." [4]

Though Kropotkin's data have for many reasons proved unacceptable to those trained in later times, the aspect of his findings that has stood up under later investigation is the demonstration of how extensive is cooperation among members of the same species, and how far down in the biological scale these patterns of social behavior reach. Ants and bees have long been renowned for their social qualities—the "social insects," they are called—as have the wolf pack and the bison herd. Later work, indeed, has demonstrated that non-social species, such as the ladybird beetles or male midges, collect in aggregates to hibernate or to await the coming of the females in mating season. Animals likewise may form part of a wider ecological community that includes not only all the different species that inhabit a given region, but also the plant life.

How important social life can be to animals is to be seen from an experiment conducted by Allee whereby goldfish, singly and in groups of ten, were exposed to fixed amounts of colloidal silver until they expired. Those exposed in groups of ten survived significantly longer than those exposed singly, because together they secreted a slime that rendered less toxic a dose that quickly killed any one of them when alone. White mice were shown to grow faster in small groups than in isolation or when overcrowded. When the mice had skin lesions in the region of the head that could only be treated by licking, the isolated mice went uncured until transferred to a cage where their fellows could treat them. The fact that they were able to huddle together when the temperature was lowered promoted their growth, since they could keep each other warm and thus give to the growth process the energy they would otherwise have to expend keeping warm.[5]

When we study animal societies, we find many analogies to human aggregates. The mechanisms of dominance and submission operative in them, the factors of competition and cooperation

[4] P. Kropotkin, 1916, pp. 1-3.
[5] W. C. Allee, 1938, *passim*.

within a group and between groups, the complexity of their social relations, all contribute significantly to their successful functioning. The most dramatic example of dominance and submission is found in the research of Schjelderup-Ebbe on birds of various sorts. Among these creatures, he stated, "There exists . . . a definite order or precedence or social distinction," which, he maintained, has "proved to be founded upon certain conditions of despotism." [6] This is what has come to be known as the *peck-order*. The "despotism" he described comes after the animal has passed the chick stage. Among chicks, though there is competition for food, for example, there is no pecking. Later, however, their "spirit of competition," which was regarded by this student as instinctive, "begins to turn into envy," especially when they must compete against other members of the flock who are older, stronger and better established. Old thus dominate young, males dominate females. Such other factors as the time of the year, illness, and the degree of acquaintance the animals have with one another are also operative.

The peck-order of barn-yard fowl has been carefully analyzed. In studying this problem each bird is identified by a marker so that its contacts with every other member of the flock can be recorded. Sometimes the results show that more than one bird has power, or a bird that dominates most of the others submits to one that is relatively weak because, let us say, at the first encounter of these two the dominant bird was ill and the other was able to prevail. In one flock of eighteen ducks of the same sex studied by Schjelderup-Ebbe the pecking hierarchy was clear:

1	bird	pecked	17	others
1	"	"	16	"
1	"	"	15	"
1	"	"	14	"
1	"	"	13	"
1	"	"	12	"
1	"	"	11	"
1	"	"	10	"
2	birds	"	8	"
1	bird	"	7	"
1	"	"	6	"
2	birds	"	5	"
2	"	"	3	"
1	bird	"	1	other
1	"	"	0	" 7

---

[6] T. Schjelderup-Ebbe, 1935, p. 949.
[7] *Ibid.*, pp. 965–6.

The fate of the lowest-ranking birds is not pleasant to contemplate. "They spend time in out-of-the-way places, feed after others have fed, and make their way around cautiously, apparently with an eye out to avoid contacts. The lowest-ranking birds may appear lean, and their plumage is somewhat more rumpled because they have less time to arrange it." [8]

It is not to be assumed, however, that this kind of dominance is the rule in all social aggregates. Even the social orders found among birds seem to vary from species to species. Allee asserts that the peck-order of the common chicken is far more rigid than in any other species studied by him. On the basis of his research on pigeons, he concludes: "It frequently becomes difficult to decide which bird stands higher in the social order." Though "social hierarchy among chickens is based on an almost absolute peck-right which smacks strongly of the despotism of which Schjelderup-Ebbe writes, these other birds have an organization based on peck-dominance rather than on absolute peck-right." That is, though "one becomes fairly sure which bird . . . will dominate in the larger number of their contacts . . . the result of the next meeting between two individuals is not to be known with certainty until it has taken place." [9]

Groupings of animals, then, are *organized*, though the degree and type of organization varies. Some are so loosely and so sporadically organized that one may use the designation "society" only with extreme reservation. Many others, however, not only in organization but in functioning are, in every sense of the word, a social unit. For, like human societies, such aggregates constitute unified groupings whose members, both in their internal and external relations, have a sense of "belonging" by identifying themselves with a given locality, recognizing their fellow members as such, and reacting against strangers.

Membership in such a social group rests on acceptance by at least a number of its members. In most cases, acceptance is achieved merely by the circumstance of being born into the group and of growing to maturity under its shelter. Yet not only is the infant brought to maturity in the group but his relations to his fellows are defined for him. On the basis of his field study of the gibbon, Carpenter reports:

> The integration of primates into groups is believed to be a complex process involving mutually reciprocal patterns of naturalistic behavior which are modified and made specific by learn-

[8] W. C. Allee, 1938, p. 182.
[9] *Ibid.,* pp. 186–9, *passim.*

ing or conditioning. Almost every phase of behavior of which a primate is capable enters to some degree into the determination of its "gregariousness" and the qualities of its complex social behavior.[10]

Relations between individuals, in all societies, change with age, with strength, with obligations assumed, and with status achieved. The modifications in the behavior of the hamadryad baboon mother, which contrasts with her prematernal behavior, as described by Zuckerman, makes the point. While a female baboon usually behaves with extreme passivity, as when males are struggling for her, after the birth of an offspring, she snatches up her baby at the first sign of danger and moves to a place of safety with it.[11]

Experimentation has not proceeded far enough to determine to what extent the individual in animal societies follows instinctive drives in achieving integration into his group, or to what extent it is aided by what Yerkes and Yerkes call "social stimulation" to enlarge on inborn tendencies. There is ample evidence, however, that anthropoid apes can be taught to eat substances foreign to their normal diet. The factor of imitation probably enters in such cases, even though there is reason to believe that monkeys and apes are not as imitative as popular ideas would hold. It is to be noted that most of the observations made on this aspect of anthropoid and monkey behavior have come out of experimental situations. To what extent this tendency would function in the wild cannot be stated.

One important factor in all social life is the identification of the individual with his group. This means that the outsider, until he is accepted, leads a life of considerable hardship. Köhler has given a most vivid description of this process in his classic study of chimpanzees. His group, he says, was "a vaguely organized community" of individuals "*used to each other.*" He continues:

> One day, a newly-bought chimpanzee arrived, and at first was put, for purposes of the sanitary control, in a special cage a few metres away from the others. She at once aroused the greatest interest on the part of the older animals, who tried their best with sticks and stalks put through the bars to indicate at least a not too friendly connexion with her; once even a stone was thrown against the wire-netting at the newcomer. . . . When the new-comer, after some weeks, was allowed into the large animals' ground in the presence of the older animals, they stood for

[10] C. R. Carpenter, 1934, p. 199.
[11] S. Zuckerman, 1932, pp. 237, 260.

a second in stony silence. But hardly had they followed her few uncertain steps with staring eyes than Rana, a foolish but otherwise harmless animal, uttered their cry of indignant fury, which was at once taken up by all the others in frenzied excitement. The next moment the new-comer had disappeared under a raging crowd of assailants, who dug their teeth into her skin, and who were only kept off by our most determined interference while we remained. Even after several days the eldest and most dangerous of the creatures tried over and over again to steal up to the stranger while we were present, and ill-treated her cruelly when we did not notice in time. She was a poor, weak creature, who at no time showed the slightest wish for a fight, and there was really nothing to arouse their anger, except that she was a stranger.[12]

The sequel is of equal interest:

Sultan, who had played less part in the above-mentioned assault, was the first to be left alone with the newly-arrived female. He at once began to busy himself with her, . . . but she was really very shy after her bad treatment. However, he went on trying to make friends, . . . until at last she gave way to his invitations to play, to his embraces, and—rather shyly—to his childish sexual advances. When the others came near and he was any distance away, she called him anxiously to her. . . . Whenever she was frightened, they at once put their arms round each other. Two other female apes, however, likewise soon broke away from the muttering group, and played with the new-comer . . . until at last only Chica and Grande, who up till now had shown no friendship for each other, united by a mutual aversion . . . led their own life in distant spots of the stockade, away from the new-comer and the renegades.[13]

Some of the reasons why societies are formed have been indicated in the preceding pages, where it has been shown how animal aggregates can achieve survival in a manner not possible for individuals. The degree to which their communal organizations are dictated by biophysical reasons, such as the need to care for the young, or whether other factors enter, need not concern us here. What we do know is that the tendency to live in societies is one that man shares with other animals.

3

Human and infrahuman societies have much in common both in form and function. The localization of the group, the fact

[12] W. Köhler, 1925, p. 301. Reprinted by permission.
[13] *Ibid.,* pp. 301–2.

of differentiation within it on the basis of age, or size, or some other trait, its cooperative aspect, the identification of the members of the "in-group" as against those outside it are all characteristic of human as well as animal aggregates. Such functions as care of the young, protection against enemies, the integration into the community of those born into it or received as adults from outside also characterize them all.

What differentiates human societies from others is that man is the only animal that has culture. The statement of the difference as phrased by Zuckerman is particularly cogent.

> Cultural phenomena may not, in the last resort, prove to be absolutely different from physiological events. But there is a significant distinction between the physiological responses of the animal and the cultural behavior of man. The effective stimuli involved in the behavior of animals are mainly inherent in immediate physical events, which are in no way the by-products of the activities of pre-existing animals of the same species. Man, on the other hand, amasses experience through speech, and the effective stimuli underlying human behaviour are largely products of the lives of pre-existing people. The environment within which human beings live is mainly the accumulation of activities of previous generations. Culture, in this sense, is an essentially human phenomenon.[14]

The same position has also been taken by Schneirla, who points out that, among ants, "the learning process is stereotyped and rote in character, and as a process is limited to the individual and the given situation," so that unlike human societies, where knowledge is cumulative, "the special learning of each society dies with it." Because of this, Schneirla concludes, we must "recognize the existence of a qualitatively different process of individual socialization on the human level, influenced very differently by psychological factors according to cultural pattern and social heritage, rather than in dependence upon the direct function of hereditary organic agencies as on the insect level." [15]

These statements express the uniquely human quality of culture, or, as we have phrased it, the fact that man is the only culture-building animal. Here also are other expressions of the distinction we have drawn between society, an aggregate of individuals, and culture, the body of learned behavior in accordance with which their lives are lived. Yet this is not enough. We must

[14] S. Zuckerman, 1932, p. 19.
[15] T. C. Schneirla, 1946, pp. 390–9.

draw still a further distinction between the processes involved when an individual is integrated into his society and what occurs when he learns the customary ways of thinking and acting that make up the culture that distinguishes his society from other human groupings.

The process by means of which an individual is integrated into his society is called *socialization*. It involves the adaptation of the individual to the fellow members of his group, which, in turn, gives him status and assigns to him the role he plays in the life of the community. He passes through various stages, each distinguished by certain permitted and prohibited forms of behavior, such as playfulness in the young or the manipulation of power among the elders. As sexual maturity is reached, he again participates in a family grouping, but now as parent, protector and teacher. He will also figure as a member of certain groupings not based on kinship at all but on sex or age differences.

Because man alone has the ability to develop and transmit learned behavior, his social institutions exhibit a variety and a degree of complexity greater than the social forms of any other *single species* of animal. By his ability to communicate with his fellows in the symbolic and conceptual forms of speech, he alone has been able to ring the innumerable variations on even such a basic social structure as the family. If we consider the group life of any species of infrahuman animals, we find that their social structures are far more uniform and thus much more predictable than those of man. For each of their generations learns only behavior common to all its contemporaries, whereas man builds on the experience of all who have gone before him.

For animals and man alike, *conditioning*, in its broadest sense, is the essential process involved. Animals can, of course, learn. Countless experiments have shown that canaries brought up among other birds will vary their song, or that cats can be brought up to play with rats rather than to kill them. In one experiment of this latter kind, Kuo even conditioned cats to be afraid of rats; nine of the twenty kittens reared in isolation from rat-killing cats themselves became rat-killers.[16] Yet conscious learning cannot be discarded as a factor, and for kittens brought up under normal circumstances the example of the mother cat is of appreciable importance.

That older animals teach their young is recognized far beyond the limits of scientific inquiry. Such a tale as the following, from Dutch Guiana, shows how recognition of the factor of

[16] Z. Y. Kuo, 1930.

teaching and learning among animals can be expressed in homely form:

> Kitten and little Rat were great friends. Every day they went to play together. But Rat did not know that he was Cat's favorite food, and Kitten did not know that Rat was his favorite food. But one day, when little Rat came home, his mother asked him, "With whom do you play?" He said, "With friend Kitten." And at the same time, when Kitten went home, his mother asked him, said, "With whom do you play?" He said, "With little Rat." Then Rat's mother said to him, "You must not play with Kitten any more, because you are his favorite food." And at the same time, too, mother Cat was saying to Kitten, "You stupid fellow, don't you know that he is your tidbit? When you play with him, you must strike him." The next day, no sooner did they come out on the street than Kitten called to friend Rat, said, "Aren't you coming to play with me any more?" At once little Rat answered him, "Yes, brother. There are wise people in your village, and there are wise people in my village, too!" [17]

The socialization of men is understandably more complex than that of animals, because human social institutions take on such varied and changing forms. This means, moreover, that the process of socialization is only a part of the process by means of which men adjust to their fellows in working with the total body of traditions—economic, social, technological, religious, aesthetic, linguistic—to which they fall heir. Here learning takes on special significance that must be fully grasped if its all-important role in shaping the way of life of a people is to be adequately appreciated. [18]

4

The aspects of the learning experience that mark off man from other creatures, and by means of which he achieves competence in his culture, may be called *enculturation*. This is in essence a process of conscious or unconscious conditioning, exercised within the limits sanctioned by a given body of custom. From this process not only is all adjustment to social living achieved, but also all those satisfactions, themselves a part of social experience, that derive from individual expression rather than association with others in the group.

Every human being goes through a process of enculturation,

[17] M. J. and F. S. Herskovits, 1936, p. 281.
[18] For statements of the psychocultural approach to this problem, see N. E. Millar and J. Dollard, 1941.

for without the adaptations it describes he could not live as a member of society. Like any phenomenon of human behavior, this process is most complex. In the earliest years of an individual's life, it is largely a matter of conditioning to fundamentals—habits of eating, sleeping, speaking, personal cleanliness—whose inculcation has been shown to have special significance in shaping the personality and forming the habit patterns of the adult in later life. Yet the enculturative experience is not terminated at the close of infancy. As an individual continues through childhood and adolescence to adult status, he is continuously exposed to this process of learning, which can be said to end only with his death.

The difference between the nature of the enculturative experience in the early years of life and later is that the range of conscious acceptance or rejection by an individual continuously increases as he grows older. By the time he has reached maturity, a man or woman has been so conditioned that he moves easily within the limits of accepted behavior set by his group. Thereafter, new forms of behavior presented to him are largely those involved in culture change—new inventions or discoveries, or new ideas diffused from outside his society about which, as an individual, he has to "make up his mind" and thus play his role in reorienting his culture.

In truth, we are here touching on one of the most fundamental aspects of the enculturative process, an aspect whose full significance will be probed when we take up such a problem as the relation of the individual to culture, or the question of conservatism and change in culture, the reconciliation of which, it will be recalled, involved the resolution of one of our apparent dilemmas in the understanding of culture. However, the basic principle involved is clear: *The enculturation of the individual in the early years of his life is the prime mechanism making for cultural stability, while the process, as it operates on more mature folk, is highly important in inducing change.*

It is because of the earliest enculturative conditionings that, as we have pointed out, "human beings learn their cultures so well that most behavior rarely rises to the level of consciousness." In our earliest years we are being continuously conditioned to conformity, whether through the exercise of techniques of punishment and reward, as in the inculcation of the moral code of society, or by imitation, as in learning motor habits, such as the gestures, or the cadences of speech. Infantile protest, such as occurs when a child refuses to learn to speak, is not absent. But such protests are individual ones, made against the restraints placed on the infant's freedom of behavior. It is significant that the infantile protest is not rationalized. It cannot be, for the linguistic—that is, the symbolic—equipment of the infant does not permit this.

In other words, learning, by inculcating in the new member of society the enculturative disciplines essential for his functioning as a member of his social group, contributes to social stability and cultural continuity. As the individual grows older, these early conditionings become so effective that they settle into the routines of daily behavior. Then the continuing enculturation to which he is exposed is in very large measure a reconditioning process, which lies on the conscious level. A man or woman knows the ways of behavior that are traditionally acceptable to his group in a given situation—in one society, that he must step off a path and turn his back on a passing elder to show respect, in another, that the thing to do with the property of a dead person is to burn it.

But should he have contact with another people who hold that respect is shown by facing a superior rather than by turning away from him, then even with the greatest freedom of choice, an alternative has been presented that must be grappled with. If he accepts the new mode for himself he may meet with resistance at home. But unless he is prevented from carrying on the new way of showing respect, his persistence will make of him a center from which a possible deviation from the sanctioned form of polite behavior radiates, and his fellows will be continuously faced with making the choice he has already made.

The resistances to revisions in economic behavior called into play by the spread of Euroamerican culture over the world demonstrate how this process works. The destruction of the property of the dead, or any other form of destruction of property, is frowned on in our culture. Great pressure to change such customs has been brought upon native peoples by administrators who have no concept of what the social significance of the destruction of property may be. Whether they have succeeded or not, the psychological processes of the natives in making an adjustment to this dictum is of a different order than the early conditioning process to which these same individuals were exposed as infants.

The enculturative experience of later life, however, is only intermittent. It thus presents a further contrast to the continuous conditioning to which the infant and young child are exposed. Nor do these enculturative situations, for the adult, cover as many segments of culture as for the young. The adult knows his language, the systems of etiquette that regulate behavior, the ways of facing the supernatural, the musical forms of his culture—all things that the child must learn. For the adult, enculturation has been completed except where new situations must be met. He projects the decisions he must reach in his daily round against the background of knowledge his culture has provided him. This permits an adult human being to react to the stimuli presented to him by his culture with a minimum of need to traverse ground already covered. Enculturation is thus the process that permits most behavior to be carried on *below the level of conscious thought.* In nontechnical language, it can be taken for granted in the manner in which we accept without question even such complex manifestations of our own culture as automobiles, electricity, and symphony orchestras, to say nothing of the art of writing or such a fundamental technological device as the wheel.

Chapter **Eighteen**

Culture and the Individual

The concept of enculturation affords us a bridge between culture as something that exists by and of itself, and culture as the total behavior of the individuals through whom it is manifest. We have seen that, in the process of enculturation, an individual learns the forms of conduct acceptable to his group. He does this so well that his thoughts, his values and his acts rarely conflict with those of other members of his society. In consequence, the life of the group can be reified into a series of institutions, capable of objective description as though they existed independently of the people who live in accordance with them.

This is the way most ethnographic studies of culture are presented. It is possible, for example, to state that in East Africa cattle are prized as tokens of status and wealth and not killed for food, or that in certain South American Indian cultures a man takes to his hammock when a child is born to his wife. Yet statements of this kind are but summations of the characteristic and thus predictable behavior of *people* in these situations. It is an East African man who contemplates his cattle with pride or envies his neighbor who has a larger herd; it is a South American Indian woman who carries on her work after childbirth while her man is being petted in his hammock. In short, the individual must never be lost sight of in considering the institution.

In the course of the enculturative experience, the individual tends to be molded into the kind of person his group envisages as desirable. Complete success is never achieved; some persons are more pliant than others, some resist the enculturative discipline more than their fellows. Yet, by and large, all become sufficiently alike so that, as one travels over the earth, one finds that just as cultures differ from each other, so people seem to differ from one society to the next.

Here lies the core of one of the critical problems in the study of culture—how enculturation affects the development of individual personalities. Does the process of growing up in a given society tend to encourage aggressive drives, so that successful competition within the group and warfare with other groups bring the greatest rewards to an individual? Or are gentler procedures held desirable, so that the most cooperative individual is best adjusted within the group, and diplomacy and compromise rule in contact with outsiders? Are inconsistencies in sanctioned behavior within a society the sources of frustration, or are institutions harmoniously blended so that an individual can live an adjusted life with a minimum of inner conflict?

How deep-seated the reactions to influences of this sort can be is to be perceived when we give a moment's thought to two conflicting patterns in the United States. On the one hand, the American is born into a society whose ideology is based on the concept of equality of opportunity, typified by such a commonly stated article of faith as, "Every boy has a chance to become president," or by the prominence of the success story in popular literature. Yet the handicaps posed by economic or social class lines, or by the circumstance of ethnic or racial origin, cannot be denied. To untold persons who have been indoctrinated with the concept of equality of opportunity, these contradictions present a conflict between ideals and experience that produces at best a tortured cynicism, and at worst the psychoses that result from the frustrations the individual has experienced.

The relation between culture and the individual, as seen in terms of the enculturative process, yields a profound sense of the plasticity of the human organism. Here we see how broad is the range of possible behavior permitted by man's biological heritage. From this, too, we derive the principle that any human being can master any culture, even in its subtlest aspect, provided he has the opportunity to learn it.

But it must not be concluded that the individual is solely a passive element in the process. In his early enculturation, it is true, a person is mainly the recipient of attention that ensures his adaptation to the patterns of behavior sanctioned by his group. Yet the sense of security that comes to him from the care he receives during his infancy, or the insecurity he feels under neglect, the degree to which he experiences a rigorous training in the exercise of physiological functions or is permitted freedom—such differences in the development of the individual may, in turn, have far-reaching consequences for society. The infant whose sense of security is invaded by a feeling that he is not accepted will grow up compensating for this deficiency. He may seek to impose his will on his fellows, by whatever means he finds at hand, until he becomes a tyrant like the Zulu chief Chaka.[1] The theory that holds that the history of a people is shaped by the dominant personalities who appear from time to time—the "great man" theory of history—was based on such facts. This theory is now discredited because it oversimplified a complicated process. But we can see how much it drew, all unwittingly, on the results of interaction between an individual and his group, as this is determined by his experience in the course of his enculturation to its standards of conduct, its system of values, its institutionalized forms of behavior.

It will be remembered that in the opening pages of this book the closeness of the relation between anthropology and psychology was stressed. This suggests that we should reconsider the formula, long accepted and still heard, that anthropology is concerned with groups, psychology with individuals. Under this formula culture was studied by anthropologists as a series of institutions, without reference to the place or function of the individual. Psychologists were held to be interested in individual human beings, whose mental processes were to be analyzed with but little, if any, reference to the cultural setting in which they were found.

It is a middle ground of common concern, long neglected, that we treat here. Such fundamental processes as motivation and adjustment cannot be separated from the situations in which they take place, nor can they be studied without reference to individuals who are motivated and who must make their adjustments. But while individuals respond to approval, seek security, strive to conform to accepted modes of behavior, or reach pre-eminence, their culture dictates what ends they will seek and what they must

[1] T. Mofolo, 1931.

do to achieve them. Our interest here, in short, is in the *psychology of culture,* or *psychoethnography* as it is called, which is the study of the individual as he is enculturated to the established norms of behavior already present in his society when he becomes a member of it.

2

The schools of psychology that have most stimulated the study of the individual in his cultural setting are behaviorism, the Gestalt or configurational approach, and psychoanalysis. Other influences can, of course, be found. Before 1920, various anthropologists, such as Franz Boas, A. A. Goldenweiser, C. G. Seligman, and W. H. R. Rivers, stressed the importance of taking psychology into account. The behavioristic school, which emphasized the principle of the conditioned response, provided anthropologists with conceptual and methodological tools they were quick to grasp and use.

To what extent the behavioristic point of view has been absorbed into the anthropological approach toward culture is to be seen in our discussion of enculturation in the preceding chapter. In vast proportion, the learning process *is* a conditioning process, or, in later years, one of reconditioning. If this were not so, a human being could not function, for his time would be spent in assessing each situation he might meet, instead of responding "without thinking," as we say. To see this, we may consider the problem of crossing a busy street. It is a dangerous business, and we recognize its dangers when we have to pilot a partially enculturated child across one. Adults, however, thread their way through traffic with but little thought, unless they travel to countries where the traffic moves in the opposite direction to that which they are accustomed; on the left, let us say, rather than the right. Only in such situations is the effectiveness of cultural conditioning realized, and the efficiency and freedom with which it endows us grasped.

Gestalt or configurational psychology, which followed and, in a sense, grew out of behaviorism, has been less specifically employed by anthropologists, despite its considerable influence on their thinking. The core of its position is the stress it places on the essential unity of any human experience. This point of view was particularly congenial to an anthropology that was increasingly realizing the integration of every culture, and laying more and more stress on the artificiality of attempts to divide a culture into sub-units without taking this integration into full account.

Gestalt, or later "field-theory," psychology, through the work of Lewin and of Brown underscored the importance of the fact that to differentiate the individual from his culture leads inevitably to a distorted perspective on behavior. To be effective, all those elements that, at a given moment, figure in the total setting of an individual or of a group must be considered. In this, of course, the culture in which the life of the subject is lived assumes a place of greatest importance.

The writings of Sigmund Freud and his disciples have had a profound influence on the anthropological study of the individual in his culture. The emphasis placed by Freud and his followers on the role of the experiences of the first years of life in shaping the human personality has stimulated anthropologists to study the life and training of the child in nonliterate societies. Freud's refusal to accept the taboo on discussing sex that permeated Euroamerican nineteenth- and early twentieth-century thinking resulted in a recognition by anthropologists of the importance of sex habits and the inclusion of their study in programs of research. The light thrown by the Freudians on the problem of motivation has stimulated a re-examination of many forms of behavior that represent rephrasings, "rationalizations," of objectives whose real character would not earlier have been admitted.

Freud's writings were accepted by anthropologists only slowly. One reason for this was the stress he laid on dream symbolism. Enthusiastic disciples of Freud, attempting to impress on native thinking a symbolism derived from the conventions of late nineteenth-century Vienna, where Freud worked, made apparent the inacceptability of such interpretations. Anthropologists had had too long experience with this sort of argument, for the study of many cultures had taught them that no specific form of any institution has universal scope.

Interestingly enough, the one book in which Freud purported to use anthropological materials, *Totem and Taboo*, did most to make anthropologists hostile to Freudian psychology. Freud had found that the attraction a mother holds for her son, which he named the Oedipus complex, was paralleled, on the level of the unconscious, by a dual attitude toward the father. This was well documented in Freud's analytical materials. He showed that it arises out of infantile jealousy of the father's relation to the mother; a jealousy, however, by no means untempered, since, at the same time, many bonds of affection exist between father and son. As a result of these findings, Freud advanced one of his most valuable concepts, that of *ambivalence*, which describes how at

late 12 *Carved ivory container from Benin, West Africa (height, 3⅛ in.). (A)
Section showing Christ on the cross, the spirit of the Holy Ghost (doves), Mary
and Saint John; (B) opposite side, showing Saint Andrew and Saint Peter. See p.
53. (Photographs by Mary Modglin, Chicago.)*

A B

C D

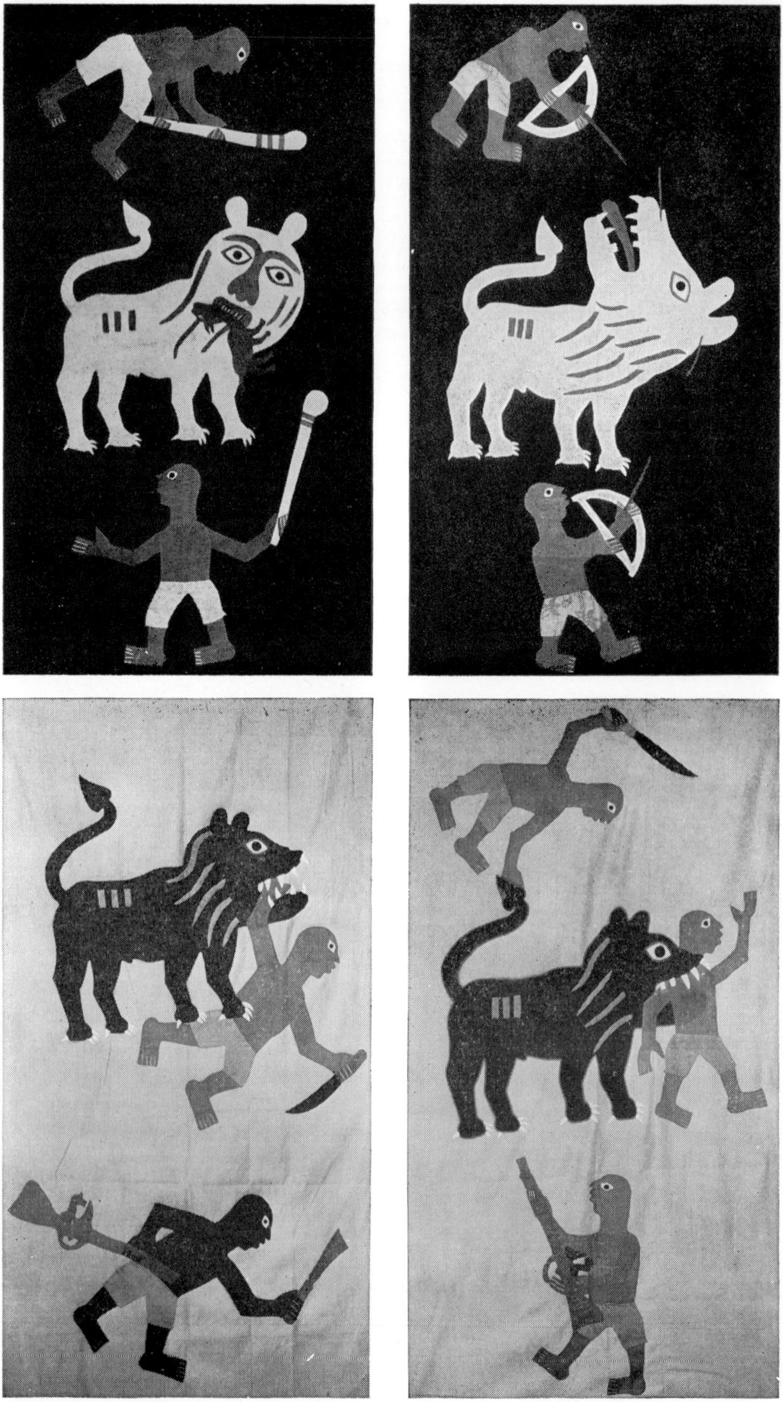

Plate 13 *Dahomean appliqué cloths, showing changes (A–D) in design over four generations of cloth sewers.* *See p. 256.*

any given moment one may be both attracted to a person or object and repelled by it, loving and at the same time hating it.

Struck by the implications of this mechanism for an understanding of the human mind, Freud turned to other cultures for materials to test its universality and to probe its origins. But without firsthand knowledge of any society but his own, without even knowing what studies of nonliterate peoples might throw light on his problem, he turned to secondary sources, compilations by writers trained and untrained. Furthermore, he did not seek comparative materials in these works, but evidences of origins, a quest now recognized as unattainable.

The competition between a man and his sons, he held, arose out of a situation that he believed to have existed in the earliest days of man's life on earth. In the primeval family, the "Old Man" ruled unquestioned, by right of brute force, and all women of the horde were his. As his sons grew older, they rebelled, and one day combined forces to murder their progenitor. Moreover, they made of his body a cannibalistic feast so as mystically to take his power for themselves. Returning to the women, who now, because of remorse for their deed they denied to themselves, they symbolized what they had done by holding sacred an animal that thus became a "natural and appropriate" substitute for the father, not to be eaten. Hence the phenomenon of ambivalence in the human mind, manifested in the wider social scene by the totemic symbols of many peoples, since the totem is a symbol at once sacred and loved, and yet tabooed and thus to be avoided; and of the prohibition against incest, universal in human societies.

B. Malinowski's chief contribution to the psychology of culture was his demonstration that Freud's findings reflected the time and place in which he worked, and that in the setting of certain types of family relationships, the Oedipus complex, as Freud enunciated it, did not exist.[2] Among the natives of the Melanesian Trobriand Islands, he found the family structure is of the type where descent is counted on the side of the mother, so that a child does not belong to his father's family at all and it is the mother's elder brother who directs the boy's life, thus releasing the father to be a friend and playmate. With the uncle as the one who punishes, who thwarts the child as the father does in Euroamerican families, Malinowski found many examples of reactions of the Oedipus variety directed against the mother's brother, but none against the father.

The significance of this study was not that it invalidated an

[2] B. Malinowski, 1927, *passim.*

important element in the Freudian system. Rather, it came increasingly to be realized that it, and researches that came after it, gave the Freudian system a wider relevance than it could otherwise have. This is exemplified in D. Eggan's analysis of an extended sequence of the dreams of a Hopi Indian, in which she exploits a psychoanalytic technique that has rarely been used by students concerned with the impact of the cultural setting on the personality of the individual. This neglect, she points out, has been caused both by the reaction of anthropologists against the "seemingly arbitrary use of symbols in dream interpretation" and by the amount of time and training necessary for the collection and adequate analysis of data of this kind. Yet, as she says, "if . . . the assumption is justified that dreams are a probable universal form of mental activity, at once idiosyncratic and culturally molded . . . ," then the analysis of dreams in terms of their manifest content, derived from the culture of the dreamer, shows "cultural stresses, as well as cultural supports," which shape his total reaction to the situations in which his life is lived. The forms of the dreams, though couched in an imagery quite different from that with which Freud dealt, nonetheless demonstrate how the observed "dream mechanisms . . . work on problems which are of more than passing concern to the individual," and reveal, among other things, "the frequency of the Freudian symbols at the manifest level, . . . as well as the incidence of those symbols to which the group itself attaches significance." [3]

Freud's postulate that the personality structure is dynamic and not fixed, the result of the total experience of the individual, has been seen to be basically sound. Malinowski's findings, and the studies of others, such as that of Eggan just cited, merely underscore the fact that the forms of personality disorders and their compensating mechanisms discovered by Freud to exist in certain circles of nineteenth-century Viennese society could not be expanded into universals having cross-cultural validity. Realization of the need to strike deep into the memories of infancy in understanding the human personality, one of his major contributions, has, as we have observed, led to studies of child care and child development as a key to the problem. But these, like other studies, it came to be realized, could only be made in their full cultural context, since no reaction of any human being could be understood without reference to its cultural framework. Similarly, the nature of many culturally sanctioned forms of behavior could be

[3] D. Eggan, 1949, pp. 177-8 and *passim;* 1952, pp. 477, 484, and *passim.*

understood only by referring to the common experiences of those who acted in accordance with them.

Here psychoanalysis joins gestalt psychology in establishing the unity of human experience, and thus forces the conclusion that culture cannot, in fact, be separated from people. Sapir, preeminent in this movement in anthropology, and one of the first to stress the importance of studying the individual in relation to his culture, has phrased the point tellingly:

> In spite of the oft asserted impersonality of culture, . . . far from being in any real sense "carried" by a community or a group as such, . . . it is discoverable only as the peculiar property of certain individuals, who cannot but give these cultural goods the impress of their own personality. . . . Culture is not, as a matter of sober fact, a "given" at all. It is so only by a polite convention of speech. As soon as we set ourselves at the vantage point of the culture-acquiring child, . . . everything changes. Culture is then not something given but something to be gradually and gropingly discovered.[4]

3

Three approaches to the study of the interaction between the individual and his cultural setting may be distinguished. The first, or *cultural configurational* approach, seeks to establish the dominant integrative patterns of cultures that encourage the development of certain personality types. The second, or *modal personality* approach, lays emphasis on the reactions of the individual to the cultural setting into which he is born. The aim of those who employ this method is to discern the typical personality structures to be found in a given society. The third, or *projective* approach, employs the various "projective" methods of analysis, especially the Rorschach series of ink blots, to establish the range of personality structures in a given society.

These three approaches represent no more than emphases on different aspects of the same problem. They are perhaps best described as successive steps taken in the analysis of the role of the individual in culture and the impact of culture on the human personality. The differences between them may be briefly phrased as follows: (1) *The cultural configurational approach is essentially ethnological.* The reference here is always to institutions, to the cultural patterns that set the framework within which develop the predominant personality structures of the group. (2) *The modal*

[4] E. Sapir, 1949, pp. 594-5, 596.

personality approach lays its stress on the individual. It derives from the application of psychoanalysis to the comparative study of broad problems of social adjustment. The contrasts between these two approaches may be said to arise out of their sources, the first from conventional ethnology, the second from orthodox Freudianism. (3) *Both the individual and culture figure where projective techniques are used.* The use of a standardized test to which all results can be referred provides a methodological tool for assessing the personality structures of the individual members of a given group in terms of their enculturation to the institutions and values of their culture.

The cultural configurational attack is most often thought of as exemplified in the writings of R. Benedict and M. Mead, though one of its earliest and its most concise statements is that of E. Sapir, from whom most anthropological study of the individual in his culture has stemmed. He says:

> The socialization of personality traits may be expected to lead cumulatively to the development of specific psychological biases in the cultures of the world. Thus Eskimo culture, contrasted with most North American Indian cultures, is extraverted; Hindu culture, on the whole corresponds to the world of the thinking introvert; the culture of the United States is definitely extraverted in character, with a greater emphasis on thinking and intuition than on feeling; and sensational evaluations are more clearly evident in the cultures of the Mediterranean area than in those of Northern Europe.[5]

Though he states here that "such psychological characterizations of culture . . . in the long run . . . are inevitable and necessary," Sapir later gave over this approach as his interest moved from the classification of whole cultures in psychological terms to the dynamics of personality formation.

The contribution of Mead derives principally from her field researches in the Southwest Pacific.[6] In Manus, an island off the coast of New Guinea, she related the social conditioning of the individual to the sharp breaks between childhood and adult patterns of behavior, and described the tensions induced by the need to adjust to such sharply differing situations. Later she studied the personality types of men and women in three New Guinea societies. Here the conclusion she reached was that it was culture that molded what had previously been held to be biologically de-

[5] E. Sapir, 1949, p. 563.
[6] M. Mead, 1939.

termined patterns of dominance and submission between the sexes. The individual was conceived as the resultant of the socio-cultural forces to which he was subject; and thus disappeared in the group.

The tendency to submerge the individual in studying differing psychological "sets" of different cultures also characterized the work of Benedict.[7] In outlining the traits of the cultures used to exemplify the types she describes, she drew on her own field research among the Zuñi Indians of the American Southwest, on Mead's investigations, on those of Boas among the Kwakiutl Indians of British Columbia, and on Fortune's study of the inhabitants of Dobu. These types she named Appolonian, which is broadly equivalent to Sapir's introverted type, and Dionysian, equivalent to the extraverted. The Zuñi Indians are given as an example of the first type. Their restraint in personal relations, the submergence of the individual in the group, their slowness to anger, and the absence of hysteria in their religious rites are some of the traits held to mark them off as having this type of culture. On the other hand, the passion of the Kwakiutl and the suspiciousness of the Dobuans, the extravaganza of the rites that mark the economic waste of the Kwakiutl potlatch as a psychological adjustment to a frustrating situation, and the use of garden magic in Dobu to extend the personality and establish the ego are characteristics that cause these cultures to be classified as Dionysian.

Like all pioneer effort, this position proved to have the defects of its virtues. It was pointed out that, in stressing cultural types, the variation in individual behavior, within the limits of the sanctions set by a culture, was lost sight of. The question was raised whether all the institutions of any culture could be expected to be in accord with the over-all pattern provided by the Apollonian-Dionysian classification, or any similar typological scheme. In the process of assigning cultures to these classifications, it was asked, must not the assumptions made by the observer and the selectivity of his observations as influenced by these assumptions dominate his judgment?[8] Papers by Li An-che on Zuñi, by Boas on the Kwakiutl, by Fortune on the Arapesh documented these reservations.[9] Li, a Chinese anthropologist, whose own physical traits made him inconspicuous among the Indians,

[7] R. Benedict, 1934.

[8] For a discussion of the methodological problem involved here, see Chap. 28 below.

[9] Cf. Li An-che, 1937, pp. 62–9; F. Boas, 1936, p. 267; 1938, pp. 684–5; R. F. Fortune, 1939, pp. 36–8.

found them, as people, to be quite different from the picture of themselves they had presented to white students. Boas observed how, among the Kwakiutl, the chief who indulged in the frenzied boasting of the potlatch could also, within his family, debase himself before the child who would one day be his successor. And Fortune pointed out that in one of the New Guinea tribes studied by Mead, the Arapesh, the conception that there is little aggression shown either by males or females required modification in the light of materials indicating that this people had well-established patterns of warfare.

The influence of the cultural configurationist point of view is, however, to be seen in the next development in this field, wherein, as has been indicated, certain psychoanalytic concepts were used to account for the differences in the personalities of peoples living in societies where different ways of life prevail. The Kardiner-Linton postulate of the "basic personality structure," held to prevail in each society, may be regarded as an extension and refinement of the Benedict-Mead hypothesis. Basic personality structure is conceived as a norm, not as a type, and is derived from the emphasis laid on the study of the individual. Yet stress placed on the varied influences that differing institutions of different cultures exert in the process of personality formation shows how this earlier work made available to the psychoanalyst Kardiner a sense of the possible variation in human institutions as a primary factor in explaining why peoples differ.[10]

Kardiner defines an institution as "any fixed mode of thought or behavior held by a group of individuals" that can be communicated, is generally accepted, and the violation of which causes disturbance. It is the reaction of the individual to the institution that produces the resultant behavior we call the personality. Institutions are classified as primary and secondary. The primary institutions arise out of the "conditions which the individual cannot control"—the food quest, sex customs, various training disciplines. The secondary ones are derived from the satisfaction of needs and the release of tensions created by the primary institutions, and are exemplified by the deity that, for a people, resolves the anxieties created by their need for assurance of a continued food supply. What distinguishes this approach from its predecessor is thus its dynamic character, since the basic personality structure is derived from an analysis of the institutions and their effect on people in one culture after another.

The data employed to document this hypothesis were de-

[10] Cf. A. Kardiner, 1944, p. 7.

rived from Kardiner's probing of various field workers for materials out of their field experience that would throw light on the personalities of the peoples they had studied. Such materials every field worker has, but rarely publishes—casual observations of nursing practices, how a man behaved in a quarrel, the playthings of children, gossip about why a couple in the village failed to make the customary adjustment in marriage. The stress laid on the institutions centering about the food quest and social structure, as well as on sex customs, represented a distinct advance over the conventional psychoanalytic preoccupation with data restricted to this last category. Objections, however, were raised to the slighting of elements in culture not related to its socioeconomic problems, such as aesthetic aspects, or the phases of religion concerned with other matters than the food quest and family continuity.

The study carried on by Du Bois [11] in the island of Alor was designed to provide field data that could be used to test the basic personality hypothesis by means of techniques of "psychocultural synthesis"—"cultural analyses, combined with the better established psychological processes of the analytical school." In order to do this, details of Alorese life, concerning such matters as infant care, the handling of early and late childhood and adolescence, marriage, sex, and the psychological aspects of religion, were studied in addition to the more general ethnographic research into the customs of the people. Eight autobiographies were also obtained from four men and four women, who were encouraged to recount their dreams in daily sessions with the ethnographer. Children's drawings were collected, and various tests, including thirty-seven Rorschachs, were given. On the basis of these data, Kardiner evaluated the personalities of the subjects in the light of their cultural setting, and his conclusions were independently checked by an expert in Rorschach analysis. That the correspondences in these independent evaluations of a field worker's data, gathered to study the culture-personality equation, were as numerous as they proved to be, indicates that fruitful cooperation between anthropology and psychiatry is to be expected in further research. It also points toward the advisability of cross-disciplinary training to make it possible for the same individual to carry on the various phases of research and analysis demanded by this method of psychocultural synthesis.

It is here that the use of the Rorschach and perhaps other "projective" techniques, such as the Thematic Apperception Test,

[11] C. Du Bois, 1944, p. 5.

will prove to be most effective. Hallowell has made the most consistent use of the first of these, and we may with profit cite his exposition of its usefulness in the study of individuals in different cultures, wherein he summarizes the nature of the method, how it is employed, and its potential contribution to the study of the relationship between personality and culture.[12]

> [The] raw data for personality appraisal in the Rorschach technique are obtained from the verbal responses the subject gives to a standard series of ten representationally indefinite but symmetrically structured ink-blots, presented to him one by one in a set order. Five of the blots are entirely black, but with variegated tonal values, three are in colors, and two combine black with red. . . . By means of an initial suggestion that he say what they might be, the subject is motivated to invest the stimulus fields successively set before him with representational values, rather than to see them as meaningless forms or empty designs. Whatever he says is written down by the administrator of the test."

Through this process of interpretation—much after the manner we may see a horse's head in a cloud of the summer sky—these ink-blots permit the subject to express himself in ways of his own choosing. That is, "it is *he* who projects meaning into objectively meaningless forms; it is *he* who gives few or many answers, selects the whole card or a part of it for interpretation, makes use of the color or ignores it. . . ." This is why such tests are called *projective*. This process of projecting meaning into forms otherwise meaningless allows the investigator, through analyzing the results, to reach conclusions about the personality structure of the individuals he is studying.

From the cross-cultural use of this method we may expect not only a picture of the characteristic personality structures of different groups, but a knowledge of the variation in such structures within each society as well. This is especially important since, given a sense of variability in psychological responses, we shall have a surer grasp on the problem of what constitutes normal and abnormal behavior. These are only two of the questions to which, as Hallowell points out, tests such as the Rorschach can make their contribution. "It is not a substitute for other methods of approach," he states in summary, "but it nicely supplements them." The Rorschach and other tests of its type are thus an important addition to the battery of techniques that must be brought to bear on the problem of the interaction between the individual and the situation in which he finds adjustment or maladjustment.

[12] A. I. Hallowell, 1945b, pp. 198–9.

4

The attention that has come to be given to the problem of the individual in his culture clearly constitutes a major advance in the study of man. But the work done in this field represents only a beginning, and methods, no less than documentation, are in their infancy. Let us briefly summarize what has been done, outline what needs to be done, and list some of the cautions experience suggests as anthropology treads the difficult path toward understanding this phase of its study of man.

The problem has been well stated, and its significance clearly recognized. That the life of man is one; that "culture" is a construct that describes the similar modes of conduct of those who make up a given society; that, in the final analysis, behavior is always the behavior of individuals however it may lend itself to summary in generalized terms—these are some of the ways in which this recognition is to be phrased. Though it makes the studying of culture even more complex than earlier researches have indicated, this only encourages us to feel that it is a clear step in the direction of reality.

It is a further gain that the problem is being attacked by the use of various methods, and that the terminology applied to it is under continuous refinement. The ascription of personality *types* to given cultures has given way to the study of the *range* of personalities in a society. The concept of *basic* personality has come to be thought of as *modal* personality. And there has been the further recognition that even within a culture, characteristic personality sub-types may develop from the differing situations of the lives of persons who play different roles in a given group. These are what Linton terms *status personalities*, defined as "status-linked response configurations." [13]

The need still exists, however, for the study of the individual in culture by other methods, in addition to the dominant psychiatric-psychoanalytic techniques that have been used in most studies, especially as this had to do with the cross-cultural study of the range of manifestations given by human behavior in such of its non-psychiatric aspects as perception, motivation, and memory. How important this approach can be is apparent from Hallowell's brief discussion of its implications in the field of perception alone.[14] The great advance achieved by means of the concepts and methods of psychiatry and psychoanalysis has been indicated, but,

[13] R. Linton, 1945, p. 130.
[14] A. I. Hallowell, 1951.

in the enthusiasm its contributions have engendered, there has been a tendency to overlook the handicaps under which it labors. Yet it would be unrealistic not to recognize that psychiatric techniques are devised to be applied to individuals and to achieve therapeutic ends. To adapt them to the study of societies composed of adjusted as well as maladjusted individuals involves a reorientation that has by no means been reached. The need for such a reorientation is to be seen in the classification of entire cultures in psychopathological terms such as paranoid or schizoid. It is to be seen in the description of behavior norms in terms of concepts derived from the study of neurotic states. It is to be seen in the extraordinary stress laid on analyzing cultures in terms of the frustrations they impose, and the comparative neglect of the channels to adjustment offered by every way of life.

A classification of the range of adjustment in a non-European group, given by Hallowell for his Saulteaux subjects on the basis of their Rorschach protocols, effectively makes the point we have just raised. Among these people, who have to make extraordinarily severe adjustments because of frustrations induced by contact with the whites, the percentages were:

Well adjusted	10.7%
Adjusted	33.3
Poorly adjusted	44.1
Maladjusted	11.7

In comparison, 50 per cent of the Inland Indians who had had least contact with whites were found to fall into the categories of "adjusted" and "well adjusted." Among those with most contacts, 60 per cent were poorly adjusted or maladjusted, and this group also included the more extreme cases of failure to adapt.[15] From the point of view of the problem of understanding the interaction between the individual and his total setting, it is apparent that emphasis on the study of processes of adjustment is as essential as it is to discover the circumstances that make for maladjustment.

5

Whether the anthropologist can study the problem of personality in nonliterate societies without himself having been psychoanalyzed has been much discussed. One has not heard as much about whether the practicing psychoanalyst concerned with cross-cultural studies must have first-hand experience of societies where sanctions, goals, and systems of motivations and control

[15] A. I. Hallowell, 1945b, p. 208.

are entirely different from his own. The fact is, however, that only a few of the psychoanalysts who have shown interest in these problems have themselves conducted field research to test their hypotheses among groups outside the orbit of Euroamerican culture. This is almost as true, moreover, of students whose approach to the psychology of culture is that of academic psychology as it is of those who utilize the techniques and concepts of the analytic school.

One suggestion that has been advanced seems to offer a common-sense resolution of the difficulty that inheres in work on a problem that lies so broadly athwart two fields of science. "Some sort of immediate compromise" should be reached, it is stated, "in which anthropologist and psychologist will be willing each to learn as much as possible from the other and to define some of his problems and methods accordingly." [16] To the extent that some anthropologists have worked in psychological laboratories or have undergone analyses, and that some psychologists, especially in the more academic tradition, have tested their hypotheses in field research, this "immediate compromise" is being approached. Examples of this latter category, such as the studies by Dennis on Hopi children or by Campbell on the Negroes of the Virgin Islands may be cited.

It is of importance also that the initial attack on the study of the individual in culture be made from the point of view of the total configuration of the body of customs in which he lives. Opler phrases this view as follows:

> Out of the ethnologist's sojourn in the field are emerging two orders of problems and two sets of interests. One deals with total cultural patterns, those generalized and inclusive statements which any member of the group, whatever his own behavior and personality, would have to admit represent the traditions and recognized usages of his people. The other interest is that which . . . seeks to learn the relationship between the larger pattern of the culture and the world of intimate meanings, attachments and behavior patterns each individual builds up for himself.[17]

The approach of cultural orientation is too fruitful to be lost through an exclusive emphasis on the study of the individual.

Out of a comprehension of cultural orientations emerges the importance of culturally sanctioned continuities and discontinuities in the process of growing up. Such a contrast in our own cul-

---

[16] F. C. Bartlett, 1937, p. 402.
[17] M. E. Opler, 1938, p. 218.

ture as that between the responsibility of the adult for his act and the lack of responsibility of the child represents a patterned discontinuity that is by no means found in all cultures. It sets the stage for a difficult adjustment that each individual member of our society must make. Similarly, dominance of a father over his children, which is also the rule among ourselves, is to be contrasted with conventions where father and children are on a plane of relative equality. A situation of father-child equality makes for no such discontinuity in growing up as exists in a situation where the father is dominant. This difference we would expect to find reflected in the personalities of those who live in the psychological atmosphere of the one type of society as against the other.[18]

How a study of the cultural setting may disclose psychological mechanisms that direct individual behavior and channel aggressions through disciplined avenues of expression is to be seen in such an institution as the *apo* rite practiced by the Ashanti of the Gold Coast, West Africa. During the *apo* ceremony, it is not only permitted, but held imperative that those in power hear the derision, reproaches, and imprecations of their subjects for the injustices they have committed. This, the Ashanti believe, assures that the souls of the rulers will not suffer harm by reason of the repressed ill will of those they have angered, which otherwise would cumulatively have the power to weaken, and even to kill them. The effectiveness of this obviously Freudian mechanism in releasing repressions calls for no elaboration. It clearly throws much light on how institutionalized forms of behavior correct imbalance in the development of the individual personalities involved.[19]

In a comparable manner, the concept of *fiofio* held by the Negroes of Dutch Guiana reveals the type of adjustment these people make to certain tensions that are always set up by group life. In this case, an unresolved quarrel between kindred or intimates is believed to exert its influence long after the fact of its occurrence has been erased from conscious thought. Let one party to the quarrel accept a gift or favor from the other, and illness or some misfortune will befall one or both of them. Only when, after consultation with a diviner, the cause has been revealed, and the public ceremonial retraction, termed *puru mofo* ("withdraw from the mouth"), has been performed will the evil be removed. Otherwise, death is believed to result. "To have honest dislikes is natural enough and, says the native, these do a man no harm; it is only

[18] R. Benedict, 1938.
[19] R. S. Rattray, 1923, pp. 151-69.

when quarrels are masked in surface friendliness and an ancient grudge is harboured that it is dangerous to make an exchange of belongings or accept any gesture of affection." [20]

Such socially sanctioned mechanisms that permit the release of inhibitions and the resolution of conflicts are the means whereby the adjustment of the individual is, to a considerable degree, attained. They are aspects of those consensuses of belief and behavior that, as elements in culture, constitute the matrix within which the personality structures of individuals develop, and in which they must function.

[20] M. J. Herskovits, 1934, p. 82.

Chapter **Nineteen**

Cultural Relativism and Cultural Values

All peoples form judgments about ways of life different from their own. Where systematic study is undertaken, comparison gives rise to classification, and scholars have devised many schemes for classifying ways of life. Moral judgments have been drawn regarding the ethical principles that guide the behavior and mold the value systems of different peoples. Their economic and political structures and their religious beliefs have been ranked in order of complexity, efficiency, desirability. Their art, music, and literary forms have been weighed.

It has become increasingly evident, however, that evaluations of this kind stand or fall with the acceptance of the premises from which they derive. In addition, many of the criteria on which judgment is based are in conflict, so that conclusions drawn from one definition of what is desirable will not agree with those based on another formulation.

A simple example will illustrate this. There are not many ways in which the primary family can be constituted. One man may live with one woman, one woman may have a number of husbands, one man may have a number of wives. But if we evaluate these forms according to their function of perpetuating the group, it is clear that they perform their essential tasks. Otherwise, the societies wherein they exist would not survive.

Such an answer will, however, not satisfy all those who have undertaken to study cultural evaluation. What of the moral questions inherent in the practice of monogamy as against polygamy, the adjustment of children raised in households where, for example, the mothers must compete on behalf of their offspring for the favors of a common husband? If monogamy is held to be the desired form of marriage, the responses to these questions are predetermined. But when we consider these questions from the point of view of those who live in polygamous societies, alternative answers, based on different conceptions of what is desirable, may be given.

Let us consider, for example, the life of a plural family in the West African culture of Dahomey.[1] Here, within a compound, live a man and his wives. The man has his own house, as has each of the women and her children, after the basic African principle that two wives cannot successfully inhabit the same quarters. Each wife in turn spends a native week of four days with the common husband, cooking his food, washing his cloths, sleeping in his house, and then making way for the next. Her children, however, remain in their mother's hut. With pregnancy, she drops out of this routine, and ideally, in the interest of her child's health and her own, does not again visit her husband until the child has been born and weaned. This means a period of from three to four years, since infants are nursed two years and longer.

The compound, made up of these households, is a cooperative unit. The women who sell goods in the market, or make pottery, or have their gardens, contribute to its support. This aspect, though of great economic importance, is secondary to the prestige that attaches to the larger unit. This is why one often finds a wife not only urging her husband to acquire a second spouse but even aiding him by loans or gifts to make this possible.

Tensions do arise between the women who inhabit a large compound. Thirteen different ways of getting married have been recorded in this society, and in a large household those wives who are married in the same category tend to unite against all others. Competition for the regard of the husband is also a factor, when several wives try to influence the choice of an heir in favor of their own sons. Yet all the children of the compound play together, and the strength of the emotional ties between the children of the same mother more than compensates for whatever

[1] Cf. M. J. Herskovits, 1938b, Vol. I, pp. 137–55, 300–51.

stresses may arise between brothers and sisters who share the same father but are of different mothers. Cooperation, moreover, is by no means a mere formality among the wives. Many common tasks are performed in friendly unison, and there is solidarity in the interest of women's prerogatives, or where the status of the common husband is threatened.

We may now return to the criteria to be applied in drawing judgments concerning polygamous as against monogamous families. The family structure of Dahomey is obviously a complex institution. If we but consider the possible lines of personal relations among the many individuals concerned, we see clearly how numerous are the ramifications of reciprocal right and obligation of the Dahomean family. The effectiveness of the Dahomean family is, however, patent. It has, for untold generations, performed its function of rearing the young; more than this, the very size of the group gives it economic resources and a resulting stability that might well be envied by those who live under different systems of family organization. Moral values are always difficult to establish, but at least in this society marriage is clearly distinguished from casual sex relations and from prostitution, in its supernatural sanctions and in the prestige it confers, to say nothing of the economic obligations toward spouse and prospective offspring explicitly accepted by one who enters into a marriage.

Numerous problems of adjustment do present themselves in an aggregate of this sort. It does not call for much speculation to understand the plaint of the head of one large compound when he said: "One must be something of a diplomat if one has many wives." Yet the sly digs in proverb and song, and the open quarreling, involve no greater stress than is found in any small rural community where people are also thrown closely together for long periods of time. Quarrels between co-wives are not greatly different from disputes over the back fence between neighbors. And Dahomeans who know European culture, when they argue for their system, stress the fact that it permits the individual wife to space her children in a way that is in accord with the best precepts of modern gynecology.

Thus polygamy, when looked at from the point of view of those who practice it, is seen to hold values that are not apparent from the outside. A similar case can be made for monogamy, however, when it is attacked by those who are enculturated to a different kind of family structure. And what is true of a particular phase of culture such as this, is also true of others. Evaluations are *relative* to the cultural background out of which they arise.

2

Cultural relativism is in essence an approach to the question of the nature and role of values in culture. It represents a scientific, inductive attack on an age-old philosophical problem, using fresh, cross-cultural data, hitherto not available to scholars, gained from the study of the underlying value-systems of societies having the most diverse customs. The principle of cultural relativism, briefly stated, is as follows: *Judgments are based on experience, and experience is interpreted by each individual in terms of his own enculturation.* Those who hold for the existence of fixed values will find materials in other societies that necessitate a re-investigation of their assumptions. Are there absolute moral standards, or are moral standards effective only as far as they agree with the orientations of a given people at a given period of their history? We even approach the problem of the ultimate nature of reality itself. Cassirer [2] holds that reality can only be experienced through the symbolism of language. Is reality, then, not defined and redefined by the ever-varied symbolisms of the innumerable languages of mankind?

Answers to questions such as these represent one of the most profound contributions of anthropology to the analysis of man's place in the world. When we reflect that such intangibles as right and wrong, normal and abnormal, beautiful and plain are absorbed as a person learns the ways of the group into which he is born, we see that we are dealing here with a process of first importance. Even the facts of the physical world are discerned through the enculturative screen, so that the perception of time, distance, weight, size, and other "realities" is mediated by the conventions of any given group.

No culture, however, is a closed system of rigid molds to which the behavior of all members of a society must conform. In stressing the psychological reality of culture, it was made plain that a culture, as such, can *do* nothing. It is but the summation of the behavior and habitual modes of thought of the persons who make up a particular society. Though by learning and habit these individuals conform to the ways of the group into which they have been born, they nonetheless vary in their reactions to the situations of living they commonly meet. They vary, too, in the degree to which they desire change, as whole cultures vary. This is but another way in which we see that culture is flexible and holds many possibilities of choice within its framework, and that

[2] E. Cassirer, 1944, p. 25.

to recognize the values held by a given people in no wise implies that these values are a constant factor in the lives of succeeding generations of the same group.

How the ideas of a people mediate their approach even to the physical world can be made plain by a few examples. Indians living in the southwestern part of the United States think in terms of *six* cardinal points rather than four. In addition to north, south, east and west, they include the directions "up" and "down." From the point of view that the universe is three dimensional, these Indians are entirely realistic. Among ourselves, even in airplane navigation, where three dimensions must be coped with as they need not by those who keep to the surface of the earth, we separate direction from height in instruments and in our thinking about position. We operate, conceptually, on two distinct planes. One is horizontal—"We are traveling ENE." One is vertical—"We are now cruising at 8000 feet."

Or take a problem in the patterning of sound. We accept the concept of the wave length, tune pianos in accordance with a mechanically determined scale, and are thus conditioned to what we call true pitch. Some persons, we say, have absolute pitch; that is, a note struck or sung at random will immediately be given its place in the scale—"That's B flat." A composition learned in a given key, when transposed, will deeply trouble such a person, though those who are musically trained but do not have true pitch will enjoy such a transposed work, if the *relation* of each note to every other has not been disturbed. Let us assume that it is proposed to study whether this ability to identify a note is an inborn trait, found among varying but small percentages of individuals in various societies. The difficulty of probing such a question appears immediately once we discover that but few peoples have fixed scales, and none other than ourselves has the concept of true pitch! Those living in cultures without mechanically tuned and true instruments are free to enjoy notes that are as much as a quarter-tone "off," as we would say. As for the patterned progressions in which the typical scales and modal orientations of any musical convention are set, the number of such systems, each of which is consistent within its own limits, is infinite.

The principle that judgments are derived from experience has a sure psychological foundation. This has been best expressed by Sherif in his development of the hypothesis of "social norms." His experiments are fundamental, and his accessory concept of the "frame of reference," the background to which experience is referred, has become standard in social psychology. Because of its importance for an understanding of cultural differences, we shall briefly describe the work he did in testing his hypothesis that "experience appears to depend always on *relations.*"

The subjects were introduced into a dark room where a dim light appeared and disappeared when an electric key was pressed. Some subjects were brought into the room, first alone and later as members of groups, while others were exposed to the group situation before they were tested individually. Though the light was fixed, the autokinetic response to a situation like this is such that the subject perceives movement where there is none, since being in a room that is perfectly dark, he has no fixed point from which to judge motion. Judgments obtained from each subject *individually* conclusively demonstrated that individuals subjectively establish "a range of extent and a point (a standard or norm) within that range which is peculiar to the individual" when no objective standard is available to them, and that in repetitions of the experiment the established range is retained. In the group situation, diversity of individual judgments concerning the extent of movement by the light became gradually less. But each group establishes a norm peculiar to itself, after which the individual member "perceives the situation in terms of the range and norm that he brings from the group situation."

The general principle advanced on the basis of these results and those of many other relevant psychological experiments may be given in the words of Sherif:

> The psychological basis of the established social norms, such as stereotypes, fashions, conventions, customs, and values, is the formation of common frames of reference as a product of the contact of individuals. Once such frames of reference are established and incorporated in the individual they enter as important factors to determine or modify his reactions to the situations he will face later—social, and even non-social, at times, especially if the stimulus field is not well structured [3]

—that is, if the experience is one for which precedents in accustomed behavior are lacking.[4]

In extending Sherif's position in terms of the cross-cultural

---

[3] M. Sherif, 1936, pp. 32, 92–106.

[4] A psychological basis for relativism, deriving from gestalt psychology, has been proposed by S. E. Asch, 1952, pp. 364–84. He fails to consider in this connection Sherif's critical experiment cited above, and does not seem adequately to have distinguished (1) between intracultural and cross-cultural relativism, and (2) between absolute values and universal aspects of culture.

factor, but with stress laid on the influence of culture on the perceptive processes in general, Hallowell has stated:

> Dynamically conceived, perception is one of the basic integral functions of an on-going adjustment process on the part of any organism viewed as a whole. . . . In our species, therefore, what is learned and the content of acquired experience in one society as compared to another constitute important variables with reference to full understanding, explanation or prediction of the behavior of individuals who have received a *common* preparation for action.[5]

And he quotes from a paper by Bartlett, the psychologist: "Everybody now realizes that perceptual meanings, which have an enormous influence upon social life, vary from social setting to social setting, and the field anthropologist has a golden opportunity to study the limits of such variation and its importance." [6]

Numerous instances of how the norms posited by Sherif vary may be found in the anthropological literature. They are so powerful that they can flourish even in the face of what seems to the outsider an obvious, objectively verifiable fact. Thus, while recognizing the role of both father and mother in procreation, many peoples have conventions of relationship that count descent on but one side of the family. In such societies, it is common for incest lines to be so arbitrarily defined that "first cousins," as we would say, on the mother's side call each other brother and sister and regard marriage with one another with horror. Yet marriage within the same degree of biological relationship on the father's side may be held not only desirable, but sometimes mandatory. This is because two persons related in this way are by definition not considered blood relatives.

The very definition of what is normal or abnormal is relative to the cultural frame of reference. As an example of this, we may take the phenomenon of possession as found among African and New World Negroes. The supreme expression of their religious experience, possession, is a psychological state wherein a displacement of personality occurs when the god "comes to the head" of the worshipper. The individual thereupon is held to be the deity himself. This phenomenon has been described in pathological terms by many students whose approach is non-anthropological, because of its surface resemblance to cases in the

[5] A. I. Hallowell, 1951, pp. 166-7.
[6] *Ibid.*, p. 190.

records of medical practitioners, psychological clinicians, psychiatrists, and others. The hysteria-like trances, where persons, their eyes tightly closed, move about excitedly and presumably without purpose or design, or roll on the ground, muttering meaningless syllables, or go into a state where their bodies achieve complete rigidity, are not difficult to equate with the neurotic and even psychotic manifestations of abnormality found in Euroamerican society.

Yet when we look beneath behavior to meaning, and place such apparently random acts in their cultural frame of reference, such conclusions become untenable. For *relative to the setting in which these possession experiences occur, they are not to be regarded as abnormal at all,* much less psychopathological. They are *culturally* patterned, and often induced by learning and discipline. The dancing or other acts of the possessed persons are so stylized that one who knows this religion can identify the god possessing a devotee by the behavior of the individual possessed. Furthermore, the possession experience does not seem to be confined to emotionally unstable persons. Those who "get the god" run the gamut of personality types found in the group. Observation of persons who frequent the cults, yet who, in the idiom of worship "have nothing in the head" and thus never experience possession, seems to show that they are far less adjusted than those who do get possessed. Finally, the nature of the possession experience in these cultures is so disciplined that it may only come to a given devotee under particular circumstances. In West Africa and Brazil the gods come only to those who have been designated in advance by the priest of their group, who lays his hands on their heads. In Haiti, for an initiate not a member of the family group giving a rite to become possessed at a ceremony is considered extremely "bad form" socially and a sign of spiritual weakness, evidence that the god is not under the control of his worshipper.

The terminology of psychopathology, employed solely for descriptive purposes, may be of some utility. But the connotation it carries of psychic instability, emotional imbalance, and departure from normality recommends the use of other words that do not invite such a distortion of cultural reality. For in these Negro societies, the meaning this experience holds for the people falls entirely in the realm of understandable, predictable, *normal* behavior. This behavior is known and recognized by all members as an experience that may come to any one of them, and is to be welcomed not only for the psychological security it affords, but also for the status, economic gain, aesthetic expression, and emotional release it vouchsafes the devotee.

3

The primary mechanism that directs the evaluation of culture is *ethnocentrism*. Ethnocentrism is the point of view that one's own way of life is to be preferred to all others. Flowing logically from the process of early enculturation, it characterizes the way most individuals feel about their own culture, whether or not they verbalize their feeling. Outside the stream of Euroamerican culture, particularly among nonliterate peoples, this is taken for granted and is to be viewed as a factor making for individual adjustment and social integration. For the strengthening of the ego, identification with one's own group, whose ways are implicitly accepted as best, is all-important. It is when, as in Euroamerican culture, ethnocentrism is rationalized and made the basis of programs of action detrimental to the well-being of other peoples that it gives rise to serious problems.

The ethnocentrism of nonliterate peoples is best illustrated in their myths, folk tales, proverbs, and linguistic habits. It is manifest in many tribal names whose meaning in their respective languages signifies "human beings." The inference that those to whom the name does not apply are outside this category is, however, rarely, if ever, explicitly made. When the Suriname Bush Negro, shown a flashlight, admires it and then quotes the proverb: "White man's magic isn't black man's magic," he is merely reaffirming his faith in his own culture. He is pointing out that the stranger, for all his mechanical devices, would be lost in the Guiana jungle without the aid of his Bush Negro friends.

A myth of the origin of human races, told by the Cherokee Indians of the Great Smoky Mountains, gives another instance of this kind of ethnocentrism. The Creator fashioned man by first making and firing an oven and then, from dough he had prepared, shaping three figures in human form. He placed the figures in the oven and waited for them to get done. But his impatience to see the result of this, his crowning experiment in the work of creation, was so great that he removed the first figure too soon. It was sadly underdone—pale, an unlovely color, and from it descended the white people. His second figure had fared well. The timing was accurate, the form, richly browned, that was to be the ancestor of the Indians, pleased him in every way. He so admired it, indeed, that he neglected to take out of the oven the third form, until he smelled it burning. He threw open the door, only to find this last one charred and black. It was regrettable, but there was nothing to be done; and this was the first Negro.[7]

This is the more usual form that ethnocentrism takes among many peoples—a gentle insistence on the good qualities of one's own group, without any drive to extend this attitude into the field of action. With such a point of view, the objectives, sanctioned modes of behavior, and value systems of peoples with whom one's own group comes into contact can be considered in terms of their desirability, then accepted or rejected without any reference to absolute standards. That differences in the manner of achieving commonly sought objectives may be permitted to exist without a judgment being entered on them involves a reorientation in thought for those in the Euroamerican tradition, because in this tradition, a difference in belief or behavior too often implies something is worse, or less desirable, and must be changed.

The assumption that the cultures of nonliterate peoples are of inferior quality is the end product of a long series of developments in our intellectual history. It is not often recalled that the concept of progress, that strikes so deep into our thinking, is relatively recent. It is, in fact, a unique product of our culture. It is a part of the same historic stream that developed the scientific tradition and that developed the machine, thus giving Europe and America the final word in debates about cultural superiority. "He who makes the gun-powder wields the power," runs a Dahomean proverb. There is no rebuttal to an argument, backed by cannon, advanced to a people who can defend their position with no more than spears, or bows and arrows, or at best a flint-lock gun.

With the possible exception of technological aspects of life, however, the proposition that one way of thought or action is better than another is exceedingly difficult to establish on the grounds of any universally acceptable criteria. Let us take food as an instance. Cultures are equipped differently for the production of food, so that some peoples eat more than others. However, even on the subsistence level, there is no people who do not hold certain potential foodstuffs to be unfit for human consumption. Milk, which figures importantly in our diet, is rejected as food by the peoples of southeastern Asia. Beef, a valued element of the

---

[7] This unpublished myth was told F. M. Olbrechts of Brussels, Belgium, in the course of field work among the Cherokee. His having made it available is gratefully acknowledged. A similar tale has been recorded from the Albany Cree, at Moose Factory, according to information received from F. Voget.

Euroamerican cuisine, is regarded with disgust by Hindus. Nor need compulsions be this strong. The thousands of cattle that range the East African highlands are primarily wealth to be preserved, and not a source of food. Only the cow that dies is eaten —a practice that, though abhorrent to us, has apparently done no harm to those who have been following it for generations.

Totemic and religious taboos set up further restrictions on available foodstuffs, while the refusal to consume many other edible and nourishing substances is simply based on the enculturative conditioning. So strong is this conditioning that prohibited food consumed unwittingly may induce such a physiological reaction as vomiting. All young animals provide succulent meat, but the religious abhorrence of the young pig by the Mohammedan is no stronger than the secular rejection of puppy steaks or colt chops by ourselves. Ant larvae, insect grubs, locusts—all of which have caloric values and vitamin content—when roasted or otherwise cooked, or even when raw, are regarded by many peoples as delicacies. We never eat them, however, though they are equally available to us. On the other hand, some of the same peoples who feed on these with gusto regard substances that come out of tin cans as unfit for human consumption.

4

Cultures are sometimes evaluated by the use of the designations "civilized" and "primitive." These terms have a deceptive simplicity, and attempts to document the differences implied in them have proved to be of unexpected difficulty. The distinctions embedded in this set of opposed terms are, however, of special importance for us. "Primitive" is the word commonly used to describe the peoples with whom anthropologists have been traditionally most concerned, the groups whose study has given cultural anthropology most of its data.

The word "primitive" came into use when anthropological theory was dominated by an evolutionary approach that equated living peoples, outside the stream of European culture, with the first human inhabitants of the earth, who may justifiably be called "primitive" in the etymological sense of the word. It is quite another matter to call present-day peoples by the same term. In other words, *there is no justification for regarding any living group as our contemporary ancestors.*

The conception implicit in such usage colors many of the judgments we draw about the ways of life of native peoples with whom the expansion of Europe and America has brought us into contact. When we speak or write of the living customs of American Indian or African or South Seas peoples as being in some way earlier than our own, we are treating their cultures as though they were unchanging. As we have seen, however, one of the basic generalizations about culture is that no body of custom is static. No matter how conservative a people may be, we find on investigation that their way of life is not the same as it was in earlier times. Remains of the past dug from the earth give ample evidence that continuous, though perhaps slow, change was the rule. Hence we must conclude that no group that exists today lives either as its ancestry or our own lived.

With time, the word "primitive" gathered other connotations that are evaluative rather than descriptive. Primitive peoples are said to have simple cultures. One widely accepted hypothesis holds that they are unable to think except in terms of a special kind of mental process. Perhaps as a summation of all these, it is asserted that primitive cultures are inferior in quality to the historic civilizations. Such terms as "savage" or "barbarous" are applied to them in this sense, deriving from a presumed evolutionary sequence of "savagery," "barbarism," and "civilization."

One example can be taken from the extended investigation into the nature and processes of change in civilization by the historian A. J. Toynbee. He speaks of those peoples outside the "base-line" of "the modern Western national community" as the "external proletariat," whose contacts with a "civilization" tend to debase it. In the United States, the "external proletariat" was the Indian. The powerful influence exerted by the Indian in modifying the ways of life of the American frontiersmen, through the "barbarization" of European custom, as he terms it, astonishes Toynbee. Many similar instances concern him, as, for example, the influence of the "barbarians of West Africa" on modern art.

> This triumph of a Negro art in the northern states of America and in the western countries of Europe represents a . . . signal victory for Barbarism. . . . To the layman's eye the flight to Benin [a center of African art] and the flight to Byzantium seem equally unlikely to lead the latter-day Western artist to the recovery of his lost soul.[8]

For all the philosophical grounding and immense scholarship in Toynbee's massive work, it is apparent that these attitudes but demonstrate the biases of the writer. Borrowing is a basic mechanism of cultural interchange, and results inevitably from any con-

[8] A. J. Toynbee, 1934–9, Vol. V, pp. 373, 479–80, 482.

tact of peoples. Quite as often as not a dominant group are deeply influenced by the customs of those over whom they rule. Toynbee's astonishment is based on what he calls the "initial disparity in spiritual culture" between the "incomers from Europe" and the Indians. Evidence is vast that the portrayal of the savage as a creature living in anarchism, without moral restraint and without sensibilities, is a vulgar caricature. What happened in America does not "astonish" the scientific student of culture. The mutual borrowing by colonists of Indian customs and by Indians of European custom should be taken for granted, despite disparity in size of the groups in power and even in capacity to survive under attack.

Some of the characteristics held to distinguish "primitive" or "savage" ways of life are open to serious question. What, for example, is a "simple" culture? The aboriginal Australians, customarily held to be one of the most "primitive" peoples on earth, have a kinship terminology and a method of counting relationship based on it so complex that for many years it defied the attempts of students to analyze it. It puts to shame our own simple series of relationship terms, where we do not even distinguish between paternal and maternal grandparents, or older or younger brother, and call literally dozens of relatives by the same word, "cousin." The natives of Peru, before the Spanish conquest, made tapestries of finer weave, dyed in colors less subject to deterioration, than any of the deservedly prized Gobelin tapestries. The world-view of the Africans, which has so much in common with the Hellenic world-view, or the epic myths of the Polynesians, impress their complexities on all who take the trouble to become acquainted with them. These, and untold other examples, show that "primitive" folk do not have ways of life that are necessarily simple. Such instances also demonstrate that "primitive" peoples are neither childlike, nor naïve, nor unsophisticated, to cite favored adjectives that are often used by those who have either had no first-hand experience with such peoples, or have not taken the trouble to come to know them through reading contemporary accounts of their ways of life.

That "primitive" peoples fail to distinguish between reality and the supernatural, as the theory concerning their presumed "prelogical mentality," put forward by the French philosopher, L. Lévy-Bruhl [9] held, is similarly proved untenable by the facts.

[9] Lévy-Bruhl, 1923, 1926. It is a tribute to the intellectual honesty and greatness of this scholar that when convinced by the data of the invalidity of this concept, he was willing to renounce it, though it had for many years

For the facts about many cultures demonstrate that all peoples *at times* think in terms of objectively provable causation, just as *at times*, they indulge in explanations that relate a fact to an *apparent* cause. What the comparative study of culture, based on first-hand contact with many peoples, has taught is that all peoples think in terms of certain premises that are taken for granted. Granted the premises, the logic is inescapable.

Most of the life of any people is lived on a plane where ideas of causation or explanations of the universe enter but rarely. In these homely aspects of life, what we would call a "hard-headed sense of reality" is manifested. Thus, except for the names, the following passage from the autobiography of a Navaho Indian, telling of the last illness of the narrator's father, rings entirely familiar to ears accustomed to the reasoning of a mechanistic tradition.

> Old man Hat said, "I don't think I'll get well. I don't think I'll live long. That's how I feel about myself, because of the way I look now. I look at myself, and there's nothing on me, no flesh on me any more, nothing but skin and bones. That's why I don't think I'll live long. . . . About eating, you know I can't eat anything that's hard, only things that are soft, something I can swallow. But I don't take much, only two or three swallows. But I drink plenty of water." Choclays Kinsman said, "Even though you're that way, my older brother, you'd better keep eating all the time. By doing that it'll give you strength. If you don't you'll surely get weak. Even though you're so weak now and not able to eat, try to eat and swallow something. Somehow or other you might get over your illness. If you quit eating food, then you'll sure be gone." That's what he said, and then he left, and I went out with the herd.[10]

We readily recognize the common-sense reasoning in this passage. Let us look at another instance where the explanation of a phenomenon is based on a premise at variance with what we regard as scientific fact. We take as our instance a widely spread West African belief that the youngest child is sharper of wit than his older brothers and sisters. This belief is based on the observation that children tend to resemble their parents, and the fact, further observed, that as a man or woman grows older, he grows in experience. These facts may seem unrelated to us, but not to

been identified with his name. Before his death in 1940 he set down his reasons why he no longer regarded the idea of "primitive mentality" as valid, in notebooks posthumously published, where he sketched his ideas for his next book. (Cf. L. Lévy-Bruhl, 1949, pp. 49–50, 61–2, 129, 157.)

[10] W. Dyk, 1938, p. 269.

the West African. He reasons that greater age permits them to pass on to their younger, and especially their youngest child, a surer, more alert awareness. Such a child is thus expected to surpass his older siblings in astuteness. The *logic* of this reasoning is impeccable. It is with the *premises* that we must differ, if we would challenge the conclusion.

In truth, it must be recognized that all human beings think "prelogically" at times.[11] The pattern of scientific thought on which we pride ourselves is followed by relatively few persons in our culture. Nor do these persons think logically all the time. When they are actually at work in their laboratories, they employ the rigorous logic of science. But outside it, other categories of reasoning come into play, as when a scientist thinks in terms of "luck" in social ventures or pays homage to some symbolic representation of power or grace.

The assumption that all those called "primitives" or "savages" have many characteristics in common when they are contrasted to "civilized" peoples is another expression of the tendency to evaluate cultures. In actuality, the range of behavior among all those many peoples termed "primitive" is much greater than among those few called "civilized." Thus we find "primitive" peoples with money economies like "civilized" ones, others who practice barter, and still others who are economically self-sufficient and do not trade at all. Numerous marriage forms and family types, including monogamy, are found in "primitive" societies. Some have totemism, but more do not. Some have a clan system, many do not. Some count descent through both parents, as we do; some count it only on the father's side; some count it on the mother's. And so we could continue with institutions of all kinds, and much customary behavior, meeting always with variety. Whatever the word "primitive" means, then, it comprehends no unity of custom, tradition, belief, or institution.

In anthropological works, the words "primitive" or "savage" do not have the connotation they possess in such a work as Toynbee's or in other non-anthropological writings. Anthropologists merely use the word "primitive" or "savage" to denote peoples outside the stream of Euroamerican culture who do not possess written languages. By reiterating this meaning, it was hoped that it would no longer convey such meanings as simple or naïve, or

---

[11] This point of view was also accepted by Lévy-Bruhl, who in his posthumously published notebooks states: "From a strictly logical point of view, no difference between primitive mentality and our own can be established."—L. Lévy-Bruhl, 1949, p. 70.

serve as a catchall to describe, except in the simple matter of absence of writing, such differing civilizations as those of the Siberian reindeer herders or the Lunda Empire of the Congo.

Several terms to replace "primitive" have been suggested. "Non-historic," which is one of these, implies that absence of written history is the equivalent of having no history at all, which, of course, cannot be said of any people who exist in time. "Pre-literate" has found more favor, but here the objection is that the prefix *pre-*, derived from the "contemporary ancestor" concept, implies that peoples without written languages are at a stage antecedent to the one in which, presumably, they will devise, or at least acquire, writing. The third form, *nonliterate*, simply describes the fact that these peoples do not have written languages. It is sometimes confused with "illiterate," but the use of this word should be guarded against, since it carries a distinct connotation of inferiority in ability or opportunity or both. "Nonliterate," because it is colorless, conveys its meaning unambiguously, and is readily applicable to the data it seeks to delimit, is thus to be preferred to all the other terms we have considered.

The question that inevitably comes to mind is whether any single criterion such as the presence or absence of writing is adequate to describe the many peoples it seeks to comprehend. Its adequacy has been indicated by its demonstrated usefulness, though it is evident that no one characteristic is ideally satisfactory for designating entire cultures. It is to be recognized that certain other characteristics commonly go with an absence of writing. Nonliterate peoples are found on observation to be relatively more isolated, to have smaller numbers, and to be less addicted to rapid change in their sanctioned modes of behavior than those that have writing. In recent generations, moreover, Euroamerican culture has had to be set off not only from nonliterate cultures but from the literate cultures outside Europe and America as well, because of the presence in European and American culture of a technology based on power-driven machinery and the scientific tradition. But it must be recognized that none of these differences, except perhaps this last, is as clearly manifest as is the presence or absence of writing.

5

Before we terminate our discussion of cultural relativism, it is important that we consider certain questions that are raised when the cultural-relativistic position is advanced. "It may be true," it is argued, "that human beings live in accordance with the ways they have learned. These ways may be regarded by them as best. A people may be so devoted to these ways that they are ready to fight and die for them. In terms of survival value, their effectiveness may be admitted, since the group that lives in accordance with them continues to exist. But does this mean that all systems of moral values, all concepts of right and wrong, are founded on such shifting sands that there is no need for morality, for proper behavior, for ethical codes? Does not a relativistic philosophy, indeed, imply a negation of these?"

To hold that values do not exist because they are relative to time and place is to fall prey to a fallacy that results from a failure to take into account the positive contribution of the relativistic position. For cultural relativism is a philosophy that recognizes the values set up by every society to guide its own life and that understands their worth to those who live by them, though they may differ from one's own. Instead of underscoring differences from absolute norms that, however objectively arrived at, are nonetheless the product of a given time or place, the relativistic point of view brings into relief the validity of every set of norms for the people who have them, and the values these represent.

It is essential, in considering cultural relativism, that we differentiate absolutes from universals. *Absolutes* are fixed, and, as far as convention is concerned, are not admitted to have variation, to differ from culture to culture, from epoch to epoch. *Universals*, on the other hand, are those least common denominators to be extracted from the range of variation that all phenomena of the natural or cultural world manifest. If we apply the distinction between these two concepts in drawing an answer to the points raised in our question, these criticisms are found to lose their force. To say that there is no absolute criterion of values or morals, or even, psychologically, of time or space, does not mean that such criteria, in differing *forms*, do not comprise universals in human culture. Morality is a universal, and so is enjoyment of beauty, and some standard for truth. The many forms these concepts take are but products of the particular historical experience of the societies that manifest them. In each, criteria are subject to continuous questioning, continuous change. But the basic conceptions remain, to channel thought and direct conduct, to give purpose to living.

In considering cultural relativism, also, we must recognize that it has three quite different aspects, which in most discussions of it tend to be disregarded. One of these is methodological, one philosophical, and one practical. As it has been put:

As method, relativism encompasses the principle of our science that, in studying a culture, one seeks to attain as great a degree of objectivity as possible; that one does not judge the modes of behavior one is describing, or seek to change them. Rather, one seeks to understand the sanctions of behavior in terms of the established relationships within the culture itself, and refrains from making interpretations that arise from a preconceived frame of reference. Relativism as philosophy concerns the nature of cultural values, and, beyond this, the implications of an epistemology that derives from a recognition of the force of enculturative conditioning in shaping thought and behavior. Its practical aspects involve the application—the practice—of the philosophical principles derived from this method, to the wider, cross-cultural scene.

We may follow this reasoning somewhat further.

In these terms, the three aspects of cultural relativism can be regarded as representing a logical sequence which, in a broad sense, the historical development of the idea has also followed. That is, the methodological aspect, whereby the data from which the epistemological propositions flow are gathered, ordered and assessed, came first. For it is difficult to conceive of a systematic theory of cultural relativism—as against a generalized idea of live-and-let-live—without the pre-existence of the massive ethnographic documentation gathered by anthropologists concerning the similarities and differences between cultures the world over. Out of these data came the philosophical position, and with the philosophical position came speculation as to its implications for conduct.[12]

Cultural relativism, in all cases, must be sharply distinguished from concepts of the relativity of individual behavior, which would negate all social controls over conduct. Conformity to the code of the group is a requirement for any regularity in life. Yet to say that we have a right to expect conformity to the code of our day for ourselves does not imply that we need expect, much less impose, conformity to our code on persons who live by other codes. The very core of cultural relativism is the social discipline that comes of respect for differences—of mutual respect. Emphasis on the worth of many ways of life, not one, is an affirmation of the values in each culture. Such emphasis seeks to understand and to harmonize goals, not to judge and destroy those that do not dovetail with our own. Cultural history teaches that, important as it is to discern and study the parallelisms in human civilizations,

[12] M. J. Herskovits, 1951, p. 24.

it is no less important to discern and study the different ways man has devised to fulfill his needs.

That it has been necessary to consider questions such as have been raised reflects an enculturative experience wherein the prevalent system of morals is not only consciously inculcated, but its exclusive claim to excellence emphasized. There are not many cultures, for example, where a rigid dichotomy between good and evil, such as we have set up, is insisted upon. Rather it is recognized that good and evil are but the extremes of a continuously varied scale between these poles that produces only different degrees of greyness. We thus return to the principle enunciated earlier, that "judgments are based on experience, and experience is interpreted by each individual in terms of his enculturation." In a culture where absolute values are stressed, the relativism of a world that encompasses many ways of living will be difficult to comprehend. Rather, it will offer a field day for value judgments based on the degree to which a given body of customs resembles or differs from those of Euroamerican culture.[13]

Once comprehended, however, and employing the field methods of the scientific student of man, together with an awareness of the satisfactions the most varied bodies of custom yield, this position gives us a leverage to lift us out of the ethnocentric morass in which our thinking about ultimate values has for so long bogged down. With a means of probing deeply into all manner of differing cultural orientations, of reaching into the significance of the ways of living of different peoples, we can turn again to our own culture with fresh perspective, and an objectivity that can be achieved in no other manner.

[13] Instances of the rejection of relativism on philosophical grounds, by writers who attempt to reconcile the principle of absolute values with the diversity of known systems, are to be found in E. Vivas, 1950, pp. 27–42, and D. Bidney, 1953a, pp. 689–95, 1953b, pp. 423–9. Both of these discussions, also, afford examples of the confusion that results when a distinction is not drawn between the methodological, philosophical, and practical aspects of relativism. For a critical consideration of relativism that, by implication, recognizes these differences, see R. Redfield, 1953, pp. 144 ff.

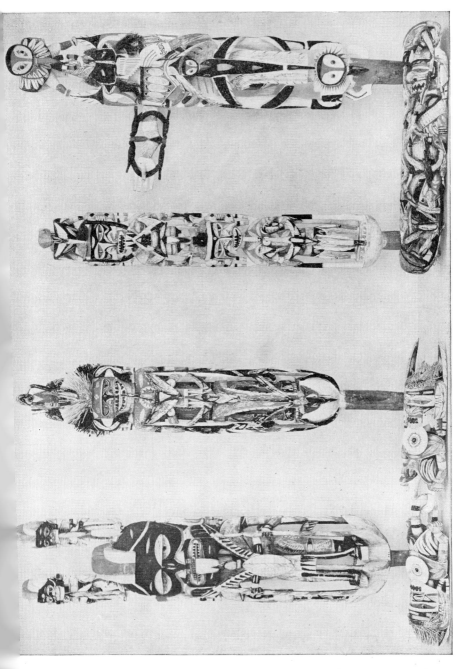

te 14 *Ceremonial carved wooden statues from New Ireland. See p. 264. (Photo-ph courtesy Chicago Natural History Museum.)*

Plate 15 *(A) Bush Negro comb; (B) clothes beater; (C) tray. See p. 264.*

Chapter **Twenty**

The Ethnographer's Laboratory

The field is the laboratory of the cultural anthropologist. To carry on his field work, he goes to the people he has elected to study, listening to their conversation, visiting their homes, attending their rites, observing their customary behavior, questioning them about their traditions, as he probes their way of life to attain a rounded view of their culture or to analyze some special aspect of it. In this, he is the ethnographer, the collector of data, which he will later, on his return from the field, analyze and relate to other materials.

Traditionally, the anthropologist has carried on field studies among nonliterate, "primitive," peoples who are outside the historic stream of Euroamerican or other literate cultures. Often these nonliterate peoples live in the far places of the earth, and to reach them the student may have to cope with difficulties of transportation, with disease, or with physical harm. But this aspect of the cultural anthropologist's work, like its "romantic" elements that appeal to laymen who would escape from the problems of everyday life that confront them, has been greatly overstressed. In the main, field work is like all scientific routines. While intensely stimulating, it makes vigorous demands on the patience, the perseverance, and the sense of humor of the scientist.

The anthropologist studies the peoples among whom he works because from them he can obtain data that will throw light on the essential problems of the nature and functioning of culture, and of human social behavior. Our data must be sought out over the face of the earth, for only by so seeking them can we study such problems as the effect of climate, race, innate psychic endowments or other factors on human culture, its range of variation in form, its processes of change. It was indeed only after a broad base of descriptive data had been established that we were able to discern the primacy of culture in shaping behavior, one of the most important achievements of our science.

That anthropologists study the wide range of peoples they do, does not, however, mean that cultural anthropology can be defined as the science that studies "primitive" peoples. Anthropologists came to study non-European peoples because the need for comparative materials was increasingly felt. But "the study of man and his works," if it is to live up to its mandate, cannot be expected to rest content with a delimitation of this sort. Any stream of investigation has a way of spilling over the retaining walls of definition. The need to follow data wherever they may lie has in recent years brought about the increasing utilization of the methods of anthropology in the study of literate folk, at home as well as in the far places. The first break in the retaining wall came in the 1920's, when the analysis of an American Midwest community by the sociologists Robert and Helen Lynd was prefaced with an introduction by the anthropologist Clark Wissler,[1] in which he pointed out that this work was an application of anthropological method to a community that was a unit in our literate, mechanized society. The controversy that ensued need not concern us here; the fact is that the experiment established a trend, so that today anthropologists often study literate groups, employing many of the same techniques and the same concepts that figure in their study of non-Euroamerican societies.

A firm grasp on methodological relativism is essential to the ethnographer who is to carry on field research successfully. This cannot be too heavily stressed. A basic necessity of ethnographic research is the exercise of scientific detachment, which in turn calls for a rigid exclusion of value judgments. Just as the chemist devotes himself to understanding, not judging, the elements he is analyzing and their behavior in relation to each other, so the

[1] R. S. and H. M. Lynd, 1929, p. vi.

student of culture must observe, describe, and analyze the traditions of the people he is studying. To do this is not easy and requires special training for, as we have seen, our ethnocentrism demands that we evaluate, judge, and attempt to shape what differs from our own ways into the pattern that seems to us the only correct and, indeed, the only possible one. The anthropologist in the field, however, must accommodate himself to understanding ways of obtaining a living that never include a machine technology and sometimes neither agriculture nor domesticated animals. What is more difficult, he must adjust his reactions to describe, in terms of the values of the people he is studying, customs as repugnant to his personal experience as infanticide, head-hunting, various "unpleasant" dietary and sanitary habits, and the like.

2

Descriptions of actual methods used by anthropologists in the field are rare, though increasing attention is being given to the technical problems of methodology.[2] Since it is in its method that cultural anthropology makes one of its most important contributions to science, and since it is a basic postulate of scientific procedure that the means whereby a given body of materials is obtained be stated clearly and specifically, it is of interest to analyze this omission. The ethnographer's difficulty in describing in any detail the methods he used in a specific field study arises out of the difference between his materials and those of the laboratory scientist. In earlier days there was little apparatus for the student of human culture to describe. In all cases the success of his work, in very great measure, depends on his sensitivity to the human situations he encounters, rather than on his skill in manipulating test tubes or balances or incubators. Any report he can phrase would, ideally, have to run with the presentation of his data, since each item of his materials is gathered under circumstances that differ from those in which every other item was obtained. It would, in short, almost require another book.

Let us see how this works out by citing a passage from such a book, written as an experiment in presenting method through describing the experiences of the ethnographers in gathering the data that are also given. The particular passage introduces a chapter that tells how information was gathered regarding the kinship structure of the Saramacca tribe of Bush Negroes who live in

[2] See A. L. Kroeber (ed.), 1953, section entitled "Problems of Process," pp. 401–87.

the forests of Dutch Guiana in northern South America, such as would conventionally appear in the section of a monograph entitled "Social Organization."

We were aroused early after our night of stories. The women were moving about, getting their morning meal before daybreak came to give them light for their harvesting. There was much they had to do. Late that afternoon they would be returning to their villages, for the next day was sacred to the Earth Mother, and no work could be done in the fields. Today, added to the round of harvesting were the preparations for the return to their village. The rice that had been cut during the week would have to be carried there for drying and winnowing, and yams and peanuts and beans were to be brought in. . . .

Soon our men, too, began to stir, and, as we came out of our hammocks, Bayo and Angita entered the clearing. They were just now returning from the dance at Pa'aba. . . . With Angita was a man we had not seen before, holding a small child by the hand.

"This is Awingu, my brother-in-law," said Angita in explanation. "His eyes trouble him. I brought him to you for medicine."

After an exchange of courtesies demanded by the visit, we turned to the child.

"Is this your child, Awingu?" we asked.

His answer came promptly. "No, he is not my child. He is my wife's child. I made him."

Here was a fine distinction. He made him, but the child was not his.

Just then our cook came up with a small present for the child, but, since he would not take it from his hands or ours, Angita gave it to him.

"Thank you, father," he said to Angita.

Angita looked down affectionately at the youngster. "Two, three years more, Awingu, and he will be ready to go and live with his father at Gankwe. Do you remember your father at Gankwe? It was he who showed you how to make a gun from a reed. And you made it well. . . ."

There appeared, then, to be yet another father, for it was clear that Angita was not speaking of himself when he referred to the Gankwe father who had showed the child how to make a play gun.

All this, in itself, however confusing to a visitor, is by no means an unusual phenomenon. Different peoples have their own sanctions for establishing kinship and their own designations for relationships. In the city we had been told many tales of the manner of life of these Negroes of the bush. And the "matriarchate," as the custom of counting descent through the mother was termed, had often come up when these people were being discussed.

"Among them only the mothers count, because among savages, who can tell who the real father is? That is why a child calls many men 'father,' " we had heard variously explained and elaborated.

Yet here was a man who said without hesitation, "No, he is not my child. He is my wife's child. I made him." And the very next instant the child called Angita father, and Angita referred to still another man as the father who would in a few years take the child with him to live and train him for manhood.

Any number of questions came to our minds, but at daybreak a stranger coming to the planting ground of a village not his own is the least willing of talkers.

"This is not your child, Awingu," we took the occasion to remark when we were saying goodbye, "Yet he seems to like you very much."

"*Ma, tye! Ma Neng'e!*—Mother of all Negroes! what would you have? I am his father!"

The man showed by his amused expression that this was a story to carry back to his village. Only the politeness due a stranger kept Awingu and Angita from laughing aloud at this strange question. But Awingu was a thoughtful fellow. "Tell me," he said, after a while, "in your white man's country, don't children care for their fathers?" [3]

The discussion then continues with a description of how, on various occasions, three different women claimed the man named Angita, who was a fine wood carver, as a son, and how social reality resolved this biological impossibility and thus yielded further understanding of Bush Negro kinship:

Later that day, when our boat found itself abreast of the dugout which Angita was poling, we lost no time in questioning him.

"Angita," we called, "is the woman who gave us the rice your mother?"

He nodded.

"But what of Tita, who said she was your mother, too?"

He was a quick-witted lad, and he saw at once what we had in mind. He said with a laugh, "You are asking about my true, true mother, the one who made me? It is not this one, and it is not Tita, who made me. It is Kutai."

"But who are the other two?"

"They are her sisters." [4]

[3] M. J. and F. S. Herskovits, 1934, pp. 124–6.
[4] *Ibid.*, pp. 127–8.

By such devious ways the ethnographer obtains fact after fact. As digested after his return from the field, the experience would be presented in his monograph by no more than such a generalized statement as: "The social organization of the Bush Negroes is unilateral, descent being counted on the maternal side, with controls within the family exercised by the mother's eldest brother. Kinship nomenclature is classificatory, mother and mother's sisters being called by the term 'mother,' father and father's brothers being called 'father.' Biological parents have no distinguishing appellation, being identified by a child as the parent 'who made him.'"

In 1922 B. Malinowski's early work, *The Argonauts of the Western Pacific*, first gave explicit expression to the necessity for including a statement of field procedure in a report of the results of field work. Malinowski also enunciated in this book the principle of the "participant observer"—that is, that the ethnographer should, "in the main, . . . live . . . right among the natives." This was a real departure from the usage of many earlier students of culture who, even though they went to the field, were content to remain in an island capital, a missionary compound, or an official resthouse, and question natives, technically termed "informants," about ways of life that were spread before them at their doorsteps to be observed, if they would but go and look at them. In formulating this doctrine, Malinowski was generalizing from experience gained within a single society, where custom permitted participation in their life, though even in his case the people never completely accepted him. As he phrased it: ". . . they finished by regarding me as part and parcel of their life, a necessary evil or nuisance, mitigated by donations of tobacco." [5]

It is apparent that even here, whatever the adaptation to his presence that was achieved, the stranger remained a foreign element that might, so to speak, induce a state of indigestion in the body politic. In other societies, where participation in the life of the people by an outsider is regarded with disfavor, this participant-observer technique cannot be applied. The difference is well illustrated by a report of field work by Evans-Pritchard among the Nuer of East Africa, which followed research by the same student among the Azande, another tribe living in the same general area:

> Since among the Nuer my tent was always in the midst of homesteads or windscreens and my inquiries had to be conducted

[5] B. Malinowski, 1922, pp. 6–8.

in public, I was seldom able to hold confidential conversations and never succeeded in training informants capable of dictating texts and giving detailed descriptions and commentaries. This failure was compensated for by the intimacy I was compelled to establish with the Nuer. As I could not use the easier and shorter method of working through regular informants I had to fall back on direct observation of, and participation in, the everyday life of the people. From the door of my tent I could see what was happening in camp or village and every moment was spent in Nuer company. Information was thus gathered in particles, each Nuer I met being used as a source of knowledge and not, as it were, in chunks supplied by selected and trained informants. Because I had to live in such close contact with the Nuer I knew them more intimately than the Azande, about whom I am able to write a much more detailed account. Azande would not allow me to live as one of themselves; Nuer would not allow me to live otherwise. Among Azande I was compelled to live outside the community; among Nuer I was compelled to be a member of it. Azande treated me as a superior; Nuer as an equal.[6]

Since the ethnographer is only one factor in the field situation, the ideal method is not always the one he can employ. The group under study must always be taken into account, for it is their preconceptions, their prejudices, their fears that dominate the scene. This factor of prevailing attitude is one toward which the ethnographer cannot direct too sensitive a concern. It is the essence of the human element in his study, and is to be handled with the greatest delicacy possible. He achieves this by an honesty of purpose that is manifest in his every act. He plays fair, and shows restraint. He does not go where he is not welcome. He asks permission before intruding into a house, or attending a rite of any kind. He realizes that, though the rituals of death and the beliefs concerning the dead they reveal are important for his research, the death of a member of a family causes deep grief among the surviving relatives, and he remains away from the funeral unless he is wanted there. If he is wise, he knows that, by exercising these restraints, he will, in the long run, gain in the respect and confidence of the people, and his materials will ultimately be the richer for this sensitivity. Above all, in living in a community, he will respect the place assigned to him by that community.

The ethnographer pitches his tent or finds a house where he can be as close to the people he studies as they will permit. But it is their reactions, not his wishes, that will dictate how close he

[6] E. E. Evans-Pritchard, 1940, p. 15.

can come to them, and how much he can participate in their lives in making his observations. As a scientist he will arrange these observations in his notes and his published reports in accordance with his concept of culture and the nature of his problems. The conditions under which he obtained them, if not published, should at least be in his notes, where they can be referred to if questions of method arise in discussing a moot point. The results of his work will give other anthropologists a further reference point in their studies of the range of cultural behavior, while those planning field research in the same general region can obtain a useful idea of what they may expect to encounter during their investigations.

Perhaps because of the fewness of available anthropologists and the great number of societies whose ways of living have still to be studied, the further scientific procedure of checking the data of one student through independent investigation of the same phenomenon by another is for anthropology in its infancy. The need for studies of this kind is, however, becoming increasingly recognized, and a number of reinvestigations of cultures have been made. The most extensive of these is the analysis of Redfield's 1926 research in the Mexican village of Tepoztlán, done some two decades later by Lewis.[7] The differences in the findings of these two students pose certain methodological problems of the first order, whose overt recognition in itself constitutes a major gain for anthropological science. Of these problems, Lewis mentions the "personal factor," the changes that occur in any community over two decades, and differences "in theoretical orientation and methodology," which in turn influence "the selection and coverage of facts" and how these facts are organized.[8] Such variables in field research must be weighed, together with still other biases that may enter into investigations, in analyzing results. The consideration of them will undoubtedly figure increasingly, especially in comparative studies where the question of the validity of the data assumes such importance. Signs are also not lacking that these methodological problems are being more and more subject to analysis in the teaching of field method and in the planning of ethnographic research.

3

Arrived at his destination, settled in his village, the ethnographer faces the problem of how to get at his materials. Whether he is among natives of a South Seas island or working

[7] O. Lewis, 1951, *passim*.
[8] *Ibid.*, p. 431.

in a Middle Western American community, to achieve entree into the group is at once the most difficult and most important step in his research. It may be possible to come with an introduction from someone, either a member of the group or a friendly outsider, who will vouch for the ethnographer to someone of position and prestige and thus gain for him initial cooperation. This is the optimum situation; at the other end of the scale is the situation of the student who must make his way alone, perhaps even without the aid of an interpreter, and break down indifference and hostility.

The question is one of establishing workable human relations, which is difficult even under the most favorable conditions. We have all had the experience of finding ourselves in a strange community—of walking the streets alone, in a setting that differs only little from our accustomed one, but with a feeling of wanting to know what is happening here, who these people we brush by may be—of being an outsider. If we project ourselves into a situation where the physical environment differs from ours, where the language is incomprehensible, the food, the clothing, the houses, the very physical type of the people are strange, we can gain some insight into the initial problems the ethnographer must meet. Such a simple experience as walking through a public market in a tropical capital can be disturbing. The experience has not *sorted itself out.* The student feels merely the strangeness of a scene to which his own past offers no clues to proper behavior or to comprehension of the behavior of others. Is this argument that he witnesses a forerunner of violence, or only the usual way of bargaining? Is the laughter of that market woman directed toward himself, or is she laughing at what her neighbor has just said to her?

This *sorting out process* is crucial to success in field work, and it applies to people no less than to cultural behavior. To the newly arrived ethnographer, personalities in the community are blurred, and only later do individuals emerge. Customary habits are meaningless when an act observed cannot be projected to its intended end, as it can later when some degree of familiarity with the ways of life of the people has been attained. At this point, the student begins to make friends—and to be disliked as well as liked. Field experience soon teaches that no matter how different in physical type or cultural tradition a people may be, there will always be some individuals among them for whom he will have a warm personal regard, and with whom his relations will be close and meaningful. But there will also be those who will baffle him, and whom he may find uncongenial. And these reactions will be mutual. They are, above all, not to be feared or avoided, for they have much to teach the ethnographer about the personality of these individuals and the tensions in the group. Often, too, the man or woman whose confidence is the most difficult to gain has valuable insights to give the student; and though negative reactions may test his patience, they are of value in the notebook.

How information is obtained depends, once more, on the kind of study being conducted, the kind of people being studied, the kind of life they lead. The exclusive use of observation as against report is not desirable, nor should entire reliance be placed on an informant. One must, first of all, be seen. To walk through the village or into the countryside is an aid in one's first days in a community. Curiosity will bring some of the inhabitants to one's dwelling, contact will be established. In societies where the people have had experience with Euroamerican culture, a native can be induced to come for a stated number of hours a day to "talk," at the going rate for whatever kind of labor he has been accustomed to perform. In societies where such contact has not been experienced, observation and casual conversation may, for many weeks, be the only sources of information. But informants are essential if a rounded knowledge of the culture is to be had. Field trips are not of indefinite duration, and not every happening in the repertory of a culture will occur even during an extended period of field work. In a small community a birth, a wedding, a funeral may not take place during the ethnographer's stay, or he may not be permitted to witness it if it does occur. Yet an account of such important rites, and of the conditions that introduce variants of these rites, must be included in the description of any culture.

The answer to difficulties of this kind lies in the use of an informant. The very best use of an informant is to discuss with him events that have been witnessed, preferably those that were witnessed in his company. In time he can be relied upon to give descriptions of those typical events in the life of the people that have not been witnessed, that occur in the winter, for example, when field work has had to be carried on during the summer. Eventually, where the rapport between informant and ethnographer is close, the work becomes almost a collaboration, the informant furnishing leads and going to men of repute in his own family and outside it for answers to questions that have arisen in their discussions or that the ethnographer has posed.

Because every culture presents many facets, and different people in the same society view their common ways of life differently, it goes without saying that reliance on one informant is never advisable, even though it is inevitable that one or two persons will figure more in this capacity than others. For example, if a rite is described separately by several informants, and then is visited three or four different times, it will be found that only in outline do all these agree. This shows us the extent to which the factor of variation in culture, whose significance will become apparent later in this book, must continuously be taken into account in field work.

Of equal importance is the realization that an informant gives more than information about happenings. From him one obtains points of view, expressions of opinion that reveal the value systems, the bases of judgments, the socially accepted motivations that inspire or explain behavior. This is another reason why observation is never of itself sufficient. There are many untrained persons who come to know and enjoy the rites of native peoples. It is instructive to inquire of them the meaning to the people of the rituals they can describe so well in outer form. They are invariably at a loss for an answer. Behavior rarely enough reveals its motivating drive even in our own culture; it never does in a strange culture.

For many years it was an axiom of field work that only the elders could give the student a "true" picture of a culture. Today we know better. Culture is as culture does, and the range of accepted variation in behavior permits, where it does not require, men to behave differently from women, young people from those who are older. The best procedure is therefore to talk to both men and women, young and old; to observe a wide range of persons in as many situations as possible. In one West African community, the names and roles of the gods of a given pantheon as told by the chief priest proved to differ in many respects from the account given by a new cult-initiate; and this, in turn, differed from that of a lay person. Yet all these were "true" as far as the tellers were concerned. The principle that, to understand a culture, exoteric information is as important as esoteric—that what is of common knowledge is as significant as what is held secret—was enunciated many years ago. But the challenge to uncover what is secret is hard to resist, and the value of the commonplace has only recently come to be recognized.

The use of as many informants as possible to supplement observation is important for checking information, whether for omissions, distortions, or untruths. It must be remembered that individuals in all societies exhibit traits of discursiveness, and of reticence. Distortions may arise out of fear, or caution, or even forgetfulness of everyday patterns so ordinary as to be thought not worth mentioning. One of the most skilled ethnographers has expressed it in this way:

> Although distinctive customs were often pointed out to me lest I fail to observe them, on the other hand customs that were lapsing were not mentioned, merely from indifference. Such *costumbres* or *creencias* were the ways or beliefs of only a few old men or of some of the women, not worth noticing. In a conservative, secretive community the social detective learns much from the efforts to conceal. In Mitla I was to learn that in social as in personal life the idea that there is nothing important to conceal may result in almost complete concealment.[9]

One person will remember what another has forgotten. Or, where a society enjoins reticence, one will reveal what another feels must be left unsaid. A well-directed question will elicit explanations that, on another occasion, the same individual will avoid by a skillful parry. The result of inquiry among as many persons as possible will be a many-sided body of materials. Such a method will, if carefully employed, give depth to comprehension, and enhance the insight with which generalizations on the sanctioned forms of behavior are drawn.

4

Though not many anthropologists have recounted in specific terms how they went about their research on particular field trips, certain procedures advanced by field workers have come to be recognized as useful techniques of field work. Like the method whereby the ethnographer becomes a participant observer, which we have already taken into account, these methods have arisen out of trial-and-error field research. As with the participant-observer method, the usefulness of each of these techniques varies with the situation in which the field researcher finds himself, with the type of culture he is studying, and with his particular problem.

The oldest of these methods is what may be termed the *Notes-and-Queries* approach. This takes its name from the title of a publication, initially prepared by a committee of the Royal Anthropological Institute for the British Association for the Ad-

[9] E. C. Parsons, 1936, pp. 14–15.

vancement of Science, which first appeared in 1875 and has gone through five revisions, the sixth edition appearing in 1951. A comprehensive questionnaire, covering all phases of material and nonmaterial culture, was originally based on the following assumptions: that the civilizations of nonliterate peoples are in danger of extinction and we must obtain as much information about them as we can while they are still in existence; that there are not enough trained anthropologists to do this; that, therefore, the services of untrained persons, such as colonial officers, missionaries, traders, and travelers must be utilized with the greatest possible effectiveness. This method, used by an observer without anthropological training, results in the gathering of many facts, but yields little information either about how these facts are interrelated in the total cultural matrix, or about the human element in the daily life of a people. In the hands of the trained anthropologist, however, *Notes-and-Queries* is a helpful check on points he may have overlooked, and it is this quality that caused the editors of the sixth edition to design it as "a handy *aide-mémoire* to the trained anthropologist doing field work" as well as a work fulfilling its earlier function.[10]

A special technique that has been effectively employed is the *genealogical method*, associated with the name of W. H. R. Rivers, who first worked it out at the end of the last century.[11] This method has proved useful because, despite its simplicity, it provides a broad range of information concerning the social structures and other institutions of the people being studied. In using it, only the simplest kinship terms are employed—father, mother, child, husband and wife. The informant is asked the *name* of those who stand in these relationships to him, after it has been made clear that biological kin are meant, and not those, such as cousins, who in what is called the classificatory system would be termed "brothers" or "sisters." He is asked what he calls each, what each calls him, and thus the kinship terminology is built up. Then, by using the given name of each of these persons, the process is repeated and the system extended.

Rivers indicated some of the objectives that can be attained by its use. By recording "the social condition" of each person and the "locality to which each . . . belongs," there emerges a sense of class lines and local groupings, how these are represented in marriage alliances, and the lines that draw localities together or hold them apart. Clan organization is clearly shown, and whether

[10] Royal Anthropological Institute, 1951, p. 27.
[11] W. H. R. Rivers, 1910.

descent is counted on the side of the father, or mother, or both. This, in turn, reveals how incest lines are drawn. Rivers states:

> The genealogical method makes it possible to investigate abstract problems on a purely concrete basis. It is even possible by its means to formulate laws regulating the lives of people which they have probably never formulated themselves, certainly not with the clearness and definiteness which they have to the mind trained by a more complex civilization.

Instead of asking the informant to generalize about what a hypothetical person would call his elder brother's younger daughter, one merely takes the term actually used by someone who has an elder brother who has more than one daughter. If the term is fixed, it will always appear the same. If not, the range of usage will emerge in the differences found in the listings.

As with other techniques, this genealogical one is not everywhere effective or even workable. In some societies, as Rivers himself says, an obstacle may be "the existence of a taboo on the names of the dead, and this can sometimes only be overcome with difficulty." Among groups where enumeration of any kind is feared, whether for magical or political reasons, the attempt to obtain genealogies would arouse suspicion and set up resistances. Finally, this method is far more applicable to studies of small isolated settlements of a Melanesian island or an American Indian tribe than the great aggregates of Indonesia or Africa, where the complexity of marriage lines and other interrelationships is such as to make it difficult, if not impossible, to achieve the satisfactory sampling of the population needed to justify pertinent inductions.

The technique of employing the *hypothetical situation* enables the student to probe many elements in a culture of which a people are reluctant to speak, or which they take so for granted that they do not mention them except in connection with a relevant series of happenings. As defined, this method consists "of devising . . . situations in the life of a people in terms of hypothetical persons, relationships and events, which, being in accord with the prevalent patterns of the culture, are used to direct and give form to discussions with informants and other members of the group being studied." [12] Thus, where happenings are invested with possible sinister magical significance, as in the case of childbirth, or where economic questions involving facts an individual is unwilling to reveal about himself or another person are concerned, discussion can take place freely where the one involved,

[12] M. J. Herskovits, 1950, p. 32.

by definition, does not exist. It is scarcely surprising that talk of hypothetical situations and persons often leads to discussion of real ones; in more instances than not, to the description of happenings in the experience of the informant himself. In all cases the values and goals of the culture will be revealed through their reflection in appraisals of the problems hypothetically posed by a member of the society. The manner in which this technique can be employed to overcome difficulties encountered in using the genealogical method is apparent; but its utility is greater because of its flexibility and the wide range of situations to which it can be applied.

In *village mapping* not only are the relationships of every individual in a community to every other person recorded, but the ecological setting and the lines along which physical contact takes place are indicated. Ideally, each dwelling, each communal building, each storage pit or other accessory structure, each public open place where groups collect, each shrine, each field, each industrial center, such as a forge or a pottery, is located. The inapplicability of this method, too, to larger settlements is apparent; it is equally evident that where it can be applied it can yield a great deal of information concerning the life of a group.

A question often raised when methods of field investigation are under discussion concerns *the use of the native language.* That those going into the field should be linguistically equipped to render in accurate transcription the names of people and places and deities, titles of various sorts, and critical texts such as invocations or words to songs is accepted as a minimum requirement. This was one of the principal contributions to field methodology of the American anthropologists, who under the leadership of F. Boas amassed an impressive body of textual materials in native Indian languages. But work of this kind does not equip the student to carry on a conversation, or to understand a conversation that is overheard. Here is encountered the full play of idiom, of imagery, of nuance in thought patterns, of allusion, and of elliptical expression. The ethnographer must be very sure of his command of the tongue in which he proposes to carry on his research, or he will but skim the surface of the thought processes about him, too often misinterpreting what is told him or what he hears.

A happy medium is found in the "pidgin" dialects that have sprung up in many parts of the world. Usually these are relatively easy to learn, and sufficiently rich to be usable in questioning informants or carrying on casual conversation. Among peoples where such a dialect exists it is a rare, remote village where someone is not to be found who speaks it. These dialects are often derived from Indo-European tongues, such as Melanesian pidgin, Negro-English, or Negro-French. But even where this is not the case, as in Swahili (Bantu-Arabic), or Chinook (Northwest Coast of North America), these "jargons" are simpler to handle than the complicated languages of the peoples who speak hybrid tongues as accessory to their native forms.

The other alternative is the interpreter. The use of an interpreter presents many problems. He has to be won over by the ethnographer; he must not only be made to understand what is at issue, but must be enthusiastic about the work. Translation is at best a difficult task, and especial care must be had that questions to be transmitted are phrased clearly, passed on correctly, and the replies properly rendered. An interpreter can become a most valuable informant, and will often expand on a reply or himself proffer significant information. The independent use of more than one interpreter is essential, since this ensures a more adequate check on the materials transmitted and gives a sense of the range of belief and behavior in the culture.

Ideally, one makes use of any linguistic device that is at hand. A pidgin dialect is spoken if one exists. At the same time, every attempt is made to master the native language to the greatest degree possible. This does not mean that interpreters are not also to be employed, for they, too, can be of aid. Competence should move forward on all fronts. Knowledge of a key word in the native language may be a check on the validity of the interpreter's performance. A question in pidgin may clear up a moot point which the use of the native language alone would not clarify. As one field worker put it: "I used an interpreter until I found myself discussing my problems with him in his language. Then I felt I could go on by myself." In the final analysis, the object is to record the data as adequately as possible. Whatever techniques contribute to this end are justified.

Biographies and *autobiographies* of natives reveal many things about a culture. Most of all, they afford a corrective to exclusive preoccupation with institutions. Cultural behavior is institutionalized, but the range of accepted variation in individual conduct must be analyzed if the institution and the culture are to be seen in perspective. Intangibles such as values, goals, and other motivating drives come out in such documents, as does the play of differing personalities within a society.

We have already illustrated the homely processes of thought by a passage from one of these autobiographies. There are a considerable number of such works, some brief and some extensive. All of them merit careful study. The same is true of biographical materials, especially where, as in the treatment of the Zulu ruler Chaka,[13] the author of the biography is a member of a tribe related to that of his subject. Here, in short, is another tool that permits us to penetrate the life of the individual in his cultural setting, at hand for the student who would assess to the fullest the function and meaning of culture.

5

Points of detail in field method need not concern us here. Matters such as when notebooks may be used and when they are best left behind, how notes should be organized and whether they should be reworked in the field, the use of the field diary, the employment of still and motion-picture cameras and of recording instruments—these are the affair of the specialist, and are increasingly presented in technical reports of research.[14] Such matters are the equivalent of the test tubes and microscopes of the student who works in the laboratories of the physical and natural sciences. Their importance is clear, in terms of the more fundamental considerations that arise out of how the research worker conceives his problem, and his basic approach toward its solution.

In ethnographic field work, this conception and this approach derive from the fact that the problem is essentially a human one. This is why honesty of purpose is so important, for the ethnographer is being observed far more intensely by the people he has come to study than he can ever observe them, and a false step is soon detected. This is also why the greatest sensitivity is essential. Even where opposition to his investigation develops, alertness to the values of a people, the ability to give way gracefully at the right moment, a feeling for canons of conduct and politeness can resolve a difficulty and win an ultimate advantage. Here, too, a sense of humor is of great usefulness, for it gives perspective when horizons seem to press irritatingly close about one.

With honesty, sensitivity and humor, then, field work, for all its difficulties and frustrations, becomes an exciting adventure. There are few ethnographers who do not talk with affection of their friends among the people with whom they have worked. They look back on their periods of field study with a feeling that

---

[13] T. Mofolo, 1931, *passim.*
[14] For a discussion of mechanical aids in field research, see H. Rowe, 1953, *passim.*

here has been an experience that more than any other has brought breadth and comprehension, not only of a particular culture, but of human culture as a whole. There is no logical reason why the student of comparative culture, who never leaves his study, should not make a contribution to the understanding of the nature of cultural institutions. But results from this type of analysis have in the main proved unsatisfactory where there has been no contact with the living reality of culture, with people who behave in ways that are never baffling when seen in their total setting.

Part Four

Cultural

Structure

and

Cultural

Dynamics

Chapter **Twenty-one**

Culture Traits, Complexes and Areas

The idea of the culture trait, as the smallest identifiable unit in a given culture, seems on first acquaintance to be relatively simple, but it has implications that will trap the unwary. For culture, in its totality or in any phase of it, is so well integrated that it is extremely difficult to know when a "smallest identifiable unit" is to be regarded as such because of its objective form, or because it is thought of by a people as an indivisible part of a larger whole. In brief, the question turns on another aspect of that relativism we have already seen to be so important where any kind of definition is involved.

An example, taken from our everyday life, will show how this difficulty arises, and how it is to be met. We can regard the family dwelling quarters as having both material and nonmaterial aspects. Among the material elements are the rooms into which the house or apartment is subdivided, the stairs, various kinds of furnishings and appliances used for the preparation of food, for cleansing the body, and for cleaning the dwelling place. The nonmaterial traits include the attitudes of the members of the household toward themselves, each other, and the world outside; the skills that enable them to employ the material devices that perform such functions as we have just described; the forms of behavior that every family devises as their own intimate means of communication or amusement.

Now out of this let us take one element, the table and six chairs that comprise the dining-room set. These are a unit, just as the dining room is a unit in the house or apartment. That is, each is a trait of a larger complex, and validly to be regarded as such in terms of its relation to the whole of which it is a part. The very fact that this table and its satellite chairs are to be designated by a single phrase—our dining-room set is in the center of the dining-room—is significant in this context. In drawing up a list of traits of our culture that would attempt to "approach completion," would we set down the dining room as a part of the dwelling complex, or the dining-room set as a part of the dining-room complex?

Objections to either of these possibilities at once present themselves. We recall that though the table-and-chair grouping is a unit when thought of as a set, the fact that it includes a table and six chairs means that it is by no means the smallest identifiable one in this context. The table is not only to be physically separated from the chairs, but any element on occasion can be psychologically abstracted from the table-plus-chairs unity, as when there are too many guests to be accommodated on the living-room chairs and those from the dining room are used for the purpose.

Let us for the moment give the table a unity of its own. Here, at least, is a physical whole that can be identified as such. But, says the literal-minded logician, though the table is a unit, is it not itself a gathering of sub-units? We may disregard those elements that are removable, such as the boards to be inserted when the table is extended so as to provide more seating space. Reduced to its physical unity as a table, it still consists of pieces of wood that were separately shaped, assembled with nails and cleats and glue, and covered with some type of veneer. Is not one of these nails, or a cleat, or the mechanism that permits the halves of the table to slide apart, a trait in its own right?

The problem sketched here has been faced, placed in perspective, and discussed by all who have used the concept of the culture trait. Thus, Driver and Kroeber state:

> Essential parts of a trait cannot of course be counted as separate traits: the stern of a canoe, the string of a bow, etc. Even the bow and arrow is a single trait until there is question of an arrowless bow. Then we have two traits, the pellet bow and arrow bow. Similarly, while the sinew backing of a bow cannot occur by it-

self, we legitimately distinguish self-bows and sinew-backed bows; and so, single-curved and recurved bows, radically and tangentially feathered arrows, canoes with blunt, round or sharp sterns, etc.[1]

Or, as Kroeber puts it in a later discussion, a trait is to be thought of as a "minimal definable element of culture." [2]

When a trait is to be regarded as constituting such a minimum involves evaluation of two kinds. The decision in a given instance must be the result of an expert's study of the problem, taking into account the unconsidered view of the individuals who live by the conventions of the culture being studied, and realizing that even such an ascribed unity may shift in terms of the larger whole of which it is a part. *The form a trait assumes at a given time will thus be determined by its context, rather than by any quality inherent in it.*

It can readily be shown how a list of traits can grow as more and more details are taken into account. For this purpose, let us consider an extensive research program based on the trait-concept, the California culture-element study. In the first California trait list, published in 1935, Klimek included four hundred and thirty items. Under the heading "hunting and fishing," he lists twenty-four elements; under "death and mourning," seventeen.[3] Later studies showed the numbers of traits perceived to increase steadily.

	Total	*Hunting and Fishing*	*Death*
Klimek (1935)	430	24	17
Gifford & Kroeber (1937)	1,094	102	48
Essene (1942)	2,174	202	110

Elsewhere, Stewart [4] notes 4,662 elements for the Ute and Southern Paiute bands to the east; E. Voegelin [5] has a list of 5,263 for tribes of northeast California; while Ray,[6] working in the region north and northeast of the California tribes, increased the number to 7,633.

How the trait list grew as a result of the increasing skill and the precise objectives of this research is to be seen if we consider the treatment of such a single cultural element as the house. The

[1] H. E. Driver and A. L. Kroeber, 1932, pp. 212–13.
[2] A. L. Kroeber, 1936, p. 101.
[3] S. Klimek, 1935, pp. 23–9.
[4] O. C. Stewart, 1942.
[5] E. W. Voegelin, 1942.
[6] V. F. Ray, 1942.

findings of Gifford and Kroeber for the Pomo set up these categories:

> Assembly or dance house (14 elements)
> Dwelling house (11 elements)
> Sweat house (20 elements)

Some years later, Essene divided the topic in this way:

> Structural features
> Frame (12 elements)
> Covering (6 elements)
> Entrances, exits (17 elements)
> Fireplace (3 elements)
> Sweat house (32 elements)
> Dwellings (9 elements)

Thus not only growth, but refinement and penetration have come with experience. The process has also been well described by Ray. Before his first field trip, adaptations of the California trait-list were made to fit it for use in the cultures he proposed to study. These revisions were tested in the field and again worked over so as "to make a more logical sequence" and to fit additions to it. The new list was then held to be ready for use. Once more, however, "the list grew constantly, in spite of its previous expansion. It was frequently necessary to remove pages or whole sections and recopy them in order that interpolated elements might be put in more logical order." [7] Ray estimates that less than 4 or 5 per cent of the entries in the first list taken into the field are to be found in the culture-element assemblage published in his final report.

Despite these considerations, it is difficult to see how the concept of the culture-trait, or some equivalent, could be omitted from the study of culture. Whether approached from the point of view of outer frame or inner meaning, culture must be viewed as a phenomenon that has form. The analysis of the forms taken by cultures, in turn, requires the assumption that these forms are structured. This assumption, again, makes it necessary to observe the component elements in the structures. Thus it is not too much to state that the entire field of archaeology is devoted to studying the incidence and development of culture traits whose functional relation to one another can only be guessed; while the British social anthropologists, who reject the concept, nonetheless subdivide the structures they study into smaller units.

[7] *Ibid.*, p. 100.

Some earlier instances where culture traits were studied may be mentioned. Tylor analyzed different cultures from this point of view when he applied the principle of correlation between cultural elements in seeking to understand how institutions developed.[8] Boas' investigation into the problem of how the mythology of a people reflects their mode of life,[9] documented by materials from the Tsimshian Indians of British Columbia, could not have been carried on had he not first broken down the stories into parts, prior to rearranging them so as to give an ordered, systematic description of the culture. The comparative ethnographic studies of Nordenskiöld, Lindbolm and others of the Swedish school also accept as a basic postulate the idea that cultures are composed of elements that can be treated separately. For the cultures of the Gran Chaco of South America, Nordenskiöld maps the separate distributions of such items as wooden spades, bow-cords made from animal material, the "bird arrow," the sling, the clay-pellet bow—to name but five of the forty-four traits considered.[10] Lindblom and his associates have similarly made separate analyses of the distribution of many distinct cultural elements for Africa, including slings, stilts, fighting bracelets, spiked wheel-traps, hammocks, and string figures.[11]

Studies of culture traits can also be effectively called on to correct false notions of the presumed "simplicity" of nonliterate cultures. We may recall the listing of more than seven thousand distinguishable items in the cultures of California, Plateau, and Great Basin Indian tribes, known for the smallness of their numbers, the "sparseness" of their material equipment, the uncomplicated nature of their economic and political systems. What figures would emerge from a tabulation of this type made among the peoples of Central America, or West Africa, or Indonesia can only be conjectured. But what material we have demonstrates that the "simplest" cultures are to be seen as complex, even when no more than the raw inventories of their cultural resources are taken into account. It need hardly be pointed out that any attempt to assess the ways in which these items are interrelated would add immeasurably to the complexity of the picture.

2

The nature of the culture-complex can best be illustrated by an example from the discussion of ritual in the analysis of Pueblo Indian religion made by E. C. Parsons.

[8] E. B. Tylor, 1889.
[9] F. Boas, 1909–10, p. 393.

[10] E. Nordenskiöld, 1919.
[11] K. G. Lindblom, ed., 1926—.

"Pueblo ritual," Parsons writes, "is kaleidoscopic. There are many ritual patterns or rites, and . . . they combine in many ways. . . . Mobilized into a comparatively constant combination, a group of rites may form a ceremony, sometimes with, sometimes without, a dramatic idea. . . . Each rite or ritual element" must be seen "as a separable element or unit, in an order partly logical, partly suggested by the extent the rite is used." [12] The details of how each element is made, sanctified, and used take many pages to set down. The answer to the question, "How do rites from this list of more than fifty-five ritual elements combine into a ceremony?" is given in terms of how each item fits into the total, making it apparent that each trait contributes to the larger unities we term culture-complexes.

This characteristic integration of the culture-complex cannot better be seen than in folktales. The several characters, the settings and the incidents are independent variables which, though having the same combinations in no two versions, make of each version a unified whole. Most persons in the Euroamerican area are familiar with the Cinderella tale, of which some three hundred and fifty variants were published in one early study.[13] If we take but a single incident, the crucial one where Cinderella loses her slipper, we find that this sometimes occurs at midnight after a ball, sometimes at noon when Cinderella must flee a church service attended by the Prince. The complex represented by the tale as a whole is everywhere recognizable. It is only of incidental significance for the plot whether the feet of Cinderella's stepsisters simply fail to fit the slipper recovered after her flight, or fraud is employed when the stepmother slashes a piece from each of her daughters' heels to make the slipper fit. Whether Cinderella's residence is visited by the king's guards who must fit the slipper, or all the young women of the kingdom go to the palace to try it on, the ill-treated little girl is always identified as the owner.

It is possible to follow the manifestation of a given complex from tribe to tribe over a wide area, just as it is possible to study trait distribution. One such example is the study made by Benedict of the complex of ritual and belief that centers about the idea of the guardian spirit in North America.[14] Among all the many peoples where this complex forms a part of the culture, no two manifestations are the same, yet each shows a grouping of traits

[12] E. C. Parsons, 1939, Vol. I, p. 268.
[13] M. R. Cox, 1892.
[14] R. Benedict, 1923. The passages quoted here are from pp. 9–16.

about the central concept that gives it recognizable form and inner unity in tribe after tribe, and in area after area.

This organizing idea of the guardian spirit concept is implemented by differing rituals, and validated by the different functions it fulfills in different regions. Among the Thompson River Indians all young men of the tribe, by fasting and isolation in the mountains, strove to achieve "supernatural communication, and the acquisition of the name and power and song of the guardian spirit in a vision." For the Kwakiutl Indians of the Northwest Coast, the guardian spirit "was an hereditary caste mark," acquired in accordance with rights established through inheritance, or marriage, or by killing the former owner. "One might not see a tutelary in his vision until his family had arranged to 'pay for his ecstasy'; a marriage must have been arranged with a woman having the hereditary right to pass on the 'crest'; in addition, the elders of the group assembled in council must have given their consent."

Traits of possession by the spirit and the manner of its acquisition take on still different forms in the guardian-spirit complex of certain California Indian and Plains Indian groups. Among the Shasta these spirits were the prerogative of the healers, the shamans, men or women whose predisposition toward this calling "manifested itself in stereotyped dreams." The Crow of the Plains, on the other hand, laid no restriction of position, sex, or age on who might seek a vision that would reveal a guardian. Most often, "isolation, fasting, and self-torture" were involved, though a spirit did on occasion manifest itself to a fortunate possessor who did not have to torture himself. Having a vision indicated the road to success, and the suppliant would cut off a finger as an offering to the spirit. Yet, among the Crow, "the seeking of visions is . . . a much more general institution than that of procuring a guardian spirit." Visions of other kinds are sought, on all occasions. The beings who appear in most visions give a song, endow one with specific powers, and indicate a token for the person to find and keep about him later, just as does the guardian spirit. In short, the kind of vision quest that figures in the Crow guardian-spirit complex is by no means confined to that complex, but is found in association with many other aspects of daily life, often non-religious ones.

The integrative factor gives to a cultural complex its unity, no matter what fortuitous traits seemingly comprise it. The student, who is seeking a purely rational explanation of why certain elements found together should have been combined, is at times baffled by the apparent absence of logic in their inclusion. Why, we ask, should the guardian spirit be in one tribe for the healer alone, in another validated by rank, in a third acquired by privation and self-discipline?

In Dahomey, West Africa, a men's cooperative work group, an important economic institution, called the *dokpwe*, can be regarded as a culture-complex that is susceptible of being analyzed into many component traits. The pride with which men think of themselves as members of these groups, their organization, which includes a chief and several assistant chiefs, the work they do in hoeing fields and thatching houses are all such items. The feast that is the payment for their work, the types of songs sung while the work is done, the competitive units set up within the cooperative group are others. Still others are the tradition that the fields of a member in ill-health are hoed by this group without a compensatory feast; or that a man of position, with many wives, fulfills his obligations to his several parents-in-law by calling on the cooperative labor of the *dokpwe* to perform a yearly agricultural task for each wife's father, and to see to the thatching of the roof of each wife's mother. In the material realm, not only the hoes used in tilling the land, but the drums, gongs, and rattles that set the beat for the strokes of these hoes, as well as for the songs that accompany the work, must be taken into account.

The logic that underlies the *dokpwe* complex and most of its component traits is evident when its economic functions are considered. In a tropical country, where the transition between dry and rainy seasons is rapid, the necessary work of preparing the earth for planting can be completed in the proper time only by group effort. When, as in the case of the head of a polygynous household, a number of fields must be hoed, or when a man has large gardens, the problem would be insurmountable without an adequate labor supply to call on. That compensation is only given in the form of a feast seems to take us outside the logic of economic demands until we recall that every man, as a member of a *dokpwe*, sooner or later completes a comparable task for those who had worked for him. The songs and drumbeats are explained by the fact that the Dahomeans hold that rhythmic accompaniment stimulates greater exertion and produces less fatigue in communal labor.

Yet the *dokpwe* complex functions not only in the economic scene, but also as an integral part of Dahomean mortuary rites. The *dokpwe* members perform many of the most important dances that honor the dead at funerals. Some of these dances require great dexterity, and much prestige accrues to those whose performance is outstanding. In one, six young men, three on a side, face each other with hands interlocked, the corpse resting on the outstretched arms. Holding their arms rigid, they rhythmically throw their bodies forward so the knotted ends of the cloths they wear, that are fastened at the back, are hurled upward to strike against their ears in perfect time. Each member of the *dokpwe* clamors to participate, as he does later to help carry the corpse when it is taken by the *dokpwe* through the village to visit in farewell the places it had frequented while alive. Again, they aid in filling the grave after the body has been interred.

That the *dokpwe* is at the same time associated with the production cycle and with the rituals of death; that it combines labor with song and dance involves no contradiction in the minds of the Dahomeans. To them this seems natural and understandable. It is an ancient sanction of the right to "disturb the earth." As Benedict has stated for the guardian-spirit complex: "The miscellaneous traits that enter in different centers into its make-up are none of them either the inevitable forerunner, the inevitable corollary, or the inevitable accompaniment of the concept, but have each an individual existence and a wider distribution outside this complex." [15]

One of the most significant aspects of culture, therefore, is this fact that disparate elements, whose distribution can be individually traced, are combined and recombined into such differing expressions of a given basic concept; each complex or aggregate forming an integrated whole whose every part is not only accepted but held as symbolically essential by the people in whose particular culture it is found.

Here perhaps lies the principal difference between the culture-trait and the culture-complex. Both are useful devices in furthering the objective, scientific study of culture. But in so far as culture has meaning, and meaning gives to culture its reality, the trait is far more an abstraction drawn by the student than the complex. A tent is a tent, but those who think of tents do not consider the number of poles, or the quality and nature of the skin that covers it, or the decoration on it. The trait-complex "tent" is a unit in their thinking, and as such has the oneness of any total image. If, however, the tent forms a trait in the family complex as a living place, then its separate psychological existence is modified, and it is merged with the other traits that go to make up the complex of which *it* now forms but a part.

[15] *Ibid.*, p. 84.

We may approach this problem from another point of view by comparing the trait-lists that have been drawn up for tribal cultures as wholes with trait-lists that are made within the framework of a given complex. The logic of the tribal trait-list is that of the student's conception of the organization of culture. Trait follows trait in catalogue fashion. The relation of one trait to another is here similar to the relation of one card in a library index to the next, where alphabetical order, and not subject matter, is the guide. Such a heading in a culture-element list as "spoons," under which one finds these utensils entered as "pine, cedar, cottonwood . . . other woods, long handle, short handle, perforated, ornamented, inlaid," differs from an alphabetical order merely in the frame in which it is cast. Both are to be contrasted to the listing of traits in a complex where, disparate though they may seem, each contributes to the unity of the whole in terms of the central idea that gives the aggregate meaning to those in whose culture it is found.

3

As we move from one part of a continent to another, we find that while the cultures of no two peoples are identical, the customs of those who live close to one another tend to have greater similarities than do the customs of those groups who live farther apart. Some traits of culture, it is true, will be more widespread than others, yet the setting of similar cultural items in the total complexes of which they form parts will differ in different regions.

This simple fact derives from the fundamental principle that since culture is learned, any element in it can be taken over by any individuals or any groups of individuals exposed to different ways of doing and thinking. By the same token, it follows that peoples who live close together have greater opportunities to borrow from each other than from folk who are at a distance. This is why, when cultures are viewed objectively, they are seen to form clusters, so to speak, sufficiently homogeneous that the regions in which they occur can be delimited on a map. *The area in which similar cultures are found is called a culture area.*

The culture-area concept, as such, was first systematically treated by Wissler, when he employed it to orient his work on American Indian cultures. His definition, though it has been since sharpened, is still useful. If, Wissler says, "the natives of the New World could be grouped according to culture traits," this would give us "food areas, textile areas, ceramic areas, etc., . . . If, however, we take all traits into simultaneous consideration and shift our point of view to the social, or tribal units, we are able to form fairly definite groups. This will give us culture areas, or a classification of social groups according to their culture traits." [16]

To classify whole cultures in this or any other way is, however, by no means as simple as it seems at first glance. The individual traits into which a culture can be broken down for purposes of objective analysis may or may not have the same distributions. This becomes apparent if, for instance, we consider the distribution of certain elements in African culture. East Africa is to be delimited as a culture-area largely on the basis of the place of cattle in the lives of the people there; the Congo because of its agricultural, political, and artistic characteristics. Yet in both these areas, a wife is acquired only after the passage of wealth from the groom to the father of the bride to ensure, among other things, that a woman will be adequately cared for by her husband; while descent is counted on one side of the family rather than on both sides. The religions of Africa are customarily divided into two categories, one in which emphasis is laid on the ancestors, the other where nature deities bulk largest. Here we differentiate East Africa from the Congo, but not the Congo from the Guinea Coast or the Western Sudan.

Nonetheless, such facts do not negate experience that the cultures of an area, considered as wholes, do "hang together." Boas has cautioned that since culture areas are commonly mapped on the basis of material culture traits, "The student interested in religion, social organization, or some other aspect of culture would soon discover that the culture areas based on material culture do not coincide with those that would naturally result from his studies." [17] It is to be noted, however, that Boas himself, in classifying North American Indian folktales, allocates the several types of myths and the dominant characters to areas that do roughly correspond to the conventional culture-area scheme for the continent.[18] In the case of the "human tale," indeed, we are told that "in all probability future study will show that its principal characteristics may well be defined by the cultural areas of the continent." [19] Roberts, too, when studying the distribution of

[16] C. Wissler, 1922, p. 218.
[17] F. Boas, 1938, p. 671.
[18] F. Boas, 1914, pp. 387–400 (1940, pp. 465–79).
[19] *Ibid.*, p. 399 (1940, p. 478).

musical forms of aboriginal North America, found that the musical areas, both instrumental and vocal, "coincide with those based on other cultural traits." [20]

Culture-areas have been formally mapped in the continents of North and South America, and in Africa. The original map of American culture areas, as given by Wissler, listed the following:

	North America		*South America*
1.	Plains	11.	Chibcha
2.	Plateau	12.	Inca
3.	California	13.	Guanaco
4.	North Pacific Coast	14.	Amazon
5.	Eskimo		
6.	Mackenzie		*Caribbean*
7.	Eastern Woodland	15.	Antilles [21]
	a. Iroquoian		
	b. Central Algonkin		
	c. Eastern Algonkin		
8.	Southeast		
9.	Southwest		
10.	Nahua		

In this first mapping, the culture areas were designed essentially to differentiate concentrations of culture, or culture-centers. This was the reason why "more definite curved contours" were not used. "These boundaries," Wissler wrote, "in fact, are merely diagrammatic, serving to indicate the loci of the points where culture stands half way between that of the contiguous centers."

Kroeber, seven years later, did not fear these more "definite curved contours," as a glance at the culture-area map of the Americas (Figure 56) shows. In arranging his areas, to which he also applied a new series of names, he did not alter the number of divisions that Wissler gave. Kroeber's revised list comprises the following:

1. Arctic or Eskimo: coastal
2. Northwest or North Pacific Coast: also a coastal strip
3. California or California–Great Basin
4. Plateau: the northern inter-mountain region
5. Mackenzie-Yukon: the northern interior forest and tundra tract
6. Plains: the level or rolling prairies of the interior
7. Northeast or Northern Woodland: forested

[20] H. H. Roberts, 1925, p. 39.
[21] C. Wissler, 1922, pp. 217–57.

Fig. 56 *Culture-areas of North and South America. (After Kroeber, 1923, p. 337.)*

8. Southeast or Southern Woodland: also timbered
9. Southwest: the southern plateau, sub-arid
10. Mexico: from the tropic to Nicaragua

The South American areas of Wissler are left unchanged, except they are called Colombia or Chibcha, Andean or Peruvian, Patagonia, Tropical Forest, and Antillean respectively.[22] In a still later revision of the culture areas of North America only, Kroeber attempted a more specific correlation of culture and ecology than had hitherto been tried. He also produced a much more complex array of distinct units, at the same time achieving an over-all simplicity that was greater than in his earlier mapping, or in Wissler's original one, with eighty-four units termed areas and sub-areas, making up seven "grand areas." [23] For the purpose of classifying North American native cultures, however, these divisions are too general, while the eighty-four sub-units are too numerous to be of utility in classification. Kroeber's revision of Wissler's original map, reproduced on page 399, will thus be found most satisfactory for the uses to which culture-area classification has most often been put.

A further revision of the classification of South American Indian cultures resulted from the intensive studies and fresh information gathered in preparing the *Handbook of South American Indians*. The map (Figure 57) shows four main types which, in their distribution, are to be regarded as the equivalent of culture-areas. They are:

1. Marginal (stippled)
2. Tropical forest (cross-hatched)
3. Circum-Caribbean (broad bands)
4. Andean (black)

They thus increase in complexity and primarily take into account ecological base as well as cultural manifestation. They betoken once again how, with more adequate information, the essentially empirical character of culture-area mapping encourages continuous revision and makes it a more effective instrument for the classification of cultures. Steward [24] has used the categories employed in drawing this map to relate similar types of cultures in North and South America as a step in reconstructing the culture history of the Americas. This points a way toward utilizing culture-area classification to orient data in studies where time depth is essential.

[22] A. L. Kroeber, 1923, pp. 335–9.
[23] A. L. Kroeber, 1939.
[24] J. H. Steward, 1947.

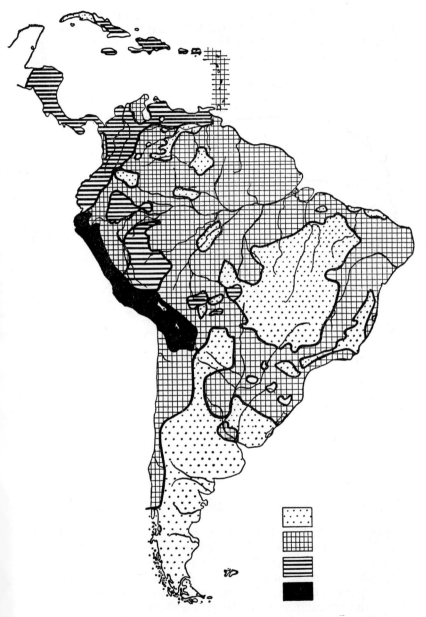

Fig. 57 *Culture types of South America.* (*After* Handbook of South American Indians.)

A map of the culture-areas of Africa was first drawn in 1924.[25] Earlier, Ratzel and Dowd had recognized the differences between the cultures of certain regions of the continent, though the former merely distinguished cattle-keeping from agricultural

Fig. 58 *Culture-areas of Africa. (After Herskovits, 1945c.)*

peoples, and the latter indicated the distributions of cultures based on different food economies. The German students, Ankermann and Frobenius, also described what was essentially a culture-area, though the purpose of their studies was not description, but historical reconstruction. This first attempt to delimit culture-areas after the procedures of Wissler followed an investigation of the East African data, and was in the nature of a test of the applica-

[25] M. J. Herskovits, 1924a.

bility of Wissler's procedure to the culture of another continent. A revision of this mapping was made a few years later,[26] so that "certain changes in accordance with the suggestions and criticisms of the earlier attempt" could be incorporated. In 1937 Hambly,[27] indicating as his objective a classification made "from the social and psychological point of view," in terms of an "ethos" envisaged as the dynamic or driving force of each culture, mapped eight areas whose "indefinite boundaries" were indicated "by shading rather than straight lines." However, these do not differ too greatly from those of the earlier attempts. The most recent revision of the original mapping [28] is reproduced on page 402. Further changes from its prototypes may be indicated. Because of the number of aspects Hottentot and Bushmen have in common, they are grouped under the name "Khoisan," "compounded of the root of two Hottentot words, *Khoi-Khoin*, the Hottentot name for themselves, and *San*, the term they use to designate the Bushmen, who have no special designation for themselves as a people." The differences between these two groups, however, made it seem worth while to retain some indication of these distinctions, so that the area is presented as:

    1. Khoisan
       a. Bushman
       b. Hottentot

The other major change is the separation of the Congo and the Guinea Coast as two distinct areas, with a slight enlargement northward of the territory encompassed by the latter, justified by scientific researches carried on since the earlier maps were published. In addition to the above, then, the areas given are:

    2. East African Cattle Area
    3. East Horn
    4. Congo
    5. Guinea Coast
    6. Western Sudan
    7. Eastern Sudan
    8. Desert Area
    9. Egypt

As in the earlier mappings, the North African coastal strip is excluded because of its close cultural affinity to Europe and and the Near East.

[26] M. J. Herskovits, 1930.
[27] W. D. Hambly, 1937. His culture-area map is opposite p. 324, Part I.
[28] M. J. Herskovits, 1945c, p. 9.

Asia has been divided into six culture-areas:

1. Siberian (Palaeo-Siberian)
2. Southwest (the sedentary cultures of southwestern Asia)
3. Steppe (the pastoral nomadic cultures of central and southern Asia)
4. China (the Chinese sedentary)
5. Southeast Asian-Indonesian (which appears to have originated in south China and to be related to the Chinese)
6. Primitive nomadic (found in isolated regions of southeast Asia) [29]

In addition, "four major areas of culture-blend" are recognized, where "distinct cultures have evolved following a fusion of two or more separate cultures." These are the Korean, Japanese, Indian and Tibetan.[30]

The culture-area concept has been successfully applied to Madagascar, whose culture, which had long been assumed to be "uniform throughout the island," was found on closer study to have "three fairly well marked culture areas . . . with the usual marginal tribes of mixed culture." These areas, which "agree in a general way with the main geographic and climatic divisions of the island," are named as the East Coast, the interior Plateau, and the West Coast and Extreme South.[31] Aboriginal New Zealand has also been mapped; eight areas have been distinguished in the culture of the Maori, these being "strongly marked" in material culture traits.[32]

It is interesting to consider how ocean regions, where the sea has been a highway rather than a barrier, lend themselves to division into culture-areas. The great regions of the Pacific, Australia and Tasmania, Polynesia, Micronesia, Melanesia and Indonesia, may be regarded as groupings in the nature of culture-areas. Systematic analysis, as Hoijer points out,[33] would undoubtedly show the need for more precise categories than these, especially in the case of Melanesia and Indonesia. The sub-continent of New Guinea, too, would require separate treatment.

4

Description of the cultures found in the areas that have been mapped is neither possible nor advisable here. An idea of them can

[29] This listing of areas is a composite taken from E. Bacon and A. E. Hudson, 1945, and E. Bacon, 1946.

[30] E. Bacon, 1946, p. 121.

[31] R. Linton, 1928, p. 363.

[32] H. D. Skinner, 1921.

[33] H. Hoijer, 1944, p. 32, pp. 40 ff.

best be gained by reading some of the detailed descriptions of specific cultures in the various regions that are readily available, and are named in the list of works given at the end of this book. Compressed presentations such as must necessarily be used to characterize culture-areas are deceptive unless read with proper background. Our concern is with the structure of culture, and in this connection the culture-area is important because it demonstrates how, in the dimension of space as in inner organization, the unities of human civilization are maintained.

Let us turn to other aspects of the culture-area that will aid us in understanding its nature, and thus its significance for the study of culture in general. We have seen how areas were mapped only after the facts about the range of cultures over an entire region were known. It will be helpful to us to probe this further. Ideally, the student considers the distribution of trait after trait in a region, discovering those cultures in which the greatest number of these traits is found. These concentrations most clearly differentiate the culture types. They represent, for the student, the peaks in the cultural landscape; about them his areas cluster.

Wissler's procedure makes this clear. Beginning his discussion of aboriginal American cultures with a delimitation of food areas, he next considers the distribution of individual cultural traits, under such headings as the methods of transportation, textile and ceramic types, decorative designs, architecture, stone and metal work, the fine arts, social institutions and ritual, and mythology. He then considers where the most dense clustering of the greatest number of similar traits occurs, and these become the centers of his areas. Traits, he points out, may be negative or positive. The absence of traits that characterize one area and the positive manifestations of traits of another are equally significant. These two categories are balanced even when the kind of culture that marks an area is being described. More importantly, however, negative as well as positive traits must be taken into account when we leave the center and search for the limits of the area.

In the Plains area Wissler counted thirty-one tribal groups. Of these he considered eleven as "manifesting the typical culture of the area," the Assiniboin, Arapaho, Blackfoot, Cheyenne, Comanche, Crow, Gros Ventre, Kiowa, Kiowa-Apache, Sarsi, and Teton-Dakota. They form a line that is roughly central on the north-south axis of the Plains area as delimited. To the eastward of them were

> some fourteen tribes having most of the positive traits . . . and, in addition, some of the negative ones, such as a limited use of

pottery and basketry; some spinning and weaving of bags; rather extensive agriculture; alternating the tipi with larger and more permanent houses covered with grass, bark, or earth; some attempts at water transportation; tending not to observe the sun dance, but to substitute maize festivals, shamanistic performances, and the *midéwin* of the Great Lakes tribes.

On the west of the axis are other tribes

lacking pottery, but producing a rather high type of basketry; depending far less on the buffalo but more on deer and small game; making large use of wild grass seeds, or grain; alternating tipis with brush and mat-covered shelters; and not as a whole inclined to the sun dance and other ceremonial practices of their eastern neighbors.[34]

These three groups of tribes, then, have cultures that, despite dissimilarities, do resemble each other. The variations from the type of culture that marks the central axis, however, are in the main manifest in "traits of the adjoining areas." This is why they are named marginal cultures—cultures, that, while sufficiently like those of the peoples whose ways of life are taken as typical, or central, differ from them in increasing degree as their habitat is removed from that of the central tribes. This is a reflection of the fact, already noted, that propinquity makes for more intensive borrowing.

In establishing and characterizing areas it is not necessary to find the points of greatest coincidence of "typical" traits. It sometimes occurs that the life of the tribes inhabiting a given region is so strikingly oriented that this focusing of interest is sufficient by itself to mark off an area. In such cases the preponderant role of a complex, *for the people who live in the area,* gives point and reason to their ways of life and is a dominating, integrating force in their existence.

Such a dominating element is found in the cattle complex of East Africa. Cattle determine a man's rank, as where, among the Bahima, chiefs were appointed to rule over a given number of cattle instead of a given region; or among the Zulu, where status is established by the derivation of the cattle that passed on the occasion of one's mother's marriage. Among the Ba-Ila, a man has an ox that he treats like a pet, that sleeps in his hut and is called by name. When this man dies, the skin of the ox is his shroud; its flesh supplies his funeral feast.

The languages of the area yield significant illustrations of the

[34] C. Wissler, 1922, pp. 218-20.

importance of cattle. Evans-Pritchard, for example, cites forty different words, each of which applies to the color of a particular kind of cow or ox.[35] The imagery in the poetry of the peoples living in this region is replete with references to their cattle. Here is a Didinga warrior song, a part of the ritual of propitiating the full moon on the eve of battle, as translated by J. H. Driberg:

> *White cow of heaven, you have fed in rich pastures*
> *and you who were small have grown great.*
> *White cow of heaven, your horns have curved full*
> *circle and are joined as one.*
> *White cow of heaven, we throw at you the dust which*
> *your feet have trampled in our kraals.*
> *White cow of heaven, give your blessing on the kraals*
> *which you have overseen that the udders of our cows*
> *may be heavy and that our women may rejoice.*[36]

The importance of cattle does not imply that the consensus of traits that mark off any culture-area from any other is absent here. Many traits that lie quite outside the influence of the cattle complex can be analyzed much as Wissler listed the positive and negative traits of the Plains Indian cultures of North America. If the coincidence of positive and negative traits in a given region is held to be necessary for considering it a culture-area, this East African region is indubitably one. Moreover, it is possible to isolate tribes where these traits, plus the overshadowing cattle complex, are found in the intensity required for a culture-center. It so happens that the long narrow East African area is divided midway by a strip of territory that harbors the tsetse fly. The presence of cattle is therefore impossible, and the cultures found there must be classified as less representative than others north and south of this strip. But along a central axis such tribes as Nuer, Lango, Bunyoro, Ankole, Nandi, Masai, and Suk form a northern series of "typical" cattle cultures, while to the south the Ila, Mashona, Basuto, and Zulu, among others, form another culture-center.

Toward the coastline of the Indian Ocean, the East African culture becomes "marginal." To the north, the traits of the East African area merge so imperceptibly with those of the East Horn and Eastern Sudan that it is difficult to justify any particular boundary. This is unlike the case westward, where the Congo

---

[35] E. E. Evans-Pritchard, 1940, pp. 41–5.
[36] J. H. Driberg, 1930, p. 44.

forests and the southern deserts impose sharp limitations on the spread of this culture based on cattle, and thus permit a clearly defined boundary to be indicated.

Hence we have an area delimited geographically and defined as to cultural content in a way that satisfies all the demands of the definition. In addition, however, the significance of cattle to the people here makes for a complex that lies uppermost in their thinking. This complex can thus be utilized to classify the cultures of the area as effectively as the conventional assemblage of traits that, however consistent as distributions, are not associated in the minds of the people whose cultures are being studied, as we shall now see.[37]

5

Certain cautions must be entered concerning the culture-area, since an uncritical employment of this useful tool can result in serious misconceptions. It is most important, first of all, to understand that the culture-area is essentially a device that arises out of the need of the student to organize his data and depict, on a broad canvas, the range of cultures over a continent or an island region. This implies that the area, as such, exists in the mind of the student and has but little meaning to those who inhabit it. The culture-area is thus not an "incipient nationality," as it has been called. It is not a self-conscious grouping at all. Rather it is a construct that those to whom it is applied would usually be the first to reject. It calls for an overview that no people can have of the wider setting in which their ways of living lodge. It necessitates fixing the eye on the broad lines of similarities and differences between cultures, not on the details seen by those who are too close to a culture. Where attention is centered on minutiae, the area vanishes into a mass of specific items.

A second caution has to do with the nature of the concepts "cultural center" and "marginal culture." These are constructs in the same way that the culture-area itself is a construct. Like it, they have the same ethnographic validity, the same lack of psychological reality. It is this negative point that gives rise to the need for a full understanding of the limitations of these two ideas. It must be emphasized that the culture-center is the place where a cluster of traits is found, not where the richest life is lived by the people of an area. Conversely, a marginal culture is one where traits from a neighboring area are to be discerned.

Some difficulty has been experienced in applying the idea of

[37] For a full treatment of these data, see M. J. Herskovits, 1926, *passim.*

culture-areas to Euroamerican groupings. Experience has shown that it is not adapted to use where the distribution of geographical differences between peoples is overridden by stratification resulting from the high degree of specialization of larger population aggregates. Area is only one of a number of criteria that can be usefully employed to distinguish cultures, and, more particularly, sub-cultures. Industrial centers do differ from agricultural regions, but all of them in the United States, for instance, have such preponderant cultural similarities that it obscures rather than brings out the significance of the differences between them to regard them as of the order of culture-areas. The typical behavior of social class or occupational group is important here. Categories derived from distinctions drawn on the basis of local differences are obviously inapplicable to such cases, and should be replaced by those that are functionally relevant.

A final point where caution is essential bears on the use of the culture-area as a dynamic device. Initially, it was purely descriptive, employed to classify the cultures found at a given period in time. This lack of time depth was stressed, and materially strengthened the usefulness of the concept. In this, the culture-area is to be contrasted to the "culture-circle" of the culture-historical school of ethnological thought. This school not only envisages geographical distributions of the "culture-complex," but strives to dissect the history of cultural development in various areas by studying a presumed stratification of these elements.

Though he works on a more limited scale and with far more precise control of his data, Kroeber has also attempted to introduce the dimension of time in studying the culture-area. There can be no differing with his contention that mere description, which has been the objective of the culture-area concept, is no end in itself; that process must be analyzed, if we are to understand the nature and functioning of culture. In achieving his end, however, he adds the concepts of cultural intensity and climax to that of area. "Intensity" is reflected in the way in which cultures and areas achieve what is termed their "level."

> A more intensive as compared with a less intensive culture normally contains not only more material—more elements or traits—but also more material peculiar to itself, as well as more precisely and articulately established interrelations between the materials. An accurate time reckoning, a religious hierarchy, a set of social classes, a detailed property law, are illustrations of this.[38]

[38] A. L. Kroeber, 1939, p. 222.

"Climax" is to be thought of as the dynamic equivalent of the descriptive term "culture-center." It is the part of the area where the tribes have "a larger content of culture; and a more developed or specialized organization of the content of the culture—in other words, more numerous elements and more sharply expressed and interrelated patterns." [39] The "above-average developments" he regards as centers from which cultural stimuli have flowed, decreasing in intensity as the marginal regions are reached and the emanations from the next center encountered.

That the idea of climax can be useful in solving that most vexing problem of the culture-area, the setting of boundaries, is evident. Whether "intensity" can be used to express in objective form the values of a people, and balance these values against one another, is quite another matter. So is the question whether the usefulness of the culture-area concept can be extended to an analysis of historic relation. At this writing, the case for its utilization in the study of such problems can in no wise be considered as established.

[39] A. L. Kroeber, 1936, p. 114.

Chapter **Twenty-two**

Patterning and Integration in Culture

In considering the pattern phenomenon, we are confronted with two differing aspects of it that, though they have given rise to much controversy, are in actuality complementary rather than contradictory. The first meaning of pattern is the form that the institutions of a culture characteristically take, as when we say that it is a pattern of our culture that church windows are of stained glass rather than of clear glass. The second meaning is a psychological one, as when we say that the pattern of behavior in churches calls for subdued speech. It is this dual significance of the pattern concept that allows us to employ it so as to move back and forth from the examination of the objective, structural aspects of culture to the study of its psychological values.

We must, therefore, draw our definition of pattern so that it will reflect these two aspects of our problem. Patterned structure, we recognize, can be described, since all structure has form and every form has describable limits. But we also recognize that patterned behavior and sanctioned responses are the raw stuff out of which the structured forms are made. We take both these aspects into account, then, when we think of cultural patterns as *the designs taken by the elements of a culture which, as consensuses of the individual behavior patterns manifest by the mem-*

bers of a society, give to this way of life coherence, continuity, and distinctive form.

How definitely the consensuses of behavior that characterize culture can be described will become apparent if we briefly sketch the patterns that, in two societies, regulate and sanction behavior in a specific phase of culture, marriage. We shall of necessity disregard deviants, but shall describe the accepted conventions as does any ethnographer who studies a culture in the field.

What is the pattern of mating, we may ask first of all, in that particular segment of Euroamerican society that exists in the United States? In the first place, marriage, on the whole, is the affair of the two contracting parties, usually adults, and is not an arrangement between family groups. Personal choice plays an important role, and financial considerations have no overt recognition. Limitations on the choice of a mate imposed by kinship or age or class lines are relatively few. Other elements in the marriage pattern may be described with equal sharpness. Marriage is preceded by a formal announcement of "engagement," marked by the gift of a valuable ring to the woman from the man. The "engagement" is a kind of interim period during which the two persons enjoy mutual priority on each other's leisure. Association, except in groups or officially, with others of the opposite sex, is not sanctioned. Also unsanctioned is the indulgence in sexual relations between the engaged couple, an item in the moral code that differs from the practices of other societies.

This engagement period is typically of greater importance to the woman than to the man, and is marked by certain social-ritual gatherings, called "showers," designated by special names in accordance with the types of gifts the guests are directed to bring, such as "linen shower," "kitchen shower." It is a mark of prestige to have several showers proffered to honor the engaged young woman, and to her material benefit. During the engagement, the principals assume reciprocal duties toward the families of their prospective spouses, particularly the parents. Visits are exchanged, birthdays and feast days calling for gifts or notes of greeting are not overlooked.

Invitations to the wedding reception that follows the actual marriage rite require that a gift be sent the couple by the recipient; marriage announcements sent after the ceremony do not call for such gifts. The marriage is predominantly a religious ceremony, though it need not be so. Secular marriage rites are carried on with less ritual than religious ones, and are regarded as deviants from the pattern. The clothing worn by the bride at the ceremony is more important than that of the groom. The symbolism of the veil and bouquet of flowers she carries, and of the color white (in the case of a first marriage) assumes great importance. The rite is followed by a feast, the most important feature of which is the cake which must be ceremonially cut by bride and groom together. Certain mild forms of hazing follow the ceremony, such as throwing rice and other objects at the newly married pair as they depart for a period of seclusion and release from customary routine. This period is termed a "honeymoon" and concludes this series of events.

Let us contrast this pattern of mating with another that is equally susceptible of being described in the same institutional terms. We may select one that is operative in the Solomon Islands, among a Melanesian people inhabiting the region about Buka Passage, a strait on the north of Bougainville.[1] Here marriage is a matter primarily of family concern, and betrothal occurs when the parties to a match are young indeed—the girl an infant, the boy less than seven or eight years of age. The boy's father opens preliminary negotiations with the mother of the girl, without the knowledge of his son, who is not informed of his betrothal until later. Betrothal, like later marriage, essentially involves the passage of valuable goods from the family of the groom to that of the bride, a transaction that is obviously of no concern to the pre-adolescent youth.

Here is a table of the events that lead up to marriage. It clearly shows how the arrangements that have to be made conform to a definite scheme. The importance of the ritual exchanges at each step, which give meaning to this series of ceremonies, are to be especially noted.

Occasion	*Transactions*
1. Betrothal, when both are children, the girl often quite a baby.	Father of boy presents spear hung with one string of *beroan* (ceremonial currency made of shell disks) to mother of girl. Betel-mixture chewed.
2. First visit of mother of boy to mother of girl. Soon after 1.	Aromatic plants brought by mother of boy to decorate girl. Betel-mixture chewed.
3. Visit of boy's mother to take back girl for her first visit. When girl is about 7 or 8 years old.	Paint for head of girl brought by boy's mother. Betel-mixture chewed.

[1] B. Blackwood, 1935, Chap. III, pp. 82–131.

4. Visit of girl's mother to see her daughter in mother-in-law's hut, 3 or 4 days after 3 above.
Girl remains with mother-in-law for a month or more.

Food and areca-nut provided by boy's mother for girl's mother and accompanying women.

If she runs away, her mother must make *menak* (ceremonial pudding of taro and coconut) for the boy's mother and must bring her back.

5. Request for handing over of ceremonial currency. At discretion of girl's mother, but usually at first signs of breast development.

Girl's mother sends food, including pig-meat, to boy's mother, the pig being a hint that it is time to produce the currency.

6. Boy's mother collects ceremonial currency from her brother and other male relatives.

Boy's mother sends pieces of pig to relatives who are expected to help provide the currency.

7. Visit of boy's people to girl's people to hand over currency, and to bring back girl for long visit. As soon as enough currency has been collected.

Agreed amount of ceremonial currency handed over for division among the girl's relatives. One string given as personal gift, secretly, by boy's mother to girl's mother. One string given by girl's mother to boy's relatives "to pay for the boy."

8. During the next few years girl spends much time with her mother-in-law, returning to her mother only for occasional visits.

9. Special visit of girl and her relatives to boy's mother to pay for *tagoan* (the front end of the house with its verandah, usually reserved for men, and occupied by women only on certain special ceremonial occasions, such as rites connected with marriage).

Girl's mother and relatives bring *menak* and a live pig to boy's relatives, and small amount of ceremonial currency.

10. Marriage ceremony. Usually not until boy has taken off *upi* (special headgear worn by boys during adolescence) and girl has been through her first menstruation ceremony.

Exchange of ceremonial baskets of taro. Much food given by bride's mother to bridegroom's relatives.[2]

[2] *Ibid.*, pp. 95–7.

We shall not detail the elements in the final ritual of the marriage pattern, though this could be outlined in much the same manner as has the long progression of events that mark finding a mate for a boy or girl and bringing them to the status of married persons. Certain general aspects of this pattern should, however, be taken into account. Plural marriage, though not the rule, is permitted. These societies know certain class distinctions, so that "it is usual for the father of a boy who is *tsunaun* [a member of the most important lineage in a village] to choose for his son's first wife a girl who is his equal in rank, but there appears to be no hard and fast rule on the subject. A *tsunaun* girl may be betrothed to a commoner if her mother agrees." The reason for this emphasizes another aspect of the pattern, since "it involves the handing over, at a later stage in the negotiations, of a larger amount of ceremonial currency than a commoner is likely to have at his disposal." [3] The virginity of a girl at marriage is taken for granted, since her betrothal occurs when she is very young. For their part, the boys are surrounded by an elaborate series of taboos and restrictions until they reach the age of marriage, restrictions that effectively prevent them from having access to the girls.

We have considered two patterns of conduct that accomplish one of the ends every society must provide for, if it is to be perpetuated, societies in which, however, the means employed to achieve the common end are so different as to coincide only in aim and accomplishment. Choice of mate is exercised by individuals in one, dictated by families in the other. In one, there is a wide range of ages at which marriage is consummated, in the other the age of the principals is relatively fixed. In one society, the passage of valuable goods during betrothal and at marriage is secondary and informal; in the other, essential and highly regularized. Yet in each, the "proper" way is explicitly recognized; and, what is more, the members of each society can describe this "proper" way, if questioned.

This is the kind of patterning of institutions that we find in all cultures, in all their different phases. Patterning, however, is not a strait jacket; it is not even a high wall that bars wandering in adjacent cultural fields. It is a model, with its outlines flexible and alterable, permitting experience to fall into meaningful forms.

2

Let us return for a moment to the individual in society. From his enculturative experience, he has learned a set of socially sanc-

[3] *Ibid.*, p. 83.

tioned behavior patterns which, while permitting the play of variables, yet keep his acts within the matrix of his culture. A society is thus composed of individuals whose behavior is to a very great extent alike in the day-to-day situations they face. Yet, as we have seen, no society is entirely homogeneous. It is composed, for one thing, of men and women; age differences also order different types of behavior, as do differences of a social, economic, or occupational nature.

The conditioning to different patterns of behavior and to different interests, goals, and meanings begins very early in life. Clothing types are differentiated when boys and girls emerge from infancy, and this extends to hair styles as well. Little girls are encouraged to play with dolls; little boys with weapons or mechanical devices. Little girls skip rope or play jacks; little boys play football or do the high jump. And while there will always be little boys who enjoy girls' games and girls who would like to play football, it is rare to find a boy who can skip rope as well as the girls or a girl who continues to remain absorbed in ball playing. The skill that comes from continuous practice, carried on because it has social approval, is just not there.

In later life, further standardized differences in characteristic activities appear. Except during adolescent and post-adolescent years, when other influences enter, a group of persons together for an evening's recreation tends to break into two. The men discuss those matters that are of concern to them, the women talk over women's affairs. On occasion they may come together for a while, as when certain matters of common concern, such as some civic enterprise, are under discussion. But men, though they are fathers, will not long be held by debate over problems of infant feeding or children's clothing, while questions of tax policy or sports will prove equally uninteresting to a woman who finds herself ensnared in a conversation of this sort.

On the level of differences in age, the boy or girl finds little to discuss with the friend of his father and mother, who is equally at a loss when he is left alone with his friend's child. This difficulty in communication only underscores the lack of common interests it implies. It also suggests that one type of cultural change takes place when the new generation shifts the pattern of procedure from that which its predecessor followed, bringing about mutual misunderstanding and irritation, especially where moral values are involved. Even where there is no emotional association, the changing patterns of belief, of interest, of taste can make for strain between the generations. Music offers numerous instances. The devotion of a young man or woman to jazz, swing and boogie-woogie will cause excessive irritation to a parent enculturated to other kinds of "popular" musical expression. On a somewhat different level, atonal progressions that come easily to the young musician and to whose values the younger listener reacts with deep emotion will tax the abilities and patience of the older generation.

Occupational or class lines similarly dictate different patternings. Speech may be an index of position, and one with a "lower-class accent" will see to it that his manner of speaking is corrected if he is ambitious to rise in the social scale. Economic differences are invariably reflected by typical differences in reaction to different situations. The eating habits of the ditch-digger and of the banker, of the janitor and of the lawyer whose office he cleans are as different as the work they do, the remuneration they receive, or the clothing they wear. It is not unlikely that there will be patterned differences in their behavior toward their wives and in the techniques they use in correcting their children; certainly, there will be differences in the kind of furnishings they have in their homes, in the use of their leisure time, in the lodges or clubs to which they belong.

The extent to which there is this differentiation of pattern in a given society depends on the size of the group, which in turn also influences its degree of specialization. The Eskimo, the Australians, the Bushmen, the people of Tierra del Fuego, or of the Great Basin region of North America, whose numbers are few, whose technologies are simple, or whose environments are rugged, have no class or occupational patterns, since their societies have no class structure and there is no specialization in production. Their sub-groupings are simply those universal ones of sex and age. In other societies, where greater resources make stratification possible, specialized patterns are to be found. The very fact that we distinguish these groups as such implies that we recognize constant differences in their ways that serve to set off one group from another in a given society.

Thus men and women in the West African culture of Dahomey have assigned to them clearly differentiated manual skills, codes of etiquette, degrees of participation in family and political councils, and economic pursuits. Men do ironworking, and the weaving and sewing of cloth; they are the hunters and wood carvers; they do the heavy agricultural work of breaking the ground, and along the seacoast they are the fishermen. The women care for the children, tend the growing crops, prepare food, sell in the markets, make the pottery. Or, to take another example, ask an elderly man for an animal tale—a fable that in its moral teaches a lesson—and he will reply that such stories are told by children; that he has long ago forgotten those he knew. Actually he does remember them, but he would not tell them except to his grandchildren. For an adult to ask him to recount these is an affront to his age.

Class distinctions in Dahomean society produce similar differences in patterned behavior. The inferior prostrates himself before the superior; the superior alone may wear sandals, walk in the shade of an umbrella, smoke the long pipe that is an evidence of his rank. The upper-class Dahomean is reserved, circumspect in speech, deliberate in his gestures, showing proud bearing in the way he wears his great toga-like cloth or handles his wand of office. He does not dance to fast compelling rhythms like the commoner. It is a saying in Dahomey that, as a man advances in the social scale, his dancing becomes more restrained, keyed to slower rhythms.

It is thus unjustified to postulate a single pattern as marking off any one culture. Such a construct disappears in the welter of differing forms of behavior dictated by considerations of sex, age, class, occupation and other distinctions. Yet, when closely observed, least common denominators in behavior do emerge. The men who are interested in football at one end of the room, their wives discussing the feeding formula of the infant at the other, are all using the same language. They have similar food preferences; they live in the same kinds of houses; read the same newspapers—the concurrences in their lives, in actuality, far outweigh the divergences. In the same way, the Dahomean chief and commoner also employ a common language; they enjoy the same musical forms; recognize and respect the same forces that rule the universe; live within the framework of a single economy.

Sapir, one of the first to recognize the psychological base of the phenomenon of cultural pattern, after asserting that "all cultural behavior is patterned," goes on to express the importance of the unifying element of comprehension. He points out:

> It is impossible to say what an individual is doing, unless we have tacitly accepted the arbitrary modes of interpretation that social tradition is constantly suggesting to us from the very moment of our birth. Let anyone who doubts this try the experiment of making a painstaking report of the actions of a group of natives engaged in some form of activity . . . to which he has not the cultural key. If he is a skilful writer, he may succeed in giving

a picturesque account of what he sees and hears, or thinks he sees and hears, but the chances of his being able to give a relation of what happened in terms that would be intelligible and acceptable to the natives themselves are practically nil.[4]

Instances of this kind of misinterpretation are innumerable. One thinks, for example, of the pleasure with which the early explorers among the Kikuyu of East Africa recorded how, in recognition of their superior position, the warriors turned out in full panoply to escort them to the place where the chief awaited them. Of the fact that this was a military measure, a sign of hostility, they were quite unaware. That is, friendly intercourse among these people takes entirely different forms. A visitor's entrance to a village is greeted with studied indifference. He sits quietly and silently by a friend, who finishes whatever he is doing, until at last he addresses to him a few casual phrases of greeting. Now not all the inhabitants of the Kikuyu village participated in the military display that greeted the early Europeans. Neither women, nor children, nor elderly men took part in it. But the act was to them decidedly a part of the patterns of their culture, and as such it was understandable, significant, predictable.

What is of signal importance is to perceive that in every society all know, recognize and can cope with the sub-patterns of their culture. A man may not be concerned with bottle formulas of infants, but he can feed the baby if he has to. His wife may not be enough interested in football to center her conversation about it, but she may enjoy seeing a game. The Dahomean elder may not care to tell fables, but he recognizes their role as an educational device for the young; the chief will not dance violently, but he will enjoy the dancing of the commoners and he will reward those whose performance is outstanding.

The conception of culture-pattern as the consensus of individual behavior patterns presents no difficulty if two things are held in mind. The first is that the concept confuses rather than clarifies unless it is thought of in multiple terms when the institutionalized modes of existence of any people are being examined. The second point to remember is that the phrase "behavior patterns" means more than overt behavior. It comprehends not only acts but the clues to action, the values that provide the motivation for action, the meaning conferred by the act. In this broad sense, then, we can conceive of a culture as composed of a series of patterns that reflect the habitual individual responses—motor,

[4] E. Sapir, 1949, pp. 546-7.

verbal, or ideational—of all those who make up the society where these responses are dominant. We can then without difficulty think of the pattern phenomenon in culture as a reflection of the common elements in the individual behavior of those who live in the culture into which they have been born.

3

It must be clearly understood that the structure of culture, as described in the preceding pages, exists only for the student. Even when men and women generalize about the customary behavior of their own group, or give the reasons that justify the institutions of their culture, they no more comprehend the structural framework that supports their manner of living than they are conscious of the rules of the grammar that give their language describable form, or the system of scales, modes, and rhythms that governs their singing.

Because the life of every group is unified for those who live it, it is essential that we perceive both the need to study how a culture is synthesized, and the usefulness of breaking down this unity into its component parts. In considering any individual way of life, we must see it as a whole that is more than the sum of its parts, but when we analyze human social behavior, we may isolate form from meaning, action from sanction. We may describe in minute detail the structure of a building, tell how it is made, by whom, and of what materials, and thus have an assemblage of traits whose distribution can be traced without the slightest reference to their functioning. Or, we can study the different uses to which structures are put by a people, indicating that some are lived in, some are used for storage, some are places of worship, and some centers of government, with equal disregard of their formal elements. We could then say, perhaps, that the range of variation in the functions of houses is here broad, there narrow, and draw our conclusions. But the human beings out of whose behavior these structures stem would have no place in our study.

The analysis of culture, first into traits and complexes, and then into patterns, has raised the question whether the patterns may not be comprehended under still broader, psychological formulations, called configurations, or themes, or affirmations. These are thought of as least common denominators of whole cultures, or of great segments of a culture, that yield clues to some of the most deeply recessed springs of behavior among a people. Whether or not they represent the master clues of all the institutions, value-systems and goals of a people is a matter on which there is as yet no agreement. Later in this chapter, we shall review the arguments advanced for the usefulness and validity of such an approach.

For the moment, we need to bear in mind that the problem of cultural integration presents two faces. One, the *functional* view, attempts to study the interrelation between the various elements in a culture; the other, the *configurational* or *thematic* attack, represents the psychological approach to cultural integration, and seeks to discover the threads of aim, of satisfactions that give to the institutional unity the particular quality, the special "feel" that everyone senses when he compares one culture with another.

The functionalist point of view, as described by B. Malinowski, with whose name this method is most closely identified,

> aims at the explanation of anthropological facts at all levels of development by their function, by the part which they play within the integral system of culture, by the manner in which they are related to each other within the system, and by the manner in which this system is related to the physical surroundings.

In terms of the functional method,

> the real identities of culture appear to lie in the organic connection of its parts, in the function which a detail fulfils within its scheme, in the relation between the scheme, the environment and the human needs. Meaningless details disappear, shape becomes alive with meaning and with function, and a testimony of irrelevant form falls away as worthless.[5]

The method is applied both in field research that aims at comprehending a single culture, and in understanding relations that are to be applied in the study of culture as a whole.

Various elements in functionalist theory have been vigorously debated. For instance, Malinowski's system derives the principal subdivisions or aspects of culture from biological necessity, and sees as the ultimate function of culture the task of satisfying these needs. It has also laid stress on the study of culture on a single time plane, and has argued against attempting to reconstruct unwritten history. We shall examine these points later. But there can be no question of the need to determine how each element of a culture influences and is influenced by those other elements with which it is associated.

The comparatively simple culture of the Bush Negroes of Dutch Guiana, South America, affords us pertinent materials for

[5] B. Malinowski, 1926, pp. 132, 139.

a presentation of this kind.[6] Their numbers are small, their villages compact, their economy direct, with no middlemen to intervene between the functions of production and consumption. Their social structures form an ascending hierarchy of immediate family, extended family and sib; on the latter governmental institutions are based. The universe is for them ruled by a series of nature deities, worshipped with song and dance. To these the forces of magic and of the dead are to be added as powerful supernatural agents. Their art, expressed primarily in the carving of highly ornamented wooden implements, is of great excellence. In the oral arts they have a full complement of myths and tales, while their musical resources in the form of singing and drumming show range, versatility, and an extensive repertory. The culture is a going concern, little influenced either by the Europeans of the coastal belt or the Indians of the interior. We consider it here, in the functional manner, in order to lay emphasis on its integrations, and without regard for its historical background of African origin, or such borrowings as it has effected from these other two cultures with which the Bush Negroes have had contact.

We can take such a simple element of the culture as the dwelling place as our starting point. The Bush Negro house, in its physical appearance, is a rectangular, gabled structure, entered by a door so low that one must stoop. The sides are woven of palm fronds in a pleasing basket-weave design; the roof is thatched; and there are neither windows nor chimney. Air enters through the interstices of the woven sides, while smoke from the fire escapes through the thatch. Here, already, we envisage purposeful functioning, in this case in terms of adaptation to the habitat. The windowless, woven sides permit enough light to enter to see what one is doing, yet leave the house cool and darkened, a refuge from the tropical sun. The smoke of the fire is an effective fumigant against the insects that would otherwise infest the thatch, and it keeps off the mosquitoes that swarm in this tropical forest.

Inside the house are many of the material possessions of the household, particularly those of the woman. In the corner lie the woven hammocks used for sleeping. Low carved stools provide seats and can conveniently be taken outdoors where a group may gather. The interstices of the wall hold small objects such as carved combs and food-stirring paddles. Against the walls rest decorated calabashes, in which possessions such as cloths are kept,

[6] M. J. and F. S. Herskovits, 1934, *passim*.

and rice, or casava meal, or in which maize is stored for immediate use. In the corners are carved canoe paddles, while suspended from the cross poles beneath the roof are still other gourds containing articles not in everyday use. Both the door and the doorposts are carved; those of a village elder with the symbol of his clan, or with other symbolic designs.

The house is a part of a complex of dwellings and accessory structures; several such complexes form the village. Certain of these structures merit special attention for a moment. One is the *gudu-wosu*—the house where a man keeps his wealth. Made differently from the dwelling house, it has latticework sides so that people can peer through and wonder at the city-bought objects, the carved drums, bush-knives, and other possessions that make the owner a person of substance and standing in the community. The floor will be of wood, raised on poles, above the ground, the door protected by a charm, a *kandu*, that would be violated by no one who valued his health, his sanity, or his life, except a relative in the male line. This type of structure, forbidden to the women, permits a man to conceal his belongings as well as to reveal them; and, in commenting on the fact, the native does not fail to phrase the advantages of both. For the wealthy man guards himself against wives who are importunate; and the man whose *gudu-wosu* tells no tales of what he may or may not have is guarded against his nagging or fault-finding wives.

Still another structure that marks the village is the *krutu-wosu*, the place of assemblage which, when death strikes, becomes the center of long and elaborate funeral rites. This is but a frame, roofed and open on all four sides. Here men and women sit during the day to discuss matters of interest, and to gossip; here the village council assembles when affairs of common concern are to be decided. This house is at the center of the village, and before it is a broad clearing, the sand meticulously swept each day. When a death occurs, the corpse is brought to lie here for a day or two on a broken canoe until a coffin can be built; and later, for the remainder of the week, in its coffin. From this house the grave diggers leave each day, and here they return to "carry the corpse," balancing the coffin atop their heads as the spirit of the dead is questioned about the cause of his death or is required to clear itself of charges that the dead person had practiced evil magic. Here, too, the old men sit with the dead the day long, playing interminably the game of *adji-boto* with its permutations and combinations of seeds as they are dropped successively in the holes of the board they use; and here the village gathers each night the dead lies there, to dance in his honor, or to tell the tales of Anansi, the trickster, that delight his spirit.

We have moved far from the simple element in Bush Negro culture with which we began. We have touched on art, on the economic base of prestige, on one aspect of the relation between the sexes, on the political system, on the rites of death, on games and dancing and folktales. The phrase "touched on" is to be emphasized here, for we have had but fleeting glimpses of the functioning culture in our exposition.

It is unnecessary to continue this account further to make plain how each element in this culture impinges on every other to make a satisfying, integrated way of life. Many of the major divisions of culture, as these are set down by ethnologists, are represented in this account. The traits of this culture we have named stand out, both alone and in the complexes with which they are associated. Yet life, as we observe it from the vantage point of our village, flows as a single current. The generalization "culture" we abstract from our observations is not haphazard or disjointed. The lines cross and recross, but they rarely become entangled. All behavior is meaningful, each act performs some function, every object has its place and its usefulness.

4

It is far simpler to trace relations between the elements of a culture as evidenced in behavior than to ferret out and subject to scientific analysis the unspoken, usually implicit sanctions that are firmly fixed in the cultural matrix. Benedict, who has given the most considered analysis of the configurationist point of view, states:

> The cultural pattern of any civilization makes use of a certain segment of the great arc of potential human purposes and motivations, just as . . . any culture makes use of certain selected material techniques or cultural traits. . . . Selection is the first requirement. Without selection, no culture could even achieve intelligibility, and the intentions it selects and makes its own are a much more important matter than the particular detail of technology or the marriage formality that it also selects in similar fashion.[7]

It is thus clear how crucial in thinking is the selectivity of cultures, which causes them to shape "their thousand items of behavior to

[7] R. Benedict, 1934, p. 237.

a balanced and rhythmic pattern." [8] Integration results when all items are selected in terms of an overall principle.

Benedict makes it plain that there are differing degrees of integration, just as there are different principles on the basis of which various societies develop the configurations of their cultures. One reason for this is a tendency to borrow cultural elements from societies having different configurations—"exposure to contradictory influences," such as is to be found "on the borders of well-defined culture areas." Or a migrating tribe that "breaks off from its fellows and takes up its position in an area of different civilization" can experience a similar disorientation of fundamental drives.

Let us now examine the configurational approach. Benedict's use of the phrase "the cultural pattern" stands in striking contrast to the manner in which other anthropologists have interpreted it, as illustrated in the first part of this chapter. Various suggestions have been made to distinguish these differing concepts by different names. One such term, that has proved useful in these pages, is *sanction*. The underlying drives, motivations, "unconscious system of meanings" that govern the reactions of a people can be thought of as the sanctions of their culture. Other designations have been brought forward which, despite their different shades of meaning, are pertinent. Kluckhohn has suggested the division of cultural phenomena into "overt" and "covert" aspects. The overt forms are those institutions and other manifest elements to which, he urges, "the technical term *pattern* be rigorously restricted." The covert culture includes the sanctions that lie on the unconscious levels of thought. To these he would apply the term "configurations." "A pattern," he states, "is a generalization of what people do or should do; a configuration is in a sense a generalization of 'why' they do or should do certain things." [9]

Opler, on the other hand, prefers to employ the term "themes" which, translated into conduct or belief, gives rise to "expressions"—"formalized" when "conventionalized and ordered," or "unformalized" when their "precise character, time, or place are not carefully defined by the culture." They may, in their direct expression, be "primary," but when given oblique or implied expression are "symbolic"; they may likewise be "material" or "nonmaterial." [10]

[8] *Ibid.*, p. 223.
[9] C. Kluckhohn, 1941, pp. 124-8.
[10] M. E. Opler, 1945, pp. 198-200.

These discussions reflect the ferment that has followed a desire to revise terminology and approach to account for the fact that there is more to culture than its expressions in behavior or the reification of behavior into institutions. They have especially followed on the widespread use of such expressions of cultural mysticism as "the genius of a culture," or its "spirit," or its "feel," which has emphasized the need for the systematic examination of cultural differences and the factors that lend themselves to such formulations. The terms that have been suggested are, of course, more than mere designations. They are handles to the conceptual tools for our research, on which alone their validity must rest. Let us see how they have been, or can be employed.

We may first consider a configurational study in which a single aspect of culture, in this instance medicine, is analyzed. Data from an American Indian, a Melanesian, and an African culture are utilized as part of a broader configuration. In each case the pattern of curing is shown to conform to the broader underlying sanctions of the culture. Thus among the Cheyenne the cause of disease primarily consists of the "invisible arrows shot by the spirits of wells, the mule-deer and other spirits," and treatment is in terms of the "small ceremonial," whereby the expulsion of the intruded object is believed to be accomplished. The Dobuans of Melanesia envisage no supernatural being as bringing on illness, but trace the cause to witchcraft or sorcery. Thus they shape their cures to meet the supernatural dangers that are reported to be so important a manifestation of the basic drives in their culture. The Thonga of South Africa, on the other hand, are reported as conceiving of disease largely as "the outcome of . . . a taboo-situation," the transgression of a rule laid down by the ancestors. On the basis of these differing configurations, the principle is enunciated that,

> the differences between primitive medicines are much less differences in "elements" . . . than differences in the medical "pattern" which they build up and which is conditioned fundamentally by their cultural pattern. . . . Disease may be regarded in its narrowest physiological limits . . . or may become a symbol for dangers menacing society through nature or through its own members. It may seem a mere incident or reach the rank of a goddess. Society unconsciously gives these different places to disease in the course of history.[11]

Kluckhohn illustrates the meaning of the term "covert culture" by telling how, during the early days of his research among

[11] E. H. Ackerknecht, 1942.

the Navaho Indians, he approached eleven persons with a request for information about witchcraft. In seven instances, the response was "Who said I knew anything about witchcraft?" Later he repeated the question to twenty-five informants. Sixteen of these responses took the same form. Having established the existence of this pattern, he then juxtaposed it with other, seemingly unrelated, types of response to typical situations. One is the care the Navaho take to hide their faeces and prevent others from obtaining anything else that comes from their bodies, such as hair, nails, or sputum. Another is their secretiveness about personal names. All these, when put together, form a configuration phrased by Kluckhohn as "fear of the malevolent intentions of other persons." Only rarely, we are told, does it rise into consciousness enough to permit a Navaho to state: "These are all ways of showing our anxiety about the activities of others." [12]

Opler turns to the Chiricahua Apache to document his concept of themes. One theme of this culture, he tells us, is that men are physically, mentally, and morally superior to women. Thus if a fetus has "lots of life," it is assumed it will be a boy. Women are believed less stable than men, and more likely to cause domestic strife. They are held to be more easily "tempted," whether sexually or where witchcraft is involved. Tribal councils are for males, tribal leaders are men. Men precede women on the path; at feasts men have special places, while women eat where they can. A menstruating woman is believed dangerous to men's health and the well-being of male horses. Another theme is the importance of old age, as evidenced in rituals such as the girl's puberty rites, the deference paid the old, the anxieties aroused by the belief that evil beings seek to shorten life, and the like. Yet the influence of such themes, it is pointed out, is not so great that they give society an imbalance that renders its functioning difficult. The influence of the theme of old age is held in check by the value set on performance as against wisdom and experience—a theme Opler terms "validation by participation"; male predominance is checked by the "limiting factors" that arise out of the human situations inherent in the day-to-day relations between the sexes.[13]

An example of what we have called "sanction," but which might be equally describable by any of the other terms just cited, is to be drawn from responses of West African and New World Negroes to many different kinds of situations, in accordance with a principle of indirection. Quite contrary to the too readily ac-

[12] C. Kluckhohn, 1941, pp. 124-5.
[13] M. E. Opler, 1945, *passim.*

cepted stereotype of the "extraverted" Negro, this sanction dominates their behavior and dictates the circumspectness with which
their life is characteristically lived. Indirection takes innumerable
forms. The oblique use of imagery, as exemplified particularly in
the constant employment of proverbs—in ordinary conversation,
or in arguing a case before a court, or in teaching proper behavior to the young—is one example. "Behind the mountain is another mountain," says the Haitian, when he expresses skepticism
about motives. "It is not for nothing the worm crawls from side
to side," comments a Bush Negro when he voices his suspicions
of another; or "He who has no fingers cannot make a fist," he
says to caution an impulsive person. In West Africa quarrels are
often carried on by the use of songs which, never mentioning an
adversary by name, convey their message of insult and disdain by
metaphor and allusion. Again, one does not ask a direct question.
One waits and observes, until assertion based on some command of
fact can open the way to further information. The taxation system of the native kings of Dahomey is the best instance of this
sanction manifest in institutionalized form. Here no one was asked
directly what he possessed, or how numerous was his family, or
how much maize he had grown the previous year. Devious inquiry, however, elicited all the information required by the royal
bureaucracy charged with gathering revenue, and no sources of
income for the royal treasury were overlooked.[14] Only in Guiana
has this reserve, that gives form to the sanction of indirection,
been phrased in non-symbolic terms. "I cannot say more," said
one man after he had for a time discussed a commonplace element
in his culture. "Long ago the ancestors taught us not to tell more
than half of what we know. I have said more than enough."

   Similarly probing for deeper-lying drives to culturally conditioned behavior, Hsü has differentiated Chinese and American
societies in terms of the typical response patterns of their members, the former, as he phrases it, being "situation-centered," the
latter "individual-centered." In documenting his hypothesis, he
examines "art, especially painting, fiction, the patterns of conduct
between the sexes and certain forms of aberrant behavior such as
alcoholism, drug addiction, mental illness and suicide." The utility
of employing data from the arts and literature of the two peoples,
Hsü stresses, derives from the fact that since "the creative individual, like others, is a product of a certain cultural context,"
these two facets of culture are "fundamentally what may be described as mirrors—or as the psychoanalyst says, projective

[14] M. J. Herskovits, 1938b, Vol. I, pp. 107–34.

screens—of the society to which the creative individual belongs." And since sex conduct and aberrant behavior are favorite topics for art and literature, these are called on to contrast the relevant scenes as found "on the projective screen and in reality," to the end that one may "gain a true picture of their differing mental universes" and from this, of their differing patterned reactions to the situations both must meet.[15]

5

Whether we analyze the objective manifestations of a culture or approach it along the broader avenues of its fundamental sanctions and intent, whatever the terminology we may apply to clarify our data and set them in a significant conceptual context, the fact of cultural unity, of cultural integration is established. Its outer forms frame inner meanings; sanctions mold conduct; and life as a whole goes on, permitting human beings to seek and find fulfillment.

As a scientist, the student of culture must divide his data into categories, just as the student of living organisms dissects his specimen. Culture is not an organism, so that the analogy must not be pressed too far. It is enough that the ethnologist, like the biologist in his laboratory, recognize that the subject as he studies it in its several parts is not the living totality. He takes his scientific liberties so that, when he turns again to the functioning whole, he can at least know what these parts are, how they are related to each other, how they combine to make the whole. It is in this sense that he must study structure and distribution. And it is in this spirit that, in another dimension, he again divides culture into the formal aspects, the kinds of institutions to be discerned in all cultures as we move over the earth, comparing one way of achieving a given end with another, assessing the varied means mankind uses to reach the same goals.

[15] F. L. K. Hsü, 1953, pp. 10, 15–17, and *passim.*

Chapter **Twenty-three**

The Problem of Cultural Origins

When, in 1877, Lewis H. Morgan wrote his study of the development of human institutions, *Ancient Society*, he stated a position that was to become known as social or cultural evolution. "The great antiquity of mankind on earth has been conclusively established," reads the opening sentence of Morgan's preface. "Mankind are now known to have existed in Europe in the glacial period," he continues, "and even back of its commencement, with every probability of their origination in a prior geological age." He then states what may be regarded as the essence of his hypothesis: "This knowledge changes materially the views which have prevailed respecting the relations of savages to barbarians, and of barbarians to civilized men. It can now be asserted upon convincing evidence that savagery preceded barbarism in all the tribes of mankind, as barbarism is known to have preceded civilization. The history of the human race is one in source, one in experience, one in progress." [1]

This quotation can be coupled with another that indicates a point of view which Morgan, and those who took a similar position, had to combat in establishing the hypothesis that man had

[1] L. H. Morgan, n.d., pp. v–vi.

moved through lower to higher stages of development in obtaining his present estate. He says:

> The views herein presented contravene, as I am aware, an assumption which has for centuries been generally accepted. It is the hypothesis of human degradation to explain the existence of barbarians and savages, who were found, physically and mentally, too far below the conceived standard of a supposed original man. It was never a scientific proposition supported by facts.

The "Aryan and Semitic tribes" who "represent the main streams of human progress," do so "because they have carried it to the highest point yet obtained." But before these people were their ancestors, who, "there are good reasons to suppose . . . formed a part of the indistinguishable mass of barbarians." Therefore, "as these tribes themselves sprang more remotely from barbarous, and still more remotely from savage ancestors, the distinction of normal and abnormal races falls to the ground." [2]

It is essential for an understanding of cultural evolutionism that it be regarded as more than just a reflex of the theory of biological evolution, whence it is customarily held to have been derived. Teggart has pointed out how Darwin's work, *The Origin of Species*, that appeared in 1859, was "just too late to have an effect upon the remarkable development of ethnological study in the second half of the nineteenth century." The works that initiated this development, such as the contributions of the Germans Waitz, Bastian, and Bachhofen, or the English scholars Maine, McLennan, and Tylor, appeared between 1859 and 1865. This means that they were being planned and written about the same time Darwin was carrying out his researches and organizing and writing down his conclusions. Teggart, moreover, shows that cultural and biological evolutionism differed in certain important theoretical respects. He points out that "Tylor, in 1873, and Mc-Lennan, in 1876," were "disclaiming dependence upon Darwin, and maintaining their allegiance to an earlier tradition of development or evolution. The concept of 'evolution' in ethnology is, in fact, distinct from the type of evolutionary study represented in Darwin's writings." [3] Teggart summarizes this distinction succinctly:

> In the pre-Darwinian tradition, the term "evolution" is synonymous with "development," and is intimately associated with the doctrine of the fixity of species. Ethnology has followed

---

[2] *Ibid.*, pp. 513–14.
[3] F. J. Teggart, 1941, pp. 110–11.

Comte in regarding the study of "evolution" as concerned with tracing the course of development of mankind, and with the construction of "ideal series."

This brings us to another point of importance that is also customarily overlooked in the discussion of cultural evolutionism. Most of the students of man who took part in the exciting search for the ladder by which man had climbed from his earlier savage condition—and would continue to climb to an ever-better world —were eminently men of good will. They thus permitted no assumption that a people on a lower rung, retarded in their cultural achievements, were of inherent inferior capacity. Briefly stated their position was that *cultural differences do not imply innate racial differences.*

But, we ask, was it not illogical to assume cultural inferiority and superiority and specifically to deny the racial basis of such differences? This is the case only if the unity of physical type and culture is postulated. These early students, like those who have followed them, however, realized that there was a fundamental difference between learned traits of behavior and innate physical characteristics, even if they did not have the concepts at hand to phrase these principles in this way. In some instances, as in the system of Spencer, where the presumed evolutionary line moved from inorganic through organic to superorganic (cultural) phenomena, the distinction between race and culture is not made. But when Morgan says, "With one principle of intelligence and one human form, in virtue of a common origin, the results of human experience have been substantially the same in all times and areas in the same ethnical status," [4] he uses "human form" in the sense we employ "physical type" or "race," and his phrase "ethnical status" is what we should term "cultural position."

2

Like any theory of moment, that of social or cultural evolution was the work of many minds, and took on many forms. Some, the best known of its proponents, worked on broad canvases and attempted to describe and account for the development of human civilization in its totality. Others restricted their efforts to specific aspects of culture, taking up the evolution of art, or of the state, or of religion.

Not only did these scholars study different aspects of culture, but they also differed in their interpretations of the facts they em-

[4] L. H. Morgan, n.d., p. 562.

ployed to establish their positions. It will be recalled how it was pointed out, in our discussion of prehistory, that the facts concerning the earliest manifestations of nonmaterial culture are irrevocably lost to us. Language, the form of the family, political structure, religious beliefs, value systems, music, and folklore are intangibles whose precise forms cannot be recovered when one body of unwritten tradition gives way to another.

The social and cultural evolutionists, then, were unable to maintain their classical position because their fundamental postulates were invalidated by the use of more refined techniques and the accumulation of more adequate data. Let us see what these postulates of theory and method were. We may best consider them in their broadest outline, distinguishing three outstanding elements always present in the studies of cultural evolution:

> *1.* The postulate that the history of mankind represents a *unilinear sequence* of institutions and beliefs, the similarities between which, as discerned at the present time, reflect the principle of the *psychic unity of man.*
>
> *2.* The *comparative method*, whereby the evolutionary sequence of human institutions and beliefs is to be established by comparing their manifestations among existing peoples, who are assumed to be the living exponents of earlier *stages of culture* through which the more advanced societies are held to have passed.
>
> *3.* The concept of the survival of customs among peoples regarded as more advanced in their development; these *survivals* to be taken as evidence that such societies have passed through earlier stages whose customs, in vestigial form, appear in their present ways of life.

1. Every exponent of cultural evolution provided an hypothetical blueprint of the progression he conceived as having marked the development of mankind. Of these, none is more specific than that given in Morgan's *Ancient Society*. Three principal periods in human sociocultural development were distinguished by Morgan—savagery, barbarism, and civilization. The first two of these were each held to have been divided into older, middle, and later periods, marked by conditions of society to which were applied the designations lower, middle, and upper status of savagery or barbarism.

Despite the exceptions that Morgan recognized, this system was justified for him by the readiness with which he could classify cultures in different parts of the world as falling under one or the other of these categories, excepting only the initial period of the series, termed the Lower Status of Savagery, which admittedly was hypothetical in the sense that no living peoples were to be found who could be regarded as coming under this heading. The comparability of tribes in the other categories, however, was held to form,

> a part of the accumulating evidence tending to show that the principal institutions of mankind have been developed from a few primary germs of thought; and that the course and manner of their development was predestined, as well as restricted within the narrow limits of divergence, by the natural logic of the human mind and the necessary limitations of its powers.[5]

We could scarcely ask for a clearer expression of the first principle of cultural evolutionism, the assumption of fixed stages of development resulting from the psychic unity of mankind.

Tylor expressed this point much more tentatively than Morgan:

> The thesis which I venture to sustain, within limits, is simply this, that the savage state in some measure represents an early condition of mankind, out of which the higher culture has gradually developed or evolved, by processes still in regular operation as of old, the result showing that, on the whole, progress has far prevailed over relapse.[6]

Everywhere in Tylor's argument we encounter the qualifying phrase, the recognition of the hypothetical nature of a conclusion:

> Even those students who hold most strongly that the general course of civilization, as measured along the scale of races from savages to ourselves, is progress towards the benefit of mankind, must admit many and manifold exceptions. Industrial and intellectual culture by no means advances uniformly in all its branches, and in fact excellence in various of its details is often obtained under conditions which keep back culture as a whole. . . . Even in comparing mental and artistic culture among several peoples, the balance of good and ill is not quite easy to strike.[7]

Spencer's approach, far less flexible in its employment of the evolutionary hypothesis, yields us our final examples. "That seeming chaos of puerile assumptions and monstrous inferences, making up the vast mass of superstitious beliefs everywhere existing," he says, with the determined ethnocentrism that marked his

[5] *Ibid.*, p. 18.
[6] E. B. Tylor, 1874, Vol. I, p. 32.
[7] *Loc. cit.*, pp. 27–8.

thinking, "thus falls into order when, instead of looking back upon it from our advanced stand-point, we look forward upon it from the stand-point of the primitive man." After summarizing the "superstitions" discussed at length in his earlier pages, he states: "How orderly is the genesis of these beliefs, will be seen on now observing that the Law of Evolution is as clearly exemplified by it as by every other natural process. I do not mean merely that a system of superstitions arises by continuous growth, each stage of which leads to the next; but I mean that the general formula of Evolution is conformed to by the change gone through." Thus integration of belief accompanies increase in mass and coherence, from the indefinite to the definite, so that, "Undeniably, . . . a system of superstitions evolves after the same manner as all other things." [8]

2. *The comparative method.* The second element in the system of the evolutionists, held that living nonliterate peoples bear witness to the early condition of man. It is from the consistent use of this method that we have come to regard "primitive" man as our contemporary ancestor. For the evolutionists, it should always be remembered, "primitive" man was "primeval." His arrested cultural development was thus held to make it possible for students to draw on accounts of the customs of "savage" peoples to provide examples of the early life of mankind as a whole.

Tylor has described in detail the procedures for utilizing the comparative method. We are told:

> A first step in the study of civilization is to dissect it into details, and to classify these in their proper groups. Thus, in examining weapons, they are to be classed under spear, club, sling, bow and arrow, and so forth; among textile arts are to be ranged matting, webbing, and several grades of making and weaving threads; myths are divided under such headings as myths of sunrise and sunset, eclipse-myths, earthquake-myths, local myths which account for the names of places by some fanciful tale, eponymic myths which account for the parentage of a tribe by turning its name into the name of an imaginary ancestor. . . . Such are a few miscellaneous examples from a list of hundreds, and the ethnographer's business is to classify such details with a view to making out their distribution in geography and history, and the relations which exist among them. [9]

These quotations make it clear why the term "comparative method" is employed to designate the evolutionists' analyses of

[8] Herbert Spencer, 1896, Vol. VII, pp. 423, 432–4.
[9] *Loc. cit.,* pp. 6–8.

their materials. It is also plain why this method is to be contrasted to the later point of view that cultures are integrated ways of life, not aggregates of discrete parts to be studied out of cultural context. One can, indeed, classify bows; and by arranging all bows, for example, in a single room of a museum, in the order of their complexity, exhibit them as an instance of the development of the bow, and as an example of the evolution of one phase of culture. One can also keep collections from a given people together, and use the bow to illustrate its contribution to the life of the tribe, regardless of the similarity or difference its form exhibits when compared with the bows other peoples use. That the method of studying forms rather than processes left the evolutionists particularly vulnerable will become apparent when later in this chapter we discuss the criticisms lodged against their hypotheses.

3. The concept of the *survival* was much more a feature of European evolutionism than of American. Tylor, with his interest centering on religion, folklore, and other nonmaterial aspects of culture, found it a useful tool. It was most elaborately developed by Frazer, its last great exponent. In the United States, however, the concept of survival was never much employed. This was in the nature of the case. For Tylor, Frazer and their colleagues, the living representatives of presumed earlier cultural stages inhabited distant lands, and their customs recalled customs of the English countryside. To Tylor, such customs in England and on the continent of Europe were nonfunctioning vestiges of a past given over by the intellectual circles which, in his system, represented the flowering of a way of life he characterized as "civilization." For Morgan, on the other hand, and for his American contemporaries, "primitive" man was no distant being, but an inhabitant of their own country. A belief in earlier stages did not have to be documented by them in terms of "the ordeal of the Key and Bible, . . . the Midsummer Bonfire, . . . the Breton peasants' All Souls' supper for the spirits of the dead." [10] That may be why, as a student of this concept has put it: "When survivals came to be frugally employed by Morgan . . . they were discovered, not as by Tylor, among the practices and ideas of civilized men for the purpose of restoring primitive man to a place in the developmental series. On the contrary, they were found exclusively in the culture of one primitive people, the Hawaiian . . . and were used to establish the existence of a condition still more archaic." [11]

[10] E. B. Tylor, *loc. cit.*, p. 16.
[11] M. T. Hodgen, 1936, p. 88.

The doctrine of survivals took on many forms. Its vitality is due to the considerable validity it actually does possess. The very fact that culture is a continuum that constantly changes implies a preponderance of elements in any given culture carried over from an earlier period in its history. The real methodological difficulty arises when a living custom in one part of the world is accepted as the valid counterpart of a "cultural curiosity" in another part. The concept of "social origins" was justified on this basis, and on this basis it fell into disuse. This is no reason, however, for permitting controversy to obscure the very real utility that the idea of cultural survivals—or retentions, as we shall call them—can have.

3

When we ask why evolutionism came to be rejected by so many students of man, we must not only phrase our answer in terms of method; but must take fully into account the changing climate of opinion of the times in which the opposition flourished. As the European world moved out of the Victorian epoch, as the American frontier reached the Pacific, doubts began to appear of the validity of the overall conception of progress that dominated the thought of the period when evolutionism held sway.

The doctrine of evolution was taken into the political field, where it hardened after the manner of any scientific hypothesis that becomes popular. Morgan's work was read by Karl Marx, and his notes on this book, almost unobtainable in Europe at the time, formed the basis of the socialist classic *The Origin of the Family, Private Property, and the State*, written by Marx's literary executor, Friedrich Engels. The hypothesis of stages was transmuted into a doctrine of hope for the underprivileged. In this political sense, social evolution meant that the path to the economic democracy of the socialist order was to be traced from savagery, through barbarism, and beyond the industrialized capitalistic societies of our day.

This episode in the history of social evolutionism seems, however, to have had few repercussions in anthropological thought. Anthropologists, like all scientists, continued the exploration of existing hypotheses on the basis of the new data derived from more intensive and more effective use of the techniques of field research. These findings, for example, tended more and more to invalidate the assumption of cultural inferiority and superiority. They thus struck at the root of the ethnocentrism that was fundamental in judging the "stage" which a given culture was held to have reached in its development. This is only one point we shall consider as we briefly review the grounds on which each of the three major postulates of the evolutionists was eventually abandoned by most anthropologists of the twentieth century.

1. The growing stress laid on the importance of cultural borrowing did much to undermine the postulate of unilinear evolution, a progression through which human culture, in all its aspects, was held to have passed. Diffusion, as this mechanism of cultural change was termed, was found to be responsible for so much more of all individual cultures than the inventiveness of any people could possibly account for that to work out developmental sequences by comparing the ways of life of "untouched" societies came to be recognized as methodologically invalid. What was an "untouched" society, it was asked? If borrowing was so universal in human experience, was it possible, by studying contemporary cultures of peoples assumed to have reached certain stages of their development, to be sure that the correspondences were not the result of diffusion rather than of independent development? The early evolutionists, of course, were not blind either to the existence of borrowing, or to its implications for their hypothesis. That these scholars and others of the evolutionary school felt that they could discern the working out of the lines of human progress despite these borrowings may, from the point of view of later knowledge, be recognized as methodologically ill-advised. This does not, however, justify a denial of the fact that they saw the problem and, in the light of their hypothesis, faced it.

As for the classical doctrine of the psychic unity of man, this could not stand against the growing realization that human behavior is so conditioned that it is difficult, if not impossible, to distinguish innate from learned behavior. We have seen that universals do exist in human culture, and that some of them—though not all—can be referred to the needs of the human organism. Yet we have further seen that because the manifestations of these universals of culture are so varied, the resemblances between the ways in which culture may be divided for purposes of study does no more than give us a framework on which to organize the behavior of peoples when we reify this behavior into the institutions and aspects we, as students, recognize. The psychic unity of man, *in this latter sense,* is undoubtedly a valid concept. But this proposition leads us nowhere in the study of cultural dynamics, which was the use to which it was put by the cultural evolutionists.

2. The comparative method was given over because it came to be recognized that it was a denial of cultural reality. It con-

sisted, in general, of comparing facts, torn out of their cultural context, with little reference to their meaning. It must not be thought that the use of the comparative method was limited to the evolutionists. As was the concept of survivals, it was taken over by some of the strongest opponents of evolutionism. Lévy-Bruhl, who was no social evolutionist, used this method to document his hypothesis of primitive mentality. The extreme diffusionists, both English and German, employed it constantly, in many instances even less critically than some of the social evolutionists. However, it is as unsatisfactory in the hands of diffusionists as in documenting a presumed social-evolutionary sequence. Any use of materials, that is, that fails to recognize cultural context and meaning must be rejected.

3. The culminating argument against cultural evolutionism derived from the refusal of the evolutionists to take into account those considerations of time and place that, as we have seen, are so important in any study of the dynamics of culture. Thus, according to Morgan, the system of matrilinear descent he associated with the "gens" (that is, the mother-sib) was held to characterize the Australians, and "remained among the American aborigines through the Upper Status of savagery and into and through the Lower Status of barbarism, with occasional exceptions." In middle barbarism, the Indians "began to change descent from the female line to the male, as the syndyasmian family of the period began to assume monogamian characteristics." With upper barbarism, "descent had become changed to the male line among the Grecian tribes." The monogamic family is held to have later developed because of the need to assure paternity so as to regularize the inheritance of property. "Between the two extremes, represented by the two rules of descent, three entire ethnical periods intervene, covering many thousands of years." [12]

The developmental series Morgan set up for this institution is as follows (reading from bottom to top):

Modern civilization (monogamy), with descent in the male line
↑
Grecian tribes, with descent in the male line
↑
American Indians, with change in descent from female to male line
↑
Australians (gens), with descent in the female line

But this series, from the point of view of a historical approach, is quite fictitious, since only the last two items in it are historically

[12] L. H. Morgan, n.d., p. 67.

related. In terms of actual time, the series should be arranged in this way:

Modern Civilization   American Indians   Australians
↑
Grecian tribes

Placed in this fashion, it is at once seen to be no series at all, but rather a comparison of data existing on a given time plane, arranged according to a predetermined scheme of development.

Tylor understood this point better than Morgan. In discussing the criteria that are to be used in establishing "a means of measurement" of civilization, he dismisses the matter in terms of the common sense of his times. "The educated world of Europe and America practically settles a standard by simply placing its own nations at one end of the social series and savage tribes at the other, arranging the rest of mankind between these limits according as they correspond more closely to savage or to cultured life." [13] No critic of cultural evolutionism has ever phrased his criticism in terms more telling than this honest recognition by Tylor of the ethnocentric basis on which "progress" was to be noted. Once we eschew this ethnocentrism, the method derived from it is revealed in all its weighting.

4

The positive contributions made by the earlier evolutionists to the study of culture are too often so taken for granted that they tend to be lost sight of in the controversies that are waged over specific points of method and over the philosophy of evolutionism. Whatever the theoretical points at issue, however, it should not be forgotten that these early anthropologists achieved the following:

1. They developed the concept of *culture*, and advanced the principle that culture and race must not be confused in studying the ways of life of human societies.

2. They distinguished those subdivisions of culture we today call *aspects*, and showed the usefulness, in studying culture, of considering separately the problems that fall within these several subdivisions.

3. They established the principle of *continuity* and the orderly development of culture, a principle that must underlie any realistic approach to the analysis of cultural dynamics.

[13] *Loc. cit.*, p. 26.

The revival of evolutionism, principally by White, is another index of the vitality of this hypothesis.[14] White has waged a vigorous campaign to rehabilitate the evolutionist position. In the course of his discussions, he has also sharpened and refined the concepts of the evolutionists. The basic error of those who have attacked evolution, he maintains, is that they have failed to distinguish the *evolution of culture* from the *culture history of peoples.* White denies the relevance of the psychological approach to the study of culture. He underscores the need, through a science of "culturology," of studying the ways of men in their own terms, without reference to psychological factors. Thus White, in reviewing one work, speaks of it as being notable because "it is a study of *culture,* not of the personality or reactions of the *human organism;* it is, in short, a culturological rather than a psychological study." [15]

The question remains, however, what does the study of the evolution of culture hold for the student of cultural dynamics? Whether or not unilinear development is postulated, what light does the assumption of logical sequences throw on the processes of cultural change? It would be unrealistic in the extreme to deny the existence of specific past sequences, particularly in the field of material culture. But what is the logic or the fact that supports the hypothesis of a sequence that requires descent to have been originally counted on the mother's side rather than the father's? To take another instance, we may recall how, in our discussion of religion, we saw one hypothesis after the other of the development of religion along stated lines, from assumed origins, invalidated by subsequent findings.

A further point bearing on our present topic may also be mentioned here, though its exploration must await a later chapter. The end of scientific endeavor is analysis and prediction. One can but ask how the tracing of past events, divorced from the psychodynamic factors that we have seen condition them so deeply, can reveal trends of a given culture, or of human culture as a whole, and thus permit valid prediction. The newer approach to an evolutionary method, which denies relevance to the psychological mechanisms of man, and ignores considerations of space if not of time, would seem of limited usefulness in terms of the ends of scientific anthropology.

It is, in every sense, regrettable that the study of culture was caught up in the controversies that centered about the word "evo-

14 L. White, 1949, *passim.*
15 L. White, 1946, p. 85.

lution." This usage, by and of itself, has too often become a battle cry rather than a research tool. Except in its historical meaning, it will therefore not be further used in this book. The word *development*, employed by Tylor as a synonym for "evolution," would seem to perform as useful a function, and to be free from the associations that make the analysis of possible sequences in cultural change, on the broadest scale, so difficult a subject to discuss.

Chapter **Twenty-four**

Cultural Conservatism and Change

We cannot too often emphasize the fact that no living culture is static. Rules of conduct may be rigid; the strictest sanctions may be invoked to enforce these rules; acquiescence in them may be unquestioning. Yet the observer of a society where even the greatest degree of conservatism obtains will find that, over a long enough period of time, changes have taken place.

The evidence for cultural change is overwhelming. Archaeological findings have demonstrated how change consistently marks the remains left by peoples who have inhabited the same site. The materials from lower and earlier strata are invariably found to differ from those in the upper and more recent levels. In a given Indian mound, for example, a type of pottery found in profusion near the top will gradually diminish in quantity, and finally disappear, as the excavators work more deeply into the site. But the pottery itself will not disappear. At a particular level, a new type will be sparsely found, and this will eventually replace the one that dominated the topmost strata. What such finds mean is that the topmost sherds represent the dominant pottery types when occupation of the site was terminated. Their sparser incidence in lower levels represents their developing preponderance, and documents the changes that occurred in this cultural element over the period the site was inhabited.

Another kind of evidence for the universality of change in culture can be drawn from the differing attitudes the members of ascending generations show toward the accepted ways of behavior of their society. Observations of this phenomenon by anthropologists are common, even among groups whose conservatism is pronounced. There are few cultures where the elders do not disapprove of the departures of the young from the traditions of an earlier generation, or where the young people do not deviate in some respect from certain forms of behavior approved by the older people, even if only in the accepted manner of salutation, or a new dance, or an elaboration or simplification of a ritual. This tugging of the young at the reins by which the old try to hold them on the cultural roadway they themselves have traveled is a constant in human social life. What is rarely recognized by these elders is how successful they really are, for the stability of their culture escapes them, and they are irked by the relatively minor changes introduced by the oncoming generation. That their opposition to change is, however, ineffectual, is a lesson that seems never to be learned.

The fact of change is also documented by available historic accounts. This applies not only to data on the past of literate peoples, but is equally true where the evidence permits a glimpse at the life of present-day nonliterate folk as lived in earlier times. Sometimes a cultural element, seemingly embedded deeply in the customs of the people, is found to be relatively recent in origin. For example, nothing could be more characteristic of the culture of Indians in the Pacific Northwest than the totem-pole, a kind of crest that symbolizes the mythical past of the totemic group. It seems inconceivable that early visitors to Northwest Coast villages could omit mention of these tall carved posts, but no account of them is found in such writings. Ethnologists who studied in the areas for many years assumed them to represent an ancient pattern, until research established that the totem-pole, far from being a feature of these cultures since the early times, is a development of the first part of the nineteenth century, resulting from contact with Europeans that introduced new technological devices, and that permitted a concentration of wealth and a standard of living not attainable in earlier times.

We can also document change by considering its end-results as shown in regional variants of the same general culture. In their over-all characteristics all local groups of a given region have ways of life that are similar. Each of them, however, differs from its neighbors in certain details of accepted behavior. These differences, that represent variations on the general theme, are end-results of a particular series of changes that occurred in the locality studied. Local dialects offer a rich field for investigations of this sort. They supply many evidences of the changes that must have taken place over the years, by the accretion of minute, even individual differences that were handed down in one locality and not in another.

Most new elements are introduced into a culture from outside the group. These borrowed cultural elements may be taken over and integrated into the life of the borrowers so completely as to baffle the most exacting student who seeks to determine what, in the culture he is studying, is of foreign origin. The case of maize in Africa is much to the point. We have seen that the domestication of this plant was achieved in the Americas. We know that early European voyagers introduced it into Africa, after it came to Europe. The acceptance of maize by the Africans must have brought significant changes in their food economy and their diet, though we know that there are few phases of culture where conservatism is more likely to manifest itself than in the food habits of a people. Today, in many parts of Africa, maize is not only a staple food, but it also enters importantly into the food offerings given the gods. It has thus invaded a second aspect of culture—the sphere of ritual—where, again, changes tend to be adopted with reluctance.

With the spread of European culture over the world, and especially the products of its machine technology, the acceptance of new ways of doing old things, or of modifications of old ways, or of innovations through borrowing has become increasingly accelerated. It must not be assumed, however, that nonliterate peoples have shown uncritical acceptance of what this expansion has presented to them, nor have they taken over European cultural elements without modification. On the contrary, they have done what all human groups do when presented with something new. They have responded to the innovation in terms of their prior experience, accepting what promised to be rewarding and rejecting what seemed unworkable or disadvantageous.

We must not conclude that borrowing goes in one direction. It is only because borrowing by indigenous groups from Euro-americans can be better documented historically than can instances of intertribal borrowing, that we draw on examples of this particular type of contact as frequently as we do. Perspective may be somewhat corrected by considering the vast changes wrought in Euroamerican culture as a result of borrowing by Europeans and Americans from the peoples with whom they have been in contact. Our dress, our food habits, our language, our music—to name only some outstanding aspects of our life where these influences are at once apparent—have been greatly changed since the sixteenth century as a result of such contacts.

We recognize the universality of cultural change when, beginning with the study of change in process and the analysis of existing nonhistoric cultures, we find that no two groups have exactly the same bodies of custom. Obviously, those peoples who live close together, or who, like the English and their descendants in modern Australia, have close historic contacts, will have more in common than those who live at a distance and rarely, if ever, come to know the cultures of each other. This is merely to say that groups who live in close contact have more opportunities to take over innovations from one another than to adopt new cultural elements from more distant societies. But since not everything introduced into a group will be taken over by it, we reach the basis of a dynamic explanation of local differences in culture.

Whether great or small, observed differences are but points in the historic chain of causation that has eventuated in a culture as it is to be seen at a given time. That in nonliterate societies scant documentation of change can be drawn upon does not controvert the fact that change has taken place. We have too much evidence from historic cultures, too many records of contact with nonliterate peoples that, when compared with present-day customs of the same people, document changes that have actually taken place, to question the presence of change even among peoples noted for their conservatism.

Change, then, is a universal cultural phenomenon, and the processes of change over a period of time constitute the dynamics of culture. Cultural change cannot be studied as an isolated phenomenon, for change, by and of itself, is meaningless, until it is projected against a baseline of human behavior as of a given time and nature. Above all, it must be contrasted to the phenomenon that is always opposed to it, the phenomenon of cultural stability, which, in its psychological aspects, is called conservatism.

The appraisal of either change or stability not only depends on taking both into account, but is dependent as well on the degree to which the observer achieves detachment from the culture in which he is studying change or stability. The closer the student is to a culture, the more blurred his perceptions in accurately identifying or isolating the changes that may be taking place in it. He reacts to the culture not unlike the members of the group he is studying. If conservatism is stressed as a prevailing pattern, he tends, often quite unconsciously, to gloss over changes. If the culture stresses change, as in Euroamerican society, there is a tendency to slight the vast body of stabilizing elements that, lying beneath the changes that are actually in process, give continuity to the way of life.

The most striking expression of this limitation of perspective was illustrated by our example of the attitude of elders toward the behavior of the younger generation, and the reaction of the younger members of a society to restraints laid on their innovations. From the point of view of the outsider, neither the old nor the young seem to direct their grievances toward matters of great importance. Yet when viewed close up, minor distinctions loom large. The over-all picture is only obtained when the culture is seen in more distant perspective. But even with the psychic distance of the detached observer, the student faces many problems. It is no simple task, even for the trained ethnographer, to sense the differences in individual behavior found in a society new to him. What he sees are the consensuses, the patterns. Recognition of deviations can only come later. Yet the student of culture, sensitive to change, must grasp variations as well as patterns. *For at a given moment, these variations are the expression of change in process.*

Students of culture have devoted far more attention to studying change than to analyzing stability. There are two principal reasons for this. One derives from the historical development of ideas about the extreme conservatism of nonliterate folk held by scholars in the earlier period of anthropological science. The second reason, however, is inherent in the problem. For it is much easier, methodologically, to study change than to study stability. Both these reasons must be held in mind to understand the problems of cultural dynamics; and we shall consider them in turn.[1]

Anthropologists have emphasized change in nonliterate societies to correct the view that denied change to the culture of these peoples. "Primitive" man is a creature of habit, living a way of life so fixed that his culture, it was argued, holds him as in a

---

[1] For an analysis of change which takes resistance to innovation into account, see H. G. Barnett, 1953, pp. 291–410.

vise, himself a passive, complacently imitative being, without the aspirations that were believed essential to continuous improvement. Herbert Spencer put the case as follows:

> The primitive man is conservative in an extreme degree. Even on contrasting higher races with one another, and even on contrasting different classes in the same society, it is observable that the least developed are the most averse to change. Among the common people an improved method is difficult to introduce; and even a new kind of food is usually disliked. The uncivilized man is thus characterized in yet a greater degree. His simpler nervous system, sooner losing its plasticity, is still less able to take on a modified mode of action. Hence both an unconscious adhesion, and an avowed adhesion, to that which is established.[2]

Sir Henry Maine wrote:

> Vast populations, some of them with a civilization considerable but peculiar, detest that which in the language of the West would be called reform. . . . The multitudes of coloured men who swarm in the great Continent of Africa detest it, and it is detested by that large part of mankind which we are accustomed to leave on one side as barbarous or savage. . . . To the fact that the enthusiasm for change is comparatively rare must be added the fact that it is extremely modern. It is known but to a small part of mankind, and to that part but for a short period during a history of incalculable length.[3]

Such pronouncements were, of course, made in good faith, but they were based on books, not on first hand experience with native peoples. Students who came to know "primitive" peoples as individuals much like those they knew at home, understandably felt impelled to correct these distortions. They underscored the fact of change by pointing to the changes they knew had taken place because of variation in observed custom among a given people, or that were to be read in the variety of forms a given complex might assume as it was diffused over a given area. "Primitive" man, for them, was no automaton. "Primitive" societies were demonstrated to have undergone change, despite their remote habitat, their numbers, their relatively simpler technologies.

Why anthropologists have continued to give little attention to the analysis of cultural stability, or conservatism, as such, re-

[2] Herbert Spencer, 1896, Vol. I, p. 71.
[3] Sir H. S. Maine, 1890, pp. 132–4.

mains to be analyzed. As pointed out, methodological difficulties must be faced in studying a problem couched in negative terms, as is this one of cultural stability. If we accept change as ever present, then conservatism can be thought of as *resistance to change*. But unless an anthropologist happened to be on the spot when something new was presented to the nonliterate group he was studying—an idea, an object, a technique, an art-form—and he was thus in a position to observe how first one, then another, and another individual would have none of it, he could not know that the idea, the object, the technique, the art-form had been presented and rejected. How otherwise could he witness the force of conservatism at work, repelling the new, retaining the old?

On occasion it is possible to obtain native testimony on why innovations have been rejected. Among the Navaho, the Night Way Chant is one of an elaborate group of ceremonies that not only is used for curing, but also to bring rain and foster the well-being of the community. Certain Navaho do perform portions of the dance in the summer, or in disregard of its place in the cycle, altering words, or dancing softly, or changing its name. However, Hill, who has analyzed the reasons why changes are looked on with disfavor, quotes the following passage that explains why, in this ritual, "any tampering with the general ideology behind the ceremonial is not considered permissible":

> You must be careful about introducing things into ceremonies. One chanter thought he could do this. He held a Night Chant. He wanted more old people so he had the dancers cough and dance as old people. He also wanted an abundance of potatoes so he painted potatoes on the dancers' bodies. He desired that there should be a great deal of food so he had the dancers break wind and vomit through their masks to make believe they had eaten a great deal. They surely got their reward. Through the coughing act a great many of the people got whooping cough and died. In the second change many of the people got spots on their bodies like potatoes only they were measles, sores, and smallpox. In the part, where they asked for all kinds of food, a lot died of diarrhea, vomiting and stomach aches. This chanter thought that he had the power to change things but everyone found out that he was wrong. It was the wrong thing to do and today no one will try to start any new ceremonies. Today we do not add anything.[4]

Where historical documentation exists, cultural stability can be analyzed, as has been done by certain sociologists interested in

[4] W. W. Hill, 1939, pp. 259–60.

the resistance to ideas in our own culture. Thus Stern has set down a long record of opposition to dissection as a medical technique, to vaccination, to the theories of Pasteur, to the doctrine of antisepsis—among others—that marked the reaction of medical practitioners to innovations in their field. Among the factors of this opposition may be mentioned the interests of those who felt threatened by the innovation, devotion to the *status quo*, the conservative force of the prevailing system of medical education, the resistances set up by established habit-patterns, and the adverse reaction of patients to new techniques that were painful when administered, like vaccination.[5]

As for nonliterate peoples, it was not until studies of cultures in contact were made that the problem of resistance to change could be analyzed. Where nonliterate groups had been in contact with literate ones, the elements presented to them could be discerned, and the fact of rejection established. With this in hand, study of the processes of the refusal to accept innovations could be initiated. This, however, we must leave for the moment, until we take up the study of acculturation. For the present, let us merely emphasize again that the study of resistance to change, that is, of cultural stability or cultural conservatism, is but a phase of the study of cultural change itself.

One further point, however, must be raised in balancing change against stability. This has to do with the different rates of change of one aspect of a culture against another. The point poses the question whether we are justified in labeling one culture, *as a whole*, conservative, against another that, *as a whole*, is receptive to change. The fact is that whether we document change and resistance to change historically, or infer it from distributions, we never find cultures that move at the same rate over the whole front. Thus the Australian aborigines, who are held to be prime examples of a conservative people, seem to have been far more conservative in their material culture than in their social organization and religion. We can therefore only designate them extremely conservative as a whole if we ignore the receptivity to change that must have existed at some time in their past where ideas having to do with social structures and the supernatural world were involved. Conversely, our own culture, held to be "progressive" and hospitable to change, shows unsuspected resistances in the field of nonmaterial culture, when we view it objectively in terms of its aspects, rather than as a unit. Change thus differs with the time, the culture, and the aspect of the culture. It is a point to be

[5] B. J. Stern, 1927, *passim*.

borne constantly in mind in the study of cultural dynamics, no less than in the analysis of the structure and forms of culture.

2

Conservatism and change in culture are the result of the interplay of environmental, historical, and psychological factors. All must be considered when studies of cultural processes are made. The habitat offers possibilities that may or may not be utilized by those who live in a given region. It sets limits that are elastic in the face of an increasingly effective technology. Thus it is often stated that natural barriers to communication can act as forces militating against the changes that come readily to a people inhabiting an area of easy access. And it does seem to hold that the peoples who inhabit the most remote areas of the world are actually to be counted among the most conservative groups. Yet this does not mean that the converse is true. The civilizations of the Far East are often pointed to as examples of cultural conservatism, yet they are by no means isolated—that is, they are not isolated except as viewed from the perspective of a developing European culture.

Isolation, of itself, can explain very little. Are the cultures of the isolated peoples at the tip of South America, or in the Arctic, or in the depths of the Ituri forests in the Congo Basin stable *because* these peoples are isolated, or because they are small in number, and have simple technological equipment that provides only a narrow base for change? Are the Eskimo conservative because they are isolated, or because a harsh habitat imposes limits that tend to suppress change? And what of the many opportunities for change peoples at the crossroads of the world, such as the Egyptians, have had presented to them, only to reject them?

Pertinent questions such as these are raised not to dispute the claim that geographical situation is to be considered in explaining cultural stability and change, but to assess this claim in perspective. Isolation is, at best, a difficult concept to work with, since it is only a relative term. The vast bulk of the Americas was isolated from the rest of the world for thousands of years. Yet from the point of view of the Americas, continents peopled with numerous Indian tribes who stimulated each other, it could as well be said that it was the Old World that was in isolation, not the New. Substantial proof was given of this after the fifteenth century, in the radical changes the discovery of the Americas by Europeans wrought in such important phases of European culture as food resources and dietary habits. Only after the stimulus of contact with the Americas did the European standard of living begin to rise.

As for the question whether other elements of the habitat may induce or reduce cultural change—temperature, barometric pressure, humidity, altitude, for example—the evidence is too scanty and the point too controversial to permit discussion here. Certainly a very difficult habitat, to which a people have made an adjustment, does not encourage experimentation in the field of technology. Whether it be the Nuer who inhabit the swamps of the Upper Nile in East Africa, or the Siberians in their Arctic habitat, or the Paiute of the Great Basin deserts of Utah and Nevada, there is little encouragement under such aboriginal conditions to experiment with established modes of getting a living. Yet we need hardly repeat here that this is not necessarily a matter of cultural conservatism; it is conservatism in the technological aspect of culture. Where the habitat is less harsh, experimentation in this, or any other aspect, may or may not take place. In short, it has proved extremely difficult, when all the available evidence is taken into account, to correlate any of the elements of the natural environment that have been named with universal or even consistent tendencies toward conservatism or change.

Within the limits set by the natural environment, access to the wide range of possible roads a culture may follow is given by historical circumstance. Here we must take into account two processes that will be discussed in some detail later, cultural drift and historic accident. Cultural drift is the working out of those sequences that seem logically to follow from the way in which a culture is organized, the interests of those persons who make up the society, and the ends they seek in terms of the values and goals sanctioned by their culture. Historic accident is a phrase applied to those sequences of events in the life of a people, unforeseen and, from the inner logic of the culture, unpredictable that give new directions to the changes that mark the course of their history, so that sequences that might otherwise have been expected to occur are altered.

Such stimuli can come from within a group or from outside it. A chance discovery, recognized as useful, may induce change, or it may solidify opposition to change and be the instrument for emphasizing conservatism. A journey taken by an individual member of a society may reveal techniques or ideas that he brings back to his people with similar positive or negative results. Conquest may lead to an interchange of cultural elements; or conqueror and conquered, even when living side by side, may each continue his own way of life. Imposition of the institutions and standards of a dominant group on dependent peoples having different cultures may serve to rally them to forbidden earlier ways, and result in those contra-acculturative movements that often mark the course of foreign rule.

These circumstances of history make the development of every people a tale that is never exactly repeated, either by themselves or any other group. And it is these ever-differing historic streams that at once reflect and shape the attitudes and points of view of societies that, in the final analysis, determine the degree to which each will be hospitable or hostile to innovations. This, then, is the third factor we must take into account in studying the dynamics of culture. It involves the many psychological mechanisms that underlie human behavior in general, and as such constitutes a special aspect of the enculturative process we found to be so important in understanding the manner in which human beings are conditioned to the way of life of the society into which they are born, and the very nature of culture itself.

The enculturative process, it will be remembered, is the means whereby an individual, during his entire lifetime, assimilates the traditions of his group and functions in terms of them. Though basically involving the learning process, enculturation, it was pointed out, proceeds on two levels, that of early life and that of the mature members of society. During early life, a person is conditioned to the basic patterns of his culture. He learns to handle the verbal symbols that make up his language; he masters accepted forms of etiquette; is inculcated with the ends of living recognized by his fellows; is adjusted to the established institutions of his culture. In all this, he has but little say; he is the instrument rather than the player.

In later years, however, enculturation involves reconditioning rather than conditioning. The learning process is one wherein choice can operate, wherein what is presented can be accepted or rejected. As was suggested, a change in recognized procedures of a society, a new concept, a reorientation of point of view can only come when people agree on the desirability of change. It is the result of discussion, of consideration by individuals who must alter their modes of thought and action if it is accepted, or argue preference for established custom in rejecting it.

Thus the mechanism of enculturation leads us to the heart of this problem of conservatism and change in culture. Its earlier conditioning level is the instrument that gives to every culture its stability; that prevents its running wild even in periods of most rapid change. In its later aspects, where enculturation operates on the conscious level, it opens the gate to change, making for the examination of alternate possibilities, and permitting reconditioning to new modes of thought and conduct.

3

Broadly considered, cultural change may be thought of as falling into two distinct categories. The first category comprises all change that stems from innovations originating from within a society; the second, all change that comes to it from outside. In the remainder of this chapter we shall treat of the first category, change from within, which comprehends the processes of discovery and invention, leaving our consideration of the second category, borrowing, for later pages.

It is difficult to differentiate between discovery and invention, the two mechanisms of internal innovation in any culture, which phrase this proposition. Functionally, and as observed from the point of view of the results achieved, the distinction between an invention and a discovery is not very important, for both represent means of changing culture from within, in contrast to innovations that were already functioning elsewhere before they were borrowed.

Dixon, who has examined this terminological difficulty, draws "a primary distinction" between the concepts of discovery and invention "on the basis of presence or absence of purpose." He points out that "discovery would then be limited to the unpremeditated finding of something new, whereas invention might be defined as purposeful discovery." Yet, like all others who have pondered the question, Dixon recognizes that the two forms range between,

> the purely accidental stumbling upon something previously unknown, through a more or less painstaking search for the same, to the purposeful experimenting with existing materials leading to the creation of a wholly new thing, which would never have existed but for this conscious human endeavor. The accidental discovery of a new edible plant might serve as an example of the first; the search for a new and stronger kind of vegetable fibre would illustrate the second; whereas the utilization of the elasticity of wood in the construction of the bow would represent the third.

In view of this, he refines his previous definition so as "more accurately" to "redefine discovery as the accidental finding of something previously unobserved, whereas invention is the purposeful creation of something radically new." [6]

For Dixon, need is paramount in both discovery and invention, and furnishes the bridge by which we pass from one to the other. Granted that something in the environment can be utilized for a given end ("opportunity") and its usefulness is recognized ("observation") by one with the imagination to understand its value ("appreciation," "genius"), the drive that carries man to new knowledge is necessity. Thus,

> although the casual discovery of a new food or material may lead to its use, if the foods already utilized are insufficient and there is a need for new sources of supply, a powerful spur is added to curiosity, and purposeful search is likely to ensue. Necessity is indeed often the mother of invention, and is likewise the parent of discovery as well. With the strengthening of this factor of need we pass more and more definitely into the sphere of invention, in which the need is met, not by the appropriation to use of a hitherto unused thing, but by the creation of something new and fundamentally better. [7]

In the climate of opinion of Euroamerican culture today, a thoroughgoing shift in orientation is necessary if we are to view the process of invention as operative over the whole of culture, rather than as applicable only to its tangible elements. We incline to overlook the role of the inventor of new ideas and new concepts, to disregard his function in contributing to the changes that mark the historical development of every culture.

The common use of the word "inventor" best exemplifies our thought concerning the matter. An "inventor," that is, is a person who "invents" a new machine, a new mechanical process. One who develops suggestions for a new economic system, or devises a new political scheme, or works out a new conception of the universe is, for us, no inventor at all. We may call him a theorist, a philosopher, a visionary, or, with less complimentary connotation, a revolutionist.

Yet ideas are no less powerful than things in shaping the lives of men. It would be difficult to maintain that the "inventors"— and the word is here used in its ethnological and functional sense —who devised the method of counting descent on one side of the family, or who later developed classificatory systems of relation-

[6] R. B. Dixon, 1928, pp. 34–5.
[7] *Ibid.*, pp. 36–7.

ship terminology, had less influence on the course of human culture than had the inventor of the skin tent, or of the outrigger canoe, or of the pump and bellows used in working iron.

This tendency to focus on material objects when discussing the introduction of new traits into a culture is not only bolstered by the climate of opinion of which this emphasis is a reflection. It also derives from the methodological fact that, in studying nonliterate cultures, it is easier to treat of material than of nonmaterial cultural elements. Let us consider from this point of view Dixon's criteria—opportunity, observation and "a measure of genius"—as they might apply in nonliterate society.

These criteria are obviously far more applicable to the invention of material than of nonmaterial cultural elements. The processes by which, let us say, a modal progression in music, not hitherto employed in the songs of a people, might be discovered would be difficult to fit to these specifications, except in a most general way. It is, indeed, far more acceptable to conceive of musical discoveries in terms of one of Dixon's additional factors, curiosity. To postulate a sense of need, on the other hand, does not seem to help us at all. What, it may well be asked, is the "need" to discover a new musical mode?

The factor of need, in either discovery or invention, which is widely assumed to play a preponderant role, also seems to have more relevance for material than for nonmaterial cultural elements. Nevertheless, even as regards material culture, it is possible to overestimate the significance of need in the process of invention. It is easy to urge the necessity for having some tool, some weapon, some technique that seems indispensable to the way of life of a people. Yet a need, even in the case of a material good, is subject to cultural interpretation. An invention, a discovery, which from the point of view of one society has filled an urgent need, frequently seems pointless or irrelevant to the members of a different group. Every field worker can find corroboration of this in the reaction of natives to items of his own field equipment. To the student, it seems self-evident that certain of these items should be of the highest utility to the natives, yet they arouse the curiosity of any novelty. This example, of course, concerns the phenomenon of diffusion rather than of discovery or invention; but the principle holds. Need, like so many other seemingly fixed concepts, is relative. There is need only in terms of the conception of necessity held by a people within the framework of their culture.

The proverb "Necessity is the mother of invention" is thus

seen, even in the material aspects of culture, to be a partial truth. Its inversion by Thorstein Veblen to "Invention is the mother of necessity" is equally valid. Once we move into the area of the intangibles of culture and study the range of phenomena comprehended in the materials presented in our preceding chapters, the popular view that need governs invention is seen to be quite inapplicable. What is the "necessity" for a unilateral descent system that flies in the face of the biological facts of descent? What is the need that dictates the invention of a new art style, or a new dance step?

Need may be uppermost in the minds of those specialists in the devising of new objects who, in our culture, we call "inventors." But such specialists are unique to the machine age. And even in their case we may but give a moment's thought to the number of inventions that do not "take," to point the fact that what an "inventor" may conceive to be a need does not necessarily appear as such to the other members of his group.

The ascription by Dixon of genius as a factor in discovery (and invention) also calls for scrutiny. It would be unrealistic to deny differentials in ability to different individuals who make various kinds of discoveries and inventions. Yet how to determine whether a given invention or discovery involves the operation of "a measure of genius" poses an insoluble methodological difficulty, unless we use the circular definition of the word "genius" as anyone who makes a discovery or invention. In any event, its use as a criterion is of dubious utility. As in many other instances where evaluation supplements the description and analysis of culture, the relativistic point of view must come into play. If only because no two cultures are the same, every people must be granted a measure of inventive genius. Among some peoples material inventions may be paramount; among others this creative drive will manifest itself in art, or religion, or social or political institutions.

That the situations needed for a discovery or an invention that have been set forth have a limited validity is not denied. But no one of them may take precedence, nor does their enumeration exhaust the list of possibilities, whether in the field of material or nonmaterial goods. Such an enumeration, indeed, is only a beginning. Both invention and discovery are basic in the dynamics of culture. Both are at once the result and the reflection of those processes of cultural change with which we are at the moment concerned. To a consideration of these processes, then, we now turn.

4

A question that has received much attention in anthropological theory is that of independent invention versus diffusion. In essence, the matter turns on the inventiveness of man; whether, when in distant parts of the world we find similar tools or institutions or concepts, we must assume these to have been invented only once and diffused to the regions where they are to be observed, or whether we may deduce that they had originated independently in these regions.

As far as most cultures are concerned, there can be little doubt that the elements that have been borrowed predominate over those that have originated from within. Man, it has been said, is a creature who finds it simpler to take over something someone else has devised than to work out his own solutions. Notwithstanding this human leaning toward dependence on what is already at hand, or near at hand, it is unlikely that the whole of any culture represents elements borrowed from other peoples.

Harrison has phrased the matter well: "The more complex the story, the more stages in the development, and the earlier its completion, the less likely is it that there would have been an independent repetition of the process in other areas." [8] This is apparent if we consider once more the principal stone-working techniques of prehistoric times. Core tools and flaking are found both in western Europe and the Far East. When they are studied in detail, characteristic differences between the two industries can readily be observed. Yet the discovery that stones could be put to various uses, that stones of certain kinds could be worked to heighten their effectiveness as tools is of such a general nature, so lacking in complexity, that it is difficult to assume a single origin for this widespread complex.

A third possibility in accounting for cultural innovations is the mechanism termed *convergence*. Convergence was at one time held to be significant for an understanding of the process of invention because it was described as comprehending a series of minor developments in two quite different manifestations of the same general phenomenon. These developments were believed to yield results having a similar outer appearance. The principle is well known in the biological sciences. For example, desert plants develop thick integuments, and leaves tend to take the form of thorns. A classification "thorny plants" might conceivably be set up, but it would have none but the most superficial significance.

[8] H. S. Harrison, 1926, p. 118.

For desert plants having thorns are not necessarily related to each other, but to many different species which, when found outside the desert, are quite different.

Goldenweiser, in employing the concept of convergence, developed the accessory principle of *limited possibilities*. "A limitation of possibilities," he stated, "checks variety" in the development of a given cultural form. This means that the fewer the possibilities of development for a given cultural element, the greater the probability that changes occurring after its invention or discovery in different regions can be assumed to have taken the same course, independently of each other. That is: "Wherever a wider range of variability in origins and developments coexists with a limitation of end results, there will be a reduction in variability, decrease in dissimilarity, and increase in similarity or convergence." [9] One example is the oar which, though it can be made of many different kinds of materials and in varied shapes, must—"if you want a *good* oar"—be neither too long nor too short, must have a flat blade, must not be too unwieldy. In the face of these limitations, "sooner or later, in one way or another," oars had to develop as "a tool with certain relatively fixed features determined by conditions of effective use." Other examples of this process can be thought of. To give only one, there are but three possible ways of counting descent—bilaterally, or on the father's side, or on the mother's. It would be rash to assume a single origin for any of these systems, especially when we find that in a relatively restricted area, such as West Africa, more than one patrilineal people has a matrilineal group as its neighbor. Convergence thus offered an alternative to the choice between diffusion and independent invention in accounting for similarities between cultures. Yet at best it only afforded a partial answer, for with the exception of a few historical instances, most of the examples lacked precise documentation and were thus statements of probability rather than of fact.

Kroeber, advancing the hypothesis of "stimulus-diffusion," has exposed another facet of our problem. By this term he means what occurs "where a system or pattern as such encounters no resistance to its spread, but there are difficulties in regard to the transmission of the concrete content of the system." One example he gives is the invention of porcelain in Europe in the early eighteenth century. Chinese porcelain, Kroeber points out, had been known and admired in Europe for almost two hundred years. It was the desire to avoid the expense of importation that

[9] A. A. Goldenweiser, 1933, pp. 45–6.

led to the experimentation that finally produced the desired product.

The consequence is that we have here what from one angle is nothing less than an invention. Superficially it is a "parallel," in the technical language of ethnology. However, it is equally significant that the invention, although original so far as Europeans were concerned, was not really independent. A goal or objective was set by something previously existing in another culture; the originality was limited to achieving the mechanisms by which this goal could be attained. If it were not for the preëxistence of Chinese porcelain, and the fact of its having reached Europe, there is no reason to believe that Europeans would have invented porcelain in the eighteenth century, and perhaps not until much later, if at all.[10]

How complex are the processes of invention, discovery and subsequent change is apparent from these various approaches to the subject. That man is more inventive than he is customarily held to be does, however, add to our comprehension of the dynamics of culture. For the sum of these changes, great *and* small, must be very large in any culture, even when compared with what has been taken over from outside. Indeed, it is here that inventions, discoveries, and diffused elements meet, and can be grouped under the category of *innovations*. For whether discovered, invented, or introduced, each innovation responds to the propensity for conscious human experimentation and the play of human ingenuity. Small changes begin immediately on the introduction of an innovation, and the process of alteration never ceases.

[10] A. L. Kroeber, 1952, pp. 344-5.

Chapter **Twenty-five**

Diffusion and Acculturation

Systematic investigation of the problem of cultural transmission, or cultural borrowing, dates from about the beginning of the twentieth century. Before that, as we have seen, the theory of cultural evolution dominated the study of culture. It was not until the validity of this theory came to be re-examined that the significance of the mechanism of diffusion was fully recognized and its implications explored.

Three "schools" have made diffusion basic to their formulation and study of cultural history, or cultural dynamics, or both. We may first name the English group composed of Elliot Smith, W. J. Perry, and their followers, sometimes termed the "pan-Egyptian," or the "heliolithic," school. It was last on the anthropological scene and first off it, and the controversies it engendered were as heated as any in the history of anthropology. The next group is the German-Austrian "culture-historical" school. Founded by F. Graebner and E. Foy, of the Cologne Museum, it was continued by the scholars who, in the main, published their findings in the Austrian journal *Anthropos*, under the leadership of Pater W. Schmidt and his associates, W. Koppers and M. Gusinde. This has become one of the leading schools of anthropological thought on the continent of Europe, but has never achieved any degree of acceptance in English-speaking anthropological circles.

The third group, the American, can scarcely be called a "school" at all. It is historical in its approach, stressing field research and restricted reconstructions of history rather than the comparative studies, on a world-wide basis, that characterize the two preceding points of view. Most often associated with the name of F. Boas, its concepts have been developed and its field researches carried on by various of his students, such as Kroeber, Lowie, Goldenweiser, Sapir, Spier, and others. Closely allied to it in point of view and approach are the Scandinavians Nordenskiöld and Lindblom in Sweden, and Thalbitzer and Birket-Smith in Denmark, while its methods have also been received sympathetically and effectively employed in France, Belgium, and Holland.

No discussion of diffusion would be complete without a review of the position taken by the anti-diffusionist functionalist school, chiefly identified with the name of B. Malinowski. We have seen in our discussion of cultural integration that the interest of the functionalists is in the manner in which institutions, operating on a single time-plane, reinforce each other as part of a single cultural whole. Functionalists are thus concerned only with understanding how each aspect of a culture is related to every other aspect.

Malinowski, like Elliot Smith, was a great polemicist, and his severest criticisms were directed against the study of diffusion, just as the critiques of the diffusionists were directed against the evolutionists. But he was a better critic of method than of theory. In attacking "diffusionism," he coupled Graebner and Boas, or Kroeber and Schmidt, with utter disregard of the fact that the area of disagreement between Boas and Graebner, or between Kroeber and Schmidt, was certainly as great as that between any of these scholars and Malinowski himself. Indeed, in most respects the position of the Americans differed from that of the functionalists but slightly. The real line of distinction was between the Americans and the functionalists, on the one hand, and the culture-historical school and the defunct position of Elliot Smith, on the other, despite the differences that separated the two extreme diffusionist schools.

2

The rise and decline of the English diffusionist school constitutes one of the more ephemeral episodes of anthropological history. The founder of this "school," Sir Grafton Elliot Smith, was a distinguished anatomist whose work on the brain, and whose studies in paleoanthropology, brought him great and deserved distinction. At one point in his career he embarked on a study of the brains of Egyptian mummies. His research took him to Egypt, where he became impressed with the quality of Egyptian civilization. As so many others have done, he began to note how the culture of ancient Egypt comprised many elements that seemed to have parallels in the cultures of other parts of the world, and his daring theories transcended considerations of time and of space. He not only assumed that comparable cultural elements in the Mediterranean Basin, Africa, the Near East and India were of Egyptian origin, but also that those of Indonesia, Polynesia, and the Americas were similarly derived.

The most elaborate presentation of the heliolithic theory of cultural history, as the hypothesis of this school came to be called, was given by Perry in his book *The Children of the Sun*. Its title refers to one element in the complex of traits assumed to have originated in and diffused from Egypt, the belief that the ruler is descended from the Sun. Other elements in this aggregate of traits were mummification, the building of pyramids, and a high value set on gold and pearls.

Elliot Smith and his followers made of borrowing almost the sole means by which culture change could be achieved. That is, the inventiveness of mankind is reduced in his theory almost to nonexistence, and the very possibility that some traits of culture could be independently invented was explicitly denied. With this position goes the denial of multiple origin and multiple diffusions, to say nothing of the possibility of convergence. Much of the argument of Elliot Smith and Perry depends on interpretation of data, after a manner that may be exemplified by citing the instance of pyramids. When, indeed, is a pyramid really a pyramid in the Egyptian sense? Is a pyramid used as a structure on which to place a temple, as the Mexican pyramids were, a cultural fact identical with a pyramid-shaped structure reared as a monument to a dead king, and designed to contain his body for eternity? Once a unity of origin for all pyramids is assumed, then the hypothesis is held to apply to more and more tenuous cases. The stone platforms of Polynesia, the earthen mounds of the Ohio Valley are held to be vestigial or marginal forms of pyramids. And a similar interpretation is given other elements of the Egyptian "civilization." The thighbone of a dead African king, preserved for ritual uses, represents for Elliot Smith a diffusion of

Egyptian mummification. Any large single stone memorial is a megalithic monument that originated from the same source.

There is no question that every group borrows more elements of culture than it initiates; but this does not mean that mankind invents as little and copies as much as this extreme diffusionist position would hold. Conversely, because we accept the phenomenon of borrowing, this does not mean that it must be regarded as the sole mechanism whereby culture change is effected. It was the neglect to take into account the inventiveness of man, no less than the failure to recognize factors of time and space in assuming the world-wide diffusion of Egyptian culture, that caused the ultimate rejection of the heliolithic diffusionist position.

The point of view of the German-Austrian *kulturhistorische Schule* is much more sophisticated. Its carefully drawn criteria for judging the value of assumed borrowings, its insistence on caution in the use of source materials, the care with which its definitions are drawn and the wealth of its documentation are fully in accord with the demands of scholarship. For these reasons it has been widely accepted. The system of the culture-historical school, as developed by Father Schmidt, who is its recognized leader, is essentially based on a mystical view of the nature of life and human experience. It has been developed within a frame of reference and employs a terminology that differ fundamentally from the rationalistic point of view and vocabulary of most anthropological thought. How this invades the methodological approach of this school is to be seen in Schmidt's discussion of the techniques for studying the various strata into which this school divides all cultures and which, through the diffusion of their elements, are held to have produced the cultures that today exist on earth. Like all ethnographers, Schmidt recognizes the need to understand the meaning of "primitive life" to those who live it and, more importantly, to those who in past ages lived it. This we do, he tells us, by recourse to the psychological principle of empathy (*Einfühlung*), whereby one projects himself into the psychic state of the person with whom he is in relation.

This, of course, is what in some measure happens when any good field worker achieves rapport with his subjects. It is with some bewilderment, however, that we learn from Schmidt [1] that this permits the student to reconstruct the earlier cultures that through their migrations produced the cultural strata held to yield the clues to historical reconstruction of the contacts of

[1] W. Schmidt, 1939, pp. 263-5.

present-day cultures. The Pygmies, for example, are held to represent the "primitive"—that is, primeval (*Urkulturen*)—stratum of human experience. By studying them as they exist to-day, the economies, the social structures, and other aspects of this "primitive" stratum of human experience can, it is believed, be recovered. In these terms, however, it would seem that not *Einfühlung*, but the exercise of the imagination is the instrument Schmidt proposes to employ in determining the elements of cultural diffusion.

Graebner's principal contribution, both to the methodology of the culture-historical school, and to anthropology in general, was to sharpen and give objective expression to the criteria in appraising the presumed diffusion of cultural elements from people to people. These criteria, called by him the criteria of form and quantity, are basic in all studies of cultural transmission. Their meaning is quite simple. When similarities are manifest in the cultures of two different groups, our judgment about the probability of derivation from a single source depends on how numerous they are, and how complex. The greater the number of similarities, the more likelihood of borrowing having occurred; and the same holds for the complexity of a given element. This is why, for example, folktales can be used so effectively in the study of historical contact between nonliterate peoples. It will be remembered that a story is composed of independent variables, each of which can travel separately. Therefore, when we find such a complicated cultural element as a story widely distributed, the conclusion is inescapable that it must have been diffused and not independently developed in each locality where it is told.

There are, however, certain pertinent reservations to his position that Graebner did not take into account. These reservations, paramount in the work of American diffusionists, stress the factor of accessibility in place and reasonable closeness in time. Graebner held that if two elements of culture are established on the basis of the criteria of form and quantity to be the same, they must derive from the same source, wherever they are found. Furthermore, he looked for "bundles" of traits on the basis of which he could establish diffusion. The difficulty was that the items in a "bundle" bore no functional relation to one another. In a word, they existed in a unit only in the mind of the student.

An example will make this clear. Ankermann described the cultures of the Congo and West Africa in terms of the following "complex" of traits that were similar to those designated by Graebner for the East-Papuan culture of Oceania: secret societies, masks, cannibalism, cane and wooden shields, xylophones, panpipes, bark-cloth, wooden drums, and carved human figures, among others. Since these elements are also present in certain Indian cultures of South America, this collection of traits was referred to a single cultural stratum, from which it follows, for the Graebnerians, that they have resulted from the diffusion of a single historic stream. It is apparent that such a "complex" is but a grouping of psychologically unrelated traits that, as a complex, exists only by definition from the outside and has no meaning, as a complex, in the culture as envisaged by those who live in it. As Sapir puts it: "A West Coast crutch paddle will not necessarily be heard to cry vigorously for its Melanesian mate." [2]

These defects in method of handling the ethnographic data, the mystical approach to the fundamentals of human cultural experience, and the extremely hypothetical nature of its conclusions account for the rejection of the position of the culture-historical school by many anthropologists. Nevertheless, the criteria for assessing culture-contacts, drawn with such clarity in the writings of this group, give this contribution significance, whatever position concerning its point of view as a whole may be taken. Furthermore, the stress laid by the culture-historical school on diffusion was, at the time of its initial formulation, a healthy reaction to the earlier evolutionist and sociological approaches to the study of culture. The rich documentation that Graebner and Schmidt provided and the field studies carried on by many members of the "school" as, for instance, the work of Koppers and Gusinde in Tierra del Fuego, are additional reasons why this group has had the respect even of its most consistent opponents.

Yet it is patent that more than clarity of definition, based on the assumption of regularity in historic development, is necessary to explain the processes of cultural change. An approach such as that of the culture-historians can at best answer the question "what?" The "why?" of cultural dynamics, the reasons behind the acceptance or rejection of an innovation, lie as much outside the purview of this group as they did in the case of the English diffusionists. Their objectives constitute but a first step in the understanding of cultural change. This first step, as taken by the culture-historical school, can scarcely be said to have laid the ground for that analysis of cultural causation that must ultimately be the objective of the scientific study of the nature of culture and of cultural change.

[2] E. Sapir, 1949, p. 422.

3

The studies of diffusion initiated by Franz Boas form a bridge to our consideration of acculturation. Boas recognized early in his career that the fundamental question toward which the study of culture must be pointed was not so much the fact of contact between peoples as the dynamic effects of such contact in making for cultural change. He was concerned with answering the question "what?" but only as far as these answers led to that comprehension of process that is implied in the question "why?" It is, therefore, in terms of the insistence on dynamics rather than on the recovery of descriptive fact that the position of the American diffusionists and their colleagues in other countries may be characterized.

If we go through Boas' writings, we can see that his position may be distinguished from that of Elliot Smith, Perry, Graebner, Schmidt, and other more extreme diffusionists in the emphasis he laid on the following points:

1. The descriptive study of diffusion is a preliminary to the analytical study of process.

2. The study of diffusion must be inductive, in that associated traits of cultures (culture-complexes) held diffused must be considered in terms of their inner relations rather than as groupings arbitrarily classified by the student.

3. The study of diffusion must work from the particular to the general, plotting distributions of traits in restricted areas before proceeding to the mapping of their distribution on a continental, to say nothing of a world-wide, basis.

4. The approach to the study of the dynamic processes, of which diffusion is but one expression, must be psychological and reach back to the individual for the comprehension of the realities of cultural change.

None of these points is given more than lip service by adherents of the extreme diffusionist schools. As has been pointed out several times in discussing their work, one has difficulty in seeing any objectives in their research beyond the establishment of the facts about diffusion. Granted that to establish the fact of borrowing was important in the face of the belief that man everywhere independently invented the elements of his culture, it is scarcely satisfactory to go to the other extreme and urge a priori that similar elements could never have been independently invented. Therefore, Boas held, a catalogue of similar traits in different cultures could never of itself offer adequate proof of historic contact. The similarities would have to include similar traits, similarly related, to give proof of diffusion; and this, moreover, only within a restricted area, where communication between borrowers and lenders was not difficult to assume.

Above all, for Boas and those who concurred in his views, it was of the greatest importance to keep continuously in mind the psychological factors underlying borrowing. This, they held, must be done even where these factors could not themselves be studied, as among nonliterate peoples where there are no historic records. Such cultures were to be analyzed individually, then compared in detail as to organization and structure as well as to their elements. Then only could conclusions be reached on such matters as acceptance and rejection of new traits, and the reshaping, in the light of pre-existing patterns of the borrowing culture, of what had been borrowed. Conclusions, moreover, were regarded as applicable only where investigations in many areas of restricted scope justified setting them up as generalizations.

Perhaps the most systematic presentation of the ways in which the analysis of data designed to reveal the history of nonliterate peoples should be employed in the restricted fashion of the American ethnologists has been given by Sapir. Admitting that all the knowledge we have of these nonhistoric peoples are collections of data that lie mainly on a single time level, he seeks to answer this question: "How inject a chronology into this confusing mass of purely descriptive fact?" Sapir points out two limitations: that in the time perspectives of historical reconstruction, nothing like the absolute chronology of history can be achieved; and that we must be content to deal with relations between groups, and not in terms of the individuals who were the effective instruments of the processes we study.

The important problem to be faced is what Sapir terms the problem of interpreting "continuous distribution from a culture-centre," [3] but which has come to be better known as the *age-area* hypothesis. Its most elaborate documentation has been given by Wissler, who used it to analyze the historic relations between the tribes of North America. He stated it simply, as follows: "A distribution of narrow range may be suspected of being an innovation, whereas one of wide range would be of respectable age." [4]

This proposition, which has been documented by archaeolog-

[3] E. Sapir, 1948, pp. 410–12.
[4] C. Wissler, 1926, p. xv.

ical and ethnographic distributions, is exemplified in the following diagram:

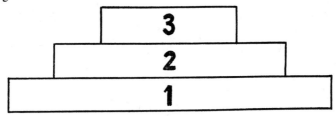

Fig. 59 *Diagram to illustrate basis of age-area concept.*

Let us say this represents the archaeological distribution of three related pottery types. In the center of the area where it is found, three strata are uncovered; over a wider range, two types will be present; while the distribution of the type found at the bottom of each of the preceding two will be still wider. The conclusion we reach, therefore, is that this kind of pottery originated in region *3*, and diffused to *2*. In the meantime, the people of *3* were developing a new type which later diffused to region *2*, displacing the original kind, which, during this time, had diffused to region *1*. At the same time, however, the people at the center developed a third type, which did not have time to diffuse before the development in all the area came to an end.

Here the idea that diffusion occurs concentrically is basic, and it is on this point that the theory has come in for the most criticism. Sapir, whose work antedates Wissler's, enters three cautions to the idea of continuous distribution. He points out: (1) that spread may be more rapid in one direction than another, (2) that the historically oldest form may have undergone such modification at the center that the actual point of origin will be wrongly determined, and (3) that population movements within the area of distribution may have had repercussions that lead to a "misinterpreted type of culture distribution." [5]

Dixon, one of the most severe critics of the age-area hypothesis, has not only challenged Wissler's basic assumptions but has also challenged the validity of the mapping of the data from which his conclusions are derived. Thus Dixon states categorically that traits diffuse "asymmetrically and erratically, and at varying rates," while he also flatly asserts that "the area of origin, the trait nucleus, is not usually the centre whence specializations spread, but that these arise in the main marginally." He concludes

[5] E. Sapir, 1948, pp. 411–12.

by stating that while the principles of the age-area hypothesis may have a certain validity within a culture-area, yet "just as soon . . . as . . . the trait passes into another environment and a different culture, the enormous and persistent power of modification which both exert, comes into play, to the ultimate and inevitable ruin of the principles hitherto active." [6]

To Dixon's cogent strictures on Wissler's use of data from the American Indians are to be added instances showing where the principle is inapplicable to facts concerning which we have the historic record. Wallis has found that "Wissler's 'principle' of centrifugal diffusion does not apply to traits of the Old World, where historic evidence is available." Taking as an example the "relative distributions in the Old World of the symbolism attaching to the number four and that attaching to the number seven," he shows that seven as a mystical number "for centuries . . . has been . . . more widely diffused . . . than the concept four, although . . . the latter is in these areas, as far as the historical record is available, the older." From this Wallis concludes that "the older trait is less widely diffused, and in neither case is the area of origin the center of the area of distribution." [7] A later demonstration that the age-area theory must be used with the greatest circumspection in making historical reconstructions is found in Hodgen's studies of "dated distributions" of how the windmill achieved its present European distribution, and how various techniques were actually diffused in medieval England. Her research has proved that the spread of these items of culture was by no means in accordance with the hypothesis. [8] Many other examples that have been overlooked in considering this "principle" could also be adduced. Thus the dog has long been held to be the oldest domesticated animal *because* of its world-wide distribution. Yet this argument overlooks the fact that the chicken, which we know to have been domesticated in relatively recent times, also has a world-wide distribution.

Does all this, then, mean that attempts to reconstruct the historic contacts of nonliterate peoples and the historic developments of nonhistoric areas should be given over? Such a conclusion is hardly justified. It would seem, all things considered, that the effort is worth the return, provided (1) *that the area selected for analysis should be one whose historic unity can be assumed,*

[6] R. B. Dixon, 1928, p. 145–6.
[7] W. D. Wallis, 1930, pp. 75–6.
[8] M. T. Hodgen, 1942, pp. 351–68; 1952, *passim.*

and (2) *that the probability, not the absolute fact of historic developments, be recognized as the aim.*

4

The flowering of the positive elements in the approach of diffusionists who were interested in cultural dynamics rather than historical reconstruction per se is to be found in the study of acculturation. The problem of defining the word and delimiting the scope of work to which the term can be applied came to the fore about 1935. At this time, a definition was presented by a committee of the Social Science Research Council as part of a Memorandum designed to act as a guide in acculturation research, which reads as follows: "Acculturation comprehends those phenomena which result when groups of individuals having different cultures come into continuous first-hand contact, with subsequent changes in the original cultural patterns of either or both groups." [9]

Within five years of the publication of this definition, however, two of its three authors had entered reservations to its phrasing. In one instance, it was indicated that "the definition makes no attempt to specify the *nature* of the phenomena which are to be treated as a part of acculturation." The determinants under this definition, it was pointed out, are "a) the particular situation under which the phenomena are present, and b) a suggested rather than clearly indicated limitation of the field of those phenomena which seem to be the results of a particular situation." The limitations imposed by the phrase "continuous first-hand contact" were also indicated—that of distinguishing "first-hand" from other contacts, and of delimiting "continuous" from intermittent relations.[10]

The other critique was directed against the use of the phrase "groups of individuals."

> It can be assumed, . . . that where contact between cultures is mentioned a certain human contact must be taken for granted as the only means by which culture can spread from people to people or from generation to generation. Yet, while it is desirable to emphasize that culture is no mystical entity that can travel without its human carriers, it is also true that it is not a simple matter always to know when "groups of individuals" are in contact."

[9] R. Redfield, R. Linton and M. J. Herskovits, 1936, pp. 149–50.
[10] R. Linton, 1940, pp. 464–5.

An instance cited to make this point can be taken from the South Seas island of Tikopia. Here "certain elements of European culture, especially in the fields of material culture and religion," have been "effecting an invasion of aboriginal patterns." The question is then raised:

> Is the visit of the mission boat once or twice a year, and the work of a single missionary (a native of another island and not himself a European!) to be regarded as an acculturating force? Certainly this person is not a "group of individuals," nor can it well be maintained that recurring visits of those on the mission boat constitute "continuous" contact.[11]

It is evident that neither duration nor intensity of contact can provide adequate criteria for differentiating acculturation from other mechanisms of cultural change. Our concern is primarily with the processes of cultural change, and only secondarily with classifying the situations in which change occurs. From this point of view, it makes but slight difference whether a given case of cultural transmission is to be termed acculturation or diffusion. Only as far as the circumstances in a particular instance affect the kind of reception accorded a given innovation do these circumstances come to be of consequence to us. We shall distinguish these designations, therefore, in terms of methodological considerations. Over the years, diffusion has come to mean the analysis of similarities and differences between existing nonliterate, and in this sense, nonhistoric, cultures. The contacts that presumably took place between peoples had to be reconstructed, and the reshaping of the borrowed elements inferred from the variations in their forms as manifest in one culture after another. Acculturation, on the other hand, has been applied chiefly to instances where transmission of cultural elements could be more fully documented either by study on the spot, or by the use of documentary data, or both. In summary, then, diffusion is the study of *achieved cultural transmission;* while acculturation is the study of *cultural transmission in process.*

This usage rests on a real methodological distinction, wherein the difference between observation and inference are paramount. Diffusion studies, from this point of view, assume that contacts have taken place between peoples because of the similarities observed between their cultures at the time they are studied. The reconstruction of the processes by means of which transmission was made effective must hence be a matter of inference from the

[11] M. J. Herskovits, 1938a, pp. 11–12.

nature of the materials. The studies of Wissler, who plotted the patterns of moccasins over the Plains and adjoining culture-areas, or Hallowell's researches into the regional variations in bear cere-monialism throughout northern North America and Asia give us a sense of how given cultural elements or complexes of elements were reworked as they moved from one tribe to another, or how a given complex incorporated varied elements as it was taken up in one tribe after another. Yet *how* all this happened, *when* it occurred, *where* it originated, and *by whom* the change was brought about, remain conjectural in such studies.

In the investigation of acculturation, however, the historic facts are known or can be obtained. In most cases, acculturation research deals with contacts in the contemporary period. The conditions antecedent to the contact can thus be discovered, the pre-contact cultures of the peoples party to it can be ascertained, and the present condition of the cultures set down. In some cases, even the personalities involved in influencing the acceptance or rejection of varied elements can be reached. Where documenta-tion is necessary, the welding of ethnographic and historical mate-rials is a matter of cross-disciplinary research, which has given rise to a special technique called the ethnohistorical method.

Where past contacts between historic peoples are the con-cern of the student, the acculturative situation can be studied by the use of documentary materials. These materials have not been used more because, as Hodgen has put it, "The scope of accultura-tion study has been unduly circumscribed by the tight but un-realistic boundaries of the formal academic disciplines." This student has shown, by her own documentary study of the spread of glassmaking and paper in England,[12] what fruitful results can follow from breaking down these unrealistic boundaries. The three steps in borrowing that she distinguishes are exposure, es-tablishment, and dissemination. Treated as a continuous process, their application to studies of contact between contemporary peo-ples should yield valuable results.

To differentiate diffusion from acculturation pragmatically as has been done here does not, however, fully delimit the mean-ing of the term "acculturation." It has been differently used by different disciplines, while certain equivalents for it found in the literature of anthropology itself have connotations that require clarification. Thus psychologists, educators, and child-develop-ment specialists have found the word acculturation useful to de-scribe the process of conditioning by means of which a child is

[12] M. T. Hodgen, 1945, pp. 466–67.

habituated to the ways of life of its group. It will be obvious, however, that in this sense it is roughly the equivalent of the word enculturation that, in these pages, has been used to describe this process. As far as can be ascertained, those who use the word acculturation in this way have employed it without defining its meaning with any degree of precision. In child-study reports, acculturation is often given the significance of several other terms, and it is a commonplace to find papers in which *acculturation, socialization, education,* and *conditioning* are used insofar as context would indicate, as synonyms.

While the question of proper or improper usage does not enter when a term is variously employed by different disciplines, it must be taken into account when connotations of an evaluative character are introduced, especially where research deals with contacts between what are termed higher or lower, or active and passive, bodies of tradition. For evaluations of this nature, injected into scientific study in any field, lessen objectivity and by this very fact render scientific analysis difficult.

Let us, for example, consider the position of Malinowski that the study of African culture-contact is one of "an impact of a higher, active culture upon a simpler, more passive one." To the study of the resultant situation, he holds, "the conception of culture change as the impact of Western civilization and the re-action thereto of the indigenous cultures is the only fruitful approach." [13] His disregard of the fact that in African culture-change the native exerts his influence upon the resultant borrowing, whether intertribal or from Europeans, is inadmissible to those who take the position that under any contact all peoples party to it borrow from one another.

Since both explicitly and implicitly Malinowski's work stressed the values in the life of nonliterate peoples and the necessity of studying every culture in terms of its own orientations, we must seek our explanation of his point of view elsewhere than ethnocentrism. The essentially anti-historical point of view of functionalist theory, derived as it was from field-work in a single, small, relatively static South Seas culture, may be said to be one reason; another, that Malinowski's concern with the phenomena of culture-contact was to develop techniques for solving the practical problems of African colonial administration.

The first of these reasons caused Malinowski to evolve the concept of the "zero-point" in culture, the point from which change in a static way of life began. It is difficult to believe that

[13] B. Malinowski, 1945, pp. 15, 17.

he did not develop this concept merely to be able to demolish it, for there is no "point" at which any culture is static. What is done in studies of culture-contact is to take some period in the history of a given culture, usually antecedent to the particular contact being investigated, as a base line from which to triangulate change and thus provide the framework within which the resultant dynamic processes can be analyzed. This technique Malinowski and his students, like all others concerned with contact studies, were forced to employ; though his ahistorical approach made it difficult for him to place change in Africa in its proper perspective, as only one phase of the age-long process of cultural transmission.

Malinowski's preoccupation with administrative problems led him to overemphasize the weakness of African ways of life in the face of the impact of European culture. The very works of his students, that he himself cites, contain abundant proofs of the extent to which African culture, despite the pressures brought against it, has withstood these onslaughts. This same preoccupation, too, caused him to neglect the phenomenon of interchange of cultural elements under contact. In contact between Europeans and Africans, this interchange has at least been sufficient to make the life of Europeans living in Africa quite different than it is in Europe, a fact of theoretical, no less than practical, implications.

More acceptable than the evaluative phrasings we have just considered is the word transculturation that first appeared in 1940. Ortiz, the Cuban scholar, gives these reasons for its use:

> I am of the opinion that the word *transculturation* better expresses the different phases of the process of transition from one culture to another because this does not consist merely in acquiring another culture, which is what the English word *acculturation* really implies, but the process also necessarily involves the loss or uprooting of a previous culture, which could be defined as deculturation. In addition it carries the idea of the consequent creation of new cultural phenomena, which would be called neoculturation.[14]

Though Ortiz misapprehends the terms of reference in the use of the word acculturation, he does not make the mistake of ascribing to it an ethnocentric quality it has never had. Were not the term "acculturation" so firmly fixed in the literature of anthropology, "transculturation" might equally express the same concept. It is so used by some anthropologists who write in Spanish, but in Brazil, the Portuguese *aculturação* is the accepted designation.

[14] F. Ortiz, 1947, pp. 102-3.

Aside from questions of terminology, what is important is that the term acculturation does not imply that cultures in contact are to be distinguished as "higher," or "more advanced," or as having a greater "content of civilization," or to differ in any qualitative manner. The evidence shows that the transmission of culture, a process of cultural change of which acculturation is but one expression, occurs when any two peoples are in historic contact. Whatever the nature of the contact, mutual borrowing and subsequent revision of cultural elements seem to result.

5

Types of contact between peoples differ in many respects. They can occur between entire populations, or substantial segments of these populations, or they may arise from contact between smaller groupings or even individuals. Where the representatives of one group bring to another a particular facet of their culture, the elements borrowed will self-evidently be those of the facet presented. When men of two nonliterate groups meet periodically to follow game, for example, one would not anticipate the women's sphere of either culture to be much affected. Where the representatives of Euroamerican culture in contact with a native people are missionaries, relatively little change in native technology would be expected.

Contacts are also to be classified as friendly or hostile. So much stress has been laid on the more dramatic instances of hostile contact, that the less striking—but probably more numerous— examples of friendly association between peoples has tended to be lost sight of. An outstanding contribution that has called attention to the importance of studying this latter type of contact is the analysis by Lindgren of the "culture contact without conflict," occurring between the Reindeer Tungus and certain Russian Cossacks in northwestern Manchuria. She defines the condition of this contact in terms of two salient facts:

> 1) I heard no Tungus or Cossack express fear, contempt, or hatred in relation to the other group as a whole or any individual composing it. . . . 2) No instance was recorded of the use or threat of force in the relations between these communities, although the reminiscences of the elderly cover most of the period of contact.[15]

Cultural interchange is not absent in hostile contact between peoples, however. The mutual borrowing under contact between

[15] E. J. Lindgren, 1938, p. 607.

Euroamericans and natives has often been achieved despite a lack of friendly relations between the parties to the interchange. Bushman "clicks" now characterize the language of the Zulu and other Bantu-speaking peoples of southeast Africa, whose cattle the Bushmen have systematically raided for many generations. The lesson to be drawn from such examples is that cultural interchange results from any kind of contact; that the factor of friendliness or hostility is of itself not crucial.

It is essentially out of contacts involving dominance of one people over another that contra-acculturative movements arise—those movements wherein a people come to stress the values in aboriginal ways of life, and to move aggressively, either actually or in fantasy, toward the restoration of those ways, even in the face of apparent impotence to throw off the power that restricts them. One of the best documented instances of a contra-acculturative movement has been given by Williams, who has described the rise and subsequent career of what he termed the "Vailala Madness," naming it after the town on the Gulf of Papua, New Guinea, where the movement originated in 1919.[16] This cult arose as a reaction to the situation of foreign domination, and was based on a doctrine of the early return of the dead. It had its prophets, and was marked by possession and violent dancing. Though it was anti-white, and predicted the day when olden times would return and the invaders would be wiped out, it led to the destruction of certain rituals and sacred objects of earlier times the substitution for them of Christian and secular European elements. Twelve years later the Madness had abated, leaving only the tradition that the miracles predicted by the prophets had actually taken place.

Three further types of contact are to be noted. One is where contacts are between groups of equal or different population sizes. Another is where groups differ in the complexity of their material or nonmaterial culture, or both; or where their cultures are of an equal degree of complexity. Finally, we encounter those situations where a group having one way of life comes into the habitat of another, or where the receiving group achieves its contact with the new culture in a new habitat.

The significance of these factors is apparent, though of the three situations, the first, where population size is involved, is likely to prove of least importance. There are too many instances where small groups have influenced large ones, or where a large group has failed to influence a small one, for this to stand as a

[16] F. E. Williams, 1923 and 1934.

factor of major significance. Unequal complexity in various aspects of culture may be referred to difference in population mass, and in this sense the size of the groups concerned may be accounted a factor in the resulting process, albeit a secondary one. The most important point to be held in mind in assessing the role of cultural complexity is that by and of itself, and aside from the prestige factor that may be introduced, greater complexity in a culture does not necessarily carry conviction to those whose traditional background is of a simple nature. A more complex culture can offer more things to be borrowed than a simpler one. But this very richness may confuse, or even remain unperceived by, a people whose ways of life are pitched in a different key. Though on first glance the spread of European dominance over the world seems to refute this, analysis shows that such a conclusion is premature. It is doubtful, as a matter of fact, whether the native peoples of the world, by and large, have taken over much more of Euroamerican culture than the Western world has borrowed from them.

More interesting is the problem presented by the third type of contact. Do a people who move into the habitat of another take over more of the culture they find, or does a migrating group give more of its culture to those among whom they settle? Many examples of both kinds of exchange are to be cited, so that the balance must be struck in terms of the particular peoples involved, and the particular situation encountered. Negroes who were brought to Brazil influenced the culture of the dominant Portuguese, themselves migrants, and subject to Indian influence as well. These varied influences are to be seen merged in such widely differing aspects of modern Brazilian life as the cuisine, the social structure, beliefs of various sorts, current musical forms and linguistic usages, to say nothing of the extensive retentions of African belief and behavior by the Africans themselves.[17] In North America the Negroes took over far more of the dominant European patterns than they gave to the resulting culture. As a third example of differing results from the same forced migration, Haiti can be mentioned. Here, in spite of two centuries of early French domination, the present-day life of the peasants retains more African traits than French, and but little if anything that can be referred to the customs of the autochthonous Indians.

The situations in which acculturation occurs are, in a sense, but an aspect of the types of contacts that have been sketched. The first kind of situation to be envisaged is where elements of

[17] G. Freyre, 1946, *passim;* A. Ramos, 1940, Chaps. I–VIII, *passim.*

culture are forced on a people, or where acceptance is voluntary. The second situation is where no social or political inequality exists between groups. In the third situation, three alternatives are presented—that is, where there is political dominance but not social; where dominance is both political and social; and where social superiority of one group over another is recognized, without there being political dominance. In contacts between non-literate peoples, indeed, it is to be doubted whether considerations of this kind have been important. In such cases, all parties to contact tend to be small and, because firsthand contacts are restricted in large part to neighboring peoples, borrowing is on a more modest scale. It is more a matter of taking over details of culture than of integrating many elements that come from strikingly different ways of life. The examples of contact without conflict indicate that more borrowing has probably occurred where dominance did not enter than where it did.

Some students of culture-contact have approached acculturative situations with the idea of analyzing the resultant cultures into their component parts, seeing which are borrowed and which represent retentions of older traits. Others have criticized this approach, holding that this treats borrowing as "a mechanical pitchforking of elements of culture, like bundles of hay, from one culture to another," as Fortes [18] has phrased it. To break down cultures of mixed origin into traits, they maintain, is to reduce the living reality of a way of life into lifeless and, what is worse, meaningless components. For them, the arithmetic of culture-contact is never a process of addition. The borrowed element is always merged with what was present before the contact. As a result, a culture of multiple origins is different from any of the bodies of tradition that have contributed to it. The dynamics of acculturation, they say, are creative. To study the results of acculturation by tracing traits to their origin is to distort the picture and falsify the results.

In acculturation studies, however, as in the study of any phase of cultural dynamics, cultures are analyzed into component elements only as a methodological device. For while the ideal of studying the results of contact between peoples in terms of whole cultures is well worth pursuing, the principal difficulty in this approach lies in the fact that workable methods of achieving it have as yet to be devised. On the contrary, the really significant studies of culture-contact have been those where one aspect, even one trait, has been taken at a time, perhaps to be combined later

[18] M. Fortes, 1938, p. 62.

into a comprehensive portrayal of the results of the acculturative experience.

One of the best examples of this flexibility in method is to be found in Parsons' study of the Mexican community of Mitla. The description of the life of this people, with two exceptions we need not name here, is drawn in terms of the accepted categories of the ethnographic monograph, while Parsons' summary chapter breaks down the institutions already described into their Indian or Spanish sources, and considers the amalgamations of custom that are seen to derive from both cultural streams. Some quotations, given as "partial answers" to the "basic queries" of why the traits that have been studied survived, and why certain elements that might have been expected to be found are not present, reveal how telling this approach can be.

> Traits may be preserved merely because of ignorance of anything different; in other words, certain parts of two contacting cultures may not be in contact at all.
>
> Intermarriage is a more obvious factor in cultural breakdown or cultural assimilation, whichever way you look at it, particularly when the woman belongs to the dominant culture.
>
> Ignorance of custom, whatever it is due to, is a great protection to custom.
>
> . . . An old custom . . . [may survive] . . . because it is agreeable to the new one.[19]

There are some situations in which the study of acculturative change can be made only in terms of how separate elements have fared in the interchange. Chinese migrants to the South Seas who return to their home, Hsü points out,

> have not shown fundamental changes from the home culture but they have taken on many single items of the alien cultures. In addition, new ideas and ways of life have either been taken on by some emigrants in the South Seas or are being broadcast into the home communities by a few "progressive" reformers. The latter insist on the abolition of the joint family, on the free choice of life partners, on the suppression of superstitions and so forth.[20]

Obviously, the problem for study here is how each of these centers of change in Chinese communities is achieving acceptance or rejection of the particular elements where reform is being advocated. There would be little profit, at this point, in studying the changing culture as a whole.

[19] E. C. Parsons, 1936, pp. xii, 511–19.
[20] F. L. K. Hsü, 1945, p. 55.

In essence, the reason why the study of acculturation in terms of whole cultures is so difficult is that borrowing, even in the most intimate contacts, is selective. This principle of selectivity is basic not only to a discussion of acculturation but to the study of any phase of cultural change. The need to study the nature and processes of cultural selectivity led anthropologists from the hypothetical reconstruction of presumed processes of change to the analysis of changes actually taking place. The principle of selectivity is as important in understanding why innovations from within a society become a part of its culture or are discarded, as it is in helping us comprehend why elements of one culture presented to another are taken over, or refused, or give rise to contra-acculturative movements that seek to restore the sanctions of a precontact way of life.

Selectivity, moreover, accounts for the great variation in the degree to which peoples undergoing contact do take over elements of each other's culture. A variety of historic factors enter to facilitate acceptance or to steel resistance to innovations. Thus Willems has shown that the "horse complex," as he terms it, was taken over by the Germans who settled in southern Brazil not only because of the higher standing of *gaucho* [cattlebreeder] culture in the hierarchy of Brazilian regional cultures, but also due to certain cultural associations that the average German immigrant attached to the saddle horse. This latter point is illuminating.

> It should be remembered that the German peasant cultures . . . do not have the horse as a riding animal. . . . The saddle horse represented and still represents one of the outstanding cultural traits of Germany's rural aristocracy. Here as elsewhere in Europe the large farmer . . . controls the activities of his field hands by using a horse from which he gives his commands. Landless fieldworkers and smaller landowners never own saddle horses.[21]

As a result of this and other prestige factors centering about the horse, it has come about that, while the Brazilian Germans have retained many elements of the culture they brought with them, they have taken over the horse-complex of southern Brazil, including the extensive Portuguese vocabulary associated with this animal.

An example of contact with a minimum of borrowing is found on the island of Trinidad, where British Indians and Negroes have lived in contiguity since the first half of the nine-

[21] Emílio Willems, 1944, pp. 156-7.

teenth century. The immigrants from India, brought as inden-
tured workers on the plantations, settled in Trinidad, and their
descendants now form a colony almost one hundred and seventy-
five thousand strong. "They speak their own language, dress in
the Indian manner, cultivate their irrigated rice patches, and
otherwise follow the modes of life of the parts of India from
which they derive." The Negroes, on the other hand, have become acculturated to many patterns of the Europeans who constitute the economically, politically, and socially dominant minority of the island's population. The Negroes, from the first,
resented the importation of the "coolies" from India as an economic threat; the Indians looked on the Negroes as "savages,"
according to Charles Kingsley, who was on the scene in 1871.
The Indians have taken over something of Negro magic, but the
Negroes seem to have accepted nothing from the Indians.[22]

Contact, therefore, can result in minimal borrowing, with or
without external pressure, or it can range to almost complete
acceptance of the ways of life of another people. In any given
case, the aspects of culture that are transmitted, or the transfer
of the sanctions of an older custom to a new cultural form are
the result of particular historical circumstances which influence
the psychological motivations underlying the selectivity that
comes into play.

The historical and psychological aspects of borrowing are,
of course, only to be distinguished on the conceptual level. While
all peoples are exposed to elements of cultures other than their
own, what they will in a given instance take over and what they
will reject is determined by their pre-existing culture and the
circumstance of the contact. The enculturation of later life, as
we have seen, is the mechanism through which change is
achieved. The adult member of a group must make a decision
whether or not he will accept something new; or, if something is
forced on him, he must devise ways to retain what he has been
taught are the right and proper kinds of belief or behavior. As
Hallowell has put it: "Readjustment on the part of individuals
may influence the thinking, feeling or behavior of other individuals and perhaps lead to readaptation in the mode of life of
the group." One of the least studied but most important problems
in acculturation research, as he points out, derives from "the drives
that have motivated individuals toward readaptation and how
these drives are rewarded." [23]

[22] M. J. and F. S. Herskovits, 1947, pp. 19–20.
[23] A. I. Hallowell, 1945a, pp. 177, 185.

How important historic depth can be in aiding the student to comprehend the dynamics of cultural change is to be seen in such studies as those in which Keesing has assessed the effects of three centuries of contact between Menomini Indians and the whites in the light of the present ways of life of these Indians; [24] or in which Lewis, using the techniques of ethnohistory, has made a similar study of one group of Blackfoot, particularly as these people were affected by the fur trade; [25] or in which Goldfrank, here as in the case of the Dakota, has investigated the changes in the cultural configurations and basic incentive-drives of another subdivision of this people.[26] These and many other researches that not only accept "adulterated" cultures as valid objects of study, but make their principal aim the search for an understanding of how such cultures arrived at the state in which they are to be observed, all reflect a profound reorientation in anthropological thinking.

In summary, the search for "pure" cultures, "uncontaminated" by outer contact, has been almost entirely given over, while the hypothetical nature of reconstructions of unrecorded history has come to be clearly understood as an exercise in probability. The use of historical documents and the field study of peoples whose cultures are changing under contact have, above all, demonstrated that culture-change is a single problem, whether studied in process or through the analysis of accomplished cultural facts in terms of the distribution of variant forms of the same element. With this unity of the problem of cultural dynamics established, then, we may next examine certain aspects of the organization and the psychology of culture that, as part of the same problem, throw further light on the mechanisms of cultural stability and cultural change.

[24] F. Keesing, 1939.
[25] Oscar Lewis, 1942.
[26] E. Goldfrank, 1945.

Chapter **Twenty-six**

Cultural Focus and Reinterpretation

Cultural focus designates the tendency of every culture to exhibit greater complexity, greater variation in the institutions of some of its aspects than in others. So striking is this tendency to develop certain phases of life, while others remain in the background, so to speak, that in the shorthand of the disciplines that study human societies these focal aspects are often used to characterize whole cultures.

The hypothesis of cultural focus refers the dynamics of culture to the only instruments through which change in culture can be achieved—the individuals who compose a society where a way of life is undergoing change. The emphasis individuals lay on the sanctions, the values, the goals that comprise the motivating drives to their behavior gives meaning to what they do at a given moment. We must thus turn to these changing emphases and drives if we are to comprehend more adequately the changes in the artifacts, the institutions, the organized systems of belief of a culture at a given time, and mark it off from what it was at a different time or from the other cultures that exist coterminously with it.

We have seen that no individual, however wide his range of

cultural responses, and even in the most stable, conservative culture, knows all the elements in the mode of life of his group.

> Not every musician is a virtuoso, nor does he control the full range of orchestral instruments; and in the same manner no one individual controls his culture or is even conscious of its total resources, and no group, as a group, places the same emphases on all facets of the entire body of custom of which its members are the carriers.[1]

That is, the differences in cultures that allow us to designate a culture by its outstanding interests, convey the fact that the concerns of the persons who go to make up the group at a given time are more centered in some aspects of their culture than in others.

Of the varied aspects that compose any given body of custom of a people, those that dominate are least apt to be taken for granted. They will be most often talked about, and will thus be closest to the levels of consciousness for a greater part of the time than elements that are of less interest. From the point of view of culture, objectively considered, these aspects of a culture will manifest the greatest degree of variation. "A people's dominant concern may be thought of as the focus of their culture; that area of activity or belief where the greatest awareness of form exists, the most discussion of values is heard, the widest difference in structure is to be discerned." [2]

If we follow a step further, the relevance of these points in the analysis of cultural dynamics will become clear. The things that outstandingly mark the culture of a people—technology (present-day Euroamerican culture), supernaturalism (medieval Europe), or economics as directed toward the attainment of prestige (Melanesia)—also tend to dominate their lives. Because such matters are important to them, people will think and talk a great deal about personalities, events, and possibilities lying in this aspect of their culture. As a result of this interest and the concomitant discussions that are carried on, possibilities for realignment will emerge, and emerge with enough frequency so that resistance to the idea of something new will be minimized, whereas a suggestion of change in a phase of life taken for granted and seldom discussed will meet with considerable hostility. We can therefore state that the greatest variation in custom, manifest in the greatest complexity of form, can be looked for in the focal

---

[1] M. J. Herskovits, 1945a, p. 164.
[2] *Ibid.*, pp. 164-5.

aspects of a culture, and that this represents either potential or achieved cultural change.

The fact that the interests of a people tend to center on a particular phase of their culture has been established by studies reported in many monographs, whose emphasis on certain institutions as against others reflects the emphases laid by the society itself. We do not refer here to monographs restricted to a particular phase of a given culture, but rather to the rounded presentations of culture. We may take, as an instance of this, the Todas of India. "The daily life of the Toda men is largely devoted to the care of their buffaloes and to the performance of the dairy operations," says Rivers at the outset of his pioneer work.[3]

> The milking and churning operations of the dairy form the basis of the greater part of the religious ritual of the Todas. The lives of the people are largely devoted to their buffaloes, and the care of certain of these animals, regarded as more sacred than the rest, is associated with much ceremonial. The sacred animals are attended by men especially set apart who form the Toda priesthood, and the milk of the sacred animals is churned in dairies which may be regarded as the Toda temples and are so regarded by the people themselves. The ordinary operations of the dairy have become a religious ritual and ceremonies of a religious character accompany nearly every important incident in the lives of the buffaloes.[4]

The buffaloes figure in all aspects of life. They form the economic base of the culture. They, or their milk, play prominent parts in the rituals of birth, childhood, marriage, and death, especially in funeral rites. The gods are thought of as having dairies and buffalo herds as do mortals, and buffaloes have an important place in Toda mythology. As we read Rivers' account, there is little question that the buffaloes, and the religious complex centering about them, give point and meaning to the Toda men and, to a lesser extent, women in whose lives they function so incessantly. The dairy is the central point of the focal aspect of culture, the one where, if our hypothesis is valid, we should expect greatest variation. And this is what is actually found, as is evident from the "comparison of procedure of different dairies" given by Rivers. The "increasing elaboration and complexity from the lowest to the highest grade of dairy," he says, is "one of the most striking features of the ritual in all its branches."[5] Likewise, the

---

[3] W. H. R. Rivers, 1906, p. 31.
[4] *Ibid.*, p. 38.
[5] *Ibid.*, p. 232.

milk from buffaloes of various grades, that belong to different dairies, has different degrees of sanctity. Various villages have special rites; the groupings into which the two Toda sibs are divided are distinguished by the degree of complexity of their dairy rituals.

As always in scientific procedure, the test case is the one where a special condition alters the customary situation. This permits us to understand and evaluate the role of elements whose functions are lost sight of in the ordinary, undisturbed course of events. In this sense, therefore, it is instructive to consider what happened to the one Toda sib-village, the site of whose sacred dairies was taken over for part of the parade ground of a British cantonment. This unfortunate group, alone of the Toda, experienced the destruction of what is described as "the heart of the Toda cult." They alone were deprived of access to the all-important places that, for a sib, are "one, inalienable and irreplaceable." The case is the more significant because the other sibs were undisturbed in the process, and thus form a contrast which tests the statement that "Toda culture is so highly integrated, so tightly knit about the care and cult of the buffalo, that unless the buffalo cult breaks down, other influence can hardly penetrate." [6]

The sib whose territory was needed for military purposes were able to keep buffalo in the new location, but they could not maintain rituals associated with the buffalo cult. Because of this, the statement that "only this solitary settlement has taken to raising potatoes, only they keep cattle as well as buffalo" takes on special importance. "Deprived of the hub of their ritual," we learn, "this group has lost its zest for buffalo care and has taken over certain non-buffalo traits." In contrast to this, "the other Toda sibs continue to maintain their ritual, retain the old economic pattern, remain impervious to foreign ways." [7]

Another instance of cultural focus comes from the study, made by Bascom, of the Micronesian island of Ponape, in the Eastern Carolines. The inhabitants of this island have lived under the control of four foreign powers—Spain, Germany, Japan, and the United States. They are primarily agriculturalists. In addition to yams they raise coconuts, from which copra is derived, breadfruit, taro, and bananas. They have pigs, and gather wild foods, while fishing adds to their subsistence resources. Of all these, coconuts are the most important from an economic point of view —they are "the primary agricultural crop in the commercial

[6] D. G. Mandelbaum, 1941, p. 22.
[7] *Ibid.*, p. 23.

economy of Ponape." Yams, however, which "have never had a real place in the commercial economy," are "because of their importance in both the prestige economy and subsistence" to be regarded "as the primary agricultural crop. . . ."

As in all Micronesian and Polynesian islands, rank and prestige are so important that they must be regarded as focal, and in Ponape the yam is the instrument that symbolizes the rank-prestige preoccupation of the people. Thus the yam, rather than the coconut, is the primary agricultural crop, despite the fact that under the acculturative situation of contact with ruling powers whose economy is on a money base, the principal cash crop, coconuts, might a priori be expected to dominate. As far as the interests of the Ponapeans go, however, only through yam growing can a man better his status.

It has been indicated that greater range of variation and more content are found in focal elements of culture than in those outside them. A crude measure of this is at hand in the Ponapean data. Fourteen different native varieties of coconuts are recognized and named. One hundred and fifty-six varieties of yams, however "were recorded, with descriptions as to size, shape and color and, for most varieties, the period of their introduction" into the island—that is, under what regime they had been imported or developed. "The total number of native varieties planted on Ponape probably runs well over two hundred." The reason why botanical identification of these varieties is difficult— why, indeed, it is so hard to arrive at any accurate figure regarding their number—is because of the secrecy that surrounds yam growing.

The reason for this secrecy is that the prestige competition, which "is a fundamental factor to the understanding of the Ponapean's motivations and his attitudes toward work" centers about yams. So strong is this that families will go hungry rather than touch the large yams that may be in their gardens. When the Section feasts are given, these large yams are displayed. The man who consistently brings the largest yams is not only respected and praised by his fellows, but is selected to assume a Section title that may be vacant, or is promoted to a higher title, if he already has one.

The secrecy about yam growing is reminiscent of the American business-man's attitude toward the technical and financial details of his organization. Larger operations bring him prestige and enhance his position, and he resents an outsider "prying into his affairs," as the saying goes. So on Ponape, as concerns yams: "A Ponapean may speak openly about the number of coconut trees or the amount of money he has, or even boast about them; but his answers to questions about the number and kind of yams he has planted are evasive and often deliberately falsified. He conceals this information so that he may surprise the others when he produces his yams at a feast, in the hope that he may be able to surpass them." More than this, "It is impolite to look at another man's yams, and any one caught doing so will be shamed by gossip and ridicule." How successful as yam growers the Ponapeans are is evident from the criterion of size they use—that is, the number of men it takes to carry a given yam. This makes its point when it is realized that a yam weighing one hundred kilograms (two hundred and twenty pounds) has been produced.

A few other indications of how yam growing claims the interest of this people can be given. One of Bascom's informants was able to name ninety native varieties of yams without stopping. Many Ponapeans are able to name the man who first planted a given variety of yam, and in what District and Section he lived. The contrast with bananas in this regard is impressive. The banana worm destroyed all the older native varieties of bananas, and during the period of Japanese rule new types were introduced. Though this was only a comparatively short time before the research described here, the name of the man who introduced them had been quite forgotten. A new variety of yam, brought to a feast, however, occasions much excitement, and the man who exhibits it obtains even more prestige than if he had brought a very large tuber. He usually gives it his own name. He grows it in secrecy so that when he "unveils" it he will have cuttings to present to the many persons who will want them.[8]

2

These examples are sketched to demonstrate that the greatest variation in form is to be found in the aspect of a culture that is focal to the interests of a people. This variation, by implication, suggests that the focal aspect has undergone greater changes than other elements, a point we may now examine by considering several cultures where the process can be observed in operation as a result of the circumstance of acculturation. In such cases we find that where cultures are in free contact, the focal aspect will be the one where the new elements are most hospitably received.

[8] W. R. Bascom, 1948, *passim.*

On the other hand, in situations where one people is dominated by another, and pressure is brought against customs lying in the focal aspect, retention will be achieved by devious ways.

For an example of how cultural focus affects borrowing under free interchange, we may turn to a description of the mutual influence exerted by the indigenous Arab culture of Palestine and the European ways of life of the Jewish groups who settled there. Patai, who has analyzed the course of this acculturation,[9] shows how, at first, the early Jewish settlers adapted themselves to prevailing Arab patterns, in dress, house types, and other aspects of culture. The swelling flood of newcomers from Europe after the World War I, however, gradually tipped the balance, so that Palestine came to take on a European character. Then, for various social and economic reasons, the Arabs came to borrow from the Jews.

Patai describes how attitudes toward agriculture, which is focal in Jewish but not in Arab concerns, affected the degree of conservatism or change in this aspect of culture among the two groups. The Arab agriculturalists, the *fellahin*, occupied an inferior place in Arab society. They inherited their position from their fathers, but were much more interested in life in the towns than on the farm. Those who remained in the country continued to live much as their ancestors did. The agricultural work of the *fellah* involved "an amount of inevitable toil, necessary for his subsistence," but was "neither a matter of ideological enthusiasm, nor of as much interest as carried by many other aspects of his life."[10]

In contrast, agriculture was, and still is, the center of Jewish interest. "To be a farmer in Palestine was from the very beginning the highest ideal." New Jewish villages are made up of recruits from the towns and of immigrants who have had prior agricultural training. "Members of the second generation leave the village for the town very rarely, while they much more often take the contrary course and, leaving the town-homes of their parents, go to the land." The founding of a village is as important to the Jews of Palestine as the news of a new variety of yam is to the Ponapeans. To be a member of a village from its founding is to attain great prestige, and many young people are strongly motivated by this honor. Conversely, it is resented when a member of a village community leaves the group.

West African cultures and their New World derivatives af-

[9] R. Patai, 1947, *passim*.
[10] *Ibid.*, p. 31.

ford an instance of retention of an original focus under forced acculturation. These West African societies, unlike those other nonliterate groupings considered previously in this chapter, are among the largest in the nonliterate world. Their technological equipment is advanced, their economies complex, their political systems sophisticated and their social structures well organized and administered. Their art has become famous, their folklore is noted for its subtlety, and their music is at the base of the reorientations in Euroamerican musical style which has manifested a shift from exclusive emphasis on melody to stress laid on rhythm. The focus of these cultures, however, is on religion in all its manifestations—belief-systems, world-view, and ritual. The greatest stimulus to thought and creative expression lodges here, and the greatest variety of form is found.

In the New World, this focus on religion stood the Africans and their descendants in good stead. Perhaps because belief was focal, and thus encouraged experimentation and the acceptance of innovations, an adaptation was achieved that eventually surmounted and conquered the tragedy of slavery as in the case of almost no other people that has experienced so far-reaching a disruption of their culture. For while their religion gave meaning to life, their belief was not committed to any rigid dogma. In West Africa, tribal gods had been freely borrowed, and there was no reason why the Christian concept of the universe and the powers that rule it, which the Negroes encountered, could not equally well be incorporated into their system of belief.

In the New World, this willingness to accept the gods of other folk thus made for significant psychological and institutional adaptations. These adaptations, which retained African belief while taking over European forms, or which added the beliefs of the masters to aboriginal belief, are found to this day in New World Negro societies. That the changes in aboriginal religious custom did not come about only in deference to the superior power of the European's deity is to be seen where Africans had contact with Indians, as in Brazil and Guiana, Cuba, and Haiti. Here full attention is paid the autochthonous spirits who ruled the new land, despite the fact that in these countries full-blown African religious forms have been retained. This is to be seen in the Caboclo (Indian) cult of the Brazilian *Africanos*, or the "Indian spirits" (*ingi winti*) of the Dutch Guiana Bush Negroes, or the "indigenous spirits" (*loa créole*) of the Haitian *vodun* worship.

The changes that were made in African forms of religion in

this process of survival under the harsh regime of slavery, and that to a lesser degree permitted the retention of Africanisms in other than religious aspects of life, bring us to a second hypothesis regarding cultural change. This has to do with the process of reinterpretation, to which we now turn.

3

Reinterpretation marks all aspects of cultural change. It is the process by which old meanings are ascribed to new elements or by which new values change the cultural significance of old forms. It operates internally, from generation to generation, no less than in integrating a borrowed element into a receiving culture. But it is in the latter process that the phenomenon is most easily to be studied.

Syncretism is one form of reinterpretation. It is most strikingly exemplified by the reconciliations that have been effected by New World Negroes in the focal aspect of aboriginal African culture, religion. Outstanding here is the identification, in Catholic countries of the New World, of African deities with the saints of the Church. The means whereby the identification has been achieved varies. In Haiti, for example, Legba, the trickster of the West African Dahomeans and Yorubans, is identified with Saint Anthony. This saint is depicted in the chromolithographs acquired by the devout as the patron of the poor, while Legba is conceived as an old man who wanders about, clad in tatters. Damballa, the Dahomean rainbow-serpent, to give only one more example, is identified with Saint Patrick, who is portrayed in his familiar role, and therefore has serpents about him.

Instances of religious syncretism elsewhere can be cited. Thus among the Hausa of West Africa, where aboriginal belief is in contact with Mohammedanism, the pagan *'iskôkî* are identified with the *jinn* of the Koran.[11] In the New World, where Africans came into contact with Protestantism, retention of individual gods was impossible, since no identification with subsidiary beings could be effected, as under Catholicism. Reinterpretations thus took the form of emphasis on the power of the Holy Ghost; or stressed the importance of the River Jordan, the equivalent of the rivers that, in Africa, the spirits must cross to reach the supernatural world. In ritual, spirit possession continued, but by the Holy Ghost, while the place accorded baptism in running water reinterpreted the significance in Africa of the river and sea cults.

[11] J. Greenberg, 1946, pp. 60–1.

In organization, the function of the "mourning groun'" became that of the initiatory rites of African cult groups.

The fact that retentions of aboriginal African custom achieved through reinterpretation bulk so large in the focal aspect of New World Negro religions does not mean that substantial numbers of reinterpretations are not found in other elements of these cultures. "Bury leagues," with their elaborate funerals, conceptions of the place and role of the dead, forms of kinship nomenclature, the economic and social position of women, traditions of polite behavior, lodge organization—these are but a few of the phases of New World Negro cultures that have persisted in reinterpreted form in various parts of the Americas. In the field of social organization these reinterpretations have been so far-reaching as to change a culture that, in Africa, was dominated by men, to one in which the women play the dominant role.[12]

Language offers a broad documentation of the process of reinterpretation. Indeed, much of philological research, broadly interpreted in cultural terms, can be regarded as the study of the phenomenon. One or two examples of Indo-European reinterpretations can be given to make the point. It is recounted how, during the Napoleonic Wars, the French soldiers were greatly feared by the Russian peasants. The French troops, wanting to make friends, would go about repeating the phrase *bon ami*, "good friend." Because of this, the French became known as *bonamicheski*, "bonamis," a word that for the Russians took on the meaning "scoundrel." In Europe generally, the word "smoking" is used for a man's dinner coat. In the nineteenth century, at formal dinners, men did not smoke when women were present, while at all-male parties, where a dinner coat rather than full evening clothes was worn—"smokers," as they were called in English—smoking was the rule. In France, therefore, to be invited to an affair *en smoking*—with accent on the final syllable—means that dinner clothes are to be worn.

The Maya Indians who live in the territory of Quintana Roo in Yucatan, Mexico, have syncretized native gods and various beings worshiped in Catholic rituals in a manner analogous to that of the Christian Negroes of the New World and the Mohammedanized Hausa of West Africa. Among these Maya, the role of the cross represents the most striking aspect of this syncretization. "The cross is the most sacred symbol of the group,"

---

[12] M. J. and F. S. Herskovits, 1947. See pp. 5–17 for a discussion of this process.

writes Villa. "It acts as an intermediary between God and man, for wherever stands a cross, there are the eyes of God. The cross does not, however, communicate directly with God, but through His Son, Jesus Christ, also called John of the Cross." Crosses have power to work miracles, are blessed and sprinkled with holy water, decorated, and dressed. Certain kinds of wood, which are held to have especially great power, are particularly important, and there is a hierarchy of crosses. Domestic crosses, which hold the "lowest rank and sanctity," protect the immediate family. These humble protectors have no shrines, except when a family cross gains prestige by the wonders it comes to have the reputation for working, whereupon this miraculous cross then becomes public, so to speak. Village crosses have greater powers, and on occasion may come to act in their own right. La Santísima (The Most Holy) is the name of the most sacred of these crosses. It has its own altar, cult, and votaries, and masses are said for it. It has become "the guardian of the moral and religious order of the subtribe and the protector of its people from danger and distress." [13]

The concept of reinterpretation, however, has a broader applicability than just to change in culture under contact, for the internal development of a culture also responds to the process of reinterpreting pre-existing elements in terms of new cultural reorientations. Originally, for example, the French word *chauffeur* meant a stoker, a fireman; but its use as the term for driver of an automobile has not only taken its place in French, but in this sense is a full-fledged member of the vocabulary of English and other languages. A "factory" in earlier English was a place where a "factor," the agent of a business concern, carried on his work. It then became a "manu-factory," where goods were made. We still have the word "manufacture," but a "factory" is today reinterpreted as the place where a business concern fabricates the articles it sells.

The principle of reinterpretation sharpens certain propositions regarding the dynamics of culture that are well established in anthropological thought. Linton has suggested that "every element of culture has qualities of four distinct, although mutually interrelated kinds: i.e., it has *form, meaning, use* and *function*." [14] Barnett, building on this formulation, points out that each of these qualities can vary independently as cultural elements change. New meaning can be read into an old form, or a new principle

[13] Alfonso Villa R., 1945, pp. 97–9.
[14] R. Linton, 1936, p. 402.

can be applied despite the retention of a previous function.[15] In the terminology used in this book, these changes may be called cultural reinterpretations, the reading of old meaning into new forms, or the retention of old forms with new meanings. It is apparent, in this connection, that the concept of reinterpretation is also of significance for the hypothesis of "stimulus diffusion" that has been advanced by Kroeber. In many of the cultural changes that fall under such a category the principle of reinterpretation is fundamental.

Fenton provides still another example of reinterpretation, showing how it can act as a mechanism in the retention of a custom under changing conditions, in his study of the patterns of suicide among the Iroquois Indians. In early days of European contact, the attitude of these people toward suicide was ambivalent, but under the influence of Christianity it came to be condemned. This hardening of attitude was enhanced by "a definite concept of allotted life and exclusion from the land of the dead," the former a belief introduced by the outsiders, the latter a development of indigenous beliefs. Yet, although attitudes toward self-destruction have changed, the "fundamental suicide patterns" have remained stable. "The same motives, the same methods, and similar beliefs concerning the fate of souls prevail. Danger of capture and torture ceased with the wars, and blood revenge is giving way to white law enforcement on the reservation: The onus is shifted but throughout avoidance remains the dominating motive." Fenton then concludes: "Pattern then serves as a cultural continuant for custom, antecedents have already defined the situation for the individual, and once a fundamental pattern becomes established it tends to persist despite substitution within its framework." [16] That is, the earlier pattern, with the passage of time, is reinterpreted so as to be in accord with change in the total setting of the culture as a whole.

4

The significance of the concepts of cultural focus and reinterpretation becomes apparent when we consider the usual answer to the question, "Why do a given people take over one new idea or thing presented to them, and reject another?" Customarily it is stated that those elements that are in accord with the preceding patterns of the culture will be accepted, while those that are not will be rejected. Sometimes the answer is expressed in terms of the

[15] H. G. Barnett, 1942, *passim.*
[16] W. N. Fenton, 1941, pp. 134–5.

cultural base, with the implication that when a culture is ready for an innovation, the innovation will make its appearance. This, it will be recalled, is the answer of the cultural determinists to the problem of the acceptability of inventions, and is usually documented by reference to the multiple independent inventions of our own culture.

It is evident, however, that the answer to the question must, in the final analysis, come from the study of change in process. Data derived from distribution studies can be used to test our hypotheses, but hypotheses themselves, as instruments of scientific investigation, must arise out of the direct observation of the changes, whether internal or stimulated by contact, that are actually taking place.

The question raised concerning the differential selectivity of a people faced with a cultural innovation still needs to be answered. It is doubtful whether the answer will be given, except in general terms, for many years to come. This is the ultimate quest of most social scientists, as of many students whose concerns are entirely of a practical nature. The problem presents itself every time a new commodity is placed on the market, for the market survey is but one attempt to study this problem of acceptance or rejection of an internal change. In every attempt to introduce, in a foreign society, a new idea, a new technique, a new kind of goods, the question must be faced.

If our question cannot be answered, however, it can be refined and clarified. It is toward this end that the discussion in this chapter has been directed. The hypotheses of *cultural focus* and of *reinterpretation*, derived from the study of cultures where change in process has been under observation, have a significance that transcends their applicability to the situations in which they have been studied. These concepts reorient the approach to the fundamental problem of cultural change. The answers to the question, "Why do a given people take over one new idea or thing presented to them, and reject another?" are customarily phrased only in terms of culture itself. Its formulation in terms of focus and reinterpretation introduces a needed psychological perspective. This approach, it should once more be emphasized, is essential if the motivations that cause a people to accept or reject a possible innovation are to be comprehended, and if the process of cultural change is really to be understood.

Chapter **Twenty-seven**

The Mechanisms of Cultural Variation

We have seen that individual differences in behavior can be discerned only when the way of life of a people is known. It takes time and experience to comprehend what limits are set for approved deviations from the ways in which, broadly considered, the members of a particular society react to a situation.

It was out of the difficulties in perceiving individual differences in strange cultures that the idea arose that "primitive man" lived in a cultural strait jacket. The quotations in an earlier chapter from Herbert Spencer and others bearing on this point will be recalled, and it is not too much to say that this conception dominated anthropological thought until well after the end of the nineteenth century. Students, using the comparative method, drew on accounts of travelers, missionaries, and others, who wrote in terms of generalized custom, and early field-workers tended to be unaware of the existence of individuals in the societies they studied. Much early field-work, it will be remembered, aimed at recovering cultures that were in the process of disintegration, often under Euroamerican contact, as in the case of the American Indians; here individual differences were lost in the reminiscences of the survivors who acted as informants.

Still another cause for the neglect of individual differences in earlier anthropological writing was the feeling that anthropology, as the science of custom, was to be distinguished from psychology, the discipline that studied the individual. Sapir stated the point well, in indicating how anthropology, under these terms, emphasized

> those aspects of behavior which belonged to society as such, more particularly societies of the dim past or exotic societies whose way of life seemed so different from that of our own people that one could hope to construct a generalized picture of the life of society at large, particularly in its more archaic stages of development.[1]

Names of informants were given, it is true, but there was little attempt to indicate how their statements on a given point may have differed. Says Sapir:

> I remember being rather shocked than pleased, when in my student days I came across such statements in J. O. Dorsey's "Omaha Sociology" as "Two Crows denies this." This looked a little as though the writer had not squarely met the challenge of assaying his source material and giving us the kind of data that we, as respectable anthropologists, could live on. It was as though he "passed the buck" to the reader, expecting him by some miracle of cultural insight to segregate truth from error.

But Dorsey, as Sapir points out, was ahead of his time. He knew his Indians well, and recognized that they, as individuals, differed in their behavior and in the interpretations they gave of this behavior, as do the members of any human group. "Apparently Two Crows," says Sapir, "a perfectly good and authoritative Indian, could presume to rule out of court the very existence of a custom or attitude or belief vouched for by some other Indian, equally good and authoritative."[2]

More recently the point has been succinctly phrased by Ashton, in a passage where he points out that,

> culture is not a homogeneous, integrated whole. There is obviously a central pattern which gives a particular culture its general character and distinguishes it from other cultures; but it is not a rigid pattern nor yet all-embracing. It has all sorts of deviations and exceptions, some of which are due to individual aberration or choice, to changes of time, place or circumstance, while others are due to differences between whole sections of the community.[3]

[1] E. Sapir, 1938, p. 7.
[2] *Ibid.*, pp. 7–8.
[3] H. Ashton, 1952, p. viii.

A demonstration of the validity of this position is to be found in Roberts' study of variants in the songs of the Negroes of Jamaica. With the precision that the analysis of musical forms lends to the investigation of cultural phenomena, she shows how, both in melody and words, individual songs differ in their rendition from district to district of the same part of the island, and from singer to singer. Her data derive from variants of the "John Crow" (or "Cyam Crow") song, which she recorded in the northwestern part of Jamaica. John Crow is the vulture, the turkey-buzzard. The name given him is, in all likelihood, an Anglicized version of the name *Yankoro*, given this same bird in West Africa; his other name is probably derived from "carrion-crow," pronounced in the manner of the Jamaican Negroes. The point of the song, which is of a common African and New World Negro type, is that it ridicules the greed of the ungainly bird who in his haste to get the food from "Missa Wright's cow," fell rather than flew, and "broke his diaphragm ['diagram' in the song], or wind, as it was explained." [4] The author goes on: "From this small incident has sprung all the train of happenings that may be found in the different versions, and doubtless many more."

Even in three of these songs, recorded in neighboring settlements, despite similarities in melodic line and rhythm and in the motifs of the verses, minor variants are to be observed. The other songs, which show wider dissimilarities, are from communities farther removed. They illustrate how a single cultural item can continue to extend its limits of variation as the region in which it is studied is widened. We cannot consider here the variation in individual performance. The rendition of this song by each singer, we are told, was quite constant. Yet Roberts also gives instances that demonstrate differences in repetitions of a given song by the same singer.

Where, then, does ethnographic "truth" lie? There is scarcely need to repeat here what has been often stated in earlier pages concerning the problem of establishing truth when describing cultural phenomena. We need only emphasize here that ethnological truth is not fixed, but variable. What the ethnographer must ascertain, then, is *the limits within which a culture recognizes and sanctions variations* in a given belief or a given mode of behavior.

Having set down this principle, it is necessary to explore some of its implications. As with so many seemingly obvious principles that guide research and analysis in the field of culture, unsuspected complexities appear in probing even a simple point.

[4] H. H. Roberts, 1925, p. 178.

It is essential, for example, that the difference between *ideal* and *actual* behavior be clear to the field student, and that this distinction be held in mind in reading accounts of the ways of life of any people. The chief difficulty here is that the members of a society do not necessarily agree about what constitutes ideal behavior. Different members of the same community will give different versions of what is sanctioned by their group, while actual observation will reveal broad differences in behavior that reflect the variety of accepted sanctions.

An example of how this search for ethnographic truth is complicated by the deviations found in actual practice will both clarify the problem and indicate how it is to be faced. Our instance may be taken from the acculturative syncretisms between African belief and Catholicism in the culture of the Brazilian Negroes. As in other New World Catholic countries, ancestral African beliefs have been reconciled with Christianity, as a result of the forced conversions of slavery times. We have seen how the descendants of these Africans worship the African gods, and are simultaneously professing and practicing Catholics. As in all Catholic countries, Lent is a period of great importance, and so is Shrove Tuesday (Mardi Gras), the culmination of the annual carnival. Now almost everyone in this Brazilian city of Bahia, Negro or white, cult-member or not, will state with perfect good faith that Lent is no time to study cult-ceremonies, since cult-houses are closed for the observance of Lent. As one pursues his inquiry he is told, with comparable unanimity, that Holy Saturday (*Sábado da Alelúia*) is the day when, with elaborate rites, these African cult centers reopen after their Lenten suspension of activities. Some persons are even more specific. They say that these cult rites are timed to begin at 11 A.M. when, on the day before Easter, the bells of all Bahia's many churches peal to mark the moment of the Resurrection.

Investigation showed that in actual practice, however, many cult centers continue the worship of their African gods well into Lent. Not a single center could be found in the year 1942 that suspended its activities at the beginning of that period. All cult-houses were closed during Holy Week, and even the people who live in these centers went elsewhere then, since this is regarded as a time of spiritual danger, because the gods have departed. But, again, not all the cult centers reopened on Easter Saturday. In actuality the rites that reopen them may be witnessed for a month or more after Easter Sunday. It depends largely on the plans of the priest who heads the cult-house, or on the wishes of the gods themselves, as revealed by divination, or on other circumstances.

The gods, who, as we have said, are believed to be absent while the cult-house is closed, are thought of as being "off to the wars" during the period. The rite of closing the house, called *lorogun*, has as its essential purpose speeding these beings on their way. In it the deities are "called," possess their devotees, and in some centers stage a dance which, with the intricate choreography of a mock combat, determines which spirits will "rule" the center during the ensuing year. The gods then shoulder their food sacks, visit in turn the shrines of the center to say their good-byes, and then finish the dance in the cult-house, proffering their favorite foods to the spectators before they depart.

This is an abstract of the *lorogun* rite taken from common elements in descriptions given by three different informants, plus observations of six actual ceremonies. Each informant reported, in considerable detail, the sequence of events, and the reasons why each element in this rite was carried out. But each was, in all likelihood, thinking of a particular ceremony as performed in the cult center with which he was affiliated. Among some groups, for example, the "combat" was described as between male and female deities, to see which would "rule" for the year. Among others, it was said to be between gods of different pantheons. In one center, at an actual ceremony, it was the god that first "came" to a devotee when the drum rhythms called—that is, in whose name the initial possession occurred—that was to be paramount for the year. On occasion, an informant would say, "In our center we do it this way, but in others they don't do this"; or, when presented with the conflicting statement of another informant, would shrug his shoulders, and say, "They probably do it that way in his house."

What is the "truth" of Afrobahian cult practices as regards the identification of Catholic saints and African gods, or in connection with Lent? Here, it is apparent, there is no single truth. There are many truths. But it is equally apparent that there are limits beyond which statements are not true, while there is a core of common behavior wherein a minimum of deviation is to be found. The fact that practically all cult-houses are closed during Holy Week is one such core element; the common items given in our general outline of the *lorogun* rite constitute others; yet about this core are the numerous variants, each of which has an ethnological validity that is beyond dispute. It is the same when, in other cultures, and in an entirely different realm, a person in good faith tells how in his group men show respect for their mothers-in-law by avoiding them—specifically, by not speaking to them in face-to-face conversation. More than one ethnographer has been nonplussed later to observe this same informant talking to his own mother-in-law, only to be told that here was a special instance—a child was ill, or the man's wife was in need of advice she herself could not come to get.

"Circumstances alter cases" is as good a rule of thumb in ethnography as it is in guiding everyday conduct. For it is circumstances that make for differences in individual behavior which are reflected in the variability found in the patterned sanctions that permit deviations from the norm of approved conduct, or in the recognized forms of institutions. The problem of ascertaining the range of accepted variation in custom, then, is the essence of the question of ethnographic truth.

2

The concept of culture-pattern advanced earlier in this book defined this phenomenon as the consensus of differing individual behavior patterns. The point, however, was further made that the term, in all discussions except those that describe and analyze a particular pattern, should be used in the plural sense. This conclusion was reached because we found that, even in the most homogeneous group, *institutionalized* variants in ways of meeting the same situation are always to be encountered. These differing sets of patterns reflect the fact that every society is an aggregate of sub-groups, whose particular ways of life are to be distinguished within the general sanctions of the group as a whole. The fact that these lines cross and recross, in the sense that a given individual belongs to a number of sub-groups, was seen to complicate the problem presented by the pattern phenomenon. At the same time it was pointed out that a recognition of this complexity tends of itself to clarify certain problems in the study of culture that otherwise present serious difficulties.

Underlying all these differences are those others that mark off individual from individual, and intermediately, family from family. This is why the nature of any pattern, no matter how minute or particular, or how broad, as a *consensus* of behavior, was stressed. The larger the number of persons who react to a given situation in similar—not identical—ways, the wider the effectiveness of that pattern over the society where it is found. Consensus of cultural behavior is thus but another expression of cultural variation. A culture, considered in this way, becomes an aggregate of differing individual patterns which, in their totality, reflect the fact that the behavior of any member of a particular society will be more like that of any fellow member than like that of any outsider.

Linton has suggested a useful series of concepts to denote certain degrees of similarity and difference in behavior to be found in a culture. The first of these he calls "universals," which are those beliefs and forms of behavior to be expected of any normal member of a society: language, types of clothing and housing, the way a group orders its social relations. The second category comprises the "specialties," which are composed of those particular aspects of behavior that characterize the members of specialized groups within the larger social whole; those differences we have indicated as marking off the activities of one sex from those of the other, or of different kinds of craftsmen. Next come the "alternatives," the forms of behavior recognized by a society as valid, but which cut across class or occupational or sex lines. A man may choose one color or another in decorating a basket he is making, or may phrase an assertion with one set of words or another; a game may be played in various ways; marriage may be sanctioned by observing different forms. Finally, we have "individual peculiarities," experimental forms of behavior, which represent the contribution of the individualist. Linton points to these as the source of innovation in culture. Every contribution to a way of life, as he says, must have been started by someone. At the outset, it is an individual peculiarity which, regarded benevolently by the members of the society when it is introduced, passes into more general use.[5]

If we apply the concept of variability to Linton's series, we find that there are levels of difference not unrelated to these categories. Thus the variations that mark off the belief and behavior of every member of any group from that of any other are, in a sense, the "individual peculiarities" of Linton's scheme. However, as a statistical concept, this most general level of variation defines the limits of acceptable behavior permitted by a group rather than the extreme deviations that are stressed by Linton in describing his category. From the point of view of cultural variability, an extreme deviation, if accepted, merely widens the range of variation in a culture. If it does not "catch on," or is suppressed, it is to be put down as an innovation that departed too widely from accepted custom.

Individual variation, however, may exist without involving innovation. The nearer the individual's particular kind of be-

[5] R. Linton, 1936, pp. 272–5.

havior is to the average type, the less marked it will be from that of his fellows. But no two persons, even those who do not question their culture at all, will perform the same operation, or conceive the same accepted belief, in identical terms. It is just as important for a comprehension of cultural form and process to understand this fact as it is to recognize the role of the individual idiosyncrasy that constitutes an extreme departure from the norm. In its totality, this range of permitted deviation is an index of cultural homogeneity or heterogeneity. To recognize that there is no culture where all members of a group react in the same way to a given situation is but to say that variation is a universal in culture, no less than any of its other aspects. This means that, no matter how imperfect the instrument for analyzing it, variability must be taken into account in all studies of culture. The recognition of the fact of variation in cultures, however expressed, thus becomes one of the most significant steps in the development of anthropological science.

3

The points that have thus far been made concerning variation in culture may be summarized in the following propositions:

1. Culture is an expression of the behavior of a people and of the sanctions that underlie behavior.

2. The behavior and belief of no two individuals is identical; hence these must be thought of, and studied, as variable rather than rigidly structured.

3. The total range of variation in individual belief and behavior found among the members of a given society, at a given time, thus defines the culture of that society, and this holds true for the sub-cultures of smaller units within the social whole.

However,

4. Belief and behavior in any society are never haphazard, but vary about established norms.

5. These norms are to be derived inductively from the consensuses of the observed beliefs and modes of behavior of a given group; they comprise the patterns of a culture.

Finally,

6. Other things being equal, the smaller the group, the more homogeneous its patterns of belief and behavior will be.

7. Specialist groups, however, may be expected to exhibit a greater range of variation in the field of their specialties than groups of equivalent size among the population as a whole.

This approach to the problem of the nature of culture and its organization, though conceived in statistical terms cannot, in view of the methodological problems involved, be treated in mathematical form. What is important to recognize, as we read the ethnographic literature and discussions of anthropological theory, is the significance of the problem of *cultural homogeneity* and *cultural heterogeneity*. For the present, the methods of quantitative analysis are best utilized in the study of those aspects of culture, such as certain elements in musical style, in the graphic arts, or in the economic life of a people, that are susceptible of mathematical treatment. However, the student must always be on his guard against the spurious sense of accuracy that derives from the unwarranted use of statistical method. There is much in culture of which qualitative description quite effectively gives a lively and significant sense of the range of differences found in one group or sub-group as against another. It is hardly necessary, for example, to resort to counting to know that the cultures of the tribes of the Mackenzie Basin are more homogeneous than those of Java. But, as we shall see when we consider the nature of cultural laws and the problem of prediction, it is important to conceive of their differences in homogeneity as comprising differing degrees of variation in the expressions of belief and behavior that define the life of the members of such groups.

It should be evident that the very conception of a culture as the summation of the variables in belief and behavior of a people is of importance in approaching almost any problem of cultural dynamics. In the study of culture, as in so many fields of science, the differences that are to be discerned between the individual units of any category of phenomena must be recognized as a primary mechanism of change. The role of the extreme deviant in widening the range of variation in a culture has been mentioned. This, in turn, may set up a dynamic reaction that leads to other deviations which push the frontiers of accepted convention ever further, and this is fundamental to the process of cultural drift, to a discussion of which we shall turn shortly.

Propensities to change can, indeed, be envisaged as a function of the variable attitudes toward innovation that are found in a given society or in different societies. This idea is inherent in the concept of a culture as differently oriented from other cultures in terms of its different cultural focus. Consequently, when we say religion is focal to West African culture, we are expressing the fact that the concerns of the people center in this more than in other aspects of their experience, and we imply a patterned receptivity to change in this focal aspect that is not present in social organization, for example, or technology. That is why, when we speak of one aspect of culture, or of one whole culture as more "fluid" than another, we mean that it exhibits a greater degree of patterned acceptance of variation than one we call "conservative."

4

As a concept, *cultural drift* follows logically from the idea of a culture as the consensus of the variables in the beliefs and modes of behavior of a people. We have seen that the presence of deviations from norms of concept and conduct, even when so small as to go unrecognized, is important in giving to a culture an inner dynamic that in time may result in alterations of the most profound character. These variants, however, do not all have the same dynamic significance. They tend to be random variations, in the sense that they represent all kinds of departures from all sorts of norms. They are dynamically significant only when they begin to accumulate, and thus give direction to cultural change.

As an instance, we may take the habit of men, in Euroamerican culture, to wear about their necks strips of cloth, or neckties, as they are called. This is the norm. Some of these ties are longer than others, some are tied as bows and others as slipknots. Some are more brightly colored than others. Different kinds of neckties will be in order on different occasions. A person mourning the death of a relative will wear a dark-colored tie tied in a slipknot, and not a bright-colored one, or a bow tie. On the other hand, a man wearing formal clothes will wear only bow ties, though degrees of formality of the occasion will be indicated by whether the bow is black or white. If it is a black one, this has no reference to mourning, but denotes a lesser degree of formality than does a white one.

We find a recognizable swing in fashion, over the years, from knotted ties to bow ties, yet the fluctuations have had to do with the type of tie, not with the incidence of wearing ties. The variations concerned color and form; the question whether or not to have neckties was not raised. Lurking in the background of this consensus, however, was a more radical deviant—the tieless man. The fact that the necktie was associated with status was of some significance here, for persons of substance and position have been reluctant to discard this symbol. Nonetheless, it began to be noted that the lower-class individual, the workman, gained a measure of comfort by not wearing additional widths of constricting cloth about his neck.

Some men of status came to veer toward this particular deviation. As more and more did this, especially during the summer heat, clothing manufacturers began to take cognizance of the trend and to design shirts that could be worn open at the neck or closed, with or without a necktie. Whatever the final outcome of this inclination toward "necktielessness"—which, incidentally, is part of a wider dress-reform complex that includes brighter colors and greater informality of clothes in general—it provides a good example of how at one time a particular deviation will be of greater significance than another. That is, we see, in this minor and perhaps frivolous detail of Euroamerican culture, a manifestation of *that process of cumulative variation we define as cultural drift.*

The term "drift" represents an adaptation of Sapir's concept of linguistic drift, a concept that he developed out of his observation of variability in linguistic expression. Every person, he observed, manifests idiosyncrasies in his particular speech habits. Yet in a social class or in a local area, the speakers of a common language form "a compact, relatively unified group" in contrast to other such groups. "The individual variations are swamped in or absorbed by certain major agreements—say of pronunciation and vocabulary—which stand out very strongly when the language of the group as a whole is contrasted to that of the other group." [6]

If we translate this into the terms of our discussion of variability in culture as a whole, we would say that the individual differences in belief and behavior of persons who belong to one subgroup or local community within a particular society are submerged in the consensuses that characterize the sub-cultures of the two groups, and thus make it possible to distinguish them from each other in terms of their typical patterns of thought and conduct. In language as in the rest of culture, however, not all of the idiosyncrasies, the random deviations from the norm, are of the same consequence. Change is brought about by a process whereby certain deviations from established norms are taken over by a number of people, thus initiating and continuing a tendency that becomes a trend.

The concept of drift, the piling up of minor variations that are in consonance with pre-existing tendencies, is associated with the idea of cultural focus. We have advanced the hypothesis that change is more likely to occur in the institutions lying in the focal aspect of a culture than in those found in other of its aspects. If we grant that change is not haphazard, but directional, then the

[6] E. Sapir, 1921, pp. 157-8.

increased range of variation in the focal aspect of a culture would not only continuously tend to produce a wider range of variants in line with the direction in which the institutions were moving, but would also make for more decided change than in other aspects. If, further, the specific focal aspect is the one that gave a culture its "flavor," then the outstanding changes that mark the development of cultures in terms of the succession of focal interests manifested over long periods could be referred to the fact that drift is not a simple unilinear phenomenon. This would further reflect the fact that the broad stream which comprises any culture has varied currents, of which now some, now others will be the more rapid.

It will become evident when the problem of prediction of cultural change is discussed how potentially significant is this concept of Sapir's. For though the phenomenon of cultural drift can, as yet, only be studied in terms of its past manifestations, it is nonetheless easier to project lines of established developmental drift than if the concept were not there to sharpen our perceptions. In the main, this can be done only for details of culture, not for larger subdivisions or a culture as a whole. Sapir's demonstration of the drift, in English, toward the use of the pronoun "who" for "whom" is a case in point. "Whom did you see?" he observes, though actually "correct," may seem "incorrect" to many who feel uncomfortable when they employ the phrase. They prefer the "colloquial" usage "Who did you see?" and their preference marks the drift that will make this the "correct" usage of the future. This, it is shown, is only part of a broader trend that makes it possible to predict that English of the future, in this detail as in certain other aspects—in "Come quick!" for "Come quickly!"—will but embody the continuation of tendencies that the discerning backward look can isolate, see in present usage, and project into the future.

In 1934–5, Eggan made a field study of culture change among the Tinguian of the northern Philippines, following earlier field research by the Coles [7] which provided a detailed description of Tinguian culture as it existed twenty years earlier. Since the study of culture change among the Tinguian involved many elements in a highly complex relation, Eggan studied changes in the culture of this people in relation to the changes that had occurred in the cultures of their neighbors. These tribes, "with similar basic cultures" are the Ilocano, Apayao, Bontoc, Ifugao, and Igorot. They all inhabit villages and their economies are based on rice cultiva-

[7] F. C. Cole, 1922.

tion; but on this pattern "considerable variations" are to be seen.[8]

The regularity of change in social, political, and religious institutions as one moves from the interior tribes to those of the coast or from the coast to the interior, to which Eggan applies the term "cultural drift," is striking. In the interior, village organization is simpler than among the tribes nearer the coast. Kinship structures show a similar kind of directional variation, from the sib system of the Ifugao to the European-like family forms of the Ilocano. There is a corresponding reduction in the range of obligations one must fulfill to kinsmen, and a consequent increase in the importance of social units based on territorial ties. Controls shift from the family heads of the Ifugao to the ward and *barrio* and village heads or councils, while "customary law decreases in complexity and development until it practically vanishes." Class lines, based on economic resources, are more sharply drawn as one moves from the interior to the coast, and the per capita wealth increases. Marriage customs show similar regularity in the differences to be observed as one moves from tribe to tribe. These vary from the relatively free choice exercised by the Ifugao and Bontoc to the arranged marriages of the Tinguian and the Ilocano. As might be expected, the ease with which separation or divorce is achieved shows a similar series of differences, as do their frequency.

What, then, of cultural drift? The case of the presumed instance of Spanish repression of head-hunting among the Tinguian is to the point. This is supposed to have made trade and other kinds of relations possible in a wider area than previously. Yet, according to Eggan, "a closer examination of the situation among the Tinguian and their neighbors . . . suggests that the Tinguian had themselves developed an effective mechanism for stopping head-hunting." In the days preceding Spanish rule, this people had not only compacted to maintain the peace with neighboring villages but had also developed agreements, validated and strengthened by intermarriage, with the peoples inhabiting villages over the mountains eastward.

> These were rigidly enforced by the headmen and made trade and travel possible over a wide area. The relative ease with which head-hunting was stopped in the Tinguian region, compared with the difficulties encountered in the Ifugao and Bontoc areas, seems as much a result of the shift in type of local integration as of the efforts of the Spanish authorities.

[8] This and following quotations on this study of drift in culture are from F. Eggan, 1941, pp. 11–18.

In terms of the concept of cultural drift, this would seem to imply that where the policy of the dominant political power was in harmony with a pre-existing tendency, the success of the effort was not difficult to achieve. On the other hand, it proved much more difficult where no tendency had been established. This is apparent in the other aspects of these cultures. "The Spanish worked in vain to christianize the Tinguian, while the Americans have struggled to break down the class system through the introduction of free public education and universal suffrage." The Spanish succeeded best in the coastal area, the Americans best in the interior.

In both regions, each unwittingly was building on pre-existing custom. Their successes or failures were due to the fact that they were able to utilize a pre-existing momentum of prevailing patterns that was the end-result of established drift, or that they had to counteract the unsensed, but nonetheless powerful force of these cumulative drives. On the coast, where class lines had long existed, the Spanish had but to superimpose a new class, their own, atop the ones they found, and thus a pre-existing system was continued. On the other hand, the democracy of the interior peoples resisted this innovation but was amenable to the efforts of the Americans which, in turn, were not acceptable to the coastal peoples.

Here we are presented with an interaction between established drift and outer compulsions, which means that an additional factor has to be taken into account. This factor is the one we have called historical accident. Therefore it is well for us, at this point, to turn to a consideration of the nature and significance of this concept. With our analysis in hand, we may then assess the manner in which accidental happenings act to reinforce or counteract the drifts already present in the cultures where they occur.

5

Historic accident is the term to be applied to abrupt innovations that arise from within a culture or result from the contact of peoples. It must be made clear, at the outset, that the use of the word "accident" in no way implies an absence of causation. It is, rather, that happenings of this kind occur outside any sequence of events that might ordinarily have been anticipated. In this sense, the concept in no way begs the question of causation, as some writers have claimed. Rather it recognizes the multiplicity of factors that can act as causes, and phrases an acknowledgment of the fact that no causal sequence is self-sufficient.

It is unfortunate, in a sense, that the commonly accepted use of the word "accident" brings to it the connotation that an unforeseen event is one having undesirable consequences. In applying it to the study of culture, it must be made clear that no such evaluative meaning is to be attached to the word. Many happenings outside the range of probability, which we would term historical accidents, have operated to make more effective the efforts of a people to live their lives more adequately, with better inner adjustment, and on a higher material plane than would otherwise have been possible. The many food plants that were introduced into Europe after the discovery of the New World, from the point of view of the people of Europe, and even from the point of view of the motivations that led to the discovery of the Americas, are to be thought of as a series of cultural accidents. It would be difficult to argue that their effects were other than beneficial. And if, as will soon become apparent, we apply the term historical accident to unlooked-for results of developments that take place within a culture, then the number of such beneficent happenings increases apace.

Where the concept of historical accident is used by anthropologists, it signifies those abrupt, unforeseeable changes in a culture that have been introduced from outside. This is quite understandable, since occurrences of this kind offer much clearer examples of the nature and consequences of historic accident than do internal changes. Outer influences making for abrupt change can be richly documented in instances of culture-contact, where the acceptance of new elements by a people shifts lines of development, and moves them into new channels. Internal accidents of history are exemplified, however, in the unforeseeable consequences of a given discovery or invention, and are much more difficult to study; and this obtains whether or not a chain of antecedent developments can later be discerned as leading to the particular discovery or invention.

An example of how the unanticipated impact of a foreign culture effected changes of the kind we call accidental, which is often cited and that merits some scrutiny here, is that of Japan. The visit of Commodore Matthew C. Perry in 1852, which, as Euroamerican terminology has it, "opened the door" of Japan to the rest of the world, caused a flood of ideas and material objects to enter into this hitherto isolated country. The subsequent cultural changes need only be mentioned for their significance to emerge.

It is important, of course, to understand that these impulses did not affect all aspects of Japanese culture equally. Some it altered so fundamentally that older forms were discarded. This was especially true in technology, urbanization and industrialization. Some—certain basic sanctions of family structure, aspects of rural economy and technology, religious life, and status orientations—were altered very slightly, if at all. What did occur was that, given the initial happening and subsequent impulses from other cultures, the course of development of Japanese culture was deflected into channels that no one in Japan could have foreseen, even though some scholars outside that country might have predicted the future course of events on the basis of their knowledge of world history.

The accidents of history that occur within a culture are far more difficult to document than those unpredictable results of contact that are everywhere to be perceived merely for the looking. Historians, however, recognize the fact of such "accidental" happenings in their writings; especially where a powerful individual makes decisions whose consequences, often affecting the lives of multitudes, could not have been foretold. Of a somewhat different type are the unforeseen consequences that have followed on discovery or invention, a point we have already mentioned.

Consider, for example, the invention of the automobile. As we have seen in discussing the problem of the nature of invention, this in itself is to be regarded as the sum of a long series of minor developments that flowered in the "horseless buggy" of the initial stage of the motorcar. This series would include the change in form from a true horseless carriage to a vehicle designed for higher speeds in the light of aerodynamic principles. The linguistic lag implicit in the statement, "I *drive* a car," a carry-over of the idiom "to drive a horse" is matched by the reluctance of car users to accept cars where the motor is at the rear, functionally a far more reasonable place for it than in front. With facts such as these we are not concerned, however. Both they, and other aspects of the technical development of the motorcar are part of a series of events that represents a regular sequence in the history of our culture, a logical working out of the impulses that began with the invention of this particular machine. Nor is prediction too difficult as regards the automobile, provided the factor of probability is taken into account. Thus it should surprise no one if cars with motors installed at the rear actually do become current.

What was unpredictable in the development of the motor-car were some of the consequences of its invention that lay entirely outside the technological field. The concentration of people in the center of cities diminished and eventually ceased, and the ensuing rise of the suburb and the satellite town took place because of the distances that the automobile made it possible to traverse. Change invaded other spheres of life in unexpected ways. A process of secularization that took men and women out of the churches onto the golf links was accelerated. The effect on competing transportation media was another unlooked-for consequence, since the ability to cover long distances in reasonable time by routes of one's own choosing and at relatively low cost made this kind of travel appealing. As a result, the railways were hard put to it to survive, and were forced to consider new ways of meeting this unanticipated incursion into their business.

These are only a few of the more obvious repercussions of the invention of the automobile. Many more, some of them affecting details of the moral code, of family life, of the inner organization of cities, for instance, could be given. From the point of view of the people living in 1900, they were as unpredictable as were the changes wrought in the lives of Africans since 1900 as a result of the impact of European culture. In terms of the criteria that have been advanced, however, all must be thought of as historic accidents. That one originates within a society, another outside it, is not important as far as the results of such occurrences are concerned. Their effect is to shift the lines along which the development of a culture had been taking place, so that an established trend—a "drift"—is deflected in a new direction.

In nonliterate societies historical accidents arising from events within the group are, to be sure, more difficult to document than in literate ones. The discovery of fire, or the domestication of animals, must have been occurrences that were of the order of historic accidents; so were the discovery of ironworking, or the wheel, or the loom. The chicken, domesticated in southeast Asia for purposes of divination, became primarily a factor in the food-producing economy of many peoples. The invention of powder, used in China for fireworks, became in western Europe an instrument of destruction. Within a society or through diffusion, a discovery, an invention, a borrowing that is incorporated into a culture may have effects that seem quite outside the range of probability. It thus initiates a series of events that we call accidental. In these terms, then, the accidents of history become prime factors to be taken into account in our search for a comprehension of the nature and processes of culture.

6

The concepts of cultural drift and historic accident bring us one step further toward attaining an understanding of how cultures develop, especially as this concerns the selective nature of change. If we recognize the importance of differential variation in providing a basis both for change and selection, then drift is to be regarded as the expression of the process whereby some variants come to be of more importance than others to a particular people at a given time. If this were the whole story, the study of culture would be much simpler than it is. Given the analysis of drift, it would be possible to plot future growth within far more restricted limits of probability than is actually possible.

Historic accidents, whether originating from within or without, intervene in the process. Yet the established drift must not be thought of as a passive element in change, for even where historic accidents of far-reaching consequence emerge, existing selective tendencies exert their influence. Sweeping changes imposed through conquest are met by reinterpreting older values in terms of new forms, or old forms may be carried on in secret if the demands of the conqueror involve too great changes in earlier custom.

Drift, whose outstanding expression is in the focal aspect of a culture, thus influences what is to be taken into a culture, whether from innovations arising out of inner variation or introduced from outside the group. Similarly, drift, together with focus, offer an explanation why diffused elements are reinterpreted to assume forms and meanings in accord with established patterns. Finally, these two concepts aid us in perceiving how the unpredictable events of history, even when their initial shock demoralizes the people who experience them, are eventually assimilated.

The significance of these concepts, however, transcends just these points in the study of culture. They have a bearing on questions that bring into play the fundamental assumptions of anthropological science. They are pertinent to problems of the organization of data and to problems of law and prediction in history, to a discussion of which we now move.

Chapter **Twenty-eight**

---

*The Problem of Law and Prediction
in Culture*

When a phenomenon has been described and named, an important step in the scientific process has been taken, since data must be recognizable and capable of delimitation before they can be systematically studied. However, experience has taught that as soon as a description or a definition becomes the statement of a position, it may come to be a major preoccupation of scholars and thus defeat the end for which it was devised. When classes that represent a system of terminology and a set of definitions harden into dogma, they become an obstruction rather than an aid to scientific analysis.

The danger point is not difficult to determine. It is reached when cases that do not fit the definition are brushed aside as "exceptions." The method of science, however, which is to test hypotheses by ascertaining the extent to which the facts verify postulates, admits of no "exceptions." For, in science, "exceptions" are the critical cases, and constitute the real challenge to the research worker. If they are numerous enough, they negate the hypothesis. If they are not so numerous, they must be studied with special care to determine how the hypothesis is to be revised in accordance with the facts. In the laboratory, controls can be manipulated until recalcitrant data of this kind can be explained. The problem of coping with the "exception" is therefore the technical one of employing instruments at hand, or devising new instruments, to alter the conditions under which the experiment has been carried on. But such experimentation is impossible in the disciplines where the data cannot be manipulated in the laboratory, as in the study of culture.

Where the controlled experimentation of the laboratory sciences cannot be had, historic controls must be sought. That is, situations of various kinds must be found where differing circumstances make it possible to test hypotheses in terms of achieved results that are to be referred to differing series of ascertainable historic events. Above all, in applying the methods of science to the study of culture, it is essential to investigate the "negative" manifestations of the phenomenon. If we would understand totemism, for example, we must be careful not only to describe, classify and analyze as many examples of it as are to be found, but also to study as carefully as possible cultures where totemism is not present.

This was the issue on which controversy turned in the period between 1910 and 1920, resolved by Goldenweiser's analysis, which established the broad criteria under which totemic phenomena of varied kinds were to be comprehended. What gave rise to the controversy was the familiar problem of classification. The customs of the Australians had come to be set up as the essential criteria of totemism. But many "exceptions" to totemic forms of this sort began to be found elsewhere in the world. What, then, were these "exceptions"? They either were phenomena of a different order, or the definition of totemism was in error. The definition was broadened—but this has not settled the question why, though many groups have totemic beliefs, by no means all societies have them; or why these beliefs can function so differently in the many societies where they are found. Only minute analysis of data from societies in varied settings, with historical backgrounds of differing degrees of similarity, including those where totemism is absent as well as where it is present, can yield answers to the basic problem of the development and functioning of totemism in human society.

For many years, problems of classification dominated the study of language. The common designation of language as "isolating," "agglutinative," and "inflectional" that continues to be encountered, has been considered in our discussion of linguistics.

As was seen, this classification has proved no more satisfactory than other classifications drawn on the basis of types of grammatical forms, or complexity of structure, or any other single criterion. For such classifications, as Sapir says, "do not so much enfold the known languages in their embrace as force them down into narrow, straight-backed seats." He notes four reasons why attempts to classify languages have been unrewarding. First, to find a satisfactory basis of classification is most difficult. In the second place, to generalize from "a small number of selected languages," even so varied as Latin, Arabic, Turkish, Chinese and "perhaps Eskimo or Sioux as an after thought," is "to court disaster." Third, "The strong craving for a simple formula," such as that which gives to word structure the importance we have noted, has motivated those confronted with the many varieties of linguistic expression that speech forms manifest. Finally, Sapir cites the biases of an ethnocentrism that has caused students of language to judge languages different from their own as inferior tongues, and to classify them accordingly.[1] Sapir's conclusions regarding the kinds of classification that can aid in linguistic study are of great interest, for as was seen in this revised taxonomy, it is dynamics, rather than the inert forms themselves that dictate significant linguistic classification.

In the field of religion, to take another example, we are wont to read of entire belief-systems that are described as "animistic" or "monotheistic," or dominated by "fetichism." Experience, however, has taught us that such simplifications are barriers rather than aids to comprehension, for they mask the variation in worldview and ritual that marks the religious life of all peoples. Animistic beliefs are indeed widespread, but what do we mean when we categorize a people as "animistic"? Does this mean they have no conception of deities? That they do not practice magic? That they have no idea of impersonal power operating in the universe?

Our earlier discussion of the difficulties in drawing a definition of the phenomenon of religion makes the answer we must give to these questions self-evident. As categories to describe any religion, they are too simple, their validity deriving only from the fact that they do designate certain kinds of belief and behavior we call religious. The problems we seek to solve in this aspect of culture, however, concern the nature of the religious experience, the way in which its many manifestations are interrelated, its function in the total life of a people. These are dynamic problems that look beyond mere classification. It was in

[1] E. Sapir, 1921, pp. 129-31.

such dynamic terms, indeed, that the definition of religion as a process of "identification with a greater force or power" was drawn. The forms in which this process manifests itself must, as in every aspect of culture, afford the basis for analysis. The first step must be to reduce their variety to some kind of order. But, as we saw in examining this aspect of culture, the classification of religious forms is only a first step. Beyond form lies process, and here, as in all phases of the study of culture, the key to understanding is to be sought in dynamics, not descriptions.

Other classifications of cultural phenomena have proved unsatisfactory because they have arisen out of an ethnocentrism that dictates the lines along which they are drawn. One such type has been cited for language, where divergence from Indo-European forms has been the basis for classifying speech systems as "higher" or "lower" in a scale of value. Such classifications, however, run counter to the postulate of scientific method that precludes value-judgments as bases for classification; they are thus by that very fact rendered inacceptable. "Better" and "worse" are designations that, in scientific research, can only be defined in terms of specific ends. One chemical may be worse than another in that it kills while the other does not; as a chemical, however, it is to be analyzed as any other compound, not judged. In the field of culture, as long as a cultural institution, a linguistic system, or any other item functions satisfactorily in the lives of those who employ it, its position as a valid datum in the study of culture is established. It can only be "better" or "worse" in the mind of the student, and his patterns of thought will inevitably reflect the value-system in the course of his own enculturative experience.

2

Thus far, our discussion has made the following points:

1. Classification is an important first step in the study of data, but may not be regarded as an end in itself.

2. The factor of variation must be taken into account when classifying data, so that the resulting classifications will have a flexibility that those based on the concept of "type" cannot have.

3. To devise a series of categories of a complex phenomenon, based on a single criterion, is to over-simplify the data and thus vitiate the validity of the resulting classes.

4. To base classifications on value-judgments is to employ criteria that will not stand the test of scientific analysis which takes into account all the facts.

These propositions describe the limits within which acceptable classifications of data can be achieved. In turn, they lead us to the crucial point that classifications of the materials of culture, based on *form*, are but a step in achieving an understanding of *process;* that is, in achieving a comprehension of dynamics. This point bears importantly on another characteristic of the many classificatory systems that have been advanced in the study of culture, their *polarity*. In most classifications, that is, concepts are contrasted as extremes of a scale on which differing manifestations of a phenomenon may be placed. This was basic in all classificatory systems that developed out of attempts to place data in an evolutionary sequence. The economic sequence of food gathering, hunting, herding, agriculture was held to represent a change from simpler to more complex methods of gaining a livelihood. For Tylor, animism was contrasted with monotheism as ends of a series between which were placed what he held to be the earliest and latest forms. When the concept of impersonal power called "mana" was discovered among the Melanesians, it was given precedence in this sequence under the name "animatism," since it was held to exemplify an even earlier "stage" in the development of religion. In the same category is the continuum that has as its poles cultural extroversion and introversion, or that designates the extremes of cultural "types" as Apollonian and Dionysian.

This brings up the question of the *ideal type*. In classifying materials must one confine oneself to actual manifestations of the data in setting up series of classifications that are arranged from simple to complex, let us say, or from inward to outward orientation, or from large to small, or on the basis of any other paired opposites? Classifications arranged on a scale between polar extremes are, on analysis, found in most cases to derive essentially from conceptualizations of the data by the student. A culture that is officially monotheistic may on investigation reveal animatistic beliefs, plus belief in magic, and animistic beliefs as well. There is an advantage in separating data in terms of these categories as a first step toward furthering our understanding of their nature and functioning. But to place a culture where all are present on a scale ranging from animatism to monotheism is to reflect the position of the student rather than to describe the orientations and inner relations of the data themselves in the culture being studied.

The appeal of series arranged between polar conceptions lies in their logical character; for they are always logical. But if this is their strength, it is also their weakness. As has been stressed many times in earlier pages, the historical development of every culture has its own logic. The logic of history, however, does not admit of the neat arrangement of data between the opposites that classifications of this kind presuppose. Historical logic differs from culture to culture, from historic stream to historic stream. It is an inner logic that, to the observer who marks only the form it takes, may seem untidy, even illogical. It is, in short, a logic of process that, because of the factor of variability, is manifest in many forms. And since we here again encounter a point that is crucial for the comprehension of the nature of law in the study of culture, we will leave it for the moment, to return to the problem of classification in terms of cultural phenomena ranged on a scale between two polar concepts.

Let us consider one of the most carefully drawn and best-documented examples of this kind, in which all of the four criteria for a valid system of classification are complied with; the system that opposes the concept of the "folk society" to that of the "modern urbanized society." This mode of classifying cultures has been documented by first-hand investigation in Yucatan. The research has been carried out in accordance with careful field method, and has yielded important ethnographic data. The system is set up as a framework within which problems of dynamics can be attacked; it takes into full account the fact of cultural variation; it does not rely on a single criterion; no value-judgments are implicit in it. It is, however, based on criteria of form, and arranges the data on a scale between the polar concepts of differing types of societies. It thus affords an excellent opportunity for analyzing the aspect of the problem of classification in terms of polar types with which we are concerned at the moment.

The problem, as stated in the work in which it was first given full expression [2] is as follows: "The chief objective of this investigation is . . . to define differences in the nature of isolated homogeneous society, on the one hand, and mobile heterogeneous society, on the other, so far as these kinds of societies are represented in Yucatan." The documentation is drawn from four communities in the region, which vary in size and complexity as one moves from the city to sections where Euroamerican culture has least penetrated. The statement of the problem is expanded in these terms: "Are some of the differences among these four communities instances of what often happens when an isolated homogeneous society comes in contact with other societies?"

The characteristics held to mark a folk society are as follows: It is small and isolated. In contrast with its isolation from other groups is the intimacy of communication among its members.

[2] R. Redfield, 1941, pp. 17–18.

The people who make it up are much alike in physical type, no less than in their customary modes of behavior; they have a "strong sense of belonging together." There is not much division of labor in a folk society, but it is a group economically self-sufficient. It is "a little world off by itself." The basic sanctions of life are understood by all, and there is a minimum of criticism leveled against accepted modes of conduct; abstract thinking is not found to any extent. The social structures are tightly knit and family relationships are clearly distinguished. There is little legislation; custom is king. The sacred quality of life is outstanding and extends to such cultural items as food or utensils, which in urban culture are regarded as secular. Magic is another reflection of what is termed the folk mind. "The man of the folk society tends to make mental associations which are personal and emotional, rather than abstractly categoric or defined in terms of cause and effect." Finally, "there is no place for the motive of commercial gain. . . . There is no money and nothing is measured by any common denominator of value." [3]

In many respects these traits parallel those ascribed in the literature to peoples called "primitive," or what, in this book, has been defined as "nonliterate," especially when to the absence of writing is added the factor of nonindustrialization and an absence of mechanization. What, then, is the point at issue? It lies in the fact that while terms such as "primitive" or "nonliterate" are used to indicate, in a kind of anthropological shorthand, a condition that marks off some peoples from others, nothing more than this is connoted. It is important to seek to understand why some peoples have writing and others do not; but we do not set up an ideal category of the nonliterate society in order to contrast it with a literate one. The function of writing, in making for elaboration of culture, is a problem on which we have touched; but so is the problem of population size and its relation to specialization, which we have seen to be so important a factor in differences between cultures in one aspect after another.

There are small and large literate and nonliterate societies, wherein the degree of specialization varies greatly. Even in Guatemala, a country that is relatively close to Yucatan, as Redfield himself notes in the best tradition of scientific method, Tax has shown that "a stable society can be small, unsophisticated, homogeneous in beliefs and practices" and yet have "relationships impersonal, with formal institutions dictating the acts of individuals, with familial organization weak, with life secularized, and with

[3] R. Redfield, 1947, pp. 296–306.

individuals acting more from economic or other personal advantage than from any deep conviction or thought of the social good." [4] It is also to be noted that in discussions of the folk society, African data are nowhere taken into account. In West Africa, however, many urban communities are to be found that range from one hundred thousand inhabitants (the approximate size of Merida, Redfield's Yucatan "city") to over three hundred and fifty thousand. These populations have complex specialized economies exhibiting, as we have seen, the use of money and the presence of profit motivation. Yet in these cities relations are as personal as in any "folk society," and religion is the focal aspect of the culture. In short, here we have the anomaly—anomaly, that is, in terms of the concept of the folk society—of urban, *sacred*, communities.

The ideal type of any phenomenon, as most of those who work with such concepts point out, cannot by definition fit any particular case. The greater the number of criteria, the more difficult will be the applicability to any given instance. We must again point out that this follows from the fact that in such systems the orientation is in terms of categories based on *form*, rather than problems phrased in terms of *process*. Herein lies the real difference between the concept of "folk society" and of "nonliterate" peoples. The first is a category that dominates the data; the second is merely a convenient handle to describe materials destined to be examined in the light of differing situations that have arisen out of the historic process. Let us again emphasize that this particular polar ideal form of the "folk society" has been used here because it is a sophisticated and carefully documented example of the classificatory approach. That it, like others, leads to difficulties only strengthens the point made, namely, that classification must not be accorded too prominent a place in scientific study.

3

As we have seen, one reason why culture cannot be studied in the same way as organic and inorganic phenomena is the difficulty of obtaining laboratory controls. This is true not only of the study of culture, however. The astronomer or the historical geologist also deals with the data that cannot be manipulated. One can no more take a star or a mountain into a laboratory than one can take a human society. Recourse must be had in such disciplines to historic controls that manifest themselves in sequences of related events. In astronomy and geology the sequences are more

[4] S. Tax, 1939, p. 467.

regular than in culture. But the difference is one of degree and not of kind, just as is the greater difference—again, of degree and not kind—between historic controls and those that are set up in the laboratory of the physicist or the zoologist.

The difference between the student of culture and the laboratory investigator is not that the former is a kind of historian and the student who works in a laboratory is a scientist. It is, rather, that the laboratory of the student of culture *is* an historical one. It is the circumstance of historical happenings that, over the world, sets up situations that are used by the anthropologist to test his hypotheses in a way quite analogous to that in which the chemist sets up his test tubes or the physicist his balances, or the way in which the geologist seeks out stratified outcroppings of rock to ascertain the facts about the development of the earth. The anthropologist, it is true, deals with far more variables, and with variables much less subject to control, than do his fellow scientists. But crude as they may be, the controls—the historic situations in which at least a number of variables are held approximately constant—are there. To the extent these historic controls reduce the number of variables, to that degree they permit the anthropologist to use the circumstances of history to investigate, as any other scientist, the data with which he is concerned.

The distinction between science and history has long figured in discussions of anthropological theory, turning largely on the question whether anthropology is an historical or a scientific discipline. Such a formulation at once raises the problem whether the aims of anthropological study should be to recover the story of the development of human culture and of particular cultures, or whether the ends of research should be to disclose broad principles of form and structure and interrelations that will lead to the enunciation of valid "laws" of culture.

The degree to which these two approaches are held to be mutually irreconcilable alternatives or are regarded merely as facets of a single objective has varied from time to time, from scholar to scholar. In 1896, Boas formulated the point as follows:

> The immediate results of the historical method are . . . histories of the cultures of diverse tribes which have been the subject of study. I fully agree with those anthropologists who claim that this is not the ultimate aim of our science, because the general laws, though implied in such a description, cannot be clearly formulated nor their relative value appreciated without a thorough comparison of the manner in which they become manifest in different cultures. But I insist that the application of this

method is the indispensable condition of sound progress. . . . When we have cleared up the history of a single culture and understand the effects of the environment and the psychological conditions that are reflected in it we have made a step forward, as we can then investigate in how far the same causes were at work in the development of other cultures.[5]

Radcliffe-Brown has approached the problem of history versus science in a different manner. "Using the word science to mean the accumulation of exact knowledge," he says, "we may distinguish two kinds of scientific study, or two kinds of method. One of these is historical. The other method or type of study I should like to call the inductive, but there is a chance that the word might be misunderstood. I will therefore call it the method of generalization." He suggests that, in effect, anthropology must be thought of as encompassing two sub-disciplines. One he calls "ethnology," the other "comparative sociology." The first of these, he states, "is concerned with the relations of peoples," and is "a historical and not a generalizing science." "It is true," he says, "that in making their historical reconstructions the ethnologists often assume certain generalizations, but as a rule little or no attempt is made to base them on any wide inductive study. The generalizations are the postulates with which the subject starts, not the conclusions which it aims to attain as the result of the investigations undertaken." On the other hand, comparative sociology is "a science that applies the generalizing method of the natural sciences to the phenomena of the social life of man and to everything that we include under the term culture or civilization."[6]

It is apparent from the preceding discussion that the question whether anthropology is history or science does not present us with two mutually exclusive alternatives. Our task, therefore, is to weigh the two possibilities in terms of methods and achieved results, rather than to go to either extreme of the scale that moves from description to generalization.

We may observe how historic controls can be used in our search for generalizations, by following a problem wherein the resources of the laboratory of history are utilized. This concerns the investigation of the ways of life of Negro societies in varied parts of Africa and the New World, where historical relations can be ascertained. The "laboratory" is of vast geographic scope, and has a time-depth of from three to four centuries. It comprises

[5] F. Boas, 1940, pp. 278–9.
[6] A. R. Radcliffe-Brown, 1932, pp. 143–4.

the western part of Africa south of the Sahara, and the western part of the Congo Basin; it includes the eastern coastal strip of North America, most of the southeastern part of the United States, the West Indies, Central America and most of South America.

From the regions of Africa just named, great numbers of Negroes were brought to these reaches of the New World, where they made lives for themselves in accordance with the possibilities of their condition of servitude. They were not passive agents in the process, but the limits imposed on them in making their adjustment were of a special kind, that laid more specific and more severe restrictions on them than are ordinarily operative in contact between peoples. We have, then, a first of those "controls" that permits us, after the manner of science, to be more precise in analyzing the ensuing cultural changes.

The cultures of Africa from which the Negroes derived, like the cultures of any area, differ from each other to varying degrees. Beneath this variation in detail, however, are certain broad patterns in which they are quite similar. In some New World countries, for reasons that can be isolated and analyzed, certain of these specific African cultures came to predominate, and recognizable retentions of these customs are present. Elsewhere, especially where tribal conventions became increasingly difficult to maintain, the underlying patterns came to the fore. Under such conditions, generalized Africanisms, blended with the patterns of the dominant groups so subtly that only the most careful dissection can reveal historical derivations, are to be found. Yet despite all this, there is to be discerned an African base-line from which degree, direction, and type of cultural change are to be plotted.

The African retentions in New World Negro societies are found to vary in accordance with the dominant social, political, economic, and religious patterns of the European group with which the Negroes in a given New World area came into contact. In Brazil it was a Portuguese culture; in the rest of South America, in Central America, and in Cuba, a Spanish one; in Haiti and other islands of the Antilles and in Louisiana, a French way of life—all predominantly Catholic in religion. In most of the United States and much of the West Indies, the English predominated. In the Virgin Islands, Danish traditions, in part of the West Indies and in Dutch Guiana the culture of the Netherlands prevailed. All these latter countries are predominantly Protestant in religion. Each group, whether Catholic or Protestant, had its own set of attitudes toward the Negroes. The economic situation, though principally based on a plantation system, was by no means a constant. Not only did skilled Negro artisans everywhere constitute an elite, but in some regions of South American the Negroes did not work on plantations at all but were imported to labor in the mines.

The basic apparatus set up for this research was an integrated program of historical and ethnological investigation. The base-line of African culture for our analysis had first to be established. This was done in two ways. Studies of the cultures of New World Negroes pointed to certain regions of Africa because they were found to have the same or similar institutions, conventions, often details of custom, such as specific names of places, persons, and deities found among specific African tribes. Field research in these regions of Africa provided further data, which brought to light Africanisms hitherto overlooked in the New World. At the same time, the historical documents dealing with the slave trade, and the writings of travelers and others who recorded their impressions of life in the New World during the days of slavery, made it possible to establish the historical validity of the relations that the comparison of ethnographic findings in African and New World Negro communities had revealed. These documents also were found to give a firm historical record of the ways of life of the Europeans who came to the New World. In telling of their customs, and particularly in their accounts of plantation life, these documents yielded much insight into the nature and mechanisms of the early phases of those adjustments to the New World setting that have become established in the present-day scene.

With the base-line from which to plot cultural change established, the next step was to organize the materials according to some comprehensive scheme of classification. In accordance with the principles stated above, the scheme employed in classifying the materials of New World Negro cultures was drawn in terms of the historical framework of the problem. That is, a *scale of intensity of Africanisms* was set up on which the data were ranged, country by country, from most African to least—that is, to most European. That American Indian elements had to be taken into account in analyzing the New World scene in general was recognized, but those were found to enter significantly only in restricted instances.

The classification of the data shown in the accompanying table reflects the working hypotheses and methodological devices out of which it derives. The fact that the degree of retention is given by aspect of culture rather than in terms of whole cultures represents a recognition of the variability of cultural elements not only in form, but in the extent to which, in a given historical situation, they are subject to change. This is the hypothesis that

SCALE OF INTENSITY OF NEW WORLD AFRICANISMS[7]
(Only the greatest degree of retention is indicated for each group.)

	Technology	Economic Life	Social Organization	Non-kinship Institutions	Religion	Magic	Art	Folklore	Music	Language
Guiana (bush)	b	b	a	a	a	a	b	a	a	b
Guiana (Paramaribo)	c	c	b	c	a	a	e	a	a	c
Haiti (peasant)	c	b	b	c	a	b	d	a	a	c
Haiti (urban)	e	d	c	c	b	b	e	a	a	c
Brazil (Bahia)	d	d	b	d	a	a	b	a	a	a
Brazil (Porto Alegre)	e	e	c	d	a	a	e	?	a	c
Brazil (north—urban)	e	d	c	e	a	b	e	d	a	b
Brazil (north—rural)	c	c	b	e	c	b	e	b	b	d
Jamaica (Maroons)	c	c	b	b	b	a	e	a	a	c
Jamaica (Morant Bay)	e	c	b	b	a	a	e	a	a	a
Jamaica (other)	e	d	d	d	c	b	e	a	b	c
Trinidad (Toco)	e	d	c	c	c	b	e	b	b	d
Trinidad (Port-of-Spain)	e	d	c	b	a	a	e	b	a	c
Cuba	e	d	c	b	a	a	b	b	a	a
Honduras (Black Carib)*	c	c	c	c	c	a	e	b	?	e
Virgin Islands	e	d	c	d	e	c	?	b	?	d
Gulla Islands	c	c	c	d	c	b	e	a	b	b
United States (rural South)	d	e	c	d	c	c	e	c	b	e
United States (North)	e	e	c	d	c	c	e	d	b	e

a: very African
b: quite African
c: somewhat African
d: a little African
e: trace of African custom, or absent
?: no report
* Carib Indian elements are strong in this culture.

was explored in discussing the problem of cultural focus and cultural drift. It derived, in turn, from the assumption that culture can be studied as the series of related but independent variables we term aspects. Again, in this table the fact is recognized that in

[7] Adapted from M. J. Herskovits, 1945b, p. 14.

the New World, local differences must be taken into account; that larger regions must be treated in terms of their sub-areas. This is a reflection of the ecological approach to culture, as worked out in the many distribution studies that have established the importance of the local variant out of which the larger units are conceptually to be built up. Finally, and perhaps most important of all, is the fact that this table represents a scale of intensity of Africanisms only as far as the *greatest degree of retention* is concerned. This derives from the acceptance of the hypothesis of individual variability within a culture.

The broad attack on the particular problem of New World Negro acculturation that has been sketched is thus seen to afford a method whereby accepted postulates can be tested, and new hypotheses devised on which to base further investigation. The problem, as it has been outlined, has in the main been concerned with the cultural matrix out of which the observed cultural variations from the basic patterns have arisen. The resulting data thus set the stage for a further attack, in terms of the new constants that can be employed as further controls in the analysis of the differential behavior patterns, and in terms of the differing degrees of individual variation to be found in these Negro societies of the New World. The investigation can also proceed to the study of similar historically related sets of cultures elsewhere,[8] so as to test in these situations the comparability of the dynamic processes, and the generalizations derived from them, found in the historic culture sequence examined here.

A framework analogous to that used for the analysis of the mechanisms of cultural change and their expression in new cultural forms in the relation between African and New World Negro cultures can be paralleled in other "laboratory" situations, elsewhere in the world. The Jesup North Pacific Expedition not only studied the historic relation between the cultures bordering on the North Pacific, but had also as its purpose a comprehension of how the elements common to the area had been changed as they traveled from people to people. The study of the Plains Sun Dance treated of tribes living in a restricted area, between which diffusion could be assumed, so that the resulting variation in cultural elements could be analyzed—the fundamental hypothesis thus being that the phenomena under examination derived from a single historic stream.

[8] As, for example, the approach of G. M. Foster, 1951, to the study of the relation between Spanish culture and the Hispano-American cultures of the New World.

That later acculturation studies could be carried on with assurances of the historic relations involved rather than assumptions of them, only meant that the conclusions drawn could be the more securely based on historic fact. Redfield's study of cultural differentials in four related communities, though conceived in terms of the establishment of ideal classifications of culture, may be thought of as falling in this category. We have seen how Eggan's study in the Philippines had to do with a series of historically related groups. Of a similar nature is Hunter's analysis of the Pondo in southeastern Africa, consisting of comparative studies of the life of this people on the reserves, as farm workers, and in the towns.[9] In his analysis of the relation between personality and culture, Hallowell combines the use of ethnohistory with projective psychological techniques for assessing the underlying similarities between related Algonkian and neighboring peoples.[10]

It is important that in most studies made of cultures where the historic factors are under control, the resulting generalizations are of a dynamic character. They are, indeed, to be differentiated in just this way from the generalizations derived from the use of the older comparative method wherein similarities between cultural elements or relations were studied without reference to whether or not they eventuated from the play of like historic forces. Such earlier generalizations are preponderantly concerned with cultural forms.

It has been just such generalizations that have given the anthropologist the unwelcome task of repeatedly questioning the conclusions of his fellow social scientists by reference to cross-cultural data. This use of cross-cultural materials, more than anything else, has sounded the death knell of theories about "human nature." "Human nature" was that chameleonlike force in man variously held to cause him to seek profits, or to be a monogamist or to have polygamous tendencies, or to strive to better his standard of living, or to do any of those things that seemed obviously basic to students of Euroamerican society. The anthropologist, however, beginning, "But, in Kamchatka . . ."—or in Senegal or Ecuador or Pukapuka—would proceed to give instances where men and women, presumably activated by this same "human nature," eschewed profits, or were polygamist or monogamist, or seemed to be content with their lot. It can, indeed, be said that the philosophy of cultural relativism, which has come to dominate most anthropological thought and, indeed, social science in gen-

[9] M. Hunter, 1936.
[10] A. I. Hallowell, 1947, pp. 195–225.

eral, had its beginnings in the refutations of "human nature" that mark the literature of cultural anthropology.

4

If the actual course of events in human history represents only one possible development, can we encompass the alternatives in any formulation that will permit the study of culture to achieve the end of scientific research, prediction? Answers to this question have ranged from an insistence that the regularities in culture already to be discerned justify the development of those generalizations that are a first step toward prediction, to an emphasis on the unique historical character of every culture, and the conclusion that to discern regularity in the diversity of custom is a hopeless task.

Yet is this dichotomy, a kind of rewording of the problem of science versus history in the study of culture, really an accurate statement of the alternatives? The fact that we have found, in the case of history as against science, that there is no opposition, that the scientist can use historical sequences as an aid in developing his generalizations, indicates other possible resolutions of the difficulty. It was seen that classification is an essential step in the analysis of data; and that, as long as the classes of data hold to the facts and do not go beyond them, they are an aid in clarifying materials and preparing the way for further analysis. In the same manner, we have seen how history provides the laboratory in which the scientist of culture works, and how basic insights into the nature and processes of culture have been obtained by utilizing these resources.

The resolution of the apparent dilemma that arises when we stress the uniqueness of each culture can, therefore, be formulated in the following terms: *Cultural forms are the expression of unique sequences of historical events, but they are the result of underlying processes that represent constants in human experience.* This means that "laws" of culture must be statements of process. Their results are expressed in the most diverse forms, which are alike only as they represent the end results of the play of similar processes.[11] Thus we may say that borrowing will result from contact between peoples. But what in a given case will be borrowed— whether material objects or ideas, whether technology or religion —and in what amount, will differ from one case to the next. We can, of course, go further than this. Calling on such concepts as

[11] For an application of this principle to the cross-cultural analysis of dreams, see D. Eggan, 1952, pp. 479-80.

focus and reinterpretation, we can generalize that, in a particular case, borrowing will be selective, and that elements taken over by one people from another will assume new forms that are determined by the pre-existing cultural matrix.

Problems of dynamics, it should be made clear, are not the exclusive domain of cultures in contact. They may be studied within a single culture, analyzed at a given period in its history, as well as by research into the results of contacts between cultures, or of the factors that have operated to make for retentions and reinterpretations of cultures lying within a given historic stream. Herein are to be found the most important contributions of the functionalist approach and of the modern use of the comparative method. The interrelations between the institutions of a culture and the manner in which they function so as to affect the totality of a culture are not inert, fixed, and static. Inner relations are as dynamic as outer ones. There is no more important approach to an understanding of the nature and processes of culture than the analysis of how one element in culture, by its very form, affects other elements with which it is in association.

The number of "laws" that frame the research of anthropologists is actually very considerable. Many of these are so fundamental that they are largely taken for granted. Such a "law" is that which holds culture to be learned and not inborn. The fact that culture is learned leads to the generalization of cultural borrowing which, taken together with its subsidiary refinements, has played so important a role in the study of culture. From this principle, also, has been derived the hypothesis of enculturation as the mechanism whereby cultural stability and change is achieved. That culture responds to its natural setting in accordance with the forms of its technology is another such generalization; or, in the field of economics, that specialization increases with the increase of the surplus represented by the degree of production in excess of subsistence requirements of a people. When we say kinship structure influences behavior toward blood and affinal relatives, or that religion is the reflection of a world-view—that man makes his gods in his own image—or that folklore functions as an educational device, we are again only setting up generalizations that guide our approach toward the study of culture and our conception of how human beings respond to it.[12]

Once full account is taken of the fact of variation, then the reconciliation of range in cultural form with regularity in process is well in hand. It submits the phenomenon of culture, whatever

[12] For a critique of this point of view, see D. Bidney, 1953b, pp. 275-9.

its manifestations, to scrutiny after the manner of the established methodological procedures of all science. Even such a concept as historic accident is seen to fall into place as one of the armory of weapons employed by the student of culture. For the accidental occurrence that alters the course of the development of a body of tradition is, from this point of view, no accident. It is but another expression of the fact that the experience of no people duplicates that of any other—that is, that the course of history varies as it is expressed in the way of life of one group after another.

Just as we study culture in terms of accepted generalizations that are in reality more numerous than we make explicit, so prediction has been achieved to a greater extent than is commonly suggested. The analysis of the enculturative process leads to the concept of the regularity of behavior within a society. Where a degree of regularity is present, to that degree prediction can be achieved. Therefore, the generalization that through the learning process the developing human organism becomes a being whose behavior is overwhelmingly in consonance with the sanctioned patterns of his culture, leads to an acceptance of the further generalization that we can predict the behavior of the individual conditioned to live in accordance with these patterns. This does not mean that every detail of behavior can be predicted; the fact of probability and the resulting variation must always be taken into account. We can, however, not only say than an Australian aborigine will, in a given familial situation, react differently than a Crow Indian or a Mushongo of the Congo Basin, or a banker in any city of the Western world, but we can also predict, within fairly narrow limits, what his behavior will be.

The degree to which prediction can be envisaged with reasonable accuracy becomes appreciably less as we move into those situations where cross-cultural factors enter. Yet even here, workable propositions can be stated. Given two cultures in contact, for example, it is apparent that borrowing will not go beyond the limits of form described by the differences between the elements and institutions of the cultures concerned. Moreover, it should be possible to predict, with some degree of validity, wherein the two particular cultures will give way, and where they will resist change the most. Such predictions depend largely on how precise is our knowledge of the situation being studied, not only as concerns the outer forms of the cultures involved but also the inner sanctions that activate the dynamics of each culture party to the contact.

For a time, however, prediction of cultural change will undoubtedly be more successful within cultures than cross culturally. Predictability will become greater only as we are able to increase the degree of probability that a given process, operating within the framework of a particular situation, will eventuate in certain forms rather than in others. But, in the final analysis, the forms themselves, as noted by the student, will always be variable. It is thus the task of the scientist concerned with culture to probe beneath form to process. To this end, he must utilize the laboratory situations provided by the many sequences of unique historic events to formulate and test those generalizations that, as process, reveal the regularities in culture that make of it a subject for scientific analysis.

Part Five

Conclusion

Chapter **Twenty-nine**

Anthropology in a World Society

The problems that anthropologists have studied were, until recently, remote from the concerns of everyday life. Theoretical preoccupation with cultural evolution, or diffusion, or the description of cultural curiosities could hardly be reconciled with problems of conflict and adjustment that were pressing for attention both within expanding cultures and where cultures were in contact. The desire of anthropologists to study only "uncontaminated" ways of life, and a consequent obliviousness to the manifestations of cultural change that went on about them, gave to their work a quality not unlike that of laboratory investigations in the exact and natural sciences.

This was science at its purest. Those who studied nonliterate man, and those others who had daily dealings with him, not only had no contact with each other, but avoided one another. Official policies regarding native peoples were determined, often with the best intent, without any consultation with anthropologists who were in a position to know what the effects of a given measure might be. On the other hand, the anthropologists, the only persons who might speak for the native, remained silent. Their search for the fundamental principles of human civilization kept them far removed from the hubbub of public debate, even though, as individuals, they might resent the effects of procedures that were demoralizing the natives they knew.

With time, however, it became increasingly understood that to implement practical policies required knowledge of native customs and insights into the sanctions of native life. Indirect rule, a device for colonial administration that placed the immediate direction of tribal affairs in the hands of tribal rulers, under the supervision of colonial officers, called for knowledge of native law, native rules of land tenure, native political institutions, native social structures that the anthropologically untrained political officer was unequipped to obtain. At first, such officers were "seconded" as government anthropologists after a period of special training, and men like R. S. Rattray and C. K. Meek and P. A. Talbot were enabled to study the peoples of the Gold Coast and Nigeria, or F. E. Williams the peoples of New Guinea. Later, C. E. Mitchell, in East Africa, tried the experiment of creating a team of an academically trained anthropologist and a political officer as a step in the utilization of practical anthropology, after a series of articles in the journal *Africa* in which he debated the problem with Malinowski.

Similarly, in the United States, the policy of the Indian Office after 1933, which became committed to a program of respect for Indian tribal patterns while integrating Indian societies into the socio-economic matrix of American life in general, called for information not available in previous studies and gave rise to new kinds of research. The established methods by which anthropologists had been able to penetrate beneath cultural form to cultural sanction were called on to provide the base for implementing policies which would place the ordering of Indian affairs in the hands of the Indians. These studies came more and more to be made by professional anthropologists, who either joined the Indian Service or were attached to it for varying periods of time as consultants and research experts. They covered economic and political studies that are the primary interest of the administrator, the fields of religion, art, systems of value, and personality structure, as well as native patterns of education and other modes of social control.

This approach spread over the Americas. In Mexico, Central America, and South America, government officers in charge of departments touching on the lives of the vast Indian populations there introduced policies of training and using experts in cross-cultural study. In Mexico a center was established for the express purpose of furthering the study of indigenous peoples of the

Americas, and perfecting techniques of integrating these peoples into the total life of the countries where they live. This movement not only consciously aimed at welding scientific findings and administration, but it took the further step of incorporating the natives in it. This led to the appointment of Indians as reservation superintendents in the United States, and is manifest in the growing number of Indian members of government departments dealing with Indian affairs in Latin America.

In the United States, the application of the findings of anthropology to matters of practical concern did not stop with the use of anthropological concepts, techniques, and points of view in attacking the Indian problem. It was argued, rather, that anthropological methods might be applied to problems of the literate majority groups as well. Problems of personal relations in industry were studied in an initial effort stimulated by the introduction of anthropology into the Harvard University Graduate School of Business Administration. In 1941 the Society for Applied Anthropology was formed, having as its ends "the promotion of scientific investigation of the principles controlling the relations of human beings to one another, and the encouragement of the wide application of these principles to practical problems."

The problems studied by these applied anthropologists are on the whole indistinguishable from those that are investigated by students in social psychology, sociology, personnel research and related fields. This is of no importance in itself, except insofar as it underscores the concern of this approach with social problems and what, to all intent, is the exclusion of other cultural phenomena included in the total range of human learned behavior. It can be reasoned that in studies conducted in a single culture, much can be taken for granted that must be made explicit in other cultures. The danger in such studies is that, as anthropological projects, the lessons of method and the conceptual postulates that derive from cross-cultural research will be lost sight of in the complexities of the problems within our own society. Nor can we overlook the dangers that the anthropologist investigating interpersonal relations in industry may fail to take into account the economic stresses that those who deal with industry as a whole accept as primary.

The development of applied anthropology along all the lines sketched above was accelerated by the circumstance of global warfare. The Axis powers, during the tense prewar years of the 1930's, were quite alive to the potentialities of using anthropological techniques in the colonial situation and were prepared to employ them among native peoples who might come under their rule. They therefore instituted training centers for future colonial rulers, in which ethnology and comparative linguistics had a prominent place. The racist dogmas of the Nazi political creed also brought physical anthropologists into the arena of public debate as never before.

That anthropological science was put to use in all these cases is an historic fact that must, however, be placed beside the complementary fact that distortions of their science were fought by the majority of anthropologists everywhere, in many cases at the expense of liberty and even life. The uses to which those who control power put the findings of science are, unfortunately, beyond the control of scientists. The findings of scientists, when published, are a matter of public record. How to obviate the misuse of these findings, as was done here in the instance of anthropology, or as is done in utilizing the work of the physical scientists for destructive rather than constructive purposes, is a major problem of our society. We can here but note that it applies to anthropology no less than to any other discipline.

Among the powers opposed to the Axis, not until the actual onset of war brought problems that anthropologists alone could cope with were they called to active participation. Especially in the United States, where experience in large-scale contact with peoples of greatly different ways of life was relatively slight, was it essential to have expert aid in lessening the frictions. Conquest brought the need to govern peoples with differing cultures, whose conventions could not be flouted. Occupation officers had to be trained to respect customs far different from any, perhaps, they had even heard of. Anthropological linguists were called on to devise methods of teaching men who had never spoken any language but their own how to handle a foreign idiom. Native peoples in tropical countries unaffected by the war, as in South and Central America, had to be induced to work to provide raw materials when normal sources of supply were cut off. At home, the problem of adapting the people to unaccustomed items of diet had to be faced, and was faced as a problem of the type which, in this book, is called re-enculturation.

The growing sense of urgency for instituting some form of supernational control, as a measure to prevent future wars, extended the call for anthropological participation in practical affairs. But the implications of this participation are many, and the questions they raise have been found to be far more numerous than the answers that have been given them. We may, therefore, look into some of these questions in assessing the contributions anthropology can be expected to make in a world society.

2

In most of the exact and natural sciences, the realization of the social responsibility of the scientist to see to it that his findings are not misused has added a third tier to the existing structure whose base is fundamental research and teaching, and whose second story is the application, in the engineering sense, of the results of scientific investigation to the solution of practical problems. Anthropologists, together with other scientists, have newly awakened to this sense of social responsibility. But in their case the second story that did not exist for them in earlier years has likewise been added to the single-storied structure of fundamental research they had erected. It follows, then, that the questions raised in this chapter take a special form, and that debate over the issues they present involves the clarification of points that in other disciplines have come to be taken for granted.

As for the basic contribution of anthropology to our knowledge of man and his works, there is little argument except over questions of method and theory. All who accept the fundamental postulates of science and admit the need for scientific analysis of all aspects of the natural world and human experience in it take this for granted. That anthropologists have not studied more peoples or have not encompassed in their research a greater range of cultures and problems inherent in their study is a matter of lack of available personnel, not of a failure to realize the need, or of a desire to study the problems. That the efforts of anthropologists have been effective is apparent in the steady development of the resources of the discipline. This is to be seen in all phases of anthropological science—in the increase in the available data, in refinements in method, and in the constantly growing number of anthropologists equipped to carry on the necessary researches. Quietly, without debate, in centers of learning, in museums over the world, this process goes on. New cultures are under investigation, new problems are being studied, while the training of students in the basic concepts of anthropology makes these known ever more widely, and leads to the more intensive disciplining in anthropological method and theory necessary for those who contemplate making anthropology a career.

This, it must be repeated, is fundamental. But the issues whether or not anthropology should be applied to the solution of practical problems, and how the use of its findings should be controlled, have been the subject of much discussion. The problem of applying anthropology has been made the more complicated by the fact that, as has been indicated, this issue posed for anthropologists, for the first time, the question of pure as against applied science. Now this is a commonplace in the natural and exact disciplines. The biologist does not attempt to do the work of the physician who draws on his laboratory findings. The builder of bridges uses the work of physicists, but would not attempt to carry on their researches. Anthropologists, however, have attempted to do basic research and applied anthropology at the same time, with resulting confusion not only regarding the division of labor, but also concerning fundamental values, ultimate aims, and the ethics of anthropological science.

Anthropological contributions to the solution of practical problems can take various forms. Anthropologists can advise, as official members of a government organization, regarding the solution of problems of immediate concern. Questions of native rules of land ownership, or of status prerogatives, or of religious customs may be analyzed by them so as to permit an administrator better to comprehend the complexities of a situation with which he must deal in reaching a decision. Of broader scope is the evidence anthropologists can assemble on larger questions of policy, such as the degree to which, in a world economic and political system, varied cultures can be integrated so that a minimum of friction will follow when cultures that have quite different orientations are in intimate contact. On the broadest plane of all, the most immediately related to the cross-cultural research that yields the basic data of anthropology, is the investigation of those general principles of cultural form and dynamics without a knowledge of which it is impossible to achieve the world-wide adjustment of different peoples.

All these, of course, involve a weighing of ends by the anthropologist—not as anthropologist, but as citizen. There are few anthropologists who work with organs of government who do not have a conviction that in this way they can lessen friction and minimize the demoralization that has too often marked the history of native peoples under Euroamerican rule. The anthropologists who have felt that anthropology has no place in such a system point to the palliatives that take the place of reorientations they feel will alone restore a sense of dignity and worth to natives who have lost the freedom to determine their own destiny. Those who take this position hold that the expropriation of land, the lack of adequate economic return for labor, and the reduction of free peoples to conditions of degradation resulted from the play of historical factors, especially of an economic order, that no amount of expert advice could alter. They point, for example, to the spread of the American frontier with the ruthless wiping out of large portions of the Indian population as a prelude to the beggary to which the remaining tribesmen have been reduced.

On the other hand, where policies toward native peoples and minority groups with whom the anthropologist works support the ends in which he can believe, it is understandable that he often feels that he can not only respond when called on by administrative agencies for advice, but is under obligation to make his expert knowledge available to them. Thus, in the United States, anthropologists gave their aid to the Indian Bureau when an earlier policy of calculated demoralization of Indians gave way to a policy of building on pre-existing patterns so as to integrate these people into American life by restoring to them economic independence and cultural autonomy. In similar fashion, the policies of the Mexican government, pointed toward achieving comparable ends, have received similar anthropological support.

It is in the nature of the case that the anthropologist is best fitted to see the strains and stresses of underprivileged groups, or of natives who no longer control their own lives. He sees these stresses and strains from the less pleasant, underside of the situations in which they live. He sees the problems of the native as no administrator, however gifted, can possibly see them. Where, then, he is in a position to aid in obtaining for the natives he knows some reinstatement of the human rights they have been deprived of, he customarily welcomes the opportunity. As one who has the relation to native peoples peculiarly his by reason of the nature of his work among them, his biases as a human being are usually what they would be expected to be. He is their friend and, where possible, their spokesman in the high places where their voices would not otherwise be heard.

A further objection that is raised to the participation by anthropologists, as such, in the solution of practical issues must be considered before we leave this aspect of the matter. This concerns the significance, for anthropology itself, of the development of practical or applied anthropology. Does not the diversion of anthropologists to the doing of the tasks applied anthropology has come to have assigned to it take them away from the study of problems of the nature and functioning of culture that should be a first charge against anthropological effort? Evans-Pritchard, who argues for the appointment of anthropologists to the staffs of colonial administrations, leaves no room for doubt about the relative place of pure as against applied anthropological science:

> How should an anthropologist best employ his knowledge and, which comes to very much the same thing, his time? I would suggest that he can best use his knowledge for the purpose for which it was collected, namely the solution of scientific problems. . . . An anthropologist within his own scientific field will use the knowledge he acquires by research to solve anthropological problems and these may have no practical significance whatever. It may be held that it is laudable for an anthropologist to investigate practical problems. Possibly it is, but if he does so he must realize that he is no longer acting within the anthropological field.[1]

Another discussion of the topic runs:

> Both administration and science recognize that the more knowledge there is available for use, the better can be its application. Science consists of a graded series of abstractions from the more particular to the more general; it attempts to become more and more general, supposing that the more general a proposition is, the more it takes into account all phenomena, the more valid it is. . . . For example, if one wishes to apply anthropological knowledge to a given Indian tribe, science would hold that knowledge about that tribe is less important than knowledge about all Indians, or generalizations about human nature and society. . . . It is a misapprehension that . . . the anthropologist is primarily concerned with the community he is studying. Typically, and ideally, he is not. He studies that community to gain understanding of all communities, and of culture and society in general.[2]

In a word, as a scientist, the anthropologist must achieve that detachment toward his data that is the mark of the scientific search for truth. In this search he must realize, as it has been stated elsewhere, that

> the search for truth must come before all else. The debt we owe the society that supports us must be made in terms of long-time payments, in our fundamental contributions toward an understanding of the nature and processes of culture and, through this, to the solution of some of our own basic problems.[3]

3

It is from this point of view that the greatest contribution of anthropology must be envisaged. If a world society is to emerge

[1] E. E. Evans-Pritchard, 1946, p. 93.
[2] S. Tax, 1945, pp. 26-7, 28.
[3] M. J. Herskovits, 1936, p. 222.

from the conflict of ethnocentrisms we call nationalism, it can only be on a basis of live and let live, a willingness to recognize the values that are to be found in the most diverse ways of life.[4] Surely, though at times slowly, anthropology has moved toward documenting this position. The fact of cultural variability, the existence of common values expressed in different modes of behavior, the devotion of every people to its way of life—these, and many other aspects of human existence have gradually fallen into place to form a pattern for tolerance and understanding. Just as the physical anthropologists have ceaselessly combatted the concept of racial superiority, so cultural anthropology has, both explicitly and implicitly in the presentation of its data, documented the essential dignity of all human cultures.

Problems of world-wide scope, such as are presented by the need to integrate nonindustrial peoples in a world economic order, must be attacked in terms of cross-cultural analysis. To dismiss a nonindustrial tribal group as incompetent to direct their lives because their ways are different from those of the peoples who dominate the world scene is to generate resentments that may be resolved only with future bloodshed. Anthropologists are in a position to demonstrate how a people react to foreign control, even as they lie inert and powerless. They can see, all too clearly, how quickly customs can go underground or, if they do not, how demoralization can be the lot of those who experience the frustrations that go with impotence in the face of an assault on deep-seated, accepted values and goals.

Almost a laboratory study of this was afforded in the assault on democracy launched by the fascist powers during the 1930's. Democracy, it was held, was decadent, outworn. The doctrine that the individual is paramount, that the state is the servant of the citizen, was declared to be false and perverted. Rather the individual was held to exist for the state, which had no need to respect the integrity of the personalities of those who did not obey when summoned. Thus the very bases of democratic society were assailed—loudly, tauntingly, and with a challenge to the ultimate test of force. Heavily armed, the totalitarian powers continuously extended their scope and, with concentrated and calculated derision, pointed to the indecision of the democracies.

Now it is of the essence of democracy that it is an essentially peaceful way of life; that war is not glorified but something abhorred, and to be avoided save as a last resort, in self-preservation.

[4] Cf. the "Statement on Human Rights" submitted to the United Nations by the American Anthropological Association, 1947.

How could a democratic philosophy, however, maintain itself in a world where war, not peace, was the declared aim of the most heavily armed nations, with governmental systems geared efficiently to a work of destruction that is the antithesis of the democratic ideal? It was a question insoluble in terms of accepted values, as the resulting bewilderment about proper courses of action revealed. Debates concerning pacifism and nonintervention aligned persons of widely differing points of view on the same side against those with whom ordinarily they would be in agreement. Only the onset of war, the resolution to put conviction to the test of force, cleared the air, and answered the doubts of millions.

In this instance, the reaction had enough power to repel the threat. Native peoples, opposing cannon with bows and arrows, have had no choice but to submit. Yet the anthropologist, as one who studies the meaning of a way of life to those who live it, need not depart from his devotion to pure science when he points out the dangers to world peace that are inherent in repressed resentments, in the force of rising native nationalisms that are a reaction to the depreciation and suppression of a people's culture. It is his contribution, as the scientific student of cultures other than his own, to underscore the need, in a world society, to give every people cultural autonomy. It is he who must point out that customs foreign to one society may be treasured by another, or stress the importance of the fact that cultural differences are not indications of cultural inferiority. Recognizing that the processes of history are not reversible, he can nonetheless, by his data, demonstrate the psychocultural mechanisms that make inevitable the devotion of every people to their culture, and he can make plain to statesmen that it is possible to reconcile cultural autonomy with participation in a world economic and political order.

Anthropology can make another, even more far-reaching contribution to this end. The quotation that opens this book, though cast in retrospect, is as true when applied to the present or projected into the future. "Each fresh start on the never-ending quest of *Man as he ought to be*," it will be remembered it runs, "has been the response of theory to fresh facts about *Man as he is.* . . . Meanwhile, the dreams and speculations of one thinker after another—even dreams and speculations which have moved nations and precipitated revolutions—have ceased to command men's reason, when they have ceased to accord with their knowledge." Irresistibly, the knowledge about man and his works that anthropologists have amassed has continued to force the revision of our ideas about the value of human ways of living, and to re-orient policy and the implementation of policy.

Cultural relativism, which whether in implicit or explicit form dominates the thinking behind moves toward building a world society, exemplifies the point made in our quotation. It is a philosophy based on the facts that throw into bold relief the hard core of *similarities* between cultures that have been consistently overlooked in favor of the emphasis laid on cultural differences. These facts show that every society has values and imposes restraints that cannot be dismissed, even though they differ from one's own. Cultural relativism, which stresses the universals in human experience as against ethnocentric concepts of absolute values, in no wise gives over the restraints that every system of ethics exercises over those who live in accordance with it. To recognize that right, and justice, and beauty may have as many manifestations as there are cultures is to express tolerance, not nihilism. As anthropology's greatest contribution, this position puts man yet another step on his quest of what he ought to be, in the light of the facts, as we know them, about what in his unity, no less than in his diversity, he is.

Bibliographies

and

Index

I. Literature Cited

The following list contains the titles of those books and papers that have actually been cited in the preceding pages. For each item the name of the author, date of publication, title of book or article, and place of publication are given. Where more than one title published by the same author in a given year is included, the items are identified by the letter following the year, as "1942a," "1942b," and so forth.

ACKERKNECHT, ERWIN H., 1942: "Primitive Medicine and Culture Pattern." *Bulletin of the History of Medicine*, Vol. XII, pp. 545–74.

ALLEE, W. C., 1938: *The Social Life of Animals*. New York.

AMERICAN ANTHROPOLOGICAL ASSOCIATION, Executive Board, 1947: "Statement on Human Rights." *American Anthropologist*, Vol. XLIX, pp. 539–43.

ASCH, SOLOMON E., 1952: *Social Psychology*. New York.

ASHTON, HUGH, 1952: *The Basuto*. London.

BACON, ELIZABETH, 1946: "A Preliminary Attempt to Determine the Culture Areas of Asia." *Southwestern Journal of Anthropology*, Vol. II, pp. 117–32.

BACON, ELIZABETH and HUDSON, A. E., 1945: "Asia (Ethnology)." *Encyclopaedia Britannica*, Vol. II, pp. 523–5.

BALFOUR, H., 1895: *The Evolution of Decorative Art*. London.

BARBOUR, GEORGE H., 1949: "Ape or Man? An Incomplete Chapter of Human Ancestry from South Africa." *Ohio Journal of Science*, Vol. XLIX (reprinted in *Yearbook of Physical Anthropology*, 1949, New York, pp. 117–33).

BARNETT, H. G., 1942: "Invention and Culture Change." *American Anthropologist*, Vol. XLIV, pp. 14–30.

1953: *Innovation: the Basis of Cultural Change*. New York.

BARTLETT, F. C., 1937: "Psychological Methods and Anthropological Problems." *Africa*, Vol. X, pp. 401–20.

BARTON, R. F., 1919: "Ifugao Law." University of California, *Publications in American Archaeology and Ethnology*, Vol. XV, No. 1, pp. 1–186.

1922: "Ifugao Economics." University of California, *Publications in American Archaeology and Ethnology*, Vol. XV, No. 5, pp. 385–446.

BASCOM, W. R., 1939: "The Legacy of an Unknown Nigerian Donatello." *London Illustrated News*, Vol. CIV, pp. 592–4.

1948: "Ponape Prestige Economy." *Southwestern Journal of Anthropology*, Vol. IV, pp. 211–21.

BEALS, R. L., 1946: "Chéran: a Sierra Tarascan Village." Smithsonian Institution, Institute of Social Anthropology, *Publication* No. 2.

BENEDICT, R., 1923: "The Concept of the Guardian Spirit in North America." American Anthropological Association, *Memoir* No. 29.

— 1934: *Patterns of Culture.* Boston and New York.

— 1938: "Continuities and Discontinuities in Cultural Conditioning." *Psychiatry*, Vol. I, pp. 161–7.

BIDNEY, D., 1953a: "The Concept of Value in Modern Anthropology," in *Anthropology Today* (A. L. Kroeber, ed.), pp. 682–99. Chicago.

— 1953b: *Theoretical Anthropology.* New York.

BLACKWOOD, B., 1935: *Both Sides of Buka Passage.* Oxford.

BLEEK, D. F., 1929: "Bushman Folklore." *Africa*, Vol. II, pp. 302–12.

BLOOMFIELD, L., 1933: *Language.* New York.

BOAS, F., 1897: "The Social Organization and Secret Societies of the Kwakiutl Indians." U.S. National Museum, *Report for 1895*, pp. 311–738.

— 1898: "The Northwestern Tribes of Canada, Twelfth and Final Report." British Association for the Advancement of Science, *Proceedings*, pp. 40–61.

— 1909–10: "Tsimshian Mythology." Bureau of American Ethnology, *31st Annual Report*, pp. 27–1,037.

— 1911: "Introduction." *Handbook of American Indian Languages* (Bureau of American Ethnology, *Bulletin* No. 40), Part 1, pp. 5–83.

— 1914: "Mythology and Folk-tales of the North American Indians." *Journal of American Folklore*, Vol. XXVII, pp. 374–410 (reprinted in *Race, Language, and Culture*, pp. 451–90).

— 1916: "On the Variety of Lines of Descent Represented in a Population." *American Anthropologist*, Vol. XVIII, pp. 1–9.

— 1927: *Primitive Art.* Oslo.

— 1936: "Die Individualität primitiver Kulturen," in *Reine und Angewandte Soziologie* (volume in honor of F. Tönnies). Leipzig.

— 1938: (ed.), *General Anthropology.* New York.

— 1940: *Race, Language, and Culture.* New York.

BOYD, W. C., 1950: *Genetics and the Races of Man: an Introduction to Modern Physical Anthropology.* Boston.

BUCK, P. H. (Te Rangi Hiroa), 1934: "Mangaian Society." Bernice P. Bishop Museum, *Bulletin* No. 122.

— 1938: "Ethnology of Mangareva." Bernice P. Bishop Museum, *Bulletin* No. 157.

BUNZEL, R., 1929: *The Pueblo Potter.* New York.

BURKITT, MILES C., 1933. *The Old Stone Age.* New York and Cambridge.

CAMERON, NORMAN, 1938: "Functional Immaturity in the Symbolization of Scientifically Trained Adults." *Journal of Psychology*, Vol. VI, pp. 161–75.

CARPENTER, C. R., 1934: "A Field Study of the Behavior and Social Relations of Howling Monkeys." *Comparative Psychology Monographs*, Vol. X, No. 2 (No. 48).

CARTER, ISABEL GORDON, 1928: "Reduction of Variability in an Inbred Population," *American Journal of Physical Anthropology*, Vol. XI, pp. 457–77.

CASSIRER, E., 1944: *An Essay on Man.* New Haven.

CHILDE, V. G., 1946: *What Happened in History.* New York.

CODRINGTON, R. H., 1891: *The Melanesians: Studies in their Anthropology and Folk-Lore.* Oxford.

COLE, F. C., 1922: "The Tinguian." Field Museum of Natural History, *Publication* No. 209, *Anthropological Series*, Vol. XIV, No. 2.

COLE, G. D. H., 1933: Introduction to K. Marx, *Capital*, pp. xi–xxix (Everyman's Library), London.

COON, CARLTON S., 1942: "Have the Jews a Racial Identity?" In *Jews in a Gentile World*, Graeber, Isacque and Britt, Steuart H., eds., New York.

COUNTS, EARL W., 1950: *This Is Race: an Anthology Selected from the International Literature on the Races of Man.* New York.

COX, MARIAN ROALFE, 1892: *Cinderella.* Publications of the Folk-lore Society, Vol. XXXI. London.

DAVIDSON, L. J., 1943: "Moron Stories." *Southern Folklore Quarterly*, Vol. VII, pp. 101–4.

DEACON, A. B., 1934: *Malekula: a Vanishing People in the New Hebrides.* London.

DE LAGUNA, G. A., 1927: *Speech: Its Function and Development.* New Haven.

DIGBY, ADRIAN, 1938: "The Machines of Primitive People." *Man*, Vol. XXXVIII, **50**, pp. 57–8.

DIXON, ROLAND B., 1916: *Oceanic Mythology (The Mythology of All Races,* Vol. IX). Boston.

1928: *The Building of Cultures.* New York.

DOBZHANSKY, T., 1944: "On Species and Races of Living and Fossil Man." *American Journal of Physical Anthropology*, Vol. II (n.s.), pp. 251–65.

DRIBERG, J. H., 1930: *People of the Small Arrow.* New York.

DRIVER, H. E. and KROEBER, A. L., 1932: "Quantitative Expression of Cultural Relationships." University of California, *Publications in American Archaeology and Ethnology*, Vol. XXXI, No. 4, pp. 211–56.

DRUCKER, PHILIP, 1939: "Rank, Wealth, and Kinship in Northwest Coast Society." *American Anthropologist*, Vol. XLI, pp. 55–65.

DU BOIS, C., 1936: "The Wealth Concept as an Integrative Factor in Tolowa-Tututni Culture," in *Essays in Anthropology Presented to A. L. Kroeber*, pp. 49–65. Berkeley.

1944: *The People of Alor.* Minneapolis.

DUNDAS, C., 1913: "History of Kitui." *Journal of the Royal Anthropological Institute*, Vol. XLIII, pp. 480–549.

DURKHEIM, E., 1915: *The Elementary Forms of the Religious Life.* London.

DYK, W. (ed.), 1938: *Son of Old Man Hat.* New York.

EGGAN, DOROTHY, 1949: "The Significance of Dreams for Anthropological Research." *American Anthropologist*, Vol. LI, pp. 177–98.

1952: "The Manifest Content of Dreams: a Challenge to Social Science." *American Anthropologist*, Vol. LIV, pp. 469–85.

EGGAN, FRED, 1941: "Some Aspects of Culture Change in the Northern Philippines." *American Anthropologist*, Vol. XLIII, pp. 11–18.

1950: *Social Organization of the Western Pueblos.* Chicago.

EINSTEIN, CARL, 1920: *Negerplastik.* Munich.

EVANS-PRITCHARD, E. E., 1937: *Witchcraft, Oracles, and Magic among the Azande.* Oxford.

1940: *The Nuer.* Oxford.

1946: "Applied Anthropology." *Africa*, Vol. XVI, pp. 92–8.

FENTON, WILLIAM N., 1941: "Iroquois Suicide: A Study in the Stability of a Culture Pattern." *Anthropological Papers*, No. 14 (Smithsonian Institution, Bureau of American Ethnology, *Bulletin* No. 128), pp. 80–137.

FIRTH, RAYMOND, 1939: *Primitive Polynesian Economy*. London.

1951: *Elements of Social Organization*. London.

FIRTH, ROSEMARY, 1943: "Housekeeping among Malay Peasants." University of London, *Monographs on Social Anthropology*, No. 7.

FORDE, C. D., 1934: *Habitat, Society, and Economy: a Geographical Introduction to Anthropology*. London.

1937: "Land and Labour in a Cross River Village, Southern Nigeria." *Geographical Journal*, Vol. XC, pp. 24–51.

FORTES, M., 1938: "Culture-Contact as a Dynamic Process." International Institute of African Languages and Cultures, *Memorandum* No. XV, pp. 60–91.

—— and S. L., 1936: "Food in the Domestic Economy of the Tallensi." *Africa*, Vol. IX, pp. 237–76.

—— and EVANS-PRITCHARD, E. E. (eds.), 1940: *African Political Systems*. London.

FORTUNE, R. F., 1939: "Arapesh Warfare." *American Anthropologist*, Vol. XLI, pp. 22–41.

FOSTER, G. M., 1951: "Report on an Ethnological Reconaissance of Spain." *American Anthropologist*, Vol. LIII, pp. 311–25.

FRAZER, SIR J. G., 1910: *Totemism and Exogamy* (4 vols.). London.

1935: *The Golden Bough: the Magic Art and the Evolution of Kings* (2 vols.) (3d ed.). New York.

FREYRE, G., 1946: *The Masters and the Slaves*. New York.

GALLOWAY, ALEXANDER, 1937: "Man in the Light of Recent Discoveries." *South African Journal of Science*, Vol. XXXIV, pp. 59–120.

GARROD, DOROTHY A. E., 1938: "The Upper Palaeolithic in the Light of Recent Discovery." *Proceedings of the Prehistoric Society*, Vol. IV, pp. 1–26.

GATES, R. RUGGLES, 1944: "Phylogeny and Classification of Hominids and Anthropoids." *American Journal of Physical Anthropology*, Vol. II (n.s.), pp. 279–92.

GAYTON, A. H., 1946: "Culture-Environment Integration: External References in Yokuts Life." *Southwestern Journal of Anthropology*, Vol. II, pp. 252–68.

GLUCKMAN, MAX, 1943: "Essays on Lozi Land and Royal Property." Rhodes-Livingstone Institute, *Papers*, No. 10.

GOLDENWEISER, A. A., 1910: "Totemism: an Analytical Study." *Journal of American Folklore*, Vol. XXIII, pp. 179–293 (reprinted in Goldenweiser, 1933, pp. 213–332).

1922: *Early Civilization*. New York.

1933: *History, Psychology, and Culture*. New York.

GOLDFRANK, E., 1945: "Changing Configurations in the Social Organization of a Blackfoot Tribe during the Reserve Period." American Ethnological Society, *Monographs*, No. VIII.

GOODWIN, G., 1942: *The Social Organization of the Western Apache*. Chicago.

GREENBERG, J., 1946: "The Influence of Islam on a Sudanese Religion." American Ethnological Society, *Monographs*, Vol. X.

GREGORY, W. K., 1929: *Our Face from Fish to Man*.

HADDON, A. C., 1894: *The Decorative Art of British New Guinea*. Dublin.
1914: *Evolution in Art* (new ed.). London and New York.
1925: *The Races of Man and Their Distribution*. New York.
HALLOWELL, A. I., 1942: *The Role of Conjuring in Saulteaux Society*. Philadelphia.
1945a: "Sociopsychological Aspects of Acculturation," in *The Science of Man the World Crisis* (R. Linton, ed.), pp. 171–200. New York.
1945b: "The Rorschach Technique in the Study of Personality and Culture." *American Anthropologist*, Vol. XLVII, pp. 195–210.
1947: "Some Psychological Characteristics of the Northeastern Indians." Peabody Foundation for Archaeology, *Papers*, Vol. III, pp. 195–225.
1951: "Cultural Factors in the Structuralization of Perception," in *Social Psychology at the Crossroads* (John H. Rohrer and Muzafer Sherif, eds.), pp. 164–95. New York.
HAMBLY, W. D., 1937: "Source Book for African Anthropology." Field Museum of Natural History, *Publications*, Nos. 394 and 396, *Anthropology Series*, Vol. XXVI (2 parts).
HARRIS, J. S., 1944: "Some Aspects of the Economics of Sixteen Ibo Individuals." *Africa*, Vol. XIV, pp. 302–35.
HARRISON, H. S., 1925: "The Evolution of the Domestic Arts." *Handbook of the Horniman Museum*, Part 1 (2d ed.). London.
1926: "Inventions: Obtrusive, Directional, and Independent." *Man*, Vol. XXVI, **74**, pp. 117–21.
HERSKOVITS, F. S., 1934: "Dahomean Songs." *Poetry*, Vol. XLV, pp. 75–7.
1935: "Dahomean Songs for the Dead." *The New Republic*, Vol. LXXXIV, No. 103, p. 95.
HERSKOVITS, M. J., 1924: "A Preliminary Consideration of the Culture Areas of Africa." *American Anthropologist*, Vol. XXVI, pp. 50–63.
1926: "The Cattle Complex in East Africa." *American Anthropologist*, Vol. XXVIII, pp. 230–72, 361–80, 494–528, 633–64.
1928: *The American Negro: a Study in Racial Crossing*. New York.
1930: "The Culture Areas of Africa." *Africa*, Vol. III, pp. 59–77.
1934: "Freudian Mechanisms in Primitive Negro Psychology," in *Essays Presented to C. G. Seligman*, pp. 75–84. London.
1936: "Applied Anthropology and the American Anthropologists." *Science*, Vol. LXXXIII, pp. 215–22.
1938a: *Acculturation: the Study of Culture Contact*. New York.
1938b: *Dahomey: an Ancient West African Kingdom* (2 vols.). New York.
1945a: "The Processes of Cultural Change," in *The Science of Man in the World Crisis* (R. Linton, ed.), pp. 143–70. New York.
1945b: "Problem, Method, and Theory in Afroamerican Studies." *Afroamérica*, Vol. I, pp. 5–24.
1945c: *Backgrounds of African Art*. Denver.
1946: "Folklore after a Hundred Years: a Problem in Redefinition." *Journal of American Folklore*, Vol. LIX, pp. 89–100.
1949: "Who are the Jews?" in *The Jews, Their History, Culture, and Religion* (L. Finkelstein, ed.), Vol. II, pp. 1,151–71. New York.
1950: "The Hypothetical Situation: a Technique in Field Research." *Southwestern Journal of Anthropology*, Vol. VI, pp. 32–40.
1951: "Tender and Tough-Minded Anthropology and the Study of Values in Culture." *Southwestern Journal of Anthropology*, Vol. VII, pp. 22–31.
1952: *Economic Anthropology*. New York.

HERSKOVITS, M. J. and F. S., 1934: *Rebel Destiny: among the Bush Negroes of Dutch Guiana.* New York.
1936: *Suriname Folklore.* New York.
1947: *Trinidad Village.* New York.
HERZOG, G., 1938: "Music in the Thinking of the American Indian." *Peabody Bulletin,* May, pp. 1–5.
HILL, W. W., 1939: "Stability in Culture and Pattern." *American Anthropologist,* Vol. XLI, pp. 258–60.
HODGEN, M. T., 1936: *The Doctrine of Survivals.* London.
1942: "Geographical Distribution as a Criterion of Age." *American Anthropologist,* Vol. XLIV, pp. 345–68.
1945: "Glass and Paper: an Historical Study of Acculturation." *Southwestern Journal of Anthropology,* Vol. I, pp. 466–97.
1952: "Change and History." *Viking Fund Publications in Anthropology,* No. 18.
HOEBEL, E. A., 1940: "The Political Organization and Law-Ways of the Comanche Indians." American Anthropological Association, *Memoir* No. 54.
1946: "Law and Anthropology." *Virginia Law Review,* Vol. XXXII, pp. 835–54.
HOGBIN, H. I., 1937–8: "Social Advancement in Guadalcanal." *Oceania,* Vol. VIII, pp. 289–305.
1938–9: "Tillage and Collection: a New Guinea Economy." *Oceania,* Vol. IX, pp. 127–51, 286–325.
1946–7: "A New Guinea Childhood: from Weaning till the Eighth Year in Wogeo." *Oceania,* Vol. XVI, pp. 275–96.
HOIJER, HARRY, 1944: "Peoples and Cultures of the Southwest Pacific," in *The Southwest Pacific and the War,* pp. 31–68. Berkeley and Los Angeles.
HOLMES, W. H., 1886: "Origin and Development of Form and Ornament in Ceramic Art." Bureau of American Ethnology, *4th Annual Report,* pp. 443–65.
HOOTON, E. A., 1946: *Up from the Ape* (rev. ed.). New York.
HSÜ, FRANCIS L. K., 1945: "Influence of South-Seas Emigration on Certain Chinese Provinces." *Far Eastern Quarterly,* Vol. V, pp. 47–59.
1953: *Americans and Chinese: Two Ways of Life.* New York.
HUNTER, M., 1936: *Reaction to Conquest.* London.

JENKS, A. E., 1900: "The Wild Rice Gatherers of the Upper Lakes." Bureau of American Ethnology, *19th Annual Report,* pp. 1,019–1,137.

KARDINER, A., 1944: "Elaboration" of "The Problem," in *Alor,* by C. Du Bois, pp. 6–13.
KEESING, F., 1939: "The Menomini Indians of Wisconsin." American Philosophical Society, *Memoirs,* Vol. X.
KLIMEK, S., 1935: "Culture Element Distributions: I. The Structure of California Indian Cultures." University of California, *Publications in American Archaeology and Ethnology,* Vol. XXXVII, No. 1, pp. 1–70.
KLUCKHOHN, C., 1941: "Patterning as Exemplified in Navaho Culture," in *Language, Culture, and Personality: Essays in Memory of Edward Sapir,* pp. 109–30. Menasha (Wis.).
KÖHLER, W., 1925: *The Mentality of Apes.* New York.

KOENIGSWALD, G. H. R. VON, 1952: "*Gigantopithecus blacki* von Koenigswald, a Giant Fossil Hominid from the Pleistocene of Modern China." American Museum of Natural History, *Anthropological Papers*, Vol. XLIII, Part 4, pp. 295–325.

KROEBER, A. L., 1923: *Anthropology*. New York.

1936: "Culture Element Distributions: III. Area and Climax." University of California, *Publications in American Archaeology and Ethnology*, Vol. XXXVII, No. 3, pp. 101–16.

1939: "Cultural and Natural Areas of Native North America." University of California, *Publications in American Archaeology and Ethnology*, Vol. XLVIII, pp. 1–242.

1940: "Stimulus Diffusion." *American Anthropologist*, Vol. XLII, pp. 1–20.

1952: *The Nature of Culture*. Chicago.

1953: *Anthropology Today: An Encyclopaedic Inventory*. "Prepared under the Chairmanship of A. L. Kroeber." Chicago.

KROEBER, A. L. and KLUCKHOHN, CLYDE, 1952: "Culture: a Critical Review of Concepts and Definitions." Peabody Museum of American Archaeology and Ethnology, Harvard University, *Papers*, Vol. XLVII, No. 1, pp. 1–223.

KROGMAN, W. M., 1945: "The Concept of Race," in *The Science of Man in the World Crisis* (R. Linton, ed.), pp. 38–62. New York.

KROPOTKIN, P., 1916: *Mutual Aid: a Factor of Evolution*. New York.

KUO, Z. Y., 1930: "The Genesis of the Cat's Response to the Rat." *Journal of Comparative Psychology*, Vol. XI, pp. 1–30.

LANG, ANDREW, 1887: *Myth, Ritual, and Religion*. London.

LEAKEY, L. S. B., 1934. *Adam's Ancestors*. New York.

LÉVY-BRUHL, LUCIEN, 1923: *Primitive Mentality*. New York.

1926: *How Natives Think*. London.

1949: *Les Carnets de Lucien Lévy-Bruhl*. Paris.

LEWIS, OSCAR, 1942: "The Effects of White Contact upon Blackfoot Culture, with Special Reference to the Role of the Fur Trade." American Ethnological Society, *Monographs*, No. VI.

1951: *Life in a Mexican Village: Tepoztlán Revisited*. Urbana (Ill.)

LI AN-CHE, 1937: "Zuñi: Some Observations and Queries." *American Anthropologist*, Vol. XXXIX, pp. 62–76.

LINDBLOM, K. G. (ed.), 1926—: *Smärre Meddelanden*. Stockholm, Statens Ethnografiska Museum.

LINDGREN, E. J., 1938: "An Example of Culture Contact without Conflict: Reindeer Tungus and Cossacks of Northwestern Manchuria." *American Anthropologist*, Vol. XL, pp. 605–62.

LINTON, R., 1924: "Totemism in the A. E. F." *American Anthropologist*, Vol. XXVI, pp. 296–300.

1928: "Culture Areas of Madagascar." *American Anthropologist*, Vol. XXX, pp. 363–90.

1936: *The Study of Man*. New York.

1940: (ed.), *Acculturation in Seven American Indian Tribes*. New York.

1945: *The Cultural Background of Personality*. New York.

LLEWELLYN, K. N. and HOEBEL, E. A., 1941: *The Cheyenne Way*. Norman (Okla.).

LOWIE, R. H., 1920: *Primitive Society*. New York.

LUNDBORG, H. and LINDERS, F. J., 1926: *The Racial Characteristics of the Swedish Nation*. Stockholm.

LUOMALA, KATHERINE, 1946: "Polynesian Literature," in *Encyclopedia of Literature* (J. T. Shipley, ed.), pp. 772–89.
LYND, ROBERT S. and HELEN M., 1929: *Middletown: a Study in Contemporary American Culture.* New York.

MACCURDY, G. G., 1924: *Human Origins* (2 vols.). New York.
MAINE, SIR H. S., 1888: *Lectures on the Early History of Institutions.* New York.
  1890: *Popular Government.* London.
MALINOWSKI, B., 1922: *Argonauts of the Western Pacific* (2 vols.). London.
  1926: "Anthropology." *Encyclopaedia Britannica,* Supplementary Vol. I to 13th edition, pp. 131–42.
  1927: *The Father in Primitive Psychology.* New York.
  1944: *A Scientific Theory of Culture, and Other Essays.* Chapel Hill (N.C.).
  1945: *The Dynamics of Culture Change.* New Haven.
MANDELBAUM, D. G., 1936: "Friendship in North America." *Man,* Vol. XXXVI, **272,** pp. 205–6.
  1939: "Agricultural Ceremonies among Three Tribes of Travancore." *Ethnos,* Vol. IV, pp. 114–28.
  1941: "Culture Change among the Nilghiri Tribes." *American Anthropologist,* Vol. XLIII, pp. 19–26.
MARETT, R. R., 1912: *Anthropology.* London.
  1914: *The Threshold of Religion.* New York.
MARTIN, PAUL S., QUIMBY, GEORGE I., and COLLIER, DONALD, 1947: *Indians before Columbus.* Chicago.
MARTIN, R., 1928: *Lehrbuch der Anthropologie* (3 vols.). Jena.
MASON, OTIS T., 1895: *The Origins of Invention.* London and New York.
MAUSS, MARCEL, 1923–24: "Essai sur le Don, forme archaique de l'échange." *L'Année sociologique* (n.s.), Vol. I, pp. 30–186.
MCGREGOR, J. H., 1938: "Human Origins and Early Man," in *General Anthropology* (F. Boas, ed.), New York, pp. 24–94.
MEAD, MARGARET, 1939: *From the South Seas.* New York.
MÉTRAUX, A., 1946a: "Ethnography of the Chaco." *Handbook of South American Indians* (Bureau of American Ethnology, *Bulletin* No. 143), Vol. I, pp. 197–370.
  1946b: "South American Indian Literature." *Encyclopedia of Literature* (J. T. Shipley, ed.), pp. 851–63.
MILLAR, N. E. and DOLLARD, J., 1941: *Social Learning and Imitation.* New Haven.
MOFOLO, THOMAS, 1931: *Chaka: an Historical Romance.* London.
MONTAGU, M. F. ASHLEY, 1945: *An Introduction to Physical Anthropology.* Springfield (Ill.).
MORANT, G. M., 1939: *The Races of Central Europe.* London.
MORANT, G. M., and others, 1938: "Report on the Swanscombe Skull." *Journal of the Royal Anthropological Institute,* Vol. LXVIII, pp. 17–98.
MORGAN, L. H., *Ancient Society.* Chicago, n.d.
MORTON, DUDLEY J., 1927: "Human Origin: Correlation of Previous Studies of Primate Feet and Posture with other Morphologic Evidence." *American Journal of Physical Anthropology,* Vol. X, pp. 173–203.
MOVIUS, HALLAM L., JR., 1942: *The Irish Stone Age.* Cambridge.
  1944: "Early Man and Pleistocene Stratigraphy in Southern and Eastern

Asia." Peabody Museum of American Archaeology and Ethnology, Harvard University, *Papers*, Vol. XIX, No. 3.
MURDOCK, G. P., 1945: "The Common Denominator of Cultures," in *The Science of Man in the World Crisis* (R. Linton, ed.), pp. 123-42. New York.
MURDOCK, G. P., and others, 1945: "Outline of Cultural Materials." *Yale Anthropological Studies*, Vol. II (2d ed.).
MYRES, SIR J. L., 1916: "The Influence of Anthropology on the Course of Political Science." University of California, *Publications in History*, Vol. IV, No. 1.

NADEL, S. F., 1942a: *A Black Byzantium: the Kingdom of Nupe in Nigeria.* London.
   1942b: "The Hill Tribes of Kadero." *Sudan Notes and Records*, Vol. XXV, pp. 37-79.
   1945: "Notes on Beni Amer Society." *Sudan Notes and Records*, Vol. XXVI, pp. 1-44.
   1951: *The Foundations of Social Anthropology.* London.
NORDENSKIÖLD, E., 1919: "An Ethno-Geographical Analysis of the Material Culture of Two Indian Tribes in the Gran Chaco." *Comparative Ethnographic Studies*, I. Göteburg.
NUMELIN, RAGNAR, 1950: *The Beginnings of Diplomacy: a Sociological Study of Intertribal and International Relations.* London and Copenhagen.

O'NEALE, L. M., 1932: "Yurok-Karok Basket Weavers." University of California, *Publications in American Archeology and Ethnology*, Vol. XXXII, No. 1, pp. 1-182.
OPLER, M. E., 1938: "Personality and Culture: a Methodological Suggestion for the Study of their Interrelations." *Psychiatry*, Vol. I, pp. 217-20.
   1941: *An Apache Life-Way.* Chicago.
   1945: "Themes as Dynamic Forces in Culture." *American Journal of Sociology*, Vol. LI, pp. 198-206.
ORTIZ, F., 1947: *Cuban Counterpoint: Tobacco and Sugar.* New York.
OSGOOD, CORNELIUS, 1940: "Ingalik Material Culture." Yale University, *Publications in Anthropology*, No. 22. New Haven.

PARSONS, E. C., 1918: "Nativity Myth at Laguna and Zuñi." *Journal of American Folklore*, Vol. XXXI, pp. 256-63.
   1936: *Mitla: Town of the Souls.* Chicago.
   1939: *Pueblo Indian Religion* (2 vols.). Chicago.
PATAI, RAPHAEL, 1947: "On Culture Contact and its Working in Modern Palestine." American Anthropological Association, *Memoir* No. 67.
PETTITT, GEORGE A., 1946: "Primitive Education in North America." University of California, *Publications in American Archaeology and Ethnology*, Vol. XLIII, pp. 1-182.

RADCLIFFE-BROWN, A. R., 1931: "The Social Organization of Australian Tribes." *Oceania Monographs*, No. 1.
   1932: "The Present Position of Anthropological Studies." British Association for the Advancement of Science, *Report of the Centenary Meeting*, pp. 140-71. London.
   1940: Preface to *African Political Systems* (M. Fortes and E. E. Evans-Pritchard, eds.), London.

RAMOS, A., 1940: *O Negro Brasileiro* (2d ed., rev.). São Paulo.
RATTRAY, R. S., 1923: *Ashanti*. London.
  1929: *Ashanti Law and Constitution*. Oxford.
RAUM, O. F., 1940: *Chaga Childhood*. London.
RAY, VERNE F., 1942: "Culture Element Distributions: XXII. Plateau."
  Anthropological Records, Vol. VIII, No. 2, pp. 99–257.
REDFIELD, R., 1941: *The Folk Culture of Yucatan*. Chicago.
  1947: "The Folk Society." *American Journal of Sociology*, Vol. LII,
  pp. 293–308.
  1953: *The Primitive World and Its Transformations*. Ithaca (N.Y.).
REDFIELD, R., LINTON, R., and HERSKOVITS, M. J., 1936: "Memorandum on
  the Study of Acculturation." *American Anthropologist*, Vol. XXXVIII,
  pp. 149–52.
REISNER, G. A., 1923: *Excavations at Kerma*. ("Harvard African Studies,"
  Vols. V and VI). Cambridge (Mass.).
RICHARDS, A. I., 1939: *Land, Labour, and Diet in Northern Rhodesia*. Lon-
  don.
RIVERS, W. H. R., 1906: *The Todas*. London.
  1910: "The Genealogical Method of Anthropological Inquiry." *The
  Sociological Review*, Vol. III, pp. 1–12.
ROBERTS, H. H., 1925: "A Study of Folk Song Variants Based on Field Work
  in Jamaica." *Journal of American Folklore*, Vol. XXXVIII, pp. 148–216.
ROSCOE, J., 1911: *The Baganda*. London.
ROWE, JOHN H., 1953: "Technical Aids in Anthropology: a Historical
  Survey," in *Anthropology Today* (A. L. Kroeber, ed.), pp. 895–940.
  Chicago.
ROYAL ANTHROPOLOGICAL INSTITUTE, 1951: *Notes and Queries on Anthro-
  pology* (6th ed.). London.

SAIT, EDWARD M., 1938: *Political Institutions: a Preface*. New York.
SAPIR, E., 1921: *Language*. New York.
  1938: "Why Cultural Anthropology Needs the Psychiatrist." *Psychiatry*,
  Vol. I, pp. 7–12.
  1949: *Selected Writings of Edward Sapir*, in *Language, Culture, and
  Personality* (D. Mandelbaum, ed.). Berkeley.
SAPIR, E. and SWADESH, M., 1939: *Nootka Texts*. ("William Dwight Linguis-
  tic Series," Linguistic Society of America.) Philadelphia.
SCHAPERA, I., 1930: *The Khoisan Peoples of South Africa*. London.
  1940: *Married Life in an African Tribe*. London.
SCHJELDERUP-EBBE, T., 1935: "Social Behavior of Birds," in *A Handbook of
  Social Psychology* (C. Murchison, ed.), pp. 947–72, Worcester (Mass.).
SCHMIDT, W., 1931: *The Origin and Growth of Religion*. New York.
  1939: *The Cultural Historical Method of Ethnology* (S. A. Sieber, tr.).
  New York.
SCHNEIRLA, T. C., 1946: "Problems in the Biopsychology of Social Organiza-
  tion." *Journal of Abnormal and Social Psychology*, Vol. XLI, pp. 385–
  402.
SCHULTZ, A., 1936: "Characters Common to Higher Primates and Char-
  acters Specific for Man." *Quarterly Review of Biology*, Vol. XI,
  pp. 259–83, 425–55.
SHERIF, M., 1936: *The Psychology of Social Norms*. New York.
SKINNER, H. D., 1921: "Culture Areas in New Zealand." *Journal of the
  Polynesian Society*, Vol. XXX, pp. 71–8.

SMITH, J. RUSSELL, 1925: *North America.* New York.
SMITH, M. W., 1940: *The Puyallup-Nisqually.* New York.
SPECK, F. G., 1914: "The Double-Curve Motive in Northeastern Algonkian Art." *Canadian Geological Survey, Memoir* No. 42, *Anthropological Series,* No. 1. Ottawa.
1935: *Naskapi.* Norman (Okla.).
SPENCER, HERBERT, 1896: *The Principles of Sociology* (3d ed.). New York.
STAYT, H. A., 1931: *The Bavenda.* London.
STERN, B. J., 1927: *Social Factors in Medical Progress.* New York.
STEWARD, JULIAN, 1947: "American Culture History in the Light of South America." *Southwestern Journal of Anthropology,* Vol. III.
STEWART, OMAR C., 1942: "Culture Element Distributions: XVIII. Ute-Southern Paiute." *Anthropological Records,* Vol. VI, No. 4, pp. 231–360.
STURTEVANT, E. H., 1947: *An Introduction to Linguistic Science.* New Haven.
SULLIVAN, LOUIS R., 1928: *Essentials of Anthropometry: a Handbook for Explorers and Museum Collectors* (revised by H. L. Shapiro), New York.

TAX, S., 1939: "Culture and Civilization in Guatemalan Societies." *Scientific Monthly,* Vol. XLVIII, pp. 463–7.
1945: "Anthropology and Administration," *América Indígena,* Vol. V, pp. 21–33.
1953: "Penny Capitalism: a Guatemalan Indian Economy." Smithsonian Institution, Institute of Social Anthropology, *Publication* No. 16.
TEGGART, F. J., 1941: *Theory and Processes of History.* Berkeley.
THIEME, FREDERICK P., 1952: "The Population as a Unit of Study." *American Anthropologist,* Vol. LIV, pp. 504–9.
THOMPSON, STITH, 1929: *Tales of the North American Indians.* Cambridge (Mass.).
1932–6: *Motif-Index of Folk-Literature* (F F Communications Nos. 106–9, 116–17; "Indiana University Studies," Vols. XIX–XXIII).
TOYNBEE, A. J., 1934–9: *A Study of History* (6 vols.). London.
TREMEARNE, A. J. N., 1912: "Notes on the Kagoro and other Nigerian Head-Hunters." *Journal of the Royal Anthropological Institute,* Vol. XLIII, pp. 136–99.
TSCHOPIK, H., JR., 1946: "The Aymara." *Handbook of South American Indians* (Bureau of American Ethnology, *Bulletin* No. 143). Vol. 2, pp. 501–73.
TURNEY-HIGH, H. H., 1942: "The Practice of Primitive Warfare." University of Montana, *Publications in Social Science,* No. 2.
TYLOR, SIR E. B., 1874: *Primitive Culture* (2 vols.) (1st American, from the 2d English ed.). New York.
1889: "On a Method of Investigating the Development of Institutions . . ." *Journal of the Royal Anthropological Institute,* Vol. XVIII, pp. 245–69.

UNITED NATIONS EDUCATIONAL, SCIENTIFIC AND CULTURAL ORGANIZATION (UNESCO), 1952: *The Race Concept: Results of an Inquiry.* Paris.

VAN GENNEP, A., 1920: *La Formation des légendes.* Paris.
VEBLEN, THORSTEIN, 1915: *The Theory of the Leisure Class.* New York.
VILLA R., ALFONSO, 1945: *The Maya of East Central Quintana Roo* (Carnegie Institution of Washington, *Publication* No. 559). Washington.

VIVAS, ELISEO, 1950: *The Moral Life and the Ethical Life.* Chicago.
VOEGELIN, ERMINIE W., 1942: "Culture Element Distributions: XX. Northeast California." *Anthropological Records,* Vol. VII, No. 2, pp. 47–251.
  1946: "North American Native Literature," in *Encyclopedia of Literature* (J. T. Shipley, ed.), pp. 706–21. New York.

WAGLEY, C., 1941: "Economics of a Guatemalan Village." American Anthropological Association, *Memoir* No. 58.
WALLIS, W. D., 1930: *Culture and Progress.* New York.
WATKINS, M. H., 1943: "The West African 'Bush' School." *American Journal of Sociology,* Vol. XLVIII, pp. 666–74.
WEIDENREICH, F., 1943: "The Skull of Sinanthropus Pekinensis." *Palaeontologica Sinica,* new series D, No. 10, whole series 127.
  1945: "The Puzzle of Pithecanthropus," in *Science and Scientists in the Netherlands Indies.* New York, pp. 380–90.
WEINER, J. S., OAKLEY, K. P., and CLARK, W. E. LE GROS, 1953: "The Solution of the Piltdown Problem." *Bulletin of the British Museum (Natural History):* Geology, Vol. II, No. 3, pp. 141–6.
WERNER, A., 1930: *Structure and Relationship of African Languages.* London.
WHITE, L., 1946: "Kroeber's Configurations of Culture Growth." *American Anthropologist,* Vol. XLVIII, pp. 78–93.
  1949: *The Science of Culture: a Study of Man and Civilization.* New York.
WHITING, J. W. M., 1941: *Becoming a Kwoma.* New Haven.
WILLEMS, EMÍLIO, 1944: "Acculturation and the Horse Complex among German-Brazilians." *American Anthropologist,* Vol. XLVI, pp. 153–61.
WILLIAMS, F. E., 1923: "The Vailala Madness and the Destruction of Native Ceremonies in the Gulf Division." Territory of Papua, *Anthropological Report* No. 4. Port Moresby.
  1930: *Orokaiva Society.* London.
  1934: "The Vailala Madness in Retrospect," in *Essays in Honour of C. G. Seligman,* pp. 369–79. London.
  1936: *Papuans of the Trans-Fly.* London.
WINGERT, PAUL S., 1950: *The Sculpture of Negro Africa.* New York.
WISSLER, C., 1922: *The American Indian* (2d ed.). New York.
  1923: *Man and Culture.* New York.
  1926: *The Relation of Nature to Man in Aboriginal America.* New York.

YERKES, R. M. and A. W., 1935: "Social Behavior in Infra-human Primates," in *Handbook of Social Psychology* (C. Murchison, ed.), pp. 973–1033. Worcester (Mass.).
YOSELOFF, T. and STUCKEY, L. (eds.), 1944: *The Merry Adventures of Till Eulenspiegel.* New York.

ZEUNER, F. E., 1944: "Review of the Chronology of the Paleolithic Period." *Conference on the Problems and Prospects of European Archaeology* (University of London, Institute of Archaeology, *Occasional Papers,* No. 6) pp. 14–19.
ZUCKERMAN, S., 1932: *The Social Life of Monkeys and Apes.* New York.

II. *A List of Selected Titles*

This list is in three parts. In the first part are given the titles of anthropological periodicals that carry articles wholly or partly in English. They are important because it is in such journals that announcements of new discoveries, discussions of theory, and reviews of books are found. The second part is comprised of American and English monograph series, wherein are contained much of the working materials for comparative studies, particularly reports of the results of field work, presented in the detail necessary for scientific analysis. Finally, there is given a suggested list of readings from the literature of anthropology in English. These books might be regarded as a good working library for those interested in doing further reading on the subject. Some of the titles are also in the first bibliography, since they have been cited in the pages of this book; there are others, however, which have not been used there but should find a place in any list such as this.

I. *Periodicals*

Journal of the Royal Anthropological Institute (1872)
Folklore (1878)
American Anthropologist (1888)
Journal of American Folklore (1888)
Journal of the Polynesian Society (1892)
Journal de la Société des Américanistes (1895)
Man (1900)
Anthropos (1906)
International Journal of American Linguistics (1917)
American Journal of Physical Anthropology (1918)
Sudan Notes and Records (1918)
Man in India (1921)
Africa (1928)
Anthropological Quarterly (formerly *Primitive Man*) (1928)
Human Biology (1929)
Oceania (1930)
American Antiquity (1935)
Ethnos (1936)

Applied Anthropology (1941)
America Indígena (1941)
African Studies (1942)
Acta Americana (1943)
Southwestern Journal of Anthropology (1945)
Word (1945)
African Abstracts (1950)

II. *Monograph Series*

American Anthropological Association, *Memoirs*
American Folklore Society, *Memoirs*
American Ethnological Society, *Monographs*
American Museum of Natural History, New York, *Anthropological Papers*
Bernice P. Bishop Museum, Honolulu, *Bulletins* and *Memoirs*
Columbia University, *Contributions to Anthropology*
Chicago Natural History Museum, *Fieldiana, Anthropology* (earlier entitled *Anthropological Series*, Field Museum of Natural History)
International Congress of Americanists, *Proceedings*
International Congress of the Anthropological and Ethnological Sciences, *Reports*
London School of Economics, *Monographs on Social Anthropology*
Peabody Museum of American Archaeology and Ethnology, Harvard University, *Papers*
Philadelphia Anthropological Society, *Publications*
Public Museum of the City of Milwaukee, *Bulletins*
Rhodes-Livingstone Institute, *Papers*
Royal Anthropological Institute, London, *Occasional Papers*
Smithsonian Institution, Bureau of American Ethnology, *Annual Reports* and *Bulletins*
University of California, *Publications in American Archaeology and Ethnology*
University of California, *Anthropological Records*
University of London, *Monographs on Social Anthropology*
University of Washington, *Publications in Anthropology*
Viking Fund, *Publications in Anthropology*
Viking Fund, *Yearbook of Physical Anthropology*
Yale University, *Anthropological Studies*
Yale University, *Publications in Anthropology*

III. *Books and Monographs*

1. General Works

BEALS, RALPH L. and HOIJER, HARRY, *An Introduction to Anthropology*, New York, 1953
BIDNEY, D., *Theoretical Anthropology*, New York, 1953
BOAS, F., *Race, Language, and Culture*, New York, 1940
—— (ed.), *General Anthropology*, New York, 1938
EVANS-PRITCHARD, E. E., *Social Anthropology*, London, 1951
GILLIN, JOHN, *The Ways of Men*, New York, 1948

GOLDENWEISER, A. A., *Early Civilization*, New York, 1922
HADDON, A. C., *History of Anthropology*, London, 1910
HOEBEL, E. A., *Man in the Primitive World*, New York, 1949
KROEBER, A. L., *Anthropology* (2nd edition), New York, 1948
———, *The Nature of Culture*, Chicago, 1952
——— (ed.), *Anthropology Today: an Encyclopedic Inventory*, Chicago, 1953
LABARRE, W., *The Human Animal*, Chicago, 1954.
LINTON, R., *The Study of Man*, New York, 1936
——— (ed.), *The Science of Man in the World Crisis*, New York, 1945
LOWIE, R. H., *The History of Ethnological Theory*, New York, 1937
MARETT, R. R., *Anthropology*, London, 1912
MURDOCK, G. P., *Our Primitive Contemporaries*, New York, 1934
REDFIELD, R., *The Primitive World and Its Transformations*, Ithaca (N.Y.), 1953
TITIEV, M., *The Science of Man*, New York, 1954
TYLOR, SIR E. B., *Anthropology*, New York, 1881
WHITE, LESLIE A., *The Science of Culture*, New York, 1949
WISSLER, C., *Man and Culture*, New York, 1923

2. Biological Backgrounds

ALLEE, W. C., *The Social Life of Animals*, New York, 1938
HOOTON, E. A., *Up from the Ape* (2d ed.), New York, 1946
HOWELLS, W. W., *Mankind So Far*, New York, 1944
KÖHLER, W., *The Mentality of Apes*, New York, 1925
WEIDENREICH, F., *Apes, Giants, and Men*, Chicago, 1946
ZUCKERMAN, S., *The Social Life of Apes and Monkeys*, New York, 1932

3. Prehistory (Old World and New)

BURKITT, M. C., *The Old Stone Age*, New York, 1933
CHILDE, V. G., *The Dawn of European Civilization*, New York, 1939
COLE, F. C. and DEUEL, T., *Rediscovering Illinois*, Chicago, 1937
HOWELLS, W. W., *Back of History*, Garden City (N.Y.), 1954
MACCURDY, G. G., *Human Origins* (2 vols.), New York, 1924
MARTIN, PAUL S., QUIMBY, GEORGE I., and COLLIER, DONALD, *Indians Before Columbus*, Chicago, 1947
SHETRONE, H. C., *The Mound Builders*, New York, 1930

4. Race and Physical Type

BARZUN, JACQUES, *Race: a Study in Modern Superstition*, New York, 1937
BOAS, F., *The Mind of Primitive Man* (2d ed.), New York, 1938
BOYD, W. C., *Genetics and the Races of Man: an Introduction to Modern Physical Anthropology*, Boston, 1950
COUNTS, EARL W., *This is Race: an Anthology Selected from the International Literature on the Races of Man*, New York, 1950
DUNN, L. C., and DOBZHANSKY, T., *Heredity, Race and Society*, New York, 1946

Haddon, A. C., *The Races of Man and Their Distribution*, New York, 1925

Klineberg, Otto, *Race Differences*, New York, 1935

Montagu, M. F. Ashley, *Man's Most Dangerous Myth: the Fallacy of Race* (2d ed.), New York, 1925

5. Linguistics

Bloomfield, L., *Language*, New York, 1933

Hall, Robert A., *Leave Your Language Alone*, Ithaca (N.Y.), 1950

Sapir, E., *Language*, New York, 1921

Sturtevant, E. H., *An Introduction to Linguistic Science*, New Haven, 1947

6. The Ordering of Society

Eggan, Fred, *Social Organization of the Western Pueblos*, Chicago, 1950

Evans-Pritchard, E. E., *Kinship and Marriage among the Nuer*, Oxford, 1951

Firth, Raymond, *Primitive Polynesian Economy*, London, 1939

Forde, C. D., *Habitat, Society, and Economy: a Geographical Introduction to Anthropology*, London, 1934

Fortes, M. and Evans-Pritchard, E. E., *African Political Systems*, London, 1940

Herskovits, M. J., *Economic Anthropology*, New York, 1952

Llewellyn, K. N., and Hoebel, E. A., *The Cheyenne Way*, Norman, Okla., 1941

Lowie, R. H., *Primitive Society*, New York, 1920

Murdock, G. P., *Social Structure*, New York, 1949

Nadel, S. F., *The Foundations of Social Anthropology*, London, 1951

Radcliffe-Brown, H. R. and Forde, C. D. (eds.), *African Systems of Kinship and Marriage*, London, 1950

Rattray, R. S., *Ashanti Law and Constitution*, Oxford, 1929

Richards, A. I., *Land, Labour, and Diet in Northern Rhodesia*, London. 1939

Rivers, W. H. R., *Kinship and Social Organization*, London, 1914

Schapera, I., *A Handbook of Tswana Law and Custom*, London, 1939

7. The Individual in His Culture

Dennis, W., *The Hopi Child*, New York, 1940

Du Bois, C., *The People of Alor*, Minneapolis, 1944

Dyk, W. (ed.), *Son of Old Man Hat*, New York, 1938

Honigmann, John J., *Culture and Personality*, New York, 1954

Hsü, Francis L. K., *Americans and Chinese: Two Ways of Life*, New York, 1953

Kardiner, A., *The Individual and His Society*, New York, 1939

Kluckhohn, C. and Murray, H. A., *Personality in Nature, Society, and Culture* (2d ed.), New York, 1953

Leighton, Dorothea and Kluckhohn, Clyde, *Children of the People*, Cambridge, Mass., 1947

MALINOWSKI, B., *Sex and Repression in Savage Society*, London, 1927
OPLER, M. E., *An Apache Life-Way*, Chicago, 1941
RAUM, O. F., *Chaga Childhood*, London, 1940
SACHS, WULF, *Black Hamlet*, London, 1937; New York, 1947

8. Religion

EVANS-PRITCHARD, E. E., *Witchcraft, Oracles, and Magic among the Azande*, Oxford, 1937
FORDE, C. D. (ed.), *African Worlds*, London, 1954
HOWELLS, W. W., *The Heathens: Primitive Man and his Religions*, New York, 1948
LÉVY-BRUHL, LUCIEN, *The "Soul" of the Primitive*, New York, 1931
LOWIE, R. H., *Primitive Religion*, New York, 1924
MARETT, R. R., *The Threshold of Religion*, New York, 1914
PARSONS, E. C., *Pueblo Indian Religion* (2 vols.), Chicago, 1939
RADIN, PAUL, *Primitive Man as Philosopher*, New York, 1927
RIVERS, W. H. R., *Medicine, Magic, and Religion*, London, 1924
UNDERHILL, RUTH, *Papago Indian Religion*, New York, 1946

9. The Arts

BOAS, F., *Primitive Art*, Oslo, 1927
DIXON, ROLAND B., *Oceanic Mythology*, Boston, 1916
LANG, ANDREW, *Myth, Ritual, and Religion* (2 vols.), New York, 1887
LEACH, MARIA, *Standard Dictionary of Folklore, Mythology, and Legend* (2 vols.), New York, 1949, 1950
SHIPLEY, JOSEPH (ed.), *Encyclopedia of Literature* (2 vols.), New York, 1946
THOMPSON, STITH, *Tales of the North American Indians*, Cambridge (Mass.), 1929
———, *The Folktale*, New York, 1946
TRACEY, HUGH, *Chopi Musicians*, London, 1948
WERNER, ALICE, *Myths and Legends of the Bantu*, London, 1933
WILLIAMS, F. E., *Drama of Orokolo*, Oxford, 1940
WINGERT, PAUL S., *The Sculpture of Negro Africa*, New York, 1950
——— and LINTON, R., *Arts of the South Seas*, New York, 1946

10. Cultural Dynamics—Evolution, Diffusion, Acculturation

BARNETT, H. G., *Innovation: the Basis of Cultural Change*, New York, 1953
DIXON, R. B., *The Building of Cultures*, New York, 1928
GOLDENWEISER, A. A., *History, Psychology and Culture*, New York, 1933
HERSKOVITS, M. J., *Acculturation: the Study of Culture Contact*, New York, 1938
———, *The Myth of the Negro Past*, New York, 1941
KROEBER, A. L., *Configurations of Culture Growth*, Berkeley, 1944
LINTON, R. (ed.), *Acculturation in Seven American Indian Tribes*, New York, 1940
MALINOWSKI, B., *The Dynamics of Culture Change*, New Haven, 1945

MORGAN, L. H., *Ancient Society*, Chicago, n.d.
PARSONS, E. C., *Mitla: Town of the Souls*, Chicago, 1936
PERRY, W. J., *Children of the Sun*, London, 1923
REDFIELD, R., *The Folk Culture of Yucatan*, Chicago, 1941
SCHMIDT, W., *The Cultural Historical Method of Ethnology* (S. A. Sieber, tr.), New York, 1939
SUNDKLER, BERGT G. M., *Bantu Prophets in South Africa*, London, 1948
TEGGART, F. J., *Theory and Processes of History*, Berkeley, 1941
WISSLER, C., *The American Indian* (2d ed.), New York, 1923

11. Descriptive Works

A. North and South America

BIRKET-SMITH, K., *The Eskimos*, London, 1936
JENNESS, DIAMOND, *People of the Twilight*, New York, 1928
KLUCKHOHN, C. and LEIGHTON, D., *The Navaho*, Cambridge (Mass.), 1946
LOWIE, R. H., *The Crow Indians*, New York, 1945
McILWRAITH, T. F., *The Bella Coola Indians* (2 vols.), Toronto, 1948
MEANS, P. A., *Ancient Civilizations of the Andes*, New York, 1931
MORLEY, S. G., *The Ancient Maya*, Stanford (Cal.), 1946
SMITH, M. W., *The Puyallup-Nisqually*, New York, 1940
SPECK, F. G., *Naskapi*, Norman (Okla.), 1935
STEWARD, JULIAN (ed.), *Handbook of South American Indians* (*Bulletin No.* 143, Bureau of American Ethnology), Vols. 1–6, 1946–50
VALLIANT, GEORGE C., *Aztecs of Mexico*, New York, 1944
WISDOM, C., *The Chorti Indians of Guatemala*, Chicago, 1943

B. Africa

ASHTON, HUGH, *The Basuto*, London, 1952
COLSON, E. and GLUCKMAN, M., *Seven Tribes of British Central Africa*, London, 1951
EVANS-PRITCHARD, E. E., *The Nuer*, Oxford, 1940
FORTES, M., *The Dynamics of Clanship Among the Tallensi*, London, 1945
———, *The Web of Kinship Among the Tallensi*, London, 1949
HERSKOVITS, M. J., *Dahomey: an Ancient West African Kingdom* (2 vols.), New York, 1935
KABERRY, PHYLLIS M., *Women of the Grasslands*, London, 1952
NADEL, S. F., *A Black Byzantium: the Kingdom of Nupe in Nigeria*, London, 1942
RICHARDS, A. I., *Land, Labour, and Diet in Northern Rhodesia*, London, 1939
ROSCOE, J., *The Baganda*, London, 1911
SCHAPERA, I., *The Khoisan Peoples of South Africa*, London, 1930
STAYT, H. A., *The Bavenda*, London, 1931

C. Oceania and Australia

BLACKWOOD, B., *Both Sides of Buka Passage*, Oxford, 1935
FIRTH, RAYMOND, *We, the Tikopia*, New York, 1936
KABERRY, PHYLLIS, *Aboriginal Woman*, London, 1939

MALINOWSKI, B., *Argonauts of the Western Pacific* (2 vols.), London, 1922

OLIVER, DOUGLAS L., *The Pacific Islands*, Cambridge (Mass.), 1951

SPENCER, B. and GILLEN, F. J., *The Arunta*, London, 1927

WILLIAMS, F. E., *Papuans of the Trans-Fly*, London, 1936

WILLIAMSON, R. W., *Social and Political Systems of Central Polynesia* (3 vols.), Cambridge (England), 1924

———, *Religious and Cosmic Beliefs of Central Polynesia* (2 vols.), Cambridge (England), 1933

D. *Asia*

BARTON, R. F., *The Kalingas*, Chicago, 1949

BOGORAS, W., *The Chuckchee* (3 vols.), New York, 1904–09

COLE, F. C., *The Peoples of Malaysia*, New York, 1945

ELWIN, V., *The Baiga*, London, 1939

HSÜ, FRANCIS L. K., *Under the Ancestors' Shadow*, New York, 1948

HUTTON, J. H., *The Sema Nagas*, London, 1921

RIVERS, W. H. R., *The Todas*, London, 1906

SELIGMAN, C. G. and B. Z., *The Veddas*, Cambridge (England), 1911

Index

Alor, study of culture and personality in, 341

Alternatives, concept of, 503

Ambivalence, derivation of concept of, from anthropological data used by Freud, 334–5

American Anthropological Association, "Statement on Human Rights," 545

American Folklore Society, categories of folklore to be studied in America as set up by, 272

American Indians, *see* Indians

Americans, response-patterns of, contrasted to Chinese, 428–9

Americas, special archaeological problems of, 47

Anatomy, relation of, to physical anthropology, 11

Animatism, hypothesis of, as earliest form of religion, 211

Animism, as "minimum definition of religion," 210

as part of world-view of peoples, 215

forms of, in machine culture, 212

incidence of, in human societies, 212

presuasiveness of belief in, 215

Ankermann, B., cited, 465

Anthropogeography, development of, 97

Anthropological methods, use of, in study of problems of industry, 539

Anthropologists, basic tasks of, 543–4

contributions of, to solution of practical problems, 542–4

Anthropology, and psychology, interdisciplinary training in, 345

as pure and applied science, 543–4

as synthesizing discipline, 7

basic contribution of, 546–7

cultural, development of, 5

non-validity of definition of, as study of "primitive" peoples, 368

relationship of, to history, philosophy, and psychology, 12

to humanistic disciplines, 9–10

to social sciences, 8–9

scope of, 3–4

special techniques in study of, 6–7

customary differentiation of, from psychology, 498

defined, 5

divisions of, 3

Anthropology (*continued*)

early, as pure science, 537

growth in scientific resources of, 541

historical and generalizing, subdisciplines of, 524

physical, relationship of, to biological sciences, 10–11

primary aims of, 544

relationships of, to psychology, 332–3

social, 8

synthesizing character of, 11–12

unity of, 3–5, 12

Anthropometric measurements, used in classifying races, 54–7

Apache, educational methods of, 184

extended family among, 176

themes in culture of, 427

Apes, anthropoid, present distribution of, 15

Apollonian, as culture-type, 339

Apo rite, of Ashanti, psychological significance of, 346

Applied anthropology, acceleration of development of, by World War II, 539–40

debate concerning value of, 542–4

Arapesh, warfare among, 340

Archaeologists, reconstruction of prehistory by, 31–4

Archaeology, American, use of historic documents by, 48–9

as social science, 30

of North and South America, particular problems of, 47

prehistoric, relationship of, to other disciplines, 11

scope of, 3

special fields of, 4

special techniques of, 6

Armies, of nonliterate peoples, 208

Army, organization of, in Ashanti Kingdom, 200

Art, definition of, 235

degree of integration of, in Euroamerican and nonliterate cultures, 234

development of, in Palaeolithic, 239–41

evolutionary approach to study of, 241–4

formal aspects of, 257

graphic and plastic, relation of, to cultural anthropology, 9–10

influence of habitat on, 100–1

Palaeolithic, realism and conventionalization in, 239–41